"Children's Voices"

Learn, Earn
& Become Famous!

Eleanor J. Marks
2015 Holocaust Essay Contest

Sponsored by Bernard Marks
Sacramento, California

Copyright © 2015, Bernard Marks

Printed in the United States of America
I Street Press
Sacramento Public Library Authority
828 I Street
Sacramento, CA 95814

Marks, Bernard, Editor
        "Children's Voices" Learn, earn & become famous! / Eleanor J. Marks Holocaust Essay Contest

ISBN: 978-1-941125-67-0

1. Holocaust, Jewish (1939-1945). 2. Jews – Persecution – Germany. 3. Jews – Persecution – Poland. I. "Children's Voices". II. Eleanor J. Marks Holocaust Essay Contest, 2013. III. Bernard Marks.

ISSN: 2377-2565

Cover design by: Bernard Marks and Gerald F. Ward
Text interior design by: Gerald F. Ward

Pictures of:
Shannon Negrete; Alison Bradus; Rylie Roldan; Mia Sanchez;
Robin Beglinger; Marion Conus; Morgan Folger; Dominic Cupps

2 3 4 5 6 7 8 9 10

2015 Eleanor J. Marks Holocaust Writing Project

History:

The essay-writing project began in 2008 at Congregation B'nai Israel, Sacramento, California with only four entries. In 2012 the project was opened to 6th-12th grade for public, religious and private schools in California as well as European schools. In 2014 undergraduate students from colleges and universities all over the world were eligible to participate. Over the past seven years the writing project grew to over 300 entries.

Purpose:

The Eleanor J. Marks Worldwide Holocaust Essay Writing Project honors her memory by promoting remembrance and study of the Holocaust. It is also intended to enhance education in the schools through the annual essay-writing project.

The annual scholarship awards are given to winning students in each participating school:

> One award of $150.00 to a student 6th –12th grades in each school
> One award of $75.00 for runner-up in each school,
> One award $150.00 for undergraduate college/university student.
> Special awards of $50.00 selected by the founder, Bernard Marks

Thirty (30) or more judges evaluate the essays and determine the award recipients in each school.

Eleanor J. Marks Holocaust Essay Writing Project

Established 2008

Eleanor (Ellie) Marks (1931-2008), of blessed memory, was the wife of Bernard (Bernie) Marks.

Goals & Rules:
The goal of this annual writing project is for students to understand the Holocaust means and why we say, "Never Again."

The annual project commences no later than November 1 of each year. Essays are due no later than February 28 and must be submitted electronically in Microsoft Word® document to < **dov52@att.net or hagibor52@gmail.com** >

To accomplishing the task in a timely manner, the Judging Committee for 2015 consisted 25 community members. (See Judges names starting on page 562.)

Presentation of the award will be made during the Yom HaShoah (Day of Remembrance) Community event on May 1, 2016.

Awards:
1) $150.00 to one student from each school from grade 6 –12th , grade
2) $75.00 to one the runner up in each school grades 6 – 12th grade
3) $150 to the selected undergraduate essayist from a College/University
4) Special awards of $50.00 are selected by the founder of the Eleanor J. Marks Holocaust Project

PREFACE

How do you honor the victims of the Holocaust? The answer for Bernie Marks is to not let their spirit or memory fade. He does this by sharing their courageous stories with each new generation. His amazing personal story of survival, orchestrated by his father, illustrates how Bernie was able to endure the horrific death camps of the Nazi regime. This treasure of a man now gives first-hand accounts of the shocking truth behind genocide in an effort to ensure that these atrocities never happen again.

Obviously, as time goes on, the remaining survivors of the Holocaust become ever more rare. The value of Bernie's personal stories is irreplaceable and the youth understand this truth. When a slight man in his 80's can single-handedly engage 450 eighth graders, you know his message is riveting and very well received. After an assembly with Bernie, you will find a multitude of students lining up to simply shake his hand, ask additional questions, and/or take a picture. The students' "rock-star" treatment of Bernie validates the impact his message has on all in attendance.

Bernie Marks also continues to spread the truth of the Holocaust through an essay writing project that honors the memory of his late wife Eleanor J. Marks. This project allows students an opportunity to write an essay about Holocaust victims and the story behind their bravery and struggle to survive. As students research and compose their tributes to these everyday heroes, their awareness grows. At the same time, those who read their essays will understand that it takes purposeful action to prevent similar events. Bernie's message is clear that we must do all that we can to prevent the Holocaust and other events of genocide around the globe from happening again or continuing to take place.

Ron Rammer
Principal
Robert L. McCaffrey Middle School
Galt, California

INTRODUCTION

Near the end of my three-year-long graduate school experience, I was required to take a comprehensive examination on everything I had learned about German history. I recall stepping into the testing room with so little clue as to what would be asked of me. When I opened my blue book, the question that I saw was shorter than I expected: "Germany was the birthplace to the science, literature, and music that would help define culture and progress in the modern era. If this is so, how did Germany also become the birthplace of the Holocaust, an event that came to define so many of the horrors of the modern era?"

The answer was, and is, not an easy one. Simply put, while we think we know what we stand for as a society, humanity can be a fleeting thing. As a culture that prided itself on a nationalized pension plan, the speed of its automobiles, and the splendor of its medieval architecture, so much of Germany's sense of right and wrong faded overnight. Far from placing the west and its traditional bloc of democracies into the shoes of Interwar Germany, the simple take away should be that, as Americans, our own humanity and sensibilities for decency are just as susceptible to the wicked caprices of extremism and racial arrogance that affected Germany in 1933.

It is for this reason that cultivating a strong sense of humanity at the earliest of ages is imperative for a healthy democracy. And while learning from the past is engaging the past, this robust collection of essays provides a window into the bravery and sacrifice of those who stood willing to resist. To resist an ailing moral paradigm takes the strength of holding fast to one's own convictions, while thousands of voices are attempting to convince you otherwise.

What's more, with 70 years having passed between the Holocaust and today, the very act of writing enables tomorrow's leaders to explore the horrors of a broken society, giving them both a context for vigilance and a primer for understanding the earliest of warning signs.

Finally, this compilation showcases the talents and insights of some of today's finest young writers. The essays are written with a passion and dedication that should make the reader feel as if the future is in the hands of those who are willing to learn from the past and guard the sanctity of our collective future.

James C. Scott MA, MLS
Information Services Librarian

Table of Contents

CHURCHILL MIDDLE SCHOOL, CARMICHAEL, CA

DALLAS RANCH MIDDLE SCHOOL, ANTIOCH, CA

EUROPEAN SCHOOLS

C. K. MCCLATCHY HIGH SCHOOL, SACRAMENTO, CA

SHELDON HIGH, SACRAMENTO, CA

SAN JUAN HIGH SCHOOL, CITRUS HEIGHTS, CA

Brookfield School, Sacramento, CA

Dr. Jo Gonsalves became Brookfield's instructional leader in 2007. Prior to joining the Brookfield Faculty, she taught middle school and high school English and Science in Sacramento area private and parochial schools for 11 years. She also served as Assistant Principal of Academics at St. Francis High School in Sacramento for 4 years before accepting her current position to lead Brookfield School. Dr. Jo was drawn to Brookfield School because of its reputation for excellence and its commitment to serving the area's brightest and most motivated students, a population that is grossly underserved in most schools today, but is so important to the betterment of our society's future. If you ask Dr. Jo what she sees as her personal mission as Brookfield's principal, she would tell you, "My purpose is to provide a safe and happy environment, combined with a rigorous and creative academic program, and emotional and social support so my bright students have the best opportunity to reach their potential. I see each of my students as a future leader."

Dr. Jo's Professional Credentials include:
BA in English from UC Davis
Departmental Citation for Excellence, UC Davis CA Clear
Single Subject Credential: English, General Science CA
Adminstrative Services Credential Doctorate in Eduational
Leadership, St. Mary's College of California

Dr. Tracy is the middle school English teacher at Brookfield School in Sacramento, California. As a grades six through eight teacher, she focuses on making her students excellent readers, writers, and world citizens. Students write essays as part of a curriculum involving historical fiction and nonfiction about the Holocaust. It is very important that each new generation learns what happened in the Holocaust, so that we can never forget.

Dr. Trinity Tracy
6th - 8th grade English Teacher
5th - 8th grade Speech and Debate Teacher
Debate Team Coach

POWER TO DO WHAT'S RIGHT

Alexander Vasilyev

 A hero is someone who takes risks and action to do what society considers right. Carl Lutz is an example of a hero. Carl Lutz is considered a Holocaust hero because he saved countless lives, risked his own life to do so, and never gave up on his effort to do so. Charles Lutz was born on March 30, 1985, in Walzenhausen, Switzerland. He was a Swiss diplomat famous for saving Jews in Hungary. He served as Switzerland's vice-consul, and was put in charge of representing the United States. He was also an amateur photographer who helped tie up many loose ends of the Holocaust.

The first reason that Carl Lutz was a hero is because he saved countless lives. He is credited with saving over 62,000 Jews, which is considered to be the second largest rescue operation for Jews during World War II. Lutz tried his best to persuade the Hungarians to stop deportations. "After the Arrow Cross Party came to power in Hungary in October 1944, Zionist Youth activists, with the assistance of Carl Lutz and his office, protected countless lives of Hungarian Jews" (jewishvirtuallibrary). When the Germans established two ghettos, one for document-holders, Carl Lutz obtained organized buildings to house over 3,000 Jews. Only six people died.

The files and reports of Carl Lutz revealed many of Hungary's business interests. All of the reports were enhanced by pictures that Lutz took. He wrote reports that had to do with the illegal Jewish immigration to Palestine and also guarding the interests of the Germans who lived in Palestine after the beginning of World War II. He helped tie up loose ends. Due to this, we have much recorded evidence of the Holocaust.

The second reason that Carl Lutz is a hero is that he risked his life in saving the Jews. Just by participating in the act of helping Jews already made him an enemy of Germany. It was extremely forbidden to take photos in Budapest at that time. On one occasion Lutz tried to photograph a group of Arrow-Cross party thugs beating a woman in the street. They immediately noticed him, took his gun, and had a gun pointed at him. He was able to save himself only by showing his diplomatic pass and giving away the film roll. After this experience he left the camera in his residence when going out. He was very shocked by how close it was for him. Carl Lutz was in an indirect association with Raoul Wallenberg, who actively stood in the way of SS soldiers. Raoul many times told SS guards that they cannot take the Jews without going through him. Standing against the Nazi party was dangerous for anyone.

The final reason that he is a hero is that he never gave up on his efforts. There were many situations where the odds were against Carl's cause. An example of this is in November 1944, when Adolf Eichmann ordered the forced march of Budapest's

Jews to the Austrian border. Lutz and other diplomats attempted to rescue as many Jews as possible. Even after the German invasion of Hungary in March 1944, he continued his efforts to find escape routes and to issue rescue passports with the help of the Red Cross and other neutral countries. He ended up issuing more than 50,000 rescue passports to Hungarian Jews in order to save them.

Although he was commanded to leave the city before the Red Army arrived, Lutz chose to stay in Budapest with the Jews who he had protected until after the occupation by the Red Army. He waited until his cause could be carried out. He made sure that he finished it through to the end. He never gave up in rescuing the Hungarian Jews. This is the final reason why we consider Carl Lutz to be a hero of the Holocaust.

In conclusion, these are the three reasons why Carl Lutz was a hero. The three reasons are that he saved countless lives, risked his life in doing so, and never gave up on the efforts. He saved countless lives and reduced causalities of Jews by thousands. He opposed the Nazi party to save Jews, risking his life for a good cause. He never gave up on his efforts to save the Hungarian Jews, especially when the situation seemed very grave.

There were many Holocaust heroes during World War II, but Carl Lutz definitely stands out the rest. He wasn't scared, and he didn't give up. He stayed strong until the end and his cause was successful in saving lives of Jews. This was not an easy task, but in the end he managed to achieve it. Due to his heroic achievements, we respect him as a hero. World War II definitely had heroes in different places doing many things, but no hero would be as daring and as dedicated as Carl Lutz was to his cause. This is why Carl Lutz, an amateur photographer and a politician, was considered a hero.

Works Cited

http://www.yadvashem.org/YV/en/exhibitions/our_collections/carl_lutz/index.asp
http://www.jewishvirtuallibrary.org/jsource/biography/Carl_Lutz.html

HERO

Brandon Liong

Knud Christiansen was a hero from Denmark who saved thousands of lives during the Holocaust. Those lives happened to be Jews. Knud Christiansen was born on January 25, 1918. He was not only a hero but a superior athlete who competed in the Berlin Olympic Games in 1936. Because of his strength and durability, he rowed Jews across the Øresund to their safety during the Holocaust.

Knud Christiansen had a fiancé who lived in Berlin and wrote letters home describing the rise of Hitler and the Nazi power. He soon traveled to Berlin as a member of the Danish rowing team to compete in the 1936 Olympic Games, but also to see what actually was going on. Soon, Knud and his fiancée, Karen, married on 1938. Unfortunately, in April 1940 Germany occupied all of Denmark. In September, 1943 it became clear that the Germans were to execute all Jews in Demark.

One night, Knud saw steamers on the harbor and he knew immediately that they were coming for the Jews. He warned his Jewish neighbors to spend the night at his apartment. Unfortunately the next day, they decided to return to their home and were caught. They were shipped to an internment camp called Horserod. He was willing to offer them a tub of butter just to release his Jewish neighbors. Unfortunately they did not budge on releasing them any time soon.

Knud had to do something and soon arranged a meeting with Mr. Werner Best, the German Reich minister in Denmark. Knud finally got them released by promising the Germans a film that showed the Germans were allies to Denmark. Of course, that was never completed. Soon, he and his wife joined the Danish resistance along with many other Danes to save the Jews. Fortunately, Karen's father, Dr. Holger Rasmussen, was Denmark's physician of Christian X and Chief Naval Physician. He owned a village in Espergaerde, a coastal villa just north of Copenhagen, which he used as a checkpoint for Jews escaping Copenhagen. From there, Jews were able to cross the Øresund, a body of water between Denmark and neutral Sweden.

During the months of October, November, and December of 1943, Knud ferried one Jew at a time across the river using the skills he had as being part of the Danish Olympic Rowing team. Soon, the time came that large fishing boats started to help. They could now transport a great number of Jews across the Øresund. Even after all the Jews were safely evacuated out of Denmark, Knud and Karen continued their resistance efforts to keep Jews safe until the end of the war.

After 70 years, memories of the war came back to him in fragments. He immigrated to America with his wife and three of his four children and still maintained close relations with the Jewish community. Unfortunately, the hero died at age 97 on February 2, 2012. He was recognized by the Jewish community and his name was added to the list of legendary figures.

Knud Christiansen was a hero who saved many Jews from the Nazis. It all started out with his fiancée mailing him letters about the rising of Hitler and the Nazi rule. When Germany invaded Denmark, it became clear that the Germans wanted to exterminate the entire Jewish race. Knud wasn't just going to sit there and do nothing about this problem; he decided to warn his Jewish neighbors that the Germans were coming. He saw steamboats and instantly knew that the problem has started.

He protected them by allowing them to spend the night in his apartment. Unfortunately, they decided to go back to following day and were soon captured. He tried and tried again to release them from the internment camp they were staying in and it finally happened. But the war was not over; he still had the rest of the Jews in Denmark he needed to evacuate from the Nazis. He figured out a plan to transport Jews one by one by river. He crossed the Øresund River, which is a body of water between Denmark to neutral Sweden. Over time, he got large fishing boats to transfer large portions of Jews. Eventually, he evacuated all the Jews from Denmark but he and his wife continued their resistance efforts to keep Jews safe until the end of the war.

Knud Christiansen, a hero from Denmark who saved thousands of lives during the Holocaust. Those lives happened to be Jews. Knud not only helped Jews survive but also won many awards such as being on the list of legendary figures in 2005. He is a hero who many people don't know about but he is one who should stand out. Unfortunately, he passed away on February 2, 2012 but was honored deeply by the Jewish community.

Works Cited

"Christiansen, Knud - The Jewish Foundation for the Righteous." *The Jewish Foundation for the Righteous*. N.p., n.d. Web. 24 Feb. 2015.

"Danish Hero: One Rosh Hashanah Burns Bright in Holocaust." *JewishPost.com -*. N.p., n.d. Web. 24 Feb. 2015.

"FIDF Mourns the Passing of Knud Christensen - NY / Tristate - FIDF Chapters - Friends of the Israel Defense Forces." *FIDF Mourns the Passing of Knud Christensen - NY / Tristate - FIDF Chapters - Friends of the Israel Defense Forces*. N.p., n.d. Web. 24 Feb. 2015.

SWISS HEROES OF THE HOLOCAUST

Elliott Lundholm

Switzerland may not have been the best example of a nation trying to help the Jews survive during World War II. While 21,000 Jews were eventually able to find asylum in Switzerland, thousands of others were not so lucky. In the early days of the war, Swiss officials refused to allow thousands of Jews to enter Switzerland. These officials knew that the Jews were seeking sanctuary, and they may have even known that if the Jews were refused entry, a great majority would die in concentration camps. Yet, there is much evidence, that the majority of the people in Switzerland, as well of those with Swiss ancestry, wanted to help the Jewish people The Swiss heroes of the Holocaust not only risked the the lives of thousands of Jewish people, they were also instrumental in changing the policy of Switzerland's government. The selflessness and compassion of these heroes made the Swiss government realize that they had to do the right thing.

In his book, <u>The Righteous of Switzerland: Heroes of the Holocaust,</u> Meir Wagner identifies 37 men and women who risked their lives over a long period of time to save Jewish lives during WWII. All of them were heroes. All of them came up with creative ways to save lives. The heroes also protected those who helped them in this endeavor. One example is Pastor Daniel Curtet. who organized the entire town of Le Chambon, France to hide 1,000 Jewish refugees. He never told those who were housing the Jewish refugees that they were hosting Jews. Those who went out of their way to house the refugees, if caught, could sincerely say "I did not know that he was Jewish." Also, the Jewish refugees were issued new identification papers that identified them as "non-Jews," and this helped to document claims of those who were helping Jews.

Wagner's description of the Holocaust heroes is historically important and inspiring. Two of the heroes are especially inspiring. One was Carl Lutz, the Swiss Vice-Counsel in Budapest, Hungary from 1942 until the end of WW II. Lutz is credited with saving over 62,000 Jewish people. The other is Paul Grueninger, a Swiss border police commander of the St. Gallen region that borders with Austria. Grueninger recognized the Nazi injustice and defied his superiors in order to save lives.

Carl Lutz was born in Walzenhausen, Switzerland in 1895, but received his formal education in the United States. Lutz came from a very big family (one of ten children) and as teenager he attended a trade school and worked in a textile factory. In 1913, he immigrated to the United States. During his first five years in the United States, he worked as blue collar laborer. In 1918, he was able to go to school in Missouri, and by 1920 he became a correspondent student at the Swiss Embassy in Washington. He earned a BA from George Washington University in 1924, continued to work with the Swiss Embassy in Philadelphia and St. Louis until 1934. In 1935, Lutz was assigned to be the vice-consul to the Swiss consulate in Jaffa, Palestine where he served until 1942 when he went to Budapest.

The Nazis took over Budapest in 1944, and almost immediately began deporting Jewish people to concentration camps. Lutz reacted to the Nazis just as quickly. First, he entered in to an agreement with the Hungarian government and the Nazis which gave him permission to issue 8,000 protective letters allowing Hungarian Jews to immigrate to Palestine. Even though the original negotiation of this agreement made it clear that the 8,000 letters were to be issued to individuals, Lutz made certain that each letter applied to families, thereby multiplying the number of Jewish immigrants to Palestine. But Lutz believed he had to do more. He decided to issue tens of thousands of additional protective letters, and numbered each one of them between one and 8,000. Lutz also set up over 70 safe houses all over Budapest. He declared each safe house to be an annex of the Swiss legation. Jewish people in the safe houses enjoyed diplomatic immunity and were off limits to the Nazi soldiers. The biggest of the safe houses was known as the Glass House. The Glass House and a neighboring building saved over 3,000 Jews. By November of 1944, the German representative in Hungary, aware of Lutz's efforts to save the Jews, asked officials in Berlin for permission to assassinate him. Fortunately, the officials in Berlin never responded.

Lutz saved tens of thousands of lives. Yet, after the war, Switzerland was slow to recognize his achievements. In fact, when the war ended, the Swiss government criticized him for exceeding his authority and endangering Switzerland's neutral status during the war. By 1958, however, the Swiss government did recognize his heroic actions and honored him. But the other inspiring hero, Paul Grueninger, was not so lucky.

Like Lutz, Paul Grueninger acted quickly to the save the Jews from going to Nazi death camps. After the Nazis annexed Austria, and began sending Austrian Jews to the camps, many of the Jews tried to find refuge in Switzerland. Switzerland closed its border with Austria and turned back everyone without proper entry permits. Grueninger, the Swiss border commander, knew that if he turned the refugees back they would be sent to the death camps. He decided to disobey his government's instruction. Not only did he let the refugees into Switzerland, he falsified their passports so it appeared that the refugees had entered Switzerland before the date that entry into the country had been restricted. Once in Switzerland with the falsified passports, the refugees were given legal status and were aided by Jewish organizations.

When the Germans found out what Grueninger was up to, they informed the Swiss government. The Swiss dismissed Grueninger from the police force, suspended his benefits and brought him to trial. He was charged with illegally permitting the entry of 3,600 Jews into Switzerland and falsifying their registration papers. In 1941, Grueninger was found guilty of breach of duty. He was fined and his retirement benefits were taken away. Unable to find employment, Grueninger lived the rest of his life in poverty. Yet he never regretted that he was able to help the Jewish refugees. In 1954, explaining his motives, he said "It was basically a question of saving human lives threatened with death. How could I then seriously consider bureaucratic schemes and calculations?" Although the Swiss government sent him a letter of apology in in 1970, it never reinstated his pension. Grueninger died in 1972, and the Swiss government did not annul his conviction until 1995.

Carl Lutz and Paul Grueninger are inspiring examples what a

difference one man can make. Both came from rather humble beginnings. Both rose to positions of power. Both saw the need to use that power to help mankind in spite of what may happen to them.

I also love that both became so personally involved. Lutz once jumped in the Danube River to save a bleeding Jewish woman fleeing from Arrow Cross militiamen firing at Jews. Grueninger was known to use his own money to buy winter clothes for the Jewish refugees.

Neither man thought of himself, nor of the benefits of his position, nor even the how the Swiss government may ultimately view their efforts. Clearly both are among Switzerland greatest heroes.

HEROES OF THE HOLOCAUST
Khem Shergill

Paul Grueninger was a Swiss border police commander of the St. Gallon region that borders with Austria. Grueninger decided to disregard the official instructions and let refugees into Switzerland. He also falsified their registration to show that they had arrived before 1938, before Switzerland began to close off its borders. He sacrificed his peaceful life to help others. Despite the difficulties, he never regretted his action on behalf of the Jews. In 1954 he explained his motives: "It was basically a question of saving human lives threatened with death. How could I then seriously consider bureaucratic schemes and calculations?" ("Paul Grueninger, 1954 - The Righteous Among The Nations - Yad Vashem.")

At the outbreak of World War II in 1939, Switzerland immediately began to mobilize for a possible invasion from Germany. The entire country was fully mobilized in only three days. The Swiss government began to fortify positions throughout the country. In the course of the war, detailed invasion plans were drawn up by the German military command, but Switzerland was never attacked. Switzerland was able to remain independent through a combination of military deterrence, economic connections with Germany, and good fortune as larger events during the war delayed an invasion. Attempts by Switzerland's small Nazi party to effect an Anschluss with Germany failed miserably, largely as a result of Switzerland's multicultural heritage, strong sense of national identity, and long tradition of direct democracy and civil liberties. Although, for Austria it was not the same. Austria was forced to become part of the German Empire through political schemes and military dominance.

The Swiss press vigorously criticized the Third Reich, often infuriating its leadership. In turn, Berlin denounced Switzerland as a medieval rudiment and its people renegade Germans. General Henri Guisan ordered a mobilization of all militia forces. The Swiss military strategy resembled old Russian tactics during the Napoleonic Wars. The Swiss military drew their forces high up into the Alps. These positions were made for a long term retreat so they were well stocked with clothes, food, and ammunition if Germany ever decided to invade Switzerland. This strategy would lower the invading army's moral and keep Switzerland safe from invasion. If Germany had even decided to attack, Swiss units around the edges of the mountains would cause huge losses to the German invaders and force the German army to retreat. However, the Swiss military would keep control of major rail lines, so these strongholds could communicate with each other and receive any supplies or soldiers in times of need. Grueninger had orders to stop anyone who tried to enter Switzerland. These people would be Jews, who were escaping Hitler's wrath. As the situation in Austria worsened, the number of refugees who tried to illegally enter Switzerland increased. Grueninger then disregarded his orders and helped Jews seek refuge. He stated that he was saving human lives threatened with death. Eventually the German officials found out about Grueninger's scheme and informed the Swiss Council about his exploits. After the government of Switzerland found out about Grueninger's illegal actions they suspended his benefits and also brought him on trial. In total, Grueninger illegally allowed 3,600 Jews to enter Switzerland and also falsified their papers to show that they came before 1938. On the morning of April 3rd 1939 Grueninger arrived at his work as he did every day, but the Cadet Anton Schneider blocked his way following a Commander in Chief's order. Grueninger was not surprised for what happened that morning and knew that he couldn't have remained unnoticed. Meir Wagner writes in his book, The Righteous of Switzerland, that Grueninger knew that he was guilty of having allowed the illegal entry of Jewish refugees. He was forced to choose between the moral law and the law of the State. A family friend, who worked in a border post near Bregenz, a town in Austria, warned him about the risks he was taking. Grueninger was told that he was on the black list of the Gestapo and he should stay from the wrath of Hitler and his Nazi supporters. However, Grueninger did not pay much attention to this warning and continued with his "illegal" activities.

In 1939, he was caught and fined. Also, his benefits were suspended and his public image ruined. He was dismissed without benefits from the police force in 1939. The association "Justice for Paul Grueninger" was formed to suppress acts of racism and anti-Semitism with the same spirit demonstrated by the Swiss policeman. The initiatives of this association included the clearing of Paul Grueninger of the damages he had suffered and to rename a public town square close to the Police Headquarters after him. The government of St. Gallen acted accordingly. The government of the Canton of St. Gallen later paid compensation to his descendants. The government of the Canton of St. Gallen didn't elevate Paul Grueninger's name until 1995, 23 years after his death. The Yad Vashem IsraeliHolocaustmemorial honors him as one of the

Righteous Among the Nations. A street located in the northern Jerusalem neighborhood of Pisgat Ze'ev has been named after him. Paul Grüninger was the first Swiss citizen to be honored by the government of the United States of America. Sadly, Paul Grüninger died on February 22nd 1972, at the age of 81.

Paul Grueninger was a Swiss border police commander who sacrificed his career and his future for the well-being of others. He helped about 3,600 Jews into Switzerland and helped falsify their visas. Despite the difficulties, he never regretted his action on behalf of the Jews. In 1954 he explained his motives: "It was basically a question of saving human lives threatened with death. How could I then seriously consider bureaucratic schemes and calculations?" Paul Grueninger is now a Righteous Among Nations and also one of the Swiss heroes of the Holocaust. The association "Justice for Paul Grüninger" was created to fight against racism and anti-Semitism with the same spirit demonstrated by the Swiss policeman. "One of the initiatives of this association was to ask the Government of St. Gallen to compensate Paul Grüninger for the damages he had suffered and to rename a public town square close to the Police Headquarters after him." ("The Example of Grueninger.") Paul Grüninger was the first Swiss citizen to be honored by the government of the United States of America. Paul Grüninger died on February 22 1972, at the age of 81.

Works Cited

"Paul Grueninger - The Righteous Among The Nations - Yad Vashem." *Paul Grueninger - The Righteous Among The Nations - Yad Vashem*. N.p., 2015. Web. 02 Feb. 2015.

"Eastern Illinois University Homepage." *The Holocaust Paul Grueninger*. N.p., n.d. Web. 02 Feb. 2015.

"Holocaust Memorial Day Trust." *Welcome*. N.p., 2013. Web. 02 Feb. 2015.

A 1936 OLYMPIC ATHLETE AND DANISH HOLOCAUST HERO

Mathew Gunning, Co-winner

Witnessing Adolf Hitler exit the stadium during the 1936 Berlin Olympics rather than watch Jesse Owens receive a medal was Knud Christiansen's first introduction to the cruelty of Adolf Hitler when he was competing as a member of the Danish Rowing Team. He never imagined that four years later he would take a stand against Adolf Hitler. Knud Christiansen is a Danish Hero because he risked his family and business when he became a member of the Danish Freedom Fighters and the Danish

Resistance. He was willing to use his fame as an Olympic athlete and his family's connections to the Danish Royal family to help Jewish families escape. He was part of the Danish Resistance from the beginning until the end. When asked why he was willing to risk everything, he said "It was something that needed to be done." His good deeds were brought to light by Holocaust survivor, Max Rawitscher, who came out of hiding after the war and told how he evaded the Nazis thanks to Knud Christiansen.

As a member of the Danish Resistance he assisted in putting a rescue network in place to save escaping Jews. His activities ranged from saving strangers to rescuing friends. Once, he learned that close friends were going to be sent to camps, he warned them and told them to go into hiding. One of the brothers insisted on not hiding and was arrested. When he learned that his friend had been arrested, he went to the highest ranking Nazi in Denmark who was known as the "Blood Hound of Paris" because he sent so many Jews in France to death camps to ask for the release of his friend. His friend was released and it was partly attributed to his fame as an Olympic athlete and his family connections to the Denmark Royal Family. He hid large groups of Jews in his house while escape routes were set up. Because of his fame and athletic popularity he learned of a SS plan to round up all Jews at one time and ship them to either the Eastern Front or the death camps. The round up was planned for October 1, 1943 on Rosh Hashanah when 7,000 Jews were expected to be home. Knud helped spread the word all around the country. Universities closed to help students take part in rescue operations and Ministers asked congregants to help their Jewish neighbors. Knud was part of a group of Danish diplomats that negotiated with Sweden to provide asylum to all Danish Jews.

After Sweden agreed to provide asylum to all Danish Jews, Knud escorted Jews one at a time, to Sweden using his Olympic racing boats. He made 17 trips on his rowing boat before the rescuers began to use larger boats that could carry more people. In total around 7,200 Jews were rowed to Sweden over a period of three weeks. Surprisingly, he says that many German soldiers could be counted on to look the other way when the boats were on their way to Sweden. Other rescue workers and survivors have verified that boats were going back and forth under the eyes of many Germans who did nothing to stop them. However, not all German soldiers looked the other way. Sadly, two of the boats were sunk by Nazi patrols and everyone on the boats drowned.

Knud used every possible resource at his disposal to hide Jews. At one point, more than forty Jews ended up at his own apartment. They filled up his living, dining and spare rooms. He even convinced his mother to use her chocolate shop in Copenhagen to serve as a meeting place for rescue workers. Knud coordinated with a large network of friends and associates to hide Jews in every spot available. He and his wife protected resistance members and cared for wounded Allied soldiers as the war progressed. He continued to battle the Nazis until the end of the war. Several of the Danish Jews who had survived the Holocaust paid regular visits to Knud's mother's chocolate shop to leave flowers as a token of appreciation for his work during the war. Knud Christiansen and his family migrated to New York in 1970 where he lived quietly and without notoriety. He worked in a store and repaired clocks. He always had many Jewish friends.

Watching Adolf Hitler leave the stadium during the 1936 Berlin Olympics was Knud Christiansen's first time witnessing Adolf Hitler's racist actions. He became a Danish Holocaust Hero because he risked his family and business to become a member of the Danish Resistance, put a rescue network in place to save escaping Jews and cared for wounded allied soldiers. In 2005, his name was enshrined alongside twenty other Danes on the "Righteous Among the Nations" list at the Yad Vashem Holocaust Memorial Museum in Jerusalem. This remains the highest honor that the State of Israel can give to non-Jews. He maintained close ties with Jewish communities in the United States until his death. Knud died at the age of 97 in 2012.

Works Cited

Goldberger, Leo. *"The Rescue of the Danish Jews: Moral Courage Under Stress"*, New York University Press, 1983. Print

Dolgin, Robin. "Danish Hero: One Rosh Hashanah Burns Bright in Holocaust" JewishPost.com, 20/01/2015.

Rao, Jaya. "A Loser at the Olympics, He Struck Gold in Jewish Hearts Forever" The CopenhagenPost.com, 06/10/2012, 10/01/2015.

HEROES OF THE HOLOCAUST: THE GATE KEEPER

Queenie Lee, Runner-up

There were many heroes of the Holocaust. Colonel Paul Grueninger, a senior officer of the Swiss police, the President of the Swiss Policemen Association, and an active member of the Animal Protection Association, was one of them. He allowed many Jews to cross the border of Switzerland. He was born on 1891, in the city of St. Gallen, located in North East of Switzerland. In the First World War he served as Lieutenant. Grueninger was also the President of the Swiss Policeman Association.

In April 3, 1938, the government of Switzerland prohibited Austrian Jews from entering the neutral country by official law. Mr. Paul Grueninger protested against the decision. He was forced to choose: his own morality or the law of the State. He believed the Jews deserved a chance to live and forged passport dates. That way if someone checked what date they arrived in Switzerland, they came before the date of prohibition and the Diepoldsau camp, an organization in Switzerland created for helping Jews find permanent resident or transporting them to the desired destination.

He helped them in their new life, using his own hard-earned money to provide them with clothing, mainly winter wear, and housing them until they were on their feet. He lent a helping hand to over 3,600 Jews who were trying to escape from Austria to Switzerland. Grueninger also went an extra mile to help cover the tracks of these illegal immigrants. A family friend worked at a border post near Bregenz, an Austrian town, constantly warned him of the dangers and risks he was taking. He even informed Gruninger that he was on the Gestapo's black list and told him to stay far away from Germany. This was his first and only warning. He thoughtlessly decided to ignore the wise and dramatically important advice and continued his illegal activities, doing what he thought was right.

When a Jewish woman who was helped by Grueninger lost her jewels, she contacted him to look for them at a hotel that his friend owned. She then sent a letter to her relatives in Vienna about "a wonderful police Captain called Paul Grueninger. He promised me that he would look after my jewels and bring them to me from our friend's hotel" (The Example of Grueninger). The letter was seized by the Nazis. That was his last chance. He was caught and fired from the Switzerland Police Force put on trial. He was found guilty of breach of duty, stripped of his pension rights, and charged 300 Swiss francs. He lived the rest of his life in poverty because it was difficult to find work as a criminal, until the day he breathed the last breath on February 22, 1972, when he was 81 years old.

He threw away his life and envied position to help desperate Jewish refugees cross the border from Austria to Switzerland. In his life time he never received a single recognition for all the hard work that he did, that he sacrificed his occupation, and his future life, to receive nothing other than a 300 Swizz francs fine. Fifty years after the war, 23 years after his departure, in 1995, in the same room where he was found guilty, he was pardoned of his charges because the surviving Jewish immigrants who were helped by Grueninger came and gave testimony to repay their debts and thankfulness to their savior. A film named "The Affair of Gruninger" took place in the very court room that he was tried in. In the film, there were zoomed in pictures of the trial and the face of the testimonies reflected severe and awful memories.

Mr. Paul Grueninger protested against the decision that prohibited Austrian Jews from entering Switzerland. He believed the Jews deserved a chance to live and forged passport dates. He lent a helping hand to over 3,600 Jews that were trying to escape from Austria to Switzerland. He ignored his first and only warning. The second time, he was caught and fired from the Switzerland Police Force and was railed against. He was found guilty of breach of duty, stripped of his pension rights, and charged 300 Swiss francs. In his life time he never received a single recognition for all the hard work that he did, that he sacrificed his occupation, his future life, to receive nothing other than a 300 Swizz francs fine. In 1995, he was pardoned of his charges because the surviving Jewish immigrants who were helped by Grueninger and came and gave testimony to repay their debts and thankfulness to their savior. "The Affair of Gruninger," a film that was dedicated to Colonal Paul Gruninger, took place in the very court room wherehe was found guilty and innocent.

There were many heroes of the Holocaust. Colonel Paul Grueninger, a senior officer of the Swiss police, the President of the Swiss Policemen Association, and an active member of the Animal Protection Association, was one of them. This man teaches an important life lesson: do not go against one's beliefs and always do what one believes is best.

Works Cited

https://jfr.org/rescuer-stories/gruninger-paul/
http://njjewishnews.com/njjn.com/080708/sxMuseumExhibitHonors.html
http://jewishcurrents.org/tag/paul-grueninger
http://www.raoulwallenberg.net/saviors/others/example-gr-uuml-ninger/
http://www.yadvashem.org/yv/en/righteous/stories/grueninger.asp

KNUD DYBY

Riya Shergill, Co-winner

The Holocaust is one of the biggest tragedies in the history of the human race. This tragedy should never be forgotten, and Knud Dyby is one of the people who voluntarily stepped up to save the Jewish community and others from being murdered. On November 9, 1999, Knud Dyby received a medal honoring humanitarian efforts during the Holocaust that helped save thousands of lives. His heroic actions during this dark period of time showed the world that ordinary people can do almost anything. For his humanitarian efforts, he has been countlessly acknowledged by numerous Jewish organizations for his help in saving the lives of over 7,000 Jewish men, women, and children.

Knud Dyby was born in Randeis, Jutland, Denmark in the year of 1915. He soon went into the printing trade and after completing his education in a university he decided that he wanted to become a typographer. Knud Dyby was motivated to help the Jewish community fairly early in his life when he himself witnessed the true nature of the Nazis. He was only in his mid to early twenties during that period of time. When the Nazis came to power in Denmark, he almost immediately joined Nazi resistance groups, such as the Danish-Swedish Refugee Service and countless others. Later on these resistance groups became very powerful and at some points threatened to eliminate Nazi control over Denmark.

14

In the year of 1943, on August 29, Dyby and his fellow compatriots came to find out of German plans for a raid. The primary goal was to round-up all Danish Jews and send them to concentration and death camps in areas such as Nazi occupied Germany and Poland. Upon hearing this news, Dyby realized that he needed to quickly take action in order to prevent a large massacre of the Danish Jews. He began to organize a massive rescue mission. which involved the use of fishermen in Copenhagen's North Harbor. His plan was to transport the Danish Jews out of Denmark and into Sweden, since Sweden was located fairly close to Denmark.

Knud Dyby understood that the Jews had to be informed of this rescue effort in order for the plan to succeed. He discovered that the best way to inform the Jews was by going through doctors' offices. He figured that nearly everyone had a doctor of some sort, so they would be the most efficient way to quickly spread the news of the incoming raid. As an added bonus the doctors in Denmark were extremely cooperative with Dyby and offered their assistance immediately. He aimed to transport the entire Jewish population out of Denmark and into Sweden over the course of one week. He attempted to do this by organizing the city's taxi drivers and informing each of them their part in this rescue mission, this although proved to be insufficient. Dyby then thought of using police cars as his source of transport, this proved to be sufficient. The final part of mission entirely depended on the fishermen's' capability to avoid all Nazi naval ships and the Danish Coast Police. Many things were at stake including the lives of these people who were aiding the Jews, but the men and women in this operation risked their lives to help others before themselves.

Knud Dyby would secretly send Jewish people to a harbor in Denmark that was near to Sweden or into hiding spots. Then, as soon as he found an opportunity, he would send the Jews in the hiding spots down to one of the harbors. This plan took much precision and calculation; he had to make sure that nothing went drastically wrong. Soon, his companions in the resistance groups began to address him as "The Postman" because of the large amount of transport activities that were conducted because of him. One of the most famous incidences that he is well known for occurred in 1944, when he obtained 500 false ID papers for the Jews who needed them to escape to Sweden. Knud Dyby was able to accomplish this big feat with the help of some of his former police coworkers. They aided him by taking any messages that they received from people and families who were desperate to reach Sweden before the Nazi army could reach them.

Knud Dyby has won various awards over the course of his life. One of his most remarkable awards was when he was honored with the title of "Righteous Among the Nations" in Israel for his efforts to save countless lives. This was quite an honor, this prestigious award is awarded to those men and women who displayed courage, bravery, etc. and risked their own well-being during the Holocaust to help save Jews from extermination by the Nazis. Even though Dyby was honored multiple times for efforts to save the Jewish community during the Holocaust, whenever he was questioned about the subject he replied by saying that he only played a minor role in the resistance efforts. Although he spoke about his actions as ordinary and righteous, he was one of the few people who stepped out of millions of people.

At the end of the war, over 6 million Jews had been murdered by the Nazi regime party, this tragedy should never be forgotten. Knud Dyby is one of the heroes of the Holocaust who stepped up to save the Jewish community and others from annihilation. Over the course of about a week Knud Dyby accomplished something that was thought impossible, he was able to evacuate nearly every Danish Jew out of Denmark. Around 7,000 people were saved from Hitler's wrath by his heroic efforts. As in the words of Sally Ganor "If only there had been more like him..." She was right, he truly was one of the "Righteous Among the Nations."

Works Cited

"Dyby, Knud - The Jewish Foundation for the Righteous." *The Jewish Foundation for the Righteous*. Claims Conference, 2014. Web. 02 Feb. 2015.

Marin, Richard H. "Marin Man Who Helped save Thousands of Jews during World War II Dies at 96." - *San Jose Mercury News*. N.p., 2011. Web. 02 Feb. 2015.

"The Righteous Among The Nations." - *Yad Vashem*. N.p., n.d. Web. 02 Feb. 2015.

Congregation B'nai Israel, Sacramento, CA

Denise Crevin is currently the Education Administrator, Congregation B'nai Israel. After graduating from UCLA with a degree in Communication Studies, Denise received a Masters degree in Broadcast and Electronic Communication Arts from San Francisco State University. She worked as a writer for CNN Headline News in Atlanta, did PR for Marriott Hotels during the 1996 Olympics in Atlanta and then returned to the Bay Area to run a business - Service Impressions - with her husband, Dan. She is the proud mom to Ava (age 8) and Max (age 6), and enjoys volunteering for a variety of organizations including the PTO at their school, Hadassah, Girl Scouts and her college sorority, Alpha Epsilon Phi. As the daughter of a Holocaust survivor, she is glad to help review essays for the Eleanor J Marks Holocaust Essay Contest and ensure that future generations never forget.

Joe Gruen works and lives in Sacramento, CA. He is a a full-time accounting student at American River College and works part time teaching Hebrew and Judaica at B'nai Israel Congregation.

EricaCassman is a California State credentialed teacher. She taught at the elementary school level for ten years in Los Angeles before starting her family and moving to Sacramento. She is currently staying at home with her 3 year old daughter Lilah and 1 year old son Gavin. Since moving to Northern California Erica has become an active member in the Jewish community. Erica's educational background includes a Bachelor of Arts in Liberal Studies with a Concentration in Art and a Master's degree in Educational Administration, both from California State University, Northridge.

PAUL GRUENINGER: DISOBEDIENCE FOR THE SAKE OF LIVES

Dani Wiesenthal, Co-winner

Would you ever think a police officer would go against his command? Well, Paul Grueninger did, just to save the lives of thousands of Jews. "It was basically a question of saving human lives threatened with death," said Grueninger. "How could I then seriously consider bureaucratic schemes and calculations?" Some may believe he went too far since he disobeyed his orders, but others believe he is a hero to the Jewish people. However, I want you to think if performing a life-saving mitzvah in defiance of authority is crossing the line. Although he risked his job, reputation, and possibly his life, Grueninger is now recognized as a "righteous gentile" for his sacrifices.

Grueninger's Backstory

Paul Grueninger was born on October 27, 1891 in St. Gallen, Switzerland. He was a very enthusiastic lover of football as a child and played for the community team SC Brühl. Later, Paul assisted in winning the team's one and only Swiss Championship in the 1914-1915 season. Paul later decided to serve during World War I and after serving his time, settled on joining the police department. Paul was an excellent officer and rose to the top of the ranks in his hometown of St. Gallen. During the time of his position of Police Captain, the Nazis had taken over Austria, the neighboring country, in 1938. The Austrian Jews were now in the same position as the German Jews, both suffering from persecution and violence. Passports belonging to Jews were now stamped with a "J" to make sure no Austrian Jews could get through to Switzerland. The Swiss government instructed Grueninger to send the Jewish refugees back to Austria if they were trying to cross over.

Now that Austrian Jews couldn't immigrate to Switzerland, many took the risk of crossing the border illegally in fear for their lives. The journey was far from easy. Refugees captured in St. Gallen while trying to escape were brought to Grueninger cold, hungry, and upset about having to leave their whole life behind them. As more and more tried to reach freedom, the 47-year-old captain was faced with one of the hardest decisions of his life: reject thousands of innocent Jewish immigrants and return them to their home of anti-Semitism or disregard clear directions and face the punishment for the sake of Judaism. He chose to help save the lives of those who deserved to escape a life of pain, suffering, and potentially death.

In order to help the refugees, Grueninger had to alter their passports, stating that they had reached Switzerland *before* given instruction to exclude them. This act of kindness enabled the Austrians to be treated as legal citizens, being escorted to the Diepoldsau Camp. There they awaited their warrants to temporarily stay in Switzerland or depart to their final destination of freedom. The life-saving, law-breaking policeman turned in his false reports about the amount of arrivals and the status of the escapees around his area, trying his best to delay any efforts to trace any Austrians who were known to have illegally entered Switzerland. Grueninger even paid for needy refugees' winter clothes since they were forced to leave everything behind.

In 1939, the Germans immediately informed the Swiss jurisdiction of Grueninger's untruthful status report and—unfortunately for Grueninger—had him fired from the police force. His benefits were suspended and he went to court on charges of illegally permitting the entry of 3,600 Jews into Switzerland and changing their registration forms. The prosecutor included additional charges for assisting individual Jews by protecting them from discovery, helping them deposit their valuables, and more. Grueninger's trial opened in January of 1939 and was extended throughout the course of two years. In March of 1941, the court found him guilty of violation of duty. His retirement profits were forfeited, he was fined, and he had to pay the trial costs. Although the court did recognize his charitable actions, they still found that nevertheless, as a state employee, it was his duty to follow his instructions.

Shunned and forgotten, Grueninger lived for the rest of his life in difficult circumstances. Despite the difficulties, he never regretted his action on behalf of the Jews. In 1954, he explained that he would rather give the Jewish people their lives over death. He could never give in to the Swiss government's orders. In December of 1970, the Swiss government sent the ex-police officer a somewhat reserved letter of apology, but did not go as far as reopening his case and giving back his retirement savings. Only after his death were there efforts to rehabilitate him. The Swiss Council rejected the first attempt, and only as late as 1995, the Swiss federal government finally abolished Grueninger's sentence. In 1971, a year before his death, Yad Vashem bestowed the—rightfully deserved—title of Righteous Among the Nations on Paul Grueninger.

Years later, Paul Grueninger is still recognized and beloved to the Jewish population. Without him, 3,600 Jewish Austrians would be 6 feet under. That means fewer Jews to tell his story, fewer Jews to tell their story, and fewer Jews in general. Would you rather have had a 47-year-old policeman stick to his duty and obey his command? Or, that same 47-year-old policeman makes the righteous choice of straying from his strict instructions and saving over 3,000 Jews? In this case, rebelling for the sake of lives was the better choice.

DENMARK RALLIED TOGETHER: A NATION OF HEROES THAT SAVED THEIR JEWISH NEIGHBORS IN THE HOLOCAUST

Morgan Folger

On September 29th, 1943, just a few days before Rosh Hashanah, the Jewish New Year, Leo Goldberger's life was turned upside down. Leo was a young Jewish boy, and lived in Denmark with his family during the beginning of the Nazi occupation in that country. He had been lucky so far—the Nazis had not yet acted on any major plans to fulfill martial law, and uproot him from his life—but all that was about to change. Leo's family received warning that the **Nazis were planning to capture all the Jews in Denmark in** just a few days. They had very little time to formulate an escape plan or decide what to take with them in their race for safety. Leo's family voyaged to Sweden, where they lived in safety until the end of the Nazi occupation. Leo's story is not particularly unique. Thousands of Jews like him left Denmark to find safety in Sweden, and thousands managed to survive. Their escape, however, would have been impossible were it not for the generosity of the Danish people. At every stop along the way to Sweden, Leo and the thousands like him were met with help from Danish people, many of them strangers. While atrocities occurred during the Holocaust all over Europe, the whole nation of Denmark rallied together in an ultimate expression of humanity by opening their homes, offering passage to safety, and logistically planning the transportation of thousands of refugees, to ensure the safety of their Jewish neighbors.

Unlike other European countries at the time, Denmark actively and collectively worked against Nazi brutality towards Jews, so much so that the entire country of Denmark is honored by Yad Vashem with the title of Righteous Among Nations (Weiss and Brachman). The quest to safety in Sweden that the Jewish people like Leo took was along what would later be called the Danish underground. The Underground became a necessity when, in Berlin, the Nazis decided that on October 1st, Rosh Hashanah Eve, "...the Gestapo would raid Jewish homes and seize the occupants," and those captured would be transported to Tereisendstadt, a Nazi concentration camp (Weiss and Brachman). This information was passed on to the Danish people by Georg F. Duckwitz, a Nazi official who empathized with the Danish resistance movement. Duckwitz shared the details of the Nazi raid with "friends, business acquaintances, and strangers wanting to help" (Holmskov Schluter). Duckwitz risked his life by sharing sensitive Nazi information to anyone who would listen, and thousands of Jews were saved because of his risk. The news of the raid spread exponentially, and Jews all over the country were advised to leave their homes by that day to save their families. In response to the news, a "part organized, part spontaneous rescue action was mounted" (Vogelsang and Larsen). The Danes worked to organize an effort to smuggle the Jews to safety in Sweden, which was neutral ("Rescue in Denmark"). They knew it would be difficult, and, even knowing that they were risking their lives, the Danish people refused to let the Jews of Denmark be transported to their death. Every single Dane was encouraged to participate in the liberation plan; church congregants were urged by their ministers to assist their Jewish neighbors, and even universities closed the week of Rosh Hashanah so that all students could participate in the rescue plan (Dolgin). The executed journey itself was difficult. Refugees were carried across the small channel of water between Denmark and Sweden in large fishing boats, rowboats, or even kayaks. Some were placed in freight cars that were brought to Sweden on ferries (Holmskov Schluter). All along the way, smugglers had to be wary of German officials lurking on the waters to snatch anyone guilty of smuggling. The Danish people navigated through the channel, and situated themselves at checkpoints to ensure the exiled made it to Sweden safely. Approximately 7,200 Danish Jews and 680 non-Jewish family members successfully journeyed to Sweden this way ("Rescue in Denmark"). Because of this, when, on Friday night, the Nazis raided Jewish homes, they found them empty (Weiss and Brachman). Every single traveller along the Danish underground owed their freedom to the Danish men and women who organized the mission, navigated the fugitives to safety, and opened up their homes as safe houses from the Nazis.

The journey by sea to Sweden was only half of the voyage for Jewish refugees. Jews traveling the underground had to first make it to the coast, but they were uprooted from their homes, and had no where familiar to go in their escape where they would be safe. Fortunately for them, Danes welcomed escapees into their homes with open arms, and promised their safety. Gilda Valentiner, a Danish teacher and secret member of the Resistance, was dedicated to providing refuge for the Jewish children that were uprooted. In trying to escape, many families were forced to split up. In the chaos and danger of the journey, it was thought that "separate hiding places for individual members of the nuclear family" was the safest mode of transport (Grimshy and Goldberger). Because of this, many children had to be separated from their parents. Gilda would approach families that she knew were in danger and offer to keep their children safe. She would protect the children in her home, while finding a way of passage for them to Sweden. Moritz Scheftelowitz testified to Gilda's operation. He remembers that Gilda had taken in his sisters, Dora and Rita, and arranged for their passage to Sweden ("Valentiner Family"). Gilda showed nothing but respect for the children she took in. For example, when Gilda learned that some of the children were strictly observant of their religion, and were only able to eat the bread that was offered to them, she "brought them new dishes and food" that they could eat ("Valentiner Family"). Gilda played a crucial role in the lives of many Jewish children, but despite this, she remains modest. On July 28th, Gilda was recognized as one of the Righteous Among the Nations by Yad Vashem, the highest title offered to Holocaust heroes, but when asked about her extraordinary efforts, she only replied, "I only did what many Danes did, nothing special. We thought it perfectly natural to help people in mortal trouble" ("Valentiner Family"). After Gilda provided refuge and organized the transport of those they saved, they were in the hands of the many Danes who tasked themselves with navigating through the waters to Sweden.

Perhaps, while Gilda's children made their way to Sweden, they crossed paths with Knud Christiansen, a prominent Danish athlete and Holocaust hero. In 1936, Knud had competed in the Berlin Olympics as a rower for Denmark, where he lived and operated his business manufacturing leather (Dolgin). The leather industry of Denmark at the time was mostly operated by Jewish businessmen, and so, in his business, Knud came to know and be close with many Jews. After the occupation of Denmark, Knud joined the Danish Resistance, and worked to help his Jewish neighbors find safety. Knud helped large groups of Jews to churches, farmhouses, city apartments, and any other available shelter to keep them safe from arrest (Dolgin). From their, the refugees were carried by sea to Sweden. In addition to finding safeguards for Jews, Knud helped many across the channel. Knud brought Max Rawitscher, for whom he and his wife had opened up their home to, to Sweden from the shores of Denmark ("Christiansen Family"). Knud did this for various groups of Jews. He saved not only his close personal friends, but also "complete strangers" from Nazi arrest by going above and beyond for every single life (Dolgin). When Knud found out about the upcoming raid, he had warned the Philipson brothers, blacksmiths he had met, to go to his house instead of going home that night. Unfortunately, they did not believe him and went home anyway, where they were captured and thrown in a detention center. Knud refused to give up on them, and, by bribing officials and using his status as an Olympic athlete, he managed to have them freed ("Christiansen Family"). Like Gilda Valentiner, Knud was extremely modest about his heroism on the Danish underground. When asked about his work, he did not praise himself for getting involved and saving lives, but instead said, "It was something that needed to be done" (Dolgin). Much of the work Knud Christiansen and countless like him had done was improvised, however some, like Knud Dyby, helped to disseminate information and organize the transportation of refugees so that the journey went safely.

When, during German occupation, the Nazi flag was hoisted atop Amalienborg Castle, King Christian X was in an outrage, and demanded that the Denmark flag be put back in its original position over the castle. Knud Dyby was on of the Denmark soldiers who removed the Nazi flag ("Knud Dyby: Denmark"). Thus began Dyby's efforts to resist the Nazi occupation. After his military service, Dyby became an officer in the Copenhagen national police force , and this position in the police force gave him the perfect opportunity to play a key role in the Danish underground ("Knud Dyby"). As an officer, Dyby gained access to vital information that benefitted the Resistance considerably. He knew the patrol routes of the German navy, and was able to distinguish the "best sea lanes between Denmark and Sweeden" ("Knud Dyby: Denmark"). Dyby shared his knowledge with members of the underground to use in their travels to Sweden. Because of the information Dyby shared, many more Jews made it to Sweden without detection than would have been possible—but his work did not end with that. Dyby played a key role in the organization of the underground. He was the lead in convincing and mobilizing countless commercial fishermen to participate in the underground ("Knud Dyby"). These fisherman smuggled Jews to Sweden on their ships, using the information Dyby gave them about where to navigate. On land, he "organized the city's taxi drivers" to transport Jews secretly to the Denmark coast, and even used his position as an officer to arrange the use of "state police cars" to assist in the transfer ("Knud Dyby"). Because of Knud's leadership, "close to 7,000" people were saved from the Nazi regime ("Knud Dyby").

Gilda Valentiner, Knud Christiansen, Knud Dyby, and the multitude of heroes for whom their stories represent risked their futures and lives for the Jewish people of Denmark, many of whom they had never met. How they managed to save so many is relatively simple: through the Danish underground. But why they did it is a completely different debate. The decision to save the Jewish people was a collective one. Knud Christiansen remembers, "The whole time people helped one another. People took risks they weren't normally take" (Dolgin). Because the fight against the Nazis was communal, the motivation for their efforts lies in the common Danish attitudes toward Jews at the time of the occupation. Before the Nazi's rose to power, Jewish Denmark citizens lived with relative ease—"for centuries, Denmark's Jewish community lived in tranquility, without discrimination or sense of alienation," and they were "protected like every citizen under law" (Weiss and Brachman). Such a long period of time without ethnic struggle led to a culture of acceptance and tolerance. Jews were not isolated, or thought of as others in Denmark. Peter Ilsoe, a member of the Danish resistance said, "We felt that the Jews were Danes like us, and we knew we had to help them" (Weiss and Brachman). After years of not being singled out for being Jewish, the "Jew" was no longer a significant part of semitic Danish identity in society. This created a communal feeling between Danes and Jewish Danes. They were able to realize that they were all citizens of Denmark. Rabbi Ben Melchoir recalls his life in Denmark, and says, "The Danes consider us to be Danes. No one thought twice about the fact that I was Jewish" (Weiss and Brachman). The people of Denmark stood up to save their Jewish neighbors because they were their neighbors. They decided that it was more important to save their fellow Dane than to remain in silence, in safety, in immorality. For this reason Denmark was a shining example of humanity for the rest of the pitch-black, Nazi dominated Europe.

When the Nazis left Denmark, Leo Goldberger 's family left Sweden and returned to their homeland. Other European were racked by Nazi occupation, and many Jews who returned to their home countries would find a mere skeleton of their previous life. Leo and his family, however, were met with "a universal celebration of welcome" (Grimsby and Goldberger). The family was able to joyously return to their pre-Holocaust lives thanks to their Danish neighbors, who saw to it that their home and workplace was cared for and remained exactly as it was left, and the Great Synogogue of Copenhagen, which his family had previously attended, was returned to its previous condition without delay. Through the dark abyss that was Nazi occupation, the Danish people managed to not only preserve the pieces of their Jewish neighbors' lives, but also to maintain their humanity. They saved thousands of Jews from detainment, and never lost hope for those that slipped through the cracks. In 1944, a "Danish delegation" was allowed to visit the Danes that had been captured, and eventually officials of Denmark accomplished the prisoner's deportation to the unhostile Sweden (Vogelsang and Larsen). Of the 500 that were deported, 450 survived (Rescue in Denmark). Today, Denmark is considered the only occupied country to outwardly combat the Nazi regime.The Dane's efforts were not perfectly successful, unfortunately, but even with the loss of around one hundred Danish Jews, Denmark acquired the "highest survival rate in Europe during World War II," and the entire nation is considered by Yad Vashem to be Righteous Among the Nations (Vogelsang and Larsen).

Works Cited

"Christiansen FAMILY." The Righteous Among Nations. Yad Vashem, n.d. Web. 28 Feb. 2015.

Dolgin, Robyn. "Danish Hero: One Rosh Hashanah Burns Bright in Holocaust." JewishPost.com. Jewish Post, n.d. Web. 28 Feb. 2015.

"Gerda Valentiner." "Their Fate Will Be My Fate Too.." Yad Vashem, n.d. Web. 28 Feb. 2015.

Grimsby, Liv, and Leo Goldberger. " Memory and Tragedy: The Life of a Young Danish Jew during WWII." Thanks to Scandinavia. Thanks to Scandinavia, 12 June 2012. Web. 28 Feb. 2015.

Holmskov Schluter, Hans. "Danish Resistance during the Holocaust." www.HolocaustResearchProject.org. Holocaust Research Project, 2007. Web. 28 Feb. 2015.

"Knud Dyby." Knud Dyby. Humboldt University, n.d. Web. 28 Feb. 2015.

"Knud Dyby: Denmark." The Jewish Foundation for the Righteous. The Jewish Foundation for the Righteous, n.d. Web. 28 Feb. 2015.

"Rescue in Denmark." United States Holocaust Memorial Museum. United States Holocaust Memorial Council, n.d. Web. 26 Feb. 2015.

Vogelsang, Peter, and Brian B.M. Larsen. "The Fate of the Danish Jews." The Danish Center for Holocaust and and Genocide Studies, 2002. Web. 28 Feb. 2015.

Weiss, Ruchama, and Levi Brachman. "'Danes Saw Us as Friends, Neighbors, Not as Jews'" Ynet. Yedioth Internet, 03 May 2006. Web. 28 Feb. 2015.

"Valentiner Family." The Righteous Among Nations. Yad Vashem, n.d. Web. 28 Feb. 20

WERNER THEODORE "BILL" BARAZETTI - HERO OF THE HOLOCAUST

Zev Steinberg, Co-winner

The Holocaust was a very important event in history spanning from 1933, when Adolf Hitler came to power, to 1945, when the allied forces defeated the Nazis in World War II. Holocaust means "sacrifice by fire" in Greek. The Nazis believed that Germans were "superior" to Jews and other minorities, which they thought were a threat to the Germans. For instance, some of the reasons why Hitler hated the Jews was because almost half of the German private banks were owned by Jews, and most stockbrokers were Jews. Hitler also blamed the Jews for losing World War I because of the occasion when three Germans went to surrender, two were Jews. About 11 million people were killed during the Holocaust: 1.1 million children and 6 million Jews. The rest were gypsies, gays and lesbians, mentally ill and disabled persons, and others. Although there were many horrible people, there were still great heroes out there. This essay is about one of those heroes: Werner Theodore "Bill" Barazetti.

Werner Barazetti was the son of a Swiss professor of French. It was when studying law at Hamburg University that he saw Nazis beat Jewish socialist and communist students and academics in the university precinct. He was determined to help those in need or discriminated against by the Nazis. During this time a co-worker of his named Anna was sending pictures of Nazi training camps and labor camps to the press in London. Anna was eventually detected in this work, but snuck over the Czech border near her home. When Werner tried to escape, using the same route as Anna, the secret police of Germany called the Gestapo found him, beat him, and left him on the route to die. He was later found by Anna, and she took him home and nursed him back to full health. They ended up marrying each other.

During the war Werner Barazetti helped with the Kindertransport in Prague. The Kindertransport saved children from Germany, Austria, Poland, and Czechoslovakia and sent them to England. Werner organized the trains and interviewed the families of the children. He worked with Nicholas Winton, a British stockbroker, and sent him the pictures and details of each child. Nicholas Winton was in England finding the families that the children would go to when they arrived in England. Since English visas were hard to get in time, Werner got a Jewish printer in Prague to make fake papers to show the German authorities. Between 1938 and 1939, around 10,000 refugee children had arrived in England.

Werner went to Britain in August 1939. There, he changed his name to "Bill" because Werner in German means William, and a common nickname for William is "Bill." In Britain he worked for a war office unit that interrogated captured German pilots. After the war ended he got a job with the United Nations helping to establish government organizations in newly independent countries. In 1953 he became a British citizen.

During this time his story was unknown to the rest of the world. But, in 1989, he started up a conversation with an Israeli visitor who had a German accent. Werner asked the Israeli visitor why he had a German accent. The Israeli said it was because he had come to England on a Kindertransport from Berlin many years ago. Werner said he knew a little about that because he had some involvement with the transport of children from Prague. "But we had to drag the story out of him. He did not want to talk about his experiences," says Hugo Marom, another Czech Kindertransport evacuee. Their conversation was reported to another Israeli friend who had come on a Prague train as a ten year old. No one really recognized the Italian sounding name, but with some effort they finally tracked down Werner Barazetti through Nicholas Winton's diaries. The diaries are kept at the Jerusalem Holocaust memorial institute known as Yad Vashem. In 1993 Yad Vashem honored Werner Barazetti as a Righteous among the Gentiles. The Righteous Among The Gentiles recognizes people that played a big role in any part of the Holocaust. Werner died seven years later on September 24, 2000.

Some people dispute Werner Barazetti's involvement with the Kindertransport. William Chadwick wrote a book called "The Rescue of the Prague Refugees." In Chadwick's book he argues lots of points, such as, "Why did Werner not say anything until many years after the event?" This argument is pointless, Nicholas Winton mentions Werner in his diaries. I think Werner wanted to live in the present, not the past. So even though there may be a dispute about the number of children he saved — even if he did not save 669 children — he still played a big role in the Kindertransport.

Even though disputed by some, Werner Barazetti is a huge hero because he assisted in the Kindertransport. I personally believe that even if he only saved one child, he would still be a hero. Imagine being in the Holocaust and how scary that would be to stand up to the Nazis like that. To me, one child is as important as 669. All that matters is that he had the heart to save the children and was brave enough to do all of this. It would be a much better world if more people like Werner could stand up to everyday threats. Despite the danger of being killed by Nazis, Werner Barazetti stood up for what he believed in. I think that is what makes a truc hero.

Shalom School, Sacramento, CA

Leslie Kupperstein

Judaica Teacher

Melinda Ott, Teacher

THE MAN WHO EXCEEDED HIS JOB

Aaron Ichel

 Sebastian Steiger was more than just an ordinary teacher. He was a Swiss teacher during World War II who had studied at the University of Zurich and had dedicated his life to education. In 1942, he started hearing about children trying to cross the border into Switzerland to escape the Nazis, and decided he wanted to help in those efforts. So he trusted himself and put his heart in to protecting and improving the lives of those children who were traumatized by the war---both Jewish and gentile alike. This included taking care of their physical, emotional, and educational needs. He became a kind of children's "nurse" at La Hille Castle in southern France. While there, he helped shelter and hide those children who were in danger of being seized and deported by the local police or German authorities. Sebastian Steiger risked his life and reputation to ensure that the children were kept safe and tried to make life as normal as possible for them. He risked his life and reputation to ensure that the children were kept safe and tried to make life as normal as possible for all of them.

Sebastian Steiger decided to take on a bigger role in the lives of his students than that of an educator. Since he brought a medicine pack with him from Switzerland, he was able to help nurse them when they were sick. When the Gendarmes came to the Castle, his job was to hide the kids in the onion loft. Since the onion loft didn't have enough room, the older kids had to hide in a hut they built near the brooke. At night, he went to check in on the older kids and give them food. In spite of all the raids, Steiger tried as hard as he could to make the children happy. During Christmas, he bought a Christmas tree and they had a complete celebration with caroling. Despite all that, the children were still not comfortable since food was scarce and they were suffering from malnutrition. Sebastian himself even got jaundice and nearly died. He was a source of great comfort and help. He offered the children love, kindness, and the care of an adult which they needed so badly. Nevertheless, many of the kids hadn't had any news of their parents in a very long time so they were very worried and hard to comfort.

Sebastian Steiger was courageous and determined. He wasn't about to let German police intimidate him. One time when Sebastian was going shopping for pencils and paper, a German policeman approached him. The policeman asked him what he was doing, since according to the local law, he was not supposed to leave the area of La Hille. Sebastian then explained that he was a teacher at a school and was out shopping for pencils and paper. The policeman let him go, but said that he plans to further investigate Mr. Steiger. He said that Sebastian should expect to be called upon within a week. Steiger was not easily intimidated by this situation and continued his job as a teacher. This event was probably quite scary but it did not change Sebastian Steiger's commitment to help the children.

One summer day, after the raids of the Gendarmes stopped, Sebastian and some other colleagues wanted to return to their home in Switzerland. The problem was that the Gendarmes would not let people cross the border without the visas and the issuing of those took quite some time. Finally at the end of October 1944, he decided he would return to his homeland even though he did not have the necessary documents. As soon as he told the children about his plan, they became very sad. The little kids cried and begged r him not to go, but his decision to go back was final. Steiger wrote in his book: "With a sudden sadness in my heart, I took my leave of La Hille Castle and the children while it was still dark. When I reached the brooke, I looked back and saw the beautiful castle." Since the trains weren't running, he had no choice but to walk the whole way. The trip was long and strenuous. It took six whole days and nights. When he finally reached the border, he learned from the Swiss Red Cross that it would be nearly impossible to cross the border without a visa. He had no choice but to pick up work with the Red Cross Relief Column near the border. Finally, in the middle of the winter, Steiger decided to cross the border into his native country. His attempt was successful although on his way to Geneva, he was picked up by a border patrol that said that anybody who crossed the border without a visa would be taken as a refugee. Since he had no visa, they took him to the Claparde refugee camp in Geneva. After being questioned, he was released.

Before the war ended, sadly, La Hille Castle shut down and the children met a very sad fate. Twelve of them were deported and eleven did not survive. Twenty one children attempted to flee to Switzerland or Spain. Five were picked up at the Swiss-French border, and four of them had to return to France. The four children who were headed to Spain were caught trying to cross the border. One of the children, named Rosa Goldmark, was so distraught that she ended up at a mental institution where she passed away. Six children reached Palestine with the help of an American-Jewish refugee organization. Two went on to the United States.

After World War II, Sebastian Steiger became a great supporter of Israel. In 1990, one of the children rescued by him started the process of recognizing him as a Righteous of the Nations. Sebastian Steiger was awarded this recognition in 1993. Sebastian Steiger decided to follow his heart and continued to help children who suffered mentally and physically from effects of the war. Sebastian Steiger's, compassion and acts of courage as he thought of others and their well-being meant the difference in between life and death for several survivors. In gratitude for his selfless acts of kindness, Sebastian Steiger was awarded the status and recognition of a Righteous among the Nations in 1993 when he was still alive at a ceremony in Basle, Switzerland. His name is included with the names of many other heroes recognized by Yad VaShem.

RENEE FARNY

Aileen Lawrence

I, Renee Farny am sitting in a cart on a train on the way to a concentration camp. I think of how I ended up here. The train suddenly stopped. I'm here, that last place I will ever step foot on. I am walking out felling a cold gush of wind against my face. I am thinking of my friends. Martha Bouvard who was my co-worker at the Folletts Lights. She did the laundry. Leon Balland who lived next door to us. Germiane Homel, director of the fire dancers. And, Marcel Dubois and Rosli Naef, both who lead La Hille, a children's home sponsored by the Swiss Red Cross. I can't believe all they have done for me, and all we have done for the children whom we saved. I am arriving now at the barracks I will be staying at and see many ill faces all around. I feel so sorry for the children here. No one deserves this sick treatment.

I just sat down on my old, cold and dusty cot and continue to think about all the adventures I have been through. It all started in 1941 when the Swiss Red Cross took charge of our children's home, Les Feux Follets, in a territory of France, Haute-Savie. The home was for children to come to if they were traumatized by the war or needed a place to feel safe. Germaine

Hommel was the manager. In 1942 after the German troops occupied the southern part of France a lot of children, mostly from Austria and Germany came to us. They all had their own story to tell, some similar to others but still all the stories were unique. In September 1943 Rosli Nael was dismissed from her position as the principal of La Hille after the authorities found out that she was assisting in smuggling Jewish children to safety. They said it was for lack of discipline, that made a few of us chuckle but we were sad that she had to leave. I have so many good memories.

I have decided to lay down and have noticed the ceiling which has a few holes in it. Again many memories are flowing into my mind. I am remembering the time we smuggled the children across the Swiss border by saying we were going on a hike along with Leon Balland. He would wait until the border control guards were out of sight and have the children quickly cross over to safety. There was also the time that Rosli and I showed a group of four children, Margot Kern, Regina Rosenblatt, Peter Slaz and Jocques Rogh a secret escape route. We gave them money and told them this was where they needed to go to escape when the Germans came. We also hid the children who were sixteen under the onion sellers. It was an amazing time. I've only heard that Jacques Roth was safe, I'm still not sure about the others. They all deserve to be safe and start a new life that won't be scary or traumatizing.

I wonder what all the children are doing now that I'm here. I hope they are all safe. Many of them have crossed the border once the patrol officers walked by. I know they are on the other side. When they crossed the border they seemed to be safe and sound. Some of the children would wisely find their way back to us. I still remember when we decided to make Germaine Homel the Director of the Fire Dancers, but then in August of 1942 most of the Fire Dancers were arrested. After that we still had many young Jews come to us. They would come in from Saint Cergues in small groups of three or four. These children, so innocent. Sadly the Swiss authorities learned of our activities and many of my friends were fired but me, I ended up here. I think I need to rest my eye for just a little while.

Now that I am looking around I'm remembering when Germaine Homel agreed to make the Fire Dancers save the Jewish children and our sponsors, the Swiss Red Cross, had no idea what we were doing. I could have never imagined what it would have been like if the Germans had found out that we were doing this or if we hadn't decided to hide the Jewish children.

32

They probably would have all been sent here. I have now noticed my surroundings, there are elderly women in here who look as if they were beaten. The children look starved and their mothers look lethargic. I assume they are thinking of giving up. Our beds most likely have blood stains on them and the walls are light brown and all torn up. There is no heat in here and probably this place is never heated. There are two windows that have bars on them but why, we have no place to go.

I think I will lay back down and quietly start up at the holes in the roof and think about all the wonderful children I have saved. I haven't even known that until now. I was born in 1919 and who knows maybe today is the day I will die. I am happy I have had all I could. I will keep this this smile and drift asleep.

HENRY AND ELLEN THOMSEN AND THE DANISH UNDERGROUND

Aviva Spector

In April 9, 1940 Denmark surrendered to the mighty army of Germany. The Danish military was too weak to withstand the Germans and the king of Denmark wanted to prevent unnecessary loss of life. German diplomats were allowed to keep their positions in Denmark and the Nazis left the Jews in peace. In the summer of 1943, when the Germans noticed that the Danish people were trying to organize themselves against the Nazis things got tough. Life for Danish Jews was turned upside down once the Germans imposed martial law in Denmark. When Jews had to wear the yellow star, the king of Denmark, Christian X wore the star himself and asked all of the Danish citizens to wear it as well. This showed the Danes' support toward the Jews.

It is estimated that about 7,700 Jews lived in Denmark at this time. The Germans' plan was to deport all of the Danish Jews on one night, the night of October 1, 1943. Luckily for the Jews, this important secret leaked out. Just a few days before the plan was about to be executed, an important person, working at the German embassy- Georg Ferdinand Duckwitz- shared this information with Danish friends of his. The Jewish community and the Danish underground resistance were immediately notified. All over Denmark,

Jews were warned by rabbis about the Nazi plan. This Rosh Hashanah was a very different and scary one. The Jews were advised to leave their homes and hide. The heroes of the Danish underground had a huge role in helping Jews survive these terrible times.

Two Danish citizens, Henry and Ellen Thomsen started the Thomsen group within the Danish underground. The Thomsen group was an underground cell within the Danish resistance that helped Jews get to Sweden. While Denmark was under Nazi occupation, Sweden was not it was still free. The Thomsen group included many people who came from different walks of life, including teachers, businessmen, doctors, and housewives. Captains of fishing vessels were also involved in the Thomsen group and they were very important. There is a narrow sea channel separating Denmark from Sweden. Fishing boats are always out there on the water. The plan, that was executed over and over again, was that Jews will come to the area close to the Danish coast. People in that area hid them until they were able to get on a boat that would take them across the sea. Once on the other side, in Sweden, they were free because Sweden was a neutral country. Henry and Ellen Thomsen ran the Snekkersten Inn near the city of Elsinore. Henry had been a sea captain for the past 20 years. It is estimated that about 1,000 Jews fled Denmark through the Snekkersten Inn and made it to Sweden thanks to the Thomsen group and additional groups of the resistance working out of that area.

The Thomsen group encountered many challenges while the Holocaust was happening. Although the Thomsen group helped many Jews, some were caught and sent to the Theresienstadt camp in Bohemia. The Theresienstadt camp was not as bad as some of the other concentration camps but it was still a camp. Theresienstadt was not as harsh as some of the other camps, because it was used as a model camp for the Nazis. They would show it off to organizations such as the Red Cross, demonstrating that German camps were great. In addition, special rules applied to Danish Jews thanks to the strong bonds between the Jews and their fellow Danes. For example, the Danish Jews who were deported to Theresienstadt were allowed to receive packages from the Danish Red Cross. These packages could contain food and clothing. It is probably thanks to these packages that the Danish Jews did not starve to death. As the Thomsen group faced the challenge of hiding the Jews until they were out of Denmark they also faced another challenge. It was the challenge of safely crossing the sea at times that it was illegal to take boats out. Many members of the Thomsen group risked being sent to jail as they were trying to get the Jews safely to Sweden by boat. One of the members of the Thomsen group was Dr. Jorgen Gersfelt. He had trouble with driving and ran into many dramatic situations while on the road. One in which he used up all the gas in is car but luckily he was able to easily purchase more.

One of the Jewish fugitives was named Torben L. Meyer. They arrived on September 3 and were greeted very kindly upon landing. The family who greeted Torben made sure they were comfortable and cozy. Torben could not go to bed without having a cup of coffee, a cheese sandwich, and some cookies from the family. Another Jewish fugitive was Rachel Posin who was born in 1920 and arrived in Denmark in 1938. Rachel was on a train with her aunt, cousin and his wife, their son, and two Jewish friends. As Rachel says, "On the train Bertha and I were sitting opposite a man reading the *Berlingske Tidende* newspaper. He was watching us over the paper and we became nervous." When Rachel and Bertha got off the train the man handed them a card and it turned out that he was handing out cards to Jews with an address where they could get help. This man was part of the Thomsen group and like many others in the movement, he helped save another life. Many others, like Torben and Rachel, were saved by the Thomsen group.

Eventually the Gestapo caught up with Henry and Ellen. It was when the Gestapo started raiding hotels, boarding houses, and inns that things went from bad to worse. Many Jews were arrested because of this and the group started using private lodgings as hiding places. Although the Gestapo was ruthless, Henry was smart and often tricked the Gestapo. The Gestapo would come in trying to befriend Henry and he would play along, pretending to be one of them. He promised to let them know if any Jews came in to his inn. Henry had already sent the Jews to private lodgings in hope that they would not be caught in his inn. The Gestapo interrogated Henry yet he continued to be active in the Resistance. In August 1944 Henry was arrested with six other Snekkersten residents. He was sent to the Neuengamme camp in Germany where he sadly died of maltreatment four months after his arrest. He was 38 years old. In honor of Henry Thomsen and his efforts to save the lives of so many people, despite such great danger a monument of Henry was erected in his favorite place, the Snekkersten inn.

Henry was survived by his wife Ellen. Ellen made it through the war and the story of their self-sacrifice and bravery wash shared with Yad Vashem. In 1968 Ellen Margrethe Thomsen was invited by Yad Vashem to come to Israel. Yad Vashem awarded her and her husband, Henry Christian Thomsen, the title of "Righteous of the Nations". Ellen planted a tree in the Avenue of the Righteous Yad Vashen in Jerusalem.

MARCEL PASCHE AND THE PERVERSENESS OF NAZISM

Dusty Wright

In 1912 a hero was born. His name was Marcel Pasche. Marcel Pasche was a righteous gentile, who during World War II, helped the Jews avoid being taken to the concentration camps. If it were not for Marcel Pasche and his friend, Friedrich Gunther, some Jews may not have made it to safety.

Marcel Pasche was born in 1912 in the German speaking city, Berne, located in Switzerland. However, he was raised in a French speaking, more western part of the country. When he finished his school years, Marcel joined the Swiss Army, around the time social uprisings were occurring in Geneva. When his service was over, Marcel decided to study theology. He was first a student at the University of Lausanne, but in 1934 he transferred to the University of Basle. While studying there, he grew a strong dislike towards the extremist right wing ideology that was ascending. In other words, he was an anti-Nazi.

After Marcel's graduation, he was assigned to a church in Basle where he helped Pastor Pierre Bosc. Marcel then married a young woman named Mady Choffat. The couple was posted to Roubaix, near the Belgian border. It was here, on May 10, 1940, that they experienced a terrifying intrusion by the Nazi German Wehrmacht. This means that the Nazis had invaded and they were afraid.

The invasion of France by the Nazis preceded a literal wave of refugees, mostly Jews. Marcel and his wife helped where they could, but it wouldn't be long until they felt the need to flee as well. Once inside a small Peugeot, a type of car, the young couple barely made it out alive because they were escaping the German Wehrmacht that was invading. Soon after, they found refuge at Pastor Bosc's summer home. Marcel later became a pastor himself, at a reform church. He did this because a church is a place of refuge and he wanted to calm civilians.

When Marcel went to the Administrations Building of La Bourse, he showed his ID to the guard, who found common ground, revealing that he was a pastor as well. He then identified himself as Friedrich Gunther. This was the opening of a conversation that would change both of their lives. Friedrich was not a typical soldier. Actually, he was consistently fighting the Nazification of Catholic Churches. He was an interpreter, and because of his confidence, he was an important asset of his people. Marcel then became one of Friedrich's helpers.

One day, Marcel got into a rather embarrassing situation. Three young French people had escaped from their jobs in a German labor camp. Due to the fact that they were fugitives, they could not get another job. Gunther knew of a soldier who ran the ammunition dumps located at Saint-Armand-les-Eaux. The man could take care of three fugitives, giving them food cards and identification papers that said they were "Heavy Laborers". This made sure the three French fugitives avoided investigation.

Friedrich's assistance was especially important in the case of raids towards Jewish refugees. When he became aware that a raid was planned to happen early the next morning, he immediately notified the pastor. Realizing the pastor was not home, Friedrich took it upon himself to notify multiple people who would be raided using a telephone at the concierge's booth, impersonating a "High Official of The Oberfeld Kommandatur," a trick which he succeeded to achieve in multiple instances. Witnesses verified that a certain Mr. Rabinowitsch was saved as an effect.

Friedrich introduced Marcel to many people who could be trusted, like himself. Marcel once helped a young girl being sentenced to a year in prison because of her "insolence". When Marcel intervened, the sentence was reduced to only three months. None of these things would have been possible if Friedrich Gunther never made friends with Marcel Pasche.

In 1992, the mayor of Roubaix, France, offered Marcel Pasche the Medal of Honor. Marcel accepted the offer. In his speech, Marcel said,

I understood what it was that Professor Karl Barth had declared to be "the perverseness of Nazism" just five years prior to my coming to France. With the help of Pastor Friedrich Günther... I got to know Dr. Carlo Schmidt, who played a considerable role in favor of the population suffering under the occupying forces... During the four years of occupation, I was able to have recourse to a network of close and reliable Christian friends. Our notion of `enemies' was wiped away... We helped Jewish families and refugees... Numerous prisoners were freed and the lot of many remaining in prison was alleviated.

That is to say, Marcel understood that killing millions of people because they were Jewish was unjust. Marcel appreciated Friedrich taking him under his wing and introducing him to people who could be trusted. Marcel helped Jewish families and refugees by placing people into jobs and shortening prison sentences.

In conclusion, Marcel Pasche was a righteous gentile who helped multiple people. Marcel helped refugees get jobs, shortened prison sentences, and, with the help of his friend Friedrich, kept people from being raided. This matters today because the descendants of Mr. Rabinowitz would not exist. This relates to me because my great grandmother's husband helped her escape Nazi Germany, and, if it wasn't for him, then I would not exist.

MARCEL JUNOD
Edwin Carde

Without Marcel Junod's own determination to find out the real conditions in which prisoners were held, he never would have known the truth. Because of that and thanks to his courage he was able to document and expose the world to the horrific conditions at prisoners' camps. He had personally visited the Warsaw ghetto and wrote about the terrible conditions he witnessed there. Marcel published a book sharing the atrocities he had seen with his own eyes. He documented what he had learned so that the world would know.

Marcel Junod was a Swiss citizen. He was a student of medicine in the last year of his training as a surgeon. At that time the Red Cross was in need of his services. The Red Cross contacted him and interrupted his studies. He was asked to travel and help out in Ethiopia. After the assignment in Ethiopia, Marcel Junod was again asked by the Red Cross to go on a special assignment. This time he was sent to help in Spain.

In 1939, Marcel Junod moved to Berlin, Germany, still working for the Red Cross. The Germans had him under surveillance all the time and two soldiers were on duty, watching him. Even if he was spending the night at a hotel, the guards would be there, in adjacent rooms to his. In November 1939 Junod visited Warsaw, Poland. The policemen who were watching his every move were not the most cooperative. Junod would ask to stop the car so he could talk to farmers he saw along the road, about what they seen or what they know. He was digging deep for the truth. He was on a dangerous quest and the Germans regularly put obstacles in his path. They made it difficult for him and tried to keep the truth hidden. Marcel Junod wrote a book by the name of "*Le Troisieme Combatant*" (Warriors without Weapons). In the book he shares the challenges in finding the truth. This is what Junod wrote about trying to find the truth: "Gradually I learned to divine what the Germans did not show me, to understand the double sense of words. To perceive the distress conveyed in the silence of a prisoner in the presence of his forbidding guard". Junod had to convince the policemen that their cooperation is much better than him reporting that they are standing in his way. Junod talked to as many people as he could.

One day, while Marcel Junod was exploring Warsaw, a passerby by the name of Prince Lipkovsky introduced himself to Junod. Lipkovsky showed him around the city. They eventually came across the edge of a ghetto surrounded by barbed wire. Lipkovsky explained that soldiers are guarding the entrance to the ghetto day and night and that no one was allowed to enter or leave. There were three hundred thousand Jews that lived inside the ghetto. He continued and explained that boats came along a river that borders one side of the ghetto. At times these boats manage to bring to the residents of the ghetto some supplies. This was of course illegal and against the Nazi rules. The Germans made the Jews starve inside the ghetto. Food was very strictly rationed. According to official calculations the food that the people in the ghetto received wasn't even a tenth of normal human consumption. Junod was furious that the Germans were hiding this from him. He then said his thanks and goodbyes to Lipkovsky and returned to his hotel room. Junod reported about the conditions in Warsaw: "...the air was foul with a horrible smell of decomposition. . . . The side streets had often been so devastated that they were now little more than paths. Out of eighteen thousand houses eight thousand had been completely destroyed. Amidst these terrible ruins wandered crowds of miserable, trembling, and hungry people". In the spring of 1940 Marcel Junod's efforts to expose the truth paid off. The Germans had no option but to allow the Red Cross to establish a permanent delegation in Berlin.

At the end of 1941 Junod visited Germany again. He was delivering diplomatic mail to the Swiss delegation in Paris. He was stopped by the Gestapo and interrogated. They tried to prove that he was an "enemy agent".

Junod returned to his hotel and colleagues. They were determined to help as many prisoners as they could. They gathered around a large map of Germany and the countries occupied by the Nazis. They marked the spots of camps they were allowed to visit with little red crosses. Thoughts of all the camps they were not given access to troubled them greatly. They couldn't visit camps in Russia or the Polish prisons. Most troubling were the camps that were showed by mystery. They knew very bad things were happening there but couldn't do much about it. When the war was over Junod returned to his medical career. He continued his development in the Red Cross. Marcel Junod passed away in 1961 at the age of fifty six.

SAVING OF THE INNOCENT

Eitan Goore

This essay is about one of the great heroes of the Shoah. Ernest Prodolliet was responsible for saving many Jews during the Holocaust. He was a righteous man and he used his position within the Swiss consulate as overseer of visa-making to help save many people but mostly Jews. In recognition of his heroism he was honored with the title "Righteous Among the Nations" for helping save the lives of innocent people. Ernest Prodolliet truly was a courageous and selfless individual.

Ernest Prodolliet was born in Amriswil, Switzerland. He grew up to be a businessman and then became a diplomat in the Swiss government. Ernest Prodolliet lived in the harsh time of WWII when the Germans were trying to take over the world. As a diplomat, Ernest Prodolliet was in charge of the passport and visa section of the Swiss consulate in Bregenz, Austria. This means that he had the power to provide people with transit documents needed to travel to Switzerland. He helped many Jews leave Austria so that they could get to safety. People would come to Ernest Prodolliet with fake visas to distant countries like China and he would grant them transit visas to Switzerland. This meant that they could get out of Austria and into Switzerland and from there continue on. It was clear that Ernest Prodolliet knew that some of the documents he was presented with were forged however he cooperated with the Jews and helped them escape the horrible atrocities waiting for them. Every day, Jews came to the consulate in great numbers asking for help so the consul placed a guard at the gate of the consulate to ward off the refugees seeking help. Now, Ernest Prodolliet had to find a new ways to help people escape.

Eventually, when Ernest Prodelliet could no longer give Jews visas through his position at the consulate, he began having them come to his home where he would then transport them over the border into Switzerland. He did this because he wanted to save the jews. A man named Dr. Stanislaus was desperate to escape so he asked Ernest Prodelliet if he could be hidden in the back of a furniture truck in order to cross the border and get out of Austria. Ernest Prodelliet advised against this because he knew the German guards had orders to check the trucks. Even after Ernest Prodelliet warning, two of the man's friends attempted this tactic and failed. They were caught and killed. Ernest Prodelliet then saved the first man by driving him across the border in his car. This story shows that transporting Jews over the border was not easy and that Ernest Prodelliet was risking his life to save Jews.

Another story of Ernest Prodelliet's bravery happened one day when he was driving Max Wortsman over the border. It seemed that his lick had run out. When he tried to cross the border, unlike usual, the guards stopped him. He claimed that he was only going to show the man where to move once he'd gotten his valid papers, but the guards did not let him through. Instead, he was sent to court and, luckily for him, he knew all the court members because they were his friends from his old job. His punishment was not bad, just a talking to. The court members warned him not to do something like this again. After this incident, he was fired but he kept on with his endeavor of saving Jewish refugees.

Although Prodolliet was sent to Amsterdam and warned to stop his illegal actions, he was determined to continue helping Jews. In 1492 Ernest Prodolliet continued to get passports for Jews. He took advantage of the fact that he was working for the consulate to save as many Jews as he could.

Because of the change in the political environment the Swiss consulate needed to close down Prodolliet gave a woman named Gertrude Van Tijn, who was active on the Jewish council in Amsterdam a list of names and phone numbers of important people who might be able to help the Jews in need he also gave her 57,500 Swiss francs in cash to for transit and a well lived life for the refugees.

In the end, Ernest Prodelliet was deported back to his hometown, Amrswil, Switzerland. As Jewish law says "He who saves but one Israelite saves the whole of mankind." This applies to Ernest Prodolliet because the number of Jews he saved is crazy. When he returned home, he was honored by Yad Vashem and the French army. They honored him by giving him the title of "Righteous Among the Nations." This is a title that was given to righteous gentiles who saved Jews during the Holocaust. Most people who were given this title died before they were even recognized. However, Ernest Prodelliet received his while still alive. He lived a long and prosperous life. He always knew that in the end he would be a great man. Ernest Prodelliet lived to be Ernest Prodolliet Died in 1984 in his birthplace Amriswil Switzerland.

FRED AND LILETTE REYMOND

Elise Ezikiel, Winner

Fred and Lilette Reymond helped people survive the Holocaust by hiding them in their basement thus protecting them from the German police. Fred and Lilette Reymond put their lives on the line for the Jews to be safe. They helped the Jews cross the borderline between France and Switzerland. In addition they gave them money so that they could start a new life. Without the incredible efforts of Fred and Lilette Reymond many Jews would not be alive.

The Reymond's were Swiss citizens who lived in a small rural town up on a mountain. They lived very close to the borderline with France. Fred Reymond was a watch maker in the Swiss army at the age of twenty. In 1940 he was given the job of observing the activities of the German army as an intelligence officer. Since he lived up on a mountain so close to France he was in a good position to servile that Nazis and their activities in that area. He was specifically assigned to the two areas in France bordering Switzerland. His job required him to work close to the border quite often. Fred met many people, among the many Jews, who were trying to get out of France. Among those who were looking for ways out of France were British paratroopers, and young French men who were drafted by the Nazis for hard labor, activities the French Resistance, and escaped prisoners. Fred saw the great fear and suffering of these people and decided to help as much as he could and as many as he could.

Fred worked with French agents across the border. They knew of people who needed help in escaping from the Nazis. The French agents worked carefully and in secrecy. They would bring the people to a secret meeting place at the border. Fred would meet them there and literally across the border with them there was a small gate in the border fence which the Swiss were not watching over. Fred used this gate to get the people through and into Switzerland. Once inside Switzerland the journey was not yet over. Although the Swiss were neutral they did have guards and patrols along their borders. They did not want or allow people to sneak into their country. Fred had devised a plan for the people he helped. He brought them to home and hid them in his basement. Lilette, his wife, was a part of this operation. The couple hosted the refugees in their home and kept them safe. It was very dangerous for the refugees to travel during the day because there were many Swiss patrols looking for people without proper travel documents. At times the refugees spent up to thirty-six hours at the Reymonds' basement so that they left the safety of their in the middle of the night. Fred bought train tickets for these refugees and managed to get the necessary documents for them refugees in case they were topped and had to show travel documents and identity cards. When they were ready to leave, he also gave them some money for their journey.

People who witnessed the efforts of Fred and Lilette Reymond remember the hard work Lilette put in supporting her husband and the refugees. During those years there was very little food and every family received strict rations according to the number of people in their family. Lilette always had food for the refugees. It is unclear how she was able to obtain the food for so many people but she did it. She never showed the refugees how tired she was. She had enough energy to give everyone the attention they deserved although she worked night and day. Lilette always had kind words for the refugees and gave them hope.

Fred and Lilette were true heroes who helped anyone they could. They never asked questions about the refugees' backgrounds or religions. Fred had pedaled countless miles on his bike, taking short cuts through the forest and following paths that were unknown to the German or Swiss patrols to bring people to safety. Lilette had spent countless night cooking, feeding, clothing and encouraging the refugees she hid in her basement.

In 1997 on Fred's ninetieth birthday, a Yad Vashem representative in Geneva announced that the Reymonds were awarded the title of "Righteous of the nations". The ceremony took place a few months later and the two received a medal from Yad Vashem and also in honor by the local municipality. At the age of ninety-two Fred Reymond passed away peacefully (1999). His wife Lilette Reymond passed way a year later (200).

THE ANGEL OF LA HILLE CASTLE: ROSLI NAEF

Isaiah Ortego, Co-runners-up

 This is the story of children who survived the war in southern France. They lived at a children's refugee shelter by the name of La Hille Castle. The story is told through the eyes of Jacques Roth, who survived the holocaust thanks to Rosli Naef.

August 26, 1942 seemed like a normal day at La Hille Castle, the children's home in southern France. We were playing, learning, and resting. We all thought we were safe. While in our beds, at dawn, we were awakened by the startling sound of truck engines, people shouting, and yelling. A big argument was developing. The most surprising thing was that Rosli Naef (1911-1996) was yelling too. Rosli was a very calm person who never raised her voice and never broke her everlasting calmness; she was also the very caring woman who took care of us, children. We knew something very bad was going to happen. My name is Jacques Roth, I was one of the kids who lived in that children's home. The argument was over. The police men came inside the castle. All of the children, sixteen and older, were ordered to give their names over to the police men who were now raiding the castle, our home. We were told that there was a misunderstanding. We had to obey the policemen. We had to go with these scary men. Rosli, the ever the calming caretaker, assured us that everything would be alright and that we would be back.

Rosli was determined to get us back to the castle. She somehow found out we were at the camp of Le Vernet. She was speeding down the road, riding a bicycle when she punctured her tire. This didn't stop her. The woman was decided on getting us back. She managed to find a taxi. When we saw her, we all were hopeful again. Just by being there she made us feel safe again. Rosli told us that she was in contact with Maurice Dubois, the head of the Swiss Red Cross children's home, and she expected good news from him. We were saved and felt secure and comforted. Things were good until November of 1942 when Germans took over southern France.

Rosli knew there would be more raids and more attacks. She knew that the oldest kids would be taken under arrest. It was at this point that we came up with the hideouts and escape plans in case we were raided surprised by the Nazis. First of all we hired guards who watched over the castle day and night. It was their job to alert us if any "unexpected guests" were close by. If they were near and we needed to act quickly we would go to the onion loft located in the upper attic. The entrance was hidden and only known by a few carefully chosen children. The password was *shortcut*. But for Rosli this wasn't enough. She made preparations for the most endangered children to leave and escape the castle all together. She got in touch with the nearby farmers. She made arrangements for many of us to hide in their farms for a few weeks. She also made arrangements with Germaine Hommel, the head mistress of the Swiss Children's home close of the Swiss/French border. They agreed that the Swiss home would give the exhausted children shelter. We knew what we had to do and we were all prepared for the worst.

At La Hille Castle life wasn't the best. The French were starting their attacks again cooperating with the Nazi forces. Rosli though was ready; she assembled a meeting with the older children: me, Jaquez Roth, Peter Salz, Regina Rosenblatt, and Margot Kern. We were ready to escape to Switzerland. On December 22, 1942, embarking on a 350 mile journey north, we set off to the border. Rosli made sure we were provided with some food, clean underwear, and some Swiss money. Fake travel documents were provided for us that had fake French names. Finally, we made it to the Swiss children's home. After a quick rest, late at, night we were picked up by a young Frenchman and taken across the border, hiding in the darkness and shadows. Later, Rosli got dismissed from her job as headmistress, because it was found out that she was sending kids across the border illegally. She moved back to Switzerland where we were currently staying. She got a job in Geneva at the Henri-Dunant Refugee Shelter. Rosli was amazing! She got us jobs at the shelter she worked in.

Knowing that her first escape was successful Rosli sent many more kids after us. Some went to Switzerland and some went to Spain. However, on the nights of the first and second of January, another group of six kids were sent into the forest when they were caught by a patrol. Five were captured, but one girl Inge Joseph was set free because the patrol felt bad for her, she was ordered to go back to France. The five kids were taken to Annemasse, a French border town in Geneva. When Rosli Naef heard about the children being captured she knew more raids would be coming to La Hille Castle. Naef had, however, taken precautions the youngest children were sent to the nearby farms and the other children hid in the onion loft. No endangered kids were hurt or captured.

I still remember the love and care Rosli had for the refugees. She never wanted anything in return. Before she got the job at La Hille Castle she barely knew Jews existed. When she heard that her kids may be in trouble she did everything she could do to learn about us Jews. She read books, asked questions, and learned our ways and traditions.. She helped so much. I was able to stay in Switzerland until the war was over in 1945. After the war there was a movie made about her life called "La Filiere" which I got to have a role in.

In 1989 Naef was going to be named one of the "Righteous among the Nations", but she respectfully declined the title and the Medal of Honor that came with it. On October 4, 1992, while attending a ceremony for Germaine Hommel and others at St.-Cerque-les-Voirns, she finally agreed to accept the honor. Rosli Naef's story ends in Glarus, Switzerland, her birth place, where she was buried in 1996.

I think Rosli Naef is a great role model for all people anywhere. She knew that these innocent people didn't deserve to be tortured like this, especially the kids. Even though she didn't know anything about Jews she knew they were human and weren't monsters. They didn't deserve to be locked up and tortured. It doesn't matter what people believe in or how they look, people are people and should all be treated equal. She would do whatever it took whether it was hiding the kids, risking her life to protect the kids, or even have the children leave all together.

RIGHTEOUS GENTILES

Joe Fahn

In 1942, there was a Swiss man, who worked as the head of the Swiss Red Cross, named Maurice Dubois. Maurice Dubois was a righteous gentile who aided in hiding Jews in a castle, Chateau La Hille. The Swiss Red Cross was situated near Capitole square in Rue du Taur. Dubois was informed by the director of the Swiss Red Cross of the horrid conditions of the families situated in concentration camps. Soon, he then visited the site to experience the terror

46

that the about one-hundred kids in the camp were experiencing. These kids were not only treated like they were not as good as the Nazis, they also suffered from jaundice, boils, and scabies. Without delay, Dubois knew that these families a vast amount of help from any person who was willing to stand up to the Nazis.

Though Dubois knew these poor families needed help, he lacked the means. As soon as possible, he contacted Berne, and after a long talked discussion, the Swiss Red Cross started to discuss the possibilities of how to take care of these terrorized families. Maurice Dubois' wife, Eleonore, had heard of a nearby vacant castle, La Hille, in the lovely valley of the Leze River in the Ariege region. Eleonore immediately obtained a lease on La Hille because she had the idea of hiding these kids in the uninhabited castle. About ninety children were first conveyed to the castle and treated like royalty. Those kids needed the uppermost help to recover from abhorrent treatment from the Nazis. Eleonore then consistently visited La Hille, but she was not the only person who visited the castle. The French gendarmes also visited the castle frequently. No arrests had been made to the children, so they assumed they were safe. On any ordinary day, at about four o'clock before dawn," like the lightening from the sky", a massive raid operation by the gendarmes was about to occur. The gendarmes encircled the castle of La Hille. One of the older children, Walter Kamlet, wrote in his journal about this occurrence saying", the gendarmes entered by force, pistols in their hands, and stormed into the bedrooms." Do to the frightening raids, the middle and younger children were awoken from deep sleeps by the sounds of the slamming entry doors. The young boys sat on their bed anxious about how at any time the gendarmes could come storming into their room. The girls even started to cry. Next thing they know, the gendarmes ordered them to pack their belongings. After being lined up for an early attendance outside a La Hille, forty-five older children were forced into a truck that had been previously waiting on the country road on the other side of the bridge. The children later found out they were in the process of being transported off to the camp of La Vernet.

Before they were carted off, the warden of La Hille, Rosli Naef attempted to bargain with the stubborn gendarmes. Naef was a Swiss woman living in France who also worked for the Swiss Red Cross. The gendarmes didn't bother to even listen to her argument to return the children. The gendarmes declared that the refugees needed to be ready for transportation within the hour. Warden Naef was very upset and as soon as possible, she ran up to Montegut, where she had access to call Dubois about the occurrence. Dubois assured that he would do everything in his power to save the children that had been confined behind the barbed wire fence of Vernet that same morning. Without delay, Dubois traveled to Vichy and contacted the Swiss Embassy. Because he was not a diplomat, it was particularly hard to get the embassy to do something. At the same time, Eleonore traveled to Berne, to obtain authorization of the kids that had been transported to La Vernet form the Federal Government. Dubois introduced his argument by mentioning the three thousand French children that were still recovering from the effects of the war. This was amazing and brave for just one man to actually stand up and represent all of the innocent children that were injured and recovering from the effects that the crude and horrid Nazis had caused. With all the passion he could muster he explained the arrests of these forty-five children who were apparently arrested in the early morning of August 26th, 1942. He described this pernicious action as an unacceptable act by the French gendarmes. The Federal Government and Vichy Regime responded with only an apology. This was an outrage that the two agencies did not react with retaliation. Naef was informed that the kids would be released from La Vernet. The children were already standing with their bags ready to depart at the forlorn train station.

On September 2nd, 1942, the children had returned safely back to La Hille Castle. Frau Naef told them that they shouldn't be thanking her for saving them. She told them that they owed their lives to Maurice Dubois who had personally intervened with the Vichy Regime. This brave action also released three Jewish employees of the Swiss Red Cross who had previously been in a raid at another home in Haute-Savoie. Dubois did not only protect the refugees at La Hille. He also protected the Jewish children at Le Chambon-sur-Lignon in Haute-Loire.

Another Swiss gentile, Sebastian Steiger, who worked as a teacher at La Hille castle, reported that the work that Maurice Dubois and his wife had accomplished would not stop there. Eleonore consistently tried to improve the way of life at the castle. She worked to constantly improve the children's lot. She repeatedly contacted the Vichy Regime and reported the mortal danger the kids were in even after their return to La Hille. This happened because the gendarmes constantly warned them that they would frequently return to raid the castle until they surrendered. She attempted to arrange visas to be given to the children to seek refuge as a normal kid in Switzerland. However, her plea was not acknowledged.

48

Two young adults, Peter Salz and Ruth Tamir, who were among the refugee children at La Hille Castle, today live in Israel. If you would ask them today, they would remember Maurice Dubois like it was yesterday. Maurice Dubois made an immense impact on many people's lives. Dubois put his own life in jeopardy to save the innocent children who were situated at La Vernet. He did not only keep the refugees safe. He also supplied them with a good educational system at the castle. Maurice had protests outside of Laval's office against the arrests and deportations of the youths. Maurice Dubois showed me that you don't live forever so you might as well help save children who still have a long life to live.

Maurice Dubois is remembered by many people in the world. He showed the world that any person can stand up to the Nazis and start a revolt against discrimination. Usually people only remember Maurice Dubois, but Eleonore Dubois, his wife, also helped immensely. The ninety children would've never had a place to escape to if Eleonore hadn't found and leased La Hille. The refugee children will remember Maurice and Eleonore Dubois for as long as they live for risking their lives to save the lives of many people. Maurice Dubois received a medal of honor", Righteous Among the Nations," which was presented to him by the Israeli ambassador, Maurice Rivlin. Two of the children who survived the inauspicious attack personally thanked Maurice for all of his help during World War II at the ceremony.

THE FREEDOM GIVING LADY-FRIEDA IMPAKOVEN

Sivan Shamir

The gift of freedom is something that Frieda Impakoven gave to many Jews from the hands of Hitler. Wife of the famous actor and playwright Toni Impakoven, and the mother of the well-known dancer Niddy Impakoven, Frieda Kobler was born in Switzerland in 1880, the daughter of a wealthy man. She gave shelter and food for the Jews during the Holocaust. Without Frieda Impakoven many Jews would not have survived the Holocaust.

The Holocaust happened during World War II. It was a very hard time for the Jews because Hitler, the cruel ruler of Germany, tried to erase the Jews from the earth by imprisoning and killing them. Frieda came from Switzerland and believed that the Jews were innocent. Due to the fact she believed in the Jews innocence, she helped them.

In order to help the Jews, Frieda provided them with food and shelter. For example, one of the Jews that Frieda helped was Frau Wolffler, an elderly woman. Another woman that Frieda helped was Frau Knewitz. Frau Knewitz later wrote a thank you letter to Frieda which read:

> When I was in danger, you took me in, showing true friendship and hospitality. When you heard of a Gestapo raid in our area, you offered me the shelter of your house although you knew that I was Jewish. I thank you from the bottom of my heart.

This letter shows that Frieda was a very generous woman who cared about other people even though she knew that if she got caught she would be killed or sent to a labor camp. Frieda also helped her husband's sister's child Anton Muller whose father was Jewish. Frieda and her husband Toni provided him with shelter in their apartment in Frankfurt and helped him make it to Switzerland.

After the death of her husband, Frieda moved back to her native Switzerland. In 1966 she was honored by Israel's ambassador to Switzerland, who gave her the Yad Vashem "Righteous among the Nations" medal for her bravery, because she had stood up against the Nazi regime and saved many lives of Jewish people.

Frieda Impakoven's husband was sent to a forced labor camp after Hitler came to power. He was sent there because he was a sworn Anti-Nazi. Like her husband, Frieda was an Anti-Nazi, however, she didn't try showing it in the same way her husband did. Instead, Frieda kept quiet and continued to save Jews by hiding them in her own home, knowing that she might get caught.

I am a Jewish girl from Israel and all of my relatives have inspired me. That is why I would like to share my father's grandmother's story. The story is about two of my great grandmother's friends who warned her about the war. Although they didn't hide her or they weren't righteous gentiles they did help my great grandmother, Dvora, by telling her the truth, so she could escape with her kids. It was late in the afternoon, the sun was shining, birds were chirping, the grass was green, and the streets of Poland were empty. It was just my great grandmother, Dvora on the street. Dvora was walking by a factory, at about six or seven o'clock in the evening and the factory was working. This factory used to work until five o'clock in the afternoon, but today they worked until six or seven. Dvora thought it was weird but she moved on. The next evening she took a walk and saw that they were still working over the normal hours, which confused her. She thought maybe they are making something new and they needed more time to make it or maybe they just wanted the workers to work more, but all of what Dvora was thinking was wrong. The next morning she went to the market. It was a weekend. While she was in the market Dvora saw her friends (that weren't Jewish). One of them worked in the factory. She asked them if they might know what was happening in the factory and why they were working over the normal ending hours, and her friends answered her. They said that there was a war coming to Poland and that the factory was making weapons for the war and my great grandmother knew that the war was probably against the Jewish people. So she wanted to run away from Poland. And she did, by escaping through Russia.

I know this essay is supposed to be on Righteous Gentiles but this story is amazing in my point of view. It shows how even if you don't share the same belief as your friend or that you're not the same kind it can't stop you from helping your friends. Just like Frieda Impakoven.

If Frieda Impakoven wasn't a "Righteous Gentile" many Jews wouldn't have survived the Holocaust. By letting the Jews hide in her own home and risking her life by doing this, those Jews whom Frieda did save got to create families, have fun, learn, make mistakes, and most important they got to see the end of the war.

DEAR MR. ARCHIBALD
Talia Friedman, Co-runners-up

3/18/1991

Dear Mr. Archibald,

My name is Jamie Kelly, and I work for a special company that honors Holocaust survivors and rescuers. This year instead of interviewing a survivor, I decided to interview someone who helped the Jews get to safety. This summer I went to Denmark to seek the freedom fighter I needed. When I was there I met with many important writers who told me about the great people who put their lives the on the line to help those who were being exiled. I heard many names that I thought over but when I did further investigating I knew who was right for this program. I know all the people who survived the Holocaust must be quite interesting, all having different tales to tell, but I this year I want the person to be extraordinary with tales that will let young people know the importance of the people who helped those in need. Instead of going back to the writers I decided to do my own research and find the person I needed. Sure enough I found someone. Her name is Anne-Marie Im Hof-Piguet. As I dug further back into her history I was intrigued! This woman saved dozens and dozens of Jewish children.

Jamie Kelly

3/19/1991

Dear Mr. Archibald,

It's only been one day since I last wrote to you and I have been up all night studying and researching Anne-Marie Im Hof-Piguet. In June 1942, she was asked to be a relief worker at Montluel Castle (which is located in southern France). She expected to see French girls and boys who were suffering from the effects of the war; instead she saw families from Spain. When the Spanish Civil War came to an end many Spanish families fled Spain and went into France. While she was at Montluel Castle, Anne- Marie saw Jewish refugee children for the first time. This was the first time she saw people deported. She couldn't do anything but take of the small amount of survivors who were left. In May 1943, Anne-Marie went to La Hille Castle. Rosli Naef, the warden of La Hille left the day after Anne-Marie arrived. The new warden tried to continue the rescue efforts of Rosli. It was here that Anne-Marie Im hof-Piguet learned about the terrifying situation going on at the castle. Over and over again she would speak with the children, trying to understand them and soon enough she did. Outside the castle the gendarmes would arrest Jews on the orders of the German Army. She tried her hardest to calm the small children down. She found older kids hiding in out in the farms. That's all the information I have for now. I'm heading out to meet Ann-Marie Im Hof-Piguet. I am very excited to meet this glorious woman. Hopefully I will be able to find out exactly what she did to help the children

Jamie Kelly

3/21/91

Dear Mr. Archibald,

I have met with Anne-Marie Im Hof-Piguet and am so amazed. I have a new hero. Yes, I got my answer. Apparently she got worried for the children and decided to take matters into her own hands. Even though she was told by the Red Cross she should follow the orders of the gendarmes she knew she had to help the children. She told me that she tried to come up with a new escape plan because crossing the border to Geneva was no longer an option as the gendarmes were told to turn back people to France. All of this created much stress for Anne-Marie Im Hof-Piguet.

As a child she went on walks with her father in a wide forest. Luckily she knew the stone wall that separated France and Switzerland like the back of her hand. When the summer came she decided to take some time off to test her escape route. She invited another Red Cross member to come with her to try to cross into Switzerland. She was very confident that her passport would allow her to pass without any trouble. She and her friend made it to Annie-Marie Im Hof-Piguet parents' home in Switzerland. While they were there, she met with Victoria Cordier, who was ready to help any way possible. Victoria's mother and two sisters were dedicated to the idea of helping Jews cross the border. The family was kind and humble and was devoted to their Catholic beliefs.

Jamie Kelly

3/22/1991

Dear Mr. Archibald,

I ended the last letter short trying to make more of an impact. I want you and all the people in the world to know how important the people who helped to allow 13,859,800 Jews to be alive today.

Victoria and her family lived right next to the border and their house joined next to the stone wall. Because of that, the twelve children she rescued would have never made it across the border. In September 1943, Anne-Marie Im Hof-Piguet returned from her trip and came back to the La Hille. Sadly the Gendarmes were back and they would hide in the neighborhood day and night watching the castle. All the kids knew how dangerous it was if they were to be caught and that the gendarmes were waiting for them to make a mistake. Some hid in the onion loft, which was a small secret room in the castle. After three days they all decided they needed to flee. September 12, 1943, Anne-Marie decided to take a young boy across the border to Switzerland to meet his sister there. The young boy needed identification papers so she had to forge them. Addy was the first kid to cross the border safely. In the winter more children were able to cross the border, each experiencing the risk and excitement of near death. Anne-Marie met with the two sisters, who knew the trees very well. They used the trees to guide people through the forest.

The border crossings were exhausting and <u>very</u> emotional. Ann-Marie Im Hof-Piguet was very thankful to the success in getting children to her home in La Sentier. She is very proud of the fact that she and the Cordier sisters worked excellently together.

Anne-Marie took her last trip May of 1944. The group she went with almost met a disastrous situation. The group already made it to the Swiss border when a Swiss guard stopped them. The guard wanted to make them turn back but Madeleine Cordier convinced the guard to let them continue but they had to go to a refugee camp. Piguet was disappointed that group could not make it to her home but she was thankful they had been saved.

After Anne-Marie Im Hof-Piguet's last trip she married Ulrich Im Hof, a historian. She never gave up on her desire to help. Last year Yad Vashem presented her with a medal of honor.

Jamie Kelly

3/25/1991

Dear Miss. Kelly,

After reading all your letters over and over again I have decided to invest in your company. I must say that I am very impressed how much time and effort you put in this assignment. Anne-Marie Im Hof-Piguet is a very interesting woman and should be known by all people. Investing in your company will be good publicity for you and me. I am hoping that that this report will be publicized. I am hoping that people all over the world will read it. I even hope that the President of the United States could read it and then meet Anne-Marie Im Hof-Piguet. I think having Mrs. Hof-Piguet meet the President and discuss her life would make her joyful and she will see that she will never be forgotten. The fact of the matter is that Holocaust survivors and rescuers are slowly fading away, and I think having more people like you in the world will keep the spirit of freedom alive in this world.

Joshua Archibald

THE SCHNEEBERGER'S STORY

Tillie Rubin

I would like to bring to your attention the story of Arthur and Anne Schneeberger. Their story of self-sacrifice caught my attention when I was reading about the Righteous among the Nations and how they saved many Jews during the Holocaust. This is their story of victory, as told by Benjamin Wolkowicz, account of how they kept safe until the war was over.

<u>August 1939</u>

It is a beautiful day today. The sun is out and shining brightly on my face and the green trees are giving me shade. I went to the park with my parents and my baby brother Claude. My parents' best friends, Arthur and Anne Schneeberger, were also there. My dad has his own business and so does Mr.

Schneeberger. Both of them are successful businessmen. They make socks and tights in their factories. My dad and Arthur Schneeberger have a lot in common even though my dad was born in Poland and Arthur was born in Switzerland.

P.S

Did I mention my mom baked a delicious cake for my 7th birthday? Not a crumb was left!

<u>August 1940</u>

Today I am writing from my hiding place in Haute Loire. It is dark and quiet and I am not allowed to talk or move. We don't want the Germans don't find us. We are planning to go back home to Roanne. I heard that there is a special agreement between the French and Germans we will be able to return to our home and get out of hiding. I cannot wait to sleep in my own bed and play with Charles, my neighbor.

<u>January 1941</u>

I am now back in Roanne, and life is much worse than before. The Germans took my dad's factory and money away, but worst of all, my dad was sent away. My mom says he is in camp but I think it's more like prison. I miss him very much. When they came to take him I tried to go with him but he wouldn't let me. It is so different than before. I still remember the time before the war when everything was happy and joyful before the war. Now it's terrible and everyone is hiding, crying, and terrified. I just wish it could be over.

<u>1942</u>

My dad is back. He was gone for a whole year, but he doesn't talk much about his time in camp. Arthur spoke to my dad about me, staying with him and his family. I don't want to stay away from my family! I can't even imagine what it would be like. Unfortunately Arthur said yes. Now my parents are making preparations for me to leave. I think my parents are planning to give Claude a to nurse so that they can go away. This is all too much for me to understand. Do I have to memorize a new address now? All I know is 77 Rue Thomas... I trust that my parents know what they are doing. It must be serious if my father is making these arrangements. I just wish it wasn't like this and that Claude and I could be together at are home.

<u>1943</u>

The Schneebergers welcomed me as if I were their own son. Arthur and Anne have two daughters, Anny and Janine. They are both older than me, so

I don't really have anyone to talk to. Every time that Janine hears a car go by she makes me hide in a barrel in case it is the Germans.

I truly enjoy living with the Schneebergers' but I want to go back home to my own family. The Schneebergers house is about 100 meters away from the German soldiers. They are marching past our house every day. It is very frightening. Even though I know that the Germans don't know I am Jewish, I always feel like I am hiding something and that I am in danger of being caught. If the Germans find out that the Schneebergers are protecting me, they will probably kill us. I am also very worried about my parents. I miss them and don't know where they are and how they are doing.

<u>1945</u>

Today is the day I get to see my parents. The war is over and Jewish people are no longer in danger just because they are Jewish. I have been waiting for this day for what seems like forever. While I became part of the Schneeberger family, I never forgot what it was like to be with my own family.

When I will finally see my parents and will look into their, eyes I know I will start to shed lots of tears. I heard that they are alive and I am happy and relieved that they are ok.

<u>I have seen my parents!</u>

I am so joyful, and lucky. Now I can be with my parents and no longer have to stay with Arthur and his family. Even though they had saved my life during the holocaust I will always love my family. I understand that again if the Schneebergers hadn't protected me. I would probably not have survived. The Schneebergers will always be in my heart and on my mind.

Hopefully my dad and Arthur will get their businesses back and start earning money. It would be great if things could be like before the holocaust and everything will be fine but I already know that things are not always perfect in the real world.

Benjamin Wolkowicz was taken in by the Schneebergers family. This saved his life. After the war he remained in France. He shared his story and the story of the brave Arthur and Anne Schneeberger with the French committee of Yad Vashem. In 1999, their daughter Anny, represented her parents who had passed away by then, in a ceremony awarding them the recognition and medal of' " Righteous of the Nations".

Churchill Middle School, Carmichael, CA

LaDonna Ray is a middle school teacher at Churchill Middle School in Carmichael, California. She has been teaching for twenty-six years, the first twenty in elementary school. Currently, she is teaching history and English to International Baccalaureate students.

Debby Fraizer teaches 8th grade Language Arts and U.S. History at Churchill Middle School in Carmichael. She has been teaching about the Holocaust during most of her 18 years of teaching. She became part of the Holocaust Educators Network in 2014.

GERDA VALENTINER- A HERO TO THE CHILDREN OF THE HOLOCAUST

Landon Abi

"I only did what many Danes did, nothing special. We thought it perfectly natural to help people in mortal danger." This was the quote of Gerda Valentiner, a very brave and courageous woman during the Holocaust. Valentiner lived in Denmark with her parents Rosine and Axel Valentiner. Gerda was at the age of 40 when the Holocaust took place. Gerda Valentiner was a teacher before the time of this genocide. She was devoted to every child she taught, which is why she did so much to help so many kids during the Holocaust. Valentiner helped children by doing everything from giving them food to even letting them into her home and taking care of them. Overall, it was Gerda Valentiner's courage, bravery, and trust that saved so many children from the intimidation and fearfulness of the Holocaust.

Gerda Valentiner did many noble actions in her life. Valentiner wasn't born into a rich family, but she lived with a loving family. In her early years, Valentiner lived with her mom, Rosine Valentiner, her dad Axel Valentiner, and in Denmark. When Valentiner grew to be an adult, she became a teacher. She loved kids and loved just being around them. Her passion was kids. In fact Valentiner was willing to sacrifice her life for these kids and almost willing to do anything to protect the children she taught.

When news of the Holocaust reached Denmark, it hit Gerda Valentiner pretty hard. She was very nervous for the children she taught and didn't really know what to expect might happen to her and to her students when Germany invaded Denmark. Although she vowed to secretly help her Jewish students escape back to Sweden no matter what happened. So she started collecting Jewish children from their parents to have them stay at her home while she waited for a good time to bring them to the coast and have them shipped off to a boat to Sweden. She did this many times and many years starting in the year of 1943. Valentiner's house was used many times as a safe haven for countless Jewish children. Valentiner risked her life in many ways by doing this for the Jewish children, but she did it anyway and greatly enjoyed it. Giving a place to children wasn't the only action Valentiner made for these children, though. She also became more aware of the diets of some of the children who did have to endure time in the Nazi death camps of bread and soup. Valentiner wanted to give the children more of a variety in their diets, so she decided to give them additional foods and dishes to eat. Gerda Valentiner helped these kids in so many ways. She not only gave them a place to stay but also threatened her own life when Nazi soldiers came to inspect her house. Every time a Nazi soldier came to inspect her house, she made sure each child was hidden carefully so that the Nazi soldiers wouldn't arrest her or the kids. The action of transferring the Jewish children in Denmark to Sweden was pretty successful, and many lives of the children were spared because of the transferring system.

After the Holocaust, Valentiner was recognized for her brave actions and strides she made for many of the Jewish children around her. As people look back on their experiences on the Holocaust, especially children, they reflect how Gerda Valentiner helped them escape from the Nazis. For example, Moritz Scheftelowitz, the brother of one of Gerda Valentiner's students, reflects on the fact that Valentiner came to their parents and told them that their family was in danger. Valentiner had urged the Scheftelowitz kids to stay at her house so she could get everything situated and arranged for the departure of the children to Denmark. Although the escape plan didn't work the first two times, it did work the third time. The kids were then put on a boat to sail to catch the nearest train to Sweden. Looking back on the whole experience, Valentiner was still very modest about the whole thing. Once the war ended, Valentiner decided to quit her teaching job and work as a social worker for a couple of years. She also retired soon after she became a social worker at the age of 68.

In conclusion, Gerda Valentiner is a courageous, brave, and trustworthy person. She not only snuck children to Sweden, but she also gave them a place to stay and gave them things to eat. She became a mother figure to them. She didn't care if she would get chastised or killed for doing any of what she did as long as the children were safe. Valentiner was also just so modest about the whole thing. Just the fact that she was willing to risk her life to save others shows one thing: that she is a hero.

Bibliography:

Vashem, Yad. "Teachers Who Rescued Jews During the Holocaust" Yad Vashem. 5 Sep. 1997. https://www.google.com/?gws_rd=ssl#q=gerda+valentiner

THE LIFE OF HARALD FELLER

Akshay Srinivasan

A man named Harald Feller was a hero of the Holocaust. Harald Feller was a very important Swiss Diplomat during the time of the Holocaust. During Harald Feller's life he saved thousand of Hungarian Jews during the Holocaust. They called him the Hero for the Hungarians. Also known as the Hungarian Jew's savior. Harald Feller had a very long and fulfilled life.

Harald Feller lived from 1913 and died recently in 2003. During this time Feller had replaced Maximilian Jaegar who was the head of the Swiss legation in Budapest, Hungary at the time of 1914. Maximilian

Jaegar was alive from the time of 1915 to 1999. Harald Feller also supported a man whose name was Carl Lutz. Carl Lutz worked as a helper and a savior of the Jews, while being under the Swiss protection. Harald Feller worked extremely closely with other neutral groups. With these groups he kept on pressuring the Sztojay and the Horthy Government. He pressured those governments to stop and end the prosecution of the Jews. Harald Feller had also helped keep the people of the Swedish legation safe. Some members of the legation were targeted by what is known as the "Arrow Cross Party" who gave the Swiss no shelter and gave them false passports. In the time of 1944 Maximilian Jaeger was recalled to a place called Berne. Harald Feller then had to work with the chancellor of Swiss Legation Max Meir. They again escaped from the Arrow Cross Gang. Toward the end of the Holocaust Feller had hid a total of a dozen Jews in the basement of his house in Budapest, Hungary. In the time of February 1945 the Soviet policemen arrest Harald Feller and his partner Maximilian Jaeger. Harald was violently tortured and violently question by the Soviet policemen. After the arrest the Soviet cops sent Harald Feller and Maximilian Jaeger to Moscow with some other Swiss national policemen. After that on February 1945 Harald Feller was then named the interim head of the Swiss Legation. He was named that position even though he was the youngest diplomat there at the time. He then had to leave his big house and live at the office. After that Harald Feller and Max Meir were taken to Moscow. In Moscow the two of them were being interned.

After a long time of being a Swiss Diplomat he finally got to return to his home in Switzerland. Fifty-three years later, Harald Feller was recalled on September 6th, 1999 to be at a very special ceremony in Berne. Their he received his Righteous Among the Nations award in 1999. He died shortly after. Harald Feller was not only a hero, but he was a savior of the Holocaust.

The Life of Carl Lutz

Carl Lutz was not only a hero for the Holocaust but he was a hero to the Jews. Carl Lutz was born in Walzenhausean, Switzerland. He was born on March 30th in 1895. Carl Lutz died in Bern, Switzerland on February 12th 1975. From 1943 until the end of the World War II he was the Swiss vice-consul in Budapest, Hungary. Carl Lutz had a good early life, helped the Holocaust, and made an impact on our society.

Lutz had a good life at an early age and he had a great education. When Carl Lutz was a young boy he had attended many local schools inside of Switzerland. When he was 18 he immigrated to the United States of America. In the United States he worked and lived there for more than 20 years in Illinois. In Illinois he studied at the Central Wesleyan College inside of Warrenton, Missouri. After that in 1920 Carl Lutz found a job in the Swiss Legation inside of Washington D.C. As he worked for the Swiss Legation Lutz studied at the George Washington University. Then in 1926, Carl Lutz was given the position as the Chancellor at the Swiss Consulate in Philadelphia, USA. Then from 1926 to 1934 he was assigned the Swiss consulate inside of St. Louis. After that from 1934 to 1942 he was assigned as the vice-consul to the Swiss in Jaffa (Palestine).

Carl Lutz saved thousands of lives in the Holocaust. During the World War II Carl Lutz worked for the Jewish Agency for Palestine. After that he issued Swiss safe-conduct documents, which saved 10,000 Hungarian Jewish children. After that in Palestine he saved over 8,000 Hungarian Jews. By the end of the whole World War II Carl Lutz had saved over 62,000 lives from dying in World War II. After this Carl Lutz had many honors done after him.

Carl Lutz made a great impact in our society. In 1963 a street was named after him Haifa. Then in 1965 he got the Righteous Among the Nations Award. The most recent award that he received was in 2014 which was the President's Medal in the George Washington University.

Bibliography

1. "Carl Lutz." *Wikipedia*. Wikimedia Foundation. Web. 10 Feb. 2015. <http://en.wikipedia.org/wiki/Carl_Lutz>.

2. "Harald Feller." *Wikipedia*. Wikimedia Foundation. Web. 10 Feb. 2015. <http://en.wikipedia.org/wiki/Harald_Feller>.

3. Wagner, Meir, and Moshe Meisels. *The Righteous of Switzerland: Heroes of the Holocaust*. Hoboken, NJ: KTAV Pub., 2000. Print.

4. "The Rescuer and His Camera - Through the Lens of History." *The Rescuer and His Camera - Through the Lens of History*. Web. 10 Feb. 2015. <http://www.yadvashem.org/YV/en/exhibitions/our_collections/carl_lutz/>

SWISS HERO DR. PETER ZÜRCHER

Alex Bersamin

The Holocaust was a terrible tragedy that occurred in Germany, during World War II. It became a major problem when the Nazis gained control 1933. They believed that the Jewish people, as well as some other people of different belief (such as Communists), were inferior to the rest of the population, especially the Nazis themselves. Times were tough if you were Jewish, and it looked as if there would be no end to the misery brought on by the Nazis. But justice prevailed, as we all know. Even though many innocent people were killed by the Nazis' harsh actions, a significant amount were saved. So how exactly were these people rescued from the endless attacks? Allied forces came across to Germany, and found these people (who they liberated). This could not have been done, however, without the brave, unselfish heroes of the Holocaust. These special people were there for the purpose of assisting the Jewish (and other people discriminated against). They fought for the Jews, even putting their own lives on the line to rescue as many as they could. There are many that exemplify the best of the people, in this select group, and I will be informing you on one of them. Today I will be highlighting one of these heroes, who shows exemplary skill and courage.

Dr. Peter Zürcher was born in Zurich, Switzerland, 1914. He found interest in a career, and was brought to Hungary in 1940 on business. From there, he came across a job located in Budapest (under the Swiss Legation). This was in 1944, whence Peter Zürcher was appointed to a position in the Department for Safeguarding the Interests of Foreigners in the Swiss Embassy. This position was given to him by the Vice-Consul of the Embassy: Carl Lutz. Carl Lutz was also a hero, who saved countless Jewish people during the time, and did very well to protect them. So it was from this point that Dr. Zürcher would be able to save Jewish people from the Nazis. He followed his appointer's example by successfully liberating many amounts of Jewish people in the near future.

Here are some examples of Dr. Peter Zürcher's brave exploits to save the Jewish from the Nazis, while in his position on the Department for Safeguarding the Interests of Foreigners. He stopped the invasion of SS and Arrow Cross groups on the Pest Ghetto. The groups were planning on killing every inhabitant of the ghetto. Luckily, Zürcher was there to stop them, fending them off by threatening the commander with legal dealings. Most of the many people residing there, approximately 70,000 people, lived to see another day because of this action. The SS even defended the Jewish against the Arrow Cross group's attack because of Zürcher's rebuke. In January of 1945, Peter Zürcher was made aware of an attack planned by the Arrow Cross in advance. They planned to capture all the citizens in Swiss protected houses, located in the international ghetto. Immediately, Zürcher jumped into action, contacting the Minister of the Interior, Gabor Vajna, with strong protests to try and stop the attack on the Swiss houses. It worked, and the attack was canceled. The final example was when Zürcher's secretary, Maria Kormos, was stuck in a situation, and Zürcher put his life on the line to save her. The Jewish homes were shut down, and so Zürcher tried to bribe the porter into releasing Kormos. But he was denied. Zürcher still did not give up. Some people, dressed as Arrow Cross executives came and picked Maria Kormos up from the home, and took her to Zürcher as he ordered. Unable to hide her anywhere else, he risked letting her stay at his place for 6 weeks until he could devise fake papers for her to escape. She was then able to live on in freedom, all because of his valiant efforts. On October 22, 1998, Dr. Peter Zürcher was recognized by Yad Vashem for these actions to save thousands of people.

So you can see, just from this one man, how truly wonderful the heroes of the Holocaust were. They showed that no matter the cost, other's lives must be saved, or your own has no meaning. They were the ones who understood that nothing can be done unless they make it happen. Only they had the courage to stand up for the weak and innocent, and without pay. It is these people, rising to the occasion and doing whatever they can possibly do to help others, who can be called heroes. Heroes of the thousands upon thousands of people who wouldn't have been able to live otherwise. There are plenty of people who do the wrong thing, just as the Nazis did. It was a terrible tragedy, as I have previously stated. But if there is wrongdoing, then the only solution is people who stand for their rights, or others' rights, to correct the behavior of these corrupted people. And so lives on, the legacy of the Heroes of the Holocaust.

Works Cited

"Introduction to the Holocaust." United States Holocaust Memorial Museum. United States Holocaust Memorial Council, 20 June 2014. Web. 10 Feb. 2015.

"Peter Zürcher." *Funkascript ATOM*. The International Raoul Wallenberg Foundation. Web. 10 Feb. 2015.

"The Righteous of Switzerland." *Google Books*. Web. 9 Feb. 2015. < https://books.google.com/books?id=-MtaXNRtrB0C&pg=PR41&dq=peter zurcher switzerland&hl=en&sa=X&ei=_s3JVNioM4K3ogSOh4GABQ&ved=0CCUQ6AEwAQ#v=onepage&q=peter zurcher switzerland&f=true>.

"Zurcher Family." *The Righteous Among the Nations*. Yad Vashem. Web. 9 Feb. 2015.

HOLOCAUST ESSAY

Amy Kerfoot

There is segregation everywhere we go. Whether it is because of race, religion, or sex, segregation is still a big part of our world. There have been many times that segregation has created a war, but one of the biggest and cruelest examples is the Holocaust. The definition of the Holocaust is the destruction or slaughter on a mass scale, especially caused by fire or nuclear war. The Jewish Holocaust put many children to their dismal demise by locking them in gas chambers when parents thought they were going to get a better education. The leader of the Nazis was a German politician by the name of Adolf Hitler. But there were people who chose to stand up and make a difference, Benedikt Brunschweiler, Abbe Albert Gross, and Paul Grueninger.

One of the many heroes was Benedikt Brunschweiler. Brunschweiler was a representative of the ICRC (International Committee of the Red Cross). He arranged to keep the refugees in Abbey buildings for the last months of World War II. In the camp of Abbey, many people found joy in music, even though the conditions were very gloomy. There were about 3,000 people in the Abbey buildings, most of them were children, and they found safety at the end of the war in Abbey. Brunschweiler was also a merchant. He was sent by Friedrich Born, a delegate of the International Red Cross, to go to Pannonhalma. Brunschweiler hide the refugees in the Benedictine Monastery. There were Jewish mothers and children hiding in the monastery.

Another hero was Abbe Albert Gross. He was born in Lausanne. Albert Gross ran the Fribourg Foyer Saint-Justin. In May 1942, Albert Gross arrived at Gurs Camp. The Bishop of Fribourg sent Albert Gross as representative of Swiss welfare organization. This organization was called Caritas.

The camp gave Catholic spiritual comfort. Through out the 13 months he spent in the camp he started to aid other people who had different religions, some which included Jews. To aid the Jews he had to do illegal activy to insure comfort to the Jews. There were many Jews who owed their life to Abbe Albert Gross. Some of those people were Georges Vadnai, Weizberg Dora, her father, and sister. Georges Vadnai became Chief Rabbi of Lausanne.

In Gurs, Father Albert Gross saved George Vadnai's life. Father Albert Gross took Vadnai to the barracks where the fate of the Jews had not been decided yet after Father Albert Gross saw Vadnai on the list to be deported. Vadnai was put on the refugee category of "non swage." Seven-hundred-fifty Jews were selected for deportation on the night of 3rd to 4th of March. George Vadnai had to go the "selection committee." His Yugoslav citizenship maked sure that he had to get deportarted. It tried to make Vadnai admit his nationality, Hungarian, where he was born in 1915. This information would spare him his deportation. "I have to sit in a group that will leave the next bus Oloron-Drancy [...] Beside me, a door opens, a priest comes in. I learn of a fellow prisoner that it is Father Albert Gross * [...] whose effective interventions and rescue operations are known to everyone. Without hesitation I approach it: "Father, I introduce myself: I'm the Vadnai Rabbi. I serve God in another temple as you, but I hope it will not prevent you give me a hand; I have just been selected for deportation selection committee."

In the Grus, Father Albert Gross found many more Swiss. The first foreign sent to the camp was a nurse by the name of Elsbeth Kasser. She was admitted in 1940 December. She created a clinic and opened a school with seven classes in the three years she was there. The actions of Father Albert Gross was not just based on the Gurs camp. He organized crossing the Lake Geneva for two or three refugees and has contributed to making false papers.

Another hero was Paul Grueninger. He was the Swiss border police commander of the St. Gallen region. Switzerland was not letting the Jews go through Switzerland. Grueninger broke the law to let the suffering and desperate refugees go into Switzerland. To legalize the refuge's status he forged their registration. He made their passports say that they had been in Switzerland before March of 1938. He did this because that was when refugees were allowed to come into Switzerland. This made the refugees to be treated as legals. They were taken to the Diepoldsau camp. In the camp they were aided and waited to see if Switzerland would be their new home or if they had to go the final destination. Grueninger lied about how many refugees were in the camp and even used his own hard owned money to buy the refugees winter clothes, because many of the refugees has to leave their belongings behind. Grueninger was exposed by the Germans and he leave the police force. He was put on trial for aiding, permitting entry, and foreign registration papers of 3,600 Jews.

Although nothing can make up for the terrible events of the Holocaust there are people who showed as heroes and saved many people's lives. The Holocaust showed who was a true hero and who couldn't stand up for what was right.

Kerfoot 4"Albert Gross." *Albert-Gross*. 1 Jan. 2001. Web. 25 Feb. 2015. <http://www.ajpn.org/juste-Albert-Gross-1331.html>.

"Hungary: Posthumous "Righteous among the Nations" Awardbestowed on War-time ICRC Representative." *Hungary: Posthumous "Righteous among the Nations" Awardbestowed on War-time ICRC Representative*. ICRC, 1 Jan. 2010. Web. 25 Feb. 2015.

"Paul Grueninger - The Righteous Among The Nations - Yad Vashem." *Paul Grueninger - The Righteous Among The Nations - Yad Vashem*. Yad Vashem The Holocaust Martyrs' and Heroes' Remembrance Authority, 1 Jan. 2015. Web. 25 Feb. 2015. <http://www.yadvashem.org/yv/en/righteous/stories/grueninger.asp>.

"Remembering Raoul Wallenberg." *PolskieRadio.pl*. Web. 25 Feb. 2015. <http://www.polskieradio.pl/123/2137/Artykul/607370,Remembering-Raoul-Wallenberg>.

Sawer, Patrick, and Edward Malnick. "Westminster Abbey to Honour Music of the Nazi Camps." *The Telegraph*. Telegraph Media Group, 25 Jan. 2015. Web. 25 Feb. 2015. <http://www.telegraph.co.uk/news/religion/11367391/Westminster-Abbey-to-honour-music-of-the-Nazi-camps.html>

HEROES OF THE HOLOCAUST

Angelina He

The Holocaust was a persecution and murder of 6 million Jews by the Nazis. This all started in 1933, when the Jews who lived in Europe had a population of over 9 million. During World War II, the Jews lived in European countries that Nazi Germany would occupy. Soon, two out of every three European Jews were killed, as a part of the "Final Solution," which was a plan to kill all the European Jews. The Nazi tyranny started spreading all over Europe, while the Germans kept killing and persecuting millions of Jews, homosexuals and other people who weren't "normal."

The Germans also sent out Polish and Soviet citizens to forced labor camps, and targeted lots of political opponents and religious people (*"Introduction to the Holocaust"*). Incarceration and maltreatment were two ways many of those people died. In the final months of the war, people started "death marches" to prevent the liberation of prisoners. Soon, the Allies finally stopped the German armed forces and the war was over (*"Introduction to the Holocaust"*). Throughout the Holocaust, there were lots of heroes who were brave and strong enough to stand up to the Germans. Margareta Tobler, Emma and Walter Giannini, and Anne-Marie Im Hof-Piguet are the people I recognized as heroes. In my essay, I will be talking about those four people who saved innocent children's lives during the Holocaust.

Margareta (Gret) Tobler worked as a Kindergarten teacher at the Swiss Red Cross children's home at the La Hille castle in southern France. But what she did for the two children matters more. She single-handedly took two young Jewish girls across the border to Switzerland. Gret wrote her own account of their journey, and it was also documented by Anne-Marie Im Hof-Piguet in her book, *"La Filière."* The two girls who escaped from La Hille were: Toni Rosenblatt, age 12 and Inge Bernard, age 15. They both had earned visas to leave France and go to Switzerland, but they couldn't leave France legally ("*The Righteous of Switzerland*"). That's when Gret stepped in. On December 10, 1943 at 2:30 in the morning, they left the castle, and walked for three hours until they reached the train station of Saint-Jean-de-Verges. They then took a train to Toulouse, which then led them to take another train to Carcasonne. Later that night they managed to fit into an express train to Lyons, and then they caught another train to Annemasse. From Annnemasse, they walked along the border to St.-Cergue-les-Voirons. Soon they had arrived at the Red Cross children's home "Les Feux Follets" and they stayed a few nights there until they found a way out ("*The Righteous of Switzerland*"). Over the course of a few days, they found three places to escape from, but they were either heavily guarded or had a barbed wire fence up. Finally, Gret found a way out with no guards or a barbed wire fence, Inge was the first one across, and she was safe on Swiss soil. The next day, Gret and Toni made it across too. All of the Swiss guards were surprised that they made it to there.

Walter and Emma Giannini were both Swiss citizens, who worked for the Swiss Children's Relief. This organization was working with the Swiss Red Cross, and had opened up a home for children from needy families. Lots of children were admitted into Faverges for a three-month cure of supplementary feeding. In the beginning of 1942, they took in Jewish parents who were looking for refuge in France. There were two girls who stayed behind after the three-month cure. Those two girls were Rose Spiegel and Berthe Silber (*"Giannini Rescue Story"*). Berthe was a 12-year-old girl, who was the daughter of a Belgian Jewish family that fled to Eauze, and was put into Faverges on June 25, 1942. Later in August, she got a letter stating that her parents and her little sister had been arrested, and she didn't see her family again after that. Walter and Emma were determined to get those two girls out of France. They took a train to Annemasse, and then they walked along the border until Walter had found an opening, which led them safely to Switzerland. ("*Giannini Rescue Story*") The girls had found refuge with the Gianninis and their close friends, the family of Sina Jecklin. A few months later, Emma gave birth to a newborn baby, which meant that she was pregnant throughout the journey to Switzerland. Thinking upon that, there were lots of dangerous scenarios that could have hurt Emma and her baby, but she and Walter overcoming those dangers helped save the lives of Berthe Silber and Rose Spiegel.

Anne-Marie Im Hof-Piguet was born on April 12, 1916. After she graduated at the University of Lausanne in 1940, she temporarily worked as a teacher at the Swiss Red Cross. The Germans soon expanded their territory and Anne-Marie feared the worst about what is going to happen when they came. Her fears were answered when they came in November 1942, and the French were on their side, trying to invade La Hille castle to take children from ages 16 to 17. The next year in February 1943, the French police had arrested five residents, and three of them were deported, then in June three more teenagers were arrested. Anne-Marie was fed up about the French taking away these people, so she was planning to smuggle them across the border, and lead them into a wooded mountain valley called, Risoux ("*Anne-Marie Im Hof*"). The first time that they were going to cross the border was very dangerous, with the forbidden border was very well organized and there would be lots of heavy security, it would be difficult to cross. She had taken eight young people across the border the first time. Now, the last time across the border in May 1944 would be a very memorable one. This time she took with her Paul Schlesinger, his mother Flora, Walter Kamlet, Sebastian Steiger, and Victoria and Madeleine Cordier. After landing into some troubles with the police, they finally reached their destination ("*Anne-Marie Im Hof*"). Over the time period of two years, Anne-Marie had saved 14 innocent lives. She married Ulrich Im Hof, two years before the war ended and once the war was over she worked as a teacher in the canton of Vaud and Basel.

These four people did amazing things to save innocent children's lives. They were honored as heroes because they were some of the many people that were brave enough to go against the Germans' hold on the Jews. Margareta (Gret) Tobler helped two girls escape from France to Switzerland. She displayed lots of courage to go and disobey laws to take the girls away from the war, which saved their lives. Walter and Emma Giannini were a brave couple working together to also save two girls' lives, with Emma risking the loss her own unborn child to save the other two girls. She and Walter defied the rule of the Germans, standing up to them. And lastly, Anne-Marie Im Hof-Piguet saved 14 girls by helping them to escape. These four people did great things risking their own lives to help save others, and that's why we honor them as heroes.

Works Cited

Anonymous, Just and Persecuted during the Nazi Period in the Communes of France. "Anne- Marie Im Hof." *Anne-Marie-Im-Hof*. Anonymous, Just and Persecuted during the Nazi   Period in the Communes of France, 2008. Web. 06 Feb. 2015.

United States Holocaust Memorial Museum. "Introduction to the Holocaust." *United States   Holocaust Memorial Museum*. United States Holocaust Memorial Council, 20 June 2014. Web. 06 Feb. 2015.

Wagner, Meir, and Moshe Meisels. "The Righteous of Switzerland." *Google Books*. KTAV Publishing House, 2001. Web. 25 Feb. 2015. Used pages 85-86.

Yad Vashem. "Giannini FAMILY: Rescue Story." *Yad Vashem*. Yad Vashem The Holocaust Martyrs' and Heroes' Remembrance Authority, 2015. Web. 06 Feb. 2015.

PAUL GRUENINGER

Anna Cohen

The Holocaust was a horrible time for millions of people who were tortured, shot, starved, and worked to the bone, and they had no way to protect themselves from the dominant Nazis. This went on for a very long while and over that time over 6 million Jews were killed. The Holocaust left a stamp on everyone, showing to all what true torture is. However, in this horrible outbreak rose some heroes who we remember now and forever for their bravery and courage. Many risked their lives to save even the smallest number of Jews whose lives were in jeopardy. Among these lifesavers was Paul Grueninger. This man was the Swiss border police commander of the St. Gallen region that borders with Austria. His story is rather simple, but had a large effect on thousands of Jews.

Recently, Switzerland had closed the border to everyone except for those who had proper entry permits. In 1938, Switzerland and Nazi Germany came upon an agreement to stamp the famous J in all Jews' passports, thus keeping them out. As time went on, the treatment of the Jews in Austria deteriorated, leading to a large influx of Jews trying to cross to Switzerland.

Forty-seven year old Paul Grueninger was faced with probably the biggest decision of his life. Was he to follow his directions as given, turning thousands of Jews back into a dangerous, anti-Semitic situation, or let them through, saving them all? In a thrust of courage, Paul disregarded all explicit directions given to him and let many pass across into Switzerland. He falsified all of their registrations, saying that they had arrived in Switzerland before the law was made against their crossing. In doing this he enabled them to appear as if they legally entered Switzerland and thus got sent to the Diepoldsau camp, which was aided by the Jewish organizations. When reporting, Paul reported a false number of entrees and a false status of the refugees in his district, but he didn't stop there. He even used his own money to buy warm clothes for the needy Jews, who had been forced to leave everything behind.

As expected, Paul did have to deal with the repercussions of his actions. The Germans eventually found out and reported to the Swiss authorities of Paul's falsifying the status of the refugees. He was released of his police duties and sent to trial where he was charged with illegally permitting the entry of 3,600 Jews into Switzerland, falsifying their registration papers, and most importantly shielding them from detection. Again, as expected, Paul Grueninger was found guilty. While his motives were taken into consideration, overall they reasoned that he was a state employee, and that he had disregarded critical directions given to him by the Swiss authorities.

After being found guilty, Paul had to pay the court trial, and on top of having lost his job, this brought him down quite hard. For the rest of his life he lived in very difficult circumstances, but he never regretted saving thousands of lives. The people that he helped cross the border most likely have children and possibly even grandchildren, and none of them would be here today if it had not been for Paul Grueninger. I personally know people whose grandparents and/or great grandparents were sadly in the concentration camps and I just think about how if they were killed in the Holocaust, they would not be here today. So many other families must feel the same way. I think of my peers as those who could not be here today if their relatives had passed away during this horrible time, but for some people including my peers, they have to think that they personally might not exist if their relatives didn't make it. Paul not only saved them in the present, but also in the future.

Later, Paul explained his reasoning in this simple yet powerful quote, "It was basically a question of saving human lives threatened with death. How could I then seriously consider bureaucratic schemes and calculations?"

It was not that Paul had a personal connection with each of the 3,600 Jews that he let cross the border, but an emotional one. It was an emotional connection with them and within himself. Although he was trained to do his job as it was directed, he could not turn people back to the country to face their gruesome deaths. Death was essentially staring at him right in the eyes, and he had to choose who he wanted to save, thousands of people he didn't even know, or himself. Thankfully for so many people, he chose for the lives of those thousands to be spared.

After years of living in difficulty, in 1970, Paul received a letter of apology from the Swiss government. However, steps to help Paul's recovery from the long period of hardships he faced were not taken until shortly after Paul's death.

In 1971, which was a year before Paul passed away, he was awarded the title of Righteous Among the Nations. Besides saving the lives of thousands of Jews, this was the best that he could have felt about what he had done. He then knew that people really appreciated all that he did. And we do. So thank you to Paul Grueninger for saving so many of us. We are so grateful that there was somebody out there who was willing to risk their own safety in return for thousands of beautiful souls.

On February 22, 1972, Paul Grueninger sadly passed on, yet his legacy lives on. Paul was one of the few of people who risked themselves in return for not one, not two, but thousands of lives.

THE HEROISM OF CARL LUTZ' DURING THE HOLOCAUST
Areeb Ahmed

The Holocaust is one of the darkest periods of time in history, and a hard time for the Jews. Six million innocent Jews were murdered by the Nazi regime, or Hitler's followers. The Holocaust segregated Jews, and faced them with many different obstacles and hardships. However, there were many heroes who tried to help the Jews during this time, and one of them was Carl Lutz. Nowadays kids' perspective of a hero is either in the form of a superhero or a sports athlete, not of someone who has left an impact on the world through their words or actions.

Carl Lutz was born on March 30, 1985 in Walzenhausen, Switzerland. His mother was a teacher at the Methodist chapel and taught religion, while his father owned a marble quarry. His parents had ten children, and Lutz was the second youngest child. Lutz spent his childhood and adolescence in this village, and this gave him a sense of personal responsibility and social commitment. In 1913, he moved to the United States, and he began to study the subjects of Latin and theology, and through this he got a job at the Swiss Embassy in Washington D.C. In 1935, he married his wife Gertrude Frankhauser. In 1939, when the Second World War broke, Germany asked Switzerland to represent its interest in the region. At this time Lutz was promoted to vice-consul and in 1942, he went to Hungary to serve his duties as a vice-consul. Carl Lutz can be considered a hero as he saved thousands of Jews from getting killed and deported by the Nazis, he went against the German and Hungarian government to save these Jews, and went through many hardships to do all of this.

In 1944, the Nazis took over Hungary and they began to send all the Jews to extermination camps. Many of the Hungarian Jews pleaded for help. As a diplomat and a kind person, Lutz did everything in his power to help these Jews. He first began by requesting the Hungarians to stop the deportation of the Jews to Germany. The Hungarian Government's answer was that they would only do what Germany would tell them to do. His approach failed, so he began to issue thousands and thousands of Schutzbriefs, or rescue letters. These letters said that nothing can be done to these Jews as they were under Swiss protection. Using his own money, Lutz

70

rented around 76 buildings to protect and house Jews under his own protection. With the help of his wife, Gertrude, he gave them food and also provided them with medical treatment" (Yad Vashem). Many of the diplomats and consuls had left Budapest by 1944, except for Raoul Wallenberg, the Swedish diplomat, who was also in favor of helping Lutz and the Jews.

Besides just helping these Jews, Carl Lutz also went against the German and Hungarian government. "When Lutz first pleaded with the Hungarian government to protect the Jews, they refused. Later, he managed to convince them to give him permission to save 8,000 Jews. However, Lutz realized that there were many more Jews to save. As mentioned before, he issued protective passports to Jews so they could migrate to Palestine. The first time he sent 10,000 Jews to Palestine. He fooled the Hungarian government since he told them he would send only 8,000, but actually he sent 10,000" (Holocaust Heroes). Every single time, when he made the passports he would only make a small amount of passports as then this would not surpass the government. This shows how cunning Lutz was, and how he used his sharp skills to save many lives. "He went against the German government in these ways. When Germany took over Hungary, it became their property. However, they let the Hungarian government still run their country themselves" (Famous Stories). Lutz didn't really challenge the German government but he took advantage of them. However, if you think about it, Lutz was dealing with Germany, a superpower at that time. The numbers of Jews that Lutz saved was not enough to be noticed by the German governments and thus he was able to save many lives.

"Besides saving the Jews, and challenging the Hungarian and German governments, Carl Lutz also went through many hardships. There were many gangsters and thugs who were after Lutz for trying to save the Jews. Often Lutz saved himself by showing them his diplomatic pass and saying that if they would kill him, the Swiss government would not spare them" (Yad Vashem). Also, Lutz loved photography; and many times he would go out and take pictures of what was going on. Often this hobby of his got him into trouble. At times, he would get arrested or mugged for trying to take shots of Jews and the ghettos they lived in. The only way he would be saved is by his diplomatic pass. Also, when Lutz put the Jews into 76 different buildings, he used his own savings and money to rent these buildings and provide food and medical treatment for these Jews. Neither did USA nor Switzerland fund him for trying to save these Jews. He had no financial support from either country. The Red Cross was willing to do anything to help Lutz, but they also survived on a very meager financial situation. Lutz had to use his own money to carry out these tasks for the Hungarian Jews. Also, when the war was over, "Lutz did not even receive any credit from Switzerland for saving the Jews. This put him in a very mentally unstable condition and he stayed in a mental hospital in Zurich for a little while" (Holocaust Heroes). After many years, the

Yad Vashem society gave him and his wife recognition for what they did during the Holocaust.

Carl Lutz indeed was a true hero for the things that he did. He is credited for the largest escape during the Holocaust. He saved many Jews using his issued passports. He also challenged the Hungarian and German governments. He also went through many hardships to save these Jewish citizens. Besides, just going through many different hardships, he did not even receive credit from his own country for trying to save the Jews. He indeed suffered a lot, but if it wasn't for Carl Lutz, many lives would have been lost.

Bibliography

Holmes, Marian. "Five Rescuers of Those Threatened by the Holocaust." *Smithsonian.* 24Feb. 2009. Web. 6 Feb. 2015.

Tenembaum, Baruch. "Carl Lutz." *The International Raoul Wallenburg Foundation.* Web.   5   Feb. 2015.

Tschuy, Theo. "Donate Now." *Yad Vashem Search Results.* Yad Vashem, 1 Jan. 1986. Web. 5 Feb. 2015.

Zadikow, Dara. "Lutz, Carl - The Jewish Foundation for the Righteous." *The Jewish Foundation for the Righteous.* Claims Conference. Web. 5 Feb. 2015.

FRIEDRICH BORN

Brendan Barlow

In 1942, the International Committee of the Red Cross (ICRC) became aware that genocide was taking place in Europe. They were informed by a number of sources that the Nazis intended to eliminate the Jews. However, the official policy of the ICRC did not allow them to step in and stop the deportations and killing of the Jewish people. In 1944, Friedrich Born became the Swiss delegate to the ICRC in Budapest, Hungary. He had learned about the deportation of Hungarian Jews to the concentration camps and was determined to do as much as he could to try to save as many people as possible. Years after his death, Friedrich Born was awarded Righteous Among Nations in 1987 for his bravery and ingenuity for saving thousands of Jews despite the policies of the ICRC.

Friedrich Born was born on June 10, 1903 in Langenthal, Switzerland. He initially came to Budapest as a trader with the Swiss federal department of foreign trade. This was before his appointment in 1944 to the International Committee of the Red Cross (ICRC). Soon after the occupation of Hungary took place in March of 1944, Born became aware of the deportation and various other measures being taken against the Hungarian Jews by the Nazis. He realized the speed at which the Nazis were deporting and exterminating the Hungarian Jews and that it would take no more than two to three months for them to exterminate the total population of Jews in Hungary. He wrote a number of letters and reports that he sent to ICRC headquarters in Geneva describing, "the terrible things that were being prepared and done." Born knew he wanted to do something to help so he began by approaching the Hungarian government and asking to visit two camps in Hungary where Jews were placed before being transported to Auschwitz. He found men, women and children in incredibly crowded conditions. There were not even close to enough toilets or sanitary facilities for the number of people being housed. There was very little food and water as well. Born became alarmed and asked that the ICRC intervene immediately to stop the suffering. He wanted them to "protest officially against the persecution of the Jews and request that the harassment would cease without delay." The ICRC did not reply to Born's request, so he decided to act on his own initiative and do whatever was within his power to save as many people as possible.

Born set up and ran a special department of the ICRC from the Budapest office. The goal he started with was to bring together and protect at least six thousand Jewish children from all around the country. His plan had been to have the Spanish Red Cross take care of them and then transport them to North Africa where they would be safe. They were never able to carry this plan out but the focus of this department became the rescue of Jewish children. They setup safe houses, or children's homes, that operated with the protection of Swiss diplomats and the ICRC. Through this program, thousands of Jewish children and their nurses were saved. The men and women of the Jewish Pioneers and the Zionist Movement supported these shelters. Despite the fact that the ICRC was supposed to remain neutral, Born was clearly aware of and involved in these "illegal activities." According to Peresz Rowas, a member of the Hungarian resistance movement during the war, Born began issuing special identity cards to members of the resistance movement that confirmed that they were Christian and working for the ICRC. This allowed them to save as many Jews as possible from being deported to Auschwitz by using their "official" documentation.

Born's ingenuity extended to many more plans he was able to implement in order to save more of the Jewish population. He asked for hospitals to be established. There were many Jews hospitalized there as a way from being deported and killed in the concentration camps. He also increased the number of ICRC delegates needed in Hungary so he could hire Jews. This gave at least 3,000 Jews protection from deportation. In late 1944, the German authorities began forced marches of tens of thousands of Jews from Hungary to Austria and Germany. Born again protested adamantly. Some of his protests fell on deaf ears in the government but he was able to place thousands of Jews under the protection of the Red Cross, which saved them from being forced into the death marches. He risked his life and his freedom by continuing to work with resistance fighters and by opposing the government and the ICRC. Many of the measures that Born had taken were no longer effective once the Arrow Cross Party had taken over in 1944. Despite Born's vigorous objections, the Nazis deported 50,000 Jews immediately. When Born was unable to prevent these deportations, he distributed relief supplies to the deportees. He was able, however, to stop the last convoys from leaving with about 7,500 Jews.

Born took his position with the ICRC at a time when the world around him was in chaos. He was aware of the horrors taking place and seemed determined to make a difference. This was not by any means an easy task. Even the ICRC, whose job was to look out for human rights, did not show the kind of resolve that Born did to stop the atrocities that were taking place. Born showed an amazing amount of courage and determination. He fought against every obstacle he came up against, risking his own freedom and his life to help and save thousands in need.

Bibliography

Bugnion, François. "Dialogue with the Past: The ICRC and the Nazi Death Camps." *Dialogue with the Past: The ICRC and the Nazi Death Camps*. N.p., 5 Nov. 2002. Web. 08 Feb. 2015.

Wagner, Meir, and Moshe Meisels. *The Righteous of Switzerland: Heroes of the Holocaust*. Hoboken, NJ: KTAV Pub., 2000. Print.

"Friedrich Born." *The International Raoul Wallenberg Foundation*. N.p., n.d. Web. 09 Feb. 2015.

SWISS SAVIORS

Colin Brannan

During World War II, Europe was a vile place. Europe, the epicenter of fighting for this repugnant war, was ravaged by food shortages, bombings, loss, sadness, and death. Many of these wrongs follow the great mistake of war naturally; bombs will be launched, bullets will be fired, and lives will be reaped like ripe grain at the harvest. But many people remember World War II as being particularly evil. People may think that World War II was evil because it introduced techniques for mass death, involved the most countries of any war to date, or lost the lives of countless soldiers forced to fight in filthy, disgusting trenches while gunfire blazed across the open land above. However, the primary reason that World War II is remembered for its horrors to this very day is because of the Holocaust.

The Holocaust was the mass murder of all "enemies" of the Nazis throughout Europe. These "enemies" were primarily Jewish, although many groups were persecuted, including Gypsies, Catholics, homosexuals, Jehovah's Witnesses, and the disabled. Of the approximated 11 million people killed during the Holocaust, 6million were Jewish. One major piece to understanding the Holocaust lies in Nazi concentration camps. It was in these camps that prisoners faced fates almost worse than the death that awaited them. Prisoners slept without mattresses or pillows, were forced to do exhausting labor with minuscule rations to sustain themselves, were experimented on by Nazi doctors without their consent, and were tortured and tormented constantly. After enduring these things for as long as their captors saw fit, the prisoners would be permitted to take a "shower." Once the prisoners had undressed and taken off all jewelry, they were herded into gas chambers where they were killed. After all of the prisoners had died, their dead bodies were burned in mass crematoriums, their ashes being buried *en masse* in fields. Truly, the Holocaust is one of the worst things that any faction of society has ever endorsed, if not the worst. People around the world saw the Holocaust as a terrible event, even without realizing the full horror of the actions taking place. Thus, many people and groups worked tirelessly to help any prospective "enemies" of the Nazis to escape from Nazi-controlled territory, even with the threats of imprisonment or death ever-present. These brave souls came from all places and all backgrounds, all united in the goal of helping. This being said, two Swiss Red Cross Workers were particularly important in helping the persecuted to escape from the Nazis with their lives: Auguste Bohny and Friedel Bohny-Reiter, who later would become husband and wife.

Auguste Bohny, an army veteran, was 33 years old when his services became needed in the saving of the persecuted children of Europe. Bohny had previously joined a group known as *Les Secours Suisse aux Enfants*. This group originated in France and worked to relocate persecuted children from the Nazi territory to safe places throughout Switzerland. *Les Secours Suisse aux Enfants* had a main base located in Le Chambon-sur-Lignon, a village located in a mountainous yet green territory near France's Southern border with Germany. Auguste came to this base to help create additional housing for the many persecuted groups that were being hidden there, but quickly assumed control of the compound. Auguste proved himself to be a creative man, coming up with clever solutions for food and medical supply shortages. Auguste was also quite kind, shown by the numerous positive accounts that many children who had stayed at his compound gave when reflecting on the Holocaust later in life. Auguste also became allies with other protection groups in the area. In fact, he and the leaders of a group very similar to his, the Trocmés, became good friends. Auguste helped over 800 children to reach safety while working for *Les Secours Suisse aux Enfants*.

Friedel started her relocation career later then Auguste, originally planning on being a nurse in her adulthood, but joining *Les Secours Suisse aux Enfants* in 1940, as the war was beginning. Friedel's home base for *Les Secours Suisse aux Enfants* was located in Riversaltes, a camp closer to the South of France than Auguste's. Here, there were many Jews, Gypsies, and Spanish refugees, all fleeing from France's Southeastern border with Germany. Friedel did her best to make life enjoyable for these people by organizing children's activities, providing medical help, and handing out extra food. When Jews began to be deported in 1942, Friedel moved the children out of her camp and into the more secretive camp run by Auguste. By 1943, Friedel was working full time at Auguste's base. There, they helped to save anywhere from 3,000 to 5,000 Jews.

After the war ended, Friedel did indeed go on to be married to Auguste. They were some of the few rescue workers to survive the Holocaust and all of its destruction. Compared to the millions of people who died during the Holocaust, saving about 5,000 people might not seem very significant. But, combine the number of people that the Bohnys saved with the people that all other rescue workers saved, and the people who were allowed to live skyrockets. Plus, think about the terrors of the vile concentration camps created by the Nazis: any single life saved from that torture justifies any number of battles fought, any amount of money given for support, and any time donated to the cause. We all owe our thanks to Auguste, Friedel, and all others like them, who put their lives on the line to save others from death.

Bibliography

"Conspiracy of Goodness Cont. - How Rescue Developed." *Israel Issues*. The Twenty Ten Theme, 06 Mar. 2013. Web. 09 Feb. 2015.

"Friedel BOHNY-REITER." *Friedel BOHNY-REITER*. Ed. Blyth Spirit. Anglophone Direct, 2010. Web. 09 Feb. 2015.

"The Righteous Among The Nations." *Yad Vashem*. The Holocaust Martyrs' and Heroes' Remembrance Authority, 2015. Web. 09 Feb. 2015.

Rosenberg, Jennifer. "Holocaust Facts." *What You Need to Know About the Holocaust*. About.com, 2015. Web. 01 Feb. 2015.

THE THOUGHT GIVEN BY PAUL GRUNINGER

George Liu

Things looked grim for Jews residing in Germany in the 1940s. The Holocaust was a terrifying and cruel event which began with the Jews' exclusion from society and ultimately grew into the largest genocide in history. While the Nazis caused destruction and killing, however, some kind-hearted people were able to find it within their ability and will to help a victim of Hitler's acts of evil. Among these people was Colonel Paul Gruninger, a Swiss border-police commander that helped Jews escape to safety in this time of need.

Gruninger was born on October 27, 1981, in St. Gallen of northeastern Switzerland. He played football, taking the Bruhl St. Gallen team to the championships in 1915, studied in Roschach, and served as a colonel during the First World War (Tenembaum) ("Paul Gruninger"). He was also an involved supporter of an association for animal protection (Tenembaum). Before the Holocaust, not much distinguished him from a man. When he was older, he worked as a senior higher-rank policeman managing the border between Switzerland and Austria. As the Holocaust grew, he experienced that Jews had been fleeing into Switzerland in hopes of survival. After the annexation of Austria to Germany in 1938, the number of fleeing refugees grew overwhelmingly large, so border-police like Gruninger were ordered to turn back Jews wanting to enter Switzerland ("The Policeman Who Lifted the Border Barrier"). The significant moral decision for these policemen became whether to disregard orders and save lives or to refuse refugees entrance and turn them back to their country where anti-Semitism would lead to inevitable consequences for them.

Most people willingly did as they were told and began refusing entrance to desperate Jews. Paul Gruninger, however, was different. At great personal risk, he allowed Jews to illegally enter Switzerland. To avoid arousing suspicion, he fabricated the numbers in his reports about the entering refugees and changed the dates on passports to show that they had entered legally before the restriction date of March 1938. He even went as far as to purchase clothing for the Jews who had left everything trying to escape ("The Policeman Who Lifted the Border Barrier"). A woman who experienced his acts of compassion wrote a letter as follows to a friend: "There is a wonderful police Captain called Paul Grüninger. He promised me that he would look after my jewels and bring them to me from our friend's hotel." Gruninger is described as a very good and kind man, and it is also found that he took additional actions to help Jews such as retrieving the jewelry this woman left behind (Tenembaum). About three-thousand six-hundred Jews escaped to Switzerland with Gruninger's help before he was captured with the information in the above letter, which had unluckily been intercepted ("The Policeman Who Lifted the Border Barrier") (Tenembaum). When brought to trial, the case was debated for two years before he was found guilty of violating the orders given while on duty, fraud, and aiding individual Jews such as when he purchased clothes and food for them. Gruninger's sympathy for anxious Jews earned him a jail term, hefty fines, and loss of his job and retirement funds ("The Policeman Who Lifted the Border Barrier"). In his later life, he struggled to make a living as an ostracized ex-convict ("Paul Gruninger | Switzerland"). His good name was never cleared until some twenty-three years after his death when his court case was reopened (Tenembaum).

Still, Gruninger regretted nothing that he did. He explained in 1954, "It was basically a question of saving human lives threatened with death. How then, could I seriously consider bureaucratic schemes and calculations..." (Tenembaum). While others simply followed orders, Gruninger was made different through one certain experience: his meetings with the people whose lives he handled. No one else had witnessed the crying and begging of needy Jews, and had just given orders to return them to Germany and Austria (Beem). But Gruninger had listened to these people and met with them face-to-face when they came to his office on their knees (Beem).

He was able to look past himself and help these people, and happily bear the penalties, something very few during that time (or modern-day society, for that matter) did. It may seem like an obvious choice for people today as to what to do in Paul Gruninger's situation. However, few people made these good moral decisions during the Holocaust, and it can still very difficult to follow through with what's right in any society.

Public objections several years later allowed honor to properly be bestowed to Gruninger's name. A town square and a street were given his name, and Yad Vashem praised him as a *Righteous Among the Nations* (Tenembaum). In our modern society, we admire the popular and famous singers and athletes. But what have they done to be involved in problematic world affairs? It is really those people who sacrifice their reputation or anything they have to make a difference that we should respect, and Paul Gruninger will remain a perfect model for the kindness and selflessness that we should demonstrate. There is no consideration quite alike to the thought given to those Jews who needed it by Paul Gruninger.

Works Cited

Beem, Darren. "Seeing, "Beautiful Souls" and Changing My Heart." *Momentary Delight.* WordPress, 15 November 2012. Web. 8 February 2015.

"Paul Gruninger." *Wikipedia, the Free Encyclopedia.* Wikimedia Foundation, Inc., 5 November 2014. Web. 6 February 2015.

"Paul Gruninger | Switzerland." *The Jewish Foundation for the Righteous.* The Jewish Foundation for the Righteous, n.d. Web. 7 February 2015.

Tenembaum, Baruch. "The Example of Gruninger." *The International Raoul Wallenberg Foundation.* The International Raoul Wallenberg Foundation, n.d. Web. 6 February 2015.

"The Policeman Who Lifted the Border Barrier." *Yad Vashem.* Yad Vashem the Holocaust Martyrs' and Heroes' Remembrance Authority, n.d. Web. 6 February 2015.

SWISS HEROES OF THE HOLOCAUST

Harish Vasanth

The Holocaust is an event where Hitler sent multiple Jews into concentration camps where they got tortured mercilessly. The reason why Hitler made this decision is because in Germany the Jewish people were taking up many jobs of the Germans. Hitler was unhappy about this. Along with that, he also considered Jews inferior to Germans. So, to open up jobs, He sent all the Jews into concentration camps to let German citizens take those jobs. Hitler made many countries deport their Jews so that they can be sent into concentration camps. This decision is also known as the Final Solution. Many people were unhappy with this decision. They did not want Jews to be tortured by Hitler. People from many countries, like

Switzerland and Denmark, took a stand against this inhumane treatment. One person who attempted to stop this treatment was Paul Grueninger. He was in the Swiss police force. He decided to save the Jews. He disobeyed his government's orders by allowing many Jewish refugees to illegally enter Switzerland without proper entry permits. He falsified their registration by making it seem that they had arrived before March 1938, when entry into the country became restricted. The Germans figured out about what he was doing and informed the Swiss authorities about his exploits. The government of Switzerland kicked him out of the police force and also put him in court trials. The court trials went on for two years but ended with him being guilty. He was fined and had to pay for the trial costs. His retirement benefits were forfeited. For the rest of his life he lived with difficulty. He never felt bad for what he did as saving lives is a great deed. However, in December 1970, the media protested and the Swiss sent a reserved letter of apology to Paul Grueninger.

Carl Lutz was the Swiss vice-consul in Budapest, Hungary during World War II. Once the Nazis took over Budapest in 1944, they began deporting Jews to the death camps. He soon negotiated a special deal with the Hungarian government and the Nazis. He gained permission to issue 8,000 protective letters to Hungarian Jews for immigration to Palestine. He also set up 76 safe houses for the Jews saying that they were annexes of the Swiss. Among the safe houses was the Glass House, which protected 3,000 Jews. Together with diplomats from other countries, such as Raul Wallenberg, he worked relentlessly to save the innocent Jews from their death. In total, he saved tens of thousands of Jews. He died in Bern, Switzerland, in the year 1975.

Another man who saved the Jews was Friedrich Born. He was a Swiss delegate of the International Committee of the Red Cross, or the ICRC. He was living in Hungary before he became a Swiss delegate. He quickly became aware of the deportation of Hungarian Jews. Following the strategy of Carl Lutz (the Swiss vice-consul) he made it seem that 3,000 Jews were workers for his offices, granted them protection, and designated many buildings as protected by the ICRC. He also managed to distribute 15,000 protection documents that prevented the deportation of the Hungarian Jews. After the war, he returned to his regular life and kept the memories of his actions to himself.

Aimée Stauffer-Stitelmann was a woman who saved 15-20 lives of Jewish people during the Holocaust. In 1938, Germany annexed Austria, and the Swiss government began imposing strict border controls to prevent a future attack by Hitler. Many Swiss people were losing their jobs, fined, or even imprisoned for helping Jews get across the Swiss border to escape the Nazis. She was 17 years old at the time and was born in Paris and held both Swiss and French passports. She was able to move across the border. While she rescued Jewish children, she also helped a small amount of resistance fighters. She was later penalized by the Swiss government for violating border laws by helping Jews return to France in 1945. She was working to receive a pardon by the Swiss for her actions during World War II in 2004, and later died in 2006.

Eduard Benedek Brunschweiler was a Swiss national who was appointed by the ICRC to manage the Benedectine Archabbey of Pannonhalma on their behalf towards the end of the Second World War. In 1944, Archabbot Kelemen Krizoztom wrote to the Committee with a proposal that the Archabbey should be at the disposal of the ICRC. Friedrich Born took this opportunity to help protect the historical buildings and use them to provide shelter for Jewish refugees. Born obtained agreements from both the Hungarian government and the Germans that the abbey was neutral. In October 1944, Born appointed Brunchweiler to take charge of the operation. He managed to make a meeting with the German Reich ambassador to Hungary, concerning arrangements for the stay of the refugees. The ambassador accepted but stated that the percentage of Jewish children sheltered should not get too high. As the Red Army, or the Soviet army, approached Pannonhalma, the refugee population had reached 3,000 people. Soon, the Red Army took control and expelled the ICRC from the area. Eduard Benedek Brunschweiler saved a good amount of people and gave them homes.

These people saved the lives of many Jews during the Holocaust. Without them, many Jewish people would have been tortured in concentration camps or even died. They are some of the Swiss heroes who saved the lives of many innocent people during the Holocaust.

CARL LUTZ, UNKNOWN HERO

Harrison Bernales

From the years 1939 to 1945, World War II was happening. The combatants where the Axis: Germany Italy and Japan. The opposing forces where the Allies, which consisted of almost everybody else. Also, during the time period theHolocaustwas happening. TheHolocaustwas a mass murdering of gays, disabled people, communists and Jews. Eleven million people died. Although the number could have been much more if it was not for people like Carl Lutz, who risked their own lives in selfless missions to save many more. Carl Lutz is a hero.

In 1895, Lutz was born in Walzenhausen. He attended local schools like most. At the age of 18, he moved to the United States in Illinois where he stayed for 20 years. While in Illinois, he started saving up for college. Eventually he attended the Central Wesleyan College, which is located in Missouri. In 1920 Lutz moved to Washington D.C. because he had found a job with the Swiss Legation. While there he went to George Washington University and earned his Bachelor's. In 1926 Lutz moved to Philadelphia because he became chancellor at the Swiss consulate. Then he was assigned to St. Louis. In 1934 Lutz was assigned to Jaffa, Palestine (which is now part of Israel). In 1942 he was sent to work in Budapest, Hungary. In 1944 the Nazis took over Hungary. Lutz noticed that when the Nazis took over they started deporting gay, disabled, communist, Gypsy and Jewish people away to camps. Lutz devised a plan to save them and made a deal with the Hungarian government and the Nazis. He was allowed to give 8,000 protective letters to 8,000 Jews. But Lutz did something different with these letters. Instead of giving them to 8,000 people, Lutz gave one to every family he could find so that a whole family could leave on just one pass. This way he could save many more people. Lutz also claimed land for Sweden in 76 houses so that the Germans could not touch them. This way the Jews could be safe there. Lutz kept doing things such as this. It has been found out that many German officials also wanted him assassinated. While doing things like this, Lutz saved over 62,000 Jews. That makes him a hero.

The Butterfly

The last, the very last,
So richly, brightly, dazzlingly yellow.
Perhaps if the sun's tears would sing
against a white stone...
Such, such a yellow
Is carried lightly 'way up high.
It went away I'm sure because it wished to
kiss the world goodbye.
For seven weeks I've lived in here,
Penned up inside this ghetto
But I have found my people here.
The dandelions call to me
And the white chestnut candles in the court.
Only I never saw another butterfly.
That butterfly was the last one.
Butterflies don't live in here,
In the ghetto.
By Pavel Friedmann

The poem *The Butterfly* by Pavel Friedmann is a poem about his time in the ghetto. It talks about how he is dying and he will see his dead relatives. The butterfly is a symbol for life. Pavel was just a child when he was sent to Auswitz and killed. Many people in theHolocaustnever saw another butterfly again. But because of people like Carl Lutz, many people did see another butterfly, or life. Some even saw many more. It's because of people like Carl Lutz that some survived. And Carl Lutz also had his own personal life. He had a wife, and he also had his own life. The whole time there was a very high likelihood that both of them would die. But he continued on anyway knowing it was the right thing to do. And just because it was the right thing does not mean he had to do it. But would you risk you and your family's own life to attempt to save others? To be honest, I know I would not and you probably would not either. Almost nobody would. That is part of what makes Carl Lutz special. Also, Lutz had no extremely rare talents or abilities, just his own courage and judgment. And it was his courage and judgment that saved thousands and thousands of people.

Carl Lutz was a hero and a great person overall. He was born like everybody else, went to normal schools like most, went to college like most, got a job like most, and still achieved the extraordinary. He battled terror of dying, greed of fame, and denial of the events happening. But he denied all these things unlike most. He did his job and more. He stuck his neck into the fray so that others could live during one of the most dangerous times on our planet, World War II. He is one of the righteous among the nations, and he earned that title and more. Over 62,000 people could have told you that. Carl Lutz also had a wife and friends, and he was in danger of losing them if he lost his life. He might have never seen them again, but luckily he did. But he went in knowing about these dangers and knew that he would receive no payment. He did not want payment. To him, his payment was that he knew he was saving lives and helping people survive. That is why Carl Lutz is a hero.

Works Cited

"Carl Lutz." *Wikipedia*. Wikimedia Foundation, n.d. Web. 08 Feb. 2015. <http://en.wikipedia.org/wiki/Carl_Lutz>.

A, N. /. "Carl Lutz." *Jewishvirtuallibrary.org*. N.p., n/a. Web. 28 Jan. 15. <http%3A%2F%2Fwww.jewishvirtuallibrary.ord%2Fjsource%2Fbiography%2FCarl_Lutz.html>.

KNUD CHRISTIANSEN: THE LITTLE KNOWN HOLOCAUST HERO

Jishnu Sen

Holocaust, the systematic annihilation of the Jews by the Nazis during World War II shows how cruel man can be. By the end of the war, over 60 percent of the Jewish population in Europe had died. Under the autocratic rule of Adolf Hitler, Germany saw the rise of the Nazis, who were anti-Semitic and did not believe that the Jewish people deserved to live. The Nazis also hated homosexuals, Gypsies, and the disabled. Hitler believed in Aryan supremacy. At the beginning of World War II,

Nazi Germany had taken over almost all of Europe and were arresting Jews and sending them to concentration camps were they were tortured, and forced to live and work in unhealthy environments for little or no pay. These camps were brutal and few survived them. The Nazis also constructed several death camps, to which thousands of Jews were deported from the concentration camps, and then killed by lethal gasses.

Out of the many European countries that the Nazis had taken over, the occupation of Denmark was unique because of the partial autonomy they were given by the Nazis due to Denmark's neutral status in the beginning of the war. During this time of occupation, a theologian and professor of church history at the University of Copenhagen named Hal Koch started to give public lectures about how the toleration of Nazi occupation contradicts with the nation's Biblical ideals and democratic belief. Koch roused the spirits of many Danes and brought back the pride of Denmark. Denmark as a nation was special due to its love for democracy, as well as its deep ideals that all the people of Denmark were righteous citizens, no matter who they are. In 1943, as the German occupiers demanded more and more from the Danes, they started to refuse to meet those demands. Shortly after, Danes began to show active resistance toward the Nazis. This effort was called the Danish Resistance. In response, Germany immediately retracted the little freedom that the Danes initially had and fully took over the Danish government. Later in 1943, Dr. Werner Best, Hitler's representative in Denmark, declared a "state of emergency." This meant that curfews, and other strict laws would be imposed on the Danish people. Then in September of 1943, Werner Best informed a high ranking Nazi official named George F. Duckwitz of a plan that Adolf Hitler called the "Final Solution." The plan was to conduct a massive round-up of the 6,500 Jews in Copenhagen on Rosh Hashanah, the Jewish New Year. The fact that every Jew in Copenhagen was expected to be at home on Rosh Hashanah made it an ideal day. For unknown reasons, Duckwitz immediately informed Danish officials of this plan. These Danish officials relayed the information to Copenhagen's main rabbi, Marcus Melchior, who announced that nobody should stay home on the day of Rosh Hashanah during service at the local synagogue.

As the information about the Rosh Hashanah round-up became public, many non-Jew Danes rushed to help the Jewish Danes. One of these Danes was Mr. Knud Marstrand Christiansen. He was a well-known Olympic rower who lived in Copenhagen. Christiansen had first seen an example of Hitler's discriminatory ideals when Hitler walked out of the stadium as a black man named Jesse Owens won gold.

Christiansen grew up in Denmark, and met his wife-to-be Karen Rasmussen shortly after the 1936 Berlin Olympics. They both hated the Nazis' cruel and irrational ways. Soon after marrying Karen, Christiansen joined the Danish Resistance against the German occupation of Denmark. They protected and sheltered thousands of Jews in their own homes. Christiansen ferried dozens of Danish Jews to safety in Sweden using his Olympic rowboat. His wife risked her life every day by publishing a newspaper that translated Dutch BBC broadcasts into German, so that the people of Denmark could know about the daily advances of the Allied forces. Karen also took care of the Danes who were hiding from the Gestapo and SS (Schutzstaffel). Christiansen lived in a luxurious apartment in Copenhagen, the capital of Denmark, which was very close to the port and that allowed him to know when Nazi troops were entering and leaving Denmark. One night, Knud saw German freighters through his apartment window. Knud realized that the freighters would be used to deport Danish Jews. He immediately warned his friends, the Philipson brothers, not to go home that night, lest they get captured. They ignored him and were promptly caught by a group of Nazis. When Knud tried to tell the Nazi soldiers that the Philipsons were not full Jewish, the guards ignored him, and threatened Knud with severe consequences should he return. So, Knud decided to go to Werner Best, Hitler's envoy in Denmark. Best struck a deal with Christiansen. This deal stated that if Christiansen were to participate in a Nazi propaganda film, then the Philipsons would be released. Though the film was never made, the Philipsons were released from the death camp. When he learned about the plan to deport the Jews to the death camps on Rosh Hashanah, Christiansen rushed to hide them from the SS and Gestapo, two branches of the Nazi Secret Police. Risking his and his family's life, Christiansen started to hide the Jews in his own home. Due to Knud's high status in Denmark, he was also able to hide the Jews in churches, hospitals and other large buildings. Knud helped Jewish friends, as well as complete strangers. Knud also helped the Danish Resistance by recruiting other Danes eager to help the Jews. His father-in-law had bought a large house near the beach, which he was using to shelter Jews escaping from the Nazis who were waiting for a boat to Sweden. Knud moved to the United States soon after the war.

After many years, on Christiansen's 65th birthday, aHolocaust survivor named Max Rawitscher released details on Knud's heroic deeds. Twenty-five years later, Yad Vashem, a Jewish organization created to remember the Jews who perished in the Holocaust, recognized Knud and his wife Karen as Righteous Among the Nations, which is an award that is given to non-Jews who risked their lives to help Jewish people.

Throughout the entire war, out of the 6million European Jews who perished, only about 100 were Danes. The very fact that 95 percent of Danish Jews survived the war shows just how much a nation that believes in itself can do against an onslaught of cruelty and barbarism.

HEROES OF THE HOLOCAUST

Isabella Donato

There are many well-known heroes of the Holocaust, but do we really stop to think about the everyday heroes that not everyone has heard of? In my essay, I'd like to recognize three lesser-known heroes; Anna Christensen, Ester Handberg and Helga Holbek. All three Holocaust Heroes have two things. One, all of them are Danish, and two, they made the List of the Righteous Among the Nations from Denmark. This title is given to individuals, non-Jewish, whose lives resorted to rule under the Nazi Party during World War II to save Jews prior to their murder. In these next paragraphs, I'll describe the heroic deeds these three individuals did to contribute to the ending of the Holocaust.

I'll start with Anna Christensen. She was a member of the International League for Peace and Freedom, in Nyborg, Denmark, and aided in the rescue of 40 Jewish children over the years. Anna enrolled the Jewish children she saved in the local school, but, after the German invasion on April 9, 1940, the authorities were too frightened to allow it. Now the children had no school, so she turned her cellar into a classroom. Christensen taught general subjects such as math and language and the group leaders took care of the rest. When the Jewish children suddenly became in danger, Christensen organized hiding places for the children. She inspected the homes to which they were sent to make sure they children would be safe. Twice a week and occasionally on festival days, all the children met up. She often cooked traditional dishes for the children, gave them motherly love, and lifted their spirits, despite the dark and dismal times of the war. In the fall of 1943, Anna Christensen, with a little bit of help from the Danish underground movement, smuggled them out of the country and into Sweden to keep them safe. After the war was over, she kept in contact with each and every one of the Jewish Children, or "Her Children" as she called them. In summary, this is the story of a woman who risked her life so some scared, Jewish children could be happy, and have some parts of a normal education, despite running away from the Nazis.

Next up is Ester Handberg. Her story starts in the fall of 1943, when he saved the lives of 11-year-old Alit Strassman along with her parents, sister, and a little brother. The Strassman family knew the Handbergs before the war began when the Strassmans, who lived in Copenhagen, had sent their five children to vacation on the island of Fyn, to spend time with the Handberg couple who had no children of their own. When the Germans occupied Denmark, Mrs. Handberg said they would help the Strassmans if they required assistance. On October 1st, 1943, a neighbor told the Strassmans to get out of the neighborhood. Mrs. Strassman took three of her children

85

and traveled to Fyn to stay with the Handberg couple. When the Strassmans arrived on Fyn, the Handbergs arranged for the parents to be put up in a pension, while the three children stayed with the Handbergs. When it became too dangerous for them to stay with the Handbergs when Nazis began to occupy the neighborhood, the Handbergs moved the Strassmans to a farm about 50 kilometers away from the Handbergs. At this point, Ester Handberg had started to make arrangements for the transfer of the family to Sweden. Even though there were personal risks, Ester Handberg organized everything on the escape route. She arranged safe houses for the family, and a night in the hospital under false names before they went on a boat to safety. After the war, the Strassmans returned to Fyn, to thank Ester, and they kept in touch for a long time until Ester's death. In conclusion, Ester Handberg risked her home and life to save a very close family to her and he succeeded, making her a Holocaust hero.

The last story in my essay will be Helga Holbek's. Like Anna Christensen, Helga also rescued Jewish children. She was a senior member of the International Commission for the Assistance of Child Refugees and was in charge of supervising 16 refugee children in France. Helga and her Norwegian friend, Alice Resch, took care of 50 Jewish children who had been taken from the Gurs concentration camp and placed in an orphanage. Holbek risked her life time and time again not just for the sake of the children. She also conducted an illegal operation to save the Hungarian Jewish painter, Sigismund Kolozsvary, and his wife Matyi, who were interned in Gurs concentration camps for a long time. Even though they had no identification papers, which were crucial in that day and age, she managed to give them safe houses to live in until she smuggled them to Switzerland. Helga Holbek was a very kind and generous woman, who saved many lives.

In conclusion, these three people, though their deeds were small in comparison to some others, were able to shed some light in the dreary days of the Holocaust, and many things can be learned from their life stories. No matter how small of an impact you make, it amounts to so much bigger. I never really believed that, but after writing this essay, Anna, Ester and Helga proved to me that everything and anything can make a difference.

Works Cited

"The Handberg Family." *Yadvashem*. N.p., n.d. Web. 9 Feb. 2015.
<http://db.yadvashem.org/righteous/family.html?language=en&itemId=4015203>.

"The Helbek Family." *Yeshved*. N.p., n.d. Web. 10 Feb. 2015.
<http://db.yadvashem.org/righteous/family.html?language=en&itemId=4015287>.

"Liste Der Gerechten Unter Den Völkern Aus Dänemark | Fundstellen Im Internet | Cyclopaedia.net." *Liste Der Gerechten Unter Den Völkern Aus Dänemark | Fundstellen Im Internet | Cyclopaedia.net*. N.p., n.d. Web. 09 Feb. 2015.

"The Righteous Among The Nations." N.p., n.d. Web. 09 Feb. 2015.

"THE RIGHTEOUS AMONG THE NATIONS."

Jessica Cai, Co-winner

 During the Holocaust, millions of Jews were killed due to Hitler's reign of terror. However, some kind and compassionate people were willing to risk their lives to step up and do what was right by providing the Jews with protection, love, and support. They later emerged as heroes and heroines of the Holocaust. In spite of this, one of these heroines, Elisabeth Eidenbenz, thought of herself as a normal woman even putting herself below others.

But what was she really? She was a teacher, a nurse, and the founder of the Mothers of Elne. And although she herself didn't realize it, Elisabeth was a savior and the heroine of many, protecting the lives of more than 600 children and their mothers.

Elisabeth Eidenbenz was born on June 12, 1913. She was a young woman who taught in Denmark and Switzerland and was the daughter of a Zurich pastor. When she made the life-changing decision to join the Association to Aid Children in War, she had no idea what she'd be doing or where she'd be going. Elisabeth was first sent to Madrid to help in an aid team, but then decided to train as a nurse. She moved to southwest France to care for the many thousands of Spanish refugees who were fleeing after the Spanish Civil War. The refugees were detained and put into already overfilled internment camps after crossing the border. With so many people, the living conditions were terrible. The hospital was so crowded that workers only admitted those with serious illnesses or injuries, kicking out many pregnant women who were on the verge of giving birth. Most of these women, even in their stage of pregnancy, were forced to live in and give birth in stables. More than 90% of these infants died and many of the new mothers also died or fell ill due to the fact that almost none of the women knew anything about how to deliver babies. On top of that, the stables were dirty and in terrible condition. It was no place for a pregnant woman, a new mother, or a newborn baby to live. All of this had happened because the hospital had given room to others at their expense, and as a result, the women really had nowhere else to go. They had been relying on the hospital staff, but the staff had kicked them out of the hospital and abandoned them. After finding out about this and seeing their terrible living conditions, Elisabeth was appalled and resolved to find a place where the women would be given proper care and could comfortably stay. She converted an old abandoned castle in Elne into a maternity home for the women. She established this place in November 1939 at the age of 24. Elisabeth persuaded officials to allow the women to stay at her maternity home for superior medical care, living conditions, food, and water before, during, and after their child was born. Later, this extended to Gypsy and Jewish women who were expecting or had just had a child. Elisabeth later repaired and restored the home using money given to her from the Swiss Red Cross.

Everything was well until November 1942, when the Germans began increasing their efforts to find and round up Jews. Every time the Germans, or the Gestapo, had gone to her maternity center seeking Jews, Elisabeth had convinced them to leave. However, on one occasion, they had refused to leave, and although Elisabeth offered to go in their place, some women were seized and sent straight to the gas chambers. In spite of this, Elisabeth's efforts saved some 600 children and their mothers from being killed.

I see Elisabeth Eidenbenz as a heroine not only because of what she did, but also because of the sentiment and the way that she did it. When she found out about the women's terrible living conditions, Elisabeth took it upon herself to help them rather than waiting for others to do something. Elisabeth not only did all this for the women, but was also very compassionate through it all, always trying to lift their spirits and give them hope. When she created her maternity home, she named each room after a different city in Spain. This way, the women could remember where they came from and know that there were better days ahead, just like the ones they had in the past. Elisabeth was also willing to do anything and sacrifice everything for the women that she had promised to protect. On one occasion, the Gestapo had gone to the maternity home demanding to take away a Jewish woman named Lucie. The Gestapo told Elisabeth that if she did not give up Lucie they would take her to the gas chambers instead. Elisabeth said that she would take her place. However, Lucie refused to let her do that so she gave herself up. This shows that Elisabeth was completely willing to make the ultimate sacrifice and give her life for theirs. She did not hesitate. Elisabeth put her heart and soul into what she did, and she sincerely cared about each and every one of the women and children that she was sheltering. This is the attitude of a true hero. If Elisabeth had not done what she did, many more women and children would've died. Elisabeth was willing to do anything, including give up her life, to protect the women and children that she had sworn to care for, love, and protect.

Works Cited

"Elisabeth and Her Maternité." *Elisabeth Eidenbenz and the Maternité Suisse D'Elne*. N.p., n.d. Web. 08 Feb. 2015.

"Elisabeth Eidenbenz, La Enfermera Que Burló a La Gestapo." *EL PAÍS*. N.p., 26 May 2011. Web. 08 Feb. 2015.

"RECOGNIZE SOMEONE?" *Photo Archives*. N.p., n.d. Web. 08 Feb. 2015.

SWISS HEROES OF THE HOLOCAUST

Kajol Gupta

In 1933 the Jewish population in Europe was over 9 million, but by 1945 Nazi Germany and their collaborators killed nearly a third of this population. Between 2-3 million prisoners died of disease, neglect or maltreatment (ushmm.org) The Holocaust was a tragic time and every single person who helped out made a difference, whether they helped one person or many they are heroes of the Holocaust. Paul Grueninger, Anna Risen and Harald Feller made a difference, small or big and they are heroes of the Holocaust, the only hope the Jewish had.

Paul Grueninger was a Swiss border police commander of the St. Gallen region which borders Austria, during the time of the Holocaust. As the situation in Germany got even worse the number of people trying to get into Switzerland illegally increased. Paul Grueninger, then 47 years old, had to decide whether to send the refugees back to their country where they would face violence and turmoil or disobey the clear instructions given to him, suffering the consequences. Grueninger chose to take the high road and disregarded the instructions given to him. He even changed their passports to show that they had arrived in the country before March, 1938 which is when entry had been limited. Because he changed their passports, these immigrants were now allowed to enter legally. He even paid from his own pocket for some of the refugees to buy winter clothes because they had to leave their things behind. He saved 3,600 Jews from the danger they were to face in their country. The Germans informed Swiss authorities about Grueninger's actions and he was put to trial for the illegal entry of Jews. His trial dragged over two years and in March 1941 the court found him guilty. His life was difficult after his trial because he no longer had an income but he never regretted what he did. The Swiss government annulled his conviction in 1995, when he had already died (yadvashem.org).

Another Swiss hero, Anna Riesen, saved a young doctor named Joachim Flescher from a great deal of torture. Joachim had left his home at 17 to move to Vienna to study medicine and grew up to be a successful psychiatrist in Vienna. Anna Riesen had just replaced her sister as Joachim's assistant and it was getting harder and harder for Joachim to find work because he was a Jewish doctor. A year after Anna arrived, Germans occupied the North of Italy and the extermination camps began. Almost all Jews caught were murdered. Joachim managed to hide with one of his patients and Anna took care of him, providing him with food, etc. They later came up with a plan. Joachim would return to his own apartment and Anna told the Swiss officials he had fled, and she was moving into his apartment. She was also given a Swiss certificate of protection to place on the door. For the next six months Joachim did not leave the apartment or even approach the windows in fear of being seen.

There were many instances when there was danger. One time two Italian fascists came to the apartment and interrogated Anna and Joachim hid behind a closet. He hid with her in that house until July 4th 1944, then he started doctoring again and moved to the U.S. in 1949. Anna joined him in 1950 and they were married. They had two daughters, Diana and Sylvia. Joachim died in 1976 (yadvashem.org).

Harald Feller was yet another hero of the Holocaust, he was a 30 year old Swiss diplomat in Budapest, Hungary. Nazi Germany took possession of the country in March 1994 and all Jews were made to wear the yellow-star badge. They were concentrated in ghettos and transit camps. Harald Feller was involved in numerous rescue operations, saving Jews. He used illegal methods in order to save Jews that put his life in jeopardy. He also hid many people in houses like the Jewish Hungarian writer Gabor Devecseri, together with his wife Klara Huszar and their one-year-old son, several soldiers who deserted the Hungarian army and other Jews. He also later managed to rescue the Halasz couple, parents of Klara Huszar, and they were brought to his house to join their family. At the end of December, Feller was arrested by an Arrow Cross gang and tortured (yadvashem.org).

The Holocaust only brought turmoil, injustice and pain, and at a time like this it is absolutely necessary to have heroes to save the dying Jews, all heroes big or small are heroes. They risked their lives to save innocent Jews being prosecuted and they are truly heroes, people like Anna Riesen who saved only one life or people like Harald Feller and Paul Grueninger who saved many.

HELPING IN DARK TIMES: SEBASTIAN STEIGER'S EFFORTS

Katie Knapp

The Holocaust was the darkest time in World History. It is the darkest of times when people truly stand out in their effort to help others. Back then life was not easy, for the horrific Nazis squashed any idea or protest that disagreed with their beliefs, one of which being that the entire Jewish faith should be wiped out. Under these horrid conditions, most of the heroes had to do their work silently, working secretly to try to help others who were suffering in the Holocaust. In those dark times, a hero is made by helping those in need. If their actions made a difference in the oppressed peoples lives, that meant the world to the resistance. Sebastian Steiger was a hero in many ways. Sebastian himself was not one of the oppressed, for he was a Christian, but he worked to help those in concentration camps. He was one of the heroes in Europe who were in the resistance, working to save lives and rescue those in concentration camps. As a teacher, he smuggled children past the borders, and helped rehabilitate the children he rescued. He made a difference in the childrens' lives by being someone to talk to, a trusted adult figure. His life's work was to teach, and he

90

lived up to his goal. He is considered a hero for rescuing, rehabilitating, and teaching the children in the Holocaust.

Rescuing anyone from the Holocaust was risky business. Helping meant death, so why did people continue? The risky tasks were put into action because people felt feelings of passion, a need to help. Steiger had heard about a girl who traveled thousands of miles to get to freedom and it caused him to think about whether he should help. Ultimately, he knew that he had to help rescue the children who were not safely in refuge in Switzerland. He volunteered with Red Cross, which suggested he move to France. While volunteering, he worked at the French border as a teacher and rescued children. Often, he had to lie about what he was doing. Steiger sacrificed himself to protect others. Luckily, he was not caught and faced with the horrible punishments. Sebastian was a trained teacher, so he was trusted by the government. Every time he had any problem, he would explain that he was Swiss. That got him out of trouble because he was viewed as harmless by having origins of the neutral country without alliances in the war. In this way, he risked everything he had to save the lives of Jewish people. This made Sebastian Steiger a hero because he took a risk and made a leap of faith that he was doing the right thing by saving the Jewish children. He went out of his way to help and made a decision that sacrificed himself, instead of standing in silence while the Nazi Party terrorized the world. In result, Steiger changed and saved the lives of many children. He was one of the many people who responded to the crisis and rescued children from the Holocaust.

When tragedy hits, physical damages are the most mourned; but the mental damages are what makes a tragedy relevant. The Holocaust was the biggest genocide in human history. The worst part was that is wasn't natural harm. It was a human beings causing harm to others. Any person living or working in the concentration camps was damaged. Sebastian Steiger helped the children who were survivors of the concentration camps. After the war, he served as a counselor to talk to the children involved and effected by the Holocaust. Steiger saw himself as more than just a teacher. He felt he was their nurse and a person who was trusted by the children as an adult. As a result he felt he could connect with them easier and help them in their process to recover from the aftermath of the Holocaust. As a Red Cross teacher, he spoke and taught the children what they missed when their everyday lives were ruthlessly taken away. His compassion helped others recover from their trauma. He worked tirelessly for 25 years to help the adolescents whose lives were sadly interrupted.

The third way Sebastian Steiger was a hero was how he continued being a teacher after he helped the children during the Holocaust. As soon as the Nazis invaded where he was living and studying, he stopped teaching regularly to secretly help the children involved in the Holocaust. Steiger never once changed his passion and he achieved so much by doing this. He may not have taught officially, but he was teaching the children who missed out on a proper education. Even after the Holocaust, he continued teaching until he was 74. Admirably, Sebastian truly cared for the children he taught and took them on trips for swimming while looking out for them. In many ways, he wanted to better the world by rehabilitating the children of the Holocaust. It was his life's work to educate and help others flourish. This is what made him, and all other teachers who helped the children of the Holocaust heroes, because even after the tragedy occurred, he still helped.

In all, Sebastian Steiger was a brave hero. He may not have been able to help the mass millions in the Holocaust who suffered, but he helped hundreds personally. Universally, his care for the children made a huge impact in their own lives. In his 70s, he experienced a heartfelt reunion with the children he saved. His action against the monstrosities of Adolf Hitler was a ripple in the tidal wave that stopped his movement. Sebastian Steiger was driven by his passion to teach and help, which helped the children of the Holocaust. No matter how small any actions were, it still made a difference in a child's life, and that is what makes Sebastian Steiger a hero.

Bibliography

Kavanaugh, Sarah. "Holocaust: Responses to the Persecution and Mass Murder of Jews." *Google Books*. Ed. David Cesarani. Oxford University Press, 1997. Web. 24 Feb. 2015.

Wagner, Meir. "The Righteous of Switzerland." Google Books. KTAV Publishing House, 2001. Web. 5 Feb. 2015.

"RECOGNIZE SOMEONE?" Photo Archives. N.p., n.d. Web. 24 Feb. 2015.

"NEWS - News of the Lodges." Sebastian Steiger Dies. B'nai B'rith Europe, 2012. Web. 10 Feb. 2015.

TWO CARING HEARTS

Mairead McManus

Definition of Holocaust: destruction or slaughter on a mass scale, especially caused by fire or nuclear war. The definition ofHolocaust says it all. It is an event that kills people, animals, anything that you can find wrong in enough to kill it, and then you attack it. TheHolocaust that occurred in 1933 happened to be targeting Jewish people and their beliefs. Eleven million people were killed because of what they believed in. That would be like killing the entire country of Portugal because they spoke

Portuguese or Spanish. Out of those 11 million people, 6 million were Polish citizens. Of that 6 million, 3 million were Polish Jews and the other 3 million were Polish Christians. The remaining 5 million ranged from citizens of Hungary, Czechoslovakia, Ukraine, Holland, Russia, France, and believe it or not, even Germany. Hitler wanted all Jews out of his sight, which was his mission. Although he thought that he could determinate all of the Jews in Germany, very few managed to survive, but their stories are incredible and will never be forgotten. These are the stories of Elisabeth Eidenbenz and Irene Sendler.

Elisabeth Eidenbenz was born in Zurich on June 12, 1913. She was 20 years old when the Nazis attacked. She taught in Switzerland and Denmark as a teacher before she decided to join the Asociación de Ayada a los Niños en Guerra, or the Association to Aid Children in War. When she joined this association, she arrived in Madrid on April 24, 1937, but was then relocated to the South of France. There she decided that she should make a maternity home for all the mothers who were sick, and who were pregnant. Elisabeth converted an old mansion into a maternity home, with the help of the head of the association and 30,000 Swiss francs to refurbish the roof and three floors. She called it the "Elne Maternity Home;" where 597 children were born in her home. The process of coming into the maternity home was quite simple, four weeks before your due date you were admitted, and four weeks after you were discharged. If there were empty spots, you got lucky and you might have been able to stay a little longer, especially during the winter.

The Gestapo, which was the secret police of Nazi, Germany and German-occupied Europe came, one time to try to get any Jewish citizens to the gas chambers, but Elisabeth sent them away, saying that none of the mothers were Jewish. They came a second time, asking for someone specific. They had asked for a lady by the name of Lucy. Lucy's child had died long before then, but she stayed at the home providing milk for the other mothers. If Lucy didn't come out, they said that they were going to take Elisabeth instead. Lucy couldn't take up that offer of having Elisabeth taking her place to die, so they both went to the gas chambers at Mauthasen.

Elisabeth Eidenbenz saved nearly 400 Spanish children, and 200 Jewish children. Out of those 600 kids there were Spanish republicans, Jewish refugees, and Gypsies who were fleeing from the Holocaust. Elisabeth is the reason why all of those moms and children got to see the light at the end of the tunnel. Just by acting out of the kindness of her heart, she saved nearly 600 people from the Nazis. She would have rather given up her life than have the lives of the people in her maternity home be extinguished.

Another woman by the name of Irene Sendler had some of the same ideas as Elisabeth. She wanted to help out as much as she could, even if it meant putting her life on the line.

"Every child saved with my help is the justification of my existence on this earth and not a title to glory." This quote was written from Irene Sandler to the Polish Parliament. When you read this quote, it tells you a lot about who Irena Sendler was. She was somebody who wasn't boastful or who liked to brag. She was just a person who wanted to help.

Irena Sendler was born in 1910 in Warsaw, Poland. Her father was the only doctor in her small hometown of Otwock, and before he died from typhus he told her, "If you see someone drowning you must try to rescue them, even if you cannot swim." Her father cared mostly for the Jewish people in her town, so when World War II erupted, she didn't want any business except with the Jews. She was so determined to help her friends that she made fake documents and started planning her rescue if anything were to go wrong. When the Nazis set up walls in the ghetto depriving the citizens of food and water, Irene went along with her plan to save all of the Jews who were held captive behind the wall. Together with her army of friends, they smuggled aid into the city made up of four walls, and hid Jewish orphans in garbage cans, empty carts and wagons, in the sewers, and out through secret passageways.

Her plan had a lot of risks about it, especially if a child got interrogated by the Gestapo and he or she recited their name wrong or if they couldn't remember a Catholic prayer they would be killed on the spot. The kids were put under a lot of pressure, having to wake up in the middle of the night to learn the prayers, and learn how to behave in a Catholic church. It was tough, but they made it alright.

Irene was very smart, keeping their Jewish names on secret pieces of paper kept locked away for when theHolocaust ended so the children could be reunited with their families if they survived. When the Nazis came to her door, she threw the piece of paper with the childrens' real names at a friend, but was taken to jail for not giving up information. Luckily she escaped, just barely missing her execution day.

With Irene Sendler's brain, wisdom, and courage she was able to save more than 2,500 lives of the innocent children taken by the Nazis. This women, although she was reckless, is one of the smartest women I have ever read about. It would be a dream if I could even get to see her. Sadly, this dream will never happen because she left the world on May, 12, 2008.

These two women were selfless. They didn't care that they could possibly die if they were caught doing the helpful acts that they did. They were willing to put themselves in front of people who they didn't even know, just to help. In my eyes, these women are what define the word hero.

Bibliography

On 7Th December 1939, Josep Molina Came Into The. *Memorial Democràtic*(n.d.): n. pag. Web. 8 Feb. 2015.

"Elisabeth and Her Maternité." *Elisabeth Eidenbenz and the Maternité Suisse D'Elne.* N.p., n.d. Web. 08 Feb. 2015

"Adolf Hitler and The Holocaust." *Adolf Hitler and The Holocaust.* N.p., n.d. Web. 05 Feb. 2015.

"List of Countries by Population (graphical)." *Wikipedia.* Wikimedia Foundation, n.d. Web. 09 Feb. 2015

"Irena Sendler: In the Name of Their Mothers." *PBS.* PBS, n.d. Web. 09 Feb. 2015

DAGMAR LUSTRUP: DANISH HERO

Neil Frydendal

Dagmar Lustrup, an active member of the Women's Peace Organization in the Thisted area, saved 20 Jewish teenagers who she didn't even know, most from Czechoslovakia, from the Germans during World War II. That's why she was an everyday hero. She was a selfless, strong, and committed housewife who denounced Hitler and the Third Reich Holocaust with all her heart. She believed it was her duty to save those 20 Jewish kids from being killed in one of Hitler's gas chambers. She followed her conscience. Dagmar Lustrup knew the risks, but despite this, she helped the children anyway. She was more concerned with the children's safety than her own.

Dagmar Lustrup was born in Kalundborg, a city in Denmark, around 1894. This is also where she met her husband-to-be, Jesper Lustrup, a journalist and editor for The *Maribo Journal*. In 1917, the two became a couple and went to Thisted, where Jesper Lustrup became the editor of the local newspaper: The *Thisted Amts Tidende*. It later became known as The *Thisted Dagblad*; he was editor for 45 years. Sadly, or happily (depending on how you look at it), they had no children. In 1977, Dagmar Lustrup became a widow.

Based on the accounts of Aryeh Weiner, Zvi Oscar Strauss, and Nomi Sagie, some of the teenage kids who Lustrup saved, it can be gathered that this is what happened: the kids belonged to Zionist pioneer organizations at that time. After Czechoslovakia (now the two separate republics of Czech and Slovakia) became occupied by the Germans in 1939, they arrived in the Thisted area. Dagmar Lustrup took in the teenagers and arranged for their accommodations in private rural homes in three areas near Thisted. The goal was that they would be trained in agriculture and farming and later travel to Palestine. The Protestants farmers agreed to give them agricultural training. She organized the groups on the farms, caring not only about physical needs, but also social activities. Twice a week she arranged for them to meet in person and stay in contact. Apparently, the Germans offered at one point to let the children pass through Germany unharmed to get to their destination. The parents of many of these kids wrote coded letters to Dagmar Lustrup begging her to not send their kid(s) through Germany. Lustrup stayed firm on the matter: she was not giving up the children. The Germans had never faced such a stubborn Danish woman before!

Dagmar Lustrup's problem came about after April 1940, when Denmark was occupied by Germany. In November 1940, it was said that all Jews were to be expelled from the north Jutland area because it was a strategic area for the Germans. This is where the group was located, so it was a problem. It was also said that they had to leave at once. Within a day, a very violent, sad, and chaotic day, Lustrup succeeded in getting all the teenagers to a youth hostel near Odense, on Fyn Island, in central Denmark. She got all the kids together, from their foster families that had been looking out for them. She gave them to a different member of the Women's Peace Organization who would momentarily look after them and provide temporary shelter until they would leave for Palestine. The goodbyes between the foster families and the kids was the hardest part because they had grown accustomed to each other.

Somehow, a deal was made with the Germans: the kids would be sent to Sweden in a clever way that involved the Germans looking the other way while the children passed. Seven days later, on December 5, 1940, equipped with immigration certificates, the kids boarded a ship that brought them to Sweden, and via the Soviet Union, they continued on to Palestine. After the war was over, Dagmar Lustrup also went on to Palestine with compassion and great interest. The children who she saved never forgot her valiant efforts on their behalf.

In 1983, a niece of Dagmar Lustrup's, Ingrid Bisgaard heard about how Israel recognized the people who made a special effort to save Jews from death in Hitler's gas chambers. Thinking of her aunt, she then contacted the Israeli Embassy in Copenhagen. She shared to them about her aunt's actions and heroism. After Dagmar Lustrup's story was confirmed, by none other than Oscar Strauss (one of the Jewish teenagers who she saved), she was, on October 2, 1984, finally honored with the title of Righteous Among the Nations by Yad Vashem. Sadly, because of a serious illness, Dagmar could only receive her diploma and medal on August 28, 1985. Interestingly, in an interview on May 7, 1987, for her dead husband's newspaper: the *Thisted Dagblad*, she said, "I do not regard myself as a hero. We did not know then what we did. The only thing we knew was that we should not fail" (Christensen). It appears that she did not want or like the attention being brought to her for saving the Jewish teenagers. On June 26, 1990, she peacefully died a hero, at age 96, in a nursing home in Thisted.

Bibliography

Christensen, Uffe. "Dansk børne-frelser: Jeg er ingen helt." Jyllands-Posten. Jyllands-Posten, 20 February 2011. Web. 9 February 2015.

"Rescue Story Lustrup, Dagmar." Yad Vashem. Yad Vashem, 2015. Web. 9 February 2015.

HOLOCAUST ESSAY

Olivia Harimoto

The Holocaust; from 1933 to 1945, it was led by Adolf Hitler who rose in power in Germany, started the Nazi race and army; he used the Jewish people as a scapegoat and told all of Germany that Jewish people were responsible for all of their problems. They captured all the Jews, put them into concentration camps, and killed all of them by gas chambers, shootings, etc. Hundreds of thousands of Jews were terminated. Even though this was a terrible event, not everybody was cruel to the Jews; there were some people who are considered heroes for their actions during the Holocaust. Two people who stood out the most to me were Sister Jeanne Berchmans and Paul Gruninger. Due to their courageous actions, they are known as the heroes of the Holocaust.

Sister Jeanne Berchmans was a Swiss nun at the Sacre-Coeur (Sacred Heart) convent. One day, she heard a loud noise of vehicles approaching and recognized them as being German trucks. Sister Jeanne had to act quickly, so she went to the convent where three Jewish refugees, Taube Wittels, her daughter Renee, and her son Bruno were hiding. Sister Jeanne took them to an unused room on the third floor, locked the door, and put up a sign saying... "Quarantine: Scarlet Fever". She did that to save the three refugees from being taken away by the German soldiers. When the German soldiers came in and searched the whole building, door to door, Sister Jeanne Berchmans accompanied them. When they came up to the third floor and were about to open the door with the three refugees, she explained to the German soldiers that the people in the room were contagious patients suffering from Scarlet Fever. Her story had tricked the German soldiers, therefore the German soldiers left them alone and marched off. If Sister Jeanne Berchmans had not stepped up to aid that family, they would have be taken away and killed, along with Sister Jeanne Berchmans. Sister Jeanne Berchmans is considered a hero because she helped save three lives (a whole family). If it wasn't for her bravery three more innocent lives would have been taken by the Holocaust.

Another hero during the Holocaust was Paul Gruninger. He is considered a hero because one day he arrived for work as usual, but Anton Schneider, a policeman in charge of refugee files, had blocked the entrance because the chief commander had ordered him to be blocked from entering the central police station. Anton Schneider said that the chief commander had ordered him not to let Gruninger in. Although

Paul Gruninger was aware of his guilt, he protested by helping refugees travel to Switzerland and giving them citizen a citizen ID.

Paul Gruninger had been warned that whoever was working at the checkpoint near Bregenz where the German and Swiss borders meet, the Gestapo had their name on their wanted list and that they should stay away from German territory. Paul Gruninger did not take the warning seriously and continued his illegal activities. What Paul Gruninger did not know was that the Gestapo had gotten news about him helping a Jewish woman escape from Germany. The woman who Paul Gruninger helped had left her jewelry back at the hotel in Bregenz, so she wanted him to retrieve it for her. So Paul Gruninger got in touch with Ernest Prodolliet at the Swiss consulate in Bregenz, and asking him to go to the hotel, get jewelry, and send it to him. He had worked with Prodolliet on several similar rescue missions in the past, so Paul Gruninger knew that he could be trusted. In a letter to the woman's family in Vienna, she had written, "There is a wonderful police captain named Paul Gruninger. He promised to look after my jewelry and bring it to me from the hotel of our friend in Bregenz." But the letter was intercepted by the Germans, therefore the hotel owner was arrested. After a while, they informed the Swiss federal authorities in Berne about Gruninger's illegal activities. So in 1939, the Germans ordered legal punishments would be used against him. Paul Gruninger is considered a hero because of his generosity he helped a woman, knowing all of the consequences that might occur if he gets caught. Due to Paul Gruninger's actions, another innocent person was saved from being executed.

As you can see, these two people and many more did extraordinary actions out of the kindness of their hearts to save the Jewish people. They did it that even if they knew that there would be a huge punishment if they ever got caught. This is why Sister Jeanne Berchmans, Paul Gruninger, and many more ordinary people, rich or poor, were considered heroes during one of the most terrible times in history known as the Holocaust.

Bibliography

Wagner, Meir, and Moshe Meisels. N.p., n.d. Web. 6 Feb. 2015.

Baker, Colin. N.p., n.d. Web. 6 Feb. 2015.

"Nonfiction Book Review: The Righteous of Switzerland: Heroes of the Holocaust by Meir Wagner, Author Ktav Publishing House $35 (269p) ISBN 978-0-88125-698-7." PublishersWeekly.com. N.p., n.d. Web. 5 Feb. 2015.

HOLOCAUST HEROES: GERDA VALENTINER AND PAUL GRUNINGER

Shilpa Mudumbe

The Holocaust was a blemish in Europe's history. A man named Adolf Hitler was trying to make all of Germany to be free of Jews, and so he captured all the Jews and put them in concentration camps. Hundreds of thousands of people died in these camps. However, there were many people who were trying to rescue the Jews, and two of these people, also known as Holocaust heroes are Gerda Valentiner and Paul Gruninger.

Gerda Valentiner was a Danish teacher who risked her life to save hundreds of Jewish children. In October 1943, a deportation of all the Jews in Denmark was planned, so she collected Jewish children and took them to her house, waiting for the right time to transfer them safely to Sweden. She even bought new food for them to eat when she realized that the Jewish children had certain dietary restrictions that they had to follow. A man named Moritz Scheftelowitz said that Gerda Valentiner was his sister's teacher, and one night in September 1943, she came to his parents to tell them about the danger. Moritz and his sisters moved into Gerda's home, and they tried several times to leave the country. The first two attempts failed, but the third one succeeded. They departed on a fishing boat 10 kilometers from Copenhagen and arrived at Landskrona, Sweden the next morning.

When Valentiner was asked about her endeavors, she said "I only did what many Danes did, nothing special. We thought it perfectly natural to help people in mortal danger." After the war, she took a leave of absence from her teaching job and volunteered as a social worker in Jewish refugee camps in Germany and Austria. She worked there for two years, and in 1971, when she was retired, she came to Israel for a year to see the country and to learn Hebrew.

Many teachers who rescued Jews during the Holocaust said that "Their fate will be my fate too..." Whatever happened to their students would happen to them so that the kids weren't alone in this; everyone was in it together. These teachers knew that their main job was to help children by educating them, but they also felt like it was their duty to do this outside of a classroom, even if it meant giving up their life. Gerda Valentiner was one of these wonderful teachers, and she was recognized as a Righteous Among the Nations by Yad Vashem on July 28, 1968.

Another courageous hero out of many was a man named Paul Gruninger. He was a Swiss border police commander of the St. Gallen region that borders Austria. After

Germany had annexed Austria, Switzerland sealed its borders and didn't allow the entry of Austrian Jews and other people without proper entry permits. The situation grew worse, and many immigrants and refugees tried to illegally inter Switzerland, but to no avail. Paul Gruniner was observing all of this, and now he faced a dilemma: Should he turn the refugees away back to their dangerous country, or should he disregard the laws and let them in to safety?

Gruninger eventually decided to let the tens of thousands of desperate runaways in, and even took the liberty to legalize their status. He falsified their registration so that it should that they had arrived before March 1938, when the country had been closed off. These now "legal" immigrants were taken to the Diepoldsau camp where they waited for their permits for a temporary stay in Switzerland or their departure to a final destination. Meanwhile, Gruninger turned in their false reports, and he even bought with his own money some winter clothes for those who had been forced to leave all of their belongings behind. Eventually, the Germans found out about his plans, and they informed the Swiss authorities about it. Gruninger was dismissed from the police force the next year in March 1939, and he lost his police rank and pension rights. He was brought to trial and found guilty of fraud in 1940, and he was fined by court. After his arrest, Gruninger lived a life of hardship. It was very difficult for him to find a job with his criminal record, especially in Switzerland. Despite his circumstances, Paul never regretted his actions. In 1945 he explained his motives. He said, "It was basically a question of saving human lives threatened by death. How could I then seriously consider bureaucratic schemes and calculations?"

In 1970, as a result of protesting from the media, the Swiss government sent Paul Gruninger a letter of apology, but they did not reopen his case and reinstate his pension. In 1972, after Gruninger's death, steps to rehabilitate him were set in motion. Judges decided to reopen the trial, and absolved him from the charges. He was completely rehabilitating in 1996.

Although Paul's heroic actions sent him to jail, he saved nearly 3000 Jews, and his kindness certainly did not go unrewarded. In 1971, Yad Vashem presented him with the title of Righteous Among the Nations.

The Holocaust was a tragedy, an event that made humans all over the world lose their faith in humanity, but it was quickly restored when heroes, such as Gerda Valentiner, Paul Gruninger, and many more, quickly assisted many Jews toward their safety. We need more people like them with their mindset of helping others despite the consequences, because if the human race ever has to go through something as terrifying as the Holocaust, I hope that they will step up and aid those who are affected.

Bibliography

"Gerda Valentiner." *Yad Vashem*. N.p., n.d. Web. 08 Feb. 2015

"Paul Gruninger." *The Jewish Foundation for the Righteous*. N.p., n.d. Web. 09 Feb 2015

"Paul Gruninger." N.p., 2005. Web. 9 Feb 2015.

FRIT DANMARK

Shreya Chaudhary

"The Holocaust, taken by itself, is a black hole. To look at it directly is to be swallowed up by it."–David Novak. The Holocaust was a dark time in the history of the world that was started by the Nazi party led by Hitler. Millions of people in Europe were killed because they were Jewish. They were segregated and sent to concentration camps. They were fed next to nothing. About two thirds of the Jewish population was killed by the end of the Holocaust at concentration camps (where they were forced to work long hard hours), gas chambers, etc. Yet there were survivors because there were heroes. Many heroes, such as the people who ran and helped the Danish newspaper, Frit Danmark (Free Denmark), were heroes of the Holocaust who helped Jews escape being shipped off to concentration camps and being put to death. The famed illegal newspaper Frit Danmark helped many Jews escape to Sweden. Some of these heroes are Jorgen Kieler, Elsebet Kieler, and Ebba Lund.

Jorgen Kieler, born August 23, 1919, is a Danish physician. He started working with forces against the Nazis when he was in college. Over the years he did a lot of traveling for educational purposes, and during a long stay in Germany, he witnessed the cruel treatment of the Jews. He couldn't stand seeing the cruelty, and he knew he had to take action. His first course of conduct was the newspaper Frit Danmark. The newspaper was created to criticize adjustment policies and called out to others who were against this. This newspaper was run out of his apartment and he was part of the Holger Danske resistance group that published it. He and his siblings propagated the newspaper and helped gather people for the cause. Even amidst all the good he had done, Kieler still felt bad, however, for having people risk their own life and security for the cause. He also questioned the morals of his cause and if what he was doing was right several times, but he stuck to it and his doubt only strengthened his commitment to his cause. Because of what he did, he was involved with the escape of over 1,000 Jews.

His older sister, Elsebet Kieler, was with him for his cause. Elsebet first saw the cruelty of Nazi Germany when she visited it for a part of her college studies. She saw how the Jews were treated. What really broke her heart, however, were the posters she saw that said, "Jews not wanted here." She knew that she wanted to help in the fight against the Nazis. When she and her family joined the cause, she was in the middle of her college studies, but she left it all behind to help others have a better life. She, Jorgen, and their other siblings joined the Holger Danske resistance group together. She and her siblings altogether passed out things to propagate their cause and the newspaper. When her brothers wanted to take the cause to the next level and sabotage Gestapo activities, she wanted nothing to do with it, until she learned that the Gestapo were to take a group of Danish Jews to concentration camps. She realized they did have to do more. Her role was to collect money/donations for helping the Jews escape. It was used to bribe the soldiers and to pay fisherman who put their lives at risk, sailing the Jews to Sweden to be safe. The group they belonged to overall was responsible for transporting about a thousand Jews. The family reunited and she finished her stalled college education in the U.S. She died in 2006.

Another person who played a role in rescuing Jews was a women named Ebba Lund. She went under the name Helga Dansk. She is infamously known as the women who wore a red cap to save the Jews. She played a role in saving over 800 Jews, mainly on her own. Ebba Lund was about 20 when she started fighting for her cause. A regular school girl, who was from an upper middle class family. She knew she wanted to help because they were people too, and she wanted to help anyone who needed it. A passionate lover of freedom, Ebba Lund had many resources to aid her cause. She had a lot of money and many boatmen to help her. She personally provided a safe hiding place for the Jews who she helped escape, which was her parent's home in Copenhagen. Some, however, stayed in hospitals under Christian names until they were freed. She helped free these Jews, and all in daylight (unlike the many heroes who executed their plan at nighttime). Her bravery is forever associated with her iconic red hat that identified her as the women who saved many Jews. Because of her work, a group was named after her alias. It was called the Holger Danske resistance group, which was responsible for the newspaper Frit Danmark which she also played a role in. Helga Dansk's true identity was revealed over a decade later as Ebba Lund. She also received the Ebbe Munck Award for her efforts many years later in 1985.

These Danish heroes played a role in a fight of many against the Nazis and were the reason for the survival of so many Jews who could have suffered and died. Thanks to people like Jorgen Kieler, Elsebet Kieler, and Ebba Lund, vast majorities of Jews made it to safety in Sweden. They truly uphold many great accomplishments and are great examples of people who don't stay bystanders. "Thou shalt not be a victim, thou shalt not be a perpetrator, but, above all, thou shalt not be a bystander."- Yehuda Bauer.

Bibliography

Brink, Angela, Stephen Kang, and Lillian Marsh. "In Search of Humanity in Action." Humanity In Action. N.p., n.d. Web. 20 Feb. 2015.

"The Courage of Elsebet Kieler, Holocaust Resistance Fighter." AAUW Empowering Women Since 1881 The Courage of Elsebet Kieler Holocaust Resistance Fighter Comments. N.p., 5 Nov. 2014. Web. 20 Feb. 2015.

"Ebba Lund (1923 - 1999) Lund, Ebba." Dansk Kvindebiografisk Leksikon. N.p., n.d. Web. 20 Feb. 2015.

Harrison, Donald H. "'Girl in Red Cap' Saved Hundreds of Jews." Jewish Sightseeing. San Diego Jewish Press-Heritage, 14 Jan. 1994. Web. 20 Feb. 2015.

"Women Heroes of WWII." The Danish Rescue of the Jews: Ebba Lund. N.p., 13 June 2011. Web. 20 Feb. 2015.

HOLOCAUST ESSAY

Shreya Sridhar

Holocaust means "whole" and "burned," and is used to describe a sacrificial offering in history. But since 1945, this word has so much fear, and is like a scar for others. This horrible incident was caused by haters, which resulted in having over 6 million innocent Jews killed. The Holocaust was a brewing act against Jewish civilians, which proclaimed that Jews weren't worth enough to be saved. The Jewish population in 1933 in the European continent was over 9.5 million, but by 1945 almost every 2 out of 3 Jews were killed. The Nazi leader, Adolf Hitler, said that Jews were a weird race, and that they were a danger to Europe. The domination in Nazi Germany was uncontrollable, that the policy was to murder all the Jews in Europe. During 1942, camps in Auschwitz were ordered to have extermination camps, which was a labor camp that was intended to kill large groups of Jews in Treblinka, Sobibor, and Belzec. The Holocaust has burned holes in many people's lives but mainly the history of our great nation.

Elisabeth Eidenbenz

Elisabeth Eidenbenz was born on June 12, 1913 in Wila, Switzerland. This woman helped rescue 597 babies in 1939 to 1944, mostly the children of Spanish Republicans, Jewish refugees and gypsies fleeing the Nazi invasion during Spain's Civil War. This kind lady was a teacher from Switzerland, but turned out to be a nurse and the founder of the "Mothers of Elne." A few things that she prosecuted to aid people during the Holocaust by the Nazis, was how she joined the "Save the Swiss Children" program. She moved to the southwest region of France in 1939 to help the millions of the Spanish refugees who were crossing the border. After the fall of the Spanish Republic, many of these civilians moved to France. But people died of diseases, injuries, and malnutrition issues. In November 1939, she moved forward to Perpignan to take care of pregnant women, so she stayed at the ward for giving medical care and nourishment to the millions of women who were struggling with wounds. Many pregnant women were so close to losing their unborn children, or dying during childbirth. On April 24, 1937, Elisabeth came to Madrid with a team to save all the refugees, which became a group of local volunteers from Zurich who were midwife aid workers. Because of her well heartedness, she earned to be 9,565th in the nation's peace for the year of 2001. Her group came, based on the donation from Europe to save the refugees, but after the beginning of World War II, their funds seemed to "disappear" when the refugees came from France and the remnant of Europe. Most of the people who were vanishing from the refugees were the population of women. So Elisabeth's group was forced to affiliate themselves with the "Red Cross," and that prevented them from sheltering refugees. Elisabeth Eidenbenz never felt like a hero, she felt like it was a duty.

Living under the Holocaust was like a brutal carnage, but the most important thing for her during the Holocaust was saving the refugees.

Bill Barazetti

Bill Barazetti was born in Aarau, Switzerland, and saved 669 Jewish kids from Nazi officers in Czechoslovakia. Bill was a retiring champion against the struggle of Nazism, because he helped thousands of families from the pre-war in Germany face the power of discrimination. In 1933, when Hitler had full control, Barazetti met a few Jews and became friends with them, but the Nazi men took the Jews and marched them off to concentration camps. Soon, German officers found out about his identity, but Barazetti faked a death, which let him to escape to Poland, where he changed his identity again. Though, he was caught by the Gestapo, and was almost killed by abuse, but a young Czech girl, Anna, helped him recover. Eventually the got married, and arranged a way for the evacuation of Jewish children from Prague, a resident of Horn church, so they could "get away" from Nazism. Barazetti soon came to Britain himself, to interrogate the captured German pilots, so he could approach their reason for their terrible actions. Bill Barazetti placed 5,904th for the nation's peace award during the year of 1993.

To conclude, the Holocaust was an important part of history, and it ended on a big note. When comparing both Bill and Elisabeth, they helped the nation's weak areas, and looked out for others besides themselves. The death march was when the German army led camps into Austria. The death march lasted for weeks, and approximately 250,000 people died by harsh conditions. In November 1944, 70,000 Jews were relocated from Dachau to another place in Austria, and were murdered there. The Holocaust, as a whole, has much meaning to it because it makes you realize the consequence for every action you do. It really teaches you about discrimination and beliefs and in a way the Holocaust somewhat brought many people back together. Now, it's something that is ingratiated in our morals of history. Last but not least, the Holocaust definitely teaches you about humanity and equal rights and respect by challenging the notion of our civilism.

BILL BARAZETTI, KINDERTRANSPORT HERO

Simrun Heir

On Oct 9th 2000 *The Times'* obituary column reported, "A retiring hero of the struggle against Nazism, whose story came to light only ten years ago, Bill Barazetti helped thousands of victims of discrimination to get out of prewar Germany. In a Schindler-style operation carried out in conjunction with a British stockbroker, Nicholas Winton, he also played a major part in organizing the escape of children from German-occupied Prague in the spring and summer months of 1939 before war broke out (Werner Theodore Barazetti – a Swiss hero of Kindertransporte, *The Times*)."

Bill Barazetti, born as Werner Theodore Barazetti in Aarau, Switzerland was son of a Swiss Professor of French at Heidelberg University. In 1933, when Hitler came to power he was 19 and he was studying at Hamburg University where he saw the Hitler's Nazi thugs beat up Jewish, socialist and communist students in the university precinct. "We are a silent majority (Werner Theodore Barazetti – a Swiss hero of Kindertransporte, *The Times*)," was the disappointing reply he got from the dean, who was also Jewish, when he reported the incident to him. Also, that was where he met and became friends with Jews, witnessing the Nazi persecution as Jews were marched off the campus to concentration camps.

When in Prague he worked in a church based organization that helped move refugees that had flooded Czechoslovakia toward Britain and Scandinavia. About 50,000 to 70,000 people escaped with the help of this organization. In 1934 he moved to Czechoslovakia and was recruited by the Czech Secret Service as an intelligence officer. He returned to Hamburg as a spy and after a year, the Germans found out about him and the Secret Services tried to arrest him. He discovered this in time and he escaped this arrest by faking his death. He then escaped to Poland and changed his identity. Barazetti ended up getting caught by the Gestapo and was almost beaten to death. A Czech girl named Anna found him wounded on the German-Czech border. She helped him recuperate. He ended up marrying her and they had a son named Nicholas in Switzerland in 1937. He was eager to help aid in the fight against the Nazis so he sent Anna back to her village with their son when he traveled to Poland. In Poland he got forged passports and returned to Prague.

Operation Kindertransport was a nine month rescue effort authorized by the British government with the objective of saving children under the age of 17, most of them being Jewish from Nazi Germany, Austria, Czechoslovakia, and the free city of Danzig and relocating them to United Kingdom. A massive fund-raising endeavor was undertaken and the British public responded generously. In six months close to half a million pounds were raised. Between December 1938 and May 1940, almost

10,000 infants to teenagers were rescued and relocated to Britain's homes, camps and farms. Unfortunately this operation failed to reach Czechoslovakia.

Martin Blake called his friend Nicholas Winton, a 29 year old stockbroker in London, to come and help in refugee camps in Prague during the December of 1938, just after the ill-fated Munich agreement in Oct 1938 and the annexation of a large part of western Czechoslovakia. Soon the rest of the country would be under German occupation. Time was running out.

Wiston found out that there was no organization in Prague connected to Operation Kindertransport. Wiston partnered with Barazetti. They both were urgently trying to evacuate the children in Prague. Winton returned to England to get the children passports, find families for relocation, and £50-a-head fee to be deposited at the home office (£ means pound, a pound is a form of currency in England) for each kid. While Winton was making arrangements in England Barazetti was making arrangements in Prague. Barazetti was interviewing the families and sending Winton details about each child including photographs. This operation was nearly stopped when he was caught by the Gestapo again but an uncle, a colon in the Swiss Army, freed him. In March 1939 he returned to Prague and avoided arrest by staying with a different family every night among the children he was going to send to England. There was one issue with the visas for the children, it was that English visas took a long time to come through. To solve this issue Barazetti was able to get a Jewish printer, who lived in Prague, to forge papers that they could give to German authorities. These papers allowed the children to go and be transported to England. Barazetti decided to transport the children by train. There were three trains with children, each with forged papers. When the first train reached Holland their visas came in. Barazetti was able to get the forged papers back and use them for the next two trains. They was able to get out 669 children over in one airplane and seven railroad transports. On September 1, 1939 the day Poland was invaded by Hitler another train with 250 children was supposed to leave but the rescue failed as all borders controlled by Germany were sealed. Not a single one of those children were heard of again.

Bill Barazetti ended spending the rest of his life in Britain. At the age of 25 Barazetti managed to save the lives of over 600 children. At a young age he managed to make a huge contribution to the people who were oppressed by the Nazi's.

In conclusion Bill Barazetti was a hero during the Holocaust. Instead of trying to fight the Nazis on the frontlines he decided to help and save the lives of many innocent people. At a young age he was able to make a great impact on a community and many people.

Bibliography

"The Power of Good - The Nicholas Winton Story." *The Power of Good - The Nicholas Winton Story*. N.p., 28 May 2009. Web.

"Exhibits." *Kindertransport Association*. N.p., n.d. Web.

"Philosemitism." *: Werner Theodore Barazetti*. N.p., 14 Jan. 2008. Web.

"The Righteous Among The Nations." *Www.yadvashem.org*. N.p., n.d. Web.

KNUD AND KAREN CHRISTIANSEN

Tessa P. Bomk

"We can easily forgive a child who is afraid of the dark; the real tragedy of life is when men are afraid of the light"- Plato. To me, Knud and Karen Christiansen embodied the meaning of the previous quote because of their impavid actions taken against the reign of Nazi Germany.

Just a few years from the beginning of World War II, Knud Christiansen was competing in the 1936 Berlin Olympics as a member of the Danish National Rowing Team. He was one of the many athletes who witnessed Adolf Hitler shake only the hands of German contenders and disregard the accomplishments of superior competitors like Jesse Owens, an American, who won four gold medals. His fiancée, Karen, was also witnessing the "terrible brutalization" of Jews on the streets of Berlin, where she was attending a prestigious cooking school. She was eventually forced to leave the famed cooking school because staying in Berlin was a threat to her life.

A few years later, the Nazis invaded Denmark, and stayed there from April 1940 until May 1945. Knud was in Denmark the whole time, and he procured a prominent position on the Danish Nazis' "watch list." He was a part of many resistance groups including the Danish Freedom Fighters. The Christiansens lived in an upscale apartment in Copenhagen due to Knud's successful leather business. Ironically, higher ranked Nazi soldiers lived near Knud and Karen's family as a result. Around September, 1943, Knud and Karen heard word from the Nazi soldiers around their home that they would be arresting Jews in a mass roundup on Rosh Hashanah (the Jewish New Year). The Christiansens flew into action. They alerted the Danish Freedom Fighters of the Nazis' plans and ushered massive groups of Jews, about 7,000, to farmhouses, churches and city apartments, essentially using every Nazi-free space to armor the Jews from instant arrest. The Christiansens even used their own home to protect the Jewish people. Their youngest daughter, Jyttte fondly remembers her living room swarming with Jews. She was told to address the complete strangers as uncle or aunt. One of the guests at the house was the Director of the Danish National Bank. In fact, Knud, Karen, and some of the Jews who came to his home described the experience in a positive manner. Knud said, "The whole time people helped one another. People took risks they wouldn't normally take. People were so good to one another."

Along with helping complete strangers, Knud and Karen also assisted close, personal friends. For example, Knud urged two Jewish brothers, the Philipsons, who

107

they were friends with, to immediately go into hiding when he learned of the Nazi plan to arrest them. One of the brothers refused, and instead, he made arrangements for him and his brother's family to go home. The next day, the Christiansens learned that their friends were arrested and taken to a detainment camp. Knud went to a Nazi commandant and begged him to release his friend saying that he was only one-quarter Jewish. The commandant refused saying that too many Jews had gotten out of the camps because of mendacious excuses like his. But, instead of giving up, Knud risked his own life by carrying his request to the highest ranking Nazi in Denmark, General Werner Best. The general was even nicknamed "The Blood Hound of Paris" for mercilessly sending Jews in France to death camps. However, due to his fame as an Olympian and Karen's father's position as the private physician to the royal family of Denmark, General Werner Best accepted his request and even suggested that Knud be in a Nazi propaganda film which would make it seem as if Germany was allies with Denmark.

The parents of Knud and Karen were also a solace for the repressed Jews. Karen's father, the royal family's physician, bought a mansion on the shoreline to shelter large groups of escaping Jews. Knud's mother, who owned a distinguished chocolate shop in Berlin, allowed her shop to serve as a meeting place for Jewish people and the Danish Freedom Fighters. Furthermore, Knud's brother served as a lookout on a beachfront for Jews being taken from Denmark to Sweden while Knud ferried Jews across one at a time in his small rowing skiff.

Karen Christiansen continually published a newspaper called the "Die Warheit" (The Truth), which translated BBC broadcasts from Dutch to German to notify soldiers of the barbarous acts committed by Adolf Hitler and the Third Reich. Knud thought she was an extremely strong-willed and fearless woman and said of her, "My wife had a backbone made of steel."

Knud and Karen immigrated to New York City with their family in 1970. Up until his last days at age 97, Knud would still stay in shape by using the rowing machine in the Jewish Community Center. Karen died in 1992 and Knud died 20 years later in 2012. In 2005, Knud and Karen Christiansen's names were added to a list of legendary figures as "Righteous Among Nations" at the Yad Vashem Memorial Museum in Jerusalem. Although we can never undo even a single inhuman act committed by the Third Reich during the Holocaust, Knud and Karen Christiansen serve as reminders that one should not do good just to gain recognition and they were never left regretting not doing enough to help appease the havoc.

Bibliography

Rescuer Support. *Stories of Rescuers.* The Jewish Foundation for the Righteous. 11 January 2015. Web

Dolgin, Robyn. Danish Hero: One Rosh Hashanah Burns Bright in Holocaust. News Archives. Jewish Post. 11 January 2015. Web.

EMILY KNUD DYBY HOLOCAUST ESSAY

Adam Kneitel

Of the many countries taken over by Germany and purged of its Jewish residents, Denmark's response was the most dramatic. Instead of simply some small-scale hiding of Jewish neighbors, almost the entire state rushed to their Jewish countrymen's side, helping 7,220 out of its 7,800 Jewish people flee to the free country Sweden. One of the leaders of a large group that smuggled Jews and provided them with passports was a former castle guardsman named Knud Dyby.

Knud Dyby was a high-ranking police officer in the Denmark police force. He took this job after he retired from his job as a guardsman at King Christensen X, where back when Denmark was first taken over he had helped take down the Nazi flag under the King's orders, as the king refused to have any flag other than that of Denmark fly over his castle. As a policeman, when he heard from German Georg Ferdinand Duckwitz that Germany was going to implement the "Final Solution" towards the Jews in Denmark, he wasted no time in getting to work.

Using his connections with fishermen, Knud Dyby arranged for fishing boats to go out to and from Sweden. Then, the group he joined, the Danish-Swedish Refugee Service, arranged for Denmark's Jews to be notified about the escape through their doctors. He then had them hide in the hospitals until they could be taken across the sound to Sweden.

To get there, they enlisted taxi drivers. When that wasn't enough, Knud Dyby commandeered police cars. To help keep German officers and their dogs away from the boats, he invented a mixture of blood plasma and cocaine that attracted the dogs, then numbed their senses so they couldn't smell anything. Even though the boats left Denmark, their trials didn't end there. The passage between the two countries was only a few miles wide, but it was dangerous: there was ice everywhere in the cold choppy waters, and the water itself was heavily mined. In fact, they relied on the German minesweeper boats to lead the way. Halfway through, the Jews had to transfer over to a Swedish boat, and from there to the Swedish shore, where they had to avoid Swedish informants. Once there, however, they were free, as Knud Dyby had provided them with passports and fake IDs from friends in government. The system was so efficient that over 99% of Denmark's Jews survived and returned to Denmark. 61% of that, or 91% of the total population, were saved by the Danish-Swedish Refugee Service.

After the war, Knud Dyby immigrated to the San Francisco area. There, he has been recognized several times for what he has done, including the Simon Wiesenthal Center and the State of Israel, which gave him the title "Righteous Among the Nations." He lived out the rest of his days in peace until November 2011, when he died peacefully. He was an interesting case, as although the rest of the Danish-Swedish Refugee Service preferred to be listed as a whole, Knud Dyby is also on the list of the righteous on the Yad Vashem website, probably due to his award.

Although my family doesn't personally hail from Denmark, I do feel touched personally by Knud Dyby. In a continent where Jews were distrusted and turned out, people like the Danish-Swedish Refugee Service and Knud Dyby helped us. We were given shelter, a way out, and comfort in that terrible time. Although people and places like Denmark don't come around very often, we have to appreciate them when they do.

PETER ZÜRCHER AND HARALD FELLER- THE HOLOCAUST IN SWITZERLAND

Aleah H. Treiterer

Europe in the 1940s was slowly being conquered by Nazi Germany. Although countries were resisting, a lot of civilizations weren't able to escape Nazi Germany. Switzerland was taken over by the Nazis in the March of 1944. Because of this, many of the Jews were put into Ghettos against there will. Even though the Swiss had been taken over by the Nazis, there were still people resisting the evils of Germany. Two of these people were Peter Zürcher and Harald Feller, who, in the time of death, destruction, and terror, rose up to defend the lives of innocents and helped save Jews. Both Peter Zürcher and Harald Feller will always be remembered as heroes of Switzerland during theHolocaust because of their courageous actions to save many Jewish lives.

During World War Two, Switzerland tried to remain neutral, although they did end up having Nazis in their country and their government. Even though Switzerland wasn't with the allies against the Nazis, the general population was against the ideals of the Hitler. In Switzerland, the Arrow Cross was a political party that had Nazi sympathizers. It was a right wing party that was based in Hungary and it supported the Nazis during the time of World War II. When Hitler became a commanding force in Europe, the Arrow Cross allied itself with the Nazi party. Its leader was Ferenc Szalasi. Even though Switzerland was neutral in the war, the citizens still had to deal with the horrors from the Nazis and the crimes that were committed during World War II..

One hero from Switzerland was Peter Zürcher, who resisted the Nazis from the inside and prevented the deaths of hundreds of Jews. Before the war, Zürcher was a Swiss businessman and lawyer living in Wartime, Budapest. After the Nazis took over Switzerland, Zürcher became employed at the Department for Safeguarding the Interests of Foreigners in the Swiss Embassy. Because of this job, Zürcher was able to rescue a lot of Jews from being deported from their homes. One of the Jews that he rescued was named Maria Kormos. She went to him for help when she found out that she was probably going to be removed from her house. At first, he advised her to attempt to bribe the porter of her house, to prevent them from figuring out that she was a Jew. After that didn't work, Zürcher sent men dressed up as the Arrow Cross to "question and arrest" her. In reality, these men brought Maria Kormos to Zürcher where he hid her in his own flat to keep her safe. After that, he created fake documents for her and located a pension for her to live at until all of the Jews were free and safe. Another huge way that Zürcher rescued hundreds of Jews was that he managed to prevent the genocide of all of the Jews living in the Pest ghetto. Zürcher overheard the Arrow Cross organization talking about murdering the entire Pest ghetto before the Soviets took it over. In response to Zürcher overhearing this information, he decided to blackmail the commander of Arrow Cross with the threat that Zürcher will bring the commander to trial with war crimes if he goes through with his plans of genocide. In the end, the plan of Zürcher worked and so the inhabitants of the Pest ghetto were safe from being slaughtered. The commander ended up ordering his troops not to enter the ghetto and not to harm the Jews in the Swiss safe houses. Because of his actions, Peter Zürcher received the Righteous Among Nations Award in 1999. Peter Zürcher wasn't the only man who was a hero for the Jews during the Holocaust.

Another man who influenced the lives of many different Jews and allowed them to live their lives to the fullest was Harald Feller. Harald Feller was a Swiss diplomat in the 1930s. After March 1944, when Switzerland was taken over by the Nazis, Fuller was involved in many different operations with a rebel organization to rescue Jews in Switzerland. He also used different illegal methods to save Swiss citizens married to Hungarians. In addition to those actions, Fuller rescued different Jews from transit camps and brought rescued Jews over to Switzerland. Harald Fuller even used own home to help protect Jews from being captured, killed, or put into a ghetto. He hid Gabor Derecseri, a Hungarian writer, his wife named Mara Huszar, and their one-year-old son in his house, and eventually rescued the parents of Mara Huszar and joined them with their daughter. He also provided refuge, not just for Jews, but also soldiers who deserted the Nazi army. In addition, Harald Fuller helped the Jews in an indirect way. He fed useful information about the Nazis to the Zionist underground rebel group, which was a huge risk for Feller's own wellbeing. Eventually, Harald Feller was arrested by the Arrow Cross because he had helped Jews escape the clutches of the Nazis. Feller was tortured by the people who had arrested him, but he still helped the Jews. He allowed Jews to find refuge in his house even after he was captured. Harald Feller was an amazing, brave man. He survived the Holocaust, and he was thanked and honored for his actions on July 15, 1999 when he received the Righteous Among the Nations award.

Because of men like Peter Zürcher and Harald Feller, many Jews survived theHolocaust in Switzerland. Peter Zürcher ended up preventing the deaths of hundreds of Jews by blackmailing an Arrow Cross commander. Harald Feller continually helped Jews and gave them refuge in his house, even after he was arrested by the Arrow Cross and was tortured. Without men and women like Feller and Zürcher, theHolocaust would have been much worse. These two men helped influence the entire world by standing up against frightening, powerful people, and they helped represent what was right and what they believed in, no matter the consequences. The actions of Peter Zürcher and Harald Feller will always be remembered and both of these men will be revered for their courageous actions during the Holocaust.

Works Cited

"Arrow Cross Party | Hungarian Organization." *Encyclopedia Britannica Online*. Encyclopedia Britannica. Web. 21 Feb. 2015. < http://www.britannica.com/EBchecked/topic/36144/Arrow-Cross-Party >.

"Peter Zürcher." *The International Raoul Wallenberg Foundation*. Web. 9 Feb. 2015. < http://www.raoulwallenberg.net/saviors/diplomats/list/peter-z-uuml-rcher-826/ >.

"Switzerland's Rolein World War II." *History of Switzerland*. Web. 22 Feb. 2015. < http://history-switzerland.geschichte-schweiz.ch/switzerland-second-world-war-ii.html >.

"The Holocaust in Hungary." *Children in History*. Web. 22 Feb. 2015. < http://histclo.com/essay/war/ww2/hol/holc-hun.html >.

"The Righteous Among Nations." *Yad Vashem*. Web. 9 Feb. 2015. < http://db.yadvashem.org/righteous/family.html?language=en&itemId=4018455 >.

"The Righteous Among Nations, Harald Feller." *Yad Vashem*. Web. 8 Feb. 2015. < "The Righteous Among Nations, Harald Feller." Yad Vashem. Web. 9 Feb. 2015. . >.

SWISS HEROES OF THE HOLOCAUST

Alec Sumner

What is a hero? According to the Google search engine, it is a person, who is admired or idealized for courage, outstanding achievements, or noble qualities. I have to agree, especially the part where it states that a hero has courage and noble qualities. Both of these people who I am writing about today have both of those qualities. Herald Feller had many noble qualities like sacrificing himself, and putting himself in danger of being found out that he was helping Jews by Nazi Germany. Most people would be killed when being found out about aiding Jews by the Nazis. And Paul Grueninger had a tremendous amount of courage. He broke the law of Switzerland many times. He had a monumental amount of courage to break his own law, because he was an enforcer of the law.

Harald Feller, born in 1913 in Switzerland and died in 2003, was a Swiss diplomat who saved Hungarian Jews during the Holocaust. He eventually became Swiss Minister, who is basically head of the Swiss legation, like an embassy, in Budapest, Hungary. Dr. Feller started to support Consul Charles Lutz by rescuing Jews under the protection of Switzerland. He worked with some of the other friendly legations in trying to persuade the Horthy and Sztójay puppet governments to end the cruelty to Jews. He also protected members of the Swedish legation, who were targeted by the Arrow Cross, the national socialist party in Hungary, by giving them fake Swiss passports and providing shelter. Toward the end of the war, He hid dozens of Jews in the basement of his house in Budapest. In February 1945, agents from the Soviet Union arrested him and sent him to Moscow, along with the other people who helped him with his rescuing. He was returned to Switzerland in February 1946 in exchange for two Soviet soldiers who had been taken by Switzerland. He received a Righteous Among the Nations award in 1999. This award is given to people by Israel for helping Jews from Nazi Germany during World War II.

Another Swiss hero was Paul Grueninger, who was a border policeman of the St. Gallen region, a region in Switzerland that shares a border with Austria. After the takeover of Austria by Germany, Switzerland had stopped letting people come in without authorized entry permits. In October of 1938 Switzerland and Nazi Germany were discussing things, and the outcome of the discussion was the "J" stamps. The "J" stamp was a "J" that was stamped onto your passport if you were Jewish, in Nazi Germany. As the situation of the Jews in Austria got worse and the more people wanted to illegally come into Switzerland, He was faced with a ginormous decision: letting them in and breaking the law, or making them go back to a country where the policy was to treat them horribly, and inhumanely.

He decided to let the Jewish people enter Switzerland. Also, in order to legalize the refugees' status, he changed their registration, so that their passports showed that they had come into Switzerland before March of 1938, which was before restricted people coming in to the country. Changing the dates made it so the people could be treated as legal immigrants, and be taken to the Diepoldsau camp, a camp where Jewish organizations would help them get on their feet. There, the people waited for their permission to stay there or go to a different country. He was a policeman who decided to break the law, a law that he vowed to follow, and enforce, turned in false reports about the number of arrivals and the status of the refugees in his district, and stopped efforts to trace refugees who were known to have entered Switzerland as illegal immigrants. He even paid with his own money to buy winter clothes for needy refugees who had been forced to leave all their belongings behind, and had almost nothing.

The Germans informed the Swiss authorities of his efforts, and he was cut from the police force in March of 1939. His benefits of being a police officer, and the benefits for the duration of his retirement were taken away, and he was brought to trial on charges of illegally permitting the entry of 3,600 Jews into Switzerland and changing their registration papers, even though it was the right thing to do. The government added additional charges of helping individual Jews by hiding them, so they wouldn't be found by the Nazis, and helping them hide their valuables.

His trial began is 1939, and lasted for almost two years. In March 1941 the court found him guilty of breaking the law, and helping Jews. He lost all benefits, like police officer benefits, and retirement benefits, and on top of that, was forced to pay the cost of the trial in court, and was also fined a large sum of money. The court saw that he was trying to help the Jews, but they still thought that because he was a government worker, he needed to follow the law, even if it is not doing the right thing.

The rest of his life was very difficult for him because he was shamed and forgotten. Although it was a very difficult life to live afterward, he never regretted for one second saving and helping the Jews, because he knew it was the right thing to do. In 1954 he explained why he did this, and what drive him to do it: "It was basically a question of saving human lives threatened with death. How could I then seriously consider bureaucratic schemes and calculations?"

In December of 1970, because of a large amount protest in the media, the Swiss government sent him a very weak letter of apology, but still didn't reopen his case and still didn't give him his his retirement benefits back. Only after his death in 1972 were efforts made to redeem him. The Swiss Council rejected the first attempt. So not until 1995, after he was dead for over 20 years, did the Swiss Government say he was a hero. He received a Righteous Among the Nations award in 1971, a year before his death.

Bibliography

Dictionary.com. Dictionary.com. Web. 25 Feb. 2015.
< http://dictionary.reference.com/ >.

Web. 25 Feb. 2015. < http://www.yadvashem.org/ >.

"Home." - *Quincy Herald-Whig*. Web. 25 Feb. 2015.
< http://www.whig.com/ >.

"The International Institute for Holocaust Research." *Search and Research – Lectures and Papers*. Web. 25 Feb. 2015.
< http://www.yadvashem.org/yv/en/about/institute/research.asp >.

A HERO OF MORALS AND THE HOLOCAUST: PAUL GRÜNINGER

Alexander Nails

When people think of great heroes, people think about their idols such as Beyonce or Eminem. To me, a hero is someone who displays courage when they are required to show defiance for the great welfare of people. A hero has morals that they use to guide them through fear of higher power. Everyone has idols who are celebrities when our real heroes and idols should be veterans and survivors of wars, and devastations of the world. This really represents the Hero of the Holocaust I chose. He believed in taking the higher road, and helped Jewish people survive the homicide of Jews. I am Jewish and to me the Holocaust represents more than a war and an onslaught of killing. It represents all of the people who were judged, critiqued, defamed, and criticized for how they look and who they are. That isn't right. Paul Grüninger believed that every person was equal. He had the morals of people such as Martin Luther King Jr., Mahatma Ghandi, and Nelson Mandela. "The best way to find yourself is to lose yourself in the service of others." -Ghandi (Brainy Quote Ghandi).

Paul Grüninger was the officer rank of a Colonel Border Patrol Officer in September of 1938. During this time, the Swiss had declared immunity to the war, but still interfered with both sides. At this time, the war had started with the Anschluss, the Nazi Regime's blood-free takeover of Austria. With this non-official act of war, the Swiss ostracized Austrian Jews coming into Switzerland. Paul Grüninger didn't agree with this. Being the Colonel of the Patrol, he fabricated fake passes through the Swiss Border, inscribing dates from past times so Jews could cross the border then meet up with an organization to take them to another country. He saved over 3,600 lives of Jewish people in seek of a person who wouldn't hurt them or submit them to the Third Reich. With helping illegally, no one is immune to consequences of their government. On April 3rd, 1939, he was sentenced to jail for his valiant actions of saving Jews. Since Switzerland had declared neutrality. He had broken this law so he was sent to jail ruining his career and financial life. He had been under Gestapo watch for months, but he put himself before others so that every life he could save helped future greatness for the world. In the Holocaust, jobs were hard to find and even harder to apply for if you had an ex-convict label on your resumé. He never regretted his actions showing how the past defines you, but you shouldn't live in it.

That is why I perceive that he is a hero. He has dignity. Dignity isn't just obtained through words, but in actions. Dignity to me consists of courage and creating hope. Courage is going through your fear and overpowering it to try harder and succeed. When you create hope, you inspire people to see the greater good in everything no matter how dark. "We must accept finite disappointment, but never lose infinite hope." -Martin Luther King Jr. (Brainy Quotes MLK) With these two emotions he inspired he truly is a hero to everyone and someone to be remembered with how he made his mark on the history of the world. Great leaders all have their ways of motivation. For many people it was speaking. For Hitler, he inspired people with his evil motives because he knew how to make a riot. It has seemed that with all enormous nations or foreign powers, they all have had a strong speaker no matter how cruel the motive. Another war figure, Winston Churchill, was an exceptional speaker. He persuaded all of England to out every ounce of courage and power they have to win this war that had already expended millions of people as if these people were lambs to the slaughter.

Lambs to the slaughter represents the Holocaust well. The Nazis had taken culture of a people (Jews) and destroyed their life, land, morals, liberty, and love. As a Jew, we believe that every object has the ability to change and exceed its previous actions. Not through redemption, but through striving to understand what we know and apply it towards greater ideals of life. In the Holocaust, the Nazi Regime targeted cripples, Jews, and other people the Nazis thought not worth of the Aryan Nation. Personally as a Jew, I have dealt with prejudice of who I am or who my family is just because I am proudly Jewish. World War II represents that no one was safe from stereotypes of who they are and what they look like. What the Fuhrer of Deutschland (Hitler) called Judenrein (Extermination of Jews in German) of the entire world.

This is what Paul Grüninger strived to stop. He didn't judge any of the people he saved if they were worth saving, instead he saved anyone who he could find or help. He had more than heroism, he had the attributes of a man who does more than care, he showed compassion. Overall, he saved 3,600 lives and made a dark future brighter for the Jewish people.

Works Cited

"The Example of Grüninger." *Funkascript ATOM.* N.p., n.d. Web. 05 Feb. 2015

"Gruninger, Paul – The Jewish Foundation for the Righteous.' *The Jewish Foundation for the Righteous.* N.p., n.d. Web. 10 Feb. 2015.

"Holocaust Memorial Day Trust." *Paul Grüninger.* N.p., n.d. Web. 10 Feb. 2015

"Mahatma Ghandi Quotes." *BrainyQuote.* Xplore, n.d. Web. 02 Feb. 2015.

"Martin Luther King, Jr. Quotes." *BrainyQuote.* Xplore, n.d. Web. 02 Feb. 2015.

"Paul Gruninger – The Righteous Among The Nations – Yad Vashem." *Paul Gruninger – The Righteous Among The Nations – Yad Vashem.* N.p., n.d. Web. 09 Feb. 2015.

HENRY CHRISTEN & ELLEN MARGRETHE THOMSEN: HEROES OF THE HOLOCAUST

Alison Bradus, Co-winner

While some chose indifference during the atrocity that was the Holocaust, a few chose to extend a helping hand to those in need. These righteous people created such an impact on those being persecuted by the Nazis. Henry Christen and his wife, Ellen Margrethe Thomsen, were two of these important individuals. When the couple chose to let their inn become a huge meeting point for Jews trying to escape to Sweden, they changed (and saved) the lives of many.

The innkeepers lived in North Zeeland, Denmark; more specifically the village of Snekkersten. They owned the Snekkersten Inn and Seaside Hotel together. They had two young children, but despite this were able to covertly aid others. The Thomsens were politically involved with the Social Democratic Party. From the beginning of the persecution, the two were very involved in standing up against Nazis. The moment the heroes heard of the possible actions to be taken against the Jewish people, they began scheduling, planning, and helping out any and all refugee organizations and assisting illegal cargo shipments. Their main source of help to the Jewish people seeking help was providing a secret means of transportation by ship all the way to Sweden.

Luckily for the family, the village of Snekkersten was supportive of the operation for the most part. Their work would have been impossible if not for the help of other townspeople. Many other factors affected the Thomsens' ability to be such great assets to those in need. The central location of their operations, and its close proximity to the sea, made transport possible. In addition, their own boat, the Margrethe (named after Ellen Margrethe), was the main mode of transportation. The family didn't complete their feats of righteousness without the help of other townspeople. Holger Danish, Leif B. Hendil, and Knud Parkov also had a hand in their achievements. As a force of underground Danes, a meeting spot for the fishermen was organized. This happened to be at the Thomsens's inn, a soon-to-be hub in the perfect location.

The decision of the Thomsens to provide a meeting place for Jews and the fishermen transporting them turned out to be monumentally important. During the time the Thomsens were transporting people, an estimated 1,000 Jews were able to escape Denmark and continue on their journey to Sweden. When the number of people needing escape multiplied, the family purchased a boat and took care of most of the transport themselves. This meant that Henry Thomsen had to risk his life over and over again to make the voyage to Sweden. But this wasn't the only sacrifice he made.

During the Holocaust, many Jews were in fear for their lives at all times. At the Snekkersten Inn and Seaside Hotel, they could rest easy, even if only for a little while. The Thomsens offered a resting place and shelter at their hotel, in addition to the transportation. If Jews were fleeing, or hiding from capture, they were welcomed to the inn. Unfortunately, all of this undercover business did not happen without someone in town who was pro-Germany taking notice.

A citizen of Elsinore informed the police that he had seen a mass of Jewish fugitives boarding a boat near the inn. As a result, Henry Christen Thomsen was arrested and interrogated by the Gestapo. After his interrogation, he was detained in jail for around a week. Eventually, the officials came to the conclusion that they had no evidence of Thomsen illegally smuggling Jews and had to release him. Even after this frightening event, he was brave enough to continue helping fleeing Jews. But yet again, in August of 1944, the Gestapo became suspicious of him. Henry was arrested and interrogated. After the many questionings, he was eventually sent to the Neuengamme concentration camp in Germany on September 9, 1944 because the Gestapo determined he was helping Jews.

As in all concentration camps in Germany, life was extremely difficult for anyone sentenced to time there. For most, living in a concentration camp was no better than a death sentence. Sadly, the case was the same for Henry Christen Thomsen. Four months after arrival, on December 4th, 1944, Henry died at the young age of 38. As a result of the harsh conditions, he had contracted pneumonia. In the most literal sense, he gave his life for the cause that he believed in.

To be driven by such a passion and to go to extreme lengths to save the lives of others is inspiring. Even though Henry Christen and Ellen Margrethe Thomsen weren't the ones being discriminated against during the Holocaust, they still took their chance to make a change. If not for people like them, many lives wouldn't have been spared. A little kindness and hospitality could have been all some Jews needed to get through one more day. For Jewish people fleeing and in fear for their lives, a place to stay was the biggest gift they could've received at that point. When the Thomsens extended their help to hundreds of Jews, they put their own lives at risk to inspire and save countless more.

Bibliography

Ferro Fountain of The Righteous BiographiesBELARUS (n.d.): n. pag. *Ferro Foundation of the Righteous Biographies*. Illinois Holocaust Museum and Education Center. Web. 1 Mar. 2015.

"Henry Christen and Ellen Margrethe Thomsen - The Righteous Among The Nations." *Yad Vashem*. Yad Vashem, n.d. Web. 01 Mar. 2015."Paying the Ultimate Price." *I Am My Brother's Keeper*. Yad Vashem, n.d. Web. 01 Mar. 2015.

HEROES OF THE HOLOCAUST

Amy Li

Anyone can be a hero. Just by showing an act of kindness to a person in need can make you a hero. To some, it might just seem like it's just something nice to do, but to the person you helped can make you a hero in their eyes. Though, you only did something so simple, it can play a huge impact on their life. Heroes of the Holocaust showed extreme acts of kindness and they are still being recognized for the brave acts today.

In 1933, the Nazis gained their power over Germany creating the tragic event, known as the Holocaust. The Nazi party, lead by Adolf Hitler, believed that the Jews brought disgrace to their community and only the Germans were "racially superior." Europe's Jewish population had increased to over nine million people by 1933; most of which lived in countries occupied by the Nazi party. Because they thought the Jews made the country look poor and low-class, their way of solving this problem was to murder as many Jews as they could lay their hands on, possibly all of them.

By 1945, the Nazi party had already murdered over 6 million Jews. Over 6 million innocent people were killed just because of their race and/or religion. It wasn't only the Jews who the Nazi people murdered, although the majority were Jewish, but the Nazis simply executed any people they believed to be inferiors.

During the Holocaust, there were hundreds of heroes, but what Harald Feller and Bill Barazetti did made them heroes of many families. These heroes not only rescued the innocent Jews from the tragic discrimination, but they saved their lives. They could've left and protect their own lives, but they sacrificed the one life they had in exchange for the lives of many.

Harald Feller was a Swiss diplomat who helped save the Hungarian Jews. Feller was born in 1913 and as a young boy he had dreamed of working in the theater and acting industry, although his father forced him to study law. Luckily, he did take some acting lessons as a child, which helped him in his law career when he grew up. Often Feller would use his acting skills to confuse his opponents, playing scenes to distract them. Later on, Feller was sent to Hungary as the secretary and judical counselor of the Swiss legation in 1943 and replacing the position of Maximilian Jaeger, a Swiss Minister in 1944, which was his job to sort of the conflicts between Switzerland and Hungary.

Feller had saved so many Jews by taking them to safe homes protected by the Swiss. One family saved by Feller was Eva Koralnik-Rottenberg's family, which includes her mother, Berta Rottenberg-Passweg and her sister Veronica, who was born after the Rottenbergs moved into the Swiss house for a few weeks. He had taken them to the safe house along with two other Jewish women. Feller also arranged for them to go to Switzerland. He took them to the train station and they boarded the train to Vienna. By the early 1945, Feller has saved dozens of Jewish lives as well as preparing and arranging ways to take the Jewish to Switzerland.

Bill Barazetti, like Harald Feller, was another Swiss man was saved thousands of the Jews, specifically young Jewish children. Barazetti worked for the Czech secret service in Germany, trying to transport the innocent Jews in the United Kingdom, known as the Kindertransport. Barazetti's great deeds were not known until many years after he saved these children.

As a young man he studied law at Hamburg University in 1933. When the news of the Holocaust got to him, he felt determined to help these Jewish people. Barazetti worked with the Kindertransport and arranged routes and ways to rescue the children from concentration camps and prevent them from being captured by the Nazi. He loaded boats with the children and they were transferred to the United Kingdom. Nearly 10,000 Jewish children were sent from the Nazi countries, including, Germany, Austria, Czechoslovakia, Poland, and Danzig all the way to London.

One of Barazetti's co-workers, Anna, captured many photographs of the training camps established by the Nazis as a way to force the Jews to work. These photographs were sent back to London for publishing. Anna was later caught for taking pictures and ran away. Unfortunately, Barazetti used the same route as Anna later on and the German police caught him and beat him nearly to death. After awhile Anna found Barazetti and took care of him.

Over the years Barazetti has been recognized for his brave actions by Israel with the title, "Righteous Gentile." Saving the children was not only doing good deeds for them, but it was also a gift to their parents, although most of the children's parents and families were killed during the Holocaust. Barazetti's brave acts shall not be forgotten; he risked his life into helping these children.

If it wasn't for the brave heroes, not just the heroes of the Holocaust, but the brave heroes that ever lived, our world would be awful; a world with no kind people to help anyone or anything. The Holocaust was such a horrific event, leading to the death of over 11 million people. Nearly 1 million of these people were children and only about 10,000 children were transported to London. Later, the children of the Kindertransport joined the British army to fight against Germany. They later grew up and immigrated to other countries or stayed in Britain as citizens.

I greatly thankful for all the heroes in my life and I appreciate what they do for me. They've set great examples for me, even though what my heroes did was not as brave as the acts of Harald Feller's or Bill Barazetti's, they still became my role models.

ANNA CHRISTENSEN: A BRIGHT LIGHT IN A TIME OF SUFFERING AND DARKNESS

Andrea Jensen

Agony is a word we often associate with suffering and trials of perseverance. Amongst the people living in our world, a few can say they understand what this means. However, other people have faced a whole new level of suffering, at which some of us can not begin to fathom. More than 11 million people died in a horrific act of genocide led by Adolf Hitler. Let alone most of those who survived his wrath, lived to watch as their mothers, fathers, sister, brothers, aunts, and uncles lives depended upon the mercy of one man.

In 1933, Hitler decided to kill off the population of people that he considered to be inferior. Although many people were considered to be inferior, the main targets were typically people of the Jewish faith. These people were victims and targeted for murder. Some were sent directly to concentration camps, where they endured malnutrition, unfair living conditions, and brutal punishments. Meanwhile, others died from being fumigated with exhaust in gas busses, some were burned, and others died of starvation or other horrendous causes. The consequence for assisting or hiding a Jewish person or minority from the German army was very serious. A person who was even accused of hiding a minority during the Holocaust could, and most likely would be punished with death. Every individual who went through the Holocaust has a unique story to tell, and no one's is exactly like another's. One story in particular, belongs to a woman by the name of Anna Christensen. She gave the gift of grace to more than 40 Jewish children whose lives were saved by her heroic actions.

Not long after the invasion of Hitler, many men, women and children were taken captive. Groups of Jewish children were transported into countries such as Germany and Austria to prepare them to work as farmers, and to learn how to tend to agriculture. After a period of time, they were to be sent to Israel, and they would work there. One particular group of Jewish children was transported to Nyborg, Denmark. This is where Anna Christensen comes into our story. She knew that the children weren't safe in Adolf Hitler's hands. She snuck them away and enrolled the children into a local school where they would take up studies to give them an education. On April 9, 1940 the Germans invaded Denmark, and the school officials became afraid to admit the Jewish children into the school. They feared they would become a large target for attack, and they would be the next victims of Hitler's scheme to rid the nations of the 'inferiors.' Anna, having a heart filled with mercy and compassion, decided that she would undergo a very dangerous plan to give these children the love and education that they deserved. She immediately turned her cellar into a classroom, where she went against common law and risked her own life to keep these children out of harm's way. Knowing the penalty for hiding the children, she still continued through with her plan, even when the danger was increased greatly.

Eventually, the children who Anna cared for were no longer safe in her cellar by any means, and she knew that she would have to do something or else her life and the lives of the precious, innocent children would be taken by Hitler and his men. Without hesitation Anna, with the help of some friends, immediately organized hiding places for the children where they would be at a lesser risk for being executed. She made sure that each place that she and her friends would send the children to hide was inspected for safety beforehand. Then, she illegally transported the young children into hiding. However, that was not the end of her journey with the children. Christensen met twice a week with the children she cared for, and they usually gathered during festivals and other events, when Army men weren't as active or alert. They would discuss many different topics, and Anna would often make a wide variety of traditional foods for them. These children were without a mother or father figure to assure them of their well-being, and Anna stepped in and was a kindhearted woman who treated each and every child as if they were her own. In a time where complete peril and darkness seemed to consume millions of lives, Anna took it upon herself to pour into these children and give them hope and encouragement. In the fall of 1943, the time came where Anna knew that another drastic measure was necessary. With the help of the Danish Underground Movement, she illegally escorted the Jewish children to the country of Sweden, where their lives were spared.

After the war, Anna still made great efforts to keep in contact with the children whom she considered to be her own. She continued to write them all cards on the nights of festivals, to somewhat honor the tradition and memory of her and the children meeting (during festivals), when they were in hiding. In the year 1966, she visited Israel and reunited with some of her children, and was a very loved and appreciated guest. In May of the same year, she was honored and recognized as one of the 'Righteous Amongst the Nations' by Yad Vashem. Being a woman from a non-Jewish religion and saving the lives of 40 innocent Jewish children is truly an act worth being praised for. She was recognized for her valiance, kind heart, and most importantly, her fiery passion for lives of the children she saved at the risk of her very own. However, despite doing such courageous deeds for the children, she didn't expect any awards, acknowledgements, or benefits. Ms. Christensen teaches us one of the most important values one can learn: It doesn't matter who you are, your actions have an impact. It is the simplicity of love and passion that drives people to do grand things for others.

Bibliography

Unknown Author. The Righteous Among The Nations. Yad Vashem, Christenen Family: Christensen, Anna. Date Unknown. Web. 2 February 2015.
http://db.yadvashem.org/righteous/family.html?language=en&itemId=4014337

Unknown Author. The Holocaust: HOLOCAUST DEATH CAMPS, 1941-1945. History.com. Date Unknown. Web. 2 February 2015.
http://www.history.com/topics/world-war-ii/the-holocaust

SWEDISH HOLOCAUST HERO RAOUL WALLENBERG

Annamarie A. Solorzano

What is it that makes up a hero? This is not an easy question to answer with mere words. Heroes are many things. They are role models. They are hope when the cause seems lost. They are the people who fight for what is right no matter the odds. Most importantly, heroes are willing to lend a hand to those in need, notwithstanding how small or insignificant they may seem. Raoul Wallenberg was one such hero. During the Holocaust of 1933-1945, this bold young man helped save the lives of tens of thousands of Jews. Such a feat requires unimaginable strength; not physical strength, but outstanding perseverance. This is the story of how one small man was able to make a huge difference in the world.

Wallenberg first learned about the Holocaust and the horrific reign of Adolf Hitler in 1936 while working at a bank in Haifa (a city in Israel). A few years later, Raoul Wallenberg became acquainted with a Jewish man by the name of Koloman Lauer. Lauer ran a trading company, but since he was Jewish, it wasn't safe for him to travel through much of Europe. Wallenberg understood Lauer's issue completely. His superior language skills and knowledge of the country made Raoul the ideal man to take over for Lauer. In fact, he soon became co-manager of the trading firm. Raoul Wallenberg's new job took him to Budapest, the capital of Hungary. The Holocaust movement had not yet reached Hungary, however, and so was relatively safe to visit. This quickly changed. Nazis were ordered by Hitler to rid of the Jewish populace in Hungary. By the summer of 1944, hundreds of thousands of Hungarian Jews had been shipped off to the nearest death camp. This desperate situation called for a solution. A new Anti-Nazi organization called the War Refugee Board decided that since Sweden had stayed out of World War II it should send a man to help out the Jews in Hungary. One of the Swedes the government considered sending, in fact, was Koloman Lauer. Lauer then suggested his own business partner for the job. He explained that Raoul Wallenberg could speak Hungarian and German, had the right qualities, and was empathetic towards Jews. Raoul accepted the mission and hurried off to Hungary.

Raoul Wallenberg's emergency "hero quest" to Hungary had officially begun. He had to be courageous. Now was not the time to turn back, and countless Jews needed his help. Raoul quickly set up his own Anti-Nazi business. He hired about 400 former Jews to work at the office. Raoul began his work by designing a protective passport for Jews to hold. The purpose of this passport was to protect them from being deported to death camps. Miraculously, it worked. About 4,500 of these passports were given to Jews. Raoul Wallenberg personally helped to hand out the passports. However, Raoul's mission did not come without troubles. His one big obstacle was a Nazi official by the name of Adolf Eichmann. Eichmann often threatened Wallenberg. He also began shipping large masses of Jews off to death-camps by train. One time, Eichmann personally tried to kill Wallenberg but failed. Despite such death-threats, Wallenberg continued his valiant work. He offered Jewish people safe-houses disguised as Swedish public buildings. On one occasion, Raoul went so far in his efforts to deliver the protective passports as to leap on top of freight cars and hand out bundles of them. A German officer was ordered to shoot Wallenberg, but the officer actually missed on purpose because Raoul's heroic actions were inspiring. Other countries were inspired by his ideas, too. They used his "safe-house" idea to offer refuge for Jews. Some countries even designed their own protective passports. But this was not all. Raoul Wallenberg bribed and threatened his enemies to save peoples' lives. He established a group of spies, and the spies gave him precious information about what went on at the police-station. He even personally visited train-stations and argued with officers to release the Jews. Finally, Wallenberg put in one last effort. He found out via his spies that Adolf Eichmann planned to wipe out the rest of the Hungarian Jews in one large killing spree. Of course, being the kind-hearted humanitarian he was, Raoul could not live with this. He sent a last-minute note to the only one who could stop the massacre: German General August Schmidthuber. The massacre was canceled right in the nick of time. By the end of 1944, Raoul Wallenberg had successfully relinquished (according to a friend called Per Anger) about 100,000 Jews.

During the quest to Hungary, Raoul Wallenberg risked his own life many times over to save people he didn't even know. He ignored threats and poured his life into helping out every Jew he could-no matter how unimportant they were. Raoul Wallenberg was indeed an extraordinary man, one who went out of his way to save the lives of the weak, of the small. He gave Jewish people a voice, a cause, a flicker of hope. Wallenberg inspired others, even entire countries, to follow his lead. Perhaps this is the definition of a hero. Everyone can be a hero, really...they just need the courage and a reason to lead. Although Raoul Wallenberg mysteriously disappeared many years later, he was not denied a reward. Of course, Raoul did not ask for fame and fortune. True heroes don't ask for anything in return for their actions, they simply volunteer. Wallenberg's name can be found in the Guinness Book of World

Records under "Saved Greatest Number of People from Extinction." Other nations offered their own rewards for his heroics. Wallenberg even received a prize from President Ronald Reagan naming him an honorary citizen, which hadn't been awarded to anyone other than Winston Churchill years earlier. In all honesty, this shows that standing up for what is morally right is more rewarding than any other prize. Raoul Wallenberg, though one small man, made a lasting impact on the world. Who knows what the future holds for us?

Bibliography

Larsson, Jan. "Raoul Wallenberg's Biography". Raoulwallenberg.net. Swedish Institute 1995. Web. 9 February 2015.

"Raoul Wallenberg". History.com. A+E Networks 2010. Web. 9 February 2015.

"Raoul Wallenberg-A Man Who Made A Difference". Sweden.se. 14 May 2014. Web. 9 February 2015.

BILL BARAZETTI: A DISCREET HERO

Daniel Kim

Most of the people who had rescued the Jews and other religious people from the concentration camps had took pride and had no regrets in telling their stories of how they had saved the lives of many people through the actions of several brave souls. However, there was a man who had kept his association with helping the Jews as a secret until 1990. Bill Barazetti, a humble hero, who had been involved in a Schindler-style operation on a transport, had helped the Jews that were trapped in the concentration camps. Schindler was a fellow hero who also saved many people during the Holocaust. In 1939, Barazetti was along side with Sir Nicholas Winton, a British stockbroker, and the two men had played a major role in organizing the plan of having thousands of Jewish orphans, victims from discrimination and from the loss of family, to escape Germany before war was summoned to Germany. Called the Kindertransport, Barazetti and Winton had both succeeded in having three trainloads of Jewish children/orphans out of Germany between May and July. Through the difficult system of false identification for the children, which was designed by Barazetti, he had succeeded in having thousands of mainly Jewish children to safety in London.

Born on 1914, Barazetti was originally named as Werner Theodore Barazetti. He was the son of a Swiss Professor of French at Heidelberg University. As a 19 year old in 1933, Barazetti was studying about law and morals in Hamburg University when he saw a group of Nazis beat up Jewish students in the university. Seeing the harsh treatment that the Jewish students were receiving, Barazetti had a powerful desire to support the members of religious groups that appeared to be a disgrace by the superiors, something that I find to be quite bold for a student in pre-World War II. A fellow ally in Barazetti's objective named Anna, who was considered to be a perfect student from the Czech Sudetenland, was helping Barazetti's cause by taking photos of Nazi concentration camps and the cruel treatment that the religious people were receiving, and sending the photos to the press in London.

Eventually, Anna was discovered in her work, but successfully escaped to the Czech border near her home. Barazetti, however, wasn't as fortunate as Anna. Barazetti also tried to escape in the same route that Anna went on, but the Gestapo caught him, gave him some injuries, and left him to die. Fortunately, Anna founded him and nursed him back to top condition at her home. Later in 1936, the duo had married in Prague, which was a union that granted Barazetti his citizenship in Czech. The origin of the couple's wedding seems awfully similar to love stories, which I found amusing in a way. Barazetti appeared to be the perfect agent for Czech, being able to cross over to Germany without suspicion, visit the high security borderlines and report on Hitler's plans of sinister plans. He continued on his role of being a spy for Czech, until the Munich agreement of September 1938, which allowed Germany to gain some parts of Czech, along with control over the borders. The Munich Agreement was a failed negotiation of peace, as well as the possible reason why Germany wanted to gain more land from Czech, hence starting Germany's involvement with World War II.

After the Munich agreement was called out, Barazetti had decided to work on charities to help the huge flood of refugees running into Czechoslovakia, many from post-Anschluss Austria, to Britain, and to Scandinavia. About 50,000-70,000 refugees had succeeded in escaping by the organizations that Barazetti had supported. Around that time was when a British stockbroker, Nicholas Winton, decided to evacuate the Jewish children from the Nazi concentration camps. Winton appointed Barazetti as a partner for the rescue mission. Winton arrived at England, where he arranged visas, homes, and 50 pounds-per-head sponsor for each child who would be rescued. Barazetti had done the same arrangements in Prague as well. He assigned the trains that would pick up the children, had conversations with the families of the abducted children, and sent Winton the details and photos for each child in the concentration camps. Barazetti received a Jewish printer in Prague to produce forged papers required for the children in order to fool German authorities. Shortly after Germany invaded Prague in March 1939, Winton left to England and Barazetti later took over on the operation. Despite the fact that he was considered to be a criminal to the Nazis, he managed to convince German authorities to send 4 trains full of children to Britain. When the first train arrived at Holland, the visas were ready to be given to the children on the train. Barazetti was successful in the attempts to return to Prague in order to reuse the forged documents for re-use. On the Spring and Summer of

1939, Barazetti had succeeded in sending 3 trains full of children from Prague to Britain. The 4th train was ready to leave on the eve of World War II, but the train had never reached to Holland, and was never heard from again. The loss of the 4th train was a massive loss, but Barazetti had successfully rescued the rest of the children from the clutches of the Nazis, and returned as a hero.

In August 1939, Barazetti arrived at Britain, and employed in a War Office unit that interrogated German prisoners of war. After the World War, he found a job in the United Nations to establish government systems in many independent countries that were new, mainly in India. He became a British citizen in 1953. I admired Barazetti's actions after his heroic deed. Despite how I prefer him returning as a public hero, it is still nice to see him convert back to a normal life, with a job that still helps other people. Rather than state about his deed to the world, he just wanted to go back to a normal life, which was surprising to me. Barazetti's proud tale of being involved with the Kindertransport remained nonexistent in the world, until he stated about his involvement by pure chance. He was chatting with an Israeli visitor who was involved in the Kindertransport, and Barazetti stated that he knew about the Kindertransport. The Israeli visitor was determined to pursue the story of how Barazetti was involved in the Kindertransport, and tracked Barazetti's involvement through the diaries that Winton had sent to the Holocaust conference organizer, Dr. Elisabeth Maxwell. Winton admitted in how he had indeed left the entire Kindertransport organization to Barazetti after Winton left to England.

Personally, I think that Barazetti should have proudly declared his epic tale of rescuing the children, but Barazetti still kept the story to himself, mainly because he has no desire to talk about the story. Along with Sir Nicholas Winton, Barazetti has done this extremely risky task, not for fame or pride, but simply because Barazetti wanted to do what he thought was morally correct. I think that Barazetti should have confessed about his involvement in the Kindertransport, for it is indeed a proud story that Barazetti should tell others. There weren't that many people who were brave enough to help out the religious group that had been taken away from their homes. If not for Barazetti's actions, the Kindertransport would have most likely failed and possibly most of those children would have died in their escape. Barazetti had faced many life-risking challenges in order to rescue the children in Prague, but he faced the challenges with bravery in order to save the lives of nearly hopeless children during the Holocaust. Through the honorable and discreet actions of Barazetti during the Holocaust, Barazetti appears to be a very humble and impressive hero within the Holocaust.

Biography

Downey, Shane. "The Poor Mouth" : Bill Barazetti. N.p., 06 Jan. 2008. Web. 13 Feb. 2015

"Philosemitism." : Werner Theodore Barazetti. N.p., 14 Jan. 2008. Web. 6 Feb. 2015.

A RESCUER'S STORY

Emily Segale

In 1933, Nazis captured 6 million Jews and held them hostage in Germany. Jewish people were collected from all over Europe and sent to Germany where they were beaten, starved, and killed. This was known as the Holocaust. While it was an overwhelming evil time in history, theHolocaust did introduce the world to many heroes that will forever be remembered. Among them, teachers were a most influential and brave group. Gerda Valentiner, a Danish teacher, risked her own life for the sake of her students.

TheHolocaust began in 1933 when Adolf Hitler rose to power and became the ruler of Germany. Under his rule, Jews from all over the world were taken to Germany and held in small camps known as ghettos. Deportation was planned country by country and every day thousands of Jews were transferred to either concentration or death camps. There these hostages were victims of starvation, beatings, burnings, and gassing. One and a half million of the 6 million Jews who died were children. Gerda Valentiner, a teacher from Denmark, sympathized with her Jewish students and exclaimed "No more! " It was on the eve of the deportation of Jews of Denmark that Gerda took action.

The Germans had recently invaded Denmark and Norway. To escape the Nazis, many families were uprooted and forced to live a life outside of Denmark. At this time, there was a transfer that took place, moving all Jewish people from Denmark to Sweden. Sweden offered many refugee relief communities that were havens for the Jews. Gerda Valentiner was instrumental in the movement of Denmark's Jews to Sweden during October 1943.

While many teachers abandoned their Jewish students, Gerda did not. She felt it was her duty to educate her students in school and also teach them values outside the classroom, even if it meant risking their lives. During the planned week that Germany was expected to occupy Denmark, Gerda collected the Jewish children from their parents and took them home. Here she fed them and cared for them until the time came for a safe transfer to the coast where they would be taken to Sweden. While in her care, Gerda respected the principles of these children even adhering to the dietary laws of Judaism. To the extent that she could meet all their needs she even went out and bought special dishes and food that met their religious requirements. She did everything she could to rescue the children and secure them in an environment that allowed them to maintain and live by all their ideals. She had great respect for her students' religious observance.

Very few people can say they rescued tens and tens of children from being starved and killed. But, Gerda Valentiner can! What Gerda achieved was unheard of. A

Danish teacher had saved Jewish children from being slaughtered. Valentiner risked her life and her students for the hope that they would all be saved. If Gerda left the children they would remain in Denmark and be captured by the Nazis. What the hero did showed her respect for her religion and her dedication to the students. She attempted a dangerous mission that would save the people she loved most, but also put her life at risk. It is very incredible what the teacher accomplished for her students. Gerda Valentiner once said, "I only did what many Danes did, nothing special. We thought it perfectly natural to help people in mortal danger." Gerda didn't know she had changed the lives of everyone the day she saved those children. She did do something special!

There is no longer a Holocaust, but there will always be heroes like Gerda Valentiner. In 2012, December 14th, in Newtown Connecticut, a shooting occurred at Sandy Hook Elementary School. On that day, a man named Adam killed 20 children and 6 adults. Teachers who could not stand to see their students be killed and mistreated, similar to Gerda, took a stand and attempted to save the children. Unfortunately, these hopefuls were also killed. Gerda Valentiner would have helped these children and she helped hers back then. As a student, it is a good feeling to know that your teacher would protect you in times of danger. Gerda Valentiner is my hero because I know she would have saved my life from misery in Germany and the guns at school.

Heroes come in all shapes and sizes. Each hero overcomes something different and represents an impossible strength throughout. Heroes have different achievements that will always be remembered. Gerda Valentiner is the hero who risked her life in order to save her students from trouble in Germany. TheHolocaust era was one of the worst times for the entire world, but Valentiner made it a little bit better for a small group of students.

Works Cited

"11 Facts About the Holocaust." *11 Facts About the Holocaust*. N.p., n.d. Web. 11 Feb. 2015.

Rosenberg, Jennifer. "Holocaust Facts - 33 Things You Should Know." N.p., n.d. Web. 11 Feb. 2015.

Rosenberg, Jennifer. "The Holocaust." N.p., n.d. Web. 18 Feb. 2015.

"Sandy Hook Elementary School Shooting." *Wikipedia*. Wikimedia Foundation, n.d. Web. 18 Feb. 2015.

"Sweden." *Representation* 1.1 (1960): 4. Web.

""Their Fate Will Be My Fate Too.."" *Gerda Valentiner*. N.p., n.d. Web. 21 Feb. 2015.

HEROES DURING THE HOLOCAUST

Flunh Jameel

The Holocaust was an inhumane time between 1933 and 1944. Over 6 million innocent people were killed in the apocalypse of World War II. When Adolf Hitler received political power in Germany, he started the massacre of Jews, homosexuals, Gypsies, the homeless, and others who were considered inferior. Such actions began by simple prejudice against certain people, but it quickly progressed into one of the largest cases of genocide in our history. Countless people were sent to concentration camps, and others were immediately terminated. People took any chance to flee for their lives, but there were some brilliant heroes who risked their lives to support those being persecuted. Whether it was saving one person, or thousands, their efforts were greatly useful, and they will always be appreciated. One man was Knud Dyby, and he was a Danish rescuer born in Randers, Denmark. He acquired a lot of useful experience from various jobs. Another man was Harald Feller, who was born in Switzerland, and he became a Swiss diplomat in Hungary, in 1944. Knud Dyby and Harald Feller are true heroes for their bravery, humanitarian acts, and cleverness to aid those being persecuted during the Holocaust by the Nazis.

In a time when immoral destruction by the Nazis was nationwide in Germany, there were a minority of courageous people such as Knud Dyby and Harald Feller, who attempted to save others by showing great bravery. They are true heroes to me because they risked their own lives for other humans, instead of solely seeking their personal safety. Dyby's early brave action was when he participated in removing the Nazi flag that was placed over the Amalienborg Castle, and this was risky because the they could've issued a command to kill him. Also, when the Germans were in Denmark to deport the Jews, he helped transport almost 7,000 people to Sweden where they were safer. He was a well-known man, and the Germans were already in Denmark, so it was highly likely that he could've been caught. Dyby used taxi cars and police cars for their transportation, which was extremely dangerous because they had to avoid the nearby German Naval patrols, and the Coast Guard in Denmark. The Jews could've been found and killed immediately, and his life would've ended too. Despite knowing the dangers, he risked his life, but he was fortunately able to transport them to Sweden. Harald Feller, a famous Swiss diplomat, also took brave actions by saving Hungarian Jews. His courage encouraged him to take action in whatever that could help those in danger, although it was risky for him. The Nazis' political power was increasing rapidly, but these men were not afraid to help the endangered people by risking their own lives.

Next, KnutdDyby and Harald Feller were true heroes for their humane acts. When asked about about their efforts, they stated that it was natural and conscience of them to help the Jews, the Baltic refugees, saboteurs, Estonians, and other people fleeing from the Nazis. Dyby became a member of the Danish-Sweden Refugee Service that had to rescue almost 2,000 people, and the mission was successful. Also, when Dyby rescued 7,000 people to Sweden, he went to doctors' offices to tell them to inform the Jews of the rescue plan, and he assigned places near hospitals where they could remain until they were navigated to Sweden. When asked about his experience, he said that the Jews were friends, rightful citizens of Denmark, and were no different, except having a different religion. I definitely agree with him because that proves his kindness and heroism since he wanted equality for every single person. Also, Harald Feller is a hero for his humane acts since he saved many Hungarian Jews. Feller made determined attempts that liberated many Jews under Swiss protection, and he worked with other governments to support Jews near persecution, or termination, by providing them with false passports. Furthermore, Feller provided them with shelter, and one of those places was the basement of the consular residence in Budapest. These compassionate actions caused an unfortunate event because Feller was arrested and sent to Russia until 1946, where he was finally freed. He knew that such events could occur, but his moral values were greater than his own life.

Lastly, Knud Dyby's and Harald Feller's cleverness was another factor that led to the rescue of thousands of people near persecution. Harald Feller became a Swiss diplomat at a young age, and he worked cleverly close with neutral legations to help save people. In such a time, it was hard to obtain false passports, but he was able to with his wise skills, which protected many Jews. Also, Dyby had various jobs in his life which helped him acquire great knowledge that was useful during the Holocaust. These jobs include working in print trade, being a militia man, a Royal Guardsman, and finally a policeman. At the age of 26, he became a high ranking and national policeman where he acquired a lot of useful experience, training, and skill. He had plenty of jobs in his life, but the most important job as a liberator was being a policeman because he was acquainted with many people, and he had more freedom to wander around cities in this dangerous period of time. He was able to transport 7,000 people to Sweden by his knowledge, skill, and experience. In the past, he had experience with sailing, so he knew the best routes from Denmark to Sweden, and where to avoid the German navy patrol routes. He was also familiar with the best hiding places near fishing ports where refugees could remain until they were transported to safety. Furthermore, he was able to obtain copious important papers that were a necessity for Danish defenses. The information accessible to this policeman was vital when he planned rescue plans underground, and/or on sea. His careful planning and cleverness from various job experiences helped him save thousands of lives.

In conclusion, the Holocaust was a devastating apocalypse that ended the lives of almost 6 million people, but there are true heroes worthy of recognition because they risked themselves to save the innocent people. It was those appreciable heroes that provided us some hope in humanity throughout this tragic period of time. Knud Dyby and Harald Feller are two examples of many other heroes that showed great courage, cleverness, and humane acts to help those being persecuted by the Nazis. Knud Dyby was awarded a Righteous Among Nations by Israel in 2004. One of his memorable hero actions was when he helped transport Jews to Sweden safely. Also, these heroes proved their compassion through selfless humane acts. Dyby became a member of the Danish-Sweden Refugee Service, and searched for doctors' offices to tell them to inform the Jews of the rescue plan. In total, he saved almost 10,000 people. Feller saved Hungarian Jews under the Swiss protection since he was a diplomat. He was eventually arrested which wasn't very surprising, be he didn't let that stop his humanitarianism. They are great heroes for their cleverness as well, which was gained by various work experiences and tasks. These two men were courageous, clever, and they selflessly helped refugees, which proves to us that they are true heroes worthy of recognition. Harald Feller was awarded a Righteous Among Nations in 1999, with the special statement, "On behalf of all those men and women who selflessly helped refugees, and who's names will probably never be known."

Bibliography

"Knud Dyby: One of the Righteous." Ron Greenes Blog. N.p., 28 Jan. 2012. Web. 23 Feb. 2015.

Halstead, Richard. "Knud Dyby, Novato Man Who Helped save Thousands of Jews during World War II, Dies at 96." Knud Dyby, Novato Man Who Helped save Thousands of Jews during World War II, Dies at 96. Marin Independent Journal, 12 Sept. 2011.   Web. 23 Feb. 2015.

"Dr. Harald Feller." Funkascript ATOM. N.p., n.d. Web. 23 Feb. 2015.

KNUD DYBY: A RIGHTEOUS DANISH HERO

Gillian Benson

Thousands killed, families torn apart, but who knew that one person could make such a difference in the midst of chaos. During the Holocaust, in World War II, there were many heroes who contributed to saving the lives of countless Jews. One of them was a man named Knud Dyby, who was from Denmark. He was responsible, alone, for saving thousands of lives, reuniting families, and becoming "One of the Righteous." From his early life, to his rescue mission, to his passing, he will always be considered a hero.

Knud Dyby was born in Randers, Denmark, in 1915. In his early life, after his university years, he followed his father's footsteps into the printing trade and worked as a typographer. After that, he joined the military service, and was part of the King's Royal Guard. During his time in the military, he participated in removing the Nazi flag over the Amalienborg Castle, which was home to the Danish Royalty. Once he was done with military service, he became a police officer. As a police officer, he had access to important information that could be useful to the Danish resistance. He knew where the best places to hide by the docks were, and what the patrol routes of the German Navy were. He was best aware with their patrol routes between Denmark and Sweden. He was also an experienced sailor, so he knew the best sea lanes between Denmark and Sweden. In 1940, when the Germans came to occupy Denmark, Dyby joined several underground resistance groups. For three years, the Germans occupied Denmark. When the news spread that the "final solution" was approaching, and that all the Jews would be rounded up and deported, he acted quickly.

The evacuation of Jews began in October 1943. With all of the information Dyby was equipped with, he would be a big aid during this process to transport Jews. Their plan was to hide Jews, then take them by boat across the Oresund, which was the narrow water passage between Denmark and Sweden. Their hiding places would be mainly in hospitals. To get this plan in motion, they would first have to inform the Jews about the rescue plan. Knud Dyby discovered that hospitals were a good place to spread the news, because everyone had a doctor and the hospitals were agreeable. Then, they would have to bring as many Jews as they could to the harbor, at the appropriate time. But, to do so, they would need the city's taxi drivers. If that did not work, due to Knud being a police officer, he arranged for the use of police cars. While people were waiting for a boat to take them to Sweden they would hide in the hospitals. The hospitals would hold approximately 1,000 Jews. The boats would make repeated trips between Denmark and Sweden carrying mail, money, information, Jews, and more. But there were not only Jews on the boats, there were many others who were fleeing the Nazis. This dangerous act depended on if the fisherman were able to avoid the German naval patrols, the Danish Coast Guard, and the Swedish informers. Astonishingly, within only a couple weeks, almost all 8,000 Jews living in Denmark were brought to safety in Sweden. Precisely, about 7,200 Jews were saved by this courageous effort. Even though, in Mr. Dyby's words, the Germans "got mad like hell" when they found out what happened, it was all worth the risk.

Knud Dyby, alone, was accountable for as much as 80 percent of the information that went to Sweden from Denmark during the times of the evacuation. In May 1945, when Denmark was liberated, he ended his career as a policeman and moved to the United States a year later. Knud's heroism throughout the Holocaust during World War II has been recognized by multiple organizations around the world. He was honored by the Simon Wiesenthal Center, in Los Angeles, for all of his humanitarian efforts during World War II, on November 9, 1999. In 2004, Knud Dyby was awarded the title "Righteous Among the Nations" by Israel. This title is given to non-Jewish men and women who risked their lives to save Jews from the harm of the Nazis. Knud was given this award due to his bravery, courage, and humanitarian actions during the Holocaust. Even though he received many awards and honors for his heroic actions, Knud was a modest man. He said that he was only a small part of the resistance efforts in Denmark. He praised the ordinary Danish citizens who played a big role when the Germans came searching for Jews. However, he thought that the actions of the Danish people were just a natural response because Danes have always been loyal to their friends and neighbors, including the Jews. He said that Jews were never considered abnormal or outsiders, they were a part of the Danish community and were just people who happened to be involved in another religion. Everyone was considered equal.

On September 8th, 2011, Knud Dyby passed away in his home in Novato, California, at the age of 96. He made a contribution to the protection of almost 8,000 Jews in Denmark. To this day, we remember all of the heroes who saved thousands of lives during the Holocaust. All of their brave efforts to rescue the Jews from the Nazis are recognized and appreciated by people around the world. To all of the righteous heroes, we say *thank you*.

IN THE HOME OF A HERO

Gina Talcott, Co-runners-up

W.B. Yeats once wrote in a poem, "Come away, O human child! To the waters and the wild, With a faery, hand in hand, For the world's more full of weeping than you can understand." Many children were left orphaned and weeping by the Holocaust and a few organizations took it upon themselves to create a better place for these children, where even imaginary faeries were still possible. While the Nazi party took over Germany and sent people to concentration camps, smaller movements in France and Switzerland, such as the Secours Suisse and CIMAD (le Comité Inter-Movements Auprès des Evacuées), dedicated themselves to creating homes for children orphaned or interned during the war. Auguste Bohny was among those who devoted their lives to aiding these children. His actions with the Secours Suisse as director of several children's homes in Le Chambon justly numbered Bohny as one of the Righteous Among Nations honored by Yad Vashem.

Auguste Bohny studied to become an elementary school teacher. An interruption to his education called him away to spend a brief period of time in the army for Switzerland. He "had definite problems with military duty" and was "very happy ... to be able to work actively and positively for [his] country" (Oral History Interview with Auguste Bohny-Reiter) when an opportunity was presented to him to work at a children's home in France later on, instead of holding another gun. He worked closely with Pastor Trocmé, a local pastor who was very involved in encouraging the community to support the Secours Suisse aux Enfants and CIMAD in establishing the homes to help the children. At La Guêpé, a home completed before Bohny's arrival, children were able to continue their studies at Cevenol, a college in Le Chambon. Shortly after, they succeeded in opening a second home called L'Abrique after the "patois" spoken in the area, to mean that those in the home would be safe and sheltered. Homes were open to French social cases as well as Jewish and Spanish refugees, whom had been rescued from internment camps such as Gurs or Rivesaltes by other employees of the Secours Suisse, who stayed for three to six months until more permanent living arrangements could be made for them. Bohny became the director of the institutions in 1941 and they flourished under his guidance. A home named Faïdoli after a song that the children sang was opened, as well as the Ferme École, or farm school, where children could learn to work around a farm and refurbish the interior of the farm house. This also provided food, wool, and other necessary resources to the other homes in Le Chambon.

Throughout his years as director, Auguste Bohny sheltered and nurtured over 800 children. During those times, children hiding in other homes were discovered and deported to concentration camps where they were killed, but no one was ever taken from one of Bohny's homes. The Vichy police investigated the premises on several occasions, once asking for 72 of the children. However, each time one of the children was requested, Auguste, Friedel Bohny-Reiter, Auguste's wife who worked at the internment camp Rivesaltes for the Secours Suisse and who had by this point been working alongside him at Le Chambon, or one of the other employees would present false papers or speak to the officials and distract them long enough for the children or other persecuted individuals to sneak off into the woods around the homes and Le Chambon. Once the Vichy police had left and there was no longer an immediate looming threat of deportation, they would take a group of children out to sing their songs so that anyone hiding knew it was safe to come back and rejoin the group.

Bohny expended superhuman efforts to make life better for the children and lavish care upon them. One of the children under this care, Natalie Plessner, later described him as "a refined, serious person, loving and forgiving, who gave wonderful care to children who had been persecuted for their origin (as foreigners), their race (as Jews), or because of their situation (parents in the Resistance or dead)." Parents were sensitive subjects for the children at the institutions as many of them were either orphaned, had parents living (last they had heard) in concentration camps, or, for the French social cases, parents who were currently jailed. Bohny once commented that "Children who were haunted night and day by the memory of the horrors of the past came together in our institution. From the moment they came they were given an opportunity to gradually resume the ordinary, tranquil, happy lives of young people-- even though they were fearful about their parents' fate" ("Bohny FAMILY - Auguste Bohny"). To deal with this, Auguste and Friedel Bohny-Reiter brought the children together as a unit by singing frequently and attempting to relieve the worry on their shoulders. The two hoped that they could create at least a semi-normal and safe childhood for them.

In Auguste Bohny's own opinion, his actions were not heroic. On the subject of rescuing the children, Bohny declared that "We were not heroes. We lived, that's all" (Soirée CICAD). In his interview with Raye Farr, he said many times how special the community of Le Chambon was and ascribed much of his success in aiding the refugees to them. Pastor Trocmé, in particular, aroused the passion and support of the area through his sermons, which called upon people to have faith in what they believe to be right. According to Bohny, the people in Le Chambon believed that "We belong together and we will fight together" (Oral History Interview with Auguste Bohny-Reiter) and that in this "very special atmosphere ... the entire population was very connected with the refugee children and the organizations". Even a gendarme once told a Swiss student of the institution watching over the children playing ball that one of the children didn't look native to the Chambon region and that he wished to give the child an opportunity to avoid deportation should he be Jewish, as he suspected. Every holiday drew the community even closer together through meals and song and gave them new encouragement to do what was right and humane for those who had been treated poorly and suffered because of circumstance, race, or religion.

Auguste Bohny was honored by Yad Vashem on July 16, 1990. Although he was very flattered, he was even more pleased that the entire community, Le Plateau, had also been honored. His experiences in the Holocaust serve to teach a very valuable lesson, both about how one can truly make a difference in the lives of others and also about the power of a community united for a common purpose. In times of war, a hero is not necessarily a soldier fighting for honor with a gun, but simply an individual doing the best that he or she can to bring happiness into someone's life during an absence thereof. Sometimes the best cure for sorrow may be a song, and a place to feel welcome.

Works Cited

"Bohny FAMILY - Bohny Auguste." *Yad Vashem*. Yad Vashem The Holocaust Matyrs' and Heroes' Remembrance Authority. Web. 8 Feb. 2015. <http://db.yadvashem.org/righteous/family.html?language=en&itemId=4014013>.

"Soirée CICAD: August Bohny, Un «Juste» Que La Suisse Va Honorer." *CICAD*. CICAD, 27 Jan. 2008. Web. 8 Feb. 2015. <http://www.cicad.ch/fr/press-releases-and-feedback-hommage-aux-justes-suisse-press-releases-and-feedback/soirée-cicad>.

"Oral History Interview with Auguste Bohny-Reiter." Interview.

RIGHTEOUS AMONG THE NATIONS: PAUL GRUENINGER

Jack Stassi

During World War II, Germany began to look for allies. They eventually turned to Switzerland and gave them a choice, they could either side with Germany and the Nazi party or they could deny Germany's offer and be considered an enemy in the war. Switzerland had no choice; they could not risk a war with a country as powerful as Germany, so they ultimately sided with the Germans. As a result, Switzerland ended up closing off their borders to those arriving without proper entry permits, specifically illegal Jewish immigrants. In order to identify the illegal Jews trying to escape from Germany, Germany began to stamp the letter "J" on all passports issued to Jews. As conditions worsened for the Jews being prosecuted in Germany, more and more of them tried to illegally cross the Switzerland border, but every single time, they were caught and turned back to the horror that was also known as the Nazi party. This caused a man by the name of Paul Grueninger to take a stand against the atrocities being committed by the Nazis, and he knew that it was within his power to do so. In order to save the lives of so many Jews, Paul began scheming a plan, however it wasn't entirely legal at the time, and it could get him killed.

Paul Grueninger was a Switzerland police commander of the St. Gallen region that borders with Austria. Paul was forced to watch as thousands of innocent Jews were caught and sent back to the anti-Semitism that had festered in Germany's heart. Finally, Paul decided that siding with Germany had been a terrible mistake, and that what the Switzerland government was doing was wrong. Paul began to disobey the orders issued to him and started allowing illegal refugees into Switzerland by falsifying their registration documents. He made it appear that all the refugees had entered before March 1938, before the deal with Germany and the closing of the Switzerland borders. Also, in order to make the lives of the suffering refugees a little more bearable, Paul payed for new clothing for them out of his own pocket, as many had left all that they owned behind in Germany. Paul's schemes continued on and were going just as planned. Neither Germany nor Switzerland discovered him or the illegal Jews, and even better, more and more refugees were finding a haven from the encroaching grasp of Germany.

However, the crossing of illegal Jews from Germany into Switzerland did not last forever. Germany eventually did find out that Paul had been secretly allowing illegal immigrants into Switzerland by falsifying their registration documents. The Germans quickly alerted the Switzerland government, telling them that Paul had been disobeying their orders from right under their noses. After hearing this, the Switzerland government took immediate action. One day, when Paul was arriving at the office where he worked, he found his way blocked by a police officer. Paul knew right away that he had been discovered, and that both he and the Jews he saved would likely be severely punished.

Paul was brought before a court where the jury heard of the incident. Paul's case was dragged out for two long years, until he was eventually found guilty of allowing 3,600 illegal Jewish immigrants across the Switzerland border. In many ways, the punishment Paul received was far worse than death. He was discharged from the Switzerland police force, and the benefits that came from working for the police force when you retired were promptly taken away from Paul.

From that point on, Paul Grueninger's life got extremely difficult. He was ostracized from his community, as he had done something that was frowned upon back then. One of the most tragic things about the story of Paul Gruenginger is that he was never given the proper recognition and admiration for committing such a heroic act of kindness.

The war continued on for many more years, until eventually, Germany and the Nazi party was defeated by the Americans and their allies. Thousands of Jews everywhere were freed from concentration camps and Germany was plunged into an economic crisis after spending almost all their money on a war, and then losing. Paul Grueninger had lain low for many years, until protest from the media demanded that Paul be given the justice he so rightly deserved. Protest continued until the Switzerland government finally realized the error of their ways. They issued a formal apology to Paul Grueninger, but sadly, Paul's case was never given a second chance, and soon afterwards, he died.

One year before his death, Paul was recognized by Yad Vashem for what he did. Yad Vashem bestowed the title Righteous Among the Nations upon Paul. So at the end of his life, having been given full recognition for his actions, the man known as Paul Grueninger died the hero that he had been all along.

The people of today can learn a lot from the action of Paul Grueninger. Paul was faced with a difficult decision: he could either prevent the illegal Jews from crossing the Switzerland border, or he could protect them from both the Nazis and the Switzerland. In the end, Paul made the decision to allow the Jews to cross the border and escape from Germany. Paul didn't make his choice without knowing the consequences, and eventually he chose the option that would affect his life in an extremely bad way, but it also was the right thing to do.

PAUL GRUNINGER: A REAL HERO

Jared Laygui

What is a real hero? Do you think that a man who was fired from his job is a hero, or a soldier? Would your view change if you find out that the man that was fired was saving people by helping them, and the soldier was the one who was killing them? Many people today think that everybody who breaks the law does it for bad purposes or do not do it purposely, but that was not the case for Paul Gruninger. This could be seen with Paul's early life, his actions, and his legacy

Paul Gruninger was born 1881 in Saint Gallen, Switzerland. Paul Gruninger had a great life ahead of him. He was born in a wealthy city that had one of the best Universities in the country. During his early 20s he joined the local football (soccer) team, SC Brühl. He was an avid footballer and even won the team their first and only Swiss Championship. This could be stated at the least a very well self-made man. He had money, fame, and a moderate amount of power. He could have done anything, but then World War I broke out. Like many others his age, he joined the army as a lieutenant. After the war he joined the police and rose the ranks. This again shows the potential of this man and how much talent he really had. Not only was he able to attain the rank of lieutenant, a step down from captain, but he was able to change his jobs drastically and excel in it. I personally think this is a precursor for a man who can become successful and comfortable in life. Above all though he was a good man and had a very high moral standard, but that was what soon got him in trouble in the next World War.

When Germany first annexed Austria, Switzerland closed its borders calling itself as a neutral zone. Hundreds of Jews tried to escape to Switzerland, but all who tried were turned back. Paul Gruninger's action again showed how great of a person he was. Paul, who was under orders to turn back all Jews, decided to take a huge risk and instead forged their visas to permit them access to Switzerland. This was illegal, but Gruninger knew the risks. Like I said before, Paul Gruninger was a good man and he upheld his morals, and this could be said to be almost unbelievable. This never helped him in any way and in fact worked to disadvantage, due to the fact that he would have the chance of being caught by the authorities, and also how he had to spend more time to help them. Many of us today say that if we ever saw things like theHolocaust ever happen, we would do our utmost to help them, but would we really? If you think about it, most people have a tendency to be selfish and only care about themselves. We can see throughout history, especially with people's dealing with others. Sadly, this did not go unnoticed by the authorities. In 1939, he was put under investigation under the Gestapo, the German secret police. He was warned by some friends to stop, but he decided to keep on letting Jews through the border. On April 3rd, 1939 Gruninger arrived to work where he was then blocked by fellow police officers. It was then, "Grüninger recognized that his actions had been discovered." It was that day that marked the end. He was promptly dismissed from the police force and then put on trial that same year. His case dragged out for two years, but was then found guilty of fraud. He was then fined by the court and was then found jobless and without a pension from his job in the police. Even though he was found in a hard situation he never regretted his decision. In 1954, he said, "It was basically a question of saving human lives threatened with death. How could I then seriously consider bureaucratic schemes and calculations?" How heart touching this statement could be, he has literally fallen into a hard and grueling life, but he has no regrets. This personally makes me shed tears because of the injustice of the court, and how they didn't even allow him to have at least a pension for his services. This did though later change, leaving behind a remarkable legacy.

After the war had ended, Gruninger remained still in a tough situation until the media caught on to his story. In 1971, due to the pressure brought on by the media, the Switzerland government sent quote, "a somewhat reserved letter of apology, but refrained from reopening his case and reinstating his pension." I felt very happy for this man, actually having a government say sorry to him, but that did not end there. On that same year, the Yad Vashem institution gave Gruninger a medal for being

Righteous Among The Nations. Furthermore the Swiss television broadcast a show called "Captain Gruninger" as documentary commemorating his actions. His name even appeared on "the plaque of the monument in the memory of the Jews in Washington D.C [he was] the first Swiss citizen to be honored by the government of the United States of America." Is this not heartwarming to hear? Once again though, tragedy struck his life though for the last time. On February 22nd 1972, Paul Gruninger died, having no regrets whatsoever. Twenty-three years later (and 50 years after the war had ended) in the same courthouse that condemned him, he was absolved from all charges and was completely rehabilitated in the Swiss government. When you think about, it is kind of laughable that the Swiss government absolved his charges AFTER his death and he never got to see his name being cleared. In 1997, Richard Dindo released the film "The Affair of Grüninger." This film showed the Jews who were saved by Gruninger give homage to him, but what was most tear jerking thing about this film was that they showed the Jews, their faces and their expressions it could make you break way to tears.

Paul Gruninger's story was a sad and touching story of man who risked it all to protect what he believed what he deemed as morally right. You saw his successful younger years hinted at him becoming comfortable in life, his years as an officer protecting the Jews, and his life after the war. Now to answer the question I first brought out, "What is a real Hero?" A real hero isn't a person who does heroic deeds, courageous things expecting some reward, no, a real hero is someone who does the right thing, someone who would rather follow his morals than orders.

Bibliography

Bellettieri, Nora. "The Example of Grüninger." *Funkascript ATOM*. N.P., n.d. Web. 05 Feb. 2015.

Harrison, George. "Holocaust Memorial Day Trust." *Paul Grüninger*. Department for Communities and Local Government, n.d. Web. 09 Feb. 2015.

Schaeffur, Rebecca. "Gruninger, Paul - The Jewish Foundation for the Righteous." *The Jewish Foundation for the Righteous*. Claims Conference, n.d. Web. 09 Feb. 2015.

Vashem, Yad. "Paul Grueninger - The Righteous Among the Nations - Yad Vashem." *Paul Grueninger - The Righteous Among the Nations - Yad Vashem*. N.P., n.d. Web. 09 Feb. 2015.

ELISABETH EIDENBENZ: THE NURSE, VOLUNTEER, AND TEACHER

Jennifer Wu

Kids and women screaming in an abandoned building with no shoes, clothes, and food to eat are all that Elisabeth Eidenbenz saw when she went to the bombed Madrid. Mothers with their children trying to escape from the death traps that were set out for them were what she saw a few years later when the horrors of war came again. Instead of turning a blind eye to these people who were fleeing from the cruelty of the Nazis and the Nationalists, Elisabeth donated her time to join the Association to Help Children in War and convert an abandoned mansion into a maternity home for the women and kids. Elisabeth greatly increased the surviving chance of the babies born and the women who were giving birth. She gave them a fighting chance to survive in the harsh world of the war.

Elisabeth influences me from the fact that she helped people even before the Holocaust even began. Elisabeth Eidenbenz was born on June 12 of 1913 and was the daughter of a Protestant pastor. Before she joined the Association to Help Children in War, Elisabeth taught to adults in Switzerland and Denmark. Her career as a hero began when she started helping and taking care of the children and women who were trying to escape from the Spanish Civil War. She arrived in Madrid as a volunteer in an aid team, but she was relocated to the south part of France. There she discovered the Republicans who were trying to take refuge from the Nationalists, who were funded and supported by Hitler and the Germans. Appalled from the amount of women and children and the horrible condition that they were in, Elisabeth started the idea of changing the abandoned mansion she found into a maternity home for the refugees. After receiving about 30,000 francs from the Swiss Red Cross, she began her project of repairing and altering the mansion with a group of volunteers. She also managed to convince others to support her enough to where she got four trucks of food, soap, books, and volunteers to help her with her job of rescuing others. This is when the Mothers of Elne was founded. Elisabeth was soon the light and angel for the people who were trying to escape from the war.

Even though it was not required for her to help these refugees, she committed herself to helping these children and mothers. After the house was finished in November of 1939, it was officially turned into a hospital. There were delivery rooms for the mothers, a nursery room, and a room for the sick children. However, this hospital was not a drab one. Elisabeth used the money to good use and the finished building was one that amazed. The lower bottom story had the laundry room, kitchen and the storage room. At the ground level was an octagonal room where the women could sit during the day and communicate and talk and the dining room. On the next floor there was the octagonal nursery, the delivery and another room for the women who just gave birth. The second floor held the bedrooms and Elisabeth's office. There was then a stairway that led to top of the building where you could look down at the plains around you. By the time that the hospital was built, World War II had already begun and the Jewish mothers and children were flocking to Elisabeth's refuge. They were all trying to escape from the horror of the concentration camps and the other death traps that were waiting for them if they were caught by the Germans. She was devoted to the fact of only saving others and was extremely focused on that fact. However, the collection of Jews soon began. Germans began to search the house and Elisabeth had to send the mothers and children packing before they were found by the soldiers. However, sometimes, they weren't too lucky. Lucie, a Jewish mother was found in the hospital and the Germans demanded that she needed to be taken away. If she wasn't taken they said that they would take Elisabeth instead. However, Elisabeth was devoted enough to offer her life and try to fight for Lucie's life. Lucie instead, refused to let her be taken and denied the sacrifice and allowed herself to be taken. Lucie was then taken to a gas chamber with the many others to where she ultimately died.

Elisabeth Eidenbenz was still devoted to her hospital even when she was under the pressure of not receiving any more funds. The hospital used to receive funds from Europe, but when the Holocaust began the funds slowly started to end when the refugees started to pile in from the France and the rest of Europe. Because of the loss in funds, Elisabeth was forced to associate with the Red Cross, who followed the rule of "strict neutrality." She would be forced to give up on the people who she was protecting and give them up it they were called too.

Elisabeth Eidenbenz devoted her whole life to rescuing people, not only the Holocaust victims, but also the victims of other wars. For this she received many awards from different countries and organizations like the Yad Vashem Institution's recognition as Righteous Among the Nations and an award from the French government. In all, she saved about 600 people and many lived to grow into adults. She was willing to donate her entire life from the age of 20 to the age of 97 to save others. She gave hope to the many mothers that were out there running for their life. She gave life to others and sacrificed herself for other women who were in danger. She sought out to do something to change these people's lives and instead of just thinking about her idea, she actually got it done. Elisabeth Eidenbenz proved that heroes can come from anywhere and that all you need an idea of your goal, the heart to help others, and the bravery to get your idea done.

ELISABETH EIDENBENZ AND HARALD FELLER

Jessica Andryushchenko

The Holocaust was a hostile time. Many lives were in danger, were tortured, were killed, or everything all together. There were some small heroes in the Holocaust. Some people tried to help others escape from ghettos or concentration camps but failed. Escaping was one of the most difficult solutions during theHolocaust but it also was not the only one. There were people who help the Jews through this time with as much aid as possible. These people were doctors and nurses. Elisabeth Eidenbenz and Harald Feller helped Holocaust victims and survivors with the aid of medicine and special care.

One of the people who helped Jews and other groups was a woman named Elisabeth Eidenbenz. In April, the year of 1937, she came to Madrid, Spain, where she saw terrible destruction from the Holocaust and was taken aback with disgust and horror. She was disgusted from the awful situation children and women were in among the Spanish refugees. Elisabeth then came up with the idea of turning the old château abandoned on the side of the road near Montescot into a maternity home. The château, or better known as castle in English, was still in good shape. It stood up right and had most of its parts. Elisabeth recieved 30,000 francs from the Swiss Red Cross to renovate the castle as well as repair all damages the war might have caused. The building was complete in Novembeof the year 1939 and the special touch Elisabeth added was that she named each room after a city in Spain. She said that this would help young mothers-to-be remember their roots. The nursery was named Madrid, the room for sick children was named Seville, the room for expectant mothers was Corboda, and there were many more rooms like Barcelona, Bilbao, and on the list goes. This small addition was Elisabeth's unique idea to help make all the women and children feel at home and comfortable with their surroundings.The Gestapo became a problem around 1941. The German Gestapo started to brutally collect all Jews they could find after they neglected and ignored the "Free Zone." There was a notorious and completely inhumane concentration camp in Riversaltes and it soon became, with the help of Germans, an "accommodation centre" for Tziganes, Spanish refugees, and Jews. The Gestapo started to show up at Elisabeth's castle, La Maternité, and were searching for Jews. Elisabeth bravely got them to leave. The Gestapo soon enough returned, this time demanding to take away a Jewish mother named Lucie. After this event, Lucie survived but her baby did not and the baby was getting milk from her mother while it was killed. They continued to demand for Lucie and said if they didn't get Lucie they will take Elisabeth instead. Elisabeth courageously went to her room and packed up her essentials. Alongside with her was Lucie who refused to let Elisabeth sacrifice herself. She knew Elisabeth had a position here and needed to aid all these people so she went along with the Gestapo. Elisabeth Eidenbenz had so much care in her heart for the people she worked with. She helped heal people from the Holocaust and tried to protect those people from the Gestapo.

Another hero who cared and aided Jews and other groups during the Holocaust was a doctor named Harald Feller. Even though he was a doctor, he helped saved people's lives more by rescuing and not medicine. In the year 1944, Dr. Feller replaced Maximilian Jaeger and became head of the Swiss legation in Budapest, Hungary. From the very start of his position, he worked enthusiastically in his efforts to support Consul Charles Lutz, who helped saved 62,000 Jews. Dr. Feller also worked hard to rescue Jews under Swiss protection. Since he was a legation, he closely worked neutrally with other legations and their puppet governments. His main goal was to stop them from deporting and prosecuting Jews. The Arrow Cross was trying to gather their target, which were Swiss legations, by baiting false Swiss passports and shelter. Harald Feller protected them also. Near the end of the war, Feller hid dozens of Jews in a basement of a residence with the assistance of agents who lived in the house. Soviets arrested Harald Feller in 1945 along with other Swiss nationals and were sent to Moscow. Feller cared for other Jews and wanted to aid them through and out the war. He even risked a chance of being arrested because he cared.

Elisabeth Eidenbenz only cared about other people in her lifetime. Especially in the time of the Holocaust, she would take in the survivors to her maternity home and help them back to health. She would save women and children from horrible broken places and restart their lives into a better one. Dr. Feller worked as a Swiss legation with was a diplomat minister. He worked with the Swiss protection to help save Jews from the German or any other group looking for trouble. He saved them by taking them away from governments by tricking their legations or by storing them in the basement of houses. Constantly he risked his life trying to save theirs. Both of these people are true heroes for putting the Jews before themselves.

Works Cited

"Dr. Harald Feller, Swiss Minister in Budapest." *The International Raoul Wallenburg Foundation.* n.p. n.d. Web. 9 Feb. 2015.

"Elisabeth and her Maternite." *P-O Life.* Analophone Direct. n.d. Web. 9 Feb. 2015.

CARL LUTZ HOLOCAUST ESSAY

Kat Angell

Its was the year 1942 when Swiss Vice-Counsul Carl Lutz traveled to Budapest, Hungary as a man with power and a mission, who would end up doing more good than he could have ever foreseen. Carl Lutz was chief of Foreign Interests in Budapest, Hungary, and was also in charge of fourteen war-stricken, hostile nations such as the United States and Great Britain. Carl Lutz decided that on his work trip he would temporarily reside in the British Legation at Szabadság tér in Pest, Hungary. And it was here that he was put to be responsible for the protection and safety of over 300 Americans, 300 English nationals, about 2,000 Romanians, and some 3,000 Yugoslavs who were also in Hungary— only all the people whom Carl Lutz was told to look after were stranded in Hungary against their will. They had no choice like Carl Lutz did. Carl Lutz was in Hungary for only one reason: because he wanted to help the 5,600 people stranded have deserved legal protection from any unjust or unlawful dangers, such as the Germans.

It was on March 19, 1994 when the German threat became more of a concern to these people that Lutz was offering help and protection to, thousands nearly attacked Carl Lutz's office in Szabadság tér, Hungary in seek of his protection. The mass numbers of people who besieged his office every day stayed at a constant if not growing as the need for protection ensued on, more and more. Carl Lutz was a loyal and active Christian, and he believed that it was only right to provide whatever he could for these people in need of protection and saftey, even though he had already helped over 10,000 Jewish children and young escape to Palestine by this time of his being in Hungary, working to save lives. It was Carl Lutz's mission to help and care for anyone within British and Palestine interests who needed whereas he could provide protection for the Jews from the German threats.

Then, on May 15th, German deportations to Auschhwitz, a German Nazi concentration and extermination camp from 1940-1945, began deporting Jews from Hungary. This was the beginning of a very stressful and busy time for Carl Lutz and his staff, and this time was also a very dangerous time for Jews. This was when Carl Lutz decided to take action, and put all the staff of his organization, The Jewish Council for Palestine, under diplomatic protection, and rename it to "Department of Emigration of the Swiss Legation." This shifted the purpose of his organization from protecting these people on generally legal affairs to protection of hundreds and thousands of lives of helpless Jews in Hungary who had no one else to turn to. Carl Lutz turned "The Jewish Council for Palestine" into "Department of Emigration of the Swiss Legation," which was a special relief organization that became responsible

146

for the tens of thousands of endangered Jews in Hungary. By doing this, Carl Lutz increased awareness of the seriousness of the German threat enough to go from 15 staff members to 150 staff members ready to aid in the fight, all from volunteers. But along with this change came yet one more. Since the German deportations were not very legally organized on the German behalf, Lutz was able to negotiate with German and Hungarian authorities to benefit to his organization. The change being that Carl Lutz's new goal was to save as many Jewish lives as possible with his newly founded organization, "Department of Emigration of the Swiss Legation." a name to be remembered my many thousands of Jews forever, and credited with saving lives— their lives.

Right away Carl Lutz and his staff begin to issue tens of thousands of "protective letters" ensuring the protection of an individual. There was one problem present, his organization--due to a recent change--was no longer supported by any of the original Palestine certificates. But Carl Lutz could not simply give up, he had already invested way too much into this organization, so he came up with a solution. As long as they grouped these protective letters together in one Swiss collective passport, they were still legal, functioning protective letters. The only price they had to pay for their newly found loophole was that a Swiss collective passport had a maximum of 1,000 reports each. Lutz overlooked and was sure that all of the protective letters were numbered one through 8,000, so that they could be easily organized into their Swiss collective passports. All the tens of thousands of people who got a protective letter filed were under legal Swiss protection.

Lutz then worked on placing all 30,000 of the Swiss protected Jews into 76 protected houses. In these houses, they were fed and cared for on a budget, but still humanely. Lutz also insured that his company would be provided with communications from the entire underground Jewish community by young Jewish Chalutzium (pioneers). This set the organization in a steady place on a straight track to save even more lives.

Sadly, Carl Lutz died in 1975 at an astonishing age of 80 years old. Lutz hoped to see forth as his organization continued to do good while saving as many Jewish lives as possible. In 1941, of the original 742,800 Jews who lived in Hungary, about 124,000 survived the war. Carl Lutz and the organization that he founded saved about 62,000 Jews out of the surviving 124,000. "Department of Emigration of the Swiss Legation" is a named to be remembered by over 124,000 people as the organization that saved lives— their lives.

MARTHA SCHMIDT AND BILL BARAZETTI

Kianna Thornton

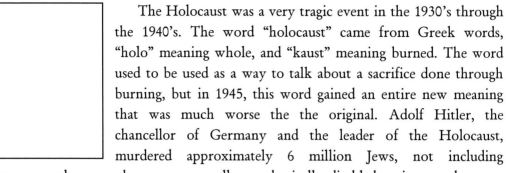

The Holocaust was a very tragic event in the 1930's through the 1940's. The word "holocaust" came from Greek words, "holo" meaning whole, and "kaust" meaning burned. The word used to be used as a way to talk about a sacrifice done through burning, but in 1945, this word gained an entire new meaning that was much worse the the original. Adolf Hitler, the chancellor of Germany and the leader of the Holocaust, murdered approximately 6 million Jews, not including homosexual men and women, mentally or physically disabled patients and groups such as Gypsies. Of these 6 million people who were murdered, about 1.5 million of them were children. Including all parties of the murderous act, the estimated amount of people who died during the Holocaust was about 11 million people.

During these times, many Jewish families had to live in concentration camps and work as well, if they survived. Some people during the Holocaust wanted to save the Jews and anyone in the concentration camps. Two of these caring people consisted of Martha Schmidt and Bill Barazetti. I believe that these two people are heroes for risking their own lives to help save and protect others and showing a kind heart in a time of cold.

Martha Schmidt was a Swiss woman, born July 24th of 1900 and survived the Holocaust. Martha had been hired to babysit the third daughter of the Cohen family named Josiane, and became bound to the Cohen family. The other two daughters, Rachel and Liliane, formed a bond between them and Martha, and started calling her "Sister Martha." Then, in 1933 M. Cohen told Schmidt that since she was Swiss, she didn't have to return to France when she was going to visit her parents in Zurich. Instead, Martha didn't want to abandon the children she was caring for, so after her vacation she traveled back to France anyway despite what the Cohen family said.

The Germans had resided in southern France in November 1942, so the Cohens and Martha had to flee because the Cohens' efforts to help Jewish children in camps, and because of this the family was at risk. The Cohen family found shelter in Italian-ruled Monaco for a year, and gave birth to their fourth daughter, Danièle. Again, Schmidt and the Cohens had to flee because the Germans had invaded Italy. The mother and father of the Cohen family decided that they wanted to separate themselves from their daughters, and put them in the hands of Martha. Schmidt and the four girls then went to live in Ste. Anthène. While in in Ste. Anthène, the Jewish girls could never leave the house they were residing in to keep their true identity unknown. In the village they lived in, the girls were known as "the Chauvins' daughters" but the residents suspected the girls to be Jewish. Schmidt took care of the

148

household chores and he education of the young girls as well as many other things to protect these children. Even after the Holocaust ended, Martha remained in the Cohen family for twenty years and became the grandmother figure to the young girls she had raised. Martha had put her life on the line to raise the Cohen children and make sure they were safe from the Germans, and showed her love to the young girls by protecting them and making sure that they were always okay.

Bill Barazetti was a young Swiss male, born in 1914 and survived the Holocaust. Barazetti had helped thousands of victims of the Holocaust. Bill helped organize the escape of children from "German-occupied Prague" before the war had broke out, and between May and July many Jewish children left the city because of Barazetti making a system of false identity papers to which the plan succeeded. Barazetti was a son of a Swiss Professor at Heidelberg University, and at 19, he studied at Hamburg University. During the time that he was in university, Barazetti saw Nazi thugs beating up Jewish students, and when he tried to protest to the Dean, nothing was solved. Barazetti worked with church-based charities that helped to flood refugees into Czechoslovakia, towards Britain and Scandinavia. A large amount of people, between 50,000 and 70,000, escaped thanks to these organizations.

In 1934, Barazetti moved to Czechoslovakia and was recruited to work in the Czech Secret Service as an intelligence officer. Because of this, Barazetti returned to Hamburg as a spy, but every year, the Germans would discover his true identity and tried to arrest him. Then he was caught by the Gestapo and was almost beaten to death, but was found by a young Czech girl named Anna. Later they married and they moved to Switzerland and had a young boy named Nicholas. Barazetti then became involved in Nicholas Winton's rescue operation to help the young Jewish children escape. Barazetti and Winton raised funds, arranged documents and recruited foster families for the children once they escape. Bill Barazetti risked his life to save many children from camps and from the Germans, and helped them to live a better life instead of what they were living at before they escaped.

In the end, both Martha Schmidt and Bill Barazetti were heroes. They risked their own lives to protect the young generation Jews and saved them from camps, or as Martha did, by protecting them from being taken away by the Germans. They showed their kindness by doing great deeds to help save the lives of young children by putting their own lives at risk in the process.

Bibliography

History.com Staff. "The Holocaust." History.com. A&E Television Networks, 2009. Web11 Feb 2015.

"The Holocaust: An Introductory History." An Introductory History of the Holocaust. N.p.,n.d. Web. 11 Feb. 2015.

"Introduction to the Holocaust." United States Holocaust Memorial Museum. United States Holocaust Memorial Council, 20 June 2014. Web. 11 Feb. 2015.

"Philosemitism." : Werner Theodore Barazetti. N.p., n.d. Web. 10 Feb. 2015.

"The Righteous Among The Nations: Barazetti Bill." The Righteous Among The Nations.N.p., n.d. Web. 11 Feb. 2015.

"The Righteous Among The Nations: Barazetti Bill Rescue Story." The Righteous Among The Nations. N.p., n.d. Web. 10 Feb. 2015.

"The Righteous Among The Nations: Schmidt Martha." The Righteous Among The Nations. N.p., n.d. Web. 10 Feb. 2015.

"The Righteous Among The Nations: Schmidt Martha Rescue Story." The Righteous Among The Nations. N.p., n.d. Web. 10 Feb. 2015.

Rosenberg, Jennifer. "Holocaust Facts - 33 Things You Should Know." About.com. N.p.,n.d. Web. 11 Feb. 2015.

"Timeline of Events." United States Holocaust Memorial Museum. United States Holocaust Memorial Council, n.d. Web. 11 Feb. 2015.

SWISS HOLOCAUST HERO'S ESSAY

Laurel Hubbell

"Compassion is the wish to see others free from suffering," as Dalai Lama once said. Every human is capable of compassion but only few reach its full extent. Sebastian Steiger and Dr. Harald Feller are two of those people and that is why I chose these Swiss heroes for this essay. Filled with compassion they helped save the lives of many children and families during the Holocaust. If they were not as compassionate, many lives would have been lost and many families scarred by their loved ones who would have perished.

Sebastian Steiger was a son of a Swiss protestant priest with five siblings. He grew up in Switzerland. First in Oltingen, then later in Binningen. He became a teacher in 1940 shortly after World War II started. During this time he was seeing many suffering Jewish refugees seeking help from his father and usually receiving the help they requested. He disliked the Swiss policy on refugees saying "I had the feeling that I was living on an enormous safe ship and had the impression of being surrounded by numerous small vessels in trouble, calling in vain for help. I could not live with the message that the boat is full." So when he heard of homes in France housing children suffering from the war he knew he too could help. He then joined the Swiss Red Cross in 1943. That job took him to Chateau La Hille in the Pyrenees, where some 100 orphan Jewish children were being secretly cared for. Little did he know that helping these children would affect his life forever. Working, with others, for two years he stayed there caring for these children, constantly dodging the daily threat from the Nazis. The children were always at risk for being taken away to concentration camps or killed. Fear and hunger was always creeping into their minds haunting them, it defiantly was not an easy life. But all he cared about was "bringing some joy back into their lives," as he once said.

Once the war ended all their lives got better, he returned to being a teacher. While about 90 of the children survived the war and settled all over the world. In 1985 there was a reunion in Israel where the children, now adults, reunited with their saviors from the war including Sebastian. Then in 2000 a commemoration ceremony, for a memorial opening in 2007 in memory of these children commenced, and Sebastian was present. Shortly after he received "The Righteous Among the Nations" medal. Dying at the age of 93 we will never lose memory of the hero who saved so many lives.

Dr. Harald Feller was also a vital part of the Jews safety during the war and the protection of many lives. Not much is known about his past but that does not affect his contributions. He replaced Maximilian Jaeger as head of the Swiss legation in Budapest, Hungary, in 1944. He was tireless in his efforts to rescue Jews under Swiss protection. Feller protected members of the Swedish legation targeted by Arrow Cross. He made them false Swiss passports and provided shelter. He found it unfair that these Jews and others were being treated so awfully. They had lost their freedom and could do nothing to regain it. Holocaust survivor Leon Schgrin once said "What I want you to take away from my life story is just how important it is to defend your freedom, at all costs. Experience has shown me that if you lose your freedom, you are condemned to fail." Not concerned by their inevitable failure Feller persevered, still helping Jews and trying to make a difference. Toward the end of the war he even housed dozens of Jews in this basement. Feeding them and essentially protecting them. But then in February 1945 the Soviets arrested Feller and sent him to Moscow along with other Swiss nationals because they aided the Jewish.

After the war he returned to his beloved Switzerland. He returned knowing he had done all that he could to help the Jews now that the war was over. In 1999 he was recognized as a hero and received his "Righteous Among the Nations" medal. No one knows when he died. But we shall never forget the contributions of Dr. Harald Feller, the lives he saved and the impact he made.

Now as I stated before everyone is capable of compassion. I should know since I went to India. There are children barefoot, freezing, begging on the streets and hungry stray dogs; I felt immense amounts of compassion for them. And everyone feels compassion when you hear a sad story or see a somber picture. Like right now just thinking of those people who suffered, were scarred, or died during theHolocaust you must be feeling some compassion. But their compassion is different from everyday compassion, they acted upon it. Instead of just thinking or talking about it, they got up and said "I am going to help these poor people." Sebastian Steiger saved the lives of about 100 Jewish children in France. And Dr.Harald Feller helped dozens of Jews, even making them fake passports. That is what really makes them heroes of the Holocaust.

I started this essay not knowing who either of these people were but now I know of their contributions to the safety of many Jewish people. I feel that without them many, many people would have been affected in a very negative way. Lives and hope would have been lost. The effect of just these two men's actions are immense. The world would not be the same without their compassionate hearts set out to help people in need.

Works Cited

Bernstein, Walter. "The Children of the Château De La Hille." *The Jewish Children of the Chateau De La Hille in Ariège- Pyrenees*. Web. 9 Feb. 2015. <http://www.ariege.com/histoire/lahille.html>.

"Dr. Harald Feller." *Funkascript ATOM*. Web. 8 Feb. 2015. <http://www.raoulwallenberg.net/saviors/diplomats/list/dr-harald-feller-362/>.

"Harald Feller." *Wikipedia*. Wikimedia Foundation. Web. 9 Feb. 2015. <http://en.wikipedia.org/wiki/Harald_Feller>.

Simon, Ernest. "NEWS - News of the Lodges." *Sebastian Steiger Dies*. Web. 9 Feb. 2015. <http://www.bnaibritheurope.org/bbeurope/en/news/news-of-the-lodges/259-sebastian-steiger-dies-a-righteous-among-the-nations>.

"The Righteous among the Nations." *Yadvashem*. Web. 10 Feb. 2015. <http://www.yadvashem.org/yv/en/righteous/statistics/switzerland.pdf>.

"This Is Me." *: NO SUCH THING AS BAD WEATHER*. Web. 10 Feb. 2015. <http://uniqueandamazing.blogspot.com/2012/10/no-such-thing-as-bad-weather.html>.

FRIEDRICH BORN: HOLOCAUST HERO

Lukas Koller

TheHolocaust was a horrible government-sponsored persecution of Jews which took place during World War II (Introduction to the Holocaust). During the Holocaust, the Germans, who deemed themselves as superior, murdered over 6 million Jews because they believed that they were inferior to them and that the Jews were a threat to them. Over the course of a few years, the Germans killed two out of every three Jews. Besides Jews, Germans also targeted Gypsies and mentally ill people. During this Holocaust, approximately 11 million people were killed at the hands of the Nazis. Although this is a huge number of dead people, many heroic individuals did their best to bring the total down. Among them was Friedrich Born of Swiss origin.

Friedrich Born was a Swiss delegate of the International Committee of the Red Cross (Friedrich Born). He came to Budapest as a delegate in the midst of World War II. At that time Hungary was under German rule, theHolocaust was enforced and

152

Jews were harassed and persecuted. Born became aware of the discrimination on Jews and soon noticed the desperations of Hungarian Jews. He was shocked. He was shocked by the inhumanity, by its breadth and extent. He was also inspired by another brilliant man, Carl Lutz, who was also saving Jews and other minorities at this time, and who was having a lot of success with this. Born was also really against segregating and discriminating minorities, and so he made it his life goal to save Jews. Born decided to use the company he worked for, the Red Cross International Committee as a mean to start helping the Jews and as a way to get the people away. By working for the Red Cross International Committee, Jewish man and woman would be able to get a protection and eventually even leave the country and escape the system. He recruited about 3,000 Jews to work for him. When they were working for him, Born provided protection and food to them and kept them away from the Nazis. Thanks to this deed, many Jews were saved from working for the Nazis and instead worked for him, a much better alternative.

Friedrich Born took advantage of his job at the International Committee of the Red Cross a second time and set up lots of safe houses of the Red Cross all across Hungary where Jews and other victims of theHolocaust could receive shelter, food, and proper care. Thanks to his job at the Red Cross he set up these houses at strategic locations across Hungary so that the victims of theHolocaust would be able to hide somewhere.

Lastly, Friedrich Born helped the Jews by issuing protection documents. Called *Schutzbriefe*, these documents made the person protected from being captured, tortured, or killed by the Nazis. Under the Red Cross, Born was able to distribute thousands of these documents to help the Jews. I truly believe Born was a man who deserves to be remembered for eons to come for his help to other Jews. This quote by Elie Wiesel describes precisely what Friedrich Born believed about the Jews he was saving.

"There is long road of suffering ahead of you. But don't lose courage. You already escaped the gravest danger: selection. So now, muster your strength, and don't lose heart. We shall all see the day of liberation. Have faith in life. Above all else, have faith. Drive out despair, and you will keep death away from yourselves. Hell is not for eternity. And now, a prayer- or rather, a piece of advice: let there be comradeship among you. We are all brothers, and we are all suffering the same fate. The same smoke floats over all our heads. Help one another. It is the only way to survive. –Elie Wiesel, Night (The Night Trilogy, #1)

This quote, I believe, writes out almost exactly Friedrich Born's thinking while saving the Jews. Born didn't care about becoming famous. He didn't care about making a lot of money off of this. All Born wanted to do was protect the victims of the Nazis' harsh and torturous treatment. Born is a man to be admired for this. I have to say that I have never studied anyone as committed to their goal as Born, especially when the goal involved putting others in front of himself. He took advantage of his job at the International committee of the Red Cross to the fullest, saving Jews and innocent victims left and right. By recruiting employees, building safe houses, and giving out protection documents, Friedrich Born was able to save about 13,000 people during the Holocaust. Born is a man who saved people from his own good will and didn't want anything for it, just a good feeling. I believe Friedrich Born is a great man who needs to be remembered as a committed, good-hearted hero.

Works Cited

"Friedrich Born." *Funkascript ATOM*. N.p., n.d. Web. 09 Feb. 2015.

"Friedrich Born." *Wikipedia*. Wikimedia Foundation, n.d. Web. 09 Feb. 2015

"Introduction to the Holocaust." *United States Holocaust Memorial Museum*. United States Holocaust Memorial Council, 20 June 2014. Web. 01 Feb. 2015.

ELISABETH EIDENBENZ: A LIGHT IN THE DARKNESS

Mariya Spiridonova

"War does not determine who is right--only who is left." These were the words of Bertrand Russell, a British philosopher. And how true this is. War takes so many people, and only the luckiest are left alive. The numbers of people dead in World War II are perhaps some of the most startling: over 60 million. Out of these people were soldiers sent to fight, and innocent men, women, and children, as well, killed in the terrible Holocaust. TheHolocaust was a truly terrible tragedy. Innocent people, most notoriously Jews, were sent to die in concentration camps and gas chambers, all orchestrated by Adolf Hitler, the German leader and dictator at the time. Who was left? Everyone was so afraid to lose their life, but thanks to brave people, who were plenty afraid to risk their life to save people but did it anyway, there *were* survivors. One of these heroes was a woman by the name of Elisabeth Eidenbenz. What exactly did she do? World War II and the Holocaust left so many people dying, starving, sick. Of course, even during times when the world is paralyzed with war and fear, and thousands of soldiers are being injured every day, there are still other medical conditions besides bullet wounds that need to be attended to- like a child that needs to be born. So many children were unborn and never got to live a life simply because the mother was too sick or malnourished tobe able to support the baby. It seemed like war wasn't about to leave any children behind. However, even in this lost time, there was hope. Elisabeth saved a

154

considerable number of these endangered children through her work, and certainly earned her title of a 'Righteous.'

Elisabeth Eidenbenz was a survivor of the entire ordeal of World War II herself, someone the war had spared. Although the war started around 1939, Elisabeth was already helping before that. Starting out life quietly and simply, she became a teacher in Switzerland, her home country in which she was born in on June 12, 1913. She wasn't very well known at all, and started her life out in the tiny area in Switzerland called Wila. She was born into a large family, her father had a fairly common job as a preacher, and her whole family was of the Christian Protestant religion. She taught for three years in Switzerland, as well as Denmark, and after that, she went to Spain and did quite the amount of volunteer work. A number of it included handing out food or other typical humanitarian aid type jobs. She saved the lives of children and their families evacuating because of minor wars or other crises, and many lives of the elderly as well in Madrid, Spain. This experience absolutely changed her. Before her trip to Spain, she had thought that she'd return to Denmark, or Switzerland, that she'd return to teaching. She planned to just spend a holiday there in Spain, helping people, and come back to her home. She never did. She was so inspired by what she could do she decided to keep going, and this was the beginning of the Mothers of Elne. After the Spanish Civil War, which ended in the year of 1939, many refugees and republicans were seeking shelter from the violence and their now lost, ruined republic. To make it even worse, World War II was right around the corner, it's beginning just a few months away, and no one knew it. Elisabeth Eidenbez, now ready to start her own volunteer group, stayed in Spain and started the 'Mothers of Elne,' or, in Spanish, *La Maternidad de Elna.*

Her goal was to keep helping people survive through hard times and hopefully, war wouldn't always determine who was left. Maybe humans would get a say, too. As mentioned before, there were many women who needed to give birth to children… but they were running. Refugees, evacuees, running from violence, chaos… many of them lost their babies or even died in the process of childbirth because of starvation, injuries and sickness. The Mothers of Elne were made to help stop this. Elisabeth found an old, long left and abandoned mansion that she could use as a sort of hospital or maternity home, where Spanish republicans fleeing the area, whether it be because of exile or another reason, could find shelter and a for pregnant woman, a place to give birth to her child. She gave it a few touches of renovation, made it look nice, with some financial help. The mansion wasn't the biggest and best and most spacious. It didn't fit hundreds of people and the volunteers couldn't serve everyone at once. It wasn't great, but it was a start, and for the Spanish republicans seeking shelter after experiencing years of ghastly violence, and for the future mothers that so desperately wanted to give life to their child, it was as if God Himself had provided them a warm, welcoming fire in the middle of a dark, dark world.

Things started out quite well. The maternity home, as small as it was, still needed financial support. Europe provided them with most of their funds, glad to donate for such a good cause. Elisabeth loved working there every day, seeing so many beautiful children come out into the world, babies' first cries, seeing people healed and cured of disease, typhoid fever, and nursed back to health, brought back from starvation. What could possibly be better than seeing that every single day? The year was 1939, and things were going great. And then, World War II happened. Deafening explosions, entire towns being burned to the ground, millions and millions of innocent people dead. Jews starving to death in concentration camps just because of their religion, bravely fighting for their lives. The Nazi Invasion, firearms, bombs crashing and widespread panic. No one could possibly have seen something like the Holocaust happening, genocide on such a massive scale. Refugees and survivors of the war and Holocaust came rushing in from all of Europe. People hurt, sick, women needing to give birth. (Mostly Jewish women). It all happened in a blur, and before they knew it, the Mothers of Elne was dangerously low on money, which was needed to buy supplies and medicine. Elisabeth hated to see her organization going down so quickly. To save her maternity hospital, Elisabeth and her volunteers partnered up with the Red Cross. That wasn't as simple as it seems. In order for the Red Cross to give them funds, the Mothers of Elne had to stop serving and taking in only political refugees, so they couldn't take in exclusively Jews anymore, they'd have to take less of them in. This was called neutrality. In order to solve this problem, the Mothers of Elne decided to keep the identities of the patients and refugees secret, so they could take anyone in. And that they did. It was a dangerous job, too. The Gestapo, the Nazi secret police, constantly came to her maternity home, searching for any Jews they were planning to kill or take to concentration camps. Elisabeth never let them take anyone away, concealing all their identities. She was determined to help all her patients survive. Once, however, the Gestapo did manage to take one Jewish woman named Lucie away, and only because Lucie gave herself up when the secret police threatened to take Elisabeth instead. Elisabeth was forever in debt and remembered Lucie her whole life. So even through hard times, Elisabeth kept her organization going. The Mothers of Elne saved over 600 children from being unborn and never living a life. There are still people alive today, people who were born and lived at Elisabeth's makeshift maternity home who still remember their experience and are forever thankful.

After World War II was over, around 1945, the Mothers of Elne weren't needed too much anymore. They were glad to have saved so many children from the horrors of war. Elisabeth still kept continuing her volunteer work, her teaching job a thing of the past. Her experiences with the Mothers of Elne were something she'd never forget. Elisabeth later worked with the Swiss Evangelical Church in 1946, and with other groups as well. For her work, she received quite a lot of awards- the 'Righteous

Among the Nations' recognition by the Yad Vashem Institution, and three awards from France, Spain, and Catalonia. The people she had saved, now grown into adults, and having survived the war, were extremely grateful to her. She lived a long, good life, and finally, Elizabeth Eidenbenz, a true hero, died on May 23rd of the year 2011.

War truly is brutal. It doesn't leave many people behind, and destroys so many innocents. But thanks to people like Elizabeth Eidenbenz, there was hope. So many mothers were lucky enough to be able to give birth even in the terrible time of World War II. There were so many people who just stood by and watched sadly as millions of innocent Jews died in the holocaust, starving to death or dying of sickness. But Elizabeth Eidenbenz took action. She created hope for the refugees and survivors of these trying times and gave them shelter. She has earned the name of a Righteous. Who knows what the Nazis would have done of they knew she was rescuing Jews? One mistake, one Jewish-sounding name slipping out when the Gestapo came by, one little hint that the patients were Jews... and it would all be over. But no. She risked her life even though she was afraid, and because of her, there are still people alive today who wouldn't be here if it weren't for the Mothers of Elne. She nobly fought for good when others just lamented the bad. To me, what Elisabeth did is the act of a hero. A true hero. She earned her title. After all, as a great Chinese proverb says, "Better to light a candle than to curse the darkness."

Bibliography

"Elisabeth and Her Maternité." *Elisabeth Eidenbenz and the Maternité Suisse D'Elne.* Anglophone Direct, n.d. Web. 13 Feb. 2015.

"Elisabeth Eidenbenz." *Whoislog.info.* N.p., n.d. Web. 12 Feb. 2015."Elizabeth Eidenbenz - SpeedyLook Encyclopedia." *Elizabeth Eidenbenz - SpeedyLook Encyclopedia.* N.p., n.d. Web. 13 Feb. 2015."Spanish Civil War | Spanish History." *Encyclopedia Britannica Online.* Encyclopedia

Britannica, 11 Oct. 2014. Web. 11 Feb. 2015.

Encyclopedia. N.p., n.d. Web. 13 Feb. 2015.

HONOR. REMEMBER. PRAISE.

Mathew D. Huh

A hero comes in all sizes. He does not have to be a knight in shining armor, nor wear a red cape. Many unsung heroes have come out of the tragedy we know today as the Holocaust. The Nazis came into power in 1933 in Germany. Since they believed that they were superior to the Jews, they started a racial cleansing which is known as the Holocaust. This tragic event, lasting from 1933 to 1945, resulted in the murder of approximately six million Jews. During this time of chaos, many non-Jewish people stepped up to help the Jewish people in their attempts to survive. Despite all the atrocities, courageous rescue attempts were made by people of all backgrounds, races, and religions. These "unsung heroes" displayed true heroism in the face of extreme peril and danger to help their fellow humankind. Attitudes of the bystanders during this appalling time ranged from denial, to indifference, to hostility towards the Jews. The heroes were all ordinary people who never planned to rescue Jews and therefore were completely unprepared. The Yad Vashem website recognizes heroes called The Righteous from 44 countries and nationalities. These heroes came from all different backgrounds. They were Christian, Muslim, women, men, illiterate, and educated. However, in this diverse group, their similarities lie in the fact that they had empathy and a philanthropic personality. They displayed courage and respect for their neighbors.

In what ways did these heroes help? Some hid Jews in their homes. The most famous story of these heroes hiding Jews was the concealment of Anne Frank. The hero in this story is named Otto Frank. He let Anne frank and her family, along with another family of four, live in a secret apartment behind his business in Amsterdam. Only after 25 months did an anonymous person betray them. However, the bravery of Otto permitting a total of 8 Jews hide on his property is unbelievable. Similarly, even with the threat of death, other heroes proceeded to hide Jews in their basements, farms, and houses. Sometimes they even presented these people as their relatives. Hiding Jews was extremely difficult for them. They had to provide food, remove their waste, and take care of daily living, all while living in terror of being found out. Some of these heroes even provided false papers and false identities so that the Jews could pose as non-Jews to escape detection. Rescuers would forge these papers for them. Even benevolent officials risked their positions, lives, and family to provide papers to protect Jews. Still other heroes smuggled and helped Jews escape to a different location or country that was more protected. Like Harriet Tubman, these rescuers would help Jews across borderlines to rescuing Jewish children. Some parents were forced to separate from their children to protected countries, such as Switzerland that remained neutral. Other heroes helped by increase their chances of survival. When they did this, they needed trusted caretakers for their children. These altruistic caretakers housed, educated, and loved these children.

One such hero was Martha Schmidt. Martha was born in 1900 in Switzerland. The Cohen family, living in France, hired Ms. Schmidt to care for their 3 young daughters. The youngest was only a few months old. These children adored her and called her "Tata." When Germany occupied their area of southern France in 1942, the Cohens were forced to flee to Monaco near Italy. Martha came with them to continue to protect the young children. There in Monaco, the Cohens had a fourth daughter. The following year, they were forced to flee again when the Germans invaded Italy. However, this time, the Cohens made the decision to separate from their children. Martha Schmidt took the children with her and hid them from public in a region in France called Auvergne. She transformed herself to be the "mother" of the four children by looking after their education, health, and lives as well as running the house. She did this for 20 years, despite the fear of being found and persecuted for hiding Jews. She put the girls' lives ahead of hers.

Martha Schmidt dedicated her life and saved the four Cohen daughters. She did this with courage and demonstrated humanity in the face of extreme peril. These virtuous and compassionate acts demonstrate what people can be capable of. This was evident to me when I visited theHolocaust Museum in Washington, D.C. last year. It was poignant to see the faces of those who had been lost. Each had their own story. I was reminded how important it is to remember these stories and keep them alive. Bernie Marks speaking to us at our school brought this important event to life. He taught me that compassion must never be a bystander. I am saddened by the thought that the next generation will not be able to experience the Holocaust survivors firsthand. Therefore, it is imperative that we keep them alive through their stories of heroism, survival and humanity. We must make sure this never happens again and be indifferent bystanders. There are still tragedies of genocide and ethnic cleansing happening today, such as in places like Darfur and Sudan. By continuing the discussions and talking about the horribleness of the Holocaust, perhaps people can be sensitive to what is happening globally. It all starts with education. It all starts with us.

HOLOCAUST HEROES

Melisanda Jaecks

The Holocaust was a tragic event that affected many different groups, but very much affected people in the Jewish religion. This affected so many people and it really was not okay that some did nothing to help the people suffering. Anyone who aided those negatively impacted are true heroes and it doesn't matter if they saved one person or one hundred. Two people that were a contributing factor to the Denmark victims were Helga Holbeck and Gerda Valentiner. The two women couldn't have been more different, but a strong tie connected them, the goodness in their hearts for risking their lives for people they didn't even know which was so brave and a really big risk to take in that the consequences could even possibly of been death. It was though with great kind hearts that they got help from people all around that helped them in small ways that meant a lot to the people receiving the help. It is in my belief to think that we were all created equal and therefore all have the same opportunities as the person next to us and if someone needs help you give it because maybe someday you will need their help, it is a give and get situation.

Miss Helga Holbeck was a Danish woman working with an American organization. She was also acquainted with the Quaker Friends Service Committee. She was a head of the delegation of American Friends. This meant she was allied with American organizations, she also helped get the children to orphanages. Working with OSE (a Jewish association) she helped children escape to safe orphanages. This lovely older woman worked with organizations privately to help sneak the children into safety. By helping children that were of the Jewish religion put Miss Helga Holbeck at high risk of being caught which include punishment and practically death. To know people like Miss Helga Holbeck had been there in Denmark to help the innocent children from receiving a fatal death at such a young age and just be able to be such an inspiration to future generations is amazing.

Miss Gerda Valentiner was a school teacher who helped students who were Jewish. She helped them with getting food and also respected their religion and was extremely sensitive and aware of their dietary restrictions. There should have been many more people such as Miss Helga Holbeck and Miss Gerda Valentiner during these groups' times of need. Although there were women willing to aid there were people that just accepted this or even supported this action against the Jewish. She aided them during October 1943. This was an extremely noble act as she was risking her life and should be recognized for this as she is. The woman was of great need for her students were almost constantly bullied if they were Jewish and wore a symbol showing their religion. They were not treated with the respect they should have been treated with. This I find so unhuman and just so awful that people would be ridiculed and sent off to almost always resulting in more lives lost too soon and shouldn't be lost at all or at least not without vain.

This research I've done for this essay made me realize not all heroes wear capes some of them are perfectly ordinary, yet extraordinary people. Anyone who helped or saved lives of people who happened to be ill-treated at this time are all people that we should be commemorating and definitely giving them credit and praise for their actions. Miss Helga Holbeck and Miss Gerda Valentiner both make the country of Denmark very proud in as their inhabitance includes people like this, with very good character traits such as their sacrifices and hardwork. These women acted on pure gut and knowing that this act on Jewish people was morally wrong. What happened was never okay, but the fact that there were people that were courageous enough to risk everything and put it out on the line to aid others in bad situations that need all of the help they can get from being racially discriminated against. Fact is that this was a terrible time when true colors were revealed in whether you helped or made the situation worse. It is nice to know that know there is no more tormenting for the people who were saved, but yet very terrifying that such a tragic event took place.

People these days complain about how tough life is for them, they should put themselves in the shoes of a person helping the Jewish community or a Jewish person and the fear they must of lived in. There has been many times in history in which one race is trying to be superior to another, but there will always be help and motivation to aid those who need it because at the end of the day we are all human and deserve to be equal and be treated with the same way you would of liked to be treated if you were in a tough situation.

Bibliography

http://www.yadvashem.org/yv/en/exhibitions/righteous-teachers/valentiner.asp

http://www.yadvashem.org/yv/en/holocaust/france/pdf/doc04.pdf
http://www.yadvashem.org/yv/en/righteous/statistics.asp

http://www.ajpn.org/juste-Helga-Holbeck-3544.html

PAUL GRUENINGER: A HERO FROM SWITZERLAND

Nathan Ng

Many people would be able to give you a general overview of what happened during World War II. Many people would tell you the highlights of the war like D-day or the Germans persecuting the Jews. However, not many people can tell you the people who helped the Jews. Some might not even think there were people who helped. Or some people thought that the numbers were few. However, there have been more than 25,000 people who have helped the Jews. People in Asian countries like Japan and China have even helped the Jews. But a hero who faced a constant threat from both Nazi Germany and his own country, Switzerland, was a man by the name of Paul Grueninger. Paul Grueninger was born in 1891, in the city of St. Gallen, in Switzerland. During World War I, he rose to the rank of a lieutenant. Towards the end of the war he was promoted to the rank of Captain in 1925. When the border for Switzerland closed for Jews, Paul Grueninger was faced with a difficult situation. Turn the Jews away or illegally help them into the country. He chooses to help them. Paul Grueninger helped the Jews by falsifying passports for the Jews saying that they were already in the country before the border block, blocking all efforts to find previous Jews who had illegally crossed the country and used his own money to buy winter clothes for the fleeing Jews who did not have them.

As the Swiss government ordered the borders to be closed on all Jews who were fleeing to Switzerland, Grueninger had two choices: let the Jews into the country illegally, or deporting them. He helped them. One way he did this was by making false passports for them so they could get inside safely without being harassed by other officers. These passports also allowed the Jews to reach Diepoldsau camp which was a safe camp run by Jews where other Jews could wait to get a permit to stay in that country or get sent to their real destination. This helped many Jews get away from Nazi Germany. As I said in the introduction, Grueninger had been a captain at the end of World War I, which was a pretty honorable position. By doing this, he choose to forfeit all of that for people he barely knew. All he knew was that they were people that needed help.

When he let the refugees cross, he also shielded them from the Germans. He helped slow them down if they grew suspicious. He also managed to hide them from his own officers. By shielding them, he helped prevent other Jews who may have made it across. He also helped the many Jews hide their possessions. Many people had brought along hidden treasures or family heirlooms that could bring them money for the hard times ahead. He helped hide all those jewels so that the Jews would not have to lose them. Though this behavior got him caught when a woman wrote to her family about how Officer Grueninger was a very kind man who helped keep their possessions safe. But by doing this, he helped protect many old family treasures that could be from and extremely long time. These treasures can be very valuable and those treasure falling into the people who don't know its value might destroy it. By shielding the Jews he also was able to protect those camps that were run by Jewish organizations. This helped insure the protection of much more Jews that may have not been helped by him

The last and I think most generous thing he did was to buy clothes for these refugees. Many of the refugees had to leave everything behind and could not take their warm winter jackets. So he bought them the winter jackets. This I think was really brave since it must have been suspicious going into the jacket shop almost every week to buy jackets for adults and kids; especially if those jackets didn't fit him. By doing this, he spent lots of money on these people he didn't even know. In addition to, he probably didn't make the most money. By doing something like this, he spent his money and probably raised a lot of suspicion by going to the shop a lot. By doing this, he was able to make many families warm. The jacket could also double as a blanket and could also be used to keep a baby warm. He also kept the sickness and disease at a minimum in the Jewish camps

In conclusion, I think this man did an extraordinary job of helping Jews. By falsifying passports, hiding the Jews and their jewelry, and buying them winter clothes; he helped the Jews in so many ways. In total, He helped at least 3,000 Jews safely cross over the border of Switzerland. However, he was eventually caught when the Germans informed the Swiss border police what he had been doing. They took away all his benefits and he had to stand trial in court. The trial took 2 years. Finally, they declared him guilty and stripped him of retirement benefits and forced him to pay for the trial costs. Then he was dismissed from the force and was forgotten. However, he never regretted his choice. However, when he died in 1972, it took 23 years, all the way up to 1995 for the Swiss government to declare him innocent.

"It was basically a question of saving human lives threatened with death. How could I then seriously consider bureaucratic schemes and calculations." Paul Grueninger, 1954

Works Cited

"Eastern Illinois University Homepage." *The Holocaust Paul Grueninger*. Web. 9 Feb. 2015. < http://www.eiu.edu/ ~ eiutps/holocaust_gruneninger.php > .

"Gruninger, Paul - The Jewish Foundation for the Righteous." *The Jewish Foundation for the Righteous*. Web. 9 Feb. 2015. < https://jfr.org/ rescuer-stories/gruninger-paul/ > .

"Paul Grueninger - The Righteous Among The Nations - Yad Vashem." *Paul Grueninger - The Righteous Among The Nations - Yad Vashem*. Web. 9 Feb. 2015. < http://www.yadvashem.org/yv/en/righteous/stories/gruneninger.asp > .

"Tag Archives: Paul Grueninger." *Jewish Currents*. Web. 9 Feb. 2015. < http://jewishcurrents.org/tag/paul-grueninger > .

"The Example of Grüninger." *Funkascript ATOM*. Web. 9 Feb. 2015. < http://www.raoulwallenberg.net/saviors/others/example-gr-uuml-ninger/ > .

"The Example of Grüninger." *Funkascript ATOM*. Web. 9 Feb. 2015. < http://www.raoulwallenberg.net/saviors/others/example-gr-uuml-ninger/ > .

MARTHA SCHMIDT: THE SAVIOR

Neha Shetty

It is difficult to find a person who is generous enough and willing to risk their life for others. It is even more difficult to find a person who is willing to risk their lives for someone unrelated by blood. But surprisingly enough, people like this do exist in the world. Some dead, some alive. One person who stands out among these people is Martha Schmidt. Martha Schmidt was a Swiss lady born in 1900. Her story took place during the Holocaust in World War II. She was hired as a children's nurse for the daughters of the Cohen family. Sadly, during the Holocaust her life became associated with the fate of the Cohen family.

The Holocaust was a genocide of Jews that started on January 30, 1933, the day Hitler became the Chancellor of Germany, and ended on May 8, 1945. The Nazi Leader was Adolf Hitler. About 6 million Jews, Gypsies, homosexuals, and other groups died. Many people died and many people survived, but there were more people who were involved in this genocide. The people who attempted to save the victims of the Holocaust. This is the story of Martha Schmidt; the savior of the Cohen family.

In 1937, the third daughter of the Cohen family, Josiane (also known as Josette), was born in Montpellier, a city in Southern France. The family decided to hire Martha Schmidt as their nurse. The Cohens also had two other daughters. The older girl was named Rachel and was 8 years old, and their second daughter was named Liliane who was 5 years old. Martha also took care of Rachel and Liliane. The girls called Martha "Tata" because Martha was difficult to say for them. This name eventually stuck and became a nickname for Martha.

In September of 1939, sometime before the Germans took over Montepellier, Martha was given her annual break. Martha took this time to stay with her parents in Zurich. The Germans took over Montepellier in the November of 1942. The Cohens were in a predicament. Mr. Cohen started getting threatening letters and was afraid of getting arrested. To prevent the family from separating, the Cohens plan to move away from Montepellier. They insisted that Martha stay with her parents and not come with them, but Martha refused. She said she was a Christian lady and believed it was her duty to help and support the Cohens sustain during their difficult times. They were Jewish and she considered them as family.

First they move to Monaco. They live there for about a year. Martha helped the family in every way she can. Here, the Cohens' fourth baby girl was born. Her name was Danielle. Once again, the Germans took over Italian zones, Monaco being one of them. The Gestapo (the police who worked for the Nazis) would come to every house in search of hiding Jews. In fear, the family moved away again, but this time it was different. The Cohens decided it would be safer if the parents separated from Martha and the children. Martha agreed and became in charge of the four girls.

First, Martha and the kids moved to a local inn in Lépin-le-lac, a small area near the lake of Aiguebelette. Once again, Martha took care of the children as best as she coulc. To make sure no one knew who they were, she changed her last name to Chauvin. All five of them become known as the Chauvin daughters. After some time, Martha realizes that Lépin-le-lac was the center of the French Resistance, an organization that supplied their allies, like Britain, with important reports. They also meddled with Germany's supplies and communication with France in hopes to defeat the Nazis. Unfortunately, this meant that the Schutzstaffel was always watching the town of Lépin-le-lac. The Schutzstaffel were men who were bodyguards for Adolf Hitler. Eventually, they became one of the most feared and powerful organizations of the Nazis. Martha knew that this was dangerous for her and the girls. Due to this reason, Martha maked arrangements to move to Auvergne, a region in central France. They rented out a small house here. Once again, Martha helped greatly. She did all the housework, household chores, shopping, educated the girls, and created a sort of security and comfort to compensate for the fear developed in the children. Martha really made a connection with the four girls during this time.

Fortunately, all the Cohens and Martha survived World War II without getting caught. After the family reunited, Martha chose to live with the Cohens for twenty years more years. She always maintained some sort of connection with the Cohens even after she stopped working for them. Martha said that she wanted to stay with them because Mr. Cohen was a great man and she would never want anything bad to happen to him, him wife, or their four daughters.

Overall, Martha Schmidt was a great woman who had a small but great role in the Holocaust. She did exceptional deeds for a small, Jewish family who was going through tough times during World War II. Schmidt displayed exemplary character and affection towards the Cohen family. She always managed to take away the fear that had been drilled into the faces and eyes of the four innocent girls. Even when she was not sure of the future events herself, she kept spirits up and remained optimistic. Martha's actions show that it does not matter whether you are not of the same ethnicity or related by blood; anyone can be family. What really matters is how you all come together as a whole, fight your battles together, and in the end find yourselves victorious.

Works Cited

Wagner, Meir, and Moshe Meisels. "The Righteous of Switzerland." *Google Books*. KTAV Publishing House, n.d. Web. 7 Feb. 2015.

"The Righteous Among the Nations." *Yad Vashem*. Yad Vashem, n.d. Web. 7 Feb. 2015.

"The French Resistance." *The French Resistance*. HistoryLearningSite.co.uk, n.d. Web. 8 Feb. 2015.

"The SS." *History.com*. A&E Television Networks, n.d. Web. 8 Feb. 2015.

BILL BARAZETTI – A HERO OF THE GERMAN HOLOCAUST

Pavithra Sundaravaradan

As history goes on and is made daily, we also need to take a large step back and look at the past of our world. We have any important events from our past, one of them being the Holocaust. The Holocaust is "the mass murder of Jews under the German Nazi regime during the period 1941–45. More than 6 million European Jews, as well as members of other persecuted groups, such as gypsies and homosexuals, were murdered at concentration camps such as Auschwitz." (Oxford Dictionary). Now normally, when we are asked to think about the Holocaust, we may think of many different things, but the first thing that usually comes up is the fact that this was an extremely dark and cruel period in history. While it might've been all of the things mentioned above, one of the things we need to mention is that fact that the people did have many heroes and these heroes did whatever it took put the lives of others before their own to ensure the safety and wellbeing of others. Now that we are informed about the major tragic event that occurred in Germany, we also need to acknowledge the righteous people of the Holocaust. These are people who are morally correct and have saved lives and have done something very great. One of these people is a man born in Aarau, Switzerland from Prague in Czechoslovakia. This valiant man managed to save 669 Jewish children from the cruel German Nazis. He is Bill Barazetti.

Bill Barazetti saved the lives of about 669 children by arranging transportation for the kids. He achieved this by arranging three transports out of Czechoslovakia. He was also the driving force for the kinder transport operation, during this mission he really risked his life in order to save families and their children. While organizing this very complicated mission, Barazetti lived under an alias, he often stayed with the families he was helping. In 1934, Barazetti made a brave decision, his decision was to move to Czechoslovakia. Here he was recruited by the Czech Secret Service to work as an intelligence officer.

After Barazetti returned to the Hamburg Area as a spy, a year later the Germans discovered his real identity and the SS attempted to arrest him. Luckily, Barazetti found out about this plan in time and had enough time to plan and fake his death. After faking his death, Barazetti escaped to Poland where he changed his identity again. But it doesn't end there, Barazetti was then caught by the "Great Gestapo," he was almost beaten to death, and after being beaten he is found on the German-Czech border he was found by Anna. Anna was a young Czech girl who helped Barazetti recuperate. Later, he ended up marrying her and they both moved to Switzerland where they had their first child together, Nicholas in 1937. But Barazetti didn't stop there, he was eager to fight the Nazis, so he finally made Anna go back to her village with their son Nicholas, while he traveled back to Poland, where he obtained an illegally forged passport and then returned to Prague.

There in the city of Prague, Barazetti got very involved with Nicholas Winton's rescue operation to help rescue and evacuate Jewish children from the city. Winton did many things for this operation to ensure that is worked successfully, he arranged documents, raised funds, and recruited many British foster families for the children so that they had a safe home to live in. Shortly before the time when the Germans invaded Prague in March of 1938, Winton left to England and Barazetti took over and took charge of the operation. Although Barazetti was a wanted man who worked under a fake name, he succeeded in persuading the German authorities in Prague to end three rail transports of children to Britain. This happened in the spring of 1939, when the war had not started yet. When this well thought out plan got approved, Barazetti obtained visas for all of the children and he organized the train for the children to escape. One of the many children that he helped was Hugo Murom, who was just 10 years old at the time and his brother, Rudolph who was nine years old at the time. These trains were dispatched just days before the war terrible war broke out. Barazetti spent the rest of his life in Britain. And on October 27th, 1993 the Yad Vashem Society recognized Bill Barazetti as Righteous Among the Nations.

After analyzing one of the many key moments in our history we can learn that there are many people on our planet who have helped make the world a better place. Bill Barazetti is a brave and strong man who helped save the lives of many Jewish families survive through some of the toughest conditions imaginable. Without a man like Bill Barazetti, the lives of many would be lost after excruciatingly painful pain. All in all, heroes do their best to put the lives of others in front theirs for the well-being of the people around them. These heroes do many things including putting their life in harm's way for others.

Works Cited

"Bill Barazetti | The Times." *The Times*. Web. 8 Feb. 2015.
< http://www.thetimes.co.uk/tto/opinion/obituaries/article2088543.ece >.

"Definition of Holocaust in English:." *Holocaust: Definition of Holocaust in Oxford Dictionary (American English) (US)*. Web. 6 Feb. 2015.
< http://www.oxforddictionaries.com/us/definition/american_english/holocaust >.

"Righteous." *Miriam Webster*. Web. 10 Feb. 2015.
< http://www.merriamwebster.com/dictionary/righteous >.

"The Righteous Among The Nations." *Yad Vashem*. Web. 9 Feb. 2015.
< http://db.yadvashem.org/righteous/family.html? Language-en & itemId=4013808

THE HEROES OF THE HOLOCAUST

Polina Davydova

TheHolocaust destroyed the Jewish heritage. Just because of their nationality, the Jewish people were separated from their families, put into concentration camps where they were forced to work day and night without knowledge about their family members, and killed. However, there were a few brave people who helped the Jewish people escape the German Nazis torture with no regrets because they knew that it was the right thing to do. Their commitment was dangerous because if the German Nazis found out about people helping the Jewish escape, the person had to join in the camps with the Jewish people where they would be tortured slowly to death or put to death immediately. They were willing to sacrifice their lives in order to save another life. These true heroes are Anna Christensen and Sigurd Larsen. I admire Anna Christensen and Sigurd Larsen for their humane actions.

Anna Christensen

Anna Christensen cared for immigrant Jewish children during the World War II. Anna Christensen provided them with motherly love and care when they were separated from their families. She kept the children well cared for and educated. She was a hero to the children when they were hopeless and disconnected with loved ones. She was a sign of hope for the children and the children looked up to her.

Anna Christensen participated in the International League for Peace and Freedom. During the war, Jewish immigrants from Germany and Austria were deported. One of the clusters of refugees fell into the hands of Anna Christensen. She was responsible for 40 Jewish children.

Anna Christensen cared for the children like a mother. Once she received the children, she first sent the 40 Jewish children off to school. However, at the time it was too dangerous to send Jewish children to school and authorities disagreed with her decision to give the children an official education. Instead, Anna Christensen decided to be their teacher herself. She housed them and took care of them as well as taught them. She and the other workers taught the Jewish children most of the subjects that normal children were taught at that time. Once the situation worsened and became more dangerous for Jewish people she hid the children in the safe homes she found for them. She continued to teach the children. Anna Christensen and the children continued to meet up and have their discussions and lessons once a week. Soon, she managed to successfully get the children out of the country into Sweden through an underground tunnel. Once the war was the over, Anna Christensen still kept in touch with the children.

Anna Christensen took care of the Jewish immigrant children when they were hopeless. She raised them during the World War II when the children were separated from their families. She sacrificed many things for those children in order to achieve her goal that interfered with danger and put her life at risk of being killed to care for the children and to keep them safe and educated. Heroes are admired for their selflessness and self sacrifice. Anna Christensen is a hero to the 40 Jewish immigrant children she rescued in times of need during the World War II.

Sigurd Larsen

Sigurd Larsen was a hero and admired for his altruism like Anna Christensen. However, he went through a more dangerous path in order to help the Jewish. Although he initially was a German Nazi who fought in the World War II, he helped the Jewish people escape. He, unlike most of the Germans was willing to go against government politics. If the German Nazis later found out that one of their people was betraying them, this would result most likely in immediate death. The world would have viewed as a humane act, however the German Nazis would have defined this a humiliation.

Originally, Sigurd Larsen became a German soldier during World War II.

However, in one of the battles he got injured. His parents pleaded to German forces for their son to not return back to the battle. Soon, Sigurd Larsen was resigned from the conflict against the Jewish. At the time, Sigurd Larsen knew a man named Joachim Marcuse. Joachim Marcuse was a Jewish man who was forced to do hard labor during the war in a wood factory. He was in need of help and he asked Larsen to help rescue him. Sigurd Larsen agreed to commit to help Joachim Marcuse escape. During their traveling journey to Sweden, he organized a hideout for three more Jewish people. Their escape was successful and they finally arrived to their destination. Sigurd Larsen feared that his illegal support to the Jewish would be uncovered by the German Nazi disciples. He then moved to Copenhagen, Denmark to live with his family.

Sigurd Larsen is a true hero. A Jewish person, Joachim Marcuse, was in need of escape. Sigurd Larsen agreed to helping Joachim Marcuse break away from Germany. This was a dangerous decision that Sigurd Larsen committed to. If the German Nazis found out that their fellow member betrayed them and helped their enemy to escape. This would cost him his life, the lives of the people he helped, and the lives of the people he loved. Sigurd Larsen was willing to go against German government agenda of destroying other nations. This is the definition of a true hero.

In the dangerous times, Anna Christensen's and Sigurd Larsen's actions became heroic. In peaceful times, caring actions are usual. In critical times, to help those who are in need is humane and dangerous. Anna Christensen and Sigurd Larsen put their lives and the lives of their loved ones in danger. They understood the risk, but they valued human life as a priceless gift which no one can take. Heroes are people who are staying humane regardless of times.

Bibliography:
"Sigurd Larsen." *Funkascript ATOM.* N.p., n.d. Web. 3 Feb. 2015.
N.p., n.d. Web.
(http://db.yadvashem.org/righteous/family.html?language=en&itemId=4014337)

GERDA VALENTINER – THE TEACHER WHO SAVED
Rachel W. Firl

We all have or had a teacher that has meant a great deal to our lives. They may have taught you how to multiply, or stopped you from being bullied. They may even have helped you out of a bad place in your life. But has your teacher saved your life? Gerda Valentiner did just that; she managed to save many of her Jewish students from being put into concentration camps and possibly from being killed by the Nazis. Valentiner was born on April 25, 1903 in Denmark and was about thirty when the Holocaust began to work its terror. She was also a part of the Danish resistance, which sparked her interest in wanting to help her students. She lived a very interesting and noble life and used her position to help those lower than she.

As many people in our world may know, from 1933 until March 8, 1945, a horrific event occurred over almost all of Europe. Nazis, members of a party run by Adolf Hitler, with the support of the German government tracked down every Jew, Gypsy, disabled, homosexual, Polish, Russian, and many other groups of people they could find, and either put them into concentration camps or killed them. The Nazis felt that "Germans were 'racially superior' and that the Jews, deemed 'inferior'" ("Introduction to the Holocaust"). The ways that these people were treated are unspeakable. Imagine one day you're going to school with your friends and you go home to your loving family. The next day, German soldiers knock down your doors and tell you to get what you can hold and go to the street to go to the sickening living conditions of a concentration camp. In the entire Holocaust, 11 million people were killed. Elevenmillion people who will never get to accomplish their dreams. The Holocaust finally ended when Allied forces went across Europe and freed a lot of people from concentration camps, until the German Government gave up and surrendered. Amazing; a happy ending to a tragic tale. But 11 million people never had the chance to see the war end. If it were not for people like Gerda Valentiner and many others, many more people would have been captured and/or killed.

There were many Jewish students who attended public schools in Denmark. During the Holocaust, they were tormented and attacked by other students, and they had to wear a yellow star on the front of their shirt. Worst of all, many Jewish students were banned from schools and taken to concentration camps where most of the time they would be killed. Many teachers did not feel it was their duty to impede on the German law to save their students. After all, they were following the law, and had been taught to feel this way about the Jewish population. And why should they risk their lives to save children they would probably never see again in a year? But a woman named Gerda Valentiner felt differently about the situation. She stepped up to the plate and did what she felt was her part in ending the Holocaust. She saw what was happening to so many Jewish children in the school she worked at, and felt it was her duty to protect as many of these children as she could. So, with the parents awed in her bravery, she took in her Jewish students and housed them in her home. Some children would eat bread only due to religious laws, so she got other types of food for them to eat. This shows that she was an incredibly selfless person, especially because food was very hard to buy because rations were set to every person.

Valentiner would know when the Germans were coming to search for Jews, so she would go and warn parents, and then take the children to her house. The Nazis would not search Valentiner's house because they had no records of her being a Jew, and nobody found out what she was doing. If they did however, Valentiner would have been killed in a heartbeat. After the children were transported to her house, Valentiner would use her connections as being a part of the Danish resistance to have someone on a fishing boat take the children to Sweden, which was a safe place to be at the time because it was a neutral country, and it was selling iron to the Germans. It is also not too far away from where they were in Denmark; about 10 kilometers away. They had to repeat this mission three times before the children could get to Sweden, but in the end they all got there safely. Their parents arrived soon after, and on the eve of Yom Kippur, a Jewish holiday, in 1943.

Gerda Valentiner risked her life for these children and their families. And although her mission turned out to be a successful one, there were many people who were put into concentration camps because they were going against everything that the Nazis stood for. Many people have thought of her as a hero, but she said that what she did was "what many Danes did, nothing special" ("The Righteous among the Nations"). This shows that she was not just a courageous and selfless person, she was also very modest. For the amazing things she had done during the Holocaust, she was awarded with the title as Righteous among the Nations by Yad Vashem, in 1968. She also has a tree dedicated to her in Denmark for what she has done for the Jewish population in Denmark during the Holocaust.

Gerda Valentiner was a righteous woman who did things many did not have the courage to do. She cared for the lowest of the low, and saved them from potential death. She deserves every award she has received, and in my opinion she should have more. At least the public should know her name. But that is not probably what she would have wanted because she felt what she did was nothing special. Gerda Valentiner was the teacher who saved.

WorkCited

"The Holocaust: An Introductory History." *An Introductory History of the Holocaust*. N.p., n.d.   Web. 02 Feb. 2015.

"Http://www.gluud.fr/getperson.php?personID=I46055&tree=gluud." N.p., n.d. Web.

"I Found Great Synonyms for "search" on the New Thesaurus.com!" *Www.thesaurus.com*. N.p., n.d. Web. 08 Feb. 2015.

"Introduction to the Holocaust." *United States Holocaust Memorial Museum*. United States Holocaust Memorial Council, 20 June 2014. Web. 01 Feb. 2015.

"The Righteous Among The Nations." *Yad Vashem*. Yad Vashem, n.d. Web. 08 Feb. 2015.

Rosenberg, Jennifer. "Holocaust Facts - 33 Things You Should Know." N.p., n.d. Web. 01 Feb. 2015.

""Their Fate Will Be My Fate Too.."" *Gerda Valentiner*. N.p., n.d. Web. 08 Feb. 2015.

"Welcome to the Purdue OWL." *Purdue OWL: MLA Formatting and Style Guide*. N.p., n.d. Web. 07 Feb. 2015.

"WikiAnswers - Why Did Germany Not Invade Sweden in World War 2." *WikiAnswers - Why Did Germany Not Invade Sweden in World War 2*. N.p., n.d. Web. 08 Feb. 2015.

VONRUFS AND ZURCHER: THE SWISS PAIR

Sabal Niroula

Many heroes were made during World War II. They fought valiantly in the battles for their alliance, or they helped from the sidelines, assisting the wounded. Then there are those who helped out the primary target of the Nazis: the Jews of Europe. Many different peoples from many different countries stepped up against Nazism and provided hiding Jews with refuge, food and other necessities. There was specifically a pair of heroes from Switzerland that, together, protected thousands of Jews from genocide. Their names were Ernst Vonrufs and Peter Zurcher.

Ernst Vonrufs

It goes without argument to say that Ernst Vonrufs was truly great man. What he did to protect those being persecuted by the Nazis was an extraordinarily kind and brave thing. In the year 1935, Ernst Vonrufs went to Budapest, Hungary in order to manage a factory. His family stayed with him there until around the summer of 1944, when the Nazis arrived in Hungary. Ernst sent his family back to Switzerland, which was where they came from, but bravely stayed behind in Hungary in order to keep managing the textile factory. The Swiss Ministry of Foreign affairs wanted to appoint two Swiss residents there in order to deal with Jewish Affairs. Ernst Vonrufs was appointed as secretary of the Department of Foreign interests, and his companion Peter Zürcher was appointed head of the Department.

At about that time, Ferenc Szalasi took over Hungary. Szalasi led the Arrow Cross party, which was a faithful Pro-Nazi Hungarian fascist party. Underneath the Arrow Cross party, 10,000 to 15,000 people were murdered, and 80,000 people were sent to concentration camps in Austria. Soon enough, it became evident that the Jews in Budapest were to be deported to concentration camps, so Vonrufs and Zürcher sprung into action under the guidance of Swiss deputy Karl Lutz.

The pair collaborated with Hungarian Fascist officials in order to assist the Jewish people of Hungary. They didn't only help the foreign Jews in Hungary, they also helped persecuted Jews as well. The Swiss pair saved many Jews by protecting them from deportation. Even when the Russians started to bomb Budapest, Vonrufs and Zurcher would carry on walking through the ghettos and protected Jewish neighborhoods. This was particularly brave of them because they kept on doing their job to protect the Jews even though they were endangered. On January 8' 1945, while the allies and the axis powers clashed, the pair headed over to the town of Sopron. They were heading to Sopron because there, the last Arrow Cross party member (Erno Vajna) resided. They were there because they wished to protect a group of Jews who were in possession of American Documents. The Hungarian Government found out about the documents, extracted them from the Jews, and then proceeded to banish those Jews to the ghetto. Those Jews were to be executed by the Arrow Cross Fascists after evacuation. They conversed with the Arrow Cross member, and that conversation saved the banished Jews' lives.

When the Russians finally breached Budapest in 1945, Vonrufs was asked by the Swiss government to stay there until Pro-Nazi Hungary broke off all its relations with foreign countries and became free Hungary. Ernst left Hungary in 1947 to return home in Switzerland to reunite with his wife and children. As you can see, Ernst Vonrufs was a great man that saved many lives during the Nazi and Fascist rules. Ernst Vonrufs was recognized as Righteous Among the Nations on December 12, 2001.

Peter Zurcher

What Peter Zurcher did protected thousands of Jews in the ghettos and thousands more who were about to be deported was extraordinary. Aside from his quests with his fellow Swiss companion Ernst Vonrufs, Zurcher helped out in many other situations, as he was the head of Swiss Department of Foreign Interests. Originally, he was a Swiss businessman in Budapest, but then he was appointed as head of the department by Karl Lutz. Zurcher was so brave that one of the people he saved, Maria Kormos, ended up working as his secretary, claiming that he risked his life for hers. Zurcher was asked for help by her when the Szalasi government closed the Jewish houses. He cleverly sent a group of men dressed in fascist uniforms to "arrest" her after "questioning." After providing false documents for her, he found a place that she could live, and she lived there until she was liberated.

Peter Zurcher also saved over 70,000 Jews in one incident. In an attempt at last minute genocide, the SS (Schutzstaffel) and the Arrow Cross Fascists allegedly attempted to enter and most likely murder some 70,000 Jews in the Budapest ghetto. He did so by threatening the SS general with trial, because if he did carry out the plans, then he would have committed serious war crimes. His threats worked, and the SS general commanded his troops not to enter the ghetto.

Another incident where Zurcher stopped what would have most likely turned out to be mass murder is when the Arrow Cross Fascists attempted to evacuate the Jews in the Swiss protected houses of the International Ghetto. It was on that day that Zurcher and Vonrufs went down to the town of Sopron to intervene. After a conversation with Erno Vajna, the leader of the Fascists, Zurcher denounced the violation of the International Rights, and ordered the immediate and conclusive termination of the attacks on the Swiss houses and their inhabitants. As you can see, Peter Zurcher saved hundreds of thousands of lives during World War II and the rule of the Nazis and the Fascist party. On October 22' 1998, Peter Zurcher was recognized as Righteous Among the Nations.

HOLOCAUST HEROINES GERDA VALENTINER AND DAGMAR LUSTRUP

Sam Feinberg

 Throughout the Holocaust, Jewish children were greatly discriminated against. They were harassed, persecuted, and forced to wear yellow stars or other markings. All Jewish children were banned from public schools, and teachers gave up on any Jewish students and disregarded them, leaving them behind. One and a half million Jewish children were taken away from their families and murdered. Some women saw the horrors that were happening and could not stand by; instead they risked their lives to help these powerless children.

Gerda Valentiner was a teacher who was part of the Danish Revolution, and in 1943 endangered her life many times to save Danish Jews from the Nazis. She would go and collect Jewish children from their parents, and take them to her home. She would then wait for the first chance she got and took them to safety in Sweden. Although she survived the Holocaust, she put the safety of others before her own, and saved many Jewish children. She was even aware of thechildren's beliefs, realizing that some had to eat kosher, and could only eat bread, so she brought them food they could eat.

One of the witnesses of Valentiner's heroic measures was Moritz Scheftelowitz. He stated that she was his sister's teacher, and Valentiner came to their home in late September of 1943, to warn his parents of the oncoming hazards. Within the next few days, he and his sisters had moved into her home and stayed there until she could move them to Sweden safely. Two of their attempts failed, but on the third try, they managed the transfer successfully. Gerda and the children climbed in a fishing boat 10 km north of Copenhagen, and reached safety in Landskrona, Sweden, on the night of Yom Kippur, 1943, the holiest day of the Jewish calendar, a day of prayers of atonement and fasting. Mortiz's parents had already arrived ten days before them. When the war ended Gerda took a leave of absence from her job and went to Germany and Austria to volunteer to do social work in Jewish refugee camps for two years.

Dagmar Lustrup, another heroine from Denmark, took part in the Women's Peace Organization in the area of Jutland, Denmark. She helped save twenty Jewish teenagers, mainly from Czechoslovakia, from being captured and murdered by the Germans. According to some of the children Lustrup saved, they all were part of Zionist pioneer organizations during the time, and wanted to learn how to be farmers to prepare themselves for immigration to Palestine. After having their home country

174

occupied by Germans, they arrived in the Jutland area. Lustrup's husband ran the local newspaper, Thisted Amtstidende, and obtained the children and had them all sent to private homes in three different areas of Jutland. It was agreed that the Protestant farmers in the area would provide the teens with agricultural training. Lustrup put together different groups on the farms, not only thinking about physical needs, but also cultural activities, similar to Gerda Valentiner acknowledging the dietary needs of those she rescued. Mrs. Lustrup arranged for the teens to meet twice a week just for social purposes.

Unfortunately, problems began after April 1940, when Germans occupied Denmark. All Jews were to be expelled from the Jutland areas in November 1940, where the children were, because the Germans needed the area for strategic purposes. They were told through a message that they had to leave immediately. In a period of just 24 hours, Lustrup was able to get all of the children to a youth hostel in Odense, on Fyn Island, in central Denmark. After a week, on December 5, 1940, they all had immigration certificates and climbed aboard a ship bringing them to Sweden, and with the help of the Soviet Union, went even further, all the way to Palestine. Lustrup made sure these teenagers were trained with the skills they needed to live in Palestine, arranged living quarters for them, and even took them all the way to Palestine, saving them from the Jews. After the war had ended, Lustrup ended up following the same path as her group, but with immense enthusiasm and passion. She survived the war and the children never forgot the sacrifices she made to help them survive.

Both Mrs. Valentiner and Mrs. Lustrup were tremendously courageous, risking their own lives to save others, truly defining them as heroines. Rather than hide away or flee from the horrifying Nazis, they chose to help children who would certainly have been killed without their help. Because of their heroic actions, Yad Vashem recognizes them as righteous among the nations, and heroes of the Holocaust.

Bibliography

"Lustrup Dagmar Rescue Story." Yad†Vashem†. N.p., n.d. Web. 8 Feb. 2015.

""Their Fate Will Be My Fate Too.."" Gerda†Valentiner†. N.p., n.d. Web. 08 Feb.2015.

KNUD DYBY

Samantha Ross, Special award

Hero. It is a word that might be used too often to describe people we think are cool because they have superpowers, or because they have money or good looks. I think it has another meaning though. It should be used for people like Knud Dyby, who had all of the courage in the world. Knud Dyby stood up to people like the Nazis, and risked his life for others.

Knud Dyby was born in Denmark in 1915. He grew up in a poor family, but was a very bright young man. He enjoyed sailing and was very good at it. By the age of 16, he had won multiple awards based on his sailing abilities. He soon went into the publishing and advertisement industry after starting a family. His two sons helped him with his business. In 1940, when the war took a turn for the worse, Dyby decided he wanted to help more. He became a police officer for the Danish police force and a member of the Danish Underground. He wanted to do whatever he could to protect his country, and the people within.

Knud Dyby was promoted to Guardsman at the Royal Palace of Copenhagen. During this time, German troops started to round up Jews, and the word on the street was that they would be sent to concentration camps. Dyby and his fellow policemen could not let that happen. He used his position in the Guardsman and being a sailor to his advantage and retained vital pieces of information for the Underground. He knew all of the patrol routes of the Germans, and the best trade routes from Denmark to Sweden. Being such an experienced sailor, he knew all of the secret coves for fishing along the way. He and several others, including ordinary citizens, quickly came up with a plan to get all of the Danish Jews to safety in Sweden. Knud Dyby and several other fishermen took their boats and smuggled Jews inside. They traveled by the cover of night to Sweden. There, the Jews were dropped off and the fishermen bought fish to make their cover look more realistic. In just a month, they evacuated 7,200 Jews. For those who could not leave the country, the hospital in Denmark took them in secretly. On their charts, the doctor said to write that every Jew had "German Measles."

Knud Dyby himself transported 1,888 people across the sea. Not all were Jewish. Some were refugees fleeing the country because they sided with the Allies. Dyby handled five fishing skippers. People were not the only thing the boats transported. They also contained weapons, mail and money. Classified information was transported to Sweden through these boats.

After the war, the Jews came home to a pleasant surprise. All of their homes were preserved. Others were not so lucky. Most of the time they came home to find their house had been destroyed or repurposed. The citizens of Denmark really came together during the war. They though that everyone was equal, and wanted to help the Jews in any way possible.

Knud Dyby risked his freedom and his life to help others. He helped people when they needed it the most and did everything in his power to keep complete strangers safe. He thought it was amazing to see how non- Jewish neighbors spent money and time with their lives on the line to make sure the Jews had a place to call home when they came back. Knud Dyby was a hero. He denied that what he did caused him to be a hero. He thought it was his duty, along with everyone else, to protect the people of his country. He said later that he enjoyed this. He loved messing with the Germans. Even though this was scary and he could be caught and killed at any moment, he helped anyway. I think that if more people had been like him, there would be a lot more heroes in this world. Although he died in 2011, his memory lives on, and after learning about him, I want to strive to be like him, to walk in his footsteps, to be a hero, just like him.

Bibliography

"Knud Dyby* Archives - The Jewish Foundation for the Righteous." *The Jewish Foundation for the Righteous*. N.p., n.d. Web. 24 Feb. 2015.

"Knud Dyby: One of the Righteous." *Knud Dyby: One of the Righteous*. N.p., n.d. Web. 24 Feb. 2015.

"Knud Dyby, Novato Man Who Helped save Thousands of Jews during World War II, Dies at 96." *Knud Dyby, Novato Man Who Helped save Thousands of Jews during World War II, Dies at 96*. N.p., n.d. Web. 24 Feb. 2015.

"Knud Dyby: One of the Righteous." *Knud Dyby: One of the Righteous*. N.p., n.d. Web. 24 Feb. 2015.

HEROES OF THE HOLOCAUST

Sarah Schuette, Co-winner

When the Holocaust began in the year 1933, millions of people died at the hands of Adolf Hitler. Over 11 million people were brutally killed, and 3 million of these people were Jews. If you were not executed then you became a slave laborer and you labored to the brink of death. Or you were a Nazi, a loyal German, and your life and well-being was spared. Not everyone was loyal to Hitler, and not everyone believed his actions were for the good. But those people who did not agree with Hitler and decided to take action and fight for the life of the many people that were being brutalized are today considered our heroes. Two of these heroes are Paul Grueninger and Rosa Naef, who risked their own safety for the lives of those in deep peril.

Paul Grueninger was a captain of the Police of St. Gallen, Switzerland in 1938. (Tenembaum, Baruch) The Holocaust had begun only a few years before. It spread into Austria through the annexation by Nazi Germany, called the Anschluss. (Tag Archives: Paul Grueninger). To survive, Jews in Austria fled to Switzerland, seeking safety from the Nazis. As an officer, Paul was stationed at the border of Switzerland. There were hundreds of people coming to cross the border from Austria, and Paul was given orders by the Swiss government to slow the number of people crossing by turning them back unless they had entry permits. (Paul Grueninger - The Righteous Among The Nations - Yad Vashem). But Paul did not agree with the idea of prohibiting these Jews from gaining safety. So he was faced with a dilemma: he had to decide whether to obey orders by turning the Jews back home or letting them through. If Paul was caught letting the people through, he would face serious consequences. He decided to take the risk.

When the next group came, Paul created fake registrations, stamping their passports to show that they had come to Switzerland before March of 1938, which was when the borders became restricted (Paul Grueninger - The Righteous Among The Nations - Yad Vashem). Along with the false passports, Paul used his own money to buy the Jews clothes for the winter, as they had left all of their belongings behind. Over the course of a year, Paul Grueninger allowed two or three thousand Jews across the border to Switzerland (Paul Grueninger - The Righteous Among The Nations - Yad Vashem). However, in 1939 his secret was discovered by Germans who then alerted the Swiss government. Paul was immediately fired from his job and brought to court where he was found guilty. For the rest of Paul's life, he struggled in poverty, but he did not regret what he had done. He stated, "It was basically a question of saving human lives that were threatened with death" (Paul Grueninger - The Righteous Among The Nations - Yad Vashem). Paul was a hero because, even knowing the consequences, he decided to help others reach safety.

Rosa Naef was born in Switzerland and knew nothing about the Jewish people until the Holocaust began. When Jews began to be persecuted, she felt the desire to learn about their background. She saw how wrong the persecutions were, and felt determined to make a difference in helping the Jews. Naef had studied nursing earlier in her life and became the head of the Red Cross Children's Home in Seyre, France. The home housed about a hundred Jewish refugee children from Germany and Austria (Wagner, Meir, and Moshe Meisels). These refugees had been separated from their families. However, Naef noticed how unsanitary the home was, and she organized for the children to be brought to the castle of La Hille. There, she created a warm environment for the children and organized their schooling. In addition, volunteers were brought in to help take care of the new residence. But the safety of the castle did not last long.

One morning, French gendarmes, or armed police officers, came to the shelter and arrested 45 Jewish children, taking them to the Le Vernet internment camp where deportation would begin (Wagner, Meir, and Moshe Meisels). Naef quickly spoke with authorities and was able to get the children back. In the next few months, Naef made safety plans for the children so the incident could not happen again. For example, she installed hideouts in the castle's attic and asked farmers in Switzerland if they would allow some of the children to hide on their farms (Wagner, Meir, and Moshe Meisels). Also, Rosa often scheduled and organized times for some of the children to flee across the border to Switzerland on foot. So when the gendarmes raided her castle again, she was ready. Naef worked for a long time in keeping the children hidden from the horrors of the Holocaust. Without Rosa, all of those children could have been arrested or persecuted. Rosa risked her own safety for years in the hope that she could help keep the children safe for as long as possible. This is why Rosa Naef is considered a Holocaust hero.

Both Rosa Naef and Paul Grueninger are considered heroes of the Holocaust because they both risked their own lives to protect Jews from certain peril. Naef gave shelter to about a hundred Jewish children, and Paul gave protection letters to Jews who were seeking safety in Switzerland. Both heroes helped Jews escape across the border to Switzerland. Their actions were small and they asked for no reward in return. They saw the Holocaust as wrong, and fought quietly for what was right. Clearly, people do not have to be famous to be heroes. Heroes are people who try to make a difference, no matter how small. Although these heroes were only two people, they were able to help save hundreds of Jewish lives. And even with the repercussions to them of getting caught helping, they never quit and never regretted what they had done. Their actions are what give them the title of Heroes of the Holocaust.

Bibliography

"Paul Grueninger - The Righteous Among The Nations - Yad Vashem." *Paul Grueninger - The Righteous Among The Nations - Yad Vashem*. N.p., n.d. Web. 17 Feb. 2015. <http://www.yadvashem.org/yv/en/righteous/stories/grueninger.asp>.

"Tag Archives: Paul Grueninger." *Jewish Currents*. N.p., 24 Oct. 2014. Web. 17 Feb. 2015. <http://jewishcurrents.org/tag/paul-grueninger>.

Tenembaum, Baruch. "The Example of Grüninger." *Funkascript ATOM*. N.p., n.d. Web. 17 Feb. 2015. <http://www.raoulwallenberg.net/saviors/others/example-gr-uuml-ninger/>.

Wagner, Meir, and Moshe Meisels. "The Righteous of Switzerland." *Google Books*. N.p., n.d. Web. 17 Feb. 2015. <https://books.google.com/books?id=-MtaXNRtrB0C&printsec=frontcover&dq=isbn%3A0881256986&hl=en&sa=X&ei=CdHjVKelBpfqoAT4s4DADg&ved=0CB8Q6AEwAA#v=onepage&q&f=false>.

CARL LUTZ –SWITZERLAND HERO

Sha Kunj

When people think of the Holocaust, they remember bad memories of the rise of Hitler and the formation of the Nazi Army. They also remember how Germany gained lots of power and tried to take over the world, which caused World War II. However, most importantly, people remember the persecution and inhumane treatment of Jews. Around 6 million Jews died because of the Nazi regimen. Although many parts of the world remained silent to these barbaric deeds, some tenacious and resolute men and women helped as much as they could to save the Jews. One of these valiant people was Carl Lutz, a Swiss diplomat whose willpower, determination, and negotiation skills saved many Jewish lives from the hands of the Nazis.

Charles "Carl" Lutz was born in Walzenhausen, Switzerland on March 30, 1895. He studied in the United States, where he joined the Swiss Consular Corps. He started as a consular employee in St. Louis, where he met Gertrude Fankhauser. Gertrude was also working at the Swiss Consulate, and he and Gertrude got married in 1934. They returned to Switzerland shortly after. Carl Lutz spent most of his time outside his home country, as he was a diplomat, and traveled to Swiss Consulates around the world such as Philadelphia, Palestine, and Israel. He quickly advanced through the ranks and became the Vice Consul.

He is widely known for saving Jews from deportation when he was posted to Budapest, Hungary in 1942 during World War II. During that time, chaos reigned in Budapest, the Hungarian capital. The Russian Red Army was constantly bombing Budapest. Arrow Cross gangs, which were Nazi supporters in Hungary, were terrorizing the Jews. They had broken into Jewish safe houses, which were set up by the Swiss diplomats. When Carl Lutz was driving in his car and saw the Jews brutally beaten by the Arrow Cross gangs he decided that his objective would not be to secure diplomatic ties with Hungary, but to save as many Jews as he could.

During this time, the Soviet Union was bombing Budapest, while Germany had almost taken over Hungary. Due to these circumstances, many of the countries around the world had cut off their ties with Hungary. Carl Lutz had a very important role of being a diplomat for Switzerland, as well as the diplomat for the United States, Great Britain, and many other countries. In his office, he was in charge of over 6,000 personnel from different countries. He was able to negotiate efficiently with Nazi commanders for Jewish safety.

After a few years, Germany had taken over Hungary in March 1944 and was trying to implement the Final Solution into Hungary. The Final Solution was the Nazi plan to wipe out all the Jews from the country via ghettos and gas chambers. Jews were being round up and delivered to ghettos by the Nazis and the Hungarian police. Over half a million people were arrested, and 450,000 Jews were deported to extermination camps. In order to counteract this calamity, Carl Lutz worked with Palestine government and received Palestine Certificates by Michael Krausz. These certificates allowed the user to be sent to Palestine and to be protected by the government until his/her departure. These would be of unfathomable value to the Jews. To put his plan in action, Carl Lutz met with the German Ambassador, Dr. Edmund Veesenmayer, and the head officer Adolf Eichmann. Lutz was in charge of about 8,000 certificates. To save the Jews from being deported, he used his diplomatic authority and considered them "family certificates". Because of this he was able to save 8,000 families under the protection of the certificates. This would put about 50,000 Jews under the protection of the Swiss.

Soon after, disaster struck. Veesenmayer and Eichmann were still planning on deporting the Jews and implementing the Final Solution, even though they agreed for the Jews to be protected by the certificates. They decreed that the passes and certificates for the Jews were void, and would no longer be accepted. When Lutz learned about their plans, he was outraged. He immediately reached out to the other diplomats and protested vehemently against the persecution of the Jews. He negotiated with the Nazis in order to revalidate the certificates. With his determination and diplomatic authority, they accepted the certificates of protection to save 50,000 Jews. This would happen many times. After a couple months, the Nazis would again declare the certificates void. Not only did Lutz protest and negotiate with the Nazis, but he also issued more certificates to save the Jews. Members under Lutz's command helped Lutz by forging protective letters for the Jews, which Lutz signed and handed to Jews. The number of letters reached around 120,000.

Pressure was mounting, as the Soviet Union was getting closer to Hungary. The Arrow Cross gangs were totally unrestrained and were rounding up Jews left and right. Lutz would have to intervene many times and would have to use his negotiation skills and diplomatic authority in order to persuade the gangs to relinquish the Jews holding the protective letters. As Russia got even closer to Hungary, Switzerland ordered its diplomats to leave the country for their own safety. Carl Lutz refused, and said it was his duty to save the Jews. He placed the Jews into protective air raid shelters and other strong buildings to be protected from the Russian air raids. As Carl was protecting the Jews from the skies, his wife Gertrude protested day and night against the Arrow Cross gangs when they would infiltrate safe houses. Gertrude would nourish the Jews and provide food, warmth, and shelter to those in need.

Finally, their hard work paid off. The Soviet Union bombed Budapest and the other key areas of Hungary. Germany was defeated and relinquished its hold on Hungary, and the Arrow Cross gangs disappeared. Budapest was liberated on January 18, 1945. More than 4,500 survivors were saved from the safe houses, and over 17,000 Jews were saved from the shelters created by Lutz and his helpers. Around 250,000 Jews that were crowded in ghettos were saved because of their protected status. This was all thanks to Carl Lutz and his relentless diplomatic efforts.

Carl Lutz was a heroic savior of the Jews whose willpower, negotiation skills, and determination saved the persecuted Jews from the barbaric deeds of the Germans. He influenced many other heroes such as Raoul Wallenberg, Peter Zurcher, and Friedrich Born to help free the Jews. His diplomatic authority and unflagging efforts inspired the other diplomats to take action. Without him, over 700,000 Jews would have died, compared to the 400,000. The world recognized Carl Lutz for his valiant deeds. He received numerous awards, and was nominated three times for the Nobel

Peace Prize. Yad Vashem proudly presented him with the Medal of Honor, Righteous Among the Nations. Carl Lutz was a great man who followed his heart and had the courage to do what was right even in difficult situations.

HEROES OF THE HOLOCAUST: CARL LUTZ AND SIGURD LARSEN

Soham Kondle

I picked Sigurd Larsen and Carl Lutz for my heroes of the Holocaust. Sigurd Larsen and Carl Lutz are both inspirational figures in the Holocaust because they saved so many Jewish people from death and agony. Take Carl Lutz for example, he saved 10,000 Jewish lives and helped them immigrate to Palestine. In the following paragraphs, I will discuss how both of these heroes had such an influence on the Jewish world and other communities.

Carl Lutz was a Swiss Vice Consul who had arrived in Budapest in early 1942. He was the Chief of the Swiss Legation Department of Foreign Interest, and was in charge of the interests of 14 whole nations. These nations included the United States and the United Kingdom. Germans conquered Hungary on the date of 19 March, 1944. In turn, this became the worse for Jews because they were starting to get persecuted more and more. Many people came to Mr. Lutz's office for protection. Lutz felt he had an obligation towards these people, and at that moment he decided to start helping them. So he did help, just at that time he had already helped 10,000 people and children by immigrating them to Palestine.

However, another problem occurred and it was even worse. On the 15th of May of 1944, the deportations to the dreaded Auschwitz camp had begun. Now more than ever, with people dying and suffering with so much built up agony and hatred towards the Nazis, Lutz felt he needed to help. He took immediate initiative by taking command and placing the staff of the Jewish council for Palestine under his diplomatic protection. Already, before the worst reached its pinnacle, this man was helping so may. He was a true and real hero.

After taking command of the staff, he decided to give it an upgrade and remodeling job. For starters, he changed the name to "Department of Immigration of the Swiss Legation." Lutz probably thought bigger equals better so better probably equals bigger, so he said he knew to create a larger and better super staff. From 15 people, Carl Lutz was able to increase his super task force to 150 people. Carl also took the great opportunity to see that Hitler's Pro-consul or the Sztojay government hadn't said or declared any threats against immigrating the Jews to Palestine. So, Lutz kept it going with the Hungarian and German authorities.

Now, Lutz had a more specific good intention. He wanted to save and preserve every single Jewish person possible. How had his motive changed? We don't know, but it was the right thing to do. Lutz had a way with disagreeing with the Hungarian government. For example, when they wanted to stuff all the Jewish people into one ghetto, Lutz firmly disagreed and placed them in 76 protected houses. This is 30,000 human beings we are talking about here, and that is a lot. In 1941, before Auschwitz and these terrible things happened there was about 742,800 Jews in Hungary. Budapest war came along, and only 124,000 people survived. Even worse, in the dates 15th of May to about the 9th of July, 437,402 people died. BAM! Then they're gone. 437,402 people died just from Auschwitz alone! What matters is that Carl Lutz, a very brave man, saved 62,000 Jews. 62,000 Jews probably doesn't sound like very many people to you compared to 437,402, but it is a lot. 437,402 dead for a massive genocide group, but 1 man saved 62,000 people. Remember Lutz's possible theory that better is directly proportional to bigger, well why did no one reprimand the Nazis for their massive genocides if better equals bigger? It's because bigger might equal better, but better equals morally right. Carl Lutz was a true hero because he did for a different maybe less great motive initially, but even with that thought he came up with a purer and cleaner intention and followed that instead.

Sigurd Larsen was another hero of the Holocaust even though he participated as a German soldier in World War I. He grew up in Berlin, and he was the son of a Danish man and a German woman. He happened to save 3 people because of it. For example, he was injured in the war and could not enlist in the army for the Germans anymore because someone of German nationality in his family had requested it. He then took up the wood trade business. This wood trade business was a way for Sigurd to communicate and help others to immigrate and escape. One of them Sigurd had met when the Jew got persecuted. This Jew's name was Joachim Marcuse, who was in his mid-thirties and was just persecuted because he was a Jew. Sigurd had immigrated people before, and Joachim had heard this through the wood trade. Joachim also wanted to get to be immigrated. Larsen thoroughly reviewed the plan and committed himself to it and he helped Joachim, Joachim's wife Gerda, and Joachim's friends Kurt Levin get away with escaping. They chose to escape to Sweden. The three hid away in a wood freight. Then, Larsen organized a wood exportation to Sweden. On December 24, 1942 Sigurd made sure to enclose the wagon for the safety of the passengers. When the escapees arrived in Sweden, they were recognized as political refugees. Larsen did not want to get caught for helping them illegally so he ran away to Copenhagen to live with his family in peace.

All in all, these men were true heroes because knowing the consequences, they willingly did it. They saw the wrong in Adolf Hitler's ways and tried to save many people. As a result, they succeeded, and helped many people build a new life. It was people like these who made the world a more humane place. If it wasn't for these types of people, the world would be in worse economic and political shape than it is in now. Nowadays, people that have a sincere motivation to help people are scarce. Now, the world is a very materialistic place and people have adapted to that. People who have these characteristics are very unaware of their surroundings. Hence, they make no move to fix it. These heroes can be found everywhere in the world, and they need to take a stand and actually help the new generation, so that the next generation will be better. The heroes that we have now need to actually help, like the Heroes of the Holocaust did. If these heroes, take a stand now every generation after will be better. I say this because at this time and era there is no Hitler-like influence to scare away these heroes to help in the public.

Works Cited

"Carl Lutz." *Funkascript ATOM*. Web. 7 Feb. 2015.
< http://www.raoulwallenberg.net/saviors/diplomats/list/carl-lutz/ >.

"Sigurd Larsen." *Funkascript ATOM*. Web. 7 Feb. 2015.
< http://www.raoulwallenberg.net/saviors/german2/sigurd-larsen-148/ >.

HOLOCAUST ESSAY: DAGMAR LUSTRUP

Taylore Givens, Special award

"For evil to flourish, it only requires good men to do nothing" Simon Wiesenthal. Dagmar Lustrup, a girl forced to grow up too fast, put through the clutches of the Nazis as she grew into a woman. Yet her initiatives and beliefs stood steadfast against the Nazi oppression. From Thisted, Denmark, Dagmar rescued twenty Jewish teenagers from the invading Germans and lived to tell the tale. Her good heart was her guide. Although she was not of the Jewish faith, she made the resolve to help these teenagers she knew and loved survive this catastrophe. Dagmar saved the lives of many through her bravery; and has been acknowledged and recognized for her honest and heroic actions.

During Lustrup's early years before her act of heroism, she was a mere ordinary Joe as you and I. Dagmar was born in Kalundborg, Denmark. Here she met and married her husband Jesper Lustrup, editor of the local newspaper. Later she and her husband moved to Thisted, Denmark, where her husband took up another local newspaper editing job. As her husband worked, she became an active member of the Women's Peace Organization of her area of Thisted, Denmark. By 1939 this organization alone had saved the lives of 300 Jewish orphans by sending them to safe agricultural farming foster homes where they could learn farming skills. This way the organization could later send these Jewish orphan children to their full liberation, to

184

travel and live as farmers in their religious Jewish haven of Palestine. Dagmar grew to become quite an active person who would formulate her own thoughts and opinions rather than rely on those of others. An honest, committed, caring, and resilient embodiment of hope among the darkness; the perfect description of our unlikely civilian hero. For she never had sought fame, she simply knew what was right, and wasn't afraid to do what was right. Because of that, I along with many others are so thankful for her contributions and initiative to step up when everyone else had stepped down. As she stated "I do not regard myself as a hero," she said in an interview for her town newspaper, on May 7, 1987; many years after her act of heroism and Hitler's defeat. "We did not know then what we did. The only thing we knew was that we should not fail." Her resilience and qualities of a modern hero that she established in her early life contributed to her future act to save several Jewish children; as Hitler and his Nazis embarked on a journey to take over the world, while leaving a trail of lives lost and families ruined known as the Holocaust.

While participating in the Women's Peace League, Dagmar became a foster home facilitator for twenty children in her area. She safeguarded and transported twenty Jewish foster children from Czechoslovakia to several farming homes. The Women's Peace League aimed for these foster children to learn farming skills, and then later they could be sent to Palestine to make a farming life out of themselves. It started off peacefully as Dagmar acted as the facilitator for her divison, of her Women's Peace League. She matched up many children with families nearby, and helped those children stay in touch by organizing weekly social gatherings for them to meet and enjoy themselves. However the foster program being facilitated by Dagmar, and many others by the Women's Peace League divisions, took a fateful turn. On April 9, 1940, the Germans had occupied Denmark, and ordered to have all the Jewish children taken from foster care. As Dagmar heard this, she realized her operation was in grave danger, especially since most of the families were not going to willingly hand over their foster children for a death sentence to the Nazis. Luckily the Nazis had no record of who was keeping foster children, so they were able to wait out the Nazis for a couple more months to devise a plan to get the children to Palestine safely. "In November 1940, word came that all Jews were to be expelled from the north Jutland area, where the group was located, because it was a strategic area for the Germans. The message came saying that they had to leave at once." The foster children, their host families, and Dagmar Lustrup were given twenty four hours to get these children out of the country or hidden well enough so they would not be forcefully sought out, taken, and killed by the Nazis. During those twenty four hours, Dagmar Lustrup transferred all the children to a safe house inn in central Denmark, where they were safe temporarily for the next two weeks. Finally on December 5, 1940 she had been able to give each of the children immigration certificates in order to safely travel out of the country. After the agricultural mentoring and apprenticeship they had completed earlier with their foster families, they sailed to Sweden, and by the Soviet Union made it to Palestine, where they were ready to build their new lives. Lustrup returned to her own home and survived the ruling of the Nazis until Hiitler's reign was finally put to a cataclysmic end. She continued to stay in touch with the twenty children she once knew, as they now have become adults. They continue to shroud Mrs. Lustrup with thanks for her efforts to save their lives, and her importance to defeating the Holocaust, even though that wasn't entirely her intent. It was simply the intent of a lady who knew what must be done and wasn't afraid to get it done. Her model of strong feminine power and resilience against a high evil are are examples of the characteristics to a modern hero which still apply as she changed and contributed a gift to the world. As the fruits of her gifts of the lives of those twenty children continue to reap and have a positive ripple effect upon mankind.

Works Cited

Christensen, Uffe. "Dansk Børne-frelser: Jeg Er Ingen Helt." - *Historie*. Jyllands-Posten, 2 Feb. 2011. Web. 4 Feb. 2015.

"The Righteous Among the Nations: Rescue Story." *Yad Vasheem*. Yad Vashem The Holocaust Martyrs' and Heroes' Remembrance Authority, 1 Jan. 2015. Web. 3 Feb. 2015.

FRED REYMOND'S HOLOCAUST EXPERIENCE

Timur Bekdjanov

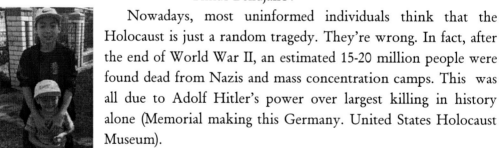

Nowadays, most uninformed individuals think that the Holocaust is just a random tragedy. They're wrong. In fact, after the end of World War II, an estimated 15-20 million people were found dead from Nazis and mass concentration camps. This was all due to Adolf Hitler's power over largest killing in history alone (Memorial making this Germany. United States Holocaust Museum).

In 1933, Adolf Hitler became the new chancellor of Germany. The same year, the first Nazi concentration camp, named Dachau, was created in present-day Bavaria. Up until the war, Dachau housed political prisoners such as communists; however once the war broke out, Dachau turned into a killing machine executing thousands of Jews, as well as some other groups of people that Hitler thought of as "unfit" for his country. These people included artists, the disabled, homosexuals, and even the sick. Prisoners died of disease, execution, exhaustion, or starvation (History). A few concentration camps, including Dachau, were liberated after the war ended. However, there were other camps that were liquidated, such as Plaszow, and everyone in these camps died (Jewish Virtual Library). According to the New York Times, there were over 40,000 camps throughout Germany just like

186

Dachau, including "30,000 slave labor camps; 1,150 Jewish ghettos; 980 concentration camps; 1,000 prisoner-of-war camps; 500 brothels filled with sex slaves; and thousands of other camps used for euthanizing the elderly and infirm, performing forced abortions, "Germanizing" prisoners or transporting victims to killing centers." This by far topped any other genocide's size, as nobody has ever had so many prisons/death camps mainly for one group of people until Adolf Hitler.

Nazi concentration camps forced people to go through torturous events such as forced labor for many continuous hours and many brutal and inhumane execution methods (Projet Aladin). The most popular methods for execution were gas chambers and death marches. For gas chambers, prisoners were put into and locked up in a dark room, where deadly gases blasted into the room until everyone died. Death marches, on the other hand, happened outside. Prisoners would be forced to march outside for hours and even days without food (Projet Aladin). Although the majority of prisoners during the war were Jews, homosexuals had the highest fatality rate because they were beaten and humiliated by the German Nazi guards (History Learning Site). Frederic Reymond (1907-1999), along with hundreds of others, helped lower these death counts by the thousands.

Although Frederic Reymond didn't live on German territory, he still helped Jewish prisoners of various concentration camps, specifically out of France, escape. Reymond, having a profession of a watchmaker, lived in Vallée de Joux, also known as present-day Vaud, Switzerland. Since Vaud is on the border between France and Switzerland, Reymond knew the region extremely well. He served in the army in 1939, and by 1940, he crossed the French/Swiss border many times and eventually became involved in many rescue missions saving concentration camp prisoners (Yad Vashem), as well as French resistance fighters (PHDN). He usually crossed the forest of Risoux before passing the Swiss border into Switzerland itself, as there was a smaller risk of running into problems (PHDN).

By carrying out these rescue missions from 1940 to 1945 (PHDN), Reymond saved many Jews' lives that would have otherwise been tragically lost in this horrific event. These Jewish prisoners lived in extremely unsanitary conditions, where they would be living a very horrific, terrifying, and inhumane life. They would be forced to work "to the death"after 1941, as a new Nazi regime's Jewish policy was taken into action, working at over 12 hours per day performing difficult and non-normal tasks, including building buildings with a very small amount of tools at hand, and even just carrying bricks from one side of a road to another as punishment (Projet Aladin). By rescuing these people, Reymond essentially saved them from pain, suffering, loss of loved ones, and humiliation yet provided them the chance for family reunification, the start of a new life, and happiness, as well as providing the world with many Holocaust survivors, witnesses, and primary source accounts of ghastly experiences of the Holocaust. In addition, since Reymond rescued so many Jewish prisoners, he remained in hiding during the war so he won't be persecuted by the German government for sneaking Jews out of their death camps (Yad Vashem). However, after the war ended, the Swiss government brought him before court for the forgery of papers, but he was found innocent, as stated on PHDN's website. Even though he smuggled Jewish prisoners out of France, Reymond never forged papers for them; he only got them across the border.

Frederic Reymond, along with hundreds of other rescuers, rescued close to 30 thousand Jewish prisoners out of German-conquered territory throughout the war (United States Holocaust Museum). Their courage and risks they were willing to take to rescue these prisoners is amazing. These rescuers looked passed the risk of being prosecuted for rescuing prisoners, especially during the greatest war of history, allowing them to fulfill such astonishing acts of courage, kindness, earning them an enormous amount of respect from people all over the world. Although he was only one person, Fred Reymond did whatever it took to rescue many Holocaust survivors from Nazi concentration camps from 1940 until the end of World War II, changing hundreds of lives.

Works Cited

"Concentration camps in Nazi Germany." History†Learning†Site Æ†Web. 6 Feb. 2015.

"Concentration Camps: List of Major Camps." Jewish†Virtual†Library Æ†Web. 5 Feb. 2015.

"Dachau." History Æ†Web. 3 Feb. 2015.

Eric Lichtblau. "The Holocaust Just Got More Shocking." New†York†Times Æ†2013. Web. 5 Feb. 2015.

"Nazi Camps." United†States†Holocaust†Memorial†Museum Æ†2014. Web. 5 Feb. 2015.

"The Aftermath of the Holocaust." United†States†Holocaust†Memorial†Museum Æ†Web. 5 Feb. 2015

."The Concentration Camps, 1933-1945."

Projet†Aladin Æ†Web. 6 Feb. 2015.

"Reymond FAMILY." YadVashem Æ†Web. 5 Feb. 2015.

"The "Righteous among the Nations" of Swiss nationality." PHDN Æ†Web. 6 Feb. 2015.

SWISS SAVIORS: FRIEDEL BOHNY-REITER AND FRIEDRICH BORN

Toby Keys

Humanity's largest genocide, known today as the Holocaust, began when a fascist German party known as the Nazis invaded and occupied much of Europe; during their occupation, they took the lives of over 11 million people, and ruined the lives of countless others. They preyed on minority groups—especially the Jewish—and held power from 1933 to May 8, 1945. The period in which the Holocaust's reign of terror took precedence in the lives of millions is largely viewed as a hopeless, horrific era of despair; however, hope was instilled in the lives of those fortunate enough to have been rescued by the *Righteous Among the Nations*, a spattering of non-Jewish heroes who had the courage to help countless men, women, and children stare death in the face. Friedel Bohny-Reiter, an ordinary citizen yet hero of countless children, and Friedrich Born, a hero of the oppressed in Budapest, Hungary, were two brave souls who risked their lives in the name of righteousness.

One of the most Righteous of them all, Friedel Bohny-Reiter was born in 1912 in Vienna, Austria. In 1941, Bohny-Reiter joined an organization that cared for children in times of war known as Schweiser Kinderhilfe (Swiss Aid to Children), which was operated by the Swiss Red Cross. This organization had been originally founded in the Spanish Civil War, but became of great use in helping many survive the Holocaust. Friedel was sent by the Swiss Aid to Children to an internment camp in the middle of unoccupied France, called Rivesaltes. She had received much training in the field of pediatric nursing in Zurich, Switzerland, before being sent on this mission. When she arrived at the camp, she began administering Jewish, Gypsy, and Spanish children medical support and food. She also provided care for Spanish refugees imprisoned at the camp. The work she did was difficult, and her life would have been jeopardized had she been discovered. She wrote "These children's eyes are the reason I stay here" in her diary, recently published in 1993. Her absolute dedication to her children is a profound sign of her righteousness; her determination to help them survive and thrive illustrates the power of love, and its ability to prevail, no matter what the circumstance.

However, Bohny-Reiter's mission was far from over. She and her organization soon realized the situation in the camp was going downhill, and once the deportation of Jews began in 1942, they knew the children had to leave the camp. Reiter was then able to start smuggling the children from Rivesaltes. She searched for places in France to send her child refugees, and eventually came across the L'Abric children's home. The head of the shelter, August Bohny, had recently an old castle known as Chateau de Montluel into another shelter for the freed when Reiter brought a group of children to him for the first time; they placed the children in the newly renovated castle, and later married each other. Friedel started sending children from camps to August and his places of refuge, which included a second house (the Faidoli) constructed due to the increasing number of smuggled prisoners. August and Friedel also provided opportunities for those they freed; they set up an agricultural training school and a furniture-making shop, and they would send refugees to these places to work. The two of them were sent to one final refugee house by Shwieser Kinderkilfe in 1943, where they continued to reside and care for orphans until the close of 1944.

Friedel Bohny-Reiter, along with her husband's assistance, saved countless children from the unspeakable horrors of the internment and death camps of the

Holocaust. The dangers the two of them faced were incredibly high, yet it seems that they didn't even hesitate to join the cause. Their selflessness and bravery were all that their children, their refugees, could rely on in those bleak, hopeless times, and to this day stand out as a beacon of the good that a couple ordinary citizens can do to face the iniquitous acts of an enemy much greater than themselves.

Friedel and her husband weren't the only ones working for the Red Cross. One man particularly stands out as a hero of the persecuted during the Holocaust. Friedrich Born was the Chief Delegate of the International Committee of the Red Cross of Switzerland in Budapest, Hungary, from 1944 to 1945. On behalf of the Red Cross, Born issued multitudes of letters that saved thousands of Jews from death marches, as well as concentration camps, in the area of Budapest. He was able to provide approximately 4,000 Jews with employment papers, which exempted them from deportation. He was also able to provide protection for 60 Jewish shelters, which housed over 7,000 Jewish children and orphans. Born was recognized by Yad Vashem as a Righteous Among the Nations 24 years after his death. Although he wasn't directly risking his life right outside internment camps, his work was anything but unimportant; he saved thousands of lives through the power of pen and paper.

The Holocaust took the lives of 11 million people, and ruined the lives of many others. Yet, the number of casualties due to this massive genocide could have been much higher had it not been for ordinary (yet brave) citizens, such as the Bohny-Reiters, and national heroes like Friedrich Born. These Righteous souls, these saviors, should always serve as a reminder of the good that we can do in the face of evil.

HERO OR INVADER?

Victoria Sullivan

During the Holocaust, Gerda Valentiner kept the Jewish children of those around her inside her home to protect them. She would collect the children from their parents and keep them in her home, well taken care of, until she could transfer them. The question is whether she was a hero in doing this, or an invader? On one side she saved the children's lives, but on the other, she took the children away from their families, and separated them. Leaving them to wonder what had happened to each other. Was she invading the family? Or was she helping them by separating them?

You could say that Gerda was doing badly towards the families whom she separated from their children by showing what bad things the family was feeling from the separation. Some of the children she saved could have wanted to stay with their parents, and some of them may have even felt suicidal in some ways afterwards. They could have felt this way in conclusion to blaming themselves for not staying

190

with their parents, if something had happened to them. What she may have actually killed some of those children by saving them? These examples support the reason why she could be seen as an invader to some people.

These are good examples of Gerda Valentiner being an "invader," but there are much more sufficient reasons of her being a hero. The entire process put her life in danger. She kept the children safe in her home, until she was able to transfer them to Sweden, where they would be safer. She kept them fed, and eventually saved their lives. She did the children, and their families a huge favor by keeping them alive. She knew what the risk was if she were to be caught, but she went ahead and continued to save the lives of these children. That is the definition of a hero. A hero basically saves the lives of others, even though they are putting their own in danger. And Gerda Valentiner was a hero, no questions asked. In no way was she an "invader" (or in other words a villain).

Gerda Valentiner was one of the many teachers who attempted to save the Jewish children of Denmark during the Holocaust. She went through many methods to save the children, putting her life at risk and the lives of those who helped her or knew about it. Gerda Valentiner had to keep children in her home, transfer them to Sweden, and keep this all a secret. Valentiner chose to protect, not only herself, but the children of those around her. She protected the children, over herself. This is what made her a hero, and these were the methods she took to make herself one.

Valentiner kept many children safe through the Holocaust, putting her own life in danger. She made sure to keep the children healthy by bringing them food. As mentioned, she would transfer the children when the time was right. She put her life at risk to save the children.

Gerda had to transfer the children discretely. She needed to make sure that nobody would catch her, and she had to be extremely careful in doing so. Gerda Valentiner went to extreme precautions to make sure that the children of others were safe. She was a true hero to the children whom she saved, and the families. One man, Moritz Scheftelowitz, shared his story of when Gerda saved him and his sisters. According to The Righteous Among the Nations, Gerda had appeared to them a few days before the events, warning his parents of the danger that was to come. A few days later, he and his two sisters moved to her home until she managed to arrange their transfer to Sweden. It took three attempts to get the children out of the country. They had finally succeeded on the third attempt by leaving by a fishing boat, and arriving after one long night. They met their parents in Sweden, whom had arrived ten days before them. In this particular example, Gerda managed to help the entire family to transfer to Sweden, reunite the family there, and save herself.

Throughout all of this activity, Gerda never really thought to save herself. She mostly just thought to save the children. This shows how unselfish Gerda was. Rather than fleeing the place as soon as she knew what was going to happen, she took the time to warn other families. Most people would flee the first chance they got, without thinking twice. This was just another way she was a hero.

"I only did what many Danes did, nothing special. We thought it perfectly natural to help people in mortal trouble." This is what Gerda modestly said after her brave rescue. Heroes tend to act like what they do, or did, isn't a big deal or don't take credit for what they had done. Gerda is one of these people who need to break out of that habit. What Gerda did was a big deal, and it had a huge impact on the lives of many families. Gerda Valentiner was in no way an "invader," but she was definitely a hero.

"I ONLY DID WHAT MANY DANES DID"

Vaishnavi Mullapudi

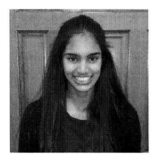

French novelist Romain Rolland wrote the inspiring quote "*A hero is a man who does what he can.*" Real heroes don't fly. Real heroes cannot lift weights that are ten times their body weight. Real heroes cannot cling on to buildings with nothing but a spider web. Real heroes are not easy to find. Heroism, by definition is greatest bravery, and flying and strength have nothing to do with bravery.

Paul Grueninger was an important but unacknowledged hero of the dreadful and awful Holocaust. The Holocaust was a major genocide during the 1940s in which over 11 million people were murdered. About 6 million of those victims were Jewish, and the other five million were mainly Gypsies (the Romani people), Poles (people from Poland), communists (people who follow communism, an economic system without social classes), homosexuals (people who find liking in the same gender), Soviet POWs (Soviet prisoners of war), and people who were either mentally or physically disabled. Out of the 11 million people who were murdered, around 1 million of them were Jewish children. At that time, there were over 9million Jews that lived in European countries, and only 3 million Jews survived the Holocaust. Only one-third of the Jews survived! Technically, the Holocaust began when Adolf Hitler was chosen as the leader of the Nazi political party in Germany. The Nazis firmly believed that the Jews were the cause of the destruction of the Germany army and German's loss of World War I.

The first step of the Holocaust was to attempt to get rid of all the Jews from the "civil society." Next, in 1933, many concentration camps were formed in order to hold Jews hostage, and places called ghettos (places meant to segregate and torture Jews) were established in 1939. In these ghettos and concentration camps, there were gas chambers that innocent Jews were put into, to be "gassed" to death. The gas contained something that would kill people after they were exposed to it. Before being put into the gas chambers, Jews were told that they were being taken to a safe place, and they had to endure an extremely dangerous and uncomfortable journey. Only if they survived this journey were they to taken to the gas chambers and very few people survived those chambers.

The number of deaths would have been much higher if it weren't for the selfless souls that we call heroes. One unknown hero and survivor of the Holocaust was a man named Paul Grueninger from Switzerland. He was born on October 27, 1891, and died on February 22, 1972, at the old age of 80. What he did in his lifetime should be considered as one of the most selfless acts in history. Paul Grueninger was a Swiss border police commander of the St. Gallen region that borders with Austria. He was also a football player, and now he is considered to be a "Righteous among the Nations," a title given to honor the non-Jewish people in the Holocaust that risked their lives in order to help the Jewish keep theirs. Paul Grueninger saved many Jews' lives by changing their visas and other documents to make it seem as if they had come to Switzerland during a time in which it was legal for Jews to enter Switzerland. Entry into Switzerland was permitted before March of 1938, so Paul Grueninger changed the visas and other documents to show that these Jews arrived in Switzerland before March 1938. By doing this, Paul Grueninger saved over 3,600 Jewish refugees. But because Paul Grueninger tried to save Jewish lives, he was fired from being a police officer, and was convicted of "official misconduct." Also, on top of that, Paul Grueninger was fined 300 Swiss francs which equals to about 324 US dollars. Paul Grueninger did not get any pension, or investment fund given to working people for retirement, and died a poor, but amazing man.

Twenty-five years after his death, Paul Grueninger was cleared of all charges and his descendants received compensation from the government of the Canton of St. Gallen. The Yad Vashem Israeli Holocaust memorial honors him as one of the *Righteous among the Nations*. Yad Vashem is a Holocaust remembrance society named after the beautiful memorial for the victims of the Holocaust in Israel.

After the taking over of Austria, all the way to Germany, Switzerland decided to close its border, and not let anyone without "proper entry permits" enter. The treatment of Jews in Austria started to become horrible, so there was a large number of Jews trying to illegally enter Switzerland. Paul Grueninger was about 47 years old during that time, and he began to face a dilemma. Should he make the Jews go back to where they came from, or should he help them escape to freedom? Grueninger chose the more humane option, and began to help the Jewish.

Paul Grueninger was a great man, whose good deeds were unheard of, and instead of being rewarded, he was put on trial for illegally allowing 3,600 Jews to enter Switzerland after March of 1938. But luckily, two years before his death, the Swiss government sent Paul Grueninger a letter with an apology, as a result of media protest. The Swiss government neither reopened his case nor sent him pension.

Finally, in 1995, the federal government of Switzerland declared Paul Grueninger's conviction invalid. "In 1971, a year before his death, Yad Vashem bestowed the title of Righteous among the Nations on Paul Grueninger."

Paul Grueninger touched my heart as soon as I realized that a well-respected man with a well-paying career left all of his luxuries to help the innocent men, women, and children who had done nothing but be born outside of Germany and who had worshipped gods separate than those worshipped by Adolf Hitler.

Works Cited

"The Holocaust." *Wikipedia*. Wikimedia Foundation, n.d. Web. 04 Feb. 2015.

"Paul Grüninger." *Wikipedia*. Wikimedia Foundation, n.d. Web. 09 Feb. 2015.

"Paul Grueninger - The Righteous Among The Nations - Yad Vashem." *Paul Grueninger - The Righteous Among The Nations - Yad Vashem*. N.p., n.d. Web. 09 Feb. 2015.

PAUL GRÜNINGER

Vikram Vadarevu, Co-runners-up

In 1933, Adolf Hitler rose to power. As Chancellor of Germany under the Nazi party Hitler was to become one of the most feared people of all time, as a consequence of his actions the Jewish genocide, known as the holocaust, and by extension World War II emerged. During this stint in history the Nazi regime took a toll on the whole of the world demographic, millions of Jews and non-Jews perished at the hands of the Nazi's beliefs During these troubling times millions died... and thousands of more would have subsided to the hands of death if not for the actions of brave men and women across Europe who endangered themselves for the sake of others. Now these humanitarians are recognized as Righteous' among the nations by Yad Vashem, among this group of resides Paul Grüninger.

Paul Grüninger was born in St. Gallen, Switzerland (Northeast bordering Austria, Vienna, and Germany) in the year of 1891, where he went on to be educated in the city of Roschach. During the World War I he served his country as a lieutenant, later joining the Police Corp in his native canton (state) earning the rank of Captain in 1925. He was also president of the Switzerland Policemen Association.

In 1938 Germany began to annex Austria, this put the Austria-Jews at risk and they began to flee. Because Switzerland had declared neutrality Grüninger received federal orders to turn back all Jewish refugees seeking asylum in Switzerland. With the sovereign country of Switzerland closing all emigration channels from Austrian-Jews, the Jewish population was regarded as illegal immigrants. All Jews were intercepted and brought to Grüninger haggard, gaunt, and deprived of comfort. This

194

presented Grüninger with a very tough decision, whether to allow the Jews to pass *illegally* or condemn them to country where the Germans have annexed anti-Semitism among the Austrian population. Grüninger decided to fallow the ethical decision he allowed the Jewish population enter Switzerland.

Paul Grüninger allowed over 3,600 Austrian-Jews to enter the country; he not only allowed them asylum but he falsified their passports to show that they entered before March of 1938 when entering the country was legal for the Jewish population. By fabricating the dates of their registration documents he allowed the Austrian-Jewish population to be treated legally within the country. He arranged for them to be sent to Diepoldsau camp, in which Jewish aid organizations helped them. Even more than allowing them into the country he expended his own money on those who needed clothes during the harsh winter months.

By doing this he allowed for these Austrian-Jewish people to have a chance at peaceful life and for them and them alone to dictate their future and what it holds to them. Though his actions were morally just he completely disregarded and infringed his federal orders and the state policy leading him to put his career and freedom on the line. This is what illustrates the enormity of his actions; he put his own person at risk for the benefit of others and so that they may live a longer more prosperous life while he suffer the consequences.

And such was the case Grüninger was to expect, he knew that eventually his actions would be found and he would have to pay for his misdemeanors to the country. He was aware of the situation for a family friend, a resident in Austria, had warned him that the Gestapo had placed him on the black list, and that he, Paul Grüninger, had been made an enemy to the regime looking for world domination. Though Paul Grüninger paid no mind to the warning, he always knew that one day, he would be caught, and so it was.

On April 3, 1939 Grüninger arrived at his office, he arrived to find that he, the chief of the station, was blocked out from the office. At once he recognized that his actions had been recognized by the Gestapo and Switzerland officials in Bern had been notified. He was notified that he had been dismissed and that his employment was terminated. His compensation and pension was withheld from him as additional punishment. He was brought to trial in 1939 under the alleged charges of allowing 3,600 Jews in the country under falsified documents as well as individual assistance in shielding, harboring, and assisting Jews. Over the course of two years his trial stretched out until in March 1941 Paul Grüninger was found guilty of breach of duty and had his benefits taken, retirement lost, and was left with a heavy fine. Paul Grüninger was ostracized and forgotten.

Though he was never given formal recognition for his heroic actions but rather given a criminal record and lack of pension Paul Grüninger never doubted his motives. In 1954 he released a statement regarding his actions, "It was basically a question of saving human lives threatened with death. How could I then seriously consider bureaucratic schemes and calculations?" This shows that he felt what he did was the ideal response to his predicament and how government oppression was ostracizing moral beliefs and humanitarian actions.

Paul Grüninger received a makeshift letter of apology from the Swiss government in 1970 as a result of the media but his pension was never reinstated and trial never appealed. On February 22, 1972 at the age of 81 Paul Grüninger, a Righteous Among the Nations, died. And it was only after his death that rehabilitation of his name commenced. The first attempt was vetoed by the Swiss Council and it was only until 1995 that the court annulled their original decision regarding Grüninger, and he was acquitted. Paul Grüninger received the Medal of Honor from Yad Vashem Institute as well as having two documentaries made about him and one book. Other honors include his Soccer club renamed itself in his honor as well as having multiple streets and schools adored with his namesake.

Overall, Paul Grüninger allowed 3,600 Austrian-Jews into Swiss territory by falsifying their documents and arranging for them to be safe. Because of his actions these people where able to pave their future themselves and they and only they had the power to dictate where they were to go. Grüninger risked his career and his life on the basis of these Jews and for that he deserves his place as a Righteous Among the Nations.

Works Cited

"Paul Grueninger - The Righteous Among The Nations - Yad Vashem." *Paul Grueninger - The Righteous Among The Nations - Yad Vashem.* Yad Vashem Institue. Web. 10 Feb. 2015

"Paul Grueninger Stiftung _Wer War Paul Grüninger?" *Paul Grueninger Stiftung _Wer War Paul Grüninger?* Web. 10 Feb. 2015

"The Example of Grüninger." *Funkascript ATOM.* Web. 10 Feb. 2015.

"HOLOCAUST MEMORIAL DAY TRUST."

Victoria Sullivan

During the Holocaust, Gerda Valentiner kept the Jewish children of those around her inside her home to protect them. She would collect the children from their parents and keep them in her home, well taken care of, until she could transfer them. The question is whether she was a hero in doing this, or an invader? On one side she saved the children's lives, but on the other, she took the children away from their families, and separated them. Leaving them to wonder what had happened to each other. Was she invading the family? Or was she helping them by separating them?

You could say that Gerda was doing bad towards the families whom she separated from their children by showing what bad things the family was feeling from the separation. Some of the children she saved could have wanted to stay with their parents, and some of them may have even felt suicidal in some ways afterwards. They could have felt this way in conclusion to blaming themselves for not staying with their parents, if something had happened to them. What she may have actually killed some of those children by saving them? These examples support the reason why she could be seen as an invader to some people.

These are good examples of Gerda Valentiner being an "invader," but there are much more sufficient reasons of her being a hero. The entire process put her life in danger. She kept the children safe in her home, until she was able to transfer them to Sweden, where they would be safer. She kept them fed, and eventually saved their lives. She did the children, and their families a huge favor by keeping them alive. She knew what the risk was if she were to be caught, but she went ahead and continued to save the lives of these children. That is the definition of a hero. A hero basically saves the lives of others, even though they are putting their own in danger. And Gerda Valentiner was a hero, no questions asked. In no way was she an "invader" (or in other words a villain).

Gerda Valentiner was one of the many teachers who attempted to save the Jewish children of Denmark during the holocaust. She went through many methods to save the children, putting her life at risk and the lives of those who helped her or knew about it. Gerda Valentiner had to keep children in her home, transfer them to Sweden, and keep this all a secret. Valentiner chose to protect, not only herself, but the children of those around her. She protected the children, over herself. This is what made her a hero, and these were the methods she took to make herself one.

Valentiner kept many children safe through the holocaust, putting her own life in danger. She made sure to keep the children healthy by bringing them food. As mentioned, she would transfer the children when the time was right. She put her life at risk to save the children.

Gerda had to transfer the children discretely. She needed to make sure that nobody would catch her, and she had to be extremely careful in doing so. Gerda Valentiner went to extreme precautions to make sure that the children of others were safe. She was a true hero to the children whom she saved, and the families. One man, Moritz Schefteolowitz, shared his story of when Gerda saved him and his sisters. According to *The Righteous Among the Nations*, Gerda had appeared to them a few days before the events, warning his parents of the danger that was to come. A few days later, he and his two sisters moved her home, until she managed to arrange their transfer to Sweden. It took three attempts to get the children out of the country.

They had finally succeeded on the third attempt by leaving by a fishing boat, and arriving after one long night. They met their parents in Sweden, whom had arrived ten days before them. In this particular example, Gerda managed to help the entire family to transfer to Sweden, reunite the family there, and save herself.

Throughout all of this activity, Gerda never really thought to save herself. She mostly just thought to save the children. This shows how unselfish Gerda was. Rather than fleeing the place as soon as she knew what was going to happen, she took the time to warn other families. Most people would flee the first chance they got, without thinking twice. This was just another way she was a hero.

"I only did what many Danes did, nothing special. We thought it perfectly natural to help people in mortal trouble." This is what Gerda modestly said after her brave rescue. Heroes tend to act like what they do, or did, isn't a big deal or don't take credit for what they had done. Gerda is one of these people who need to break out of that habit. What Gerda did was a big deal, and it had a huge impact on the lives of many families. Gerda Valentiner was in no way an "invader," but she was definitely a hero.

Bibliography

The Righteous Among us www.yadvashem.org

db.yadvashem.org

A HOLOCAUST HERO – BILL BARAZETTI

Vishnu Sreenivasamurthy

Hero. Savior. Preserver. A man who helped many throughout the Holocaust and took care of people was a heroic man known as Bill Barazetti. This man was a true hero because he saved many Jewish children and adults from Nazism during the time and he saved many lives from doing so. He helped thousands of victims who were discriminated about Judaism out of the prewar from Germany. He saved the children from Prague in Germany in the early 1900s during the spring and summer times. Barazetti set up a station called the Kinderstation which transported thousands of Jewish children out of the city to be free and safe from the Nazis. He was successful with this because he had a complicated system of having false identities for each child which tricked the people in thinking they were not Jewish. He transported the Jewish children to London and then Holland afterwards.

Barazetti started observing and watching the Nazis beat up and hurt the Jewish people outside of Hamburg University which he studied at. He was a very determined man in order to stop all the discrimination and hatred toward the Jews so he worked on an escape plan to stop the death rate throughout the city. He first got his idea of the Kinderstation by seeing one of his co-workers Anna from Czech

Sudetenland sending photos of the Nazi training camps by a courier to the press of London. But the Nazis detected her work eventually and she barely slipped past the border of Czech in order to be safe. Later on, Barazetti tried to cross the Czech border but instead he was beaten up and almost dead until Anna came and saved him and then took him home to be nursed. After Barazetti was back to health, he and Anna got married in Prague and they worked there escape plan for the children from there on. He was a very wise man, so Barazetti alliance with a special Czech agent who could cross over the German border and then report Hitler's plans and tactics back to Barazetti. After Barazetti got information from the Czech agent, he started to plan escape routes and plans with Church-based charities. So, he made refugees and campsites for the incoming survivors which were all kept in Czechoslovakia. An amazing 50,000-70,000 people were rescued and put into the refugee camps and this is why Barazetti was a great hero.

After that, a soon-to-become friend of Barazetti, Nicholas Winton, saw that children were very important, so he recommended to Barazetti to send the children over to the refugee camps rather than the adults. Soon enough Barazetti and Winton were in a partnership and they started to get information from each child in order to have a fake identity for each one. Barazetti was responsible for organizing the trains while Winton got the information about the children. They later realized that getting English visas was taking too long, so instead they took a Jewish printer and started printing forged papers in order to prove to the German authorities that the children were not Jewish. While the first train was coming to Holland, the visas were ready and they were given out to the children in order to board the train. Nearly three trains full of Jewish children were sent to camps and hostiles during the spring and summer months. A fourth train was planned to leave and take more children but after it left it was never heard of again.

Around 800 children were sent to these camps and they were Austrian, German, Czechs, and Jews. Bill Barazetti and Nicholas Winton were very important people during the time of the Holocaust by saving thousands of men and children who still live to this day. After all of these men, women, and children were saved from the horrible Holocaust, Barazetti came back to Britain after staying in Czech with his wife Anna and he was then employed to the War Office unit. After the war had completely ended, he was later employed to the United Nations (UN) to establish government organizations to new countries around the world. During the time of the Holocaust, the Kindertransport was completely unknown to everyone in the world and only after many years later they found out about his great achievements and accomplishments. The people in 1989 searched and examined the works and diaries of Barazetti and they soon came to a conclusion about how he accomplished his tough mission and who was involved within it. Many people around the world are very thankful for Barazetti making and setting up a station in order to send children to refugees and camps to keep them safe from the Holocaust.

To conclude, Bill Barazetti and his alliance Nicholas Winton were true heroes of the Holocaust because they displayed great work throughout by helping thousands of people from death. These two men had a great and important role in the Holocaust and they are now known to be very important and honorable throughout Germany and many other European countries. We can all finally say that Bill Barazetti is a true, respected, and honored man who deserves a lot of respect because he was one courageous man.

Bibliography

"Bill Barazetti | The Times." *The Times*. N.p., n.d. Web. 09 Feb. 2015.
<http://www.thetimes.co.uk/tto/opinion/obituaries/article2088543.ece>.

"The Poor Mouth." *: Bill Barazetti*. N.p., n.d. Web. 09 Feb. 2015.
<http://thepoormouth.blogspot.com/2008/01/bill-barazetti-local-hero.html>.

"Bill Barazetti | The Times." *The Times*. N.p., n.d. Web. 09 Feb. 2015.
<http://www.thetimes.co.uk/tto/opinion/obituaries/article2088543.ece>.

Dallas Ranch Middle School, Antioch, CA

Kevin Landski is a 6th grade English and History teacher at Dallas Ranch Middle School in Antioch. He has enjoyed taking courses during the summer to increase the interest and engagement of his students. He recently took a course on the Holocaust from an organization called Facing History, and has enjoyed using that material with his classes beginning in 2015. This is his sixth year teaching 6th grade.

HOLOCAUST HERO

Aleija Matthews

Did you know that Irena Adamowicz saved over 200 Jews? Irena helped save over 200 Jews from being exterminated, tortured, and worked to death by the Nazis during the Holocaust. The Holocaust is an event were the Nazis wiped out all the Jews because they wanted only people with blue eyes and blond hair to rule the world.

Irena Adamowicz was born on 1910 in Warsaw and she lived from 1910 to 1963). Irena was also a Polish non-Jew who had helped in various ghetto underground movements. Irena was a Catholic and one of the leaders in the Polish scout movements. Irena got her degree at the University of Warsaw. In 1930 she developed an attatchment to the Ha-Shomer ha-Tsa'ir Jewish Zionist Youth Movement, and she was also in its educational and social work activities. During 1942 in summer, Irena risked her life by doing perilous missions for the Jewish underground organizations in Warsaw, Bialystok, Vilna, Kovno, and Siauliai ghettos. She also carried important messages between different ghettos and boosted the morale of the Jews imprisoned in them. Irena helped establish contact between Jewish underground organizations and the Home Army (the Polish underground militia). After war, Irena stayed close with the surviving members of the Zionist pioneer movements that she worked with and aided. Irena was designated as Righteous Among the Nations by Yad Veshem. A quote from Irena Adamowicz says: "I can't go back where I came from was burned off the map I'm a Jew anywhere is someone else's land." A second quote from Irena says: "These words are dedicated to those who survived because life is a wilderness and they were savage..."

Irena Adamowicz has inspired me to become an upstander because her part in the history of the Holocaust has touched my heart. So here are some ways I can be an upstander. The first way I will be an upstander is by not going behind my parents back and talking about them in a mean way when they're not around. The second way I will be an upstander is by not being mean to other people, or my siblings. An example is calling other people names or calling my siblings names.

In the Holocaust there were a lot of heroes. Irena Adamowicz was one of the Holocaust heroes. Irena was known for being a courageous woman who helped save over 200 Jews by going to various death camps and saying that she would take Jews to different camps, but really she took the Jews that she saved back to underground ghetto rights movements where they would be safe from the Nazis. Irena also had worked and helped in various underground rights movements. This Holocaust hero risked her life doing what she believed was right. The Germans may have gotten away with the killing of the Jews, but there were many Holocaust heroes including

Irena that tried to stop them and did everything they could. The Holocaust is a depressing part in our history where the Germans killed almost all the Jews because they wanted all the blond haired, blue eyed people to rule. We will always remember all the heroes in the Holocaust who tried to save the Jews, who stood up to the Germans, our unsung heroes.

Works Cited

No Author Listed. "Irena Adamowicz" (Online) 5 February 2015, http://www.yadveshem.org

Weitz, Sonia Schreiber. I Promised I Would Tell. Brookline, Massachusetts: Facing History and Ourselves, 1993.

THE STORY OF GERDA VALENTINER
Alex Partida

Did you known that there were a lot of people who helped in the Holocaust? Gerda Valentiner was a big help to kids in the Holocaust. The Holocaust was a time when German Nazis wanted to wipe out the Jews. The focus of this paper is to share with you what nice people did during the Holocaust. Gerda Valentiner was an upstander.She risked her life for children so let's all try to be an upstander and help.

A special person named Gerda Valentiner was born in 1906.Today I'm going to tell you about the great Gerda Valentiner. Gerda helped kids when the deportation of the Jews in Denmark was happening. Gerda Valentiner was a school teacher who was also in the Danish resistance, which was a group that helped the people in Denmark. One day the deportation of the Jews was happening. So Gerda Valentiner came to her students and other kids' houses to collect them and take them to live at her house so the kids could be safe. She even bought new dishes and food for the children who only ate bread. Gerda then kept trying and trying to send the children to Sweden. On the third time Gerda sent the kids to Sweden by boat. Here is a quote from Gerda Valentiner."I only did what many Danes did, nothing special. We thought it was perfectly natural to help people in mortal danger (Their fate will be my fate too, Page 1)."

Being an upstander is important like how Gerda Valentiner took kids from her school to Sweden and saved their lives. This paragraph is about how I'm going to be an upstander and why it's so important. First, upstanding is so important so you can protect people or maybe you can save someone's life like how Gerda saved all of those kids and sent them to Sweden. Second, I'm going to be an upstander by giving back to my parents for how hard they work for me for example, buying me food, buying me clothes, and supporting me on whatever I want to do. So I'm going to give back, for example by helping them with chores, or watching my siblings if they need to do something, and helping them with anything. "She not only risked her life for the sake of those children, but also manifested great sensitivity and respect for her protégés religious observance (Their Fate Will Be My fate Too, Page 1)."

A lot of people helped in the Holocaust but most of them are unknown but one that is known is Gerda Valentiner. She helped kids got them food and shipped them to safety. The Germans could have killed many more people if Gerda wasn't there but she was and she saved some kids that could have died. Gerda helped more people than just those kids. So that shows how much bravery Gerda and all the other people who helped in the Holocaust had. People who helped in the Holocaust risked their lives for other people. I wish there was more people like her in the world. So yes be an upstander and help people like Gerda Valentiner.

Works Cited

Weitz, Sonia Schreiber I Promised I Would Tell. Brookline, Massachusetts: Facing History and Ourselves, 1993.

No author Listed. "Their Fate Will Be My Fate Too." (Online) 5 February 2015 http://www.yadvashem.org/yv/en/exhibitions/righteous-teachers/ valentiner.asp

ELISABETH EIDENBENZ: CHILD SAVIOR

Aliakhue Braimah

Do you know who Elisabeth Eidenbenz is? She helped children and mothers in need of shelter during the 20th century. She made a chateau into a maternity home and saved a lot of people. You will learn about her later on and how she was an upstander during the Holocaust, a time when a man named Hitler murdered Jews.

Elisabeth Eidenbenz was born on June 12, 1913. She was the daughter of a Zurich pastor. She had first started teaching in Switzerland and Denmark, and then she changed to the association to aid children in need. She arrived to Madrid to volunteer on an aid team but relocated again because of Spanish children didn't all fit. She changed her own Chateau into a maternity home in Montescot, outside of Elne. It was called, "Chateau d'en Bardou" named after Le n'il cigarette paper. It housed 30,000 French people and each room was named after a Spanish city. Later on, during the Holocaust, the Nazis came to the chateau to look for Jews. Elisa shooed them away but the second time they came looking for Jews, they had found a Jewish mother named Lucy. The Nazis said that if they didn't get Lucy, they would take Elisabeth instead. Since Elisa had been so great to her, Lucy sacrificed herself for Elisa's sake. They had taken Lucy to a death camp called Mauthausen. Elisabeth Eidenbenz saved a lot of people and later on died on

204

May 23, 2011 and she will be deeply missed. Later on, I will show how I will be an upstander and will learn how you can be an upstander and help people just like she did.

This is about how I can be an upstander myself. First, I will help people when they are being bullied. I will do that by comforting them and making them feel better about themselves and they won't even remember that they are sad. I will try to stop the bully by reporting them so they will stop. Upstanding is important because if people didn't help anyone, then everyone would have bad things happen to them. So remember that if you help someone then someone might help you.

You have learned all about Elisabeth Eidenbenz and her Chateau. You also learned how she helped a lot of people. You learned about how she saved Lucy (almost) from the Nazis. Then, you learned how I become an upstander. Hopefully this helped in your everyday life and made you a better person.

Worked Cited
No Author Listed. "Elizabeth and Her Maternité." (Online) February 6, 2015. **http://www.anglophone-direct.com/Elisabeth-Eidenbenz-and-the**
Weitz, Sonia Schreiber, I Promised I Would Tell. Brookline, Massachusetts: Facing History and Ourselves, 1993.

THE STORY OF AN AMAZING HOLOCAUST HERO!
Amber Jade Hawkes

Would you think that people from Switzerland would standup for Jews in the Holocaust? The Holocaust was a time during World War II in Germany when German people were killing Jews, African Americans, and Egyptians. Rosli Naf or also known as Rosa Naef was one of the few people who were upstanders in the Holocaust. Throughout this paper you will learn a lot about Rosli Naf and how she helped Jews.

Rosli Naf was an amazing person who saved several lives in the Holocaust. Rosli Naf was born in 1911 in Glarus, Switzerland and became a nurse. Rosli Naf helped many kids find a new place to live and helped take care of their needs. She assisted Dr. Albert Schweitzer in Lambarene and helped children in Swiss Aid. Jewish children fled to France when the Germans invaded Belgium, and were helped by Swiss Relief and Swiss Aid. Rosli Naf was asked to help take care of the Jewish refugee children. She went to several towns where children had been hiding in bad shelters, most of the children were sick or had some hurt legs. On Rosli Naf's way to the towns she noticed a castle where she later decided to take the children, because it was bigger and had better conditions. After about a year of living at the castle of La Hille, a police man came in the middle of the night with orders to take some of the children. Rosli Naf watched them go helplessly and so did some other local families that helped with the children. Later Rosli Naf found out that the children were taken to camp Vernet, and then she decided to go see them in the camp. When she got to the camp she was let in but she was not supposed to be let in. The guard told her she would have to stay at the camp for a while. At the camp she had free rights to the phone and was allowed to see all the prisoners. "Many refugees that I did not know all shocked and depressed wanted to talk to me. The fact that anyone could enter this closed camp gave them a glimmer of hope. I could tell my children, Mr. Dubois, very appreciated because of his visits to La Hille, was immediately moved to Vichy, and undertook everything to get the authorities release. Madame Dubois, they also knew well, had made the same purpose in Bern (Rosli Naf, page1)." Rosli Naf made calls for people to let their families know they were okay. Later just before the people in the camp were going to be killed Mr. Dubois got everyone released. Then Rosli Naf returned to the castle of La Hille to see the other children. Then in November 1942 Germans invaded France were the castle was located. The Germans had guards posted in the castle and now no one could listen to music without the German commander being told. Awhile later Rosli Naf took some children across the border into Switzerland. She went to her home but only stayed a short time because the Germans were coming, and one of the kids she brought across the border was arrested. A few months later Mr. and Mrs. Dubois and Rosli Naf went to the Red Cross and were soon sent home. "On 9 September 1943, the region was occupied by the Germans, and therefore their patrols supervised the day and night boundary. The Swiss authorities have learned their activities; Germaine Homel and Rosa Naef were fired. However, Germaine will not be discouraged and continued with Renée Bouvard Farny and Martha, to help Jewish children to cross the border. The brave woman was finally arrested and sent to a concentration camp (History, page 1)." Rosli Naf died in 1996 Glarus, Switzerland.

It's important to be an up stander because otherwise many people are going to get hurt if no one stands up to the bully. Rosli Naf inspired me to stand up for other people because our consequences are not as big as going to a concentration camp if we stand up for someone. I will stand up for my family and others. For example I will stand up for my brother when people make fun of his deafness. I will stand up to my friends if they make fun of my sister or my brothers. I will also stand up for my siblings when they bully each other by telling them to stop. Also I will stand up for my friends. For example if someone makes of my friend for being different then them or for acting weird I will tell them to stop.

People from all over the world helped Jews during the Holocaust. Not very many helped but the few that did were amazing people. Rosli Naf was one of the amazing people who helped Jews in the Holocaust. Rosli Naf never gave up on helping Jews even after she lost her job she kept helping them, until she was put in a concentration camp. Rosli Naf saved Jews and helped them go across the border to Switzerland. TheHolocaust was a very sad and horrible time in history, but everyone is thankful for the amazing people who stood up to the Germans who wanted to kill Jews.

Works Cited

No Author Listed. "History." (Online) 6 February 2015. http://www.yadvashem-france.org/les- justes-parmi-les-nations/les-justes-de-france/dossier-5119/

No Author Listed. "Notice." (Online) 6 February 2015.
http://www.ajpn.org/juste-Rosli-Naf-2036.html

Weitz, Sonia Schreiber. I Promised I Would Tell. Brookline, Massachusetts: Facing History and Ourselves, 1993.

THE STORY OF GERDA VALENTINER

Andres Chavez

The Holocaust was a terrible event to Nazis aka Germans Jews were bad so they killed them all. But Jews were no harm but Nazis wanted to torture them and kill them.

Gerda Valentiner was a teacher who was in the Danish resistance during an occupation participating in the transfer Jews to Sweden. During the terrible weeks in October 1943 when the deportation of the Jews of Denmark was planned, Gerda Valentiner collected Jewish children from their parents and took them to her home waiting for when they would be taken to Sweden.

Gerda Valentiner was his sister's teacher, and one night in September 1943 she came to her parents Ester and Reuben Sheftelowitz to warn them of the danger. A couple of days later, Rita her sister moved to Gerda's home and stayed with her until she understands to arrange their transfer. Gerda Valentiner was transferring people to Sweden and to help them not get killed and sent to a concentration camp. "I only did what many Danes did, nothing special. We thought it perfectly natural to help people in mortal danger."

In this paragraph I am going to come up with ideas to save Jews. Jews are good not bad and Germans/Nazis are bad first, Valentiner Gerda was setting good examples because she risked her life of saving Jews and being an up stander. The way I will be an up stander is standing up for my parents if my sisters are being mean to them. For example, I will treat my parents right and respect them and not talk back when they ask me to do something you just do it like the Army. Valentiner Gerda taught me to help other people. Second, I will help out family members for things to illustrate; I will help family by giving them money if they really need it to and probably give something to the homeless.

Gerda Valentiner was an up stander during the terrible event in history the Holocaust. What she did to be an up stander was she helped out people who were Jews from getting them killed by the Nazis or get sent to concentration camps. She took children to Sweden so they would not get killed by the Nazis. She also helped out older people like parents or elders and she transferred Jews from Denmark to Sweden. She took the Jews to her house and then they go and transfer them to a different country so that they won't get killed which is pretty heroic to me. After the Holocaust ended Gerda Valentiner retired from being a teacher and she volunteered as a social worker in Jewish camps in Germany and Austria. She was 68 when she retired from teaching or being a teacher at school and then she went to Israel for a year to visit the country and to learn Hebrew. On July 28, 1968 Yad Vashem recognized Gerda Valentiner as Righteous Among the Nations.

Works Cited

No Author Listed. "Gerda Valentiner" (Online) 5 February 2015. http://www.yadvashem.org/yv/en/exhibitions/righteous-teachers/valentiner.asp

Weitz, Sonia Schreiber. I Promised I Would Tell. Brookline, Massachusetts: Facing History and Ourselves, 1993.

DAGMAR LUSTRUP: HOLOCAUST HERO

Bianca Sotomayor

About 6 million Jews died during a tragic time called the Holocaust. There were people who would risk their lives to save Jews, they were called up standers. The Holocaust was a time life when Jewish people were killed in1939-1945 just because of their religion. They were sent to concentration camps and were worked to death. Dagmar Lustrup was an up stander. She saved20 Jewish teenagers from that happening to them.

German soldiers were told to leave immediately while Lustrup took advantage of the situation and saved 20 teens. Most of the 20 Jewish teenagers who Dagmar Lustrup saved were from Czechoslovakia. "According to Aryeh Weiner, Zvi Oscar Strauss, and Nomi Sagie (then Eva Bermann), some of the Lustrup children, they belonged to a Zionist pioneer organizations at that time, and wished to prepare themselves for immigration to Palestine to learn how to be farmers (Dagmar Lustrup page 1)." Dagmar found some Protestant farmers who agreed to give agricultural training. Dagmar put the kids into groups but was concerned about cultural activities and their physical needs. After their country was taken over by Germans, they went to area near Thisted, in Jutland, Denmark. Dagmar's husband owned a local newspaper stand which he gained the money for the kids' private homes near Thisted.

The reason upstanding is important is that if there were no up standers everyone would probably be pushed around or bullied. Dagmar Lustrup made me realize that if an idea is wrong and you know what is right you should do it even if you are alone. For example, I would probably make a community to help and support people who are being treated wrong. Secondly, I would gather people by protesting against the wrong idea and telling them that it is bad.

About 6 million Jews died during a tragic time called the Holocaust. Dagmar Lustrup risked her life to save twenty Jewish teenagers. She saved them by helping them prepare for immigration to Palestine by finding farmers who agreed to teach them how to be farmers. It was amazing that she saved those kids by helping get them to Palestine. In fact, "On October, 2, 1984, Yad Vashem recognized Dagmar Lustrup as Righteous Among the Nations (Dagmar Lustrup, page 1)."

Works Cited

No Author Listed. "Dagmar Lustrup." (Online) 5 February 2015. http://db.yadveshem.org/righteous/family.html?language=en&itemId=4016147

Weitz, Sonia Schreiber. I Promised I would Tell. Brookline, Massachusetts; Facing History and Ourselves, 1993.

MY HOLOCAUST SURVIVOR

Chinedu Oluo

Did you know Knud Dyby saved over 7.2 thousand Jews? Knud, helped save 7.2 thousand people from being exterminated by the Nazis. The Holocaust is an event in which the Germans killed over 10 million people. Knud Dyby was an up stander during the Holocaust.

In the early 1900 a great person was born, his name was Knud Dyby. His life started in the city of Randers, Denmark. He followed his father's footsteps by also working as a typographer, or a person who prepares the words for a newspaper when he came out of college. When he completed his military service, he decided to become a police officer. In the 1940s the Nazis attempted to hang a Nazis flag on top of the Denmark castle but, "The king refused to hang any flag but the Denmark flag above the royal castle". Knud helped with the removal of the flag and became an avid member of the Danish underground. Since he was a police officer he had a lot of information about the Danish resistance. When he learned the Germans were about to round up all the Jews and deport them, he used boats to get them to Oresund, or a 3 kilometer tunnel that goes from Copenhagen to the city of Scania so they could hide in hospitals until they could get a boat to get them to Sweden. All that information was the difference between saving no Jews and 7,200. Shortly after that he moved to the United States. He later died at the age of 96 in 2011.

My up stander helped me become a better person by reminding me that even if everyone is doing something, it might not be the right thing. For example, the Holocaust was an event that took place in the 1940s in Germany. Many people participated in it. In this paragraph I will be talking about the importance of upstanding and what I hope to do. There are two ways I'm going to be an upstander. First, If I see bullying I will try to stop it. For example, if I see a kid getting bullied I would just grab him by the arm and walk away from the situation. Next, I would ask him what he did to make the bully mad at him. If it was his fault, I would tell him he should not do it again. If it wasn't his fault, I would take to him to the office and help him file and incident report and make sure he talked to a vice principle. Also, I would talk to the bully and ask him why he bullied. If he told me, I would take him to the counselor, and tell the counselor to talk to him about why bullying is bad, and why it could hurt some mentally and physically. If I knew someone was plotting to rob a store, I would try to talk him out of it. If the person didn't listen, I would call the police and tell them to wait outside the store at the time and date he told me he was going to rob the store and tell them to deal with him accordingly.

Second, Instead of talking about my parents behind their back I will instead talk about the positive things my parents did like cooking food, providing shelter, and buying me toys. This stuff is a small example of being an upstander. One day I will hopefully be like him by saving people for a event that only time will foretell. If one day an event like this may happen I hope to save at least half the people Knud Dyby did "participated in the October 1943 rescue of almost 7,200 Jews living in Denmark."

In conclusion, the Holocaust was an event in which over 11 million people died 6 million of them were, Jews. There were many. / Weitz, Sonia Schreiber. I Promised I Would Tell. Brookline, Massachusetts: Facing History and ourselves. 1993.

GERDA JULIE VALENTINER: A TRUE HOLOCAUST HERO

Esmeralda Garcia Sanchez

"I only did what many Danes did, nothing special. We thought it perfectly natural to help people in mortal trouble (Gerda Valentiner page1)." Gerda Julie Valentiner was a member of the Resistance who helped to rescue Danish Jews from the hands of the Nazis in 1943, also known as the Holocaust. The Holocaust was a horrid, dreadful, and very frightful state-sponsored murder of approximately 6 million Jews by the Nazi regime. The word "Holocaust" is a word from the Greek language meaning "sacrifice by fire." At the time Nazis believed certain Germans

210

called Aryans were "racially superior" and that Jews were an alien threat to the so-called German racial community. Jews were sent to concentration camps and put to work and if workers were not healthy and able to work they were sentenced to death. There were many non-Jewish upstanders during the Holocaust that did the right thing and helped many Jews. One of these brave upstanders that we will never forget for their act of bravery was named Gerda Julie Valentiner.

Gerda Julie Valentiner, born in Kobenhoven, Denmark on January 27, 1903, was a very brave woman who collected young children from their parents/guardians during the Holocaust, took good care of them, and waited for the right moment to transfer them to Sweden. During this process her life was risked many times. When she realized that some of the children were religiously observant and ate nothing but bread her genuine sensitivity was manifested. Therefore she brought the children new dishes and food that they could eat. Mortiz Scheftelowitz, one of the witnesses of Gerda Valentiner's role in the rescue operation, testified that one night in late September 1943, she came to his parents, Ester and Reuben Scheftelowitz, to warn them about the danger that was to come. A couple days later Mortiz and his two sisters Dora and Rita were taken to Gerda's home and stayed with her until Gerda managed to arrange the Scheftelowitz children's transfer to Sweden. There were three attempts to leave the country. Unfortunately the first two failed, but luckily the third one succeeded. In order to leave they fished from a boat at a location of 10 kilometers North of Copenhagen. They arrived after a long night's journey to Landskron, Sweden on the eve of Yom Kippur in 1943. It had turned out that the children's parents had arrived three days before them. After war, Valentiner took a leave of absence from her job. For two years she volunteered to do social work in Jewish refugee camps in Germany and Austria. This was a great act of kindness to many people. In 1971 as a retired teacher at the age of 68 she took a trip to Israel to see the country and learn to speak Hebrew. "On July 28, 1968, Yad Vashem had recognized Gerda Valentiner as Righteous Among the Nations (The Righteous Among Nations; Valentiner Family, page 1)."

Gerda Valentiner was a very inspiring woman who was an upstander during the Holocaust.   She has inspired me in many ways to help in my classroom and community. There are two ways that I will become an upstander in my community. First, when my classroom is noisy I will not become part of the problem; I will help solve the problem. For example, instead of telling people to be quiet and making the problem worse I will simply place my finger over my lip and set a good example of the proper behavior for that specific problem in order to stop the noise. Second, I will stand up for people who are being bullied. To illustrate, when someone is picking on someone else I will tell the bully to stop, get an adult, or pull the victim out of the situation. Gerda Valentiner has inspired me to make a change in the world.

When someone needs help I will help them. When someone is put down I will pick them back up. I will do what is right. I will make a difference in my community.

There were many brave men and women who were upstanders during the Holocaust. One of these brave heroes was Gerda Julie Valentiner. Gerda Valentiner is known for taking the children from their parents, taking responsibility of the children, and planning their transfer to Sweden. This wasn't very easy but she managed it. She is known for all she managed to do during this horrific and cruel murdering of approximately 6 million Jews known as the Holocaust. The Germans thought that their people would thank them for this. They thought that this was showing their love for the Germans. Well, it wasn't this at all. It was showing the cruelness of the Germans. Many people knew that this wasn't right but they still did nothing about it. These people to this day regret that they did nothing. We are very thankful for these people who did the right thing and became upstanders. Gerda Valentiner did not save as many Jews as other people, but she is not known for how many Jews she saved. She is known for doing something. There is a message to everybody in our hero's story. Gerda's message is do something, make a difference in the world, because doing something is always better than doing nothing. You can be like one of these heroes in the future if you try. In conclusion, Gerda Valentiner is known for being brave and doing what is right. Gerda Valentiner and many other upstanders will now and forever be known as our true heroes of the Holocaust.

Works Cited

No Author Listed. "The Righteous Among Nations; Valentiner Family" (Online) 6 February 2015 http://db.yadvashem.org/righteous/family.html?language=en&itemId =4017998

Weitz, Sonia Schreiber. I Promised I Would Tell. Brookline, Massachusetts; Facing History and Ourselves, 1993.

KNUD DYBY; HOLOCAUST HERO

Giselle Schenk

Knud Dyby was an up stander during the Holocaust. Did you know that Knud Dyby saved 7,200 Jews during World War II? Knud Dyby was a royal guard at the Amalien castle before the Holocaust. After leaving his guard duties, he became an officer. About two years later the Holocaust had started. If you do not know what the Holocaust is, it was a time when Hitler wanted the extermination of Jews, mentally ill people, and Gypsys. Knud set up a hospital for the Jews whilethey waited to be rescued by a boat. Knud managed to get 1,400 Jews safely to America.

Knud Dyby also took part in taking down the Nazi flag off the Amalien Castle. As a police officer, Knud had access to information vital to the Danish resistance. He knew the best places to hide near the fishing docks. Dyby also knew the patrol routes of the German navy, specifically in the waters between Denmark and Sweden. As a sailor, Knud also knew the best sea lanes between Denmark and Sweden. As soon as Knud heard of Germany's intention to round up all the Jews in Denmark and to exterminate them, he acted quickly. "He was a member of the Danish-Swedish Refugee Service and participated in the October 1943 rescue of almost 7,200 Jews living in Denmark. (Knud Dyby | Denmark, page1)" As a member of the Danish underground, he ferried Jews from Denmark to Sweden. Knud assisted in transporting some 1,888 people to safety, a third of them were Jewish. In May 1945, when Denmark was liberated, he ended his police career and move to the United States.

There are two main things I am going to do to be an up stander. First, I will stop bullying when I see it. For example, if I see a fight I'll put a stop to it. Second, I will start to encourage my Grandma more. To illustrate, I will start helping her more often by helping her when not needed. My upstander, Knud Dyby, helped me become a better person by showing me you can choose to risk your life, to save people to make a difference, and that not all Germans were evil. The Holocaust happened cause of Hitler's evil doing; the SS men were following Hitler because they said "I was forced to." Only a few went to jail for 25 years, some were set free, most were sent to their death.

This hero is honored from everything they did in trying to protect the in the Holocaust there were so many heroes, in which some names are unknown. But the one we do remember are Knud Dyby. Knud Dyby is known for saving 7,200 Jews during World War II. Knud Dyby had saved the Jews through two ways, either through an underground tunnel, or by boat to Oresund, the narrow body of water between Denmark and Sweden. He arranged for hiding places in hospitals where Jews could wait until a boat could be found to take them to Sweden. Many people died during the Holocaust trying to save, or survive. Some people are still alive to tell their story about what they experienced during the Holocaust. The people who risked their lives to stand up to the Nazis and save thousands of Jews. They had a lot of courage to go up there and sneak people out without getting caught, or killed. After World War II was over, he moved to America. Knud Dyby died in September 2011 at the age of 96.

<u>Works Cited</u>

No Author Listed. "Knud Dyby Denmark." (Online) 6 February 2015 https://jfr.org/rescuer-stories/dyby-knud/

Wetiz, Sonia Schreiber. <u>I Promised I Would Tell.</u> Brookline, Massachusetts: Facing History and Ourselves, 1993.

THE SUPER MAN OF THE 1940S

Isabella Ionelia Rosales, Co-winner

Paul Grueniger was a hero all will remember. He 3,600 Jewish refugees during a horrible act of anti-Semitism, or the hatred of the Jewish religion, called the Holocaust. The Holocaust was a horrible historical event which involved the killing of approximately 6 million innocent people, most of them Jewish, just because of culture and religion. Apparently, Grueniger did not approve of this action. Although back at this time saving these people was illegal, Grueniger took the risk. He shows us that listening blindly to authority is not the correct thing to do. This is his story.

Paul Grueniger was a wonderful person with a story that will inspire many people to do the right thing. It all starts back in 1938, when Switzerland and Nazi Germany had a negotiation which led to the stamping of a "J" on Jewish passports in Germany. This meant that the Jews would be recognized while traveling. Since most of the area was invaded by Nazi Germany, most of the countries in Europe had closed their borders to Jews. At this time, Grueniger was a guard at the Switzerland border, and the Swiss authorities had closed their borders to Austrian Jews in particular. Grueniger's job was to make sure Austrian Jews did not cross the border. But the problem for them worsened. This meant that the number of Jews coming into Switzerland illegally would increase rapidly. Grueniger had a choice; to send the Jews back to an unknown future, or to save them at risk of losing his job and getting arrested. Thankfully, he chose to help the Jews. He did this by turning in false papers stating the incorrect number of arrivals, and tried his best to prevent other policemen from tracking refugees that they knew had entered the area. He also purchased (with his own money) food and clothing for Jews who had to leave their belongings behind. Eventually, Grueniger was caught and his trial opened in January 1939. It lasted two years. In March 1939 he was dismissed from his job and in March 1941 he was found guilty of breach of duty. Grueniger was arrested and fined. For the rest of his life it was hard for him to find a job because of his criminal record. But Grueniger thought it was worth it. He states "It was basically a question of saving human lives threatened with death. How could I then seriously consider bureaucratic schemes and calculations?" (*The Police man Who Lifted the Border Barrier*, page 1).

If you were in a situation in which you had to choose between saving yourself and helping another person, would you choose to do the right thing? You never know. This is why upstanding is important. People tend to think of themselves as a good-doing innocent person who would never kill someone just because somebody else told them to. Well, that is not always the deal. Even though the stakes were high, Paul Grueniger did not hesitate to help people in need, while others may have done otherwise. He inspired me to help make the world a better place, even though other people might discourage me. Something I will do to stand up for those who are different is to try my best to stop racism. This is a big problem but even a little help can stop it. To stop this problem, I will point out the benefits of the targeted race. For example, African Americans are often targeted even though they are perfectly equal to any other races.. There is a person named Gaby Douglas, the first African American gymnast and a three time gold medal winner. Second, I will try to stop bullying in schools. I will do this by telling an adult if I see someone getting bullied. This will help a lot because it will stop young people from growing up believing that making fun of people is the right thing. It will also help because the victim will not have such a hard experience during their child hood.

Out of the many wonderful people in the world, very few decided to do the right thing. But Paul Grueniger did. He helped by turning in false papers so Jews could cross the border and buying their necessities so that they could survive. He risked his job and freedom so that he could help others. He served time in prison and paid fines for his act. After the war, Grueniger was sent an apology and given his money back. Although he passed away in 1972, he lives in the hearts of many people today. Thanks to Grueniger, lots of people will do the right thing. Will you do the right thing if you are confronted with this type of situation, or do you just think so?

Works Cited

No Author Listed. "Paul Greuniger."(online) 16 Febuary 201
https://www.eiu.edu/~eiutps/ holocaust_grueniger.php

No Author listed. "Paul Greuniger Switzerland." (online) 6 Febuary 2015
https://jfr.org/rescuer-stories/gruninger-paul/

No Author Listed. "The Policeman That Lifted the Border Barrier." (Online) 17
Febuary 2015. www.yadvashem.org/yv/en/riteous/stories/grueniger.asp

Weitz, Sonia, Schreiber. I Promised I Would Tell. Brookline, Massachusetts: Facing History and Ourselves

PAUL GRUENINGER, A HERO OF THE HOLOCAUST

Isabella Meza, Co-winner

Did you know Paul Grueninger saved 3,600 Jews during the Holocaust? The Holocaust was when the German Nazis started to kill Jews. This event happened 1939-1945. Nazis are from the German army and they were the people who murdered the Jews. The Nazis thought the citizens would thank them for killing the Jews. Many German citizens agreed with the massacre of Jews, but those who didn't agree did nothing because they thought they would get killed. Paul Grueninger was not one of those people. He was born in Switzerland and was deeply concerned about what was happening in the Holocaust. Paul actually made a difference and did something about it. Paul Grueninger was an upstander during the Holocaust who cared for others and did not accept that innocent people were being murdered.

Paul Grueninger was an amazing person during the Holocaust, and was a Swiss border police commander. He was born October 27, 1891. His job was to send refugees without proper paper work back to Austria where they would be killed or treated unfairly. He was faced with a big dilemma if he let the Jews in, which would be breaking the law and he could go to jail, or not let them in and send them back to get killed. Paul couldn't bear sending those poor people back, so he let them into Switzerland even though it was illegal to enter. He knew his consequences and still did the right thing. He said in his exact words, "It was basically a question of saving human lives threatened with death. How could I seriously consider bureaucratic schemes and calculations (The police man who lifted the border barrier, page 1)." He was so caring; Paul even bought with his own money their winter clothes since they had to leave everything behind and gave them homes to live in. He sent them to Diespoldsau camp, were they were cared for and waited for their temporary permits to stay, or permanent permits to leave and find another place to live safely. The Germans began to catch on to his actions and told the Swiss authorities. He found out that the Germans had uncovered his actions on April 3 when he was stopped from going to work. He was fired from his job and he went to trial. The case dragged on for two years and finally he was found guilty March of 1941. Paul lived the rest of his life in hardship. Even though the rest of his life was filled with many hardships he did not regret the decisions he had made. Paul sacrificed his job and his life just to give a helping hand to the Jews in need and never regretted it; he was such a courageous man. He helped many; he was very brave because he was so willing to sacrifice everything. Paul Grueninger eventually died February 22, 1972.

Paul Grueninger was a very heroic person who not only risked his life, but his job as well. By studying and reading all about him he has inspired me to be an upstander, but nothing can compare to what he did to save the Jewish refugees. One thing I can do to be an upstander is when I'm at home I can support my parents. For example, when my siblings are saying bad things about my mom or dad I could tell them to do what their supposed to be doing and they won't get in trouble, this is just one thing I could do to be an upstander. Of course this is nothing compared to what Grueninger did, but it is still making a difference and being an upstander which means making a difference big or small. Another way that I can help is when somebody is getting hurt or bullied. For example, I could always tell an adult or a teacher, even stop the bully or help the victim. I will always be an upstander, considering how much Grueninger has done. I can't compare with what he did, but I have learned so much from him. He has been an inspiration to me and I hope he will

216

have the same effect on many people. If everybody was courageous and willing to help people, this world would change in a wonderful way. Please make a difference. I really hope learning about Paul Grueninger has made an impact on your life. I will do something about it and I hope you will to.

Paul Grueninger saved about 3,600 Jewish lives during the Holocaust. He was an amazing person who stood up for Jews. Paul Grueninger was unnoticed in his time until he died, and they reopened the case and decided he wasn't guilty. He risked everything and even knew that he was going to jail and still wanted, and did help the Jews. Paul Grueninger was a hero, savior, and a very courageous man. He let the Jews into Switzerland and bought them clothes gave them a place to stay. Paul Grueninger is just one of the many saviors and he deserves to be thanked. Paul Grueninger knew he was wrong in the name of law to be helping Jews, but knew in his heart it was right and did not care about the consequences. Thanks to Paul Grueninger and other people out there like him this isn't a world of chaos. Thank you Paul and many others who have took the risks to do what is right.

Works Cited

No Author Listed." The Example of Grueninger" (Online) 6 February 2015 http://www.raoulwallenberg.net/

No Author Listed." The Policeman who Lifted The Border Barrier." (Online) 6 February 2015 http://www.yadvashem.org/yv/en/righteous/stories/grueninger.asp

Wietz, Sonia Schreiber. I Promised I Would Tell. Brookline, Massachusetts: Facing History an Ourselves, 1993.

ANNA CHRISTENSEN; HOLOCAUST SAVER

Janae Hume

Do you know what the Holocaust is? The Holocaust was a time in history when Adolf Hitler took over Europe in the 1930s-1945. He hated the Jews. So, he had the Germans kill them. He did this because he thought it was good for his country Europe. There were places where they killed Jews called concentration camps. But there were some upstanders during the time trying to save Jews. One of them was Anna Christensen.

Anna Christensen was a nice and loving person who wanted to save the Jews. She came from Nyborg, Denmark were she "had been a member of the International League for Peace and Freedom, aided in the rescue of 40 Jewish children." "At first Anna enrolled the children openly in the local school, but, after the German invasion on April 9, 1940, the authorities were too frightened to allow it, so she turned her cellar into a classroom." Soon the exposure increased of her getting in trouble, so she asked her friends to help hide the children. First, "she inspected the homes to which they were sent." In autumn of 1943 she managed to sneak the children out of the country of Europe to Sweden.

Anna was a magnificent person because she had risked her life for the Jewish children. She has made me a better person because she had put her life on the line. To me that is a big deal. I hope to do something amazing like she did. There are two things I will do to be an upstander. First, I will be an upstander by helping my church by being a leader. For example, I will help with teach kids in God's words when I become an adult because I love talking about the Lord's word. "She was a warm and loving person, treating them with motherly affection (Anna had been)"and I plan on doing something close to what she did. Second, I plan on becoming an ecologist. For example, as an ecologist I can show how God created the world. Analogous if someone is looking at nature I could tell them that God created the world and tell them about His glories.

Anna Christensen was an upstander during the Holocaust. She protected the Jews at a time in history when Adolf Hitler was in power. Later in Israel in 1966, the children held a celebration for the fact that she saved them.

Works Cited

No Author Listed. "The Righteous among the Nations" (Online) 6 February 2015 http://db.yadvashem.org/righteous/family.html?language=en&itemId=4014337

Weitz, Sonia Schreiber. I Promised I Would Tell. Brookline, Massachusetts: Facing History and Ourselves, 1993.

THE CENSORSHIP OF GERDA VALENTINER

Kiara Lynae Evans

Children, like me, today need to understand the true meaning of kindness. That person that has kindness is Gerda Valentiner. Gerda Valentiner was a teacher in Denmark .She was born January 27, 1903.

The situation between the Germans and the Jews in the Holocaust, or the mass murder of Jews under the German Nazi regime during the period 1941–45. More than 6 million European Jews, as well as members of other persecuted groups, such as Gypsies and homosexuals, were murdered at concentration camps such as Auschwitz. Gerda was also an upstander, which means she stood up for people. When she was a teacher in Denmark she was moving from place to place getting Jews to Sweden. The week of October 1943 it was scheduled to take the Jews to Sweden. When that week had come to pass Gerda felt a generous feeling inside her to take some Jewish kids into her home. The reason Gerda did this is because she thought she should wait until the right time to send them to Sweden. When this happened Gerda had this to say: "I only did what many Danes did, nothing special. We thought it would be perfectly natural to help people in mortal danger." When she had said that she absolutely knew to risk her life for the sake of those children. At the time those children were in her home, Gerda understood the Jewish law that the kids were only allowed bread. When she realized that was the only thing they were eating she quickly went to the store and bought a whole feast for the kids.

There was this man named Moritz Scheftelowitz who went up to Gerda and said, "Ms. Valentiner you were my little sister's teacher when we were young." "Indeed I was," said Gerda with a calm but joyful voice. On the night of 1943 Gerda had grave news to give to Moritz parents, Ester and Reuben Scheftelowitz. Luckily, Gerda let Dora and Rita stay at her house until they were supposed to be transfer to Sweden. My upstander, Gerda Valentiner, helped me to be the respectful young women I am today. She was so amazing that I want to be an upstander for anybody that is in need of help. She's so caring that my family and I gathered $1,425 to save my cousin from ovarian cancer. I believe that Gerda is a strong leader with a big heart to encourage others to keep their head up and succeed. I will help people in times of need and be kind to others who are not.

In conclusion, now you understand the true meaning of being an upstander. The way Gerda showed her true meaning of being an upstander was just powerful. When Gerda was finished with teaching at the age of 68, she decided to retire and became a social worker for two years at a Jewish Camp. I am glad I got the chance to find out about Gerda Valentiner's true lifestyle of living in Denmark an being an upstander, or a person that sticks up for someone. I strongly feel I picked the right person to be an upstander.

Work Cited

No Author Listed. "Gerda Valentiner" (Online) 5 February 2015.

http://www.yadvashem.org/yv/en/search_results.asp?cx=005038866121755566658%3Au ch7z5r

Weitz, Sonia Schreiber. I Promised I Would Tell. : Brookline, Massachusetts Facing History aOurselves, 1993

SEMPO SUGIHARA; HOLOCAUST HERO

Leilana Yeung

Did you know that Sempo Sugihara and his wife, Yukiko Sugihara saved more than 6,000 Jews during the Holocaust? The Holocaust was all about the mass murder of about 11 million Jews by the German Nazis during World War II so the Germans would have a Jew-free world. Sempo and Yukiko are honored as "Righteous Gentiles" for saving the second largest amount of Jews during the Holocaust throughout the entire world. They wrote over 300 travel visas a day to help Jews get to Kobe, Japan and later on Shanghai, China. Jews helped by the Sugiharas were known as "Sugihara Saviors." It takes a lot of courage and kindness to do this kind of thing, especially for people you don't even know, but Sempo and Yukiko have all of those traits and did the right thing.

Sempo Sugihara is a Holocaust Hero. He was born on January 1, 1900 in Japan. He graduated from a Japanese training center for experts called Harbin with top marks and went to Waseda University. Since he was fluent in Russian (because of going to Harbin) he was sent to Lithuania to serve as a Japanese Consul. Part of his job was to monitor the location of the Germans so they would know if they were going to attack the Soviet Union. Thousands of Jews' lives depended on him and his wife. The Sugiharas knew that the Jews wouldn't survive here because the Germans were anticipating an attack on the Soviet Union, so they signed over 300 visas a day for the Jews to get to Japan, then later on China. The Jews took no time in getting on a train to Kobe, Japan and then to Shanghai, China. They had become Sugihara Saviors. "Today, more than 50 years after those 29 fateful days in July and August of 1940, there may be more than 40,000 who owe their lives to Sempo and Yukiko Sugihara" (Greene, "Sempo Sugihara").

Sempo risked his whole life and career to save Jews from the Holocaust. He has inspired many people around the world, including me. There are many very important ways to be an upstander that I have learned from Sempo. First, he taught me to end physical, mental, and cyber bullying. For example, if I see a person being picked on or hurt, I will pull them out of the situation and tell the bully to stop. Second, I will be an upstander at home by setting a good example for my little brothers and cousins. I will set a good example by listening to the adults and not talking bad about my family members. You should become an upstander because in the end, those small acts of kindness you do for a person will help them throughout their life and make them happy. I hope everyone can become an upstander just like Sempo and the rest of the Heroes of the Holocaust. Forty-five years after signing the visas, he was then asked why he did it. He gave two reasons: "They were human

220

beings and they needed help." He also said: "I'm glad I found the strength to make the decision and give it to them" (Greene, "Sempo Sugihara").

The Holocaust had many heroes who are unknown by many, but those heroes should be not only honored and admired, but also awarded. Sempo should definitely be one of those people. Sempo is not only known for saving Jews during the Holocaust, but doing whatever he could for his family through this rough time. Sempo is truly an inspiring man. He made Jews happy and grateful even during the horrible event. If Sempo didn't stand up to protect Jews, the 6,000 Jews he saved would be dead. Sempo should always be remembered for his acts of kindness, courage, and bravery because he fought for our freedom and the freedom of the Jews in the Holocaust. Many people wouldn't sacrifice their lives and careers to do this kind of thing, but Sempo did and we thank him for that. The Holocaust is a very horrible event, but thanks to Sempo and the many other heroes of the Holocaust, many Jews have been saved from death. Thank you to our heroes of the Holocaust.

Works Cited

Ron, Greene. "Sempo Sugihara." (Online) 6 February 2015.
http://www.jewishvirtuallibrary.org/jsource/Holocaust/sugihara.html
Weitz, Sonia Schreiber. I Promised I Would Tell. Brookline, Massachusetts: Facing History and Ourselves, 1993.

PAUL GRUENINGER; HERO OF THE PAST

Lorena Zavala, Co-winner

Did you know that Paul Grueninger had saved at least 3,700 Jewish people during the Holocaust? What is the Holocaust? The Holocaust was a time in World War II when the Nazis began killing the European Jews. Later on, concentration camps were made to torture the Jews even more. Those who hid in buildings and homes were later found and killed. Those who were lucky were able to escape this horrific nightmare and leave to other countries. And Paul helped end this horrific nightmare for some.

Paul Grueninger was born on October 27, 1891 in the city of St. Gallen. He was a football player in his youth and in the season of 1914-1915, he helped his group to win their only Swiss championship. Paul then grew up to be a Swiss police commander in his birthplace, St. Gallen. When World War II was still in its shape, the Swiss government gave strict orders to Paul that he was to turn all the Jewish refugees back to Austria. At first he did follow his orders, but later on the number of refugees increased and Paul knew he could not let them suffer any more. He ignored his orders and began taking the Jews to Switzerland. Paul made sure to add on their passports that they had arrived before the date of March 1938. He also turned in false reports of the number of refugees that arrived and entered Switzerland. Afterwards, he then could allow them to enter. With Paul's own money, he bought supplies for the needy Jewish people who had to leave their belongings behind.

Grueninger was an upstander in many different ways. He risked his very own life and job for the sake of the terrified Jews. In many ways Paul was important. For example, he was important by risking his life for the Jews. If this had not occurred, they would have been tortured until their last day. He knew what the Germans were doing was wrong, so he wanted to help end this torture. Paul was important by making the decision to save Jews rather than to keep his job. Not only did he save their lives, but he also falsified papers so that they were able to stay in Switzerland. Paul sent them to Diepoldsau camp, where they were given aid. The Jews then were given temporary permits to stay in Switzerland. Later on, the German Nazis had confronted the Swiss government about Grueninger's actions. He was later dismissed from his job and was taken to court. His trial opened in January of 1939 and lasted for over 2 years. The jury had found Paul guilty and put him in jail. Paul served his time and had paid his fines. Paul then passed away in 1972, at the age of 81. It was 1995 when the court decided to reopen his case. The judges decided to explain him from all charges. The following year, he was then 'rehabilitated'from the Swiss government. Although Paul had trouble making a living due to his criminal record, he never once regretted the decision he had made. In 1954 he explained, "It was basically a question of saving human lives threatened with death. How could I then seriously consider bureaucratic schemes and calculations? (Paul Grueninger, page 3)"

In the future I hope to be an upstander. For example, I will defend my classmates when they are getting teased on at school. I will be there to stand up for them, to make them feel better when they feel they can no longer go further. I will have their back when they need it. Second, I will be an upstander by standing up for my family. If one is name calling another, I will be there to stop him/her. I realized that you should do the right thing even though many other people could be doing the wrong thing. Some people thought it was a crime for Grueninger to help save the Jews. But in his heart, Paul knew it was the right thing and did it anyways. He has inspired many people and more to come.

So many people have become heroes because of the Holocaust. So many that most names are unknown, or 'forgotten'. Yet, to the Holocaust heroes it was not about the fame. It was about the lives that they had in their hands. None of the heroes knew that someday they would be famous. They did it because they knew it was the best thing to do in a situation like this. One of these people is Paul Grueninger. Not only did Paul save thousands of Jewish people, but he also built a stronger relationship with a part of the Jewish community. Although not many people recognize the name of Paul Grueninger, he will forever be in the hearts of those he had saved and those who were influenced.

Work Cited

No Author Listed. "The Policeman who Lifted the Border Barrier." (Online) 6 February 2015 http://www.yadvashem.org/yv/en/righteous/stories/grueninger.asp

Weitz, Sonia Schreiber. I Promised I Would Tell. Brookline, Massachusetts: Facing History and Ourselves, 1993.

THE AWESOME HOLOCAUST UPSTANDER

Miahana Hunt

Did you know that Knud Dyby saved 8,000 people during the Holocaust? The Holocaust was a horrible experience for some Jews. The Nazis beat them, starved them, and even shot them. Then, there where the bystanders. The bystanders just sat and watched the Jews get killed and beaten. But some people helped them along the way like some farmers who threw corn into the cattle cars that the Jews where in. Knud Dyby was an awesome example of an upstander during the Holocaust.

In Randers, Denmark in 1915, Knud Dyby was born. Before Germany invaded Denmark, Knud Dyby worked in printing and advertising. Then when money started getting low, he worked for the police and also he became a member of the underground participating in sabotage. In 1943 Mr. Dyby found out that Nazis were planning to round up Denmark's Jews and send them off to concentration camps. He quickly organized commercial fishermen in Copenhagen's North Harbor to transport Danish Jews in small groups to safety in Sweden. Mr. Dyby informed the Jews about what the Nazis where doing through their doctors. They asked for the help of the taxi cab drivers to transport the Jews to the harbor. When he could no longer use the taxi cars, he used the police cars to transport the Jews. Mr. Dyby was a member of the police force so he could use the police cars. The fishermen became so busy with the transports they had to buy fish in Sweden and bring it back to Denmark to fool the guards and make them think that they caught the fish so they wouldn't get suspicious.

Knud Dyby was an amazing upstander. If I were in his place I would hope to do the same thing. Knud Dyby inspired me to be an upstander too. There are two things I will try to do to become an upstander. First, I can help a person in need even if it does involve me getting hurt. For example, if someone is getting bullied I will go and grab the victims arm and walk away. Second, I will try to help my family in need. For example, if my brother/sister is in need I will help him/her. If they fell and were stuck I could help them.

Knud Dyby was an awesome person, but sadly he died on September 8, 2011 at the age of 96. He helped so many people in his lifetime and he saved many Jews. He used all his resources to find out how to help the Jews. He was an awesome and kind person. He had the courage to help people in need. I hope he will also inspire you to become an upstander.

Works Cited

Halstead, Richard, "Knud Dyby, Novato man who helped Save thousands of Jews during World War II, dies at 96." (Online) 6 February 2015 http://www.marinij.com/ci_18880546

Weitz, Sonia Schreiber. I Promised I Would Tell. Brookline, Massachusetts: Facing History and Ourselves, 1993.

HERO OF THE HOLOCAUST

Nino McWilson

Did you know Ester Handberg saved a family's life during the Holocaust? Mrs. Handberg was very concerned about the Jews and she wanted to save as many Jews she could. Ester Handberg was an up stander during the Holocaust.

The Holocaust was a bad time during the 1900's. The Germans didn't like the Jews at that time so they started killing the Jews during World War II. Adolf Hitler was the leader of the Nazi Party in German. Hitler was a dictator from 1934-1945. He did not like the Jews in his country of Germany. Hitler set up concentration camps to kill the Jews. There were many rescuers of the Holocaust like Ester Handberg.

Ester Handberg was an amazing person. She was born in Denmark in 1905, on November 6th. Mrs. Handberg risked her life by saving Jews. "On the night of October 2 a neighbor knocked in on the Strassman's door telling them to leave because the Nazis were in their neighborhood" htt://db.yadvashem.org//righteous/family.html? language=en&itemId.

She arranged for the Strassmans to go to the island of Fyn because the Nazis were in their neighborhood. The Strassmans went to Fyn Island and continued on to Sweden, which was their final destination. Mrs. Handberg arranged for several safe houses in Copenhagen, which is where Mrs. Handberg smuggled the Strassmans into through hospitals under fake names. The Strassmans stayed for a night before leaving to Sweden on a fishing boat.

Ester Handberg was an up stander during the Holocaust. "Mrs. Handberg didn't think it was right to kill Jews because they didn't do anything to them so she saved them." She risked her life to save Jews. Mrs. Handberg was an up stander in two ways. First she risked her life for others when no one wanted to help the Jews. Second she was an up stander because she smuggled Jews out of the country by boat and under fake names. Mrs. Handberg helped me become a better person and an up stander. First I will be an up stander in school. For example, I will be an up stander in

224

school. I will stop fights or I will tell a teacher. Second, I will be an up stander at home. For example, if my brother or sister is saying bad stuff about my parents I will tell them they're not right or I will tell my parents to sit down with them to explain why they should say nice things.

The Holocaust had many Heroes who are unknown by many, but many people remember Ester Handberg. Mrs. Handberg is not only known for saving Jews she is also known for risking her life. Mrs. Handberg was a savior of the Holocaust. Thank you Yad Vashem, which is a memorial place in Israel for remembering the Holocaust Martyrs and Heroes.

Works Cited

No Author Listed. "Rescuers Story." (Online) 6 February 2015. htt://db.yadvashem.org//righteous/family.html? language=en&itemId 4015203.

Weitz, Sonia Schreiber. I Promised I Would Tell. Brookline, Massachusetts: Facing History and Ourselves, 1993.

UNFORGOTTEN GENOCIDE

Olumese Z Oaiya

Do you know what the Holocaust is? The Holocaust was a time in history where Adolf Hitler took over Germany and he was very anti-Semitic (He was extremely discriminatory to Jews). So, he was having Germans kill them. There were some up standers during the time trying to save Jews; one of them is Paul Grüninger. He was courageous enough to risk his career and freedom to save 3,600 Jews. Paul Grüniger was a kind-hearted person. In this paragraph you will learn how his childhood was. Paul Grüniger was born on October 27, 1891 in St. Gallen, Switzerland. He was a determined football player and played for his local team. In 1945-1946 season of football, he led his team to win their one and only Swiss championship. After his football successes, he fought in World War I and afterwards he joined the police. He did very well in his career and rose through the ranks in his hometown.

Paul Grüniger was a police captain when the Nazis annexed neighboring Austria in 1938. Jewish members in the area now had to deal with the same persecution and violence that German Jews had to deal with. The Swiss government sent instructions to Paul that he was to turn Jewish refugees back to Austria. With official emigration locations being closed off to Austrian Jews, the Jews who feared for their life decided to make a decision between life and death and chose to risk crossing the Swiss border illegally. The journey was very challenging for the refugees. Those who were captured crossing the border in the St. Gallen area were brought to Paul starving, cold, and distraught; having being forced to leave their former lives behind. It was

225

then that Paul decided to destroy his own career to give refuge to thousands of Austrian Jews. He permitted illegal entry to Switzerland, and he falsified documents so that the Jews were issued passports classifying them as legal immigrants. Besides making them legal immigrants, he also extended a helping hand and paid out of his own pocket for winter clothes to those who had been unable to flee with them. Such kindness was not disregarded and his actions were eventually discovered. On April 3, 1939 when he arrived for work, the entrance to the police station was blocked. This was unexpected seeing as he was chief of the station. Paul immediately recognized that his actions had been discovered. Months before he had been told he was under investigation, yet Paul continued to falsify documents for Jewish refugees from Austria right up until he was arrested. For his action he was fired from his job, tried, found guilty, and fined 300 Swiss francs (314.90USD) by the court. He also served time in jail.

After Paul was convicted, he struggled to find employment after World War II and with a criminal record it was very hard to find a job. Excluded and forgotten, Paul lived the rest of his life in difficult circumstances. Despite the difficulties and hardship, he was still very optimistic about life and did not seem to have any regret whatsoever about the choices he made to save Jews. In 1954 in an interview he said "It was basically a question of saving human lives threatened with death. How could I seriously consider bureaucratic schemes and calculations?"

In December 1970 as a response to the protest in the media, the Swiss government sent Paul a somewhat reserved letter of apology, but still did not reopen his trial or reinstate his pension. Only after his death were steps to rehabilitate by the government set into motion. The first attempt was rejected by the Swiss Council; it took as late as 1995 until the Swiss federal Government finally annulled Paul conviction. After his death and recognition by Yad Vashem, Paul's legacy was subsequently restored in Switzerland. In 1995, the Swiss government finally annulled his conviction. Several streets and a school have been named after him and in 2006, SC Bruhl's stadium (the stadium he played in) was renamed Paul *Grüninger Stadium.*

Works Cited

No Author Listed. "Paul Grueniger" (Online) 6 February 2015
   http://jewishcurrents.org/tag/paul-grueninger

Weitz, Sonia Schreiber. I Promised I would Tell Brookline. Massachusetts: Facing History and Ourselves, 1993

No Author Listed. "Paul Gruninger" (Online) 6 February 2015
   https://jfr.org/rescuer-stories/gruninger-paul/

A TEACHER'S BRAVERY

Riley Hessler

Did you know that during the Holocaust over one and a half million Jewish children were deported and/or murdered? If you don't know what the Holocaust was, it was a terrible time for Jewish people. They were sent to concentration camps and were given small amounts of food and living space and over 6 million Jewish people were killed. The Jewish children were harassed and had to wear yellow stars and other markings. They were also banned from public schools. During this time, most teachers abandoned their Jewish students because they didn't want to get in trouble with the government. Gerda Valentiner, a teacher during the Holocaust, didn't abandon her students. This is about the brave Gerda Valentiner.

Gerda Valentiner was a teacher in Denmark. She was born on Jan. 27, 1906. She was also part of the Danish Resistance during the German occupation. She risked her life to help the Jewish children. She smuggled children away from their parents before they could be deported. She kept them hidden from the Nazi soldiers in her own house and fed them foods in their Jewish dietary laws. She also had to figure out how to get all the kids to Sweden or on a train to Sweden without being seen. After World War II, Gerda volunteered in Jewish refugee camps in Germany and Austria for two years. When she was asked about her bravery she said, "I only did what many Danes did, nothing special. We thought it perfectly natural to help people in mortal danger" (Their Fate Will Be My Fate Too, Page 1).

In 1971, at the age of 68, Gerda Valentiner retired and traveled to Israel. She spent a year there exploring the country and learning Hebrew.

Being an upstander is important even if you aren't loud about it. One reason is you can help the victim. For example, if I see a bully trying to do the crime of bullying I will do my best to stop it. I will first try to stop them myself. Then if I can't do it myself, I will tell an adult instead. Another reason is you can help the victim help himself/herself. For example, I will tell the victim to ignore the bully. If it still happens, I will tell them to go to the office and fill out an incident report. Then if that does not work, I will tell them to go to the principal, and ask to stop the bully.

During the Holocaust over 6 million Jewish people were killed. Over one and a half million Jewish children were deported and/or murdered. Most people turned their backs during this awful time. But there were some upstanders who risked their lives to help save the Jewish people. One of those upstanders was Gerda Valentiner. I think Gerda Valentiner was a different type of an upstander. She didn't confront Nazi soldiers, or protest them in public. She stood up to them quietly and secretly helped protect children who needed it. She bravely did what she thought was right.

227

She even risked her own life to save others. She was a brave teacher who saved countless children because she thought it was the right thing to do. If she hadn't, who knows where those people would be today.

Work Cited

No Author Listed. Their Fate Will Be My Fate Too." (Online) February 6, 2015. http://www.yadvashem.org/yv/en/exhibitions/righteous-teachers/valentiner.asp

I Promised I Would Tell, Weitz,Sonia Scheriber.   Facing History and Ourselves. Brookline, Massachusetts

A HERO FROM THE HOLOCAUST

Samira Longoria

There were many people who rescued the Jews during the Holocaust. "What is the Holocaust?" you say? Well, the Holocaust is an era where the Nazis would murder every Jew in Europe, either by working to death, or send to a death camp where they'd be killed immediately. As said before, there were many people who rescued the Jews. Gerda Valentiner, a teacher in Denmark, rescued many.

Gerda Valentiner was a teacher who helped transport Danish Jews to Sweden. When she planned out when their deportation, she took the Jewish children away from their parents and brought them to her home, waiting for the right moment to transfer them to Sweden. Gerda risked her life many times, and showed her great sensitivity and respect for the children's religious observance. When she saw that some of the children stuck to the Jewish dietary laws and therefore only ate bread, she bought them new dishes and food they could eat. One night in September 1943, Gerda came to one of her pupil's parents to warn them about the danger. A couple days later, she allowed their family to stay at Gerda's home until she planned out their transfer. Two attempts failed, but the third try succeeded. They left on a fishing boat 10 kilometers north of Copenhagen to Landskrona, Sweden. She modestly said, "I only did what Danes did, nothing special. We thought it perfectly natural to help people in mortal trouble." After the war, Gerda retired from her job as a teacher and volunteered to help the Jews in Jewish refugee camps in Germany and Austria.

Ever since Gerda Valentiner rescued the children from pain and misery, she has helped me to become a better upstander, and realized that being an upstander is more important than you think it is. I can be a better upstander in two ways: First, I will become a better by helping people when no one else is. There are many people who will see an injured person, and just walk away from them or just take photos. If I ever see one, I'll immediately call 911 and, if wounded, apply pressure on the wound and wait until the police arrive. Second, I will be a better upstander by warning others

228

about any incoming danger. Recently, there's been a shooting in Texas and Detroit, where they killed a transgender woman for no reason. Like the Holocaust, these were all hate crimes. If I see any hate crimes or hear about any, I can contact the police about this, and then send a warning about this through social media, and by telling close friends so they can spread the news. Also, being an upstander is very important because if you do not stand up for someone who may be frightened or weak, they can be beat up, or get picked on, which could lower their self esteem.

Gerda Valentiner saved and inspired many people. She saved the lives of Jewish children by taking them from their parents, bringing them to her home, planned out their deportation, and transported them to a certain area so they would not be killed. She saved many lives and risked her life many times, and without her, many lives would be taken away from innocent families. There are many others who helped the Jews during the Holocaust, and without them, more lives would have been taken away and Adolf Hitler would be successful in creating a world of his own, a world of Germans with blonde hair and blue eyes.

Works Cited

No author listed. "Teachers who Rescued Jews During the Holocaust." (Online) 11 February 2015. http://www.yadvashem.org/yv/en/exhibitions/righteous-teachers/valentiner.asp

No author listed. "Rescue Story." (Online) 11 February 2015. http://db.yadvashem.org/righteous/ family.html?language=en&itemId=4017998

Weitz, Sonia Schreiber. I Promised I Would Tell. Massachusetts: Facing History and Ourselves, 1993.

PAUL GRUNINGER

Virgilio S. Cecilio, Special Award

Do you know what amazing things Holocaust (A depressing time when European Jews were slaughtered) upstanders did to save Jews? One of those people was a man named Paul Gruninger. Paul Gruninger was a senior police officer guarding the Swiss border in August of the year 1938.While guarding the border, Gruninger permitted two- to three-thousand Jewish refugees to cross the border to neutral Switzerland illegally.

In the late 1800s an upstander was born named Paul Gruninger. Paul Gruninger was a senior police officer. In 1938, Paul Gruninger disregarded his orders and permitted thousands of Jewish refugees to enter Switzerland illegally. The year after, he was dismissed from his post, lost his police rank and pension rights. In 1940, Gruninger was taken to trial, was found guilty of fraud. He served time in jail and was fined. After released, for the remainder of his life, Gruninger struggled to make a living. It was difficult to make a living in Switzerland, having a criminal record. Paul Gruninger passed away in 1972. In 1995; about 50 years after the war had ended, 23 years after his death. The same court where Gruninger was condemned, other judges decided to reopen the trial and absolve Gruninger. "Gruninger was in charge of the Swiss border at canton of St. Gallen, disregarded the order (the order to only let people with valid passports to enter) and permitted between two to three thousand Jewish refugees to enter Switzerland illegally."

The actions Paul Gruninger took are the actions I decided to take. Paul Gruninger being an upstander inspired me to support my friends and family. Paul Gruninger helped endangered people that were going to be killed and bring them into a neutral place where the enemies wouldn't look for them. First, after reading and studying on what Paul Gruninger did to help Jewish victims, I wanted to start helping out other people or my family with stuff they weren't capable of doing. For example, I would help out my brother with stuff he isn't able to do, such as carrying something that he wasn't able to carry. Actions like this make the world a better place. Second, Paul Gruninger was an upstander who saved many Jews. Gruninger risked his life for them. To illustrate, I would help people escape the area where they were being killed. I would risk my life trying to help these people. "Gruninger decided to disregard the official instructions and to let the desperate refugees enter Switzerland. Move over, in order to legalize the refugees status, he falsified their registration, so that their passports showed that they had arrived in Switzerland before March 1938, when entry into the country had been restricted (The Policeman who lifted the Border Barrier)."

You now know what amazing things this Holocaust upstander did to help Jews. Paul Gruninger guarded the Swiss border and disregarded the official order. He permitted thousands of Jews cross the Swiss border. He falsified the passports so they could cross. After being caught he knew he was going to be sent to prison for his actions, but he was proud of what he did, saving the refugees. The actions Paul Gruninger inspired many other people to help around the world. Gruninger risked his freedom to save many other Jews so they can have their freedom. He was actions from the people he saved. He risked his whole life by helping.

Works Cited

No Author Listed. "Paul Gruninger | Switzerland" (Online) 5 February 2015.
   https://jfr.org/rescuer-stories/gruninger-paul/

No Author Listed. "The Policeman who lifted the Border Barrier" (Online) 5 February 2015. http://www.yadvashem.org/yv/en/righteous/stories/grueninger.asp

Weitz, Sonia Schreiber. I Promised I Would Tell. Brookline, Massachusetts: Facing History and Ourselves, 1993.

Holmes Jr. High School, Davis, CA

Jeanne Reeve is an English teacher at O.W. Holmes Junior High school in Davis, California where she has been teaching English for over fifteen years. Social justice and human dignity are at the heart of her Tolerance unit that all her eighth grade students experience on an annual basis. Using historical non-fiction, Mrs. Reeve encourages students to learn about the past in order to create a more peaceful future. As a 2008 co-recipient of the Thong Hy Huynh award, the Davis community has recognized her on-going commitment to students and tolerance. Mr. Bernard Marks is a key part of the Holmes community as he has inspired hundreds of students year after year to "never forget" the injustices of the past with his sobering story of survival.

SWISS OR DANISH HEROES OF THE HOLOCAUST

Erin Rairdan

In the early 1940's, Europe saw the beginning of an event that would change the world forever. It was called the Holocaust. The Holocaust lasted for three years and saw the persecution and murder of 6 million Jews under the main influence of Adolf Hitler. But it wasn't only the Jews who were attacked. The German Nazis targeted Gypsies (Roma), homosexuals, and anyone who tried to stand up for those being terribly wronged. The Nazis attributed their actions to their infamous ideology that, stated simply, proclaimed Germans (Aryans) the superior race which all other were inferior to and therefore were qualified to be "sterilized." The saddest part of the Holocaust is the fact that when the Jews began to flee from prosecution, no other country would take them in. The United States, England, and France all turned them away. But even when great world powers like England cowered in fear, other voices from all around the world piped up and called out to the Jews. These people created organizations and risked their lives to rescue the Jews from the Nazis. In fact, many notable Holocaust heroes were Swiss or Dutch.

Friedrich Born was the Chief Delegate of the International Committee of the Red Cross of Switzerland from May 1944 to January 1945. He was stationed in Budapest, Hungary at the time. During his one-year service, Born is thought to have saved from 11,000 to 15,000 Jews in the Budapest area. He accomplished this achievement under the Red Cross. Born set up Red Cross protected houses, protected over sixty Jewish establishments, and gave out thousands of Red Cross protection letters. He also saved over 7,000 Jewish children and orphans and rescued thousands of more Jews from deportation camps and death marches in the Budapest area.

Maurice Dubois also was associated with the Red Cross of Switerland. Dubois ran the Secours Suisse organization, a Swiss organization that was connected and later became part of the Swiss Red Cross. During the Holocaust, many of children were separated from their parents, who were most likely deported to Auschwitz or other camps around Europe. The Secours Suisse mainly supported these needy children in southern France with day centers, clinics, and relief programs that were dedicated to keeping the children healthy and safe. Dubois continued to safely rescue these children by taking them to the Château de la Hille in the département of Ariège for two years. But in 1942, all refugees aged 15 and up under the Secours Suisse's protection were arrested by officials and were taken to a detention camp at Vernet.

Dubois took this harshly, but through hard work, determination, and wits, he managed to recover the children and smuggle them to Switzerland.

Friedel Bohny-Reiter and her husband Auguste Bohny joined the Secours Suisse organization in 1940, and they saved many orphan or refugee children from the Nazi regime. Friedel Bohny-Reiter frequently rescued Jews from deportations from Rivesaltes, which was the city that her base camp was located. Bohny-Reiter would wait for the supervising officers to shift their attention, and then she would sneak some children to a storeroom at the Secours Suisse campsite. There they would wait as she fearlessly went back and forth, hiding as many Jewish children as she could before the trains left. Mr. and Mrs. Bohny also ran an institution in Chambon that protected about 800 children from 1941-1944. This institution was almost a rest stop for the children who stayed there for a maximum of six months or until a more stable living situation could be made. Auguste Bohny was widely acknowledged for his efforts to keep these children safe. He successfully avoided French and German police multiple times and prevented the deportation of his precious refugees at Chambon while other institutions in the area had their entire camps deported.

Another heroine who cared for children during the Holocaust was Elizabeth Eidenbenz. Though she started out a teacher in Switzerland, she then became a nurse and volunteered to help children during Spain's civil war. In 1939 she founded and was the director of the Mothers of Elne (or Maternité Suisse), an institution created to help refugee pregnant women, mothers and children. The Maternité Suisse housed Spanish refugees, Jewish women and mothers running from Rivesaltes, Gypsies (Roma), and others hiding from the Nazis. All in all, 600 children were born at Maternité Suisse during its operational period. After the war, Eidenbenz was awarded the Righteous Among the Nations medal by the Yad Vashem Institution, the Civil Order and Solidarity Medal by Queen Sophia of Spain, the Legion d'Honneur by the French Republic, and the Cross of Saint Jordi by the Generalitat de Catalunya.

The Holocaust heroes of Switzerland were brave, compassionate people who decided to stand up for others without being asked to. What might have started out a small, timid act of kindness became a bold balancing act that saved the many lives that otherwise would have been lost to discrimination. Friedrich Born, Maurice Dubois, Friedel Bohny-Reiter, Auguste Bohny, Elizabeth Eidenbenz, and all the other international heroes of the Holocaust, thank you for the lives that you saved.

SWISS AND DANISH HEROES IN THE HOLOCAUST

Gretchen Richter

There are many heroes to be remembered in the tragic and destructive events of the Holocaust. Two that stand out for me are Mr. Knud Christiansen and Moshe Kraus. These men put their lives on the line on a daily basis in efforts to save all of the Jews they could gather and protect. They are an inspiration to all who can appreciate the dedication and courage it took to carry out their actions.

One truly inspirational hero was Mr. Knud Christiansen, a member of the Danish Freedom Fighters. Christiansen was a former Olympian in rowing at the 1936 Olympics. He watched as Herr Hitler exited the stadium on protest of watching a black man receive a medal. He was a successful business man in a company producing leather and was a key member of the resistance because of his key location near a Nazi headquarters and was involved in many acts of Nazi sabotage. He could find out the plans of attack on Jews and alert other members before the plan was carried out. He was one of the first to discover an attack on an expected 7,000 Jews on October 1, 1943.

Christiansen created a rescue network for escaping Jews. He ushered large groups of Jews into safe houses under false names. Knud earned himself a position on the Nazi watch list for his persistent involvement in the resistance. He himself confronted the highest ranking Nazi in Denmark nicknamed the "Blood Hound of Paris" in hopes to free his friend from a detainment camp. His family donated many locations as safe houses and escape locations. His wife was a huge help, writing a newspaper informing people of the current events of the Holocaust. Her newspaper was entitled "Die Warheit," translating to "The Truth." She also cared for wounded soldiers involved in the cause.

When asked how long he had been a part of the resistance, he responded, "I was there from the beginning until the end." He and his family immigrated to America in 1970. He and his wife had two children and two more after the war. His name was added to an elite list of people in 2005 called "Righteous Among Nations." Mr. Knud Christiansen passes away on February 2, 2012 at 97.

Another Holocaust hero was Moshe Kraus. Moshe managed to save 40,000 Jews in his lifetime. He was responsible for the largest rescue mission ever conducted during the Holocaust. The range estimate was 40,000-100,000 Jews. Kraus created safe houses and escape routes all over but that was by far not his biggest achievement.

Moshe Kraus and Carl Lutz created tens of thousands of forged documents making Jews foreign Swiss nationals, protected by the Swiss government. The documents were handed out in the streets and all over, to wherever Kraus could reach or send people to. Kraus was given a report of 800,000 Jews planned to be killed in Auschwitz. He saw the report, added his own list detailing every person from each city and district, the reports were sent throughout Hungary and Switzerland.

Kraus was one of the head leaders in the Zionist movements in Hungary and directed the Palestine office in Budapest. He helped to alert other national governments of the deportation of Jews and successfully put a stop to it. Moshe hid thousands of Jews in 76 safe houses he contributed to purchasing, saving countless lives.

The documents granting Jews safety were all in favor of Moshe Kraus. He purchased a factory to multiply the documents by the thousands. The youth resistance and young Jews hidden in safe houses near the city got involved by helping to distribute the documents to anyone they could get their hands on. Some dressed as Nazis to pass out the papers to keep others from suspicion and shutting down the whole operation. The living conditions in the safe houses weren't the best but they were enough to survive. Red Cross provided food for the refugees forced into cramped spaces with thousands of others. Sixty-thousand to 70,000 Jews were hidden in these 76 safe houses. Kraus purchased two more factories to help multiply the documents as fast as he could, saving so many in the process.

After the Holocaust, Kraus moved to Israel and ran an institution for boys. He married a fellow Holocaust survivor and had two children. Moshe Kraus was not credited for his enormous contributions but was rewarded with the rescue of 30,000 Jews. His birth date is unknown but passed away in 1986 at 78 years of age.

In conclusion, it was not only these amazing men who put in their efforts to stop the Holocaust, it was regular citizens who took a stand for what they believed. The resistance was made out of all kinds of people from all kinds of backgrounds and lives. All of this because one man decided he didn't like certain people and wanted them dead. The fact that non-Jews were out and about every day risking their lives for people they didn't even know that are part of a religion they don't practice is amazing. That is truly what was heroic.

SWISS HEROES OF THE HOLOCAUST: ANNE-MARIE IM HOF-PIGUET

Hannah Lee, Runner-up

Anne-Marie Im Hof-Piguet worked for the Swiss Red Cross Aid for Children. But when Jewish refugees were in risk of deportation, she risked her own life to save them by smuggling them over the Franco-Swiss border.

Anne-Marie Piguet was born on April 12, 1916 to Henri-Joseph Piguet and Thérèse Nicole in Martigny in the Vallée de Joux. She studied at the University of Lausanne and received her Bachelor of Arts degree in 1940, when she volunteered for the Swiss Red Cross (AJPN.org, "Anne-Marie Im Hof-Piguet"). She had given up her dream of teaching, and instead traveled to the Château de Bellevue in Montluel, in the Department of Ain, where Jewish and Spanish children were removed from the Rivesaltes internment camp by the Swiss Red Cross, and stayed there from June 1942 to January 1943. In May 1943, after a short stay in a Toulouse operational center, Piguet moved to the Château de La Hille, in the Department of Ariège, which housed Jewish children from Germany and Austria who were either orphans or separated from their parents. Several had already escaped to Switzerland or Spain, but some had been deported (the "Righteous Among the Nations" of Swiss Nationality).

As Nazis occupied south France, they decided to round up all Jews without French citizenship above the age of 16. They raided the castle of La Hille in August of 1942, but Maurice Dubois foiled their plans. He traveled to Vichy and negotiated for their release with Prime Minister Pierre Laval. Dubois threatened to cease placing undernourished French children into Swiss Red Cross summer camps. He did not actually have the power to do so, and the Swiss Red Cross would not have supported him, but his bluff worked (The Righteous Among the Nations, "Maurice Dubois") The Jews were given their freedom, and Dubois, his wife Ellen, and Rösli Näf, or Rosa Naef, a nurse who joined Dr. Albert Schweitzer in Lambaréné and engaged in the Swiss Red Cross from 1941-1942, organized a route for them to escape into Switzerland illegally (AJPN.org, "Rösli Näf or Rosa Naef"). However, when Piguet arrived at La Hille, Jewish youths were still in danger of being arrested and sent to detention and internment camps, such as detention camp Vernet (The Righteous Among the Nations, "Anne-Marie Im Hof-Piguet").

Piguet, who had only been 26 when she entered the service of the Swiss Red Cross, was nonetheless clever and energetic. She decided to help smuggle Jews into Switzerland, and organized a secret route from La Hille, over Toulouse, through Lyon, by the children colony Montluel, passing Champagnole, to Chappelle-de-Bois, through the Risoux forest bordering her native Vallée de Joux, arriving at a rendezvous on the Swiss side of the border at the Cottage Hôtel d'Italie. She guided children on this route to safety and was helped along the way by a network of brave men and women, such as the Cordier sisters, and her own mother and father. Victoria and Madeleine Cordier lived in Champagnole and remained resolute in helping Piguet to the last (AJPN.org, "Anne-Marie Im Hof-Piguet"; Wikipedia, the Free Encyclopedia). One such example of their steadfastness was their last trip. This time, they had two refugees with them. Edith Goldapper and Inge Schragenheim had left the castle of La Hille in November 1943, and met the sisters living near the Jura Mountains in Champagnole. Anne-Marie had just gotten word that the border guards had been reinforced, and it had begun to snow in the Jura Mountains. When she warned the Cordiers, they simply kept the refugees at their home and took care of

236

them until the snow cleared in May 1944, even though food was scarce. As they were about to cross the Franco-Swiss border, a Swiss border guard stopped them, and ordered them to turn back. This would have meant arrest on French territory and immediate deportation, but Madeleine saved the day by persuading the border guard to let them pass. The refugees ended up having to go directly to a Swiss camp for refugees. Anne-Marie's family and friends also housed and supported refugees, she herself sometimes taking them to her home in Le Sentier and providing for them (Wagner, 106). Henri-Joseph Piguet, Anne-Marie's father, a forest inspector, would pick up refugees, and her mother would escort them to Zurich for refugee pastor Vogt (Wikipedia, the Free Encyclopedia). Anne-Marie, being the daughter and granddaughter of Vaud forest inspectors, knew the Risoux forest like the back of her own hand, and saved many lives that way (AJPN.org, "Anne-Marie Im Hof-Piguet").

Over the course of two years, from 1942 to 1944, Anne-Marie Im Hof-Piguet rescued a total of 14 Jewish lives, seeing them safely over the Franco-Swiss border. Among these refugees were Hans Schmutz, the son of a Swiss farmer, Paul Schlesinger, his mother, Flora Schlesinger, Walter Kamlet, Edith Goldapper, Inge Schragenheim, and eight other people, one of them a cook in La Hille, whose husband had been deported (AJPN.org, "Anne-Marie Im Hof-Piguet"; Hubler). On July 16, 1990, Yad Vashem recognized Im Hof-Piguet as Righteous Among the Nations. They presented the medal to her in person in Bern on November 28, 1991, at age 75 (The Righteous Among the Nations, "Anne-Marie Im Hof-Piguet").

There is, possibly, no one who would say Anne-Marie Im Hof-Piguet did not deserve that medal. Israel's ambassador to Switzerland, Raphael Gvir, said, as he presented the award to her that she had done everything for humanitarian reasons, and she saved many lives during World War II in spite of fear. She did what she felt was necessary despite the "clear and constant peril to her own life" (Wagner, 108). Anne-Marie Im Hof-Piguet was a clear symbol of humanity at its best, saving innocent souls from perhaps the largest and most cruel genocide the world has seen, and all at her own risk. She remains, to this day, a beacon of hope in the darkest times caused by the horrors of war.

Works Cited

"Anne-Marie Im Hof-Piguet." *AJPN.org*. Just Among the Nations, n.d. Web. 22 Feb. 2015.

"Anne-Marie Im Hof-Piguet." *The "Righteous Among the Nations" of Swiss Nationality*. N.p., 11 Dec. 1999. Web. 23 Feb. 2015.

"Anne-Marie Im Hof-Piguet." *The Righteous Among the Nations*. Yad Vashem, n.d. Web. 25 Feb. 2015.

"Anne-Marie Im Hof-Piguet." *Wikipedia, the Free Encyclopedia*. Wikimedia Foundation, Inc., 19 May 2014. Web. 23 Feb. 2015.

Hubler, Lucienne. "Im Hof [-Piguet] Anne-Marie." *HLS-DHS-DSS*. N.p., 22 Dec. 2011. Web. 22 Feb. 2015.

"Maurice Dubois." *The Righteous Among the Nations*. Yad Vashem, n.d. Web. 23 Feb. 2015.

"Rösli Näf or Rosa Naef." *AJPN.org*. Just Among the Nations, n.d. Web. 24 Feb. 2015.

Wagner, Meir. *The Righteous of Switzerland: Heroes of the Holocaust*. Hoboken: Ktav House, 2001. Print.

KNUD CHRISTIANSEN: THE LITTLE KNOWN HOLOCAUST HERO

Jishnu Sen

Holocaust, the systematic annihilation of the Jews by the Nazis during World War II, shows how cruel man can be. By the end of the war, over 60 percent of the Jewish population in Europe had died. Under the autocratic rule of Adolf Hitler, Germany saw the rise of the Nazis, who were anti-Semitic and did not believe that the Jewish people deserved to live. The Nazis also hated homosexuals, Gypsies, and the disabled. Hitler believed in Aryan supremacy. At the beginning of World War II, Nazi Germany had taken over almost all of Europe and were arresting Jews and sending them to concentration camps were they were tortured, and forced to live and work in unhealthy environments for little or no pay. These camps were brutal and few have survived them. The Nazis also constructed several death camps, to which thousands of Jews were deported from the concentration camps, and then killed by lethal gasses.

Out of the many European countries that the Nazis had taken over, the occupation of Denmark was unique because of the partial autonomy they were given by the Nazis due to Denmark's neutral status in the beginning of the war. During this time of occupation, a theologian and professor of church history at the University of Copenhagen named Hal Koch started to give public lectures about how the toleration of Nazi occupation contradicts with the nation's Biblical ideals and democratic belief. Koch roused the spirits of many Danes and brought back the pride of Denmark. Denmark, as a nation was special due to its love for democracy, as well as its deep ideals that all the people of Denmark were righteous citizens, no matter who they are.

In 1943, as the German occupiers demanded more and more from the Danes, they started to refuse to meet those demands. Shortly after, Danes began to show active resistance towards the Nazis. This effort was called the Danish Resistance. In response, Germany immediately retracted the little freedom that the Danes initially had and fully took over the Danish Government. Later in 1943, Dr. Werner Best, Hitler's representative in Denmark, declared a "state of emergency." This meant that curfews, and other strict laws would be imposed on the Danish people. Then in September of 1943, Werner Best informed a high ranking Nazi official named George F. Duckwitz of a plan which Adolf Hitler called the Final Solution. The plan was to conduct a massive round-up of the 6,500Jews in Copenhagen on Rosh Hashanah, the Jewish New Year. The fact that every Jew in Copenhagen was expected to be at home on Rosh Hashanah made it an ideal day. For unknown reasons, Duckwitz immediately informed Danish officials of this plan. These Danish officials relayed the information to Copenhagen's main rabbi, Marcus Melchior, who announced that nobody should stay home on the day of Rosh Hashanah during service at the local synagogue.

As the information about the Rosh Hashanah round-up became public, many non-Jew Danes rushed to help the Jewish Danes. One of these Danes was Mr. Knud Marstrand Christiansen. He was a well-known Olympic rower who lived in Copenhagen. Christiansen had first seen an example of Hitler's discriminatory ideals when Hitler walked out of the stadium as a black man named Jesse Owens won gold.

Christiansen grew up in Denmark, and met his wife-to-be Karen Rasmussen shortly after the 1936 Berlin Olympics. They both hated the Nazis's cruel and irrational ways. Soon after marrying Karen, Christiansen joined the Danish Resistance against the German occupation of Denmark. They protected and sheltered thousands of Jews in their own homes. Christiansen ferried dozens of Danish Jews to safety in Sweden using his Olympic rowboat. His wife risked her life every day by publishing a newspaper which translated Dutch BBC broadcasts into German, so that the people of Denmark could know about the daily advances of the Allied forces. Karen also took care of the Danes who were hiding from the Gestapo and SS (Schutzstaffel). Christiansen lived in a luxurious apartment in Copenhagen, the capital of Denmark, which was very close to the port and that allowed him to know when Nazi troops were entering and leaving Denmark. One night, Knud saw German freighters through his apartment window. Knud realized that the freighters would be used to deport Danish Jews. He immediately warned his friends, the Philipson brothers, not to go home that night, lest they get captured. They ignored him and were promptly caught by a group of Nazis. When Knud tried to tell the Nazi soldiers that the Philipsons were not full Jewish, the guards ignored him, and threatened Knud with severe consequences should he return. So, Knud decided to go to Werner Best, Hitler's envoy in Denmark. Best struck a deal with Christiansen. This deal stated that if Christiansen were to participate in a Nazi propaganda film, then the Philipsons would be released. Though the film was never made, the Philipsons were released from the death camp. When he learned about the plan to deport the Jews to the death camps on Rosh Hashanah, Christiansen rushed to hide them from the SS and Gestapo, two branches of the Nazi Secret Police. Risking his and his family's life, Christiansen started to hide the Jews in his own home. Due to Knud's high status in Denmark, he was also able to hide the Jews in churches, hospitals and other large buildings. Knud helped Jewish friends, as well as complete strangers. Knud also helped the Danish Resistance by recruiting other Danes eager to help the Jews. His father-in-law had bought a large house near the beach, which he was using to shelter Jews escaping from the Nazis who were waiting for a boat to Sweden. Knud moved to the United States soon after the War.

After many years, on Christiansen's 65th birthday, a Holocaust survivor named Max Rawitscher released details on Knud's heroic deeds. Twenty-five years later, Yad Vashem, a Jewish organization created to remember the Jews who perished in the Holocaust, recognized Knud and his wife Karen as Righteous Among the Nations, which is an award that is given to non-Jews who risked their lives to help Jewish people.

Throughout the entire war, out of the 6 million European Jews who perished, only about 100 were Danes. The very fact that 95 percent of Danish Jews survived the war shows just how much a nation that believes in itself can do against an onslaught of cruelty and barbarism.

RAOUL WALLENBERG: A HOLOCAUST HERO

Sasha Ballowe

"Whoever saves a single life, saves an entire universe" (Mishnah, Sanhedrin 4:5). Perhaps mankind's most shameful act in history, the Holocaust revealed the true nature of many – both murderers and those who allowed these crimes against humanity to go unchallenged. But the Holocaust also had heroes, courageous individuals who proved that although mankind can be unspeakably savage and cruel, there is always someone who perseveres, who proves that humanity is not lost. Raoul Wallenberg was one such hero.

The Holocaust was the Jewish genocide in Europe by the Nazis under Adolf Hitler. Striving to return Germany to greatness after a humiliating defeat in World War I, Hitler made Germany powerful again through the ruthlessness of his Nazi regime. He convinced millions of Germans that Jews were the cause of Germany's defeat. Jews were stripped of their rights and dignity, and became the victims of Germany's irrational fury. From 1933 to 1945, Hitler ordered all Jews to concentration camps, where 6.6 million Jews died.

Born on August 4, 1912 to Raoul Oscar Wallenberg and Maria Sofia Wising, Raoul Wallenberg's arrival in this world was encircled by tragedy. His father, a 23-year-old Swedish officer, died from illness eight months after his wedding and three months before the birth of his son. Three months after Wallenberg's birth, his maternal grandfather died of pneumonia. Wallenberg's remaining family focused all of their love and care on him and it was said that because of this, he grew to become an "unusually generous, loving, and compassionate person."

Wallenberg's paternal grandfather, Gustav Wallenberg, intended for his grandson to become a banker, and taught him to uphold his highly respected family's tradition of becoming successful bankers, diplomats, or politicians. However, Wallenberg decided to become an architect. He served in the military and then traveled to the United States in 1931 to study architecture at the University of Michigan. After earning his bachelor's degree in 1935, he returned to Sweden. Faced with scarce job opportunities, Wallenberg traveled to Cape Town, South Africa to work at a Swedish firm selling building material for six months. Afterward, he was given another job at a Dutch bank office in Haifa, Palestine (present-day Israel).

In Palestine, Wallenberg encountered several Jews who had escaped Hitler's Germany. He was deeply affected by their stories of inhumane treatment, and was reminded of his own half-Jewish heritage. In 1936, he formed an architect and trade partnership with a Hungarian Jew, Koloman Lauer, and then became a co-owner and international director of the Mid-European Trading Company. In the spring of 1944, people were becoming increasingly aware of just how horrifying and real Hitler's plans for the Jews were. Two escaped Jews told the public of the concentration camps and how countless Jews were being gassed to death. Gradually, the climbing death count of the Jews was becoming more widely recognized.

Because Wallenberg was a descendant of an exemplary Swedish Christian family, he was able to travel easily throughout Germany and Nazi-controlled France. Thus, he became increasingly familiar with Nazi bureaucracy and became particularly successful in his required business dealings with the Nazis. As he learned more, he became more concerned about the fate of Europe's Jews and was not hesitant to relay their frightening stories to any who would listen.

During this period, the United States assembled the War Refugee Board, an organization intending to aid the Jews and other victims of the Nazis. The WRB came to Sweden, which had an embassy in Budapest, Hungary. The WRB was looking for a volunteer to work in Budapest with the Swedish government to issue Swedish diplomatic passports to as many Jews as possible to free them from Nazi control. Wallenberg was chosen by the WRB for this task on July 9, 1944, at age 31. Some 437,000 Jews living outside of Budapest had already been deported, leaving 230,000 Hungarian Jews remaining. Wallenberg then altered the appearance of the Swedish protective passports, called the "Schutzpasses." He used the blue and yellow of Sweden's flag and the triple crown of Sweden. This passport saved the lives of tens of thousands of Jews and anti-Nazi supporters. To make the passports official and unquestionable, billboards were built all around Budapest, confirming the authority of the passports.

Wallenberg was soon the head of a special department in the Budapest embassy, and was everywhere, saving hundreds daily. So consumed was Wallenberg with his work that he only got one to two hours rest each night. In the beginning, there were around 250 people working in his department, and eventually, he had around 400 people working constantly. A legend among the Jews, Wallenberg was frequently described as a warm, calm, and collected man, whose presence meant you were saved.

He worked tirelessly to save as many as he could, using sly tactics to trick the Nazis. He persuaded the Hungarian authorities to free his Jewish staff from having to wear the Yellow Star, a standard requirement for Jews under Nazi control. This enabled his workers to move around freely while keeping their heritage hidden.

In a section of Budapest called the "International Ghetto," Wallenberg purchased thirty buildings, which he adorned with the Swedish flag and the Jewish star. These buildings were under the protection of the Swedish government. In them, he set up hospitals, schools, soup kitchens, and a shelter for 8,000 children whose parents had been lost. The buildings were normally protected, but if Wallenberg was alerted by one of his spies that a Nazi or Hungarian raid was approaching, he placed young, blond Jews in Nazi uniforms as "guards" in front of the buildings.

But even Raoul Wallenberg could not prevent every invasion. On Christmas Day in 1944, a Hungarian Nazi raid found a Swedish-protected children's shelter. All 78 children who lived there were shot or beaten to death.

Wallenberg's swift actions in installing protected shelters encouraged other neutral ministries and the International Red Cross to expand the protected shelters. Post-war, it was estimated that 50,000 Jews living in the International Ghetto survived. Twenty-five thousand Jews were directly under Wallenberg's protection.

On October 15, 1944, the legal Hungarian government fell and a pro-Nazi government called the Arrow-Cross rose to power. The Arrow-Cross attempted to complete the "final solution," and they fought more sadistically then even the German Nazis. Wallenberg continually hindered the Arrow-Cross's actions by reporting their every move. However, when supplies became scarce for the Nazis and trucks couldn't be issued to deport Jews from the city, the death marches began.

Wallenberg and Per Anger, the second secretary of the Swedish legation, drove alongside the women and children who were forced to march and gave them food, clothing, water, and Swedish passports whenever they could. On the first day, they saved 100 people with these passports. Wallenberg ordered more trucks to help and ended up rescuing 1,500 people on their way to Auschwitz.

In November, SS Lieutenant Colonel Adolf Eichmann and his Nazis were ordered back to Berlin as the Nazis prepared to surrender. All marches stopped and all "purification" was to cease. By this time, Wallenberg was a legend among the Jews. He was frequently named their "savior angel" in the hell they lived in.

Budapest had another ghetto with Jewish prisoners who lived under horrible conditions. Eichmann had a final plan to exterminate all Jews there using the SS, Arrow-Cross, and two hundred police, all of whom would encircle the ghetto. Wallenberg found out about this in the first days of January 1945, right before the attack. Wallenberg worked alongside a high ranking Arrow-Cross member, Pal Szalay, to stop the massacre. Szalay was sent to negotiate with the German general, August Schmidthuber, who led the massacre on the ghetto. Szalay threatened that Wallenberg would see Schmidthuber hanged as a war criminal if he didn't reconsider. The general withdrew his army, and 120,000 Budapest Jews were saved; they were the only large group of Jews remaining in Europe. This was Wallenberg's final victory.

In January of 1945, Raoul Wallenberg was taken by the Soviet Red Army to a Soviet prison for "espionage." He is thought to have died in 1947 in prison at age 34, although the exact circumstances of his death are unknown and remain a mystery.

Raoul Wallenberg sacrificed everything to help the Jews. His perseverance was awe-inspiring. He was sincere, courageous, and infinitely compassionate, once stating, "I will never be able to go back to Sweden without knowing... that I'd done all a man could do to save as many Jews as possible." Raoul Wallenberg will forever be a hero of the Holocaust, a man who stood firm in the face of unspeakable evil. He did not save just one life, but thousands; not just one universe, but a multitude. For that, we are forever indebted to him.

ROSA NAËF: SWISS HERO OF THE HOLOCAUST

Sithmi Jayasundara, Co-winner

Imagine a gray, stormy sky. Rain pours from thick, dark clouds, drenching the helpless people below. The sky booms with thunder and flashes with lightning. Nothing can be seen for miles. Soon, chunks of ice—hail—topple mercilessly onto the earth. Gusts of wind strike houses, trees, telephone wires, anything, but there is nothing anyone can do.

Then, suddenly, out of the blue, thin rays of sunshine burst out through the clouds, shimmering with hope. The golden beams shoot through the sky, blessing innocent faces with light and warmth.

These are our Holocaust heroes, the people who risked their own lives to save the lives of others and brought a little bit of hope and optimism into a world seized with rage and cruelty.

One of these beams of hope was Rösli, or Rosa, Naëf, a young Swiss caretaker of the children of a French orphanage, Château-de-la-Hille. Born in Glarus, Switzerland in 1911, she followed her dream to assist kids. She nurtured and provided for the malnourished children, 120 of which were Jewish children who had fled from Germany to Belgium to France. The orphanage was under the Swiss Red Cross. It had once been an abandoned castle, but Maurice Dubois, the Swiss Juvenile Assistance of the Red Cross supervisor, turned it into a children's home, a much nicer place to live than Seyre, another orphanage that Naëf used to work at. She was the one to spoke up to Dubois about its uncleanliness, which was causing illness outbreaks. She fixed up the new orphanage, establishing a school and managing everything. All was going well.

Until August 26, 1942.

The sound of engines and trucks woke up the children early that morning. They heard the shouts of arguing police. Naëf remained calm, which was unusual for her. The French police forced all the Jewish children above the age of 16 to tell them their names, and arrested them. Naëf acted like she knew nothing of what might happen to the teens. She had them get dressed and eat breakfast, and gave them some food to bring along with them. They were only permitted to bring a single small bag. With tearful goodbyes and promises that they would see each other soon, she sent them on their way. Forty-five children were arrested that day and sent to the concentration camp Le Vernet. Immediately after they left, Rosa Naëf sprang into action, notifying Maurice Dubois and instructing him to order the authorities to release the children. She then took a taxi to Le Vernet. When the children saw her, relief washed over them. Everyone was able to come home safely. Finally, everything was back to normal...for a few months.

In November 1942, the Germans took over southern France. Once again, the safety of the Jewish teens was jeopardized. Fearing arrest, Naëf planned ahead, organizing guards for the castle and a hiding place in the attic. Still more had to be done to protect the children. There was one clear option: escape.

She managed to slip some of the teens into Switzerland. She started out by finding places for them to hide if needed—local farms, another orphanage close to the border called St.-Cergues-les-Voirons. She planned this very carefully, talking to the farmers and the warden of the orphanage, preparing them. Finally, on December 22, 1942, Peter Salz, Jacques Roth, Regina Rosenblatt and Margot Kern headed off to the border with fake names, papers, and money. Their escape was a success. Margot Kern and Regina Rosenblatt worked at a Red Cross children's refugee center in Switzerland, which was where they remained in 1945, when World War II ended. Naëf continued to send teens across the border. Shortly after the first successful border crossing, seven safely made it across, while another three managed to escape to Spain. However, the plan wasn't completely perfect. Out of a group of six that was on the verge of crossing over to Switzerland, five were arrested by a patrol. Inge

Joseph narrowly avoided punishment, but was sent back to France. Eventually, after a few tries, she made it to Switzerland.

Rosa Naëf was a smart woman. She heard of the arrest and took action to save the children that were left. They were safely hidden in the attic and on farms. When an expected police raid swept through La Hille Castle, none were found.

However, no matter how hard she worked, nothing good soon came to her. Her job as the La Hille supervisor was taken away only months later, in May 1943, due to "lack of discipline," and she was ordered back to Switzerland. Infuriated with the Swiss authorities, she moved to Denmark.

Yad Vashem presented Rosa Naëf with the honor of being named Righteous Among the Nations on May 7, 1989. Ever so humble, she refused to take the medal of honor until October 4, 1992, four years before her death, at a posthumous ceremony for the St.-Cergues-les-Voirons helpers. This only proves her devotion to saving the lives of innocent Jews. Her motivation did not come from the desire for an award, nor did it come from the hope that there would be no consequences. She was aware of consequences and took action to stop that from happening. She thought ahead and devised strategies to save lives. Her efforts were remarkable and heroic, and yet she is virtually unknown, just as most Holocaust heroes are. Most people see the Holocaust as a relentless storm, which it was. But what nearly everyone misses is the sunshine, the distinct beams that struggle to peek through the clouds until their light floods the world.

Works Cited

"Rescue Story: Naëf, Rosa." *Yad Vashem*. Yad Vashem The Holocaust Martyrs Heroes' Remembrance Authority, n.d. Web. 25 Feb. 2015.

Wagner, Meir and Moshe Meisels. *The Righteous of Switzerland: Heroes of the Holocaust*. Hoboken: KTAV Publishing House, Inc., 2001. Online book preview.

PEOPLE ARE GOOD AT HEART

Sophie Lopez

The definition of Hero: ˈhirō/ *noun* a person who is admired or idealized for courage, outstanding achievements, or noble qualities. Synonyms: brave person, brave man/woman.

A hero by my definition is a person who is kind. He or she isn't perfect (no one is) but he or she tries hard. They don't have to be idolized or have noble qualities. All people have been a hero at least once in their lives; all people have done well for others before. Likewise, everyone has made good and bad choices.

The Holocaust was a time in history when 6 million Jews were tragically and unfairly murdered in World War II. Many people tried to help save Jews, and though some were successful, many Jews were put in concentration camps with only luck to help them survive the bitter lives in the internment camps and ghettos.

Several different people in the European countries and of different religious backgrounds risked their lives to help Jews. Individual acts and organized networks impacted the war and how many Jews were saved. All the people who attempted to often recognize are the Danish and Swiss people who helped save Jews.

Mr. Knud Christiansen was an athlete who competed in the 1936 Berlin Olympics as a member of the Danish Rowing Team. Germany had invaded Denmark, Christiansen's home country a few years later in 1940. Denmark was one of the many occupied countries from April 1940 until May 1945 (other countries included Norway and Finland). Christiansen was a member of the Danish Freedom Fighters, a group that worked to sabotage the Nazi war efforts, and the Danish Resistance that worked on creating a rescue network to save escaping Jews. Christiansen was an essential member to the resistance; he was one of the first to learn about the plan to arrest Danish Jews on Rosh Hashanah (10p.m. on Oct.1 in 1943) when 7,000 Jews were to be at home. To save as many people as possible, from the "round up," Christiansen hid several Jews in farmhouses, churches and apartments, including his own. Many people also helped resist the deportation of the Jewish people by opening up their homes to escaping Jews, like Christiansen's father in law. Similarly, many workers allowed their shops to be a meeting place for members of the resistance groups, like Christiansen's mother. Several people, like Christianesen's brother, were lookouts for Jews who were being ferried from Denmark into safe Sweden. Others, like Christiansen's wife, published newspapers that told the reality of the atrocities being committed against Jews (Karen Christiansen risked her life to publish a newspaper called "Die Warheit" (The Truth)). The efforts by the Danish people to save as many Jews as possible should be greatly appreciated. The Danes worked in unison, as a nation to courageously save as many Jewish people as possible; for that we should be grateful. Danish fisherman transported about 7,200 Jews (of the population of 7,800 in Denmark) to Switzerland.

Others helped the cause of saving Jews by using their job positions. In the year of 1944 in Budapest, Hungary (occupied by Germany) Raoul Wallenburg, a Swedish diplomat, Swiss diplomat Cal Lutz, and standing as a Spanish Diplomat, Italian Giorgio Perlasca gave tens of thousands of Jews certification that stated they were protected by neutral powers and worked to obtain protective papers and homes for fleeing Hungarian Jews.

Swiss Border police commander Paul Grueninger was a great help to escaping Jews into Switzerland. He commanded the St. Gallen region that borders with Austria. After the German occupation of Austria, Switzerland sealed the border to incoming newcomers unless they had proper entry permits. Unfortunately, in October 1938, Switzerland compromised with Germany to use their "J" stamp to distinguish Jews from others. The number of refugees who tried to enter Switzerland illegally swelled as the situation in Austria worsened, leaving Grueninger with a crucial decision that would change his life: Should he deny the Jewish people entry into Switzerland and turn them in to their cruel country, or suffer the consequences of being caught helping illegal immigrants?

Grueninger ignored the official rules; he allowed desperate refugees enter Switzerland. In addition to allowing them into Switzerland, Grueninger changed their registration to show that they had moved to Switzerland in 1938, five years prior, when admittance into the country had yet to be restricted. Grueninger submitted fabricated reports that did not include the illegal refugees to the other German officials. He even bought winter clothes for refugees with little of their belongings.

Grueninger was discharged from the police force after the Germans told the Swiss authorities of Grueninger's deeds. He had gained illegal entry of a total of 3,600 Jews into Switzerland and altered their registration papers.

There are many different people out in the world. Some have strong voices, some soft, some assertive, some loving. Everyone has words. Everyone has the power to speak up for liberty. Everybody has the ability to speak against wrong. Today I am not the only person writing to honor and remember the Holocaust. Hundreds of people are submitting essays about this tragic event. But more than winning an award, like any other common contestant, I hope to change the world. You may wonder, "How can an essay change the world?" There will always be problems in the world; people who are mean, rude, or judgmental exist everywhere. But there will always be kind people, people who can help, who want to improve the world, whether it's stopping a bully, raising awareness for an important cause, or inventing a cure for cancer. This Holocaust essay-writing contest is one great way to raise awareness. By teaching people about the Holocaust, we can prevent history from repeating itself. Everyone has the power to control his or her life and make the world a better place. But most of all, through all the help one can offer, we must trust human kind in kindness. We must teach and learn, so when the time comes for one to make a choice, they will make the right choice, the kind choice, the one to help others.

Human beings have made mistakes and always will. But we must believe that we can change and learn from these mistakes. Anne Frank said, "Despite all, I still believe people are good at heart." Me too, Anne. Me too.

TWO HOLOCAUST HEROES: THE POLICE OFFICER AND THE DIPLOMAT

Vinita Saxena

There are many heroes of the Holocaust: some known, and many unknown. These people helped Jews by providing them food and shelter. Helping to save the innocent people suffering from injustice was worth it, even though they had to risk their lives to do it. Among the heroes, there are Swiss heroes who were very brave and helpful in saving the lives of thousands of Jews. They had to be secretive, alert, and cautious to be able to help the Jews without telling anybody. They kept that secret until after World War II was over to be sure, but still, many were caught. Two heroes stood out among the others: a police officer and a diplomat. These two men stood up to Hitler and helped many Jews survive the Holocaust.

One of these heroes was named Paul Grüninger. He was a Swiss man who joined the police and excelled in his career, moving up in ranks very quickly. He was a police captain when the Nazis took over Austria in August 1938. The Austrian Jews were facing the same cruelty and mistreatment that the German Jews were facing. Grüninger was given specific orders to turn back the Austrian refugees that were immigrating to Switzerland, since the border was closing. He knew that the Jews who stayed in Austria would be killed, but he also knew that if he helped them in any way he would risk destroying his career and he could lose everything. Grüninger saw the Jews that had come as far as the Swiss border, were captured and taken to him. They were cold, hungry, and distressed about what was happening to them.

Grüninger looked at them and decided to risk his job and his life to help the innocent Jews whose lives were on the line just because of their religion. He knew that his career in law enforcement was over but Grüninger also knew that he could save thousands of lives if he helped. Paul Grüninger did two major things: he permitted legal entry into Switzerland, and he forged documents that stated that the Jews were legal immigrants and had come long before the border had closed. Grüninger also helped by paying for winter clothing with his own money. He had helped over 3,000 Jews by doing what he did, but he was discovered almost a year later.

When Grüninger arrived for work on April 3, 1939, his entrance to the police station was blocked. This was unusual since he was chief of the station, but he immediately knew that he had been caught helping the Jews. Months earlier he had been notified that the Gestapo was investigating him but he ignored them and continued to forge illegal documents for the Jews right up until his arrest. Because of his actions, Grüninger was fired from his job and was taken to court where he was found guilty of allowing over 3,000 Jews illegal entry into the country. He had to pay a fine and go to jail. His family had to move out of their apartment and into a room with no heating or indoor plumbing. Despite all this, Paul Grüninger's daughter said her father swore that if he ever had to do it again, he would.

After he died, the Israeli government honored him, and Switzerland officially recognized his achievements. In recognition of what he did to help the Jews, a school, many streets, and a stadium were all named in honor of Grüninger.

Another hero of the Holocaust was Carl Lutz, the Swiss Vice-Consul in Budapest, Hungary. He was chief of the Swiss Legation's Department of Foreign Interests in Budapest, and was in charge of fourteen nations. In his job he had to protect many different people in different countries. On March 19, 1944 the Nazis took Hungary. The persecution of the Jews was more and more conspicuous. Every day, many came to Lutz's office asking for protection and Carl Lutz felt that he had to protect the innocent Jews. He had already helped 10,000 Jews emigrate from Hungary. Lutz wanted to help as many people as he could, even if it meant risking his job and life.

When the deportations to Auschwitz began, Carl Lutz placed the staff of the Jewish Council for Palestine under his diplomatic safeguard and renamed it "Department of Emigration of the Swiss Legation." Many people needed to help, and with the help of volunteers, Lutz's staff increased from 15 to 150. Lutz knew that no one in the German government had officially questioned the right of 8,000 to emigrate from Hungary to Palestine, so he kept "negotiating" with the authorities in Germany and Hungary. While doing that Lutz changed his aim: he wanted to save as many Jews as he could. Lutz invented the "Schutzbrief," a protective letter that he was issuing. These letters were no longer supported with Palestine certificates. In order to hide what he was doing, Lutz only used the numbers one through 8,000, which were the original numbers of the people who were allowed to emigrate. He also interpreted the 8,000 as families, not individuals, thus saving even more Jews. Every 1,000 names were grouped into a collective Swiss passport, so that the applicants were under official Swiss protection.

Once the Hungarian government started concentrating all of the Jews into one large ghetto, Carl Lutz put many Jews in safe houses. The safe houses sheltered the Jews and provided food and water for them. Lutz and his wife Gertrud set up 76 safe houses throughout the city of Budapest. They said that they were annexes of the Swiss embassy. The most famous safe house was "the Glass House," which was a former glass factory that sheltered approximately 3,000 Jews. In the Glass House, Lutz and Gertrud issued the Jews citizenship papers, visas, and other forms of documentation that allowed them to escape the Nazi concentration camps. By doing this, Carl Lutz saved over 62,000 people by risking his life and career, but it was worth it, and he knew it. In 1963, a street in Haifa, Israel was named after Carl Lutz, in around 1964, the government issued an official Carl Lutz memorial stamp, in 1991, a memorial at the entrance to the old Budapest Ghetto was made, and in 2006, the American embassy in Budapest built a memorial to Lutz in its park.

These heroes helped to save many innocent Jews from death. They risked their careers and lives to help because they saw the bigger picture of things. They knew what would happen if Hitler continued to kill off all of the Jews and they couldn't let that happen. These two men helped in their own ways and saved many Jewish lives that would have been ended. They risked their lives to help tens of thousands of Jews even though they'd known what would happen if they got caught. These men are the heroes of the Holocaust.

Works Cited

"Carl Lutz." *The International Raoul Wallenberg Foundation*. N.p., n.d. Web. 22 Feb. 2015. <http://www.raoulwallenberg.net/saviors/diplomats/list/carl-lutz/>.

Holocaust Remembered in Stories of Rescuers." *SWI Swissinfo.ch*. N.p., 27 Jan. 2010. Web. 7 Feb. 2015. <http://www.swissinfo.ch/eng/holocaust-remembered-in-stories-of-rescuers/8175146>.

"Paul Grüninger." *Paul Grüninger*. Holocaust Memorial Day Trust, n.d. Web. 15 Feb. 2015. <http://hmd.org.uk/resources/stories/paul-gr%C3%BCninger>

Rubin, Debra. "Museum Exhibit Honors Swiss Holocaust Hero." *New Jersey Jewish News*. N.p., 12 Aug. 2008. Web. 7 Feb. 2015. <http://njjewishnews.com/njjn.com/080708/sxMuseumExhibitHonors.html>.

"The Righteous Among The Nations." *Statistics*. N.p., 1 Jan. 2014. Web. 7 Feb. 2015. <http://www.yadvashem.org/yv/en/righteous/statistics.asp>.

Marsh Jr. High School, Chico, CA

Courtny Connelly
I taught English, AVID, Leadership and social justice themes at the high school level in Oroville, California for ten years, and am currently teaching English and Academic Intervention classes at Marsh Jr. High in Chico, California. I enjoy teaching and learning. I think lessons that revolve around real life experiences and learning from our history become very powerful motivators for students to become catalysts for change. I'm so honored to have incredible students who are developing into thoughtful, responsible and productive global citizens.

IRENA SENDLER: A COURAGEOUS HERO

Rylie Roldan, Winner

"I was brought up to believe that a person must be rescued when drowning, regardless of religion or nationality." - Irena Sendler

The year is 1939; the Jewish community is being pushed into ghettos, shipped off to concentration camps and being slaughtered. In only four years about 6 million Jewish people are dead. If it weren't for a brave women whose name was Irena Sendler the death toll would be greater. During the time of theHolocaust Irena had saved about 2,500 children from the Warsaw ghetto. Irena, being a social worker, was able to obtain a permit to come inside to help the sick Jewish people.

Irena Sendler was born February 15, 1910 in Otwock, Poland to Stanislaw Krzyzanowski, and Janina Krzyzanowska. Her father was a Polish socialist as a doctor; he treated many poor Jewish people. Her father was much of her inspiration to be kind and true to her self, he was a gentle person whom cared very much of human kind. Irena went to Warsaw University; she had been suspended for one year for protesting the rule of not being able to sit next to Jewish people. In 1939 she went off and became a social worker. Her first marriage was to Mieczyslaw Sendler, she later married Stefan Zgrzembski who died before her. They had three children.

The Zegota underground was founded in 1942 as the Council for Aid to Jews in Occupied Poland. The members had asked Irena to be the head of their children department. Irena's code name was Jolanta. As the head of the children department her job was to identify and helpassist the youth. She would help smuggle the children out of the ghetto, she had to find very creative ways of sneaking the children out she used things like gunny sacks, tool boxes, or even an ambulance. As for the children old enough to learn Catholic traditions they would be sent to a church and take off the yellow stars that signified them being Jewish and would leave posing as Catholic children. Irena would be able to take up to 25 children at a time. Irena visited the ghetto every day and would return with a child every time for 18 months. Once the children were out of the ghetto Irena would put them into hiding, she would adopt them out to non-Jewish families, and she gave the children new identities. There was only one place where the true identification and location of the children were: in jars buried under an apple tree in her neighbor's yard.

Soon the Nazis became aware of Irena's actions, they sent her Powiak prison in Warsaw on October 20th, 1943, to be tortured and with the intention of her being murdered. They tortured her for days on end, but she would not give up the whereabouts of the children. Nazis were known to break limbs or burn people as a form of torture. In her case her torture was they broke her legs and her feet. She was about to be murdered when members of the Zegota paid the guard to not kill her, and her life was further spared. She was released from the jail in 1944. The Nazis kept a careful eye on Irena but she went into hiding for the rest of the war. Though in hiding she still did her rescuing, even knowing if she were to be caught it would be certain death. After the war she searched for the childrens' parents, but by then most of them were orphans.

Irena had received many awards for her courageous tasks though she thought her self no hero she was once quoted to saying *"Heroes do extraordinary things. What I did was not an extraordinary thing. it was normal."* She still won largely known recognition. In 2003 Irena won the Jan Karski award, and in 2007 she was nominated for a Nobel Peace prize. She also had a tree planted in her honor in 1963 at the Avenue of the Righteous Among the Nations.

Unfortunately Irena had died May 12th, 2008. Irena was a genuine hero to human society even if she denied it. Irena has touched many hearts with her outstanding actions. Irena is a soul to be remembered. She is a true hero, not some pop princess you claim is your hero. I know that I will definitely appreciate anybody who puts others before themselves. She had a kind heart and would sacrifice her well-being for the safety of children. She never thought herself a hero, she believed that no matter what we are all equal and everybody is equal even if they have a different skin color, belief or age. Irena has a story that most people will not be able to live up to, I feel honored to be given the opportunity to write about a lady who has saved and touched many lives. Even though most people do not know the name of Irena Sendler, I'm glad I do! It takes a special person to let their kindness and bravery shine through. Over all Irena was a fantastic lady who has inspired me, to never judge anybody by their religion, belief, gender, or sexual orientation.

Works Cited

Bulow, Louis. "Irena Sendler; An Unsung Hero." *Http://www.auschwitz.dk/sendler.htm*. Louis Bülow, 2012. Web. 23 Feb. 2015.

"Irena Sendler." *Home | Jewish Virtual Library*. N.p., n.d. Web. 11 Feb. 2015.

Kroll, Chana. "Irena Sendler Rescuer of the Children of Warsaw." *Chabadorg RSS*. N.p., n.d. Web. 27 Feb. 2015.

"Smuggling Children Out of The Ghetto." N.p., n.d. Web. 24 Feb. 2015.

T. R. Smedberg Middle School, Elk Grove, CA

Kalli Carvalho is a native of Sacramento, California. She graduated from University of California, at Davis in 1983. Her passion for teaching began in 1989, when she started her career as an educator. Since day one, Carvalho has always felt as though teaching the mandated curriculum (although critically important) is secondary to teaching life lessons that will help our young adults become compassionate, empowered citizens who will step up to change the inequities and injustices in our society and world.

This is why the teaching of the Holocaust has become one of the most important units for her 8th grade students. By using the Diary of Anne Frank, as well as the first-hand experience of honored Guest Speaker, Mr. Bernard Marks, students learn about tolerance, resilience, and resistance to ideologies which are destructive and hate-filled. The research paper (many submitted to the Eleanor Marks Essay Contest) is the culminating event, asking students to research and reflect upon the lessons taught.

When the Temple B'Nai Isreal was the target of a hate crime in 1999, Carvalho and her students took a field trip to the temple, to offer support and help to the Jewish community which was targeted.

Ms. Carvalho is a proud Greek-American who finds her joy in family, traveling to the Greek Islands, and reading. She looks forward to the future, as she is confident that the students of her past will be ready to build communities that show understanding and acceptance for all.

PAUL GRUENINGER

Kaileah Maxwell

The Swiss and Dutch heroes who rescued the Jews were brave enough to risk their own lives for others. I honestly think the best of them and look up to them. They had the courage to rescue thousands combined (even though they were strangers), they taught us how to fight the hate in our community and stand up for what we believe in, and inspired us as young people to think of others before ourselves. There are heroes from the past, present day, and I hope there will be more in the future.

Let's speak about the past. An inspirational man named Paul Grueninger was a border police commander who lived in Switzerland. When Switzerland closed its border, it caused negotiations between the Swiss and the Germans which led to the stamping of the "J" on Jewish passports. In order to save the people who crossed illegally, he turned in reports about the number of people who came across. They weren't true. He also bought clothes for the ones who weren't able to take things with them. He got sentenced to illegally saving the Jewish people and turning in false reports. "In 1971, a year before his death, Yad Vashem bestowed the title of Righteous Among the Nations on Paul Grueninger" (www.yadvashem.org).

In America, a similar thing happened. It was December 7, 1941 when military planes struck on Pearl Harbor, Hawaii. "More than two years into the conflict, America had finally joined World War II" (www. History.com). World War II lasted from 1939 to 1945. The American soldiers sent all Japanese-Americans into internment camps without being able to process what even happened. Many people were frightened, lost their families, and lost all hope in themselves, relating to the Holocaust. The young ones were scared and thought they did something wrong. Some people came back a new person, while some didn't come back at all. Heroes then didn't need a cape and a mask.

In the future, there will be more conflict. The armies are being put to work in foreign lands and it's all because of conflict and false accusations. There will be more lives lost due to it. People die every day trying to help people and save our country. We have to speak up in order to help the people who need saving because we walk right past the things that are the most important day by day.

In conclusion, many of us don't see the true hero in ourselves. There's always someone there. Heroes don't need to have their name in lights or be classified as something they're not. We don't need anyone to prove it but us. We are all equal, we are all heroes.

Works Cited

"Paul Grueninger - The Righteous Among The Nations - Yad Vashem." Paul Grueninger - The Righteous Among The Nations - Yad Vashem. N.p., n.d. Web. 12 Mar. 2015.

"Pearl Harbor." History.com. A&E Television Networks, n.d. Web. 11 Feb. 2015.

THE SCHOUTEN FAMILY

Kylee McDougall

The opposite of love is not hate; its indifference" (Wiesel). The Holocaust was a period in history where people were killed and held in poor living conditions. This event was genocide. The bravery of the Danish and Swiss during the Holocaust is a lesson to learn from because they saved lives. Our current society still faces hate and prejudice, and our future is not very hopeful without learning to be brave. Because the Swiss and Danish people saved lives, we should learn from them and become kind and selfless.

The Swiss and Danish saved lives during the Holocaust because they were selfless. The Schouten family took over 40 people into their home to protect from 1942-1943. Even though they only saved 40 lives those 40 are able to create many more lives thanks to the Schouten family. With those lives saved, today their children may do the same in today's society.

In our society today we still struggle with hate and prejudice. Until this day we still hate people for their religious belief and race. Just like Ferguson when a man was killed because of his race. If society doesn't change, it is believed something very similar to the Holocaust will happen again. If another situation like the Holocaust happens.

Our future is not very hopeful without society learning how to be brave and selfless. Like the Japanese internment camps and how the other people didn't speak up. If we don't learn how to be brave and speak up society is going to crash and burn in the future. This is why we need to become one world working together. We all need to be kind and to one another and not judge or segregate.

In conclusion, the Swiss and Danish actions are some we can learn from because it will help us now and in the future. The selflessness of the Swiss and Danish during the Holocaust is a lesson to learn from because they saved lives, our current society still faces hate and prejudice, and our future is not very hopeful without learning to not be selfless. They are heroes because their selflessness saved many lives. But today our world still struggles with hate and prejudice and very little people do anything about it. We need to correct and change our behavior now because if we don't another Holocaust like event might happen. So if you see hate, hear it, or are being hateful to anyone yourself stop take a minute and change that situation as soon as possible.

"I Am My Brother's Keeper." *Theodorus and Maria Schouten, and Their Daughter Cornelia Anna*. N.p., n.d. Web. 12 Mar. 2015. Weisel, Elie

SWISS AND DANISH HEROES OF THE HOLOCAUST
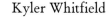
Kyler Whitfield

"The opposite of love is not hate; it is indifference (Wiesel)." The Holocaust was Genocide. The Holocaust was a period of time when the Nazis were prejudiced to Jews. The bravery of Danish and Swiss during the Holocaust is a lesson to learn because they saved lives, similar things happened in World War II, and our future is not certain if we don't change how we are. People lives are very important and the Danish and Swiss people helped save them during the Holocaust.

The Danish and Swiss people saved many lives during the Holocaust. In the winter of 1942/1943, the Schoutens took care of a little girl and protected her in danger by hiding her and others in a secret room for varying periods of time. In 1938/1939, Paul Grueninger changed many Jewish people's registration into Switzerland so that they could come into the land (http://www.yadvashem. org/). He saved 3,600 Jews from dying (http://www.yadvashem. org/). Similar things have happened since then.

Similar things have happened in America. In World War II, Japanese-American people were relocated into internment camps (http://www.history. com/). This was a violation of their civil rights. On February 19, 1942, Roosevelt signed Executive Order 9066, which forced all Japanese-Americans to evacuate to the west coast (http://www.history.com/). According to the census of 1940, 127,000 people were of Japanese ancestry and blood (http://www.history. com/). This might be the start of an uncertain future.

Our future is uncertain if we don't change how we are. If we don't change how we act toward one another we might end up completely separated on day. People seem to think that hating on a specific group will benefit them in some shape or form. If people would consider each other equal, everything would be better. This is why we have hate in America.

In conclusion, the Holocaust holds a lesson to learn from because the Swiss heroes saved lives, similar things happened in America, and our future is not certain if we don't change how we are. The bravery of Danish and Swiss during the Holocaust is a lesson to learn because they saved lives, similar things happened in World War II, and our future is not certain if we don't change how we are. So, the next time you see someone being hateful to another person, stand up for them, and protect them. You may need them one day.

Works Cited

"Japanese-American Relocation." History.com. A&E Television Networks, 2015. Web. 11 Feb. 2015. < http://www.history.com/topics/world-war-ii/japanese-american-relocation >.

Paul Grueninger - The Righteous Among The Nations - Yad Vashem." Paul Grueninger - The Righteous Among The Nations - Yad Vashem. Yad Vashem The Holocaust Martyrs' and Heroes' Remembrance Authority, 2015. Web. 12 Mar. 2015. http://www.yadvashem.org/yv/en/righteous/stories/grueninger.asp

PAUL GRUENINGER

Liliana Ramirez, Special Award

"The opposite of love is not hate; it is indifference" (Wiesel). The Holocaust was a time period in which massive amounts of people died because Hitler thought they were "imperfect." The Swiss/Danish heroes' bravery is inspirational because Swiss or Danish heroes taught us how to stand up to hate, America has too much hate in our society, and the future of us or our children depend on how society treats on another.

Swiss or Danish heroes taught us how to stand up to hate. Paul Grueninger was a border police commander of the St. Gallen region. It borders with Austria. During October of 1938 Switzerland and Germany began to negotiate and it led to the famous stamping of the "J" which was only issued to Jews. This meant that Jews were no longer allowed to enter Switzerland. Mr. Grueninger faces two options: to not let the Jews pass or to let them pass and face the consequences. Paul Grueninger bravely chose to let the desperate Jews enter Switzerland. Even more, he changed their passports' dates to March 1938, when the entry to the country hadn't been restricted. When the Germans found out about his actions they informed the Swiss authorities. He was dismissed from his police force in March of 1939. His benefits were suspended and he was brought into trial on charges of illegally permitting 3,600 Jews into Switzerland and creating false dates in the passports. Despite the difficulties, he said he never regretted doing what he did. This brave man showed us that no matter what the consequences are we must always do what's right. There are too many hate crimes in our community nowadays and we need to learn how to stand up to stop hate.

America has too much hate in society. In Roseville, California, 13 students were referred to the juvenile justice system by the police for a hate crime. The students were suspected of spreading cotton balls across the lawn of an African American classmate. This shows hate because by spreading cotton balls across the lawn it showed the racism left over from slavery. In Davis, graffiti was found in a Jewish organizational house. The graffiti phrase was found by a janitor. The phrase stated "grout out the Jews." This shows it is a hateful crime against Jews, reminding them about the hateful incident that was caused by Adolf Hitler during World War II. These are only a few cases in which hate is showed up in our community. There are so many hate crimes all around our society. Hate needs to be stopped in order to accomplish a better future for our future children and us.

Our future selves and our future children must be able to live in a better community. That cannot happen with everyone running around hating each other and committing hate crimes everywhere. It needs to stop because we need to achieve a better tomorrow. Not only for us, but also for those who we love. A world where everyone treats one another with respect and equality. Where everyone will be able to love who they want and not be judged for it. A future where our children will have friends of different colors and flavors. A place where women and men will be treated equally, where everyone is equal. A better tomorrow can be achieved, but everyone needs to put in effort to stop hate. If people saw souls instead of faces or bodies, society wouldn't be as messed up.

The Swiss/Danish heroes' bravery is inspirational because Swiss and Danish heroes taught us how to stand up to hate, America has too much hate in society, and the future of us or our children depend on how society treats one another. Swiss men and women sacrificed themselves to save many Jews' lives. We should do the same instead of committing so many hate crimes. Our future and the future of our children depend on how we treat each other. So let's create a better future together!

"Paul Grueninger - The Righteous Among The Nations - Yad Vashem." Paul Grueninger – The Righteous Among The Nations - Yad Vashem. N.p., n.d. Web. 12 Mar. 2015.

Saint James School, Davis, CA

Kathryn Baggarly

Kathryn has been an educator for 25 years, both in public and Catholic schools. She has been at St. James School in Davis, California for seven years, where she is the St. James Eighth Grade teacher and Junior High English/Language Arts teacher. Kathryn has been teaching about the Holocaust since arriving at St. James. She is a member of CVEN and the online education community of Facing History and Ourselves. Her students are deeply touched by what they learn about the Holocaust and are honored to be able to give voice to the unsung heroes of the Holocaust. She and her students are indebted to Mr. Bernard Marks and his tireless efforts to make sure we never forget.

Michele Banister

Michele has been an educator for 25 years, both in public and Catholic schools. She is the Writing and Reading Resource teacher at St. James School in Davis, California. Along with her colleague Kathryn Baggarly Michele has assisted the Junior High students with their Holocaust essays. She looks forward to many years of participation in the Eleanor J. Marks Holocaust Essay Contest.

PAUL GRUENINGER

Anne Ayotte, Co-winner

A single be ad of sweat forms along Grueninger's forehead as he grasps the refugees' passports. Of course, he must remain calm in order to falsify each report and he must not cause even the slightest bit of suspicion. Promptly, he scans each of the reports with great attention to the dates of each arrival time. He legalizes each report by exchanging the present passport arrival time with a date previous to March 1938. In spite of the fact that Grueninger has already allowed hundreds counterfeit reports, the risk of being caught gradually increases with every inaccurate report he forges. In the event that his actions are ever discovered, consequences would be certain and dire. Nevertheless, Grueninger will not send back the desperate refugees to their country, firmly ruled with violent anti-Semitism. Paul Grueninger inhales deeply before returning the passports to every individual refugee. Graciously they thank him, although they must do so without being overheard. Just as quickly as it began, the refugees are gone almost instantly. Grueninger relaxes after yet another successful act of falsifying documents for the runaway Jews.

Thus was the life of one of the greatest heroes of World War II about whom most people have never heard. Paul Grueninger was an ordinary man, whose bravery and compassion made him far from ordinary, and he suffered terrible consequences for his brave acts of compassion.

Paul Grueninger was a Swiss border police commander who supervised the St. Gallen region bordering Austria. He was given precise instructions to only allow people with proper entry permits to enter Switzerland. Grueninger was specifically told to turn all Jewish refugees with inadequate registrations back to Austria. He was also supposed to stamp a "J" in German passports to indicate any Jews crossing the border. Regardless of the explicit rules given to officials like Paul Grueninger, he disobeyed his instructions in order to sneak thousands of runaway Jews across the border. Once the Jews were treated as legal citizens in Switzerland, they would be taken to the Diepoldsau camp to be assisted by Jewish organizations. In addition to helping Jews escape their anti-Semitic countries, Paul Grueninger paid for countless refugees' clothes for contrary to the fact winter, after they had to leave their personal items and belongings behind.

After illegally sneaking approximately 3,600 Jews into Switzerland, Germans eventually discovered Grueninger's undercover actions. By 1939, he was dismissed from the police force and then brought to trial. Grueninger was charged with permitting thousands of Jews entry into Switzerland as well as falsifying their registration papers. He was also charged with helping several individual Jewish refugees hide from detection. Paul Grueninger's trial stretched over two years until in March 1941, when the court found him guilty of violating his duty. He was fined and was forced to pay trial costs as well, leaving him almost bankrupt. All of Paul Grueninger's previous benefits had been revoked and he would later face several severe consequences for his actions. Once of these consequences was poverty, which Paul Grueninger had to face throughout the rest of his life that Paul Grueninger faced countless repercussions for his acts of bravery, he never regretted his actions. He stated: "I am not ashamed of the court's verdict. On the contrary, I am proud to have saved the lives of hundreds of oppressed people. My assistance to Jews was rooted in my Christian world outlook... It was basically a question of saving human lives threatened with death. How could I then seriously consider bureaucratic schemes and calculations? Sure, I intentionally exceeded the limits of my authority and often with my own hands falsified documents and certificates, but it was done solely in order to afford persecuted people access into the country. My personal well-being, measured against the cruel fate of these thousands, was so insignificant and unimportant that I never even took it into consideration." (Yad Vashem Featured Stories: Paul Grueninger).

By the year 1970 in December, the Swiss government sent Paul Grueninger a letter of apology in order to appease the protests of the media. However he was not given the option to reopen his trial nor was he given the reinstatement of his pension. Eventually, in 1995, the Swiss federal government terminated his conviction. Numerous streets have been named after Grueninger, as well as a school in 2006. The SC Bruhl's stadium was ultimately renamed *Paul Grüninger Stadion* in Grueninger's honor.

Paul Grueninger's story remained unknown among most people; and to most, his story was never told. His great acts of selflessness and courage; however, earned him the respect and appreciation from thousands of anonymous Jewish refugees. Every report that Grueninger forged, impacted each individual life of the Jews. He accomplished incredible deeds that not only reflect his bravery, but his stronghold on his Christian faith. Paul Grueninger never put his personal welfare before the needs of the helpless runaway Jews. He trusted upon his firm beliefs and achieved remarkable things. Although Paul Grueninger was a simple and ordinary man, his compassionate acts of bravery fell far beyond ordinary.

KNUD DYBY

Patrick Stodden, Runner-up

When you ask a Junior High student to write a story about a hero they have to think, 'What makes someone a hero?' The definition of a hero or heroine is a person who is admired or idealized for courage, achievements, or noble qualities. That's a great definition, but what if no one knows about the things someone has done? Is that person still a hero? Yes. What if what they did wasn't saving someone's life or wasn't creating a revolutionary new way to preserve the environment? What if they just stood up to a bully for another child, or returned a lost pet? Are these little things not good enough to call them a hero? I believe it doesn't matter what someone accomplishes but it's the impact that it creates on the world around them. Everyone can be a hero without risking their lives; there are so many people everyday who show bravery and noble qualities with no reward. The Holocaust had so many people sacrifice their safety and comfort to help others escape from the fear and turmoil happening during this time of international distress.

Knud Dyby was born in Randeis, Juntland, Denmark 1915. His father was a printer and he trained to become a typographer after attending university. He joined the King's Royal Guard and later traveled through Germany as a police officer in 1937 and 1938, experiencing for himself the expanse of the Nazi regime. He was involved with a group named 1944 and Holger Danska. Dyby was responsible for almost 80 percent of the information that Sweden received from Denmark. He lived by what he called the three C's, compassion, conscience, and consideration.

Knud Dyby was still a member of the King's Royal Guard during the time of the German invasion of Denmark. When the Nazi flag was raised over the royal castle King Christian the Tenth demanded it be taken down. Dyby was one of the men to remove the flag. He later left service and joined the police force. In his position as an officer he had access to vital information the Danish resistance needed. He was also very involved in the Danish underground and knew the best hiding places for people at the fishing docks of Copenhagen. Dyby heard news that the Germans had a plan to deport all the Jews in Denmark so he made a quick decision, and used his knowledge of the sea-lanes between Denmark and Sweden. He participated in the Danish-Swedish Refugee Service's rescue of almost 7,200 Jews in a single week in October of 1943. Jews would be hidden in the hospitals where they would wait for one of the police cars Dyby used when the taxi drivers denied to be involved. A boat would come to take them across the resound into Sweden. Dyby himself transported 1,888 people to safety, 629 of whom were Jewish. He also had a small fleet that transported goods such as weapons, news, intelligence, and people.

Matthew 6:1-6 and 16-18 states, "Jesus said to his disciples, 'Take care not to perform righteous deeds in order that people may see them; otherwise, you will have no recompense from your heavenly Father. When you give alms, do not blow a trumpet before you, as the hypocrites do in the synagogues and in the streets to win the praise of others. Amen I say to you, they have received their reward. But when you give alms, do not let your left hand know what your right is doing, so that your almsgiving may be secret. And your Father who sees in secret will repay you.'" Knud Dyby is a perfect example of how to live this passage, he helped those around him not for the benefit of being known as a good person, but because he knew it was the right thing. Dyby showed many people that even in times of despair it's still possible to find love. In May 1945 Dyby ended his police career with the end of the war. A year after he moved to the United States. Knud Dyby passed in 2011 at the age of 96. He is remembered as a brave, courageous man.

Knud Dyby was truly an amazing person. He never feared standing up for what he believed in and he helped others when they needed it. A Junior High student or anyone who knows his story can call Knud Dyby a hero. There are so many different accounts of courageous people from the Holocaust but Knud Dyby's really stands out as something everyone can call the actions of a kind-hearted man.

Reference

https://jfr.org/rescuer-stories/dyby-knud/
http://www2.humboldt.edu/rescuers/book/album/dyby/dyby2.html
http://usccb.org/bible/readings/021313.cfm

CARL LUTZ: HOLOCAUST HERO

Piper Hechtl

The Holocaust took place during World War II. Under the regime of Nazi rule, the Nazis had persecuted and murdered million Jews. German authorities also targeted many other groups because of their perceived "racial inferiority," such as the disabled, Jews, Gypsies, Soviet prisoners of war, Jehovah's Witnesses and homosexuals. Many of these people were victims of the Nazi tyranny. As a result, many of these individuals were murdered or died of starvation, disease, neglect, or maltreatment. In the midst of these horrific tragedies arose a group of heroes. This group of individuals went out of their way to save and protect. Carl Lutz was one of those heroes. Lutz was born in Walzenhausen, Switzerland and in the year 1895. There he attended local schools up until he was about 18 years old. Once Lutz was 18, he then immigrated to the United States where he lived and worked for more than 15 years.

He worked in the state of Illinois until he earned enough money to attend College. Soon, Lutz started his studies at Central Wesleyan College in Warrenton, Missouri.

In 1920, in Washington, D.C. Lutz found employment at the Swiss Legation. There he furthered his education at George Washington University, and in 1924 he received his Bachelor's degree. Lutz lived in DuPont Circle during his time in Washington, D.C. and still continued to work for the Swiss Legation.

Soon after graduation, Lutz was appointed as chancellor at the Swiss Consulate in the state of Philadelphia, and he was then assigned to the Swiss, Consulate in St. Louis. He served in both cities from 1926 to 1934.

Later that same year, Lutz was appointed as Swiss vice-consul in Budapest, Hungary. He soon began cooperating with the Jewish Agency for Palestine. There he issued Swiss safe-conduct documents that enabled almost 10,000 Hungarian Jewish Children to emigrate to safety.

In 1944, the Nazis took over Budapest and they started deporting Jews to the death camps. Lutz negotiated a special deal with the Hungarian government and the Nazis. This deal gave him permission to issue protective letters to 8,000 Hungarian Jews for emigration to Palestine. Deliberately, Lutz used his permission for 8,000 to apply to families rather than individuals, and he proceeded to issue tens of thousands of additional letters, all of them bearing a number between one and 8,000. He set up about 76 "safe houses" around Budapest and declared them annexes of the Swiss legation. This meant that it was off limits to the Hungarian forces or Nazi soldiers. The "Glass House" was well known among the safe houses and about 3,000 Hungarian Jews found refuge in it and in a neighboring building.

One day while Arrow Cross Fascist militiamen were firing at Jews, Carl Lutz jumped in the Danube River just to save the life of a bleeding Jewish woman. With water up to his chest and his suit soaked with water, the Consul swam back to the bank with her. He then asked to speak to the Hungarian officer in charge of the firing squad, and had her declared a foreign citizen protected by Switzerland and quoted international covenants. Then the Consul brought her back to his car in front of the stunned Fascists and left quietly. They were afraid to shoot at this tall man who seemed to be important and had spoken so eloquently that no one tried to stop him.

Together with other diplomats of neutral countries, including, Raoul Wallenberg, Angelo Rotta, Friedrich Born and Lutz, himself, had worked relentlessly for many months to prevent the planned deaths of many innocent people. His colleagues and he dodged the actions of their German and Hungarian counterparts. Thanks to Lutz's diplomatic skills, he had succeeded in persuading Hungarian and Nazi-German officials into tolerating his formal protection of Hungarian Jews. Among these officials was Adolf Eichmann, a German Nazi. Since Lutz's efforts were so bold and so extensive to undermine the Nazi death machine, in November 1944, Proconsul

Veesenmeyer, the German representative in Hungary, asked to have permission to assassinate the Swiss Consul. Berlin never answered back the representative.

Maximilian Jaeger, the Swiss Minister, thoroughly supported Lutz until he left at the request of government orders as the Soviet Army approached. In the last remaining weeks before the Red Army took over the city, Lutz was helped greatly by Herald Feller, who had taken over responsibility of the Swiss Legation after Jaeger had departed. Even Lutz's wife, Trudi, also played a central supporting role during the time of her husband's activities in Budapest.

In 1975, Carl Lutz died in Bern, Switzerland. Lutz's legacy still lives on. He saved the lives of tens of thousands of people, and his achievements were not immediately recognized in Switzerland. After the war had ended, Lutz had been criticized by the government for having exceeded his authority, because officials had been fearful of endangering Switzerland's neutral status.

As a part of the Swiss national rethinking of the war years, it was in 1958 that Lutz was "rehabilitated" in terms of reputation, and that his achievements were honored. Later, in 1965, Lutz was the first Swiss national named to the list of "Righteous Among the Nations" by Yad Vashem, the Jewish people's memorial to the Holocaust. Then in 1991, a memorial dedicated to him was erected at the entrance to the old Budapest ghetto.

Finally in 2014, George Washington University in Washington, D.C. posthumously honored Carl Lutz with the President's Medal in a ceremony attended by various international dignitaries and his daughter, Agnes Hirshi.

Carl Lutz lived an honorable life. He always put the needs of others before himself, and stood up for what he believed in. Lutz and many others were heroes during a time when all hope was thought to be lost. His bravery and sacrifices left a legacy that will be remembered throughout generations.

LESSONS LIVED

Steven Noll, Co-winner

The Holocaust, a sinister, immoral plague that erupted from Germany, ravaged through Europe, devouring all kindness and justice in its path. It caused merciless devastation and destruction. Although this time in history was of dark circumstances, there were glimmers of hope and light that illuminated this inhumane age. One of these bright glimmers was an ordinary woman with extraordinary qualities by the name of Gerda Valentiner.

Gerda Valentiner, a teacher in Denmark, was known as an amiable, benevolent young lady who devoted her life to instilling knowledge into all children. She was solely committed to her students, regardless of their individual differences. Respectful, she also tolerated religions besides her own. For instance, when she came upon the realization that a few of her Jewish students were adhering to their religious dietary restrictions, and could therefore only consume bread, she purchased new food and dishes so they could eat. Small acts of compassion such as this one soon enlarged her reputation, and her confidence, and prepared her for the future, which would be much more challenging and dangerous.

When the persecution of the Jews began, many teachers immediately deserted any that were part of the Jewish faith of this group of people, including their own students. Valentiner was one of the exceptions. She was fiercely courageous, and firmly believed that she was a schoolteacher to not only educate and inspire her students, but to truly live the values of selflessness and perseverance herself. With this mindset, and the right motivation, she risked her life countless times for the sake of her pupils.

In September 1943, Valentiner unexpectedly visited the Scheftelowitz household, where she met with the family of one of her students. There, she spoke with the parents, Ester and Ruben Scheftelowitz, and warned them of the impending danger of the Nazis. A few days later, arrangements were made for the children, Moritz, Dora, and Rita, to be temporarily transferred to Valentiner's house to avoid any potential threats. Valentiner attempted to evacuate the three youths from the country multiple times. The first two trials were unsuccessful, but on the third, they managed to escape via fishing boat from a point approximately ten kilometers north of Copenhagen. After a tiresome night, the siblings arrived at their destination, Landskrona, Sweden.

One month later, in October 1943, Gerda Valentiner was given the opportunity to once again exemplify her outstanding qualities. During the following weeks, the deportation of all Jews residing in Denmark was scheduled. With knowledge of this crucial fact, Valentiner promptly enacted a plan to collect all of the Jewish students. After all of the children had been collected from their parents, she transported them to her home. There, they patiently waited until Valentiner believed that the time was right to send them to the coast, where they would be rerouted to Sweden. These two instances accurately portray this woman's inspiring characteristics in action.

Even after the grim vise of the Holocaust was released and the war officially ended, Gerda Valentiner requested a leave of absence from her occupation as a teacher, enabling her to continue her work with Jews in refugee camps, which were located in Germany and Austria.

Although Gerda Valentiner has passed, she will always be remembered as the teacher who did more than just teach lessons, she lived by them.

Fear. Fear is what allowed Hitler and his followers to manipulate the entire continent of Europe into being a part of the horrible Holocaust. Fear forced the citizens living there to join in the oppression and persecution of the Jews. Fear caused the Europeans to be unable to truly voice their opinions on the matter. Fear is what the entire Holocaust boils down to. However, during this age of death and despair, there were a select few that rose to the occasion, and were not afraid of the Nazis. Filled with courage, they did everything in their power to help save the Jewish people that they could, and one of these people was Sigurd Larsen.

Larsen, the son of a Danish father and a German mother, had resided in Berlin for the majority of his early life until about his mid-thirties. He then began operating an importing and exporting business that transferred furniture from Germany to Scandinavia. Larsen despised the Nazis so greatly that he decided to move his wife and two children to Copenhagen with him, where he would continue to maintain his business relations with Germany.

One of his associates, Joachim Marcuse, who still lived in Berlin, was Jewish. Due to the rise of Anti-Semitism in Europe, he had been immediately fired from his position as superintendent in one of the furniture companies for which Larsen also worked.. Joachim Marcuse was soon arrested and was forced to work at a labor site. Fortunately, Marcuse's skills as a carpenter were impressive enough for him to be promoted to work in a Nazi factory specializing in furniture.. After receiving word of this turn of events, Larsen immediately visited his friend to keep in touch with him. In 1941, Joachim Marcuse married a nineteen-year-old woman, Gerda Berlowitz, who was also part of forced labor. Although the couple was happy to finally be wed, their situation only worsened.

Rumors of deportation began to circulate, and expecting the worst, Marcuse promptly asked Larsen for his assistance. Agreeing, Larsen comprised a plan that although dangerous, would help the Marcuses escape from their current situation. The plan involved Larsen placing an order of furniture from Joachim Marcuse that would be delivered in the weeks prior to Christmas. During this period before Christmas, fewer German officers were assigned posts, and the surveillance and supervision of the Jews was therefore less severe. As the administrator of his small factory, Joachim Marcuse was usually authorized to load the train where the furniture was to be stored before shipment. He used this valuable opportunity to fashion a small hiding place in the vehicle to be used for his escape.

On Christmas Eve, with everything prepared, Larsen arrived with a collection of German police and customs officers, who verified that no Jews were being secretly transported. They did not realize that in the same train that they were riding on, were three Jews - Joachim Marcuse, his wife, and Kurt Levin, a good friend of theirs. They were fully equipped and supplied with food and water that would last for a large portion of the journey. During the transfer itself, the three Jews were not ever seen or heard from. Sigurd Larsen loyally remained with them for the rest of the eight-day outing, wary of the Germans, and nervous for the well-being of the three escapees.

After what seemed to be an interminable expedition, their destination, Sweden, was reached. The Jews safely evacuated the train, and were readily given refuge with the Swiss. Taking extra precautions from the possible consequences of his illegal actions, Sigurd Larsen hastily returned to Copenhagen with his family.

Although Sigurd Larsen was an ordinary craftsman and trader, he will always be remembered as an extraordinary man in character, loyalty, and most of all, fearlessness.

Saint Francis of Assissi Elementary School, Sacramento, CA

Janet Stites teaches Religion, Performing Arts, and Science at St. Francis Elementary School in Sacramento, California. She has been teaching there for 12 fabulous years.

Heather Church teaches 7th grade English-Language Arts, Social Studies, Religion, and Art at St. Francis of Assisi Elementary School in Sacramento, California. She has been teaching there for seven terrific years.

Skip Bacon earned a master's degree in theology from the University of Notre Dame. She has served as a leader in Hispanic parishes in the Chicago area for almost ten years. Skip currently serves as a Catechetical Programming Specialist and Consultant for Our Sunday Visitor, a non-for-profit Catholic publishing company. She also ministers as the Director of Faith Formation and 8th grade religion instructor at St. Francis of Assisi Catholic parish and school in Sacramento California.

AND IT BEGAN

Abby Palko

The Holocaust is an important part of history for many reasons. The Holocaust

was a time of darkness and a time where there was no justice for those who wanted to speak up about their religion. For the Jews the Holocaust was a truly a time of fear and darkness. The Holocaust was the murder of millions of Jews. Fortunately, there were people like Paul Grueninger who tried to help Jews live through this time of true darkness. Paul Grueninger was a Swiss border police commander of the St. Gallen Region that borders with Austria. Individuals like Grueninger led the way to end the prosecution of thousands of Jews during the Holocaust.

Paul Grueninger was born on October 27, 1891. Grueninger was a Swiss hero of the Holocaust which means he helped save the lives of many Jews. When he was 47 years old he was faced with a monumental moral dilemma: Turning the refugees back to their country where violent anti-Semitism was the official state policy, or facing the consequences of breaching the explicit instructions of his government and suffering the consequences. He did not want to do this so he discarded the order and change their registration so there passports said that they had arrived in Switzerland before March 1938, when entry of the country had been restricted. This fabrication of dates enabled the arrivals to be treated as legal to be taken to the Diepoldsau Camp, where, aided by the Jewish organizations, the refugees awaited their permits for temporary stay in Switzerland or their departure to a final destination.

Grueninger, the policeman who decided to break the law, turned in false reports about the number of arrivals and the status of the refugees in his district, and impeded efforts to trace refugees who were known to have entered Switzerland illegally. Something amazing he did for the refugees was he paid with his own money to buy winter clothes for needy refugees who had been forced to leave all their belongings behind. The Germans informed the Swiss authorities about what Grueninger was doing. He was kicked off the police force in March 1939, for all of the great kind acts that he did to help the Jews. All of his benefits were taken away and he was taken to trial on charges of illegally permitting the entry of 3,600 Jews into Switzerland and falsifying their registration papers. The prosecution added additional charges of helping individual Jews by shielding them from the officers finding them. Ostracized and forgotten, Grueninger lived for the rest of his life in a difficult way. Despite the difficulties, he never regretted his action of helping the Jews through this hard time in history, on behalf of the Jews. In 1954 he explained his motives: "It was basically a question of saving human lives threatened with death. How could I then seriously consider bureaucratic schemes and calculations?" In December 1970 as a result of protest in the media, the Swiss government sent Grueninger a somewhat reserved letter of apology, but did not reopen his case and reinstating his pension. Only after his death were steps to his reputation set into motion. The first attempt was rejected by the Swiss Council, and only as late as 1995, the Swiss federal Government finally annulled Grueninger's conviction. Paul Grueninger passed away in 1972.

He was not the only one who helped Jews through this time of great sadness. He was among many others who tried to make a difference and end this time of true darkness and be a light to others who could not see their future or see what God put them on this earth to do. He knew that God put him on this earth to help guide others in need that could not see the path ahead of them. Throughout his life he believed that Jews should not be treated any differently than any other religion. The sad thing is that most of the heroes of the Holocaust are not known to all people. I think that everyone, no matter their religion, should be informed about the heroes of the Holocaust and what they did for everyone to try to help and make a difference. The Holocaust was a terrible time in our history.

In the end Paul Grueninger was just like all other human beings and did not want people to die for being who they are. Grueninger did not want people to be looked at as outcasts. As you can see he would sacrifice his job, his benefits and what he has been working for all to save the lives of Jews that Nazis thought were worthless outcasts who did not deserve to be treated like an equal. He risked his own life trying to save people he did not even know. I don't know about you but that would be pretty hard for me to do. As I have told you there are many other people who risked their life and some even got there life taken away for trying to help in this sad time. In the end, Paul Grueninger was just a man who put it all on the line, to help other people he did not even know, just to make a difference in the world.

HERO ROSA

Addison Kinter

The Holocaust was made up of war, bullies and tormenting. The Holocaust was started in 1933 by Adolf Hitler when he was chosen as president for Germany. After he won he believed that all Jews should not be alive. He wanted everyone to be the same which created the start of the Holocaust. Many people saved the Jews from exhaustion and starvation those people were declared heroes. Most heroes people did not even know existed, for example Rosa Naef.

Rosa Naef was a Swiss woman. In her mid-twenties an orphanage in France named Château-de-la-Hille Orphanage hired her to take over the orphanage. In the orphanage there were 120 Jewish children who had fled from Germany to Belgium before the Holocaust started for shelter. The children lived in peace for the longest time with food, water, and the attention they needed one day that all went down. One day a couple police came in and took all the Jewish children over 16 living in the orphanage and took them to a concentration camp. She soon called a taxi to get the children from the concentration camp. She got the children back but they were still in great danger so she sent them on a train. Rosa gave them food and money before they went on the train where they would be put into another orphanage. For many the Holocaust was a time of sadness where many innocent people were killed because of the Nazis. But it is also an important part of history without it there would not be a big Jewish holiday/celebration. But as well there would not be anything to teach kids that it is okay to be different and unique in race and gender.

People did not like what she was doing so they took her out of the orphanage and returned her to Switzerland.

If I was Rosa when the police came after having peaceful days, I would have been really scared. I probably would have told someone and asked what to and not have been brave enough to drive to the consecration camp. But if I had driven to the consecration camp I would scatter the kids in empty houses that the police already looked through. If that did not work I would hide the kids throughout the orphanage. My last resort would be to send the kids on a train, like Rosa Naef, with lots of food and money.

Adolf Hitler was the prime controller of this horrible mess along with all of his Nazi followers. The Jews were punished by going to concentration camps and doing horrible jobs. Some of the jobs were farming, hauling rocks, and working for Adolf Hitler. In the building job you would build huge buildings with the risk of dying. One man fell through a building during the Holocaust and they just buried him without a funeral. If you were chosen to haul rocks you would take rocks back and forth across roads until either you passed out from the heat, passed out from exhaustion, or made it thru the day. If you worked for the Nazis that job is pretty self explanatory. If you worked for the Nazis you would make shoes, clothing, or work in a store or restaurant. Those were just some of the jobs Jews would do in the Holocaust.

The Holocaust still has an effect on us today. There is a date set aside for the holiday which was named Yom HaShoah Ve-Hagevurah, and it literally translates into "Day of the Holocaust." Yom HaShoah only lasts two days. This year (2015) it starts on April 15th and ends April 16th. It was dedicated to not only the Holocaust and its survivors, but mostly the people who persevered to survive.

The Holocaust was a horrific time of bullying. Without the Holocaust there would not be a big Jewish celebration. We also now have a better understanding that we should not treat any race, gender, or religion different like Adolf Hitler did.

AN AMAZING HERO

Angela Altamirano

Many Jewish people in Europe suffered from 1933-1945 because of one leader named Adolf Hitler. This period is known as the Holocaust. The Holocaust started with the Germans creating many laws affecting the Jews. That was not the end, because in 1935 the Germans introduced military conscriptions. Then, the Germans invaded Poland which caused World War II to begin. The Germans continued to attack many other places, and they did not stop there. They created ghettos to house the poor, and Jews, established a squad named Einsatzgruppen which killed more than 30,000 people. Few people actually helped and felt pity and mercy for the Jews, and even fewer saved many lives while risking their own. This year we are honoring Swiss and Danish heroes of the Holocaust.

There were many heroes of the Holocaust, and one of them was Paul Gruninger. Paul Gruninger was born Swiss and during the Holocaust in 1938 he became a Swiss border police commander of the St. Gallen region that bordered with Austria. Later, when Nazi Germany took over Austria they closed the border connected to Switzerland for the refugees who came with no proper information because they were Jews. Since the border closed in October 1938, Switzerland and Nazi Germany started stamping any Jew passport they gave out with a "J" so they can travel to the camps and chambers. Later in Austria when the amount of Jews trying to enter Switzerland illegally grew, Paul was debating whether he should save the refugees and Jews and face the consequences or let the refugees go back to their homes which would kill them because Nazi Germany had taken over their land. Paul thought about it and he made the decision to save the refugees and Jews.

Paul Gruninger was a good man he saved more than 3,000 Jews and refugees by changing their registration so their passport would say they came to Switzerland before the border closed (which was October 1938), because they had to limit the amount of people that could enter Switzerland. Whoever Paul saved was sent to a place called Diepoldsau camp which was run by Jewish organizations and there they were treated as undocumented. While they were at the camps they waited for their permits and they stayed in Switzerland temporarily or traveled to their destination. Since he broke the law by changing their passports Paul had to turn in many false reports to keep the refugees alive and make sure Nazi Germany will not be suspicious about how many people he had saved. Paul Gruninger had saved many lives by doing this, and he even bought a lot of the winter and warm clothes because most of the refugees had to leave their clothes and their belongings behind to travel. Paul Gruninger did many things to keep Jews safe and healthy even though he was not one of them and like all the heroes he had to face the consequences. He had to risk one life in order to save more than 3,000 lives.

Later the Germans told the Swiss Authority about Paul's lies and he had to leave the police department in March 1939. Before he left he was brought to trial in January 1939 because he allowed 3,600 Jews to enter Switzerland by falsifying their passports and making them permits but the trial did not end until March 1941. After he was put in jail which was also in 1941 he was added additional charges because he helped Jews by protecting them from death and giving them clothes and valuables. His trial was over two years long, and he was not able to retire because he lost all of his money and he still had to pay many other fines. The jury had thought about his work for the police department, but it did not help because he still did not follow the directions of Nazis about letting the Jews enter. Paul had a very hard life but never regretted his decision to save all the refugees and Jews. Paul died in 1972 and he was one of the few people who helped. Paul Gruninger was a great man who sacrificed so much and we should try to stop bullying like Paul did and stand up for what we believe in even if it means giving away all of our stuff like the Jews did.

Paul Gruninger was an amazing man, although he had to die in a hard circumstance. Paul Gruninger had a full life between saving 3,600 Jews, buying them clothes, lying multiple times to German officials, losing his job, going to court, losing all of his money, going to jail, and later struggling to live in hard circumstances. He was a great man, and he was later honored by Yadvashem a year before his death on April 20, 1971. Paul Gruninger taught us all a lesson and it is to help people and if it saves multiple people's lives it doesn't matter if you sacrifice a couple of things or lie once in a while. Paul was a hero and he was honored two years before he died by the Swiss government. They sent him a letter of apology and he got his pension back because he lost it all in court and he also got a plaque of honor in Saint Gallen. Paul was an amazing and inspiring man and we can all learn one or two things from him to stop bullying like he tried to do with the Jews and standing up to what we believe in even if we have to sacrifice a couple of things and tell a lie once in a while to save 3,600 lives just like the amazing hero Paul Gruninger.

PAUL GRUENINGER AND THE HOLOCAUST

Ariana Galvez

The Holocaust was a time during World War II where Germans killed nearly two out of every three European Jews. Other victims included about 200,000 Roma, also known as Gypsies. Even in the middle of tragedy there were amazing heroes. A Swiss hero of the Holocaust was Paul Grueninger.

Paul Grueninger was the Swiss Border Police commander of the St. Gallen region that borders with Austria. He is known for saving the lives of about 3,600 Jewish refugees where he risked his own job.

During the Holocaust, the Nazi Party had power in Germany. Through a planned, government-sponsored program, the Nazis set out to rid Europe of the 9 million Jews living there. The Nazis believed the Jews were an inferior group of people. Because the Germans believed they were "racially superior," they targeted not only the Jews, but other groups because of their race, political beliefs, and behavior. The Nazis set up labor camps and forced Jews and other people to work there. Eventually these people were sent to extermination camps where they were shot or gassed to death.

Due to Nazi regulations, Switzerland would not allow Jews to enter thecountry without proper entry permits. After Germany took control of Austria, many Austrian Jewish refugees tried to leave Austria and enter Switzerland illegally. Some of these refugees came to meet Paul Grueninger. The Swiss police commander had to make the decision if he should allow the refugees to enter the country without papers, or should he send them back to Austria and Nazi control.

Grueninger decided to help the Jewish refugees. He did not follow official instructions and he let the desperate refugees enter Switzerland. Grueninger made fake documents to help Jews enter the country legally. He changed the dates on their passports to show that the refugees had made it to Switzerland before March of 1938. This meant that they were in the country legally because they entered before the date the border was closed to refugees. Grueninger also used his own money to buy clothes for the refugees who had left their belongings in Austria. Being in Switzerland meant good things for the Jewish refugees. They were away from Hitler and Nazi rules and as legals they received help from Jewish organizations. They received permits for temporary stay in Switzerland or permits to travel through Switzerland to get to their final destination.

The Swiss authorities found out what Grueninger had done for the refugees. He was fired from the police force and lost his benefits. He was taken to court and put on trial. His trial lasted more than two years. He was eventually found guilty because he did not follow instructions. He was also charged with helping individual Jews by hiding them, and helping them hide their belongings. The rest of his life was difficult but Grueninger never regretted helping the Jews.

In 1954 he explained his choices: "It was basically a question of saving human lives threatened with death. How could I then seriously considerbureaucratic schemes and calculations." In December 1970 because the media protested, the Swiss government sent Grueninger what appeared to be a letter of apology. On April 20, 1971, YadVashem recognized Paul Grueninger as on of the Righteous Among Nations. He died in 1972. In 1995, the Swiss government abolished Grueninger's conviction and in 2014, the police department of St. Gallen decided to have Grueninger commemorated. They unveiled a plaque in Grueninger's honor at the police headquarters in Switzerland.

Although many people died during the Holocaust, many lives were saved because of people like Paul Grueninger. Because of his bravery, over 3,000 Jewish lives were saved. Paul Grueninger was a true Swiss Hero of the Holocaust.

PAUL GRUNINGER: A HOLOCAUST HERO

Brian Feldman Jr.

The *Holocaust* was the murder of 6 million European Jews from August 1933 to April 1939 by Nazi Germany. A very bad man named Adolf Hitler was the leader of the Nazi army. During this horrible time, there were a lot of bad things, but there were also some heroes who helped save many Jewish people from the *Holocaust*. One of these heroes was Paul Gruninger.

Paul Gruninger was born on October 27, 1891 in Saint Gallen, Switzerland. When he was growing up, he played football. He became the Swiss border police commander, and worked at the border between Austria and Switzerland. Switzerland closed its borders and would not allow Jewish citizens from Austria to go over the border. When the Jews tried to escape the *Holocaust*, they tried to go through Switzerland. Switzerland would not let them escape because they had a "J" on their passport which meant that they were Jewish. Paul's job was to send Jewish refugees without proper paperwork back to Austria.

Paul Gruninger felt bad for the Jewish refugees. He stopped following orders and changed their passports to show that they had arrived in Switzerland before March 1938. This was the date that Switzerland stopped letting them enter the country. When he changed the dates of their passports, the refugees were treated as legals and were taken to the Diepoldsau camp. He gave some them money and clothes because they did not have anything with them. When they had to escape many of them only had fifteen minutes to get their belongings out of the house.

When the Germans told the Swiss authorities what Paul Gruninger had done in 1939, he got in trouble. He lost his job, his pension benefits, and his valuables. He was arrested and charged with illegally allowing 2,600 to 3,600 Jews into Switzerland. He had to pay court costs and fines. He lived alone and poor but he never regretted what he did. In 1954, he said, "It was basically a question of saving human lives threatened with death". The Swiss government finally apologized to Paul Gruninger in December 1970. He was added to Yad Vashem on April 20, 1971, a year before his death. He was recognized for his bravery and was put into the Righteous among the Nations. He died on February 22, 1972.

In conclusion, the *Holocaust* was the murder of 6 million kind Jewish civilization in Europe. There was lots of bad in the world, but there were also some good too. Paul Gruninger was a good person who was a hero for many Jewish people during the *Holocaust*. By letting Jews sneak into Switzerland, he saved two thousand six hundred to three thousand six hundred Jewish people from the Holocaust.

JUST A WALK IN THE MOUNTAINS

Caroline Milar

The Holocaust was when the Nazi regime killed both Jews and non-Jews with the intent to destroy people, races, religions, and beliefs other than their own. This intention resulted in the deaths of 6 million Jews and 5 million non-Jews, a total of 11 million killings. Many advertisements convinced young men to join the Nazi regime, while others joined out of fear. Not everyone was against the Jews, though. There were many "heroes," or people who helped save the Jews from persecution from the Nazis. Some of these heroes include Oskar Schindler and Miep Gies, but what about the others? So many people risked their lives to save Jews, but only a handful of them get their own movies, biographies, foundations, documentaries and more. Luckily, Yad Vashem has the Righteous Among Nations program. The program recognizes and honors those heroes who don't get the recognition they deserve. These unsung heroes saved lives, yet so little is known or remembered about them. The Marclay Family was a group of those people.

Emile, Lina, Marguerite, and Norbert Marclay lived in Champéry, Switzerland in 1942. One September afternoon, while on a walk in the mountains, they noticed a group of people who were running. They realized that these were Jews who were trying escape to Switzerland. They had been walking in the mountains for twenty hours. They had come from Holland, through Belgium and France. The group was composed of the following seven people: the Stropper couple and their daughter Tille, the Ehrlich couple and their eldest son, and another young man named Jesha

(Yeshayahu) Shapir. The Marclays invited the fugitives to their chalet for a few days, just enough time to regain their strength and get going again. There, they were fed, cleaned up, and given new clothes so that they could look like normal people again, instead of fugitives. They were given suitcases to look like vacationers coming from the mountains, not fugitives escaping from the Nazi regime. The group of seven was then taken to the train station, where Lina and Emile Marclay purchased their train tickets to Zurich.

At Zurich, the fugitives presented themselves at the Dutch consulate, where their status became legal. Ten days later, Tille Stropper contacted the Marclay family, asking them to help a second group of Dutch Jews. One of the Jews in this second group was, in fact, Tille's fiancé. Emile and Lina agreed eagerly. Under extreme weather conditions and at a high altitude of 1,800 meters, they and Tille eventually met up with the other group at another high mountain pasture chalet. Tille had brought with her valid papers and money. The Marclays directed the group to the station, where the fugitives took a bus bound for Zurich. By helping these Jews, the Marclay Family saved a lucky fourteen out of 6 million quite unlucky Jews.

What I should be asking myself is how can I do what these amazing people did in my everyday life? I think that what I'm trying to say is, I can't go on a hike and take in some escaping Jews. Although, I know for a fact that people are being mistreated at my school. I can help those people by sticking up for them when they are getting picked on, or talking to them when they are alone, just to let them know that they are not alone. Just to let them know that they have a friend, or someone to talk to when they are lonely. If someone is sad, I can cheer them up by telling them that I will be there with them through thick and thin. I can tell them jokes, eat with them at lunch, and invite them to hang out. Why may you ask? I would do it because I care. The Marclay family gave up their time, money, and chalet for people who couldn't pay them back. They risked their lives to get those strangers to safety, and then did it AGAIN. I will never be able to do that, but I can try my best to get somewhere close. If we all treated others with supreme respect and kindness, we are saying, in a way, "What happened during the Holocaust was horrible. I never want that to happen again. By treating this person in my school, neighborhood, or anywhere like I am right now, I am insuring that what happened before will never happen again."

The Marclay family helped save the lives of Jews. I think that the reason we're entering this contest is to raise awareness for the Holocaust. It was an international catastrophe. The scariest part about it is that it could happen again. When you say something mean about someone behind their back, make fun of someone to their face, or hurt someone physically, you, in a way, are treating that person like the Nazis treated the Jews, as if they are nothing. Thanks to the kindness of the Marclay family, the lives of those Jews meant something. So just remember, those Jews were saved by a simple act. That simple act began with just a walk in the mountains.

THE HOLOCAUST AND ITS HEROES
CJ DeShong

The Holocaust was a dark and challenging time for Jews. The Holocaust is an event that lasted a long twelve years. This event was caused by Adolf Hitler and the Nazis. Hitler and the Nazis ended up killing millions of people because of their religion or race. All of the deaths were pointless. Innocent people ended up dying because of something they had no control over. Being a specific race is not a reason to be put to death. The Holocaust was a definitely one of the most horrific time periods in history. There were many heroes who were involved in the Holocaust period. Friedrich Born was one of the heroes who impacted this era the most.

"Holocaust" in Greek means "sacrifice by fire." The Nazis believed that the Jews had to be punished, so they came up with a plan to punish them. This was done for no necessary reason. They decided that they would send Jews to ghettos and killing centers away from Germany. Their plan worked and millions of people died. Fortunately the Holocaust ended when the Allied forces began to help prisoners out of their camps. This was a light in the time of severe darkness. Most of the Jews who survived had given up hope that one day they would be free. With the assistance of the Allied forces, the Nazis eventually ended up surrendering. Death was a constant force during this period. In the aftermath of the Holocaust we cannot forget the righteous heroes who died to save Jews.

The Righteous Among the Nations are a group of people who helped Jews and other faiths escape from the dreadful Holocaust. At first they started off as ordinary people, and now they are known as great heroes. These heroes were all different nationalities from different countries. The heroes rescued Jews by taking them into their homes during a search. This was a very dangerous and courageous move. In doing this the heroes had to make a choice because they could die trying to save the Jews. They put their lives at risk, but thought that their purpose was more important than the danger. The heroes had to do many creative and dangerous tactics to help the Jews escape to freedom. During this period they made false papers and identities to help Jews escape ghettos, prisons, and help children and adults get to underground bunkers. By doing this they ended up saving about six thousand Jews and other faiths from the Holocaust. Although there were many heroes during this time; the one that stands out the most to me was Friedrich Born. He was the most interesting and no doubt righteous hero to me.

Friedrich Born started off as a regular Swiss citizen. He worked for the

International Committee of the Red Cross. He is known for saving 6,000 Jewish children who were placed in homes under the protection of the International Red Cross. He had an amazing story of how he saved thousands of Jews. Friedrich Born established two sections that would deal with children. Section A was under and led by the Zionist leader, Otto Komoly. Section B was led by Reverend Gabor Sztehlo of the Good Shepherd Committee. He also established a Transportation unit that was a huge help in relief, rescue, and resistance operations. In doing this Friedrich rescued thousands of Jews from death camps. He also supplied children's homes and the people in the ghetto with food, medicine, and fuel. Friedrich Born was recognized for his actions by Yad Vashem on January 4, 1987. He truly impacted this era and made a huge difference for many who were affected.

Friedrich Born was an incredible man who had a true desire and mission to help people; especially children in who were in need. He was one of the many people that wanted to help the Jews, even if it meant giving up their lives. Friedrich Born fortunately survived, but many of the heroes who helped the Jews died. Many of the heroes weren't a part of an International Committee. Friedrich Born used being a part of an International Committee to his advantage and made establishments for the Jewish children. Friedrich Born did his part to end the dark and dreadful Holocaust.

The Holocaust lasted for twelve long years (1933-1945). It was a time that most Jews would like to forget. Although it was a horrible experience for Jews, society should never forget what was done. The Holocaust period is a good example of how we all need to stand up for what is right and overall justice. Friedrich Born was one of the Holocaust heroes who did this. I admire Friedrich Born because he could have continued on with his life instead of helping the Jews. Instead he chose to help those who needed him the most. His actions made the most impact on the Nazi's plan compared to heroes who had only saved one person.

We can all learn from the heroes of the Holocaust. If we simply stand up for the right causes and stand strong together we can continue to make the world a better place. I encourage everyone to take a stand when you see injustice. It can be something as simple as standing up for someone who is being bullied. Anyone can be a hero; even you!

HEROES OF THE HOLOCAUST

David Valencia

The Holocaust is one of the very horrible things that happened to the Jews that lived in Germany. Austria had made some negotiations with the Nazis about the Jews which had started in October 1938, and that is when the Germans started stamping the famous "J" onto the passports of the Jews. When the situation of the Jews began in Austria. It had worsened because it let a number of Jewish refugees enter Switzerland illegally. Paul Gruninger was one of the people who saved Jews from the Holocaust, and he was a Swiss police commander of Switzerland. He was a commander of the St. Gallen region that borders with Austria. Paul Gruninger was faced with a monumental dilemma because of all the Jews he had to save.

Paul had started to deny the officer's orders and let the refugees enter Switzerland. He also falsified the refugees' registration to enter Switzerland. Now their passports fooled the other officers so that they would think that the refugees were there before March 1938. Now the refugees were treated with respect instead of being treated like a Jew. He helped the Jews try to stay hidden under cover until their next departure to their next destination.

Paul decided to break the law a lot more often to save more Jews, and he turned in false reports about the number of Jews arriving and status of refugees in his district. Then other officers noticed that some of the Jews started entering the country illegally. Paul now had to use his own money to buy the refugees some coats to keep warm because it was getting cold, and the departures were all not available to leave until all the Jews that entered Switzerland were found. Most of the refugees that were found had to leave their belongings behind, and Paul was able to give the caught refugees some coats.

Eventually Paul got caught for helping the refugees and he was dismissed from the police force in March 1939. Now he was to be brought to trial on charges of illegally letting 3,600 Jews enter Switzerland and falsifying their registration papers. The charges also involved additional charges of helping individual Jews for shielding them from detection and assisting them in depositing their values. Paul's trail opened in January 1939 and dragged over two years. In March 1941 the court found him guilty of breach of duty. He was fined and had to pay the trail costs. He suffered a lot so he could save the Jews because he eventually ran out of money for himself and the Jews.

In December 1970 as a result of protest in the media, the Swiss government sent Paul somewhat a reserved letter of apology, but it did refrained from reopening his case and reinstating his pension. After his death there was steps to rehabilitate him into motion. The Swiss Council rejected the first attempt, and only as late 1995 the Swiss federal Government finally annulled Paul's conviction. In 2014, the police and justice chief in the canton of St. Gallen decided to have Paul commemorated and his daughter Ruth. Overall, I think Paul was a person who saved lots and lots of lives. He saved Jews by breaking the law and he was a trusted police commander of the Nazis. In 1971 Yad Vashem bestowed the title of Righteous Among the Nations on Paul Gruninger. He gave his own life to save Jews and that is why I think lots of people should follow in his footsteps because it is the right thing to do. If I were in his shoes I would help the Jews get to safety by getting them into a warm shelter and hide and survive the Holocaust. That is why I think he was recognized in Yad Vashem to this day. I hope other people really follow in his footsteps. Paul saved Jews but he had to give his own to save other lives of the Jews. I think Paul's story was a tragedy for him. Also I think it was very sad to other people too. He did the right to do. He was a great man. He helped the Jews until he got caught. When he got caught he had suffered more than any Jew had ever suffered. He tried to stay alive but eventually he couldn't keep up being held in prison and he died. Some of the Jews in Jail actually had a very small funeral for him because saved so many lives that were being treated unfairly. After he died some of the other Jews thought there would be some one to save more Jews. Eventually there were other people who saved Jews, but some actually survived while they were saving Jewish lives.

HERO OF THE HOLOCAUST: FRIEDRICH BORN
Desmond Greer

The Holocaust was a very gruesome and terrible time for the Jews. It was when the Nazi regime and its leader, Adolf Hitler, committed a large genocide on the Jewish population. In 1933, when the Nazis came to power in Germany, there were over 9 million European Jews. In 1945, just twelve years later, only about a third of the once thriving Jews were still alive. The Germans believed that the Jews were not 'pure' and that the world should only be filled with 'pure people' so being blinded by power, Adolf Hitler ordered the killing of millions of Jews. Being a Jew back then was worse then going to jail now. If you were a Jew you were treated with no respect. You got little to no food everyday and whatever food you did get, was low on calories. You also would never get meat, most of the time only bread and land vegetables. Sometimes, if you were not of use for the Germans or could not do work for them, you would be placed in facilities that were considered, "concentration camps," but really they would take you to gas chambers and would gas you to death which is a very bad way to die.

Through out this time Germany's army had expanded Hitler's empire to Norway, Denmark, the Netherlands, Belgium, and France. During March and April Germany conquered Norway. On April 9, 1940 Germany crossed the border into Denmark. Only about a month later on May 10, 1940 did the Germans conquer the Netherlands. Later on July 24 the Belgium government declared their neutrality, but only about two weeks later Germany declared war on Belgium because they had refused their demand of passage through Belgium. While this was going on Germany was also invading France from the west. Finally after weeks of fighting the French were finally overcome on June 18 by the now seen as the unbeatable German army.

As all this fighting and suffering was happening the Jews persevered and kept their faith alive with the only tool they had left... Hope. With the strength of a mouse and the heart of a tiger the Jews made it through one of the most horrible things in the world's history. Not every person who wasn't Jewish was against Jews. An example of one of these persons was a good, helpful man named Friedrich Born.

Friedrich Born was a righteous hero who was a saving grace to not just some Jews, but 6,000 Jewish children as well as many men and women. He was a Swiss citizen who was born on June 10, 1903 in Langenthal, Switzerland. When he grew older he began working for the International Committee of the Red Cross located in Budapest. He began to take special operations or assignments to save many Jews that were living in Nazi controlled Hungary in the year 1944. He established a transportation unit that engaged in relief, rescue and resistance missions.

Friedrich Born helped rescue many, many Jews from concentration and death camps. He also gave many adults, and children alike, living in the ghetto medicine, fuel and the most importantly, food. He was also responsible for founding lots of public institutions identified by large posters that displayed the words, "Under the protection of the International Committee of the Red Cross."

Friedrich Born also negotiated and protested against the authorities on behalf of the Jews. Because of all his many efforts and countless attempts to save Jews, he helped create and get recognized protective letters issued by the Vatican and foreign Legations. The territorial status of the institutions, camps, and buildings protected and defended by the International Committee Red Cross was also recognized.

Lots of various witnesses attested and fought for the remarkable efforts made by Born to help defend the innocent and oppressed. Of those witnesses one witness named Hanzi Brand mentioned that Friedrich Born had risked his own life for the safekeeping and help of Jews at various different times. He was not the only person to help Jews, some other great souls that helped many other Jews but Friedrich Born was one of the most impressive and successful of most of the other Righteous. Friedrich Born was finally recognized as Righteous Among the Nations on January 4, 1987.

The Holocaust was a very difficult time for the Jews, but Friedrich Born made it that much easier for the Jews. I admire his perseverance, courage, and strength to keep on fighting and pushing for fair rights for Jews. With all his efforts, with all his attempts, with all of his sacrifices for others, he has been one of the greatest, humblest, and most righteous heroes of all time. In doing this essay I have learned lots of information about the Holocaust, Jews and their religion, and about Friedrich Born, and I hope you did to. I have also learned that even if you feel small or unimportant you can still stand up for others and for what you believe in and what is right.

INSIDE THE LIFE OF JEWS

Dominic LeLouis

The Holocaust is a very dark and depressing time for our history. Jewish people were being mistreated by the Nazi Party. This took place in Germany, from 1939 until 1945. The Nazi Party was being cruel to the Jews. Jews were forced to work and create things for the Nazi Party. The Jews were also not fed very well. They were served bread or maybe a bowl of soup, and that was their meal for the entire day. The amount of calories they got per day was about 450 calories, which is about a quarter of what you need to be healthy. The Jews were mistreated, lied to, and killed because of this part of our history. Some people tried to help the Jews, and some even died for them.

Just imagine being in a small area with gates surrounding you, and people cheering and being happy outside of them. Well, that is what it felt like for the Jews. Every block, there was a fence blocking the Jews and preventing them from escaping. The Jews were not fed very well, so you would be getting about two pieces of bread a day. You would be starving the whole day, but you couldn't get food. Your family would be separated from you and maybe killed because they were too young to work. The people you love and your friends would possibly be murdered. People outside the gates were having fun shopping, eating, and celebrating parties with their friends and family. They wouldn't even bother to help you. That all changed thanks to the heroes of the Holocaust who saved many Jews from death.

Paul Grueninger was one of those heroes who saved Jews from death and suffering. Paul Grueninger moved thousands of Jews to safe places and out of torture. I can never imagine how much it felt to be a Jew at that time, and I hope it doesn't ever happen again. The Holocaust was just a very sad and dark time for our history and I hope that no one ever gets the idea again. I am proud of the Jews for not turning this time into a war even though they were being mistreated and starved. I hope something like this never happens again in our future.

Paul Grueninger was a Swiss hero of the Holocaust. He saved many Jewish people from getting murdered by the Nazis. Paul Grueninger was born on October 27th, 1891, and died on February 22nd, 1972. He was a Swiss border police commander of the St. Gallen region, which borders with Austria. Switzerland closed its border to those arriving without proper entry permits, and in October 1938 negotiations between Switzerland and Nazi Germany led to stamping "J" on German passports issued to Jews. As the situation of the Jews got worse, the number of refugees who tried to enter illegally increased. The 47-year-old official was faced with a moral dilemma. Paul Grueninger had to turn the refugees back to their country where violence was the official policy.

Paul Grueninger decided to disrespect these instructions and to let these desperate refugees into Switzerland. He falsified registration so it said that they arrived in Switzerland before March 1938, when Jews were able to enter without being sent to a concentration camp. The refugees awaited their permits for temporary stay in Switzerland or their exit to their final destination. He even paid with his own money to buy winter clothes for needy refugees who had been forced to leave all their belongings behind. The Germans informed the Swiss authorities of Grueninger's actions against them. Grueninger was fired from the police force in March 1939. "His benefits were suspended, and he was brought to trial on charges of illegally permitting the entry of 3,600 Jews into Switzerland and falsifying their registration papers." The prosecution added additional charges of helping individual Jews by shielding them from detection, assisting them in depositing their valuables. Grueninger's trial opened in January 1939 and lasted over two years. In March 1941 the court found him guilty of letting Jews into Switzerland. His retirement benefits were forfeited, and he was fined and had to pay the trial costs. Paul Grueninger felt sad and forgotten, and lived for the rest of his life in his difficult circumstances. In December 1970 media was angry at the Swiss government, and the government sent Grueninger a letter of apology, but refrained from reopening his case and reinstating his pension. The first attempt was rejected by the Swiss Council, and only as late as 1995, the Swiss federal Government finally approved of Grueninger's conviction.

The Holocaust impacts the 20th century in a dark way, but it reminds us that if we see bullying or something bad happening, we should tell someone because you can stop it before the problem gets worse. Paul Grueninger was a true hero because he saved so many Jews from being murdered and killed, just because they were Jewish. I am inspired by Paul Grueninger to stop bullying before it gets worse. Paul Grueninger made the world a better place by saving thousands of Jews. He was so brave to stand up to all those people and to let those Jews go. He risked his life to save others. Paul Grueninger is an amazing person and he will always be remembered. He tried to hard to save people. Paul Grueninger wasn't even Jewish himself, but he still saved them because he knew it was the right thing to do. I honestly think Paul Grueninger is a hero and that he should be remembered by everyone.

The Holocaust was a horrible and tragic time. Jews were being mistreated by the Germans. Some people were too scared to help the Jews, but some people had the courage to save the lives of thousands of Jewish people. Although some heroes may have not been recognized, they still saved Jews from torture. The Jews didn't fight back against the Germans, which in some ways set an example for us that violence is not the solution. They didn't fight back, and even in the hardest time and conditions, they still forgave, and up to this day, Jews are still here and helping others. The Holocaust is a terrible, dark period of our history, and I hope it is never repeated.

SAVING AND PROTECTING INNOCENT REFUGEES

Emma Simmermon

Many tragic events have happened in history, but the Holocaust may have been the most tragic. The Holocaust was one of the most gruesome and darkest times in history. It was the Nazis' attempt to exterminate all the Jewish people in Europe. The word Holocaust means "completely burnt offering to God," meaning that Jews and others assassinated during World War II were a sacrifice to God. It took place from 1933 to 1945. It started on January 30, 1933 when Adolf Hitler became the President of Germany, and ended on May 8, 1945 when World War II officially ended. Adolf Hitler, as the leader of the Nazi party and President of Germany, was in charge of the murder of 11 million people. Six million of those innocent people were Jewish. Most of the Jewish people in Europe were arrested and transported to concentration camps or to a ghetto. Life in a ghetto was unbearable. Many Jews were ultimately killed at concentration camps. Jews were treated very cruelly during this time. Jews tried to avoid Nazi capture by escaping Nazi held territory in an attempt to reach other countries. This was illegal according to Nazi law and many other countries did not allow Jews to transfer to their country. Very few Jews successfully escaped from the Nazis, but some of these people were fortunate enough to have their life saved by a hero. One of these heroes' names was Anton Buhler.

Anton Buhler is a Swiss hero of the Holocaust. He was born in 1890, and served as Secretary of the Ministry of Justice and Police and as Head of the Swiss Aliens Police. When the Nazis took over Germany, and then Austria, the Jewish people in those countries tried to immigrate to surrounding countries in Europe or countries overseas. Most of the countries did not allow the Jews to immigrate; as a result it was extremely difficult for the Jews to leave legally. Most of the Jewish people in those countries tried to escape to Switzerland because of its border with Austria and

Germany, but the Swiss authorities did not accept the Jews into their country either. The Germans even stamped the letter "J" in their passports to identify them as Jewish. If the Jews tried to escape they were sentenced to death.

On August 17, 1938, a conference of Alien Police Canton officers was held in Bern, Switzerland. Dr. Rothmund, the Head of the Police Department in the Ministry of Justice and Police, presented the argument against the refugees. Paul Gruninger and Anton Buhler were the only two officers during the conference who spoke in favor of letting the refugees enter the country. Even though Dr. Rothmund rejected their idea, Buhler and Gruninger still allowed Jewish refugees who had crossed the border illegally to remain in Switzerland. On September 30, 1938, Anton Buhler commanded his border police to allow four Viennese refugees without visas to enter Switzerland and stay in a small town named Chur. He let them stay there until they got American visas. Buhler also helped two brothers in that group open a freedom road between Switzerland and Vienna. The brothers' parents, along with other Jews, came through that same road. More people heard about it, and the number of escaping refugees grew. Approximately thirty people were saved by his actions. While the refugees stayed in Chur they were delighted by Buhler's protection. In July 1939, the Kaplan Family from Berlin arrived in Switzerland. He allowed them to stay in Chur for about eight years until they migrated to the United States. While they remained in Chur, Anton took care of the Kaplan family. He also made sure they did not get unwanted attention from other people in Chur by settling them in a no longer operating boarding house.

Anton Buhler is a Swiss hero because he was brave enough to help others when most people were too frightened to do anything. If Buhler had not taken action the Nazis would have executed, tortured, or starved those refugees. He did everything he could to make sure the refugees were safe and protected. Anton Buhler also endangered his job because he helped the Jewish people escape illegally from other countries, which was strictly forbidden at his job. Luckily, he was not removed from his position. Sadly, Anton Buhler passed away in 1973, but he is remembered as a great Swiss hero of the Holocaust.

Learning about the Holocaust today is very important for many different reasons. It helps people my age understand that being a certain religion could have changed your life dramatically during the Holocaust. Innocent Jews were treated cruelly just for being human. People were murdered, starved, and tortured because of their religion. Most people my age do not even think about how horrible it would be to live in Europe during the Holocaust. We also learn about it in order to make sure another tragic and gruesome event like this does not happen again. The Holocaust teaches us about prejudice. We also study it to be grateful for all the things we have. The Holocaust was a very dark time in history, and hopefully another tragic event like this does not happen again.

CARL LUTZ, A BLESSING

Hailey Kopp

The Holocaust was a major tragedy. It was the persecution and murder of 6 million Jews. German authorities also besieged other groups because of their perceived "racial inferiority." The Germans had also thought that Jews were an alien threat. The Holocaust devastated many European Jewish communities and eliminated hundreds of Jewish communities. Between 1941 and 1944, Nazi authorities sent millions of Jews to ghettos, killing centers, and gassing facilities. There was a hero who had risked his life bringing thousands of Hungarian Jews under Swiss protection, thus saving them from deportations to Nazi death camps. His name is Carl (Charles) Lutz.

Carl Lutz was born in 1895 and died in 1975. He was born in Walzenhausen, Switzerland. Carl had moved to the United States of America in 1913 at the age of eighteen. Carl attended George Washington University. While studying at the George Washington University, he joined the Swiss diplomatic service and became chancellor at the Swiss legation in Washington, D.C. Carl Lutz had a wife named Gertrud. She was born in 1911, there is no trace of her death.

In 1935 Carl Lutz was sent to Palestine, where he was appointed Vice Consul at the Swiss consulate in Jaffa. On January 2, 1942 Carl Lutz was reassigned to the Swiss consulate in Budapest, where he was appointed Chief of the Department of Foreign Interests of the Swiss legation. There he represented the interests of the U.S., Great Britain, and twelve other countries that had severed formal relations with Hungary because of its alliance with Nazi Germany. This mission helped more than ten thousand Jewish children and youth reach Palestine by March 1944.

On March 19, 1944, Carl began his actions rescuing thousands of Jews. Appalled by the Nazi persecution of Jews, he pressured the Hungarian government to stop the deportations that had begun in mid-May. Like I said before, Carl risked his life saving Jews from Nazi death camps by bringing them under Swiss protection. Carl issued protective letters (Schutzbriefe) to thousands of Jews, which delayed their deportation to concentration camps until they were rescued by the Allied forces. Gertrud also participated. She participated actively and passionately in Carl's rescue operations. Gertrud was active in providing food for thousands of Jews, as well as in assisting them to get medical treatment.

Carl rented 76 buildings for all the people under his protection. During the death marches of November 10-22, 1944, Carl and Gertrud followed the Jews. They were able to pull many out of the march by producing documents declaring them under Swiss protection. With the tightening of the Soviet siege of Budapest in December 1944, when all diplomatic and consular missions, except the Swedish, had left the Hungarian capital, Carl remained there at risk of his life, waiving diplomatic regulations, in order to save Jews. Carl and his wife stayed with a group of Jews they rescued for more than four weeks in a bunker under the residence of the British embassy. After the liberation in February 1945, the research into Carl's wartime actions jeopardized his career and prevented him from advancing. He was criticized on the home front for endangering Swiss neutrality.

Around when the Holocaust was over, Carl Lutz divorced his wife, Gertrud. In 1949, Carl married a woman named Maria Magdalena Grausz (Magda). Maria Magdalena Grausz was one of the Hungarian Jewish women Carl protected during the war. He also adopted Maria's daughter, Agnes. He retired from the diplomatic service in 1961.

It is sad that innocent, caring, and kind people have to deal with bad situations, even if they were doing something great. This happened to Carl. It was sad that he could not advance in his career because he endangered Switzerland by saving about 62,000 Jews. It was a blessing that Carl and Gertrud decided to try and help save as many Jews as they could even though they were risking their lives and Carl's job. Carl Lutz was recognized by Yad Vashem on March 24, 1964 and Gertrud Lutz was recognized by Yad Vashem on February 13, 1978. There are many heroes who helped save Jews, but they are not recognized. The Holocaust most likely happened because the Germans did not like certain religions or races. They thought that everything should be what they like; their religion, and their race.

The Holocaust was a very sad period during the 1940's which should never happen again. It is very important to learn about the Holocaust because it teaches us to believe in yourself and stand up for yourself. The Germans were bullies to thousands and thousands of people. Today we have bullies and sometimes people do not stand up for themselves which could cause terrible tragedies. Some of the Jews could no stand up for themselves and what happened was the end of their life. That is why today we need to stand up for anything you believe in, or just for your own self. If we stand up to the bullies now, we can make a difference in the world. We can change how people view races, religions, and other people's personalities. The world might be at peace. The world needs to be peaceful. I have learned an important word, shalom, which means peace in Hebrew.

ANTON BUEHLER AND THE HOLOCAUST

Hayden Evans

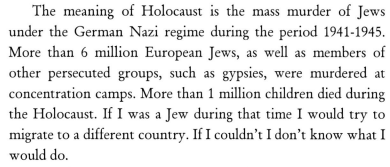

The meaning of Holocaust is the mass murder of Jews under the German Nazi regime during the period 1941-1945. More than 6 million European Jews, as well as members of other persecuted groups, such as gypsies, were murdered at concentration camps. More than 1 million children died during the Holocaust. If I was a Jew during that time I would try to migrate to a different country. If I couldn't I don't know what I would do.

Adolf Hitler became the leader of the Nazis. He became chancellor of Germany in 1933. He thought the Germans were a superior race and he thought the Germans were better than the Jews. Hitler wanted to exterminate the Jews. Hitler wanted to separate the Jews from other people. He created all of the concentration camps to kill the Jews in 1933. At first the Nazis shot the Jews, but they felt a little bad. So they made the gas chambers which made the Jews think they were taking a shower.

The most intensive Holocaust killing took place on September 1941 at the Babi Yar Ravine just outside of Kiev, Ukraine, where more than 33,000 Jews were killed in two days. Jews were forced to undress and walk to the ravine's edge. When German troops shot them, they fell into the abyss. The Nazis then pushed the wall of the ravine over, burying the dead and the living. Police grabbed children and threw them into the ravine as well.

Kristallnacht or "Night of Broken Glass" occurred throughout Germany and Austria on November 9, 1938, when the Nazis viciously attacked Jewish communities. The Nazis destroyed, looted, and burned over 1,000 synagogues and destroyed over 7,000 businesses. They also ruined Jewish hospitals, schools, cemeteries, and homes. When it was over, 96 Jews were dead and 30,000 arrested.

The Jews were isolated in their cities. The Germans soldiers made them were a yellow Star of David on their clothes so the Germans could identify them from other people. It made it easier for the Germans to round the Jews up and bring them to concentration camps. If you weren't old enough to work, you would be sent to Jewish concentration camps. When the Nazi police sent these Jewish people to these camps, gas chambers were used to kill people and children. They used Zyklon B to kill the Jews in the gas chambers. When the Nazis sent the Jews to the camps they used cattle wagons. Victims waited at switching yards for days and there were no toilets or food or water. One time the wagon took eighteen days. When it arrived, people were found dead in it.

This period in time was a horrible existence for Christians and Jews under the Nazi regime. It was especially dreadful for any Jew. If you were a Jew you couldn't stay at certain hotels, you couldn't shop at certain stores, and you would get limited amounts of food, which was very little. Thousands of Jewish people starved to death because they didn't have enough food to eat.

Many Nazi doctors tried to do medical experiments on Jews in the concentration camps. The craziest Nazi doctor was Josef Mengele. Two of his experiments were to change peoples' eye color by injecting dye into their eyes. He also put them in pressure chambers.

The Jews would have to lie, which broke the Ten Commandments. But this was an exception when you were trying to save peoples' lives. God supported them in saving others. God most likely hated the Germans because the Germans were killing the Jews just for being Jews. The Jews prayed whenever they could. I think if the Germans caught them praying they would kill that person. Some Jewish people would not fight back and would die.

When Hitler built the concentration camps people wanted to flee to other countries to be safe. Some countries let people in and one was Switzerland. Anton Buehler was a rescuer. He saved lives. He was born in 1890. He served as Secretary of the Ministry of Justice and police as head of the Swiss Aliens police. Some people wanted to come into Switzerland and it was sometimes illegal. Dr. Buehler helped them cross over the Swiss border. He started by helping four Viennese people without visas go to Switzerland into Chur. Then the Swiss Aliens police had a meeting. And only two of them wanted to let people come into their country. This was Dr. Buehler and Paul Gruninger. They started to open up a freedom road between Vienna and Switzerland because Anton Buehler was the chief of the Aliens police so he had power over them. On April 1939 at least 350 refugees came across the freedom road. Even more came later. Anton Buehler died in 1973. Anton Buehler made many friends before he passed away. The Jews called Anton a Judenfreund (Jew friend).

The Holocaust ended in 1945. The United States army helped defeat the Nazi Germany army. The armies went to the concentration camps and rescued thousands of people. Hitler committed suicide before he could be captured. The rest of the Jews who were alive thanked the Swiss, American and other armies for ending the Holocaust. I would be very thankful too if I was a Jew and just about to die in a concentration camp but was saved. That is why nobody should ever create another Holocaust.

PAUL GRUENINGER.... A TRUE HERO

Isabelle Chan

Imagine if in our everyday world being different was the difference between life and death. That's almost how life was like for Jewish people during the Holocaust. The Holocaust was the murder of many Jewish people in Nazi occupied countries in 1939-1945, mainly in Nazi Germany. The Jews were killed by the Nazis because the Nazis viewed the Jews as "inferior" and the Germans were "racially superior." During this time the National Socialist Government established concentration camps where the Jews were sent. Many Jewish people died in concentration camps due to starvation, disease, neglect, maltreatment, or the Nazis would murder them with guns or gas chambers, however during this dark time, there was still light. Paul Grueninger is a Swiss hero of the Holocaust who helped many Jewish refugees.

On October 27, 1891 a sparkle of light was introduced into the world. That piece of light was Paul Grueninger. Paul Grueninger was forty-seven years old when the Nazis took over Austria, leaving tons of Jews unsafe. Many Jews tried to cross the border between Austria and Switzerland to safety. The negotiations between Germany and Switzerland led to the stamping of the famous "J" for Jew on passports. Paul Grueninger, a Swiss border police commander of the Saint Gallen region which borders with Austria, was faced with a difficult decision: send refugees back to their unsafe home in Austria, or face the consequences of breaching specific instructions. Paul Grueninger decided to breach the instructions, and let the Jews illegally enter Switzerland. In addition to letting the Jews enter he also falsified their registration so it showed up as they had arrived in Switzerland before March of 1938. If you were a Jew and you arrived in Switzerland before March 1938 you were allowed to stay, treated as a "legal" and you were taken to a Diepoldsau camp where Jewish organizations would help you and where they could wait for a permit for temporary stay in Switzerland, or find a final destination. Paul Grueninger also sent in false reports about the number of arrivals and the amount of refugees in his district. The refugees were forced to leave everything behind. That is why when it got cold in the winter he bought many of the needy Jewish refugees new, warm winter clothes with his own money. Sadly, the Germans did find out about what he was doing to help the refugees.

The Germans then informed the Swiss authorities of Paul's exploits. The Swiss authorities dismissed him from the police force in March 1939. His benefits were taken away and he was charged for illegally letting in 3,600 Jews and falsifying their registration. Paul Gueninger's trial lasted over 2 years, and his prosecution added on extra charges of helping them in depositing their valuables and for shielding them from detection and more. Sadly, in March 1941 the court found him guilty of breach of duty. The court made him pay for the trial costs, he was fined and his retirement privileges were forfeited. They recognized his altruistic motivations, but as a state employee he had to follow instructions. Paul Grueninger lived his life under hard circumstances, but he never regretted his actions on behalf of the Jews.

HOLOCAUST ESSAY

Jessica Mendez

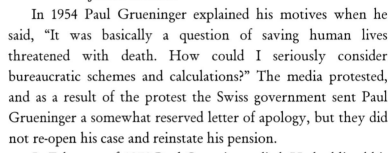

In 1954 Paul Grueninger explained his motives when he said, "It was basically a question of saving human lives threatened with death. How could I seriously consider bureaucratic schemes and calculations?" The media protested, and as a result of the protest the Swiss government sent Paul Grueninger a somewhat reserved letter of apology, but they did not re-open his case and reinstate his pension.

In February of 1972 Paul Grueninger died. He had lived his life under difficult circumstances and he died in poverty. There were many steps over the years to rehabilitate Paul's reputation. The first attempt was rejected by the Swiss Council. Later in 1995, twenty-three years after his death, the court decided to reopen his case. Finally in 1995 the Swiss federal government annulled him of his charges and conviction.

If I was put in Paul Grueninger position I do not know what I would do. It takes a true hero and a brave person to do what he did. I think I would have helped the Jews in a way, but I don't think I could have done everything he did to help the refugees. Risking your job, your life, and much more to help the Jewish refugees is a big deal and I don't think I have all the bravery that Paul Grueninger had in the 1940s.

Shortly before his death in 1971, Yad Vashem gave Paul Grueninger the title *Righteous Among the Nations*. Paul Grueninger was a very good person, with a kind, thoughtful heart. He is a true hero. In this essay you have heard about a Swiss hero of the Holocaust who did many things and put in many efforts to save 3,600 Jewish refugees from death. Without a man like Paul Grueninger there would have probably been close to 4,000 more deaths in the Holocaust. The world today has been affected by the Holocaust and by other tragedies that have happened, and it is people like Paul Grueninger that change the world by doing the right thing and saving the lives of thousands of people. Paul Grueninger may have lied in the act of saving the refugees, but he did it out of love and kindness for the refugees. We should remember Paul Grueninger for his heroic acts and for being a true hero.

The Holocaust was a very terrible time in history. During the Holocaust, the Nazis, National Socialist German workers led by Adolf Hitler, treated the Jews very poorly and gave the Jews a small food supply. The Germans would make fun of random people, especially Jews, just walking around outside. The Nazis also didn't give much food to other people. They didn't really care about other humans. A really sad thing about the Holocaust was that they would tell parents that they were sending their kids to a nice school with sports and good education, but they were really sending their kids to gas chambers. The Holocaust was not a good part of history.

There was a very important person that was involved in the Holocaust and his name is Paul Gruninger. Paul Gruninger's date of birth was October 27, 1891 and his date of death was February 22, 1972. Paul Gruninger's fate was that he survived and his nationality is Swiss. Paul Gruninger had a profession as a police officer. Paul Gruninger was very unique because he had a tree in honor of him. Paul Gruninger's file number was from the Righteous Among Nations Department. His ceremony was held in Yad Vashem and his date of recognition was April 20, 1971. Paul Gruninger was an amazing person who risked his life to save innocent people. His home during the war was Saint Gallen, Switzerland which was also his rescue place. Paul was a brave, strong, and intelligent man. He thought of others and he cared about others. Paul Gruninger was an important man. He fought for his rights! He was in charge of the Swiss border canton of the St. Gallen region, disregarded the order and permitted between two to three thousand Jewish refugees to enter Switzerland illegally. One year he lost his police officer rank and all pension rights. In 1940 Paul Gruninger was brought to trial and was found guilty of fraud. He was also a footballer. His football successes took place before the professionalization of the game and after serving in world war one. He joined the police. He excelled in this career and rose through the ranks in his hometown of St. Gallen. Paul Gruninger was a good man but such kindness did not get unnoticed and Paul Gruninger's actions were eventually discovered. For his actions Paul Gruninger was sacked from his job and brought to trial for allowing the illegal entry of 3,600 Jews into Switzerland. He was found guilty and fined by the court. After his death and recognition by Yad Vashem, Paul's legacy was subsequently restored in Switzerland. In 1995 the Swiss government finally annulled his conviction. Several streets and a school have been named after him. Paul Gruninger's efforts to help the refugees even extended to paying out of his own pocket for winter clothes for those who had been unable to flee with them. With official channels of immigration now closed to Austrian Jews, many who feared for their lives decided to risk crossing the Swiss border illegally. Paul Gruninger was recognized as a righteous among nations in 1971, a year before his death.

Above all the gory things that happened in the Holocaust, at least all the rescuers were happy that they chose the right thing to do. I know that all of those who saved people, or tried to save people, are resting in peace. The Holocaust was not a good time in history. Paul Gruninger overall sacrificed himself for many people and if they are still alive today the only reason they are is because of their Holocaust rescuer. The Holocaust in my opinion should have never happened and I wish it didn't. I know that it was a terrible time in our history and nobody wishes it was even in our history but we always have to remember our brave rescuers. Paul Gruninger was an amazing person and a hero to many people. He should be remembered forever.

HEROES OF THE HOLOCAUST

Jimmy Hernandez

World War II and the years of 1933-1945 marked a horrendous era of persecution and destruction for the Jewish community, otherwise known as "Night of Broken Glass." The Nazi party won and Adolf Hitler took control. The Germans had organized views and strange beliefs that they were racially superior. Adolf Hitler detested the Jewish people and accused them of being foreign threat to the German community. Many people including law enforcement, government, officials, and regular civilians in general were afraid of assisting any Jews due to the fact of execution or being blacklisted. One of many that became a hero to many Jews around the years of 1938 & 1939.

This hero was Paul Grueninger. Grueninger was a police officer in St. Gallen Switzerland. During the Holocaust, Switzerland closed its borders to the German Reich, and Austria. Captain Paul Grueninger illegally permitted the entry of 3,600 Jews by falsifying information. In this essay I am going to tell explain about how Mr. Grueninger struggled and sacrificed for Jews and the consequences and punishment that many as well as Mr. Grueninger experienced.

In 1939 Captain Paul Grueninger was one of many police men in charge of the Swiss Australian border, South of Lake Constance. Captain Paul saw the heartache and suffering the Jewish people were facing during the Holocaust. Mr. Grueninger decided to make a decision to help as many Jews as he could by falsely marking passports, and falsely backdating

In 1930 Captain Paul Grueninger was one of the many police men in charge of the Swiss Austria border, South of Lake Constance. Captain Paul saw the heartache and suffering the Jewish people were facing during the Holocaust. Mr. Grueninger decided to make a decision to help as many Jews as he could by falsely marking passports, falsifying, and backdating information stating that they have arrived in that country before 1938. A passport for a Jewish person allowed them the right to be able to legally cross into Switzerland. Paul Grueninger was considered a hero to the Jewish community. Paul not only aided in helping Jews cross into Switzerland, but also He used his money to buy winter clothes for refugees, who were forced to leave

296

their belongings and left behind. Paul illegally helped 3,600 Jewish men, women, and children enter Switzerland with temporary passports.

In 1939 Captain Paul Grueninger insubordination was discovered. Captain Paul Grueninger was brought to trial as a result of his actions, due to illegally helping Jewish people with false permits. He was eventually brought to trial on charges that Paul Grueninger falsified passports and registration papers. The prosecution furthermore added charges that led to additional charges of helping individual Jews by protecting them from getting detected by German Nazi officials. Grueninger also assisted them by depositing their valuables. Paul Grueninger, who was once a football player and commander of the police canton of St. Galleon was had been convicted of fraud. The trial also brought the dismissal of the police force in March 1939.

The trial lasted two years. In March 1941 the court found him guilty of breach of duty. Paul Grueninger lost his pension, and benefits. Mr. Grueninger was fined and had to pay several court fees and a prison term. The court was moved by his heroic movements, but nevertheless as a state employee he did not follow his duties. Paul lived the rest of his life in difficult circumstances as an ex-convict. Despite his difficulties Paul Grueninger did not regret any of his actions. He was exonerated in 1995 23 years after his death, Paul Grueninger is a hero and example to all of us. He sacrificed his career and freedom for others.

In conclusion, Paul Grueninger was a hero, who probably assumed he would never find himself in the situation he did. Many times people don't plan on becoming heroes or legends, but their actions and decisions impact generations over time. The decision Paul Grueninger made to help the Jewish people impacted him in a negative way at first, by losing his job, his credentials, and his freedom, but what Mr. Grueninger gained was the respect from people who did not have the courage to do the same. In 1972 Paul Grueninger passed away. Fifty five years after the war had ended Mr. Grueninger was absolved from form the charges. Justice was eventually served for Paul in 1996. Paul will always have a special place in hearts of many Jews and people everywhere.

UNSUNG HERO OF THE HOLOCAUST:

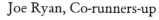

Joe Ryan, Co-runners-up

The Holocaust took part during a very horrible and gory time in history: World War II. It is still a very good thing for young adults and children to learn about. The Holocaust was the systematic murder of about 6 million Jews and other people that were"not worthy" to be in the Nazis' version of Europe by Adolf Hitler and the Nazi Party. It took place in Germany and other surrounding countries. It lasted 12 years; 1933 to 1945. The

Jews were not liked by the Nazis at all. Most of the people in those countries either didn't want to save the Jews, or were too scared to save them, even though they thought it was not proper to treat the Jews horribly, but there were some people that stood up for and saved many of the Jews. They knew that it was not right to treat Jews with disrespect, just because they were different. These people were the Heroes of the Holocaust. One of those people was Gerda Valentiner. She was a Danish hero of the Holocaust.

Gerda Valentiner was living in Denmark when the Holocaust started. She was a teacher during the time when the Nazis took over Denmark on April 9, 1940. She knew that it was wrong to treat the Jews with disrespect. She was a person who had a great respect for the Jews. She wanted to help the Jews to survive the Holocaust. Many people thought just like Valentiner, but she was one of the few people to try to help the Jewish people to survive.

Jewish kids were being treated badly at school and kicked out when they wore yellow stars that they had to wear. A lot of the teachers in Denmark left their Jewish children to possibly be killed or sent to work for Germany like slaves if they were old enough. Gerda Valentiner was one of some teachers that thought it was their job to risk their life to educate these children. Valentiner went even farther and tried to save these kids and get them out of the country to live normal lives out in the normal world where no one thought they were a disrespect to their country.

Gerda Valentiner knew that the Jews were going to be rounded up and possibly killed by the Nazis. She came to the Jewish kids in her class's homes. She told the parents about the Nazis' idea to round up the Jews. A little while later the kids were taken to her house. They were saved from going to the ghettos, transit camps, which was the Nazis' idea for keeping the Jews in order for whatever they were going to do to them. Those kids were not saved yet, though. They needed to get out of the country to be saved for good. If they didn't, they were probably going to be killed. The Jews were used to eating bread, Gerda Valentiner got them other food that they were allowed to eat. She checked the laws of the Jewish faith.

Moritz Scheftelowitz told Yad Vashem about the saving of him and his sisters. Gerda was his sister's teacher at the time. She warned their parents of the threat of the Nazis. A couple of days later, he and his sisters were transferred to Gerda Valentiner's home. They stayed there until Gerda arranged for them to be transferred to Sweden.

Now, Gerda Valentiner was challenged with a new and harder confrontation. It was another possible way to risk her life for the innocent Jewish children. She had to get the children out of the country to Sweden without the Nazis catching them. They probably had patrol boats to make sure that the Jews did not get out of the country. She needed to save these harmless, innocent children. She also had to get them out of the country fast, or the Nazis would find them.

298

You have to imagine how hard it is for those Jewish kids. They did not even know why the Nazis were trying to capture them. They probably really missed their parents, whom they would probably never see again. They only had a little bit of a chance of life. They just needed a normal Jewish life, and that was what Gerda Valentiner was going to risk her life to do.

Gerda failed two times to get the Jewish children out of the country. On the third time, she left on a fishing boat with the children. They were ten kilometers north of Copenhagen, Denmark when they set sail. It took them a whole night, and it was hard. They arrived in Landskrona, Sweden. She succeeded in getting many Jewish kids to Sweden, and many of them still remember her.

The Holocaust ended in 1945 when World War II ended. Gerda Valentiner was a great hope to many Jewish children in Denmark. She deserves to be a member of the Righteous Among Nations at Yad Vashem. She was recognized by Yad Vashem as a member of Righteous Among Nations on July 28, 1968. When she was asked about what she did in the Holocaust she said modestly "I only did what many Danes did, nothing special. We thought it perfectly natural to help people in mortal danger." After World War ll, she volunteered as a social worker at Jewish refugee camps in two countries. In 1971, when she was retired, she went to Israel for a little to see the country and learn Hebrew. She holds a place in many Jews hearts, especially Moritz Scheftelowitz. We should give a special thanks to Gerda and all the heroes of the Holocaust who helped to save Jews, because without them, the Jews would have very few survivors of the Holocaust.

A HERO FIGHTING FOR HIS DESTINY

Julie SooHoo

During World War II, the Holocaust began in 1939. This was a whole different world, not a better one, but a harsh one. In 1933, the Jewish population of Europe stood at over 9 million. Approximately 6 million Jews were killed and murdered by the Nazi regime and its collaborators. The Jews had no freedom during this time of agony, many of them died as a result of starvation, maltreatment, disease, and incarceration. The Nazi party killed many European Jews as part of the "Final Solution," which was the Nazi policy to kill the Jews of Europe. This moment of history teaches us to take action in courageous things. It is still a harsh world, butone of the most important things to remember is that heroes helped and saved other people from being killed by the Nazi party. Being a hero doesn't mean you're invincible, it means that you're brave enough to stand up, and do what's needed. The heroes of the Holocaust weren't invincible, but they were brave and courageous. One of those confident heroes was Paul Gruninger. Maybe even though Paul was never famous, he will be famous in the heart of history.

Paul Gruninger was a Swiss border police commander, and a football player in the St. Gallen region which borders Austria. He lived through a great and memorable life from October 27, 1891 in St. Gallen, Switzerland to February 22, 1972. There was an open window of opportunity, and Paul Gruninger took it.

Switzerland closed its borders for those who did not have a proper entry permit.

In October 1938, decisions were made that Jews were to be issued documents stamped with a "J" in their German passports whenever they enter Switzerland. This situation of the Jews in Austria and the refugees who would enter illegally worsened, and Gruninger was forced to send the refugees back to their country where anti Semitism was the official policy, or faced terrible consequences.

Gruninger let the desperate refugees into Switzerland after he disregarded the official instructions. He changed their status, and altered their passports to make them say the refugees arrived in Switzerland before March 1938 when entry into the country was restricted. These dates made them treated as legals, they were sent to the Diepoldsau camp, which was aided by Jewish organizations. The refugees awaited their passports, so that they can temporarily stay in Switzerland or arrive at their final destination. Gruninger turned in false reports about the number of arrivals, the status of the refugees in his district, and efforts to trace refugees who were known to have entered Switzerland illegally. He was also kind-hearted with a touch of sympathy for others. He paid with his own money to buy clothing for needy refugees who had been forced to leave all of their belongings behind.

The Germans informed the Swiss authorities of what Gruninger did. He was dismissed from the police force in March 1939. His benefits were suspended, he was brought to trial due to illegally permitting of 3,600 Jews into Switzerland and falsifying their papers. This also added additional charges of helping Jews by protecting them from detection, and assistingwith their valuables. His trial was opened in January 1939 and lasted over two years. The court found him guilty.

Gruninger's benefits were forfeited, and he was fined to pay the costs. Of course the court noticed his heroic actions, but as a police officer, it was still his duty to follow instructions. He had lived through the rest of his life with several past difficulties, but he never regretted his action in helping the Jews cross to Switzerland. He opened that window of opportunity to help others, and then he finally closed it. In December 1970, the Swiss government sent an apology letter to Gruninger, but did not reopen his case and reinstate his pension. After his death in 1971 the Swiss council rejected the idea of clearing his name.

During the day of April 20, 1971, Yad Vashem recognized Paul Gruninger as Righteous Among the Nations.

It was not until 1995, that the Swiss federal Government annulled Gruninger's guilty declaration. In 2014, police and justice chief in Saint Gallen decided to have Gruninger honored, and his 92-year old daughter, Ruth Roduner, to receive a plaque in her father's honor at Saint Gallen police headquarters.

The Holocaust was a harsh and judge-mental time in this part of history. Therewere many heroes who saved the European Jews. Unfortunately, they did not save all of those poor and defenseless Jews. Paul Gruninger was just an ordinary person to begin with, but then he put others' needs before his and became a hero. These victims dealt with many difficulties, and they went through them with sorrow and weakness. Nazi Germany made a wrongdoing to the Jews, and it should not happen again. Many of those Jews did not survive, because people were afraid of getting killed or punished for helping the Jews during this duration of mourning. Do not be afraid to do what needs to be done, be brave and show the world who you really are. The world may have fights and wars, but it also has a touching heart. If heroic motivations are made to the earth, they will be placed in that warm touching heart. Heroes do not do these actions, because they want attention. Sometimes true heroes have to sacrifice themselves for the greater good. We cannot fix the past, but we change the future and make it better. They help and save because they care.

BILL BARAZETTI, A HERO

Kylie Lapsley

The Holocaust was a time when people were discriminated, tortured, and mostly killed because of their beliefs and what they stand for. Many who were disabled or too young to work were killed by the Nazis. Even under the rule of Germany kindness and hope still existed. There were heroes who saved lives by risking their own. A hero is not a person with superpowers or extraordinary abilities. A hero is a regular person who has done extraordinary things to save other people.

The Holocaust was when people of different religions, mostly Jews, were persecuted because of their religion. People who were too young to work or had disabilities that made them not able to work were also persecuted. The people who were persecuting others for what they believed in were called the Nazis. Nazi stands for National Socialist German Workers Party, and they ruled Germany and many surrounding countries from 1933 to 1945. Over the course of thirteen years, the Nazi party murdered an estimated 6 million Jews. They killed the men, the women, and the children; the devoted and the casual Jews. After the Holocaust a struggling 3.5 million Jews were left; left without a family or hope that their lives would return to normal- that the Holocaust was just a nightmare or a bad daydream.

A person who was a hero in the Holocaust was Bill Barazetti. He was a light in the plethora of darkness that Hitler and his army had forced upon Europe. In 1914, Bill Barazetti was born in Aarau, Switzerland. When Hitler came to power in 1933, Bill Barazetti had been attending Hamburg University where he came to meet and become very good friends with many people of the Jewish religion. When the Nazis took rule in 1933, he saw many Jews marched off the campus to be persecuted. In 1934, he decided to move to Czechoslovakia where he was recruited by the Czech Secret Service to work as an intelligence officer. He returned to Hamburg for a year until his identity was discovered by the Germans. The Secret Service attempted to arrest him, but he discovered their plan and faked his death to escape to Poland. When he moved to Poland, he had to change his identity, but he got caught by the Gestapo who beat him almost to death. In bad health, he was found by a young Czech girl named Anna, who he later married and they had a son named Nicholas.

Bill Barazetti wanted to fight the Nazis, so he sent Anna and Nicholas back to Anna's village. He traveled back to Poland where he obtained a forged passport and moved back to Prague. In Prague he got involved in Nicholas Winton's rescue plan to save Jewish children from the city. In the plan Winton had to raise money, create visas, and recruit foster families for these orphaned children. In 1939, Winton escaped to Great Britain, so Bill Barazetti took over the operation. He persuaded the authorities to send three rail transports of children to Britain. After his work in Prague was finished, he spent the rest of his life in Great Britain.

Today, we use these stories as teaching opportunities. We learn about the Holocaust to teach us why this happened and how the Holocaust happened. We talk about the Holocaust, we teach about the Holocaust, we learn about the Holocaust so that the nations may never face anything like or close to the Holocaust again. Hitler put these people to death because he thought all people should be alike; that all people should be working and be the same religion. Everyone should embrace who they are and how nobody is going to be like them because you are you and nobody will ever be the same as you because we are all different. I may have black hair and you may have blonde hair, but that shouldn't affect the way everyone thinks about each other. Everyone has the right to be different and to have their own opinion, and nobody can influence that. The Holocaust taught society about accepting other people and their differences.

A HERO'S JOURNEY

Madelyn Hesse

Envision being Jewish during the Holocaust; it was painful, demanding, and completely discriminatory. Being Jewish was the difference between life and death. The Holocaust was the world's most cynical and tragic time from 1938 to 1945 in Germany, during World War II. The Holocaust was the murder of 6 million Jews and non-Jews. The Holocaust was led by Adolf Hittler, who was the leader of the Nazis. The twin goals of racial purity and spatial expansion were the core of Hitler's worldview, and from 1933 onward they would combine to form the driving force behind his foreign and domestic policy. The Jews were exterminated by gas chambers, concentration camps, starvation or killed by exhaustion. The Nazis also targeted other groups such as the Gypsies, the disabled, and some Slavic people. Darkness ruled, everyone lost hope. But some people were small lights through the darkest time. There were heroes of the Holocaust. Paul Gruninger was a hero. Paul had saved about 3,600 Jewish refugees by backdating their visas and falsifying other documents. Paul was one of the very few people who brought hope back, and was a small light during the darkest time.

Paul Gruninger was born on October 27, 1891, in Switzerland. Paul was the Swiss border police commander of the St. Gallen region that borders with Austria. Following the annexation of Austria to Germany, Switzerland closed its border to those arriving without proper entry permits. In October 1938, negotiations between Switzerland and Nazi Germany led to the famous "J" stamped in German passports given to Jews. As the situation of the Jews worsened in Austria, and the number of refugees trying to illegally enter Switzerland increased, Gruninger was faced with an overwhelming, ethical dilemma. Turn the refugees back to their country where violent anti-Semitism was the state policy, or face the consequences of breaching the explicit instructions of his government. He had to choose. He had to choose between helping the desperate Jews and break the law, or turning the refugees back to their violent country.

Gruninger decided to ignore the official instructions and to let the desperate refugees enter Switzerland. In order to do this, Gruninger falsified their registration, so that it showed they had enter Switzerland before March 1938. This then allowed the Jews to be treated as legals –taken to Diepoldsau camp, where they were aided by Jewish organizations and awaited temporary stay in Switzerland or a permanent location. Gruninger, who was a Police officer who broke the law to save 3,600 Jews, turned in falsified documents of the number of Jews who entered Switzerland, and the status of Jews in his district. Gruninger had even generously bought new winter clothes for the Jews who were forced to leave their belongings behind. To those desperate 3,600 refugees, Gruninger was a savior, a guardian angel, a hero.

Paul Gruninger was dismissed from the police force in March 1939. His benefits were suspended, and he was brought to trial on charges of illegally permitting the entry of 3,600 Jews into Switzerland and falsifying their registration papers. The prosecution added additional charges of helping individual Jews by shielding them from detection. Paul's trial began in 1939 and ended in 1941. In March of 1941 the court found him guilty of breach of duty. His retirement benefits were forfeited. Gruninger was fined and had to pay trial costs. The court recognized his, good intentions to help the innocent refugees, but as a state employee, it was his duty to follow the given instructions. Ignored and forgotten, Gruninger lived his life in difficult circumstances. Despite the difficulties, Gruninger never once regretted his decision. In 1954 he explained his motives, "It was basically a question of saving human lives threatened with death. How could I then seriously consider bureaucratic schemes and calculations?"

In December 1970, as a result of protest in the media, the Swiss government sent Gruninger somewhat of an apology letter, but didn't reopen his case and reinstate his position. After Gruninger's death, there were steps taken to redeem him. The first attempt was rejected by the Swiss council, and as late as 1995, the Swiss government finally invalidated Gruninger's conviction. Ostracized and forgotten, Gruninger lived for the rest of his life in difficult circumstances. He did the best possible thing he could have done for the desperate, ambushed Jews. He gave them their freedom. I thing I would have done as much as I could have to save the Jews, but if I could not save them I would try to help them as much as I could. Gruninger died on February 22, 1972. I would describe Paul as a marvelous, and generous man who broke the law for the 3,600 desperate Jewish refugees. Paul was a brave man who believed that what was happening was unfair, cruel, and atrocious to the innocent Jews, so he did something about it. He risked his life for those who were in trouble. Gruninger was a hero who took a risk to save the innocent Jews and he never once regretted his decision.

HEROES OF THE HOLOCAUST, GERDA VALENTINER

Malia Gay

The Holocaust was a sad period of time in which many Jews were killed violently. The Nazi party was elected into government in 1933 and was led by Adolf Hitler. They believed that people who were Jewish, elderly, or disabled in some way, did not deserve to live. The Nazis killed lots of Jews in Germany and surrounding countries from 1933 through 1945. The "Final Solution" to get rid of the Jews was to send them to concentration camps where they then put Jews in gas chambers, killing centers, or made them work to the point of exhaustion and then eventually to death. There were a few people who tried to save Jews from the Nazis. One hero of the Holocaust is known by the name of Gerda Valentiner. These heroes helped the poor, desperate Jews, but in the end there were very few survivors of this terrible time known as the Holocaust.

One specific hero that should be greatly recognized for her kindness and good deeds towards Jews was from Denmark. There was a ceremony in her honor at the Hall of Remembrance in 1968. They even planted a tree in remembrance of her at Yad Vashem. Some may refer to her as a great hero, but the ones she knew and loved referred to her as Gerda Valentiner. Her parents were Julius Valentiner and Ingeborg Margrethe Hansen. She was married to Carl Krebs. In 1943, Valentiner was a member of the Danish Resistance which helped to rescue Danish Jews from the torturing acts of the Nazis. Valentiner was a teacher and some of her students happened to be Jewish. The Holocaust was a tough time for teachers. One and a half million kids were murdered. Jewish students were forced by the Nazis to wear a mark like a yellow star to show that they were Jewish. Public schools even banned these children from attending school. There were a few teachers who did continue to teach the Jewish children. Those who did would say, "Their fate will be my fate too."

Valentiner would take Jewish children into her home after she gathered them from their parents. She was protecting the children until she was able to relocate them to Sweden through a transfer. Most transfers were illegal so that made it very difficult for her to do that. Valentiner brought them meals and items that they were able to eat. She very kindly and thoughtfully provided this specific care because she began to realize that some of these children could only eat bread. They were religiously observant and Valentiner respected the needs of these kids whom she was hiding from the Nazis.

One of the witnesses of Valentiner's rescuing process was Moritz Scheftelowitz. Gerda Valentiner was his sister's teacher. Late one night in September 1943, Valentiner warned Moritz's parents of the dangers that were soon to come. Just days later Moritz and his sisters, Dora and Rita, had moved in with Mrs. Valentiner until they could be transferred to Sweden. Moritz's sisters were later known as Diamant and Felbest. She eventually got them to Sweden on the third try in a fishing boat on a very difficult and painful overnight journey. Arriving ten days after their parents and on the eve of Yom Kippur, they made it to Sweden safely.

Gerda Valentiner once said "I only do what my Danes did, nothing special. We thought it perfectly natural to help people in mortal danger." This shows she was a humble person. After World War II, she left her job for two years to work at refugee camps in Germany and Austria. In 1971, as a retired sixty-eight year old, she traveled to Israel to learn more about the Jewish beliefs and to learn to speak the language of Hebrew. Gerda Valentiner risked her life so many times for the sake of poor children like Moritz, Dora, Rita and a several more. After hearing about Valentiner's story, I have learned that I should comfort a lonely, sad, or ill individual. Whether it is a classmate or teacher, friend or adult I can help someone in a small way that will make their day that much better. I may not be a hero, but I will always try to lend a helping hand to anyone, big or small.

Gerda Valentiner is one of the many heroes who saved not just Jewish children, but all people who were being taken by the Nazis. The Nazis from Germany were responsible for the killing of many Jews. Gerda was a teacher who brought Jewish children into her home until she was able to transfer them to Sweden. It has been recorded that she successfully transferred three kids, Moritz, Dora and Rita Scheftelowitz to Sweden. She had to take the kids to Sweden by fishing boat on an overnight trip. She was so determined to save the kids, that she would do anything to get them there, even if it meant risking her own life to bring them to Sweden. The many heroes of the Holocaust risked their lives, just as Valentiner did, for people they may not have even known. That is what makes a true hero.

THE POLICEMAN WHO SAVED MANY

Marcela Forero Pretto

The Holocaust occurred across the Allies and the continent of Europe in the time period between 1933 through 1945, ending after the United States beat Germany in World War II. It happened because a man named Adolf Hitler, who orchestrated the massacre, and convinced millions upon millions that Germans were better than Jews and other "inferior races." Those people supposedly threatened the German community, which was a cause to exterminate them. Hitler believed in the "final solution," which was the Nazi rule to murder the Jews in Europe, and eventually all over the world. Hitler's theory turned many people's opinions, causing neighbor to turn on neighbor, friend on friend, family on family, and yet some were left unconvinced of the situation. Paul Grueninger was one out of a couple handfuls of people who believed that what Hitler was doing was wrong, and risked everything to help Jews and other victims of the Holocaust.

Paul Grueninger was born on the 27th of October in the year of 1891. He died on the 22nd of February in 1972. He was an avid footballer in his youth and played for a local team SC Bruhl. In the years1914 through 1915, he helped the club win their one and only Swiss championship. He was born in St. Gallen, Switzerland, the same area where he later would work as a member of the Swiss border police. During the World War I, as a Lieutenant, Grueninger was a Swiss border police commander in charge of the St. Gallen region, which borders with Austria. In March of 1938, Switzerland closed its borders with Austria due to the occupation of Austria by

German forces. This measure prohibited any entry of Austrian Jews into Switzerland.

Refugees who were captured crossing the border in the St. Gallen area were brought to Grueninger hungry, cold, and distraught at having been forced to leave their former lives behind. Grueninger, who understood the need of Jews to escape the Germans, completely disregarded the order and used his ideal position to permit more than 3,600 desperate Jewish refugees to enter Switzerland illegally. In order to legalize the refugees' status, he had to falsify their registration so that their passports showed they had arrived in Switzerland before March 1938, when the entry into the country had been restricted. He then decided to turn in false reports about the number of arrivals and the status of the refugees in his district. He impended efforts to trace refugees who were known to have entered Switzerland illegally. He even paid with his own money to buy winter clothes for needy refugees who had been forced to leave all their belongings behind.

When he Germans found out about Grueninger's activities, they informed the Swiss authorities and accused Grueninger as the culprit of the situation. Grueninger was fired from the police force in 1939 and the Swiss convicted him of official misconduct. He was brought to trial on charges of illegally permitting the entry of 3,600 Jews into Switzerland, falsifying their registration papers and also backdating their visas. The prosecution also added additional charges for helping individual Jews by shielding them from detection, helping them in depositing their values, and giving them additional resources.

Grueninger's trial started in January 1939 and went on for two years. In March 1941, the court found him guilty of breach of duty. As a consequence he had to forfeit his retirement benefits, he was also fined and had to pay the trial costs. Due to of his criminal record Grueninger had a tough rest of his life. He mostly struggled in finding employment. All of his heroism was forgotten. However, Grueninger said he never regretted his action on behalf of the Jews. In 1954, he explained his motives: "It was basically a question of saving human lives threatened with death. How could I then seriously consider bureaucratic schemes and calculations?" It was only as late as 1995, long after Grueninger's death, that the Swiss federal government finally annulled Grueninger's conviction and his legacy was subsequently restored in Switzerland. Several streets and schools have been named after him. In 2006, SC Bruhl's stadium was renamed *Paul Grueninger Stadium*. His ceremony of death took place in Pfalzkeller, a city in Switzerland. There is a 90-minute film about him and his story made in 2013 called "Akte Grueninger." The whole movie is in Swiss.

After the dreaded war was over, Paul Grueninger got married and had a daughter named Ruth Roduner. She had to break her education at the time to contribute to the family income after the release of the father. Today, even at 93, Ruth still makes speeches about what her father did, answers questions, and fills out surveys about the subject of her father and life after him. She has two sons named Dieter Roduner, who is a secondary school teacher, and Hans Peter Krusi, who are both devoted to their grandfather and also recall with pride and joy of him. Grueninger also has a great-granddaughter named Sarah Lanz-Roduner, who is a doctor.

Paul Grueninger has an amazing story that should be shared with everyone. Sometimes you do good things, and bad things happen to you. Sometimes you do bad things, and nothing happens to you. World War II is an unfortunate, yet honest example of that. Paul Grueninger did something great and put everything on the line for the good of others. He recognized right and wrong and chose to do right, even if that meant going against the rules. What he got back from his act of kindness was a criminal record and a hard remainder of his life. Eventually his good actions were recognized and his legacy still stands. The stories of the heroes and survivors of the Holocaust need to be told so that the new generations can learn what happened and never let it happen again. The possibilities for another war are endless.

THE HOLOCAUST

Mathew Thomas

The Holocaust is the time when more than 6 million Jewish people were killed all over Europe. It was a nightmare for the Jews when the Nazis were selected to rule Germany. The Nazis led by Adolf Hitler killed more than 6 million Jews for not being a "German." There were a lot of people who tried to save the Jews too. One person is Friedrich Born from Switzerland. The Jews suffered a hard life when they were under Nazi control. Under camps like Lodz Ghettos. The children under 10 were taken to extermination camps where they killed the children who can't work.

There are a lot of people who risked their lives to save some of the innocent Jews who were killed during the Holocaust. There were many who are recognized as heroes and ones that are not recognized as heroes. Even if no one knew about them, they were still a hero. They had the courage to help their friends or neighbors maybe even family members. Jews weren't the only ones to be killed either. Many Christians and Catholics were killed as well. But the Jews are more recognized because they were the ones who were most tortured. These heroes are courageous brave, strong, and faithful people who understood that what Hitler and the Nazis were doing something that was very wrong. Pretty much no one really cared at first, because they were scared of the Nazis. But these courageous men and women are truly great people.

A specific example of one of these heroes is Swiss holocaust hero Friedrich Born. (June 10, 1903- January 14, 1963). Friedrich Born was a Swiss delegate of the

International Committee of the Red Cross (ICRC) in Budapest between May 1944 and January 1945, when he had to leave Hungary following orders of the occupying Red Army. He had already lived in the Hungarian capital city before his appointment by the ICRC, working as a trader, and originally came to Budapest as a member of the Swiss Federal Department of Foreign Trade. On 5 June 1987, the management of Yad Vashem in Jerusalem organized a ceremony during which a tree was planted in memory of Friedrich Born. Friedrich born was a great man. Because of his courage and bravery almost 11,000 to 15,000 Jews were able to live even during the Holocaust.

Friedrich Born was a Swiss delegate of the International Committee of the Red Cross (ICRC) in Budapest. He was aware of the deportation of Hungarian Jews, which began after the German Putsch in spring 1944. Following the strategy of Carl Lutz, he recruited up to 3,000 Jews as workers for his offices, giving them protection, and designated several buildings as protected by the ICRC. He also managed to distribute about 15,000Schutzbriefe (which Carl Lutz was granted permission issue 8,000 protective passes following successful negotiations with the Nazis, after which he set about duplicating the numbers on these passes to enable him to issue several thousand more. Eventually there were tens of thousands of protective passes issued bearing duplicate numbers. They were protection documents issued by the ICRC that prevented the deportation and death of many Hungarian Jews. He is credited with rescuing between11,000 and 15,000 Jews in Budapest. During his time in Budapest, Carl Lutz was supported in this work by his wife Trudi. In addition to the Glass House Memorial Room, there are monuments to Carl Lutz in Budapest located just opposite the US Embassy in Freedom Square and also in Dob utca, close to the Great Synagogue. Carl Lutz was responsible for saving at tens of thousands of lives and accordingly was recognized by Yad Vashem and awarded the title of Righteous Among the Nations by the State of Israel in 1964.)

After the war, as most of the saviors of Budapest, like Carl Lutz and Giorgio Perlasca, Friedrich Born returned to his normal life, and kept the rememberings of his actions for himself. Twenty-four years after his death, in 1987, he was designated as Righteous Among the Nations by Yad Vashem. Only one other Red Cross worker, Roslï Näf, received the same designation for also saving lives during the war. Friedrich Born was a great man. Some other great people who also helped the Jews from death and torture of the Nazis, are (lastname first): Friedrich, Jean-Edouard 1999, Giannini, Walter & Emma 2000, Gross, Abbe Albert 1989, Gruninger, Paul 1971, Barazetti, Bill 1993, Berchmans, Sister Jeanne 1991, Bohny-Reiter, Friedel 1990, Bohny, Auguste 1990, Born, Friedrich 1987, Bovet, Abbe Jean 1989, Brunschweiler, Benedikt 2007, Buehler, Anton 2001, Calame-Rosset Paul & May 1998, Dubois, Maurice 1985, Eidenbenz, Elisabeth 2001,Feller, Harald 1999, Flescher, Anna (Riesen) 2007, Francken, William & Laure 1997, Im Hof-Piguet, Anne-Marie 1990, Jaccard

Arthur & Wilhelmine, dght. Ruth Monney 2007, Lavergnat, Arthur & Jeanne 1990, Lutz, Carl & Gertrud 1964, Marclay, Emile & Lina; daughter Marguerite 2000, Naef, Rosa 1989, Prodolliet, Ernst 1982, Reymond, Fred 1997, Schaffert, Hans 1967, Schmidt, Martha 1993. By just reading this essay you will not know how hard of a time it was in Europe during the Holocaust. Every hero, just like Friedrich Born, lived every day expecting to get arrested for helping the Jews. But still knowing this they still decided to help God's people.

A JOURNEY TO FREEDOM

Michael Moreno

The Holocaust was about the extermination of millions of Jewish people by the Nazi party, led by Adolf Hitler from 1939 to 1945. The Nazis were cruel and mean to the Jews. The Nazis believed that they should hurt people who were different from them.

Jewish people were sent to camps where they were killed. The Nazis had anyone whowas a Jew at the age of ten or below go to different camps than the older people. Families were separated and never saw each other again. The Nazis had the Jews take showers that were filled with toxic gas instead of water and died. They also died from the Nazis hanging them on lamp posts. When Jews got hung on the lamp posts, they had the younger Jews watch, and the Nazis just stood there and laughed for the whole time. The Nazis did not let the Jewish people live good lives. The Jews were treated unfairly and with disrespect for seven years. Some of the Jews stood up to them. They sacrificed their lives to help other people. Only some of the Jewish people survived, the rest of them were killed. Some of the Jewish people had survived because there were people willing to help them. One of those heroes was named Paul Gruninger. Paul Gruninger was from Switzerland. He decided to ignore the official instructions and let the desperate refugees enter Switzerland. Paul risked his life for 3,600 Jews. He was born on October 27, 1891. He died on February 22, 1972.

Paul Gruninger was a very important part of the Holocaust. When he let the innocent refugees come into Switzerland, he changed their passports so it said that they had arrived in Switzerland before March 1938, when entry into the country had been restricted. This allowed the arrivals to be treated as legals, to be taken to the Diepoldsau camp, where they were aided by Jewish organizations. The refugees waited for their permits for temporary stay in Switzerland or their departure to a final destination. Paul Gruninger paid for winter clothes in order to help needy refugees that were being forced to leave their belongings behind. Paul Gruninger was dismissed from the police force in March 1939. He was brought to trial on charges of illegally permitting the entry of 3,600 Jewish people into Switzerland and falsifying their registration papers.

Paul Gruninger's trial opened in January 1939 and dragged on for over two years. In March 1941, the court found him guilty. His retirement benefits were forfeited and he was fined and had to pay the trial costs. The court recognized his motivations, but found that as a state employee, it was his duty to follow his instructions. Gruninger lived for the rest of his life in difficult circumstances. Despitethe difficulties, he never regretted his action on behalf of the Jews. In 1954 he explained his motives: "It was basically a question of saving human lives threatened with death."

In December 1970, as a result of protest in the media, the Swiss government sent Gruninger somewhat of a letter of apology but refrained from reopening his case and reinstating his pension. Only after his death were steps to rehabilitate his reputation set into motion. The first attempt was rejected by the Swiss Council and only as late as 1995, the Swiss federal government finally annulled Gruninger's conviction. Paul's legacy was subsequently restored in Switzerland. Several streets and a school were named after him and in 2006, SC Bruhl's stadium was renamed to Paul Gruninger's Stadium.

Paul Gruninger was a very important part of the Holocaust. He risked his life for 3,600 Jewish people. Even though he knew people were getting killed by getting hung on land posts, and taking showers with toxic gas instead of water, he still followed through and sacrificed his life to save Jewish people. Paul Gruninger sent the Jewish people to Switzerland and changed their passports in order for them to be free. He got sent to court following through with this action. The court found him guilty at first, but then they recognized that he was a good man, and forgave him. He paid for clothes for the Jews to wear. Paul knew he might die by doing all of these things, but he still followed through and helped the Jewish people. By doing this he got many rewards. One of the rewards was that several streets and a school were named after him. Another reward was that SC Bruhl's Stadium was renamed to Paul Gruninger's Stadium. Adolf Hitler's Mom was a Jew, so he was a Jew too. Later, Adolf Hitler killed himself because he knew someone else was eventually going to kill him. The Nazis treated the Jews unfairly. The Nazis were mean people because they believed it was right to hurt the Jewish people because they were different from them. The Nazis started coming into towns, and killing every Jew they had seen. Paul Gruninger made life a lot better for the Jews by letting them come into his country, Switzerland.

A HERO OF THE HOLOCAUST

Miguel Maestu

The Holocaust was a very dangerous time to be Jewish. It was during the time of World War II that Adolf Hitler thought that the Jews were in the way of Germany's conquest. There were many ways the Germans had tortured the Jewish people. They gave them very little food and water, they could barely survive. They rounded them up and put them in concentration camps and made them work to death. The children under the age of ten were sent to a colony to live. This was a lie. They were executed because the Germans thought they were too young to be good workers. Many Jews were killed by the Germans, and many did not survive after the events that happened. Today few survivors tell how they survived the very dangerous time of the Holocaust. Harald Peterson was one of the few who survived to tell his story.

Harald Petersen was a farmer who lived in Denmark near Copenhagen. Denmark was occupied by the Germans starting on April 9th, 1940. In 1943 he saved the lives of a Jewish couple, Richard and Erna Hausmann and their son Herman. They escaped Germany after the outbreak of the war in 1939. They went to Sweden but their resident permits could not be renewed, so they went to Denmark. Together with other Jews, they worked on farms in South Zealand, a group of islands between Sweden and main land Europe. For a short time, Richard Hausmann was employed on Peterson's farm in Kongsted. They later found work at another farm where their son, Herman, was born.

In 1941 Harald Petersen and his wife, Agnete, moved to a farm in Risby, Herstedvester, outside of Copenhagen. Again the Hausmanns found employment with the Petersens. In October 1943, when the Germans wanted to arrest all the Jews, Petersen offered to drive the Hausmanns in his car to Copenhagen, then get them on a boat to Sweden. When they arrived to Copenhagen, it took three days to find a fisherman willing to take them to Sweden. There were a total of 7,200 Jews, and 680 spouses escaped.

Petersen risked his life to save the Hausmanns. They stayed in contact with each other after the war and visited him a number of times. On one of the visits he admitted that he put up the money for their escape. Harald Petersen's birth is unknown, died in 1994, but he was remembered as a hero of the Holocaust in 1990 by Yad Vashem, Righteous Among Nations.

There have been many heroes during the Holocaust who helped and almost died trying to save Jews. Although some of them were apart of the Nazi party, they still helped the Jews escape, and they sadly did not survive. Although the people they saved knew their names, and have been telling about their stories. But not all of them were a part of the Nazi party like Harald Petersen. There were many who were arrested, fired from their jobs, and even killed. Even after the first hero was killed, the rest did not follow, instead they faced their fears, the risk of their lives being taken and the Nazi party.

CARL LUTZ - HOLOCAUST HERO

Noah Canites, Special Award

The Holocaust was the targeting, discrimination, and murder of six million Jews by a group of people who felt they were racially superior to the Jews. This group was the Nazis and they were a political party that ruled Germany. In addition, there were Germans and other people who supported the Nazi beliefs because they were scared that Jews affected the quality of their entire race. The Nazis also targeted other groups, for example, the Poles and the Russians. They feared changes to their way of life and took extreme steps to protect themselves. As a result, many people suffered and died during the Holocaust. Some Jews survived with the help of brave heroes like Carl and Gertrud Lutz. They helped more than 60,000 Jews by using Carl's position in government to save the Jews from death and providing them with safe homes in Budapest, Hungary.

The Nazis took over Budapest, Hungary in March, 1944. At that time, there were about 200,000 Jewish people living in Budapest. As vice-consul of Switzerland in Budapest in 1944, Carl Lutz saved thousands of Jews from Nazi death camps. He did this by working out a special deal with the Hungarian Government and the Nazis, who gave him permission to issue protective letters to 8,000 Jews so they could go to Israel. These protective letters were called "Schutzbrief". Instead of giving letters to 8,000 Jews, he gave letters to 8,000 Jewish families and many more than that. Jews who received these letters were treated as citizens of a foreign country and were protected with the same laws as any Swiss person. This meant they were safe in Budapest until they left for Israel where they would be protected by Great Britain. As a result of Carl Lutz's work, thousands of Jews were protected from the Nazis and the Hungarian Government.

After the Nazis took over Hungary, the Hungarian government created a ghetto in November 1944 and forced the Jews to live there. The ghetto was surrounded by guards, a high fence, and a stone wall so that no one could escape, or get into the ghetto. The ghetto was a horrible place to live in because there was no food from outside, overcrowded buildings, garbage everywhere, and diseases spreading. Carl Lutz saved thousands of Jews from the ghetto when he rented seventy-six buildings where the Jews being protected by Switzerland could live safely. These were called safe houses. One of the most famous safe houses was the Glass House where more than 3,000 Jews lived safely. It is now a museum opened to visitors who can learn about Carl Lutz and what he did for the Jews in Budapest.

In November 1944, the Nazis also started death marches from Budapest. Hungarian guards forced 76,000 Jewish men, women, and children to walk to the Austrian border. During the march, thousands of Jews died from starvation, disease, exhaustion, and cold. Others were shot along the way. Those Jews who survived and made it to the Austrian border were turned over to German soldiers, who took them to concentration camps. Carl Lutz pulled hundreds of Jews out of the death marches and sent them back to their homes in Budapest. He did this by showing the Nazis the protective letters proving these Jews were protected by the Swiss Government. By doing this, Carl rescued hundreds of Jews from death.

Carl's wife, Gertrud Lutz, was very supportive of Carl's desire to help the Jewish people and she wanted to help in other ways. One way Gertrud helped was by providing food to thousands of Jews who faced starvation. Food was very hard to get for the Jewish people. They were cut off from German-controlled stores, food sources and medical services. This meant that people not only suffered hunger, but they didn't have good health. Many were forced into ghettos and then to concentration camps. Gertrud Lutz helped these Jewish people get medical treatment by using her diplomatic powers and relationship to Carl Lutz. She helped spare many children from contracting or suffering from diseases. Gertrud played an important part in helping her husband. She was very active and, because of her efforts, rescued Jews from the death marches of November 1944. Without her help, many people would have suffered and killed by the Nazis.

The Holocaust was a terrible time in human history because it was a moment where a belief system was so strong that it looked past humanity. It created a concept of a superior race, which is a major part of discrimination and can destroy cultures. Six million innocent Jews were tortured and exterminated by the Nazis. Fortunately for many Jewish people, there were brave heroes, Carl and Gertrud Lutz, who risked their lives (and their families lives) to save thousands of Jews in Budapest, Hungary. Without Carl Lutz and his wife, these people would most likely have been tortured and killed. Carl Lutz used his authority of being the vice-consul of Switzerland to help humans. He made a very large impact to the war, German people, and thousands of Jews. Without his help, and the people who continued his efforts, Germany, Europe and the rest of the world would certainly not be the great and safe place we have today. We would live in a world that places less value on human life. In fact, many of his actions not only saved lives, but helped others in believing the importance for supporting all cultures and backgrounds. For these reasons, I believe that Carl Lutz remains as a very brave and great hero during the Holocaust.

THE TRAGEDY OF THE HOLOCAUST
Olivia Siddique

Many people in the world today are heroes and enemies. Today I would like to talk about some heroes and some enemies. The Holocaust was a sad time for many people (especially in Europe) were mistreated. The Holocaust was a death to many Europeans. This was all caused by a man of the name of Adolf Hitler. Adolf Hitler was elected president of Germany. He was elected Nazi party. He was against people that were different than him. He thought the perfect people as protestant, blonde, blue-eyed and tall, this was also known as the Aryan Race. So he got many people on his side. They became against different people. This was the start of World War II. This was a war that lasted from 1939 to 1945. Many people were taken into camps and tortured. If people were lucky people would go into hiding, but many did not survive and were taken into camps to die. Others had parents change their age, though it was deceitful it was one of the only ways to survive. Now I would like to talk about a hero, not an enemy, nor a victim, but a hero. This hero's name was Helga Hansen.

My hero, Helga Hansen, was a farmer, as was her brother, Esben Hansen, another hero. She and her brother rescued two people. They were part of the Hehalutz movement. The Hehalutz movement the training of the youth to go back to Israel. These people were Romanian. Their names were Varda and Yehiel. When the Nazis invaded Denmark on April 9, 1940, Yehiel and Varda received information from a colleague that there would be a place to hide in a nearby refuge at the Hansens'.

Helga and Esben let these two people stay with them in their farm in September. Helga and Esben believed in helping people in need. That is why Yehiel and Varda stayed with them. Whenever it was heard that the Germans were going to do a search, the Hansens would contact Vicar Arnold Gunnerson and his wife Karen who had an underground basement for the Jewish people to hide in. In October 1943 it was time for Yehiel and Varda to escape. With the help of the Hansens, Yehiel and Varda were able to go in a fisherman's boat and escape to Sweden.

I have had some thoughts after reading this story about how brave and courageous Helga and Esben Hansen were. Every day of the Holocaust these people were risking their lives just to make sure two people were safe from 1940 to 1943.

That is three years of lying and hiding, but for a good cause. When I see or hear bullying I think this shouldn't have to happen people. I bet that's what the Hansen's were thinking, and so they took a stand. I want to be like that person who helps not hears bullying. Now in my life whenever I see bullying I will take a stand just like the Hansens. I don't believe it is right for another Holocaust to happen. I don't want another Holocaust to start by someone I know or someone my age. I want to start spreading the word about not starting another Holocaust and ways it can be started. Bullying is the main one. I will tell people to stand up for bullying, and if you are a bully, stop and think to yourself what are you doing to people. The Holocaust is too important to be forgotten and restarted. In the Holocaust bullying was when people were hung, beaten, starved, over worked, burned and shot.

The Holocaust is an important time to me, it reminds me of a tragic time. Only 3 million Jewish people survived the Holocaust, and 6 million Jewish people died in the Holocaust. The Jewish people were forced into camps and were mistreated. That makes Hitler against his own mother and her own race. He must have been a very mad man. He was a bully to many. I hope you enjoyed my presentation on Helga Hansen and the Holocaust. To realize something so important can be in your past or maybe even your future. Started by something that could be stopped, but no one stopped it. To think everyday you are so lucky to live in a house and not be mistreated or torture, this was the opposite for the Jewish people of the Holocaust. They woke up every day happy to be alive. They woke up suffering. They woke up sad because they maybe separated from their love, family has died, children without parents. They woke up ready for the next obstacle. The survivors passing on their story to their family so this does not happen again. This is the tragedy of the Holocaust.

THE LIGHT

Jessica Paige Salyer

In January1933, a group called the Nazis came into power. The leader of the Nazis was Adolf Hitler. The Nazis were the ones that started the gruesome extermination of the Jews which was called the Holocaust. The Holocaust happened because the Nazis thought that they were "racially superior" and that the Jews were "inferior." The Nazis believed that the Jews were a danger to Germany and thought that if they just killed every last one of the Jews it would be a perfect Germany. I believe that this was one of the most prejudiced theories in history. During the Holocaust, they also targeted other groups because of their race.

Fred Reymond (b. 1907) was among the very brave people who put their lives in danger to protect the Jews, who were complete strangers. He helped Jews reach Switzerland in their escape from France. Reymond was well acquainted with every corner in his region as well as with the area across the border. Reymond and his family lived in Le Sentier (Vaud), a small town located between a valley and mountains. The Joux was the valley and the mountains were called Risoux, which form the border of France.

Fred Reymond was born on Christmas Day December 25, 1907. He was a keen sportsman and was a champion wrestler in his youth. Reymond was a watchmaker and a scout for the Swiss army. His wife was named Lilette. He held the post of intelligence officer. He was assigned to spy on the Germans.

One of his agents was Victoria Cordier who lived on the other side, close to the divide, in France. Reymond met many people in his surveillance including Jews who were being persecuted by the Vichy regime. Since he was active on both sides of the Franco-Swiss border, he was ideally placed to engineer the rescue of the refugees, escaped prisoners of war, and marked members of the resisitance.

Reymond could not help but feel compassion for them; he saw their anguish and misery. So he tried to find a way to help. Reymond's role was to pick up refugees in Chapelle des Bois, arrange for train tickets, and escort them through the forest of Risoux in to Switzerland. The danger of being discovered and sent back was much greater for the refugees that they saved if they moved during the daytime. Reymond and Lilette therefor took them into their house on the ridge to hide them from the Nazis for up to thrity-six hours. When they departed Reymond usually gave them some money for the onward jouney. In most cases, Reymond's French agents escorted the escapees to a secret meeting place at the border. They smuggled them in through a little gate that was unguarded by the Swiss border patrols. Along the way he expertly circumvented the heavily patrolled areas.

Most of Reymond's crossings into occupied France were by bicycle. Reymond risked being stopped by German patrols. But he was always able to evade them. His frequent clandestine border crossing caused him problems with the Swiss customs officials. They thought he was smuggling in goods across the border, and was charged on more than one occasion. But being a "smuggler" was his cover for being a secret agent. I think Fred Reymond was a very smart man because he was able to get past the Swiss customs patrol and I think that would have to take some sort of skill.

The Nazis not only took the lives of many innocent people they also took away their dignity. The Nazis were just bullies to the Jews. It is sad that they could not see what they were doing and how many innocent men, women, and children the killed just because they had this image in their twisted minds about the perfect German. They were heartless human beings who had no regard as to what they were doing. What I find most shocking is that Adolf Hitler, the leader of the Nazi party, his mother was from Jewish heritage. Yet he still went on his rampage executing the Jews. A journalist heard of the unusual story of Fred Reymond and invited him to tell his story on a Swiss television audience how he and his wife had hidden refugees in their home in the years 1942-1944 and how they arranged for their flights into Switzerland. Reymond died (1999) a brave and courageous man who stood up against the Nazis and saved many Jews. He was hope for many people who thought there was no such thing, he was their light at the end of the tunnel. I really admire Fred Reymond and his wife Lilette because even though they could have been killed trying to save Jewish people and even giving them money and a place to stay. If I were in his place I don't think I would have that much courage and fight in me. The people who he saved did not know Reymond, who was responsible for the welfare of these people on the run, risked his life, never expecting any payment or reward.

A HERO IN THE DARKNESS

Ria Chhabra

The Holocaust was a state sponsored persecution and murder of over 6 million Jews by the Nazi party, led by Adolf Hitler. To monitor Jews, the Germans would not let them go to certain places and stores. Some benches even had signs not allowing Jews to sit there. The Germans created forced labor camps for Jews during war, feeding them little or no food. They made killing centers where they heartlessly murdered thousands of Jews. Jewish children under the age of ten were considered unfit to work, and were killed. Europe 1938-1945 was a constant fight for survival if you were Jewish. Some people tried to help the Jews, even though they were not Jewish. They risked being caught and killed for helping the Jews escape the Nazis. Paul Gruninger helped Jews live by helping them escape the Nazi party.   Paul Gruninger lived through the Holocaust. The Holocaust was a very dark time full of hatred and blood. Millions of Jews died and millions of others became refugees and fled for their lives. A refugee is a person who has escaped from their home country because they have suffered or feared persecution on account of race, religion, nationality, or political opinion; because they are a member of a persecuted social category of persons; or because they are fleeing a war. The Jewish people in Europe were persecuted for their religion and many more people were persecuted for their political opinion. Back then, if you did not support Adolf Hitler, Hitler and the Nazis would come and kill you. The population was divided. Jews, children under 10 who were considered unfit to work, gypsies, and others were put on one side to be killed. Paul Gruninger saved many Jews from death. This heroic feat required him to lie to the Swiss government officials and turn away from Adolf Hitler and the Nazi party but he knew what was right and still did it anyway. His life was a battle

318

between good and bad, between right and wrong. Even though he may not be as well-known as some Holocaust heroes, he still saved about 3,600 defenseless Jewish lives. Their descendants are still alive today.

Paul Gruninger had a good life. He was a forty-three year old policeman and a talented soccer player. He lived in St. Gallen, a medium sized town in Eastern Switzerland, where he was happy. In August 1938, the Swiss government closed part of Switzerland that bordered with Austria, so Austrian Jews could not enter. Paul Gruninger was in charge of a stretch of land on that border. He was ordered to reject entry into Swiss territory if the certain person had the infamous "J" showing they were a Jew, stamped on their registration papers, or if they had no registration papers at all. Paul Gruninger knew discriminating against Jews because of their religion was wrong. He knew he was safe from the Nazis because he was Christian and in good health, but there was a voice in his head telling him to help the Jews. The Nazis were wrong and his conscience was telling him he just couldn't do what they wanted. He was going to help these poor people who cannot go anywhere without suffering, or being killed. Paul Gruninger knew that 3,600 lives depended on him. He was going to save these Jews. But how would he do this? He had no extreme power. Then he realized what he had to do. Paul Gruninger changed registration papers to say these people were not Jewish. He created false papers for those who did not have any.

Paul Gruninger really cared about the safety of these people. He paid for clothes and food for over 3,000 people with his own money. A year passed after Paul Gruninger smuggled the Jews from Austria into Switzerland, and Paul grew more and more worried the Germans would find out what he did. Suddenly, it happened. He was dismissed from his post as a police official and was called to court. He lost his rank as colonel and lost all pension rights. His trial dragged out for two years. After two years of being unsure of his fate, Paul Gruninger lost the trial. His retirement benefits were forfeited, and he was fined and had to pay the trial costs. The court recognized his true motivations, but found that nevertheless, as a state employee, it was his duty to follow his instructions. After his trial and punishment, Paul Gruninger lived a very hard life. He was known to the public as the man who battled against the Nazis and lost and was shunned. It was very difficult to live with a criminal record in that time period. In 1972, Paul Gruninger died in poverty. People still remembered him, though, and in 1995 the district court of St. Gallen removed all his charges. They revoked all their judgment against him. The government later paid compensation to his descendants and he is honored as a Righteous Among the Nations in the Yad Vashem Israeli Holocaust memorial. Lastly, to remember all he did for thousands of Jews, a street in northern Jerusalem was named after him.

Very few people across Europe were doing what Paul Gruninger was doing. Most people who were not Jewish or Gypsies were chanting, "Heil Hitler" and supporting the Nazis. Some actually believe in exterminating anyone who did not fit into a certain category, while others simply did not want to turn away from Adolf Hitler and the Nazis and risk being tortured or killed. Still, amidst all the bloodshed and darkness in the world, there stood a few, just a few, bright lights who risked everything to save these desperate lives. They may have created lists of factory workers or wrote false papers, like Paul Gruninger. When we think of the Holocaust, we should remember those who saved Jews, and the ones who died trying.

ANNA CHRISTENSEN-:HOLOCAUST HERO
Samantha Pinto

The Holocaust was a brutal time for many innocent people. The Nazi party, led by Adolf Hitler, tortured and murdered over 11million people: 6 million Jews and 5 million others. Many innocent lives were taken, and for most, hope was what kept them alive. But even in this living nightmare, there were heroes. Anna Christensen saved 40 Jewish children from the horrors of the Holocaust by hiding them and eventually smuggling them out of the country, to Sweden.

Jewish refugees from Germany and Austria began entering Denmark after Hitler came to power. A group of 40 children came, too. At first Anna enrolled the children openly in local school, but after the German invasion (April 9, 1940) the authorities were too frightened to allow it. So, Anna turned her basement into a classroom.

She taught the children the basic common core subjects, cooked traditional meals for them, and gave them a good place to stay. Anna loved the Jewish children with motherly affection, and tried her best to keep them happy. At one point, the children were separated into smaller groups, but still under Anna's care. She had asked her friends to help her keep them safe. The children only saw each other twice a week and on holidays, but they were used to seeing the other 40 children daily.

Later, Christensen and her friends worked together and were able to smuggle the children to Sweden to escape the Holocaust on a cargo ship. After the Holocaust was over, Anna still visited her "children" on special occasions and sometimes on random days. Sweet Anna Christensen still admired the young Jews, and told them often of thier bravery. She was honored greatly by the adult relatives left in the family, and they told Yad Vashhem about her. She is now recongnized as a Righteous Among the Nations Denmark hero of the Holocaust.

I can be more like Christensen by helping others even when I'm busy and need to get somewhere. There is always time to help another person or animal. Anna taught me to always stay by someone's side, even when times are hard. She also taught me to never give up, and that kindness and generostity are most important. I am a dancer, and sometimes when I'm dancing some moves are hard to grasp onto, but I still work

320

hard and perservere. Because it is important to me, I am able to do my best and try again. The children were important to Anna.

What Christensen did for those 40 Jews was very brave. Her life could've been taken by one of the Nazis. She put lots of effort into saving those kids- which is why she needed her friends' help. They all gave so much to do God's will. Sacrificing their money and time for these Jews is incredible, courageous, and kind. An act of kindness like that deserved something special. This is the reason why she was recognized as one of the Righteous Among Nations heroes.

We should all be more like Anna, more loving of our neighbors. The Nazis were just big bullies to the Jews, so when we see little Holocausts in our world, we should be someone else's hero by standing up for them and doing the right thing. We teach our children about the Holocaust to ensure it doesn't happen again, and we have been successful so far. We just need to continue persevering in being the best people we can be. So, make the world a better place and do your part.

A HARD KNOCK LIFE

Taylor Carlson

The Holocaust was the torturing and killing of the Jews by the Nazis in Europe. During the Holocaust the Nazis were bullies, and not many people stood up to them. The Holocaust started on January 30, 1933, and ended on May 8, 1945. During this sad time there were some people who stood up for the Jews, they were called heroes of the Holocaust. The hero I decided to write about is Dagmar Lustrup. She was active in the Women's Peace Organization in the area around Thisted, in Jutland, Denmark. She also saved about twenty teenage Jews, most of them from Czechoslovakia, from the hands of the Germans. She can be an inspiration to young kids, teenagers, and even adults.

These teenagers Lustrup took in as her children. Some of her Jewish children belonged to the Zionist pioneer organizations at the time. They prepared themselves for their immigration to Palestine by learning how to be farmers after their country had been taken over by Germans, in the year of 1939. Dagmar Lustrup's husband was the owner of the local newspaper in the Thisted area. The name of the newspaper was Thisted Amtstidende, and her husband received the teenagers and arranged accommodations for them in private homes in three areas near Thisted. The Protestants farmers agreed to give them agricultural training. Lustrup then organized the groups on the farms. Not only concerned about their physical needs, but their cultural needs too, twice a week she arranged for them to meet socially.

The problem arose April 1940 when Denmark was taken by Germans. In November 1940, the word came around that all Jewish people were to be expelled from the North Jutland area. That was where the group was located. This area was a strategic area for the Germans. Then the message saying the Jews had to leave at once came. In only twenty four hours Lustrup got all the teenagers to a youth hostel near Odense. That is on Fyn Island in central Denmark. On December 5, 1940, a week later, the teenagers boarded a ship with immigrant certificates. That ship brought them to Sweden, but through the Soviet Union on their way to Palestine. When the war was ended Lustrup followed the group members' fate with great interest and compassion. The teenagers never forgot Lustrup's brave efforts on their behalf.

Her story relates to my life because I try to help people, and stand up to people who are being mean. I think that Lustrup could be a model for all people. We should follow what she did and help people. I think kids should hear Lustrup's story at a younger age so they can know what to do to help people when they are older. Even kids should follow what the heroes of the Holocaust did by standing up to people who are being mean. She helped younger kids and didn't care what age she was helping. It was very nice of her to take really good care of the kids. She did a lot for them and put a lot of work into helping them.

She had some ups and downs while helping these kids, but she just kept going. Even when times got rough she still persevered. A lot of kids give up easily and stop trying. I am a drummer and a lot of drumming is hard. So sometimes when things get hard I think I can't do it, but what I will take into my drumming and my whole life is that you should keep going, nothing is impossible, and don't give up. Mostly I think kids can learn from her story not to give up in school with homework and tests.

I think that the Nazis were being cruel on the people they were bullying. There was no reason to do what they did. What they were trying to teach is the reader should not like people of a different race or religion. What they did was one day they just starting hurting and killing people for their race, or religion or both. The ads they did for the ghettos were very bad and they showed fake images where the ghettos looked nice and not cruel or bad. Overall the Holocaust was a horrible thing, and what the Nazis did was terrible.

A lot of people can relate to Lustrup's story. Some people have to be brave to do heroic things. Sometimes you may not want to be heroic, but it is the right thing to do, and it helps people. I think Lustrup was a great person and helped a lot of people. I think Lustrup got thrown into having the kids, but she handled it well and she saved them. Mrs. Lustrup was an amazing person. She was very heroic and brave, and I admire that in her. I loved her story. It was incredible and adorning. I will try harder to help people now and stand up to mean people. Dagmar Lustrup was wonderful and an incentive to me.

BILL BARAZETTI: A HERO OF THE HOLOCAUST

Tian Torres

The Holocaust began in 1933. Holocaust is a Greek word. It means "sacrifice by fire." I read information on it and it said "the systematic, bureaucratic, state-sponsored persecution and murder of 6 million Jews by Nazi regime and its collaborators." This means that almost two thirds of all European Jews were killed. The reason the Germans did not like the Jews because they were inferior; inferior means to be in a higher class than others. At first the Jewish people were forced out of their homes and had to live in special areas called ghettos. The Nazis stole their property. They were forced work in factories to make clothes and other things but were not paid. The final solution was to put them into concentration camps. In these camps families were separated and thousands of them were killed in brutal ways; an example is putting them in a room, with toxic gas in the room. The end of the Holocaust was 1945. One person who put own life at risk during the Holocaust was Bill Barazetti.

Bill started with an early childhood and a tough family problem. His grandfather got a call from a work partner and his whole family moved from Germany to Switzerland where Bill grew up. His family was not Jewish and they supported Hitler in his mission to kill Jews, especially his dad and older brother. At that time Bill went against Hitler and his family because when he was in Hamburg University he was friends with some Jews. While at college he saw Nazis beating up Jewish students. This made him angry and tried to make a protest to the college dean but the dean couldn't doing anything to stop the Nazis. After college he went to Czechoslovakia to fight against Hitler. Bill worked with some charities to help Jewish people escape from Austria into Czechoslovakia.

He was recruited by the Czech government to be a spy. The SS found out about him and Bill somehow faked his death to get away. Later he was caught by the Gestapo in Poland and he was almost beaten to death. He escaped and found a girl named Anna and married her. He later moved back to Switzerland and had a child. Bill still wanted to fight the Nazis so he left his family in Switzerland and went back to Prague.

In Prague, Bill had a disguise and a fake name. He helped another Holocaust hero named Nicholas Winton with a plan to transfer kids out of Germany that were Jewish. Bill thought out a plan to get the kids out by putting them on a train. To make the plan work, the kids needed English visas but they took a long time to get. Bill found a Jewish printer to make fake visas. Another problem was who would watch over the kids when they get off the train, so Bill got 700 families to take care of the kids when they arrive. The organization was called Winton Children and was a similar rescue mission to a project named Kindertransport. The first three trains got to Holland successfully. For the fourth train the ending was not so good though, when the last of the kids were on the train halfway to freedom the Nazis found out what was happening and stopped the train, and that was the last of what happened the kids were never heard again.

In 1939, Bill Barazetti moved to Britain. He worked at the War Office and interviewed captured German pilots. After the war, he worked at the United Nations. In 1953, he became a British citizen. Bill never talked about the war even though he got a hundreds of children out of harm's way and helped families that needed it. One day he was at a conference and someone made a comment about his German accent. During the conversation the person mentioned that he was one of the children on the refugee trains. Bill told the person that he had been part of that mission. He said he didn't want to talk about his experience because he didn't think he was a hero. He said he was just doing the right thing.

The Garden of the Righteous is a memorial place for heroes of the Holocaust which is located in Jerusalem. In 1992, Bill Barazetti was honored in the garden. Bill died of natural causes in 2000. Bill was a Swiss hero but not many know about his incredible work, but I look up to him as a role model. He shows me not to be afraid to do the right things in life, and to not give up on things that are hard. For example, Hitler was a bully but Bill was very brave and stood up to this bully and helped the Jewish people even though he knew it was very dangerous and he and his family could have been hurt or killed. I hope that if I am faced with a bully, I am brave enough to stand up to them just like Bill.

ANN CHRISTENSEN A HOLOCAUST HERO.

Vianca Khoustekian

Before we were born there was of time a great grief, an exile of the Jews, it was called the Holocaust. The Holocaust was not something small or very discrete. It was World War II, a death sentence for the Jews from 1933-1945. The Nazis invaded Europe confining the Jews and other people not allowing them to go to certain places. They were enclosed by barbed wire. Some people were saved "survivors; the lucky ones." There were also many heroes, one hero is Anna Christensen. Anna Christensen was born in Nyborg, Denmark.

The Holocaust was when World War II started. The war was started by the Nazi Party. The Nazi party killed many. Their leader Adolf Hitler was Jewish but he killed Jews (I still can't seem to understand this). The Nazis were cruel to Jews. They would give them food, but not much, and it had no fat in it. So that meant they couldn't survive very long. They did this because they needed people to work and do hard jobs all day. Could you imagine if this happened to you? Just think about all the people who didn't have a choice it was either do it or get killed. It's not just that but you couldn't pursue a dream or career. It's that you never got to have a life it's that you never got to choose what you did in your life, but some people decided that they wanted to do something bigger and save lives, and they became heroes. One of those brave life saving people is Anna Christensen.

Anna Christensen was a Holocaust hero to 40 children. If she was not there she wouldn't have been able to help save them; this is what I believe possibly could have happened. Some of the children would have gone to school to become workers. Some of those workers would have gotten too old and they would have been killed. Others would have worked for too long with not enough food and energy and they would have died working. Some children would have gone to school hidden and survived. Others might have become heroes, and saved people themselves. The last group of children would have gotten killed because the school shut down and they had no place to go. So it's a good thing Anna Christensen was there.

Anna Christensen being a Holocaust hero means that she did not just survive but she helped others hide, and survive. Anna was a member of the International League for Peace and Freedom in Nyborg, Denmark. She helped rescue 40 children from dying. This is the story of how she saved them. It all started when the children entered Nyborg, Denmark. Then she enrolled them in a school to prepare them for agricultural work. After the German invasion on April 9, 1940 they were too scared to reopen the school so Anna turned her cellar into a classroom. She taught general subjects, and group leaders taught the rest. When the danger increased for the Jews Anna organized a hiding places for the children with the help of the friends. She often cooked for the children she treated them with motherly affection. In the autumn of 1943 with the help of Danish underground movement she managed to smuggle them into Sweden. After the war was over she managed to come in contact with them. In 1966 she visited Israel as a guest of "her children." In 1966 The Righteous Among Nations recognized Ann Christensen as a Holocaust hero.

I believe the saddest thing about the Holocaust is thinking: "how many people died during the Holocaust?" The answer is a larger amount of people than you would expect, but the exact amount is 11million people, 11 million people died during the Holocaust, 1.1million of those people were children, and 6 million of those people were Jewish. Why do you think the Nazi Party killed all of these people? I can't even guess, but if I had to I would say they did it for self enjoyment.

Why didn't someone try to stop the Holocaust? I believe people did try to stop it, but they failed. It's kind of like asking why we don't try to stop bullying. We do try it's just we fail to succeed. We still try, and ask though because we know that one day we will stop bullying, like we stopped the Holocaust. Nothing is too big that you can't keep trying. We think it is so we stop trying, and give up because it's easier than to keep going, but the Holocaust heroes had to keep going or they were going to die with the people they were trying to save. Like Holocaust heroes some of us will continue to try and we will be able to stop anyting. You can do anything you want to if to are a hero, and try and never give up. Go and be a hero to the people in the world and the world around you.

THE HOLOCAUST ESSAY: FRIEDRICH BORN

Wesley Howell

The Holocaust was the slaughter of over 6 million Jews. It was a time of torture and sorrow. The group responsible for this was the Nazis. The leader of the Nazis was Adolf Hitler. He was a very bad man. He treated Jews unfairly and killed them just to make fun of them. He told lies, cheated, and killed Jews. In the Holocaust, Jews were not treated like human beings. They were treated unfairly, they didn't get a fair income, they didn't get a well-balanced meal, and they were killed for believing in certain beliefs. While all this was happening most people didn't bother to take a stand and make it stop. The few people who did were heroes. One of those heroes was Friedrich Born. He grew up in Switzerland. He was a hero for saving lives, human lives, people God created. He loved, cared for, and appreciated Jews, but most importantly he chose to do something about it. That is a kind of person people would like to hear about, and that is the kind of person that we will discuss.

Friedrich born was a Swiss hero of the Holocaust. He was born June 10, 1903, in Langental, Canton of Bern. He worked for the national committee of the Red Cross. He saved thousands of Jews. He did this by making goals for himself. Born is mostly remembered for save over 6,000 Jewish children. When he saved these children they were put under the Red Cross's care. Born helped all people who needed help even people who aren't Jewish. He still helped and cared for them. Born acted in a similar way to Oskar Shindler (another hero of the Holocaust). He let Jews work under the Red Cross's protection so they wouldn't get killed or sent to concentration camps. If any of the Nazi police men found out what Born was doing, they would kill him and send all the Jews to concentration camps or kill them too. Can you believe taking care of thousands of Jews and if anybody who was a Nazi found out you would get killed along with thousands of Jewish men, women, and children? That was the kind of courage and will power Born had to have to successfully complete his task of saving lives. He was not afraid to die.

After all Born had taken many Jews under his protection, he divided many of the children into homes upon two sections. Section A, and Section B. The leader of section A was Otto Komoly. Otto Komoly was a Hungarian Jewish engineer, officer, Zionist, and humanitarian leader in Hungary. He is credited with saving thousands of

326

children with Born during the German occupation of Budapest. He was a very committed man. The leader of Section B was Gabor Sztehlo. Gabor Sztehlo was a Hungarian Lutheran pastor, and in 1944 was appointed to represent the Lutheran church in a Calvinist-led Protestant organization responsible for providing food and clothing to Jews. In co-ordination with the International Red Cross and the Swiss Red Cross he established 32 homes in Budapest for Jewish children, and provided documents, stating that the children were Gentiles and thereby saving them from deportation or execution. He, Born, and Otto Komoly were all part of this. They all were very loving of everybody, and were very caring. They didn't let the fear of dying or torture or pain get to them. They just kept doing what was right. They stopped the people who wanted to kill Jews, and didn't let them.

Born was amazing, he established many organizations to help save Jews, such as the Good Shepherd Committee and Section T. The Good Shepherd Committee was a group of people who gathered together to help the Jews and feed them and nurse them. Section T was an operation which you helped to take care of all people in need of help. You try to help them get back on their feet or be safe.

Friedrich Born was a very kind person. He helped many Jews stay away from the Nazi memebers and politicians. As discussed earlier, he was not afraid to die for doing the right thing. I chose Friedrich Born because he really reached out to me with all the heroic deeds he did for his community and for other communities in need. He built homes for many Jewish children, thirty-two to be exact. He saved 5,000 to 11,000 Jews from the Nazis, and was willing to break the law to save lives.

Born saved many Jewish lives, especially children's lives. He had an extraordinary love for children. I believe that our world needs more people like Born to take a stand for the persecuted for the sake of righteousness. I believe, without Born we would not know much of our history because all the lives he saved were survivors of the Holocaust, and if they would have died, they would not have been able to tell their story. Friedrich Born was a very good man. He taught me a lot about how to help others in need. He is my inspiration to be there for people when others are not.

HOLOCAUST'S HERO

Daniel Phelps

The Holocaust was a very horrible and devastating event of history, but fortunately there were people who saved many Jews, cared for them, and helped stop the Holocaust. The Holocaust was the Nazi murder of 6 million Jews during World War II. This catastrophe was going on from 1933 to 1945. The center of it was in Germany, but Japan, Italy, and Romania were some other of the Axis powers. One of the heroes is Maurice

Dubois, a Swiss man who was born in 1905 and died in 1998. There were many other heroes who came from Belgium, Denmark, Holland, and a lot of other countries, but Maurice Dubois was from Switzerland. I hope that we do not need the miracle of these heroes ever again. Hopefully we have learned our lesson.

During the Holocaust, or the Shoah, the Nazis put Jews, the disabled, communists, gypsies, and many others in ghettos, forced them to work in concentration camps, and then killed them in gas chambers because of their race, religion, or culture. About 43,000 facilities in Germany, and German-occupied territories were used to concentrate and kill Jews, and other victims. World War II started when a man named Hitler believed the Germans were put down after World War I, but they were pure and powerful, and that Jews, Gypsies, disabled, communists, and non-whites were to be rid of, and that Germany should come to power. This led to, in 1933, the first slaughter of Jews in Germany, and the first concentration camps. Then in 1939, Germany invaded its first country, Poland. In Poland the Germans created ghettos and concentration camps all over. They took all boys under 13 and women to extermination camps and in 1942 started using gas chambers. This went on and on until in 1943 when the Axis powers started to wane. In 1945 the Allied forces defeated Germany and the Axis powers. The Jews' slaughter was over. But this could not have happened without the heroes of the Holocaust, because without them there would still have been more concentration camps and more lives would have been taken.

The hero I chose was Maurice Dubois. Maurice Dubois was the head of the Swiss Red Cross office of Toulouse, France in 1942. He had previously established "Secours Suisse aux Enfants," or "Save the Children Switzerland," when World War II broke out in the 1930's. Ruth Tamir, Margot Kern, Peter Salz, and Aliza Domka were German Jewish children whose parents sent them to Belgium after Kristallnacht to be safe. In 1940 when Germany invaded Belgium, these children, with another hundred, left to France. The children went from city to city and finally, were put in Secours Suisse. They were under very good care, and Maurice visited them often, and the children called him their savior. They spent two years in safety, but in 1942 when Jews without French citizenship who were 15 or older were being arrested. Aliza Domka was one of those that were arrested. After the war, 1945, Maurice went to Vichy and talked to the Prime Minister, Pierre Laval, and threatened to stop taking French citizens to the Red Cross although he knew that he could not, so the Prime Minister would free the arrested Jews. Maurice's wife was also working to get the Jews into Switzerland, because they were no longer safe in France, but the Swiss Red Cross rejected her request, so Maurice and his wife smuggled the Jews into Switzerland, endangering their life by supporting the people who carried out this dangerous mission. Many people owe their lives to this Maurice and his wife. Yad Vashem recognized Maurice as a hero on May 2, 1995.

I am truly inspired by Maurice Dubois, and his wife, because they both worked together to help and save all of these peoples' lives even if they didn't do the missions themselves or went into the action. If I was in Maurice's position I do not know what I would have done. I want to say that I would have helped the Jews, but we will never know if we were not in that position at that time. Switzerland was a neutral country during the war, but when there is a neutral country, it seems that there are more people that are moved, and or feel the need to help outside of their country's position. That is why Maurice and his wife are so inspiring. When Maurice was treating the kids, the kids called him their savior. What it would have been like to be so desperate to have been moved to all of these places, and still not be safe is a true plight to think of. Six million Jews killed, that is why we need more heroes. We need to make more heroes of ourselves so something so devastating never happens again.

This event has been one of the biggest, and most horrible events of all time. Let us work together so something like this never ever happens again. But let us not judge the Germans, because they thought that they were doing the right thing, just like we think that we are doing the right thing. While this is such a horrible event, and we keep reflecting on it, we can celebrate that it is over, and work harder to stop it in the future.

GERDA VALENTINER, HOLOCAUST HERO

Alaine Blase

The Holocaust occurred between January of 1933 and May of 1945 and made a mark and influenced our history. Holocaust in Greek means "whole burned" and was supposed to be a sacrificial offering which was burned on the altar, but it is now known as the murdering of 6 million innocent Jews and more than 1 million of them were children. As many know, it was the depressing event when the Jews were persecuted by the Nazis, who became very powerful at the time. Germany suffered social and economic poverty in the early 1930s and then blamed the Jews for this. During World War II, the Nazi party decided that they wanted to kill all Jewish people in Europe. These actions were all under the leadership of Adolf Hitler. The Jews were imprisoned in concentration camps, where they were forced to work long hours in a day and got little food. On November 9 and 10, 1938, an incident called Kristallnacht, also known as the "Night of Broken Glass," took place. The Nazis vandalized and completely destroyed Jewish homes, synagogues, stores, schools, and broke thousands of windows. They certainly did not deserve suffering and torture, so in order to prevent this from happening; we are educated from the events that occurred in this horrible time. Nobody should be treated like this at all. It was very heartbreaking and disappointing to hear about what happened during the Holocaust, but I was happy to hear that brave people, also known as heroes, stepped up. They not only saved Jews, but also risked their lives for another person's safety.

During the time of the Holocaust, many Swiss and Danish people saved the Jews, knowing that their lives would be at risk. Switzerland and Denmark were only two out of several countries involved throughout the Holocaust. Some people were neighbors with Jews and when they were being persecuted they acted as if nothing happened, but others could not stand it and got involved by rescuing or helping the Jews.

My definition of a hero is someone who stands up for what they believe in, makes the right choices, puts themselves into difficult situations, and sacrifices their lives to save others who are in danger, but does not do this for fame or glory. Anybody could be a hero even if you don't have a special costume or superpower because it's what's in the inside that matters. A few of the Swiss and Danish people became heroes and certainly inspired so many people. Today, many heroes serve our local communities such as policemen, firefighters, soldiers, doctors, and especially teachers.

Most people turned away and simply ignored their Jewish neighbors for the sake of their safety, and some even dared to partake in the persecution of many Jews and join the Nazis, who showed no mercy. Even though they were children it didn't stop the Nazis from killing them. Jewish school children were forced to wear a yellow star so the Nazis could identify that they were Jews. Numerous people were teachers left their students alone and acted as bystanders and just watched as those poor children were being judged for whom they are, mistreated, and then were killed. Only a few teachers felt like it was their job to protect their students, and stand up for them, while educating them. Those teachers were very important during that time and they are considered heroes and remember them today; they really cared and loved their students. One of those teachers was a Danish woman named Gerda Valentiner.

Gerda Valentiner lived an interesting life. She started as a teacher; she helped in the Danish resistance while the Germans were taking over Denmark during World War II. She heard that the transportation or removal of the Jews was being planned and so she gathered all the Jewish children, took them away from their parents, and brought them to her home to keep them alive and safe. Gerda was planning to transfer them to the coast and then send them to Sweden where they would be safe. Valentiner risked her life to save the lives of those children who were in great danger and even showed respect to her pupils and the religion they believed in. Many of the children strictly followed the Jewish diet and only ate bread, so Gerda created a solution by bringing new dishes and food that they could eat.

Moritz Scheftelowitz's sister was one of Valentiner's students and one night, on September 1943, she had informed her parents about the danger that would be approaching. A couple days later, Moritz and his sisters, Dora and Rita, moved to Gerda's house and stayed there until she was able to organize their transfer. They tried to leave twice, but eventually failed, the third time they tried, they succeeded. They found a fishing boat and used it from a location ten kilometers north of Copenhagen. After a long overnight journey, they finally reached Landskrona, Sweden. After the war, Gerda left her teaching job and volunteered as a social worker for two years in Jewish refugee camps in Germany and Austria. When she was sixty-eight years old in 1971 and was retired, she traveled to Israel to explore the country and to learn about Hebrew.

Gerda Valentiner was a teacher who became hero through her kindness, bravery, and courage to do what was right. I admire her for her courage to take on difficult challenges. Gerda Valentiner was a lovely person with an extraordinary personality which touched me. She had a generous heart and she treated the people she saved as family. She could have died if she got caught. Even if she knew she was going to die, she did not give up and kept going no matter what. She said, "I only did what many Danes did, nothing special. We thought it perfectly natural to help people in mortal danger." Gerda's home became an important and safe hiding place for the little Jews that she saved. Her life story will surely inspire younger children. Gerda Valentiner earned the title as a true hero of the Holocaust. Heroes do many important things which impact our world, they encourage people to make a difference and do what is right. Gerda Valentiner impacted the world by welcoming Jewish children to her home and nurtured them, while she could have just turned away, but she made the correct choice. She was recognized by Yad Vashem on January 28, 1968 and became Righteous Among the Nations.

ELIZABETH EIDENBENZ, HOLOCAUST HERO

Ana Calderon

During the Great Depression in America, something more important was happening in the greater world that would change history forever. World War II was occurring at this time and ,it changed millions of lives including those of the nine million jews who were in Europe during what is called the Holocaust. The Holocaust was a mass murder of Jews under the German Nazi regime during the 1930s and 1940s. In spite of all the darkness there was hope and help that aided many Jews during this time period. Elisabeth Eidenbenz was that hope who saved over 600 lives, 200 of them were Jewish children. The definition of a hero is someone who risked their lives for other and stays true to what they believe in. Elisabeth Eidenbenz is a true hero not only was she an inspiring role model but she fought for what she believed in no matter the risks or the dangers of it.

Elisabeth Eidenbenz was born in Wila in the Canton of Zurich on 12 June 1913. She was one of the youngest children in a very large family. Not much is known about her childhood, or her life growing up, but we do know that she was brought up in a very religious household. Her father was a Zurich pastor. She first taught in Switzerland and Denmark before she decided to join the Association to Aid Children in War. With the Association to Aid Children in War, she moved to Madrid in 1937, to help mothers and children victims of the Spanish Civil War. This was what gave her the inspiration to do the unthinkable.

At this time she moved to France where Elisabeth was equipped with a pass and was allowed to enter the camps of Argelès, Saint-Cyprien. Elisabeth organized the distribution of food to the camp of Saint-Cyprien. When she realized the situation of mothers and children amongst the Spanish refugees she was astonished and wanted to do better for them. Elizabeth decided to convert an abandoned mansion in Elne into a maternity home for pregnant refugees. She obtained 30,000 francs from the Swiss Red Cross for the repairs and renovations. She gave it a lovely touch to make her creation of the hospital. The finishing building had four levels. On the first level was the octagonal nursery. Facing south, there was a delivery room and another room for those who had just given birth. The second level had bedrooms, each with three or four beds apart from Elizabeth's room which also served as an office.

The deed of this organization was based on donations from all over Europe, but when World War II started supplies became scarce, and refugees, many of them Jewish, began to arrive from France and all over Europe. In 1942 the Maternite became the Swiss Red Crosses responsibility. Orders were given to not meddle in the affairs of France and were therefore prohibited to provide shelter for political refugees, especially Jews. Elisabeth never told the Swiss bosses that the mansion had Jews, and decided to falsify patient identities to save women and their children. In general women came usually one month before childbirth and left two months later. Some women even arrived demoralized and sick. As soon as they arrived the Swiss Red Cross went right to work and with the help of Elizabeth nobody ever knew who they really were. Because of her, mothers were able to give birth to their children and had the opportunity to escape the horrors of the war.

Elizabeth's first delivery came on a day when the midwife had eczema on her hands. She delivered forty children by herself with no help. Despite the opposition she let women who were not pregnant stay as well. When the Gestapo came to the mansion for the first time looking for Jews, Elisabeth sent them away. The second time, she was not as fortunate. They came demanding to take away a Jewish mother to one of the many camps. The Jewish mother had a miscarriage but she had stayed on to give her milk to other mothers. They threatened that if the Jewish woman was not going to give herself up they would take Elisabeth instead. Elisabeth asked for a couple of minutes to pack and go but the Jewish woman refused to let Elisabeth sacrifice herself and turned herself in to the Gestapo, including one other protegee named Esther. Thankfully the Gestapo didn't find anyone else.

The Holocaust was a very depressing time in history where many bad and terrible things happened to many innocent people. Even though many people at the time were mostly afraid to help Jews, there were some that had that missing courage needed in order to achieve something so unimaginable and that is why they are considered heroes. The ones who are there when it truly gets tough are the true heroes. The people that fight for what they believe in no matter the consequence. Elisabeth Eidenbenz is more than a hero, she was more than wonderful role model, and she is the savior of six hundred people. Most of these people were children and mothers who had the opportunity to go on with their lives because of this women who had the courage to make a difference in their lives.

Sources:
http://translate.google.com/translate?hl=en&sl=fr&u=http://www.ajpn.org/ju ste-elisabeth-Eidenbenz-1009.html&prev=search
http://www.anglophone-direct.com/Elisabeth-Eidenbenz-and-the

TIGHTS, BOATS, AND MORALS

Annelise Hernandez

A hero can be described as a person who takes risks, makes sacrifices, or goes against the odds to help those in need. Heroes are selfless beings who ask for nothing in return. Everyday heroes lacking colorful tights and supernatural powers are often overlooked.

Many of these everyday heroes lived in the time of World War II, when Adolf Hitler decided to persecute every Jew, Jehovah's Witness, Roma Gypsy, resister, priest, pastor, disabled person, African-German, communist, and homosexual. Hitler believed that people of these varieties, and others, were toxic to the population. These beliefs drove him to torture and brutally murder these people. He convinced many other people to join him in the genocide and become his followers. Hitler and his Nazis took the lives of 6 million innocent Jewish people in a period we refer to as the Holocaust. During this time of horror, there were many courageous individuals who aided the Jewish people in escaping the Nazis' pursuit. These are the everyday heroes that we forget. Knud Dyby was one of these heroes.

Knud Dyby was born on March 28, 1915 in Randeis, Jutland, Denmark. During his time at university, he studied typography and graphic arts. He sought out to follow in the footsteps of his father, who preceded him in the printing trade. He finished college in 1941. Soon after, he joined the Danish police force. It was then that Knud Dyby took action against the Nazis and their reign of terror in Denmark.

The Nazis occupied Denmark in 1940, during the opening phases of World War II. They took advantage of the Danish agriculture industry. They used resources from many European countries to support the warfare. Denmark was the only country to retaliate against the Nazis. It was discovered that Nazis were planning to gather all of the Danish Jews and send them to concentration camps. To keep the Jews from the torture of the concentration camps, Danish people began to send endangered Jews to Sweden by boat nationwide. Knud Dyby supported this effort.

Knud Dyby actively participated in the Danish resistance against the Nazis. He partnered with some subterranean resistance groups. Soon after occupying Denmark, the Germans undertook the task of raising the Nazi flag over the Amalienborg Castle. The castle was inhabited by Danish royalty. King Christian X refused to have anything but the Danish flag waving above the castle. Knud Dyby, a member of the King's Royal Guard, assisted in taking down the flag.

Knud Dyby also resisted the Nazis by saving the lives of many Jewish people. His title of police officer gave him access to information that was indispensable to the Danish Resistance. He helped them sneak Danish Jews into Sweden, which was a neutral country at the time. He coordinated places for the Jewish people to hide until a boat was free to take them across the Øresund, a thin body of water connecting Denmark and Sweden. Knud Dyby knew where to hide boats in the fishing docks so that they would go unnoticed by the Nazis. He even uncovered the patrol patterns of the German Navy. He hired taxi drivers to take the Jewish people from their hiding places to the docks. If the taxis became inadequate, Knud Dyby would use state police vehicles to drive them to the docks. Once at the docks, the people would climb aboard a boat to be sent to safety. Knud Dyby led five of these boats. The boats returned to Sweden regularly to deliver mail, money, news, and more Jewish people. He assisted in successfully transporting over one thousand threatened people to Sweden. One third of those people were Jewish. Ultimately, over seven thousand people were saved throughout Denmark.

Knud Dyby retired from his career as a policeman in May of 1945, after Denmark was liberated. In 1946, he relocated to the United States of America. He moved to the San Francisco Bay area in California. He taught others about his philosophy, the three C's: compassion, conscience, and consideration. He was a brave humanitarian and an inspiring individual. Knud Dyby died at age 96 in September of 2011.

Knud Dyby saved many lives from the wrath of the Nazis. If he had been caught helping the Jewish people, he most likely would've lost his life. The fact that he risked his own life to preserve that of others is truly remarkable. He was able to see that what Hitler was prompting was very, *very* wrong. He did what was most ethical. Knud Dyby is an excellent role model for young people today. He showed that he had tremendous virtues. Knud Dyby's selflessness, courage, and appreciation for human life is very admirable. He demonstrated that all people are equal, and all people should be treated equally.

In a world where there was chaos, destruction, and a lack of humanity, Knud Dyby fought for justice. He is the type of person many people today aspire to be. He is a reminder of the goodness in the world. He took huge risks. He made sacrifices to help others. He stood up against an army to do what is right. Knud Dyby embodies the qualities of a true hero, no colorful tights needed.

HOLOCAUST : AMAZING HERO

Ariana Lopez

The Holocaust was a time when a heinous dictator ruled in Europe convinced that he and his people were better than mentally ill people, Romas, the injured and sick, and his most hated enemy, the Jews. His name was Adolf Hitler. Hitler was a man filled with hate and prejudice. He thought that because he was Christian, Hitler was better than everybody else. Hitler convinced the other Christians that they too were better than everyone else also, of course except for their ruler Hitler. Hitler and his followers killed over 5 million innocent people for no good reason. The rest remaining, the non-Christian, were rounded into numerous concentration camps. Children were sent away from their parents into a so-called "safe" environment, only to discover later on that the children were executed and so were most of the women. The Jews were separated into concentration camps by women, children, and men. They had no contact with their other family members unless they were in the concentration camp.

Jews would live in fear of being dragged into concentration camps and even worse being executed in the middle of the street. Hitler and the police made Jews wear gold stars on their chests, indicating they were part of that religion. About 6 million Jews were killed. Add that to the 5 million, you get a total of 11 million people killed by the Adolf Hitler's Nazi regime, and its collaborators. Those people did not deserve to be killed, and probably did nothing wrong in their entire lifetime. The citizens, of course, saw what was going on. Many refused or were too scared to go against Hitler and his army, but those who did deserve to be remembered for centuries. Hundreds of people could see what Hitler was doing, and some of them made a difference in many Jewish lives. However, not many can say that they saved a life. However Theodore Barazetti and his wife, Anna, could have said they saved thousands of lives. They are truly heroes. No, no that is not good enough. They are saviors!

Theodore was born in the year of 1914. Being the son of a professor at Heidelberg University in France, Theodore was well educated as a child. When

335

Theodore got older, he attended Hamburg University in 1933 at the age of nineteen. He was studying to be a lawyer in his life. However, he did not realise how much his life was going to change in the time he was in college. Theodore witnessed a beating outside of his college. Local delinquents decided it would be a "good idea" to jump a poor innocent Jewish man because of his religion. Theodore could not stand up against more than one person, he had no choice but to walk away and pretend like he saw nothing. This is not the only time Theodore witnessed a beating. Theodore thought about this multiple times. For some reason he could not get the image of the man being beaten out of his head.

Theodore decided one day he had to make a change, not for him, but for other people. He was determined to help those in need of escape from Germany. He and his colleague, a girl named Ana who was also in college at the time, sent photographs of Jewish people in concentration camps to the media in London. They both hoped that London would realize what horrible actions that were taking place in Germany. The police finally caught on to what Ana and Theodore were doing. Ana, thankfully, crossed the border in Czech, near where they lived. However, the police caught up with Theodore right before he could make the escape. Ana found Theodore beaten up and left for dead close to the border. Poor Ana had to cure the man she loved from a brutal beating back to health.

In the year of 1936, Ana and Theodore got married in Prague. This was Ana's second marriage, her first husband sadly had gotten killed by the Nazis. A union granted Theodore citizenship to Czech. This allowed him to become a secret agent. Theodore crossed the border, entering Germany, collected data about Hitler's actions, and reported back to his boss. This work only carried out until September, 1938. Soon after he worked with churches helping refugees escape Germany. He helped a total of 5,000 to 7,000 people in these organizations escape the concentration camps. Later on a British stockbroker by the name of Nicholas Winton finally decided that children need to be evacuated immediately. Theodore was recommended for the enterprise having experience helping Jews escape from Germany. He and his colleague, another man, both collected pictures of children to transport them out of the horrible country Germany. Theodore, after the war moved to the United States. There is very little information about him after the war.

Theodore's story of the kindertransport was unknown until recently in the year of 2000. Theodore was an excellent guy who deserves a lot of credit, so does the hundreds of people who also helped the Jews. No one knows if Ana and Theodore stayed together. However I, Ariana, hope they did. Theodore's story deserves to live forever.

PAUL GRUNINGER

Brandt Poeus

The Holocaust was a horrific time in history. The Nazi-Germans executed and punished millions of Jews as well as people who were helping them. Many different countries were at war for years. There were many brave people who were helping the Jewish people. They put their lives at risk in order to save the lives of so many people. These people were heroes. Specifically, the following will be about a Swiss Holocaust hero who helped many Jewish refugees to be safe from harm. His name was Paul Gruninger.

Colonel Paul Gruninger was the senior officer of the Swiss border police in the Saint Gallen region that borders Austria. Many Jewish people who were being hunted by Nazis were fleeing to Spain and Switzerland. After Austria became a part of Germany, Jewish people were not legally permitted to cross the Swiss border. This was because Germans did not want to have anything to do with Jewish people. However, even after this, Jews kept on trying to get into Switzerland. Over time, more and more Jewish refugees tried to cross into Switzerland. Gruninger was given explicit instructions to reject all Jewish refugees. There became so many distraught, cold, and homeless rJewish people that were trying to get into Switzerland that Paul Gruninger decided to do something about it.

Paul Gruninger disregarded the new law and his explicit instructions and decided to let the many struggling Jewish people into Switzerland. After fighting in World War I and seeing all of the suffering that took place, he knew he had to stop the Jews' suffering. He preferred to save the lives of many people and risk terrible punishment rather than let thousands of people die. This was very heroic of him. In order for Paul Gruninger to "legally" allow the refugees at the border into Switzerland, he had to falsify their registration. He recorded that the Jewish refugees had entered before March of the year 1938. March of 1938 was the time in history in which entry into Austria had been restricted. Gruninger frequently turned in invalid reports that regarded the number of new arrivals and the amount of refugees trying to enter through his district to deceive the government. He also made sure to stop people from searching for Jewish refugees who were suspected to have gotten into Switzerland illegally.

When Jewish refugees got inside of the Swiss border, they were treated as legals. This was because of Gruninger's work in faking their legality. They would travel to camps such as Diepoldsau Camp where Jewish organizations got together and refugees could wait for permits that allowed them to leave for a new destination or allowed them to stay temporarily. Paul Gruninger even supported refugees with winter clothes he bought with his own money before they went to Swiss camps!

Paul Gruninger illegally allowed many Jews into Switzerland. He ended up faking 3,600 different passports so that Jewish refugees could come to Switzerland. Paul Gruninger had been helping Jews for a long time, almost a year! Before long, he began to realize that some people knew what he was up to. Gestapo, the German police force, had warned him he was under investigation months ago. He continued to falsify Jewish passports until a year after he began his exploits. When the police commander arrived at his work that day, he found the entrance to the police station blocked. He immediately knew that his actions had been found out.

Gestapo had informed the Swiss government on what Paul Gruninger had been doing for the last year. He was brought to trial for faking the passports of 3,600 Jews and illegally permitting them to enter Switzerland. The court understood Gruninger's motivation, but he had disobeyed his orders as a state employee. He was found guilty of breach of duty, fined, and lost his job as the commander of the Swiss border police. Also, because of his criminal record, had a very time finding jobs elsewhere. To make matters worse, all of his retirement was forfeited. Although he lost so many of his privileges, he never regretted what he did for the Jewish people.

Paul Gruninger was forgotten for a long period of time. He also continued to suffer from difficulties for the rest of his life. He still never regretted his actions to help the Jews. His words explaining his intention were, "It was basically a question of saving human lives threatened with death. How could I then seriously consider bureaucratic schemes and calculations?" Finally, two years before Gruninger's death, there was protest in the media regarding him. As a result of this, the Swiss government sent Gruninger a letter of apology. Nevertheless, his case was not reopened. A year before his death, Paul Gruninger was honored as one of the Righteous Among the Nations by Yad Vashem. After his death, he was finally annulled for his conviction and remembered.

A hero is someone who is remembered and honored for courage and for saving others. Paul Gruninger was a hero in and out. He saved the lives of many people, sacrificed so much he had in his life, and did not expect any reward or acknowledgement in return. This hero was one of many who served in helping many people during the Holocaust. Paul Gruninger should be remembered for generations to come.

\http://www.yadvashem.org/
http://hmd.org.uk/resources/stories/paul-gr%C3%BCninger
https://jfr.org/rescuer-stories/gruninger-paul/

A TRUE HERO, MARGARETA TOBLER

Chloe Splinter

The Holocaust was a horrible time in our world's history. Innocent people were being taken out of their homes and put into concentration camps where they were treated like animals because of their religion. Many people did nothing and just watched this happen while others took a stand and helped the victims of the war. One of these people who aided the victims was a woman from Switzerland by the name of Margareta Tobler.

The Holocaust, which occurred during World War II, was a genocide in which the Nazis, led by Adolf Hitler, exterminated Jews and others living in Europe because of their religion and ethnic backgrounds among other things. The war lasted from January 30, 1933, when Hitler was elected, to May 8, 1945 when the war was officially over. In 1933 they began building ghettos and concentration camps to hold the victims.

Approximately eleven million people were killed, 6 million of them being Jews.

About 20,000 Nazi camps were established by the Nazis. The Nazis used these camps for many purposes besides to imprison Jews as well. Some purposes included forced-labor camps, killing centers, and transit camps that sometimes served as temporary weigh stations. The camps were built to hold the "enemies of the state." Many of the people held in these camps were Social Democrats, socialists, Gypsies, German Communists, Jehovah's Witnesses, homosexuals, prisoners-of-war (POWs), criminals, and mentally and physically disabled.

Many of the victims died from exposure, exhaustion, starvation, or simply being murdered by the Nazis, whether it was by a gas chamber or physically. Some were even killed by Nazi doctors using them to perform medical experiments. Gas chambers were built to kill large amounts of victims at a time. Prisoners were shoved into a large room where they would be sealed and locked into while the Nazis released a toxic gas killing them. These rooms were often referred to as the "showers" because that is what the Nazi soldiers would tell the prisoners to trick them into going into the chambers. They were allowed meager rations of food, suffered from physical exhaustion, and were treated extremely harsh by the guards.

Switzerland and France were only two of the many countries involved in the Holocaust. Bordering France, Switzerland was know as a neutral country. Often times it provided a safe haven for many war refugees. During World War II, however Switzerland began to become a little stricter with immigration policies. Although Switzerland had become stricter, there were still some parts Jews were free to enter the country through and begin their new lives. France had very strict immigration policies, which made it hard for Jews to flee there to escape. In the early summer of the year 1940, approximately 350,000 Jews were living in France. 75,000 of them were not French citizen who had most likely fled from Nazi Germany to avoid their persecution. Not long after that, German troops began to occupy parts of France.

Born on the first of December in the year of 1915, Margareta Tobler was a Swiss child educator. During the war, Margareta resided in Montegut, Ariege, France and worked at the Chateau de la Hille, a children's home. During the war the children's home was housing more than one hundred Jewish children and adolescents who had fled from Germany and had lost contact with their family. Among these children were two girls by the name of Toni Rosenblatt who was eleven years old at the time, and Inge Bernhard who was fourteen at the time. These two girls had visas allowing them to cross the border into Switzerland until December of 1943, but were lacking the funds to pay for the train ride to get to the Swiss border and did not have permission to leave France. It seemed impossible for them to escape.

Margareta realized that they were in need of some help so she decided to help them escape herself. Margareta acquired 1,000 francs, the French currency, from her uncle who was also living in France at the time. Using that money, in the early hours of the tenth of November in 1943, Margareta secretly fled from the Chateau de la Hille with the two girls to Annemasse in an attempt to cross the border into Switzerland. Margareta did this knowing that they were taking a huge risk and could possibly get caught by the police.

After two unsuccessful attempts, Margareta found refuge for the two girls at Feux-Follets, a childrens home, near Saint-Cergues which was sponsored by the Secours Suisse aux Enfants. They were the people who ran the childrens home that the two girls use to reside at and Margareta used to work at. Knowing now how to get through the border gate easier because of their last two attempts they made one last attempt that proved to be successful. Margareta and the two girls finally made it over the border safe and sound before their visas had expired. Knowing she could possibly face huge charges against her and possibly be thrown in jail or killed, Margareta faced the odds head on and managed to smuggle two young children across the border to safety.

In contrast to the horrible acts of the Holocaust were the heroes that stood up for what they believed in. When the word hero pops into people's minds, usually the first thing they think of is a superhero, but heroes can be everyday people too. The heroes of the Holocaust were tremendous people who went against the odds and helped the Jews and other victims of the Holocaust. They did anything to help the victims from hiding them in their basement so the Nazis wouldn't find them to helping them cross the border into another country where they could live their lives more freely. Many of the heroes got caught in the act and were sent to concentration camps where they quite possibly might have lived out the rest of their lives. These heroes were not forced to help at all; their choice to get involved and try and make a difference was a completely selfless act of kindness. Being a hero meant risking their own lives in order to save another's, and that is exactly what they did.

Margareta Tobler was an exceptional human being and a woman in which we should all look up to. She was a true hero of the Holocaust without a doubt and made a difference in many peoples' lives by demonstrating a completely selfless act. She made a huge difference in those two girl's lives. While we might not be able to smuggle two children across the border to safety like she did, we can always do little things every day that will make a world of a difference to someone else.

PAUL GRUNINGER

Conner Moss

The Holocaust was a severe tragedy that happened in the early 1940s. During the Holocaust, Nazis were executing the Jewish people. Some Jewish people didn't get killed though because they hid from the Nazis. Some Jewish people asked to live with others, but they said no because they didn't want to get killed by the Nazis. Many Jewish people asked for help and the people who risked their live for Jewish people were heroes. One of those heroes is Paul Grueninger.

The Holocaust was a very dark and tragic time for Jewish people. The Holocaust in Greek means "sacrifice by fire." The Nazis killed two out of every three European Jews. The Nazis murdered 6 million Jews during World War II. They put Jews in extermination camps. Some of the camps had gas chambers for exterminating a lot of Jews at once. In concentration camps they didn't kill the slaves right away they would make them work. The Jews would usually work until they die. The freight cars that transported Jews to other places often carried horrifying conditions and many Jews died before reaching their destination. Some camps tattooed prisoners with a number when they arrive. The number was for if the prisoner was supposed to worked twelve to fourteen hour shifts. The Nazis would do roll calls before and after and sometimes it would last for hours and some prisoners died of exposure. Adolf Hitler at the time was the leader of the Nazis. After the Nazis invaded Poland they established ghettos to constrain Jews. The ghettos were formed and closed off from the outside world at different times for different reasons. Ghettos were supposed to be a place where Jews were held before they were deported. The Nazis didn't deport Jews from ghettos. Instead the people in the Ghettos were sent to extermination camps. The Nazis didn't only target Jews they targeted gypsies, homosexuals, Jehovah's Witnesses, and the disabled for persecution. Anyone who resisted was sent to forced labor or were murdered.

Paul Gruninger was born in 1891 in the city of St. Gallen. Paul was a policeman and a soccer player. He played for the team SC Bruhl. In 1914-1915 season he helped the club win their only Swiss Championship. His success in soccer took place before the professionalisation of the game after serving in World War One Paul Gruninger joined the police. Paul Gruninger illegally allowed the Jews to cross the border to Switzerland. Paul saved thousands of Austrian Jews run from persecution. Gruninger was the police captain of St. Gallen when the Nazis were neighboring Austria in 1938. The Swiss government sent instructions to Paul that he must turn Jewish refugees back to Austria. With official channels of emigration closed to Jews many feared that their lives were at risk so they decided to cross the Swiss border illegally. If they were caught crossing the border they were forced to leave their lives behind. Gruninger knew this was happening so he falsified documents so that Jews were issued with passports classifying them as legal immigrants.

The Nazis used the term "the Final Solution" for their plan to murder the Jewish people. After World War II started the Nazis began telling the Jews to wear a yellow Star of David on their clothing so the Jews could be easily recognized. Auschwitz was the largest concentration and extermination camp built it had a bout one point 1 million people were killed at Auschwitz.

When Paul Gruninger arrived for work the entrance was blocked. He knew that they discovered what he did. A couple months before he had been warned he was under investigation by the Gestapo, but he still continued to falsify documents for Jews.

In 1940, Paul Gruninger was brought to court and was found guilty of fraud. He was fined and he served time in jail. For the rest of his life he struggled to make a living. It is difficult in Switzerland to make money with a criminal record. Fifty years after the war ended and twenty-three years after he died, in the same courtroom where he was, other judges decided to reopen the trial and pronounced him from the charges.

Paul Gruninger was a hero. He was a hero because he saved thousands of people who were going to die. He put his life at risk by helping others. He lost his job and went to court to help people that he didn't even know. If he didn't help those people they all would have died.

After the war a lot of Nazi leaders were arrested and punished for what they did. The people who were responsible for brutal crimes were sentenced to death. Many problems arose after the war. One problem was the city of Berlin which was almost Russia's. The Soviet Union tried to block all routes to the city. For a whole year the allies flew in food, fuel and other things that they needed to survive. Then the Russians gave up. The Russians built a wall around Berlin to stop their citizens from escaping.

The Holocaust was a very tragic time in the world. A lot of people were killed. Most of those people were Jews. I think it is a great idea to do this essay so this cannot happen again. This essay really makes us stop and think how tragic this event really was. I don't think that something that big should happen again. It all started with one person.

http://www.eiu.edu/~eiutps/holocaust_grueninger.php

http://www.raoulwallenberg.net/saviors/others/example-gr-uuml-ninger/

PAUL GRUNINGER

Derek Yamada

World War II was a very dark time in the world. During this time many Jews were persecuted. We remember this as the Holocaust. There were people during this period who put their lives at risk. These people were considered heroes. Swiss people were some of the people who helped during this time. Paul Gruninger was considered a hero. Jews were deeply in need during this time.

During World War II many Jews were killed. We remember this as the Holocaust which was genocide in which about 6 million Jews were killed by Nazis and their alllies. Jews were put in concentration camps and ghettos. There were camps where they were exterminated. They were basically ecxluded as well from many things. It was very tough for Jews back then. But some were helped. Some people back then were brave and helped them whatever the consequences. There were even groups that tried to save Jews back then. They took them in, gave them food, shelter, clothes, and tried to help them get to safer places. These people who helped are heroes. One of these heroes was Paul Gruninger who lived in Switzerland.

Paul Gruninger was a border police officer in St. Gallen, Switzerland during World War II in September 1938. Paul was also a police captain of St. Gallen. When Switzerland closed its borders to people without proper entry permits because of Germany's annexation of Austria in March 1938. An annexation is when you add to something larger like a new territory being incorporated into a country, city, or state. The number of Jews who were trying to enter illegally enter Switzerland increased as the situation in Austria worsened because many Jews from Austria were leaving and coming to Switzerland for help. Paul decided to not follow his instructions and let refugees into the country illegally.

Paul Gruninger legalized the refugees' status that he let into Sweden illegally. He changed their passports so it showed they had entered the country before March 1938. Before then entering the country hadn't been restricted yet. Paul had helped many Jews from Austria who were fleeing because of the situation there. This allowed the Jews who entered to be treated as legals. They could be taken to the Diepoldsau Camp. Jewish organizations there would aid them as they waited for their permits to temporarily stay in Switzerland or depart to a final destination. Paul

343

also delayed his efforts to find refugees who had entered Switzerland illegally. He turned in reports about the number of arrivals and the refugees' status in his district. Paul even bought clothes with his own money for people who were needy and had been forced to leave all their possessions behind. Paul risked himself to help these Jews and let them through to Switzerland where they could get more help.

The Germans informed the Swiss of Gruninger's actions. In March 1939 Paul was dismissed from the police force. Paul's benefits were dismissed. Paul was brought to trial and charged allowing the entry of three thousand six hundred Jews and falsifying registration papers papers. Paul was also charged with helping individual Jews by shielding them from detection, assisting them in depositing their belongings, and more. The trial would last two more years and he was found guilty of breach of duty. Paul was fined, had to pay for the trial, and his retirement funds were taken away. Paul would also served time in jail. The rest of Paul's life would be difficult as well but he never regretted his actions. But he was a hero because of his actions which saved thousands of Jews who needed help.

Paul Gruninger was truly a hero. He put his job and life at risk to help Jews during a time they were deeply in need. A hero to me is someone who goes out of their way to help someone without asking whatever the consequences. A hero to me is also someone who puts themself at risk to help others in need. Paul put his job and life at risk. He went against his country's orders to help thousands of Jews get further help in Switzerland. He even gave some of them clothes. Thanks to Paul the Jews could get more help from people in Switzerland. He didn't ever regret his actions either even though they cost him a hard life later. Paul will be always be remembered as a hero because he ignored his orders to help Jews who need much help.

Paul would live the rest of his life after World War II in tough circumstances. In 1970 Paul was sent a letter of apology by the government. The government didn't reinstate his penison or reopen his case. But in 1995 which was twenty three years after his death his convictions were finally declared invalid. Even though he was dead things had been made right for Paul If it weren't for him thousands of Jews would have died. Paul will always be remembered by many as a hero for his brave actions.

Worl War II was a dark time for Jews and everybody. But there were some who rose above and helped Jews knowing the consequences. They put themselves at risk. These people are heroes. One of these heroes was a man from Switzerland named Paul Gruninger.

TEACHERS ARE MORE THAN WHAT WE SEE

Dylande Guzman

During one of the darkest times of humanity, a man named Adolf Hitler wanted to blame someone for the losses of Germany. He decide to form a group of people called the Nazis and blame the Jews for the misfortunes of Germany. To identify who were Jews the Nazis made them wear a yellow Star of David. The Nazis put Jews in inhumane concentration camps and were committing genocide. Some Jews were saved from the horrid genocide by courageous heroes. A hero is someone who fights for what they believe in and puts their lives at risk for the safety and benefit of others. If you look around you will see heroes everywhere, and maybe you are one of them. Gerda Valentiner is an incredible example of one of these courageous heroes.

Gerda Valentiner was a devoted teacher in Denmark. She loved and cared for her students very much. She respected all her pupils' religious beliefs. During World War II, she cared for her Jewish students more than ever. She took these students, their brothers, and sisters into her home so at least their parents would know they were safe. She kept them safe in her home until they could be transferred to Sweden where they would be safer. She saved many children's lives while risking her own life.

Gerda Valentiner could have faced many consequences for her heroic actions. She could have been sent to a horrible concentration camp. Also, she could have been arrested for her daring actions. Finally, the worst that could have happened to Gerda Valentiner was execution. Gerda risked facing these gruesome consequences for the sake of her students and their siblings.

Gerda Valentiner left a handprint on many of these childrens lives. One of these particular people is Moritz Scheftelowitz. His sister was a student of Gerda Valentiner. He says that one night she came over to their house warning the parents about the approaching danger. A couple days later, Moritz and his sisters were taken into Gerda Valentiner's home. She was determined to get the Scheftelowitz kids to safety. It took Gerda Valentiner three tries to get the Scheftelowitz kids to safety, but every time she failed to get them to the safety of Sweden she just persevered.

Gerda Valentiner had many great qualities just like any other hero. She was sensitive but strong. She had a great sensitivity toward her students. She cared for them very much, but she was able to build up the strength in faith to help these children. She might not have known that she was as strong as an ox. She would have fought to the death to save the lives of those children. The children could see the determination in her eyes to keep them safe. This determination gave them hope and made them feel safe. Gerda Valentiner's most important quality was her courage. She defied one of the strongest forces of evil at the time. This evil force was the Nazis.

She didn't believe what the Nazis were doing was right. Even though she didn't go to Adolf Hitler and rebel right in front of him, her act of defiance was just as big and took just as much courage. She saved the lives of innocent children that would have been worked to death or killed in a gas chamber by the Nazis. By setting this amazing example, the children she saved followed her example. There are more people like her to stand up for the innocent who can't help themselves. Gerda continued to show her courage even in the hardest of times. She said, "I only did what many Danes did, nothing special. We thought it perfectly natural to help people in mortal danger." She was so modest. She didn't consider what she was doing to be a great deed and didn't boast about it. All heroes have great qualities to get them through their tasks, but each hero's qualities vary depending on the endeavour they must face.

Gerda Valentiner displayed many heroic actions. She participated in the transfer of Jewish children from Denmark to Sweden. Also, Gerda Valentiner took the children into her loving and safe home until they could be transferred safely to Sweden. Finally, she noticed that the Jewish children would only eat the bread out of all the delicious food she gave them because they were sticking to the strict Jewish dietary laws. She decided to bring in new kosher dishes that the kids could eat and were used to. Gerda Valentiner displayed many heroic and courageous actions so the children could follow in her footsteps.

Gerda Valentiner did many great things. She was recognized by Yad Vashem for her gallant deeds on July 28, 1968. That day, she wasn't the only person recognized for her defiant and courageous feat. She stood out because not all heroes were recognized for their selflessness. We need to remember that sometimes the greatest heroes are the ones who stay in the shadows. Even though Gerda Valentiner was recognized for her silent actions, it doesn't make her less of a hero. Gerda Valentiner did these things for the children, not for her self. Gerda Valentiner was a unique hero who selflessly saved the lives of many innocent and naïve children.

HOLOCAUST HEROES

Francesca Isler

World War II was a time of sorrow and horror. Not many people stopped to help an entire population of people who were sent to concentration camps where Jews were tortured and killed because they did not fit in to what the Nazis called "normal". The Nazis not only imprisoned a religion as a whole, but also kept power and devastated the family members of the dead victims. These poor Jews were forced to work in dangerous areas, not given enough food and water, and were lied to and beaten. Adolf Hitler, the dictator of the Germans and the one to blame for the millions of lives taken, took away any and all rights away from ordinary citizens. The Jews were

346

undeserving of this type of cruelty. In the Jews' minds who were in the concentration camps, only a miracle could save them. Some were fortunate to receive a hero.

These people who did step in are considered heroes for savings as many lives as possible and put their own lives at risk in the process. Being a hero means taking action and standing up for what you believe in. People would protest, protect, and feed Jews who were being prosecuted. Without heroes the world would be full of even more war, more death, and more starvation. All heroes saved a Jew or many Jews even if it was a small piece of bread or hiding them in their house, either way someone survived. An example of this is Gertrud and Carl Lutz who were credited with leading a rescue team that saved over 62,000 Jews.

Carl Lutz was born in Walzenhausen, Switzerland on March 30th, 1895. He died on February 12th, 1975 in Bern, Switzerland. Gertrud Lutz was born on September 17th, 1910. She was betrayed by a spy and murdered on November 30th, 1945. After his studies in America, Carl Lutz acted as the Swiss consul, and as a beginner in photography, he brought his camera everywhere with him. Lutz documented his recordings of public and private events. Although true heroes do not ask for a favor or reward, most heroes are recognized. For example, in 1963 a street in Israel was named after Carl Lutz. Also, Carl Lutz was the first Swiss person to be named on the list of Righteous Among the Nations. The Righteous Among the Nations is a list of names to honor people who made a positive change during World War II.

Carl Lutz aided Jews trying to cross the border. He also helped create fake passports for Jews trying to escape the unfair treatment that had been bestowed upon them. He petitioned to make living conditions better or more bearable for those in prison camps. Lutz helped obtain permits for Jews living in local areas, and even after an invasion Carl Lutz continued to progress in finding escape routes for those who needed it. Overall, the pair issued more than 50,000 passports to Hungarian Jews in a rescue mission. Eight thousand protective letters were sent to entire families rather than individuals in order to save more families and keep them together, and around 76 "safe houses" were built for the homeless. Also, Carl Lutz created documents that enabled almost 10,000 Hungarian Jewish children to emigrate. Not only did Gertrud and Carl Lutz assist needy people, but also taught others how to set up the rescue or escape projects that reunited families and saved lives. Now with an entire party of heroes, the miracles Jews had prayed and wished for could come true. This team of heroes and heroines was the committee that saved over 62,000 people.

Cameras were now forbidden and taking pictures was also. So when Carl Lutz tried to take a picture of several thugs beating up a woman in an alley, they pointed a gun at his chest and stole his camera. The only way he was able to survive was showing his paperwork and giving up the camera roll. Soon after becoming part of the Righteous Among the Nations, his new wife, Trudi, saved his collection of photographs for the archives at Yad Vashem. Thanks to Carl Lutz, we now have the history of the decade of the 1930's and a few weeks after the war through Lutz's writings and impressive photography.

In 1932, Gertrud Lutz was first arrested because of the suspicion of communist decomposition. In 1933, she fled and looked for work underground. Then she was rearrested following the suspicion of communist decomposition writings and spent 2 years and 4 months in jail for conspiracy to commit high treason. Through prison, Gertrud Lutz organized that a family basement would be used to hide a child she saved. Her brother, Hermann Schlotterbeck, was arrested and tortured in a concentration camp in October 1944. Through all of this Gertrud Lutz continued to help everyone she could, and did not let anyone fall behind.

These two were heroes as individuals and as a whole group or family. Thanks to a rescue mission thousands of lives were saved, families were together, and the Nazis were stood up to. So now after the war, people know that a hero is brave, smart, always perseveres, and stands up for what they believe in. Carl and Gertrud Lutz made an enormous, positive change that shaped a part of history as we know it today.

HOLOCAUST VICTOR

Gabriella Koebnick

World War II was a dreadful time for many. During the war Jewish people faced persecution. Adolf Hitler, a German, came to power in Europe with the Nazis. They took and killed many Jewish people including children. This was called the Holocaust. Elizabeth Eidenbenz was a hero who stood up for what she believed in.

Elisabeth Eidenbenz was a hero to many children and their mothers. She was born on June 12, 1913, daughter to a Zurich pastor. She first taught in Switzerland and Denmark before she decided to share her talents and love at the Association to Aid Children in War. On April 24, 1937 Elisabeth arrived in Madrid as a volunteer in an aid team. Soon after, she relocated to the South of France. Shocked by the situation of mothers and their children amid Spanish Refugees, Elisabeth decided to convert a deserted house into a maternity house.

The house was in bad condition so Elisabeth got 30,000 francs from the Swiss Red Cross to help refurbish it. Adding her own touch of creativity, the house was finished and turned into a hospital by November 1939. Each room was named after a city in Spain to remind the mothers-to-be of their homeland. Pablo Casals, one of the world's best composers, left his home in Spain to live in Prades. During his visit at the hospital with Elisabeth he made a very generous donation and promised to bring even more money when he returned. Elisabeth was a hero who built a hospital and risked getting shut down all while a war was beginning.

348

Before full war began, the Nazis went to great measures to have the support of the people of Germany. They stripped Jewish people of their human dignity and rights, while educating the populations under their control that the Jewish people were malicious creatures who didn't deserve to live. Der Sturmer, a weekly Nazi newspaper, frequently said, "The Jews are our misfortune" and debuted dehumanizing cartoons of Jewish people, comparing Jewish people to satanic figures. The educational system taught children to hate Jewish people and encouraged many young people to join Hitler and the Nazi side during the Holocaust. That let the Nazis have further reinforcement against the Jewish people, placing the Jewish people at a big disadvantage at the beginning of the Holocaust. From the day Hitler and the Nazis came to power until World War II was over, Jewish people suffered terribly.

Europe, during the Holocaust, Nazis collected Jews and took them to concentration camps. When the Gestapo reached Elisabeth's hospital looking for Jews, Elisabeth sent them away. The second time she was not so lucky. They came ordering Lucie, a Jewish woman whose baby died at birth, but she stayed behind to give mothers her milk. The commander threatened that if Lucie was not given to them they would take Elisabeth instead. Elisabeth acted as a hero and asked for a few minutes to pack her bags. Lucie could not accept Elisabeth's generous offer and gave herself up. Lucie then boarded a train in a cattle wagon from Elne to Rivesaltes. She then was transferred to the gas chambers at Mauthausen. Some 20,000 others followed this route. Elisabeth was a brave soul and put her life at risk for over six hundred children refugees and their mothers.

A few weeks after Lucie was taken, Elisabeth received a leaflet from the management committee ordering her "to give up Jews, Tziganes, and Spanish refugees." Anyone who was asked to do this was not allowed to protect them from the roundups. Elisabeth knew she couldn't do anything more to protect the mothers and their children.

In the concentration camps the prisoners received very little food. The morning meal consisted of coffee or herbal tea. For lunch watery soup, perhaps a piece of turnip or potato peels. The evening meal they would get a small piece of black bread and perhaps a piece of sausage, or some cheese or marmalade. The bread was supposed to last till morning; many hid it while they slept. Hunger was one of the biggest problems in the concentration camps. Prisoners did heavy manual work, but did not have enough nutrition. If they died while working, their body became a part of the structure, and many thousands of Jews died from starvation or illnesses. Sadly the families had to be separated. Men from women, kids of both genders went with their mothers. After registration, the prisoners had to get undressed, and to get their heads shaved. Their clothes were usually taken; they were given a striped uniform. There would be no privacy or real sanitation. The prisoners had to clean themselves in dirty water and would not be given another pair of clothes for weeks or months on end. After a little meal in the morning the rest of the day would consist of work. Jews were beaten, starved, and had gruesome living conditions.

The Holocaust was a very dark time for Jewish families. A lot of people were on the Nazis' side, but some were still in favor of the Jews. These people were a light of hope for the Jewish people being severely persecuted. These men and women acted fast and were able to save the lives of numerous Jews. The people who put their lives in danger to save others were heroes. There were so many exceptional people that acted fast and deserved to be recognized. Fortunately, Yad Vashem recognized these people with the title of "Righteous Among the Nations." Although lots of Jewish people lost their lives, many were saved with the help of heroes, like Elisabeth Eidenbenz.

Elisabeth helped save over six hundred children refugees. She was not recognized for her heroic actions until after World War II. Later in her life she was awarded Righteous Among the Nations by the Government of Israel. Elisabeth died on May 23, 2011 in Zurich, Switzerland at the age of 98. She lived a full life and did a lot to contribute to society. Elisabeth Eidenbenz will always be remembered as the hero she was.

PAUL GRUENINGER

George Waltz

The Holocaust occurred from January 30, 1933 and ended on May 8, 1945. The Holocaust refers to the genocide of 6 million Jewish people in Europe. This occurred when anti-Semitic Nazi leader Adolf Hitler deemed Jews as an "inferior race" and thought they were an alien threat to German racial purity. After years of Nazi rule in Germany, during which Jews were consistently persecuted, Hitler's "final solution," now known as the Holocaust, came action under the cover of World War II, with mass killing centers constructed in the concentration camps. This led Jews to flee Nazi occupied Europe. A man named Paul Grueninger helped Jews cross the border of annexed Austria to escape Nazi tyranny.

Paul Grueninger, born October 27, 1891 and died February 22, 1972, helped the Jewish people tremendously during their time of need. Paul Grueninger was a senior officer of the Swiss police in Saint Gallen. When Switzerland closed its borders to Austria. He illegally allowed the passing of around 3,600 Jews.

Paul Grueninger was an avid soccer player. He played for SC Brühl, a local club, and helped lead the club win it's one and only championship. His success was short lived as he left to serve in World War I. After World War I Paul Grueninger became a police officer where he excelled at his job and flew through ranks in his hometown St. Gallen.

Paul Grueninger was the police captain in St. Gallen when Nazi Germany annexed Austria on August 1938. When Nazi Germany took over Austria. Austrian Jews faced the same persecution and discrimination as Jewish people who were suffering in Germany. After the peace treaty between Germany and Switzerland, Switzerland no longer allowed Jewish refugees to cross the border into Switzerland. Since official channels of immigration were closed many Jews attempted illegally to cross the border in fear of their lives. The attempt to cross the border was not easy and many Jews were caught. They would be brought to Paul Grueninger, cold and hungry having left their old lives running from the Germans.

Grueninger decided to take a risk that would destroy his career. Grueninger permitted illegal documents allowing Austrian Jews to cross the border into Switzerland. He allowed Jewish refugees to enter Switzerland and legalized their citizenship by falsely stamping their passports to show that they had entered before the date of restriction, March, 1938. This allowed them to find legal refuge at the Diepoldsau camp, where Jewish organizations took care of them and helped them gain residency permits or to travel to further destinations. Paul Grueninger also blocked efforts to trace refugees who were known to have entered Switzerland illegally, and helped to buy winter clothes, from money out of his own pocket, for needy refugees.

Finally Paul Grueninger was caught illegally falsifying documents and was dismissed from the police force in March, 1939 and soon brought to trial where he was found guilty of breach of duty and fraud, and made to give up his retirement benefits. He served time in jail and also had to pay a fine of 300 Swiss francs. Grueninger lived the rest of his life in poverty and died in 1972. Before his death Israel's Yad Vashem made him one of the "Righteous Among the Nations" in 1971. The Swiss government did not reverse his conviction until 1995. Conveniently twenty three years after Paul Grueninger's death the judges reopened and discharged him from his charges in the same courtroom where he had been condemned. In 1996 Paul Grueninger was completely absolved of charges and rehabilitated by the Swiss government.

World War II ended and the Nazi power diminished relieving Jews from persecution. The Allied occupation of Austria lasted from 1945 to 1955. Austria had been controlled by Nazi Germany as a whole part of the German state, but in 1943 the Allied powers agreed in the Declaration of Moscow that it would be regarded as the first victim of Nazi aggression, and treated as a liberated and independent country after the war. The end of the war in Austria meant the end to the persecution of Jews and the relief of Jewish brutality that Paul Grueninger was trying to save Jews from enduring.

Paul Grueninger practiced every quality of a hero. One aspect he demonstrated was Sacrafice. Paul Grueninger sacrificed his career of being a police officer and broke the law to save 3,600 Jews. His sacrifice placed him in prison, made him pay a fine, and sent him into poverty. Another quality he enacted was compassion, illegally importing Jews, finding them shelter, and paying for clothing to cloth the refugees, out of his own pocket. Paul Grueninger's compassion kick started and fueled his acts of heroism by caring for Jews when he already let them through the border. His humility, as he had to keep quite, made him a real hero. Without publicizing his heroic deeds Paul Grueninger fit the perfect definition of a hero.

The brutal truth is Paul Grueninger was about one out 1,000 who took action and helped helped the Jewish people in their time of need. Paul Grueninger can be learned from by future generations to take action and do whats right. His heroic deeds have change the course of the Holocaust giving Jews hope. If everyone stood up for what is right we would not have events like the Holocaust.

KNUD DYBY

Grace Soria

The Holocaust is regarded as one of the darkest times in the world's history. From Adolf Hitler's rise to power in the 1930s, to the beginnings of World War II in Hitler's attack on Poland, to Germany's eventual surrender in 1945, there was scarcely a bright spot in the war. The Nazis never let up on their regime, not until the very end. Learning about it today, nearly 75 years later, kids in classrooms all across America learn about the atrocities committed in the war, namely the atrocities committed by Nazi soldiers on behalf of Hitler. It is horrifying to think of all the things that the Jews suffered through, and for those of us who have never experienced something that traumatic, it is so hard to visualize that it almost doesn't seem real. But it was, and it is, and you can still see the scar the war has left on the world even today. The heroes of the war, the ones who were selfless and loving enough to risk everything to save the Jews, are often overshadowed by the sheer amount of horror. With all the terrible things that we remember today, the good deeds of the true heroes are not always touched upon. But these people are examples of a light in the dark - a ray of hope for those who had so little left. One of the greatest examples of this is a man named Knud Dyby, a former Danish policeman. People like him remind us that even when the worst of humanity takes hold, you can still find good in the world.

Knud Dyby was born in Denmark in 1915. His life before the war isn't much talked about; most accounts of what Dyby did don't mention it much, but one account mentions that he was an avid sailor, and another account from Humboldt State University says that he followed his father into the printing trade and was training to be a typographer before being drafted into the army at the age of twenty.

352

He was then assigned to be a Guardsman at the Royal Palace in Copenhagen, apparently for his good looks and the distinct military air he had about him, the kind that asserted his status as a soldier. He served his time in the military, and then immediately after signed up to become a policeman. His experience as a Guardsman helped get him into a higher position in the police force. At the time, Denmark was being occupied by Germany. In the beginning, Germany had allowed Denmark to continue being governed as it usually would be. Three years later, when the Danish government decided that German demands had simply become intolerable; the Germans finally installed a replacement government that they hoped would serve them better. But the Nazi party was met with relentless resistance from the Danish people, who didn't agree to their beliefs and refused to go along with their plans without a sound. The sabotage and other forms of resistance, as well as their apparent inability to cow the Danes into submission, angered the Nazis; they decided to do whatever they could to stop the resistance. So in September of 1943, a German diplomat named Georg Ferdinand Duckwitz announced to the Danes of the Germans' latest plan: Hitler had decided to round up all the Jews in Denmark and deport them. Of course, the Danes knew that this meant death for the Jews, and as usual, they wouldn't go down without a fight.

Dyby was only twenty-six years old when this was happening, and still a policeman at the time. He knew he needed to help, and he had all of the tools he needed to do it. As a policeman, he had access to more information than a common person; he knew things like the patrol routines of the German forces along sea routes from Sweden to Denmark that were absolutely crucial to the underground. He also was able to use state cars to transport Jews to the harbor, where they could sail to safety in a different country. His excellent training and authority proved to be useful many, many times throughout the war. In addition to the resources he had as a policeman, he also had the knowledge of an expert sailor. He provided information about sea routes and the best hiding places around the coves to underground resistance forces that focused on transporting people, especially Jews, to safety in Sweden. Not only that, but he also managed five skippers himself, and helped arrange hospital rooms for the transportees to hide in once they arrived. Between participating in transporting people on other boats to the five skippers he sailed himself, he assisted in transporting around 2,000 people, a third of whom were Jews, according to Dyby's page on the Jewish Foundation For the Righteous website. When Denmark was liberated in May of 1945, Dyby retired from the police force, and moved to the United States the next year. But the things he did from 1943 to 1945 no doubt completely changed the lives of the people he assisted; he gave them hope in the war, and granted them a future when they previously had none.

Knud Dyby died in 2011 at the age of ninety-six, but his memory lives on even today. Everything he did in the war cannot be forgotten; the hundreds of people he helped save lived because he did everything he could to help save them. He's a true hero, and it's good to know that he will be remembered as such. He truly is an example of a light in the dark. He was in the right place at the right time, and because of that he was able to touch the lives of hundreds of people he didn't even know. The most remarkable thing about this is the fact that he didn't know them; lots of these people were probably strangers to him, and yet he still cared so much about them that he risked his life and did everything he could to make sure they got to safety. He did all of this just because he knew it was the right thing to do. And while people shouldn't get a pat on the back simply because they can tell what's right from wrong, Dyby really did go beyond that. In a time when he could have met a fate worse than death for assisting these people, he hardly even cared - he just immediately started to help however he could, offering up the valuable information and knowledge he had to the underground. Lots of people wouldn't risk their life to help so many strangers, but Dyby did; and for the amount of people he saved, it's indisputable that he is a real hero.

Dyby is an inspiration. He's proof that you can find good in the worst of things. People like him should be like role models; the compassion he had for other people is nothing less than admirable. Hearing about the heroes of the Holocaust is important, because sometimes people *do* need the reminder that even when things are looking grim, there is always, *always,* a reason to hope.

HOLOCAUST HEROES

Karla Pinales-Rangel

This world is full of people, good and bad. They go about their everyday lives minding their own business without a care in the world. But do they *actually* know the world their living in? If they knew about the tragedies that occurred not too long ago would they be affected in any way? Humans these days are too caught up in updating their Twitter and posting selfies on Instagram that they don't open their eyes and realize that they should be grateful for what they have. There was a time when people didn't have this. Instead of playing Temple Run on their iPhone these poor people had to undergo hours of agonizing work in unsafe places called concentration camps.

1933 to 1945 was a bad time for the world. Jewish people were being captured and sent to camps only to be tortured and possibly killed. However, they were not alone. There were people, though only few, who made change possible. They risked their own lives to save others without asking for a prize in return. They fought for what they thought was right even if they didn't have the strength to do it. They never gave up on themselves. Today, we refer to these people as *heroes.*

Sixty-two thousand persecuted Jews were saved, the largest rescue operation of the Second World War, thanks to the help of two people, Gertrud and Carl Lutz. Carl Lutz was born on March 30, 1895 in Walzenhausen, Switzerland. He worked as a chancellor at the Swiss Consulate in St. Louis and after 20 years became a vise-consul to the Swiss Consulate General in Jaffa. While in Budapest, Hungary, Lutz became associated with the Jewish Agency for Palestine. There, he distributed Swiss safe-conduct documents that made emigration possible to about 10,000 Hungarian Jewish children. He made a deal with the Hungarian government and the Nazis to issue protective letters to 8,000 Hungarian Jews so they could escape to Palestine. Instead of giving the letters to people individually, he gave them to families thus saving tens of thousands more people. This also kept families together which was key. He also set up 76 "safe houses" that were off-limits to Hungarian forces and Nazi soldiers. After he got divorced from Gertrud, he was married to a woman named Trudi. Even though not much information is given about her, she did support Carl throughout his time in Budapest.

Gertrud Lutz migrated to the United States when she was eighteen. She obtained a job as a clerk at the Swiss Consulate in St. Louis where she met Carl Lutz. Even though Carl is mostly credited with saving all those Jews, Gertrud was by his side the whole time and she contributed to the rescuing, too. Sadly, Gertrud and Carl Lutz got divorced in 1946. From there Gertrud became a delegate of the Swiss donation. While she was the head of UNICEF, she built maternity homes and founded colleges for nannies; she became the savior of many children, and worked with feeding programs. She continued her work until she finally retired as Vice President of UNICEF.

Gertrud and Carl Lutz were truly people who seeked to spread goodness. They fought good against evil and they won. Their individual strength morphed into one was strong enough to overpower any obstacles in their way. Through hard times they still made a positive change. Even though their paths separated later in their lives, they still continued to strive for greatness and that is only something a true hero does.

When someone trusts another person to help them when they fall is truly amazing. Not everyone has the courage to accept help from others. Most people just choose to stand alone and expect to make it to the top, but you need the help or encouragement of others even if you believe in yourself 100 percent. Plus, it's never fun to be alone.

Carl and Gertrud were very courageous people. To me, they represented the SLE confident, leads and cooperates. They both kept trying and trying to help the poor Jews and they actually managed to save thousands. Also, each of them stood up for what they believed in even if authority was against them. They were both leaders because they never gave up on themselves and today people can reflect on their heroic actions. They also represent confident, embraces challenges because saving thousands of Jews from being sent to concentration camps must be pretty hard. Not a normal everyday person can do that.

Gertrud and Carl Lutz worked hard to achieve what they did. The remnants of the past must always stay in the minds of people today so we won't repeat the same mistakes. This generation needs to work harder on diversity; we mustn't exclude or harm people just because they go by a different religion or because they're a different race. We are all people and we all have feelings that need to be respected. We don't only lack diversity; we also lack people who are willing enough to become *heroes*.

PAUL GRUENINGER: THE STORY OF A TRUE HERO

Kaveh Khajavi

The Holocaust was a very dark time when Jews were being exterminated by the masses. The Holocaust started on January 30, 1933 and ended on May 8, 1945. During the Holocaust the persecution of the Jewish people was at an all time high, Jews were put into concentrations camps where millions died from inhumane living conditions, malnutrition, execution, and exhaustion. However Jews were not the only people to suffer because of the Nazis; Gypsies, Poles and other Slavs, and people with physical or mental disabilities were targeted. Others were Nazi victims because of what they did. These victims of the Nazi regime included Jehovah's Witnesses, homosexuals, the dissenting clergy, Communists, Socialists, asocials, and other political enemies. Anybody who tried to help these people shared the same fate as them. Even though it was a great risk, some very brave and kind people decided to help no matter the cost and truly have earned the title of a hero of the Holocaust.

One brave man who risked everything to help Jews was Paul Grueninger. Paul was born on October 27, 1891 and died on February 22, 1972. Paul Grueninger was a Swiss border police commander of the St. Gallen region that borders Austria. He saved about 3,600 Jews when Switzerland closed its borders to Jewish people. Paul risked everything just to help people he didn't know.

When Paul was still young, before becoming a police officer, he was a football champion. When Paul was young he was an avid footballer, and played for the football team SC Bruhl. Also in the 1914-1915 season he helped the club win their first, and only, Swiss championship. Despite this, Paul played in a time where football wasn't a professional sport. After serving in World War I, Paul decided to join the police, where he quickly moved through the ranks and became very successful.

356

While Paul was serving as the border commander in August of 1938, the Nazis annexed Austria, and Austrian Jews had to share the same fate as the German Jews. Paul was given specific instructions by the Swiss government to turn back the Jewish refugees to Austria. With the Jews in Austria facing the same persecution and violence as the Jews in Germany, for Paul it just felt wrong to deny entry to the Jews. This caused a moral dilemma for Paul, as he either had to send thousands of poor refugees back to Austria where their fates were uncertain, or let the Jews enter illegally, disregard clear instructions and risk ruining his career and life to help people he didn't know. Paul decided to help the Jews get in illegally, a choice that would ruin his life but save thousands others

Just getting the Jews past the border was not helpful enough in the eyes of Paul. Not only did he grant illegal entrance to Jews, he also falsified documents to allow Jews to receive passports that classify them as legal immigrants. He also turned in false reports about the number of arrivals and the status of the refugees in his district. He even impended efforts to trace refugees that were known to enter Switzerland illegally. Paul even went so far to paying out of his own pocket to buy winter clothes for needy refugees that were forced to leave everything they owned behind. Paul felt the need to help everybody he could not matter what the cost, even going so far to breaking many laws in the process.

Paul's acts of kindness didn't go unnoticed and eventually his actions were discovered by the Germans. Once the Germans found out about what Paul did, they immediately informed the Swiss authorities. One day when Grueninger arrived for work, the police station was blocked off and he immediately realised that they found out about what he did. He was dismissed from the police force in March 1939 and was also brought to trial on charges of illegally permitting the entry of 3,600 Jews into Switzerland and falsifying their registration papers. The prosecution added additional charges of helping individual Jews by shielding them from detection, assisting them in depositing their valuables, etc. The trial lasted two years and in the end he was found guilty and of breach of duty, his retirement benefits were forfeited, and had to pay the cost of the trial. Despite being warned that he was under investigation by the Gestapo, he continued to falsify documents for Jewish refugees until the day of his arrest.

After the end of World War II, Paul Gruninger was living in very hard circumstancs. With a criminal record and his heroism forgotten, Paul struggled to make a living for the rest of his life. Despite this he never regretted any of it and said in 1952, "It was basically a question of saving human lives threatened with death. How could I then seriously consider bureaucratic schemes and calculations?" Paul died in poverty in 1972, and in 1992 was absolved of his charges in the same courtroom he was condemned in.

Paul did many things to prove he is an amazing hero. Not only did he let thousands of Jews pass the border, he also did everything he could to help all those people. Even after losing everything, he never regret a thing he did that to help all those people he never met. Paul's kindness has inspired many people to be better, and is also a great example of how selfless everybody should be. What makes Paul Grueninger a real hero is that despite his life being completely ruined he never regretted a thing he did.

FRED REYMOND

Mariah Hudnut, Co-runners-up

It all starts with one person; one person who decides promoting wrong is ok, one mind that feels good when it hurts others. It only takes one. Prejudices have the ability to take over millions of innocent minds. And these minds can only be saved by true heroes, true souls that know right from wrong. Heroes have gut, a strength to overcome any barrier between good and evil. Heroes never give up.

The Holocaust was an unjust murder of some 6 million Jews; one that started with a single thought, a thought of hatred and disrespect. Most people chose to not be at all involved in this crime. Most ignored the murderous acts and went on with their ordinary lives. But a few did stand up and speak out. These people are today known as saviors, and among these saviors is Fred Reymond.

As any capable Swiss man of his time, Fred took part in the Swiss Militia Army. In 1940 he was commissioned to observe the German forces in eastern French communities. When Fred saw the Jews' anguish and misery, he could not help but feel their sorrow. Fred knew how terribly insane the world had become and wanted the extreme cruelty to stop. He wanted all the earth's citizens to be treated equally. Fred wanted others to know life's joys, and to do so, began to rescue Jewish refugees.

Being active on the Franco-Swiss border, Fred grew to know the woods connecting the two states quite well. With knowledge of every trail and back route in the forest, Fred devised an undefeatable plan to help save the Jewish society.

The plan began with Fred's agents, who played their role by gathering up and escorting escapees to a secret meeting place, one that changed monthly as not to draw suspicion. Occasionally British paratroopers and young French men who'd been drafted to work in German factories showed up in need of help. Though the majority of escapees remained Jewish. For quite some time Fred and his Holocaust victims met up at a little gate, unguarded by the Swiss border patrols. There, Fred sneaked the bunch through and brilliantly navigated them around all densely occupied areas. Fred knew that refugees would be at greater risk during the day, and because of this,

358

always insisted on traveling at night. Due to this restriction of night travel, Fred and his wife, Lilette, provided the refugees with up to a day's worth of protection, in order to see that each individual could escape at an appropriate hour. The couple did this out of love, genuine love. At dusk the party would set out on their journey. Fred and his gang would maneuver their way around every barrier or act of defense German patrols had put together, several times escaping only by the mere skin of their teeth. They'd cut through every back route and secret passage, always following in the trustful footsteps of Fred Reymond.

This leading role wasn't easy for Fred though. It came with drawbacks such as sleep-deprivation, forest injuries, and even sickness from being around such poor, unclean people. The job came with multiple risks as well. Fred risked being stopped and possibly arrested by German patrols multiple times in the process of crossing France's border. He put his own life at risk each time he performed this act, and not just for anyone, for strangers, people he had never encountered before in his life. By performing these illegal acts numerous times, Fred became known to the police as a "goods smuggler." This title, in a way, helped Reymond, by covering up the bigger crime he was committing. Never did he think of the extreme consequences, and never did he give up on himself. Fred did these acts because he knew they were right, not because he wanted fame or glory. Fred Reymond acted as a true hero in this crucial time and saved thousands of souls with his one helping hand.

Some fifty years later, a Swiss journalist picked up Fred's story. Reymond had kept quiet about his rescue missions until then, and might've kept quiet forever if none had questioned him. He was an amazing man who acts as a role model for millions around the globe today. We know of Fred as a modest, down-to-earth person, who refused to let fear get the best of him. Fred gave others hope; hope in life, happiness, and most importantly, in themselves. Fred was an incredible man.

Societies can group others in completely absurd ways. And these groupings are what cause wars, depressions, and true sadness. All people must remember what deep pain Holocaust victims went through. We must remember that this DID occur and that our world DID become this madly insane. This was a murder of innocent human beings, an unjust occurrence that no one in our world's history should ever be proud of. This was a time when fear overtook fairness, where no evidence was needed to support a completely illogical judgment. Only true bravery showed through to the world at this time. Only those who had faith lived on to succeed. And only true heroes are thanked today.

PAUL GRUNINGER

Mario Ramos

 The Holocaust was a horrible event when Adolf Hitler was leader of Germany and he wanted to eliminate all Jews. He tricked them in many ways and as a result millions were killed and put in concentration camps to work till they are dead and to kill even more Jews. All Jews were very terrified and did not stand up to this tragedy, very few did. One of these brave mens names was Paul Gruninger. He made a huge impact on the history of the Holocaust.

The Holocaust started on May 8, 1933. Hitler was the ruler of Germany and he hated Jews but no one knew that, not even the non-Jews. What Hitler did was he tricked the Jews in multiple ways like saying that they would take the kids to a fun camp while the parents were at work but in reality they were killed. He even said stuff like they were going to a nice place but he actually sent them to a concentration camp where they worked to death. At the camps he had them do unnecessary jobs like moving a big pile of boulders from one side of the camp to the other and they would have them do this over and over for pure entertainment. Hitler had also told German soldiers to burn down all the Jewish places of worship to the ground and take all the Jews out of their homes to work. At the concentration camps the men were separated from the women and children and a German officer would take the women and children to the "showers" where they were actually killed because the showers were actually deadly gas chambers. The United States of Americas' strong army had found out about the horrible things the German army was doing to the innocent Jewish citizens so they joined the war. Tanks came to the concentration camps and rescued all the innocent Jewish people they could and put them in good care. This ended the horrible event called the Holocaust and many of the concentration camps were destroyed but few are still standing today to remind people about the Holocaust. A big part of the end of the Holocaust was the brave Jewish citizens who stood up to Hitler's horrible army. A man named Paul Gruninger made a difference.

Paul Gruninger was born in the city of St.Gallen in the year of 1891. For education he went to Rorschach. He played football as a child and when he was older he played for his local football team named SC Bruhl. Paul was very good at football and in the years 1914 through 1915 he helped win the Swiss Championship. When Paul was older he was a Lieutenant in the Swiss army during World War I. After World War I, Gruninger became a police officer.

Every workday was the same for Paul. He would go to work and come back home no problem. All this changed on the third of April in the year of 1939. Paul had come to his place of work like any other day but a cadet prevented him from going inside. A few days later he got a notice that said that he could not let any Jewish refugees through the gate and as a result of that many people lost their jobs. They even had a J stamped on their passports. Paul protested against this and thought it was very unfair. What Paul did was very risky and he could have got himself killed but he still did it. If there were Jews past the border before they made it illegal for Jews to pass the border they were able to stay where they were and just carry on with their normal life like nothing had ever even happened. But what Paul did that made an impact on the Holocaust was that he let 3,600 Jews through the border illegally, and while he let each and every illegal Jew through the border he marked each and every one of the Jewish citizens' passports with a stamp saying that they had been past the border when Hitler and his German army made it illegal for Jews to pass the border. So if a German officer thought something was suspicious with one of the Jewish citizens that was past the border, they could just look at their passport and they could just resume their normal life like nothing had ever even happened.

Paul Gruninger is a huge hero. He had guts to do things that even the bravest person in the world couldn't do. A hero is someone who would risk his or her life just to make sure that the people around him or her are safe. That is exactly what Paul did. Paul Gruninger is a hero because he broke the law just to help Jewish citizens and in the process he knew that he could have gotten himself killed or fired from his job.

The Holocaust was a horrible time that should have never happened. Innocent people died just for being them. Since the Germans did this people ran in terror from them and did not want to do anything about it. But Paul Gruninger did stand up the the Germans and Hitler because he is a hero of history.

LIVING THE HOLOCAUST FROM THE SURVIVORS

Mason Pahule

The Holocaust, also known as the Shoah, was an important event that happened and we will never forget what happened. The Holocaust occurred around the Second World War and Nazis, members of the National Socialist German Workers' Party, killed people, mainly Jews as an act of racism. During the Holocaust, about 6 million Jews died. Between 100,000 and 500,000 helped the Nazis in the planning or the execution of the Holocaust. The Holocaust persecution was carried out in different stages. After the Holocaust, about 11million people died including Gypsies, Poles, communists, homosexuals, and mentally and physically disabled people. There were a lot of heroes during the course of the Holocaust, but one stood out to me. Friedel Bohny-Reiter was the person who stood out to me. Friedel helped many people without being asked to. She saved so many people during the Holocaust. There were only a handful of people willing to risk their life to save another, or in Friedel's case, many lives.

Friedel Bohny-Reiter was born in 1912, in the city of Vienna. Her father died around the First World War, so she was a foster child during her childhood. In 1919, she returned to Vienna and in 1920 she joined the Swiss Relief Committee children's train to Switzerland. She stayed with her foster family in Kilchberg. She attended school and she was trained as a nurse. With twenty years she was naturalized in Switzerland. After a year and half of work stay in Florence she went to work in 1941 in Switzerland by the *Swiss Association for war-affected children*. On November 12, 1941 Reiter was sent by the Secours Suisse to the Rivesaltes internment camp in the unoccupied zone of France. There, she did her best with puny resources to provide medical care, clothing and food for the imprisoned Jewish, Gypsy and Spanish children. She made an effort to save as many young children as she could in a short span of time.

Hilda Kreizer was a 16 year-old Jew waiting to be deported by a train with her younger sister and mother. Meanwhile, a police officer was assigned to make sure the Jewish people boarded the train in an orderly way. The 16-year-old knew Friedel well because Hilda was taken care of by Friedel during her work at Secours Suisse. When the police officer's attention was elsewhere, she ran to Bohny-Reiter with her sister, who had signaled them. Bohny-Reiter led them to a dark storeroom that was unlit in the camp. The storeroom had in it food from Secours Suisse. Bohny kept delivering children to the storeroom, which was safe and protected, until the train left. She sent the young children to private homes, which the parents cared and nurtured for these young kids, affiliated with her organization. She saved the childrens' lives by doing this, because their parents were sent to Auschwitz and murdered there. In her rescue actions, she ignored the leaders of Secours Suisse instructions for any activist that they had, -to obey the French government's orders and eagerly punished those who acted in any way to save and rescue the Jews.

As the camp slowly went away, she started to realize that she needed to remove as many children from the camp as possible, because yes, they would be released, but they would have nowhere to go. They didn't have a place to live or food to eat. She started to look for people to help her and she found a man named August Bohny. August Bohny had been heading the L'Abric children's home (sponsored by the Secours Suisses) in the village of Le Chambon-sur-Lignon since October 1941. In Friedel's effort to remove children from the camp, she teamed up with Bohny. In April 1942, she was asked to change an old and abandoned castle, named Chateau de Montluel near the city of Lyon, into a home for children released from Rivesaltes. When she brought the first group of children she rescued from Rivesaltes, she met

August Bohny for the first time. Together, they worked to make kids lives better and saved more lives than most people could or would have.

August Bohny and Friedel Bohny-Reiter got married later on in life. They lived happy life together and were known for what they had done. Friedel earned many awards and had many books and movies based on her and her experiences. In 1940 she was recognized as Righteous Among of Nations and 1997 the documentary, Dokumentarfilm Journal de Rivesaltes 1941–1942, was based on her. In 1994 she was awarded with the *Moral Courage Award* der *Jewish Foundation for Christian Rescuers* (present day: *Jewish Foundation for the Righteous*), gemeinsam mit ihrem Mann. Although, she won many awards, she wasn't the only one in the family that won awards. August won the *Moral Courage Award* der *Jewish Foundation for Christian Rescuers* with his wife. He was noticed by Righteous Among the Nations, Yad Vashem in 1990. He also had the *Les Camisards* in 1972, *Les armes de l'esprit* in 1989, and in 1994: La colline aux mille enfants made about him.

Friedel Bohny-Reiter saved many young children's lives and the children that were young then are the ones sharing their personal experiences about the holocaust. The Holocaust was a horrible time in our world's history and it should never happen again. It is one thing to say that it can't happen again, and another to take action and make sure it never happens again. It is this generation and the next generation's job to make sure the Holocaust never happens again. Friedel should be a role model to everyone and if everybody stands up and does exactly what Friedel did the Holocaust will never happen again. Friedel alone saved so many lives, alone, think about what the whole world can do. It should never happen again and it is our job to make sure it doesn't happen. The Holocaust was a tragic time in the world's history and the people who did it were horrible people. Friedel was a great person and she saved so many young Jewish children, she's done her part, now it's our turn.

http://en.wikipedia.org/wiki/The_Holocaust

GERDA VALENTINER, HOLOCAUST HERO

Mia Sanchez, Co-winner

There are many heroes out there like Superman, Spiderman, Batman and more, but do you ever ask yourself what a true hero is not just a fictional character but a real human hero? A hero could be a myth, or legendary figure with strength or super human ability. A hero is any person a man or woman admired for courage. A person who knows what is right and is willing to put herself in danger for others. Gerda Valentiner is a true hero, a hero who put herself in danger to help her own students.

During World War II the Nazis were persecuting Jews. The Nazis were German and their leader was Adolf Hitler. Adolf Hitler was a horrible person who was the leader who set the Holocaust. Holocaust means "sacrifice by fire" but is also the persecution of millions of Jews.

They came in power about January 1933. They believed that Germans were "racially superior" and that the Jews were "inferior" and a threat. The Nazis persecuted Jews and others who helped the Jews. To "exterminate" them they built concentration camps. To show others that the Jews were living in fine conditions and had all the necessities they needed, Adolf Hitler ordered people to make "propaganda" information which made it seem that the Jews were having fun. He put trees, market, and food, among other delights they didn't have. The camps were horrible and the Jews barely got fed and the Nazis could treat them like they were not human. The worst was the showers. The Germans would tell them, "Jews they can take a shower," but they would be murdered. They had to take off their clothes and the Nazis would pour toxic gases in the room, thought to be the showers. People were mistreated and murdered all the time. Innocent people were hung and made fun of. No one deserves that life.

Gerda Valentiner knew what was right and wrong. A quote from her is, "Their fate will be my fate too." Gerda Valentiner is a Danish hero. Before the Holocaust occurred she was a school teacher. She taught many students and in some of the classes there were Jewish children which she knew. She was a member of the Resistance which helped to rescue Jews from persecution. When she had gotten the "word" that there was a Holocaust and Jews were being persecuted she warned her students.

Gerda collected these Jewish children and took them home, waiting for the right moment to send them to Sweden, to safety. She not only risked her life for those children but also had great sensitivity and respect for their religion. She had so much respect for them that she noticed that they had dietary laws for their religion and only ate bread. Gerda started buying new dishes and food that they could eat. For a period of time there wasn't enough food for all the children and students so she didn't eat until there was more food. She treated them as her own children, as if they were hers and with all her heart she would love and protect them because they had done nothing to face this nasty threat of the tyrants.

One night in late September, 1943, Moritz Scheftelowitz came to his parents, Esther and Reuben Scheftelowitz to warn them of the impending danger. A few days later, Moritz and his sisters, Dora and Rita moved to Gerda's home and stayed with her until she managed to arrange their transfer to Sweden. There were two attempts to leave to Sweden that failed. They succeeded on their third attempt to ship about six children to Sweden. They left by a fishing boat from a location 10 km North of Copenhagen and after a troubled night's journey, they finally reached Landskrona,

Sweden and the children were safe. Gerda Valentiner told Yad Vashem, "I only did what many Danes did, nothing special. We thought it perfectly natural to help people in mortal danger." She had managed to save children's lives by sending them to Sweden for them to have a better chance, and to be safe.

By 1945 the "rule" of the Nazis was coming to an end. Germans evacuated the camps and left the Jews behind. People came to the camps to help set the Jews free. Many lived but some had died. People had tragic stories to tell. They finally got saved but couldn't return to their normal lives. Some stayed in the camps, embarrassed to what people might think or say about them. The Holocaust ended and was kind of a great ending. An ending where they got saved and yet there was much suffering before the saving.

We all wish to prevent wars and treatments like this to happen but there are wars all over the world; Isis, and Venezuela students are being killed for speaking what they think is right, all over the world we are all being persecuted in a way. We need to stop it and change our hearts to believing and knowing what is right.After the war Gerda left her teaching job. She volunteered as a social worker for two years in the Jewish refugees camps in Germany and Austria. In 1971 when she was 68 and retired she decided to go to Israel for a year in order to see the country and learn Hebrew. Gerda always had respect and love to these children and she knew that at least she needed to know their language and religion to know more of their background.

Gerda Valentiner was and is a powerful hero. She was recognized by Yad Vashem in 1968 as a Righteous Among the Nations. Although she says, she did what many Danes did. There are only about 22 heroes from Denmark recognized by Yad Vashem. She helped make a great change for people's lives. Many of us wish this slaughter did not occur, and hope nothing like it ever happens again. We can all be heroes by choosing the right choice, when you see someone being bullied in any way go and help the person. That is how the Holocaust happened no one was there to help or protect the Jews from the Nazis.

Web pages:

http://www.yadvashem.org/yv/en/exhibitions/righteous-teachers/valentiner.asp
http://db.yadvashem.org/righteous/righteousName.html?language=en&itemId=4017998
http://db.yadvashem.org/righteous/family.html?language=en&itemId=4017998
http://www.gluud.fr/getperson.php?personID=I46055&tree=gluud

BILL BARAZETTI HOLOCAUST HERO

Mira Saab

The Swiss and Danish heroes of the Holocaust saved thousands of lives and now thousands of children know their stories and how they helped in the Holocaust. A hero is a modest one who risks their life for others by putting themselves in difficult situations. He or she performs heroic deeds not for fame, and glory but for the feeling of accomplishment. One of those heroes, Bill Barazetti, was a part of the kindertransport and saved 669 children from the Nazis. Barazetti thought a lot about others and not himself first before others. He had a wife but he left her in a village so he could help children escape the Nazis and get to England safely and not be harmed on their way. Bill Barazetti saved the children to see them live and for them to tell their story of the Holocaust, not in any way for fame or for glory.

Bill Barazetti was born to a Swiss professor in Aarau, Switzerland. Later, in 1933 the year Hitler came to power, Bill Barazetti was a philosophy student at Hamburg University. At his school there were a lot of Jewish students and he became very good friends with many of them. At school, he saw Nazi thugs beat up Jews. When this happened he talked to the head teacher there and said that it wasn't right. Also, Hitler's people were marching Jews off the campus.

In 1939 Bill Barazetti saved 669 children from the Nazis workers and had them transported to England where they stayed. He went undercover back to Hamburg and when the Nazis found out, they sent him to Poland. He went undercover again and there he was also found by Gestapo and was badly beaten almost to death. When he was found by a young girl named Ann, who saved his life. They married and they had a kid, named Nicolas. He went to live with her in her village; he started working with Nicholas Winston, a man from her village that started a rescue team to save children, and started finding children from the village, foster homes in England, documents, and funds to help. When he started to work with the transport he worked with the Kindertransport, an organization that worked with children escaping the Nazis and putting them on trains and sending them somewhere, so that Jewish children would not be persecuted by the Nazis. Barazetti did this to help with the Kindertransport and not to be a bystander and let this happen. Instead he worked to save the Jewish children and help them leave the country by trains. Barazetti took a huge risk for his own health and to save children he might have known and to die a while later after the Holocaust had ended, not many would. His early life helped him take that step farther to work with the transportation of Jews to England. Bill Barazetti worked to save and help children from the Nazis and that is what makes him a Holocaust hero.

The Holocaust it a tragedy that could have not of happened if people noticed that Hitler was a horrible person. He killed millions of Jews and hundreds of other religious people, just because of his power and what he thought was right to do to the Jews even though it wasn't. Hitler had lots of money so he paid for a lot of expensive ads that made him sound like a great guy to people in Germany. He had most of the Mediterranean in his control and hundreds of internment camps where Jews and Gypsies were held captive from 1933-1945. The Holocaust was a time that made the world be upset, in Europe and here. The Nazis were selfish, heartless, and careless and didn't care for the needs of others as they should of. The Holocaust internment camps were the places that Hitler kept the Jews for years. He killed people in the streets for being Jewish and made people from the camps watch. He had some people take photos of places to show everyone how great the Jews were being treated, even though they weren't. He was Catholic so he believed that he was better than all Jews that is why he locked up all of the Jews in the internment camps, so that he could be more powerful than all of the Jews. If people died while doing their work the Nazis would just put cement over them. The Nazis had benches and signs up that said either, "No Jews allowed" or "Catholics only." They also lied to the Jews by saying that all the women and children under ten were taken to a place of happiness and beauty, when they were taking them to a place that would kill them.

The Holocaust is a time of sadness and grief that came over the Jews in Europe from 1933 to 1945. The Swiss and Danish weren't the only people helping the Jews escape Nazis and Bill Barazetti is one of thousands who helped, hundreds of children are learning today about what happened during the Holocaust. The Holocaust was a horrible time that could have been prevented and not have happened. A hero is one that protects others from harm, not for fame or for glory, but for the people's safety. Bill Barazetti did just that to help the Jewish children through the Holocaust. Bill Barazetti was a strong and willingly man to risk his life for the lives of children and people of the Holocaust. Bill did not stop to count how many kids he was saving, or telling people how great he was in front of people.

Websites:
http://www.kindertransport.org/quilts/quilt3/q0302.htm

http://philosemitism.blogspot.com/2008/01/werner-theodore-barazetti-swiss-hero-of_14.html

http://db.yadvashem.org/righteous/family.html?language=en&itemId=4013808

HOLOCAUST ESSAY

Riley Piccione

World War II started September 1, 1939, when Adolf Hitler and Nazi Germany invaded its Eastern neighbor Poland. In Europe, the war was based primarily around Germany, led by the Nazis. The Nazis were invading countries and mass exterminating Jewish people. It was a horrible time in the Jewish people's history, the Nazis exterminated roughly 6 million Jewish people during the Holocaust. The word "Holocaust," from the Greek words "holos" (whole) and "kaustos" (burned), was historically used to describe a sacrificial offering burned on an altar according the History channel's website. The Holocaust was a rough time for many people, not just Jewish people. World War II in Europe was started by a man named Adolf Hitler. Early in Hitler's life he joined a political party in Germany called the Workers' Party. This group spoke out aggressively regarding poor German economics. This group later changed into the National Socialist German Workers Party, or the Nazi party, led by the fuhrer Adolf Hitler. This group believed that the "Aryan Race," caucasian people with blond hair and blue eyes, were the supreme race. This supreme race had no flaws according to the Nazis. Hitler wanted everyone else dead. During World War II, he killed Roma Gypsies, Jehovah's witnesses, people who resisted, people who are homosexual, all priests and pastors who did not want to change their religion and be Christian, African American children, and every person in an interracial marriage had to divorce or both were sent to concentration camps.

During this horrific time in German history, most people just stood there and stood by, because anyone caught helping Nazi targets would be punished by death. A few people took action these people are heroes. A few knew that something must be done. One hero is named Paul Grueninger.

Before World War II, Paul Grueninger was a hero, but in a completely different kind of way. Paul Grueninger was a football player, a World War I veteran, and a police officer in Switzerland. In the 1914-1915 season, Paul Grueninger helped SC Bruhl, his professional football club, win the only championship they have ever won. He had to retire his football career when World War I started. He served as a lieutenant in World War I. He joined the Swiss police force after the war. He was doing well and becoming more and more famous in his city, St. Gallen. He moved up in the ranks and was promoted to border patrol.

Paul Grueninger was a man born in Switzerland on October 27, 1891. Grueninger became a Swiss border patrol officer. He patrolled the border between Austria and Switzerland. In 1938, the border was closed so that no one could enter

Switzerland unless they had the proper permits. In Austria the situation was getting worse for the Jewish people. The Nazis were rounding up Austrian Jewish people and sending them to concentration camps. Many Jewish people tried to get into Switzerland illegally from Austria. Grueninger was told by the country's officials not to let any of these refugees pass. Paul Grueninger completely disregarded their instructions and secretly let the refugees into Switzerland. He knew that if he was caught he would be punished, but he did it anyway.

Paul Grueninger falsified the paperwork so that the documents stated that the refugees entered Switzerland before March 1938, when Switzerland closed off its borders. He also falsified the number of entries and the status of refugees in his district. Paul Grueninger was such a nice man that he also bought winter clothes for the refugees, who were forced to leave their belongings, with his own money.

Paul Greninger was finally caught by the Germans and turned into the Swiss government. He was evicted off of the police force and put on trial. He was charged with illegally permitting the entry of 3,600 Jewish people into Switzerland. He also was charged with protecting individual Jewish people and helping them deposit their valuables. He was put on trial. The trial lasted two years. He was found guilty of breach of duty. His retirement benefits were forfeited. He was fined and had to pay for the trial costs. This unjust punishment forced him to live in difficult conditions for the rest of his life because he had little money. He finally received a letter of apology in 1970, thirty-two years later because of widespread protest. The Swiss government considered the idea to reimburse Paul's improperly forfeited retirement benefits in 1995. The only problem was that Paul Grueninger died in 1972.

In conclusion, Paul Grueninger was a hero who put others' lives before his own did not consider the consequences to himself. He realized that he could eventually be caught and punished, even being put to death. But, under strict instructions not to let any Jewish people go through the border and refuge in Switzerland, he still let them pass through into Switzerland. He was caught by the government and left with nothing. Even after that, he still said that he did not regret what he did and he would do it again. This is the definition of a true hero.

ONE PERSON CAN SAVE THOUSANDS OF LIVES

Samantha Lingao

There were many heroes during the Holocaust who risked their lives to help defend the helpless people from the terror of Hitler. One of them was Knud Dyby. He was a Danish hero who helped save thousands of lives during the Holocaust. With the ability to access confidential information Knud saved many people. He risked his life for strangers and is an inspiration to many people today.

Knud Dyby was born in Denmark in 1915. His father worked in the printing business, giving him a wealthy childhood. During the early stages of his adulthood Dyby followed his father into the printing business after completing college, but later decided he wanted to enlist in the military instead of taking on his father's business. Dyby was accepted to the military at age twenty and given the job of Guard due to his good looks. He would joke around at times how good looks must've been at a low back then. After his service as Guard he decided to take upon the job of a national police officer. As a police officer Knud had special access to classified information which later helped him hide the Jews.

When word was spread the Germans were planning to invade Denmark Knud Dyby, who was only twenty-six at the time and as a police officer he knew he had to help. As a devoted sailor and police officer Knud knew the best places to hide the Jews. He knew where to hide the Jews and what shorelines he could safely transport them near. When news spread the Germans were almost to Denmark, Knud, along with other people, gathered around eight thousand Jews, over the next few weeks, and smuggled them across a narrow body of water between Denmark and Sweden. Knud and several other secret organizations helped Jews along the way to ensure they were safely escorted. Places like hospitals, homes, docks, and schools were secretly filled with Jews who were waiting for help.

As well as saving the Jews Knud Dyby was an active member of the Danish-Swedish Refugee Service, an organization that helped save many other Jews and innocent victims from Denmark and Sweden and also participated in the October 1943 rescue of almost 7,200 Jews. Knud Dyby was a very generous and noble man. When a chance to stay silent and watch the gruesome event or to risk his life to save many others, Knud Dyby stood up, which made him a hero.

Knud Dyby was a hero in several ways. He was a brave and unselfish man. Risking his life for others while knowing the consequences he may receive. He didn't have to think when he heard the news that the Germans were planning on exterminating the Jews. He had a selfless heart to save the innocent. He treated strangers like family and didn't hesitate to help. He acted as if they were long time friends and family members, welcoming them into his life that had suddenly changed. He knew the right thing to do and put it to action. He stood up for what he believed was right and in doing so saved numerous people.

Even years after the war he stayed a quiet and modest man. He didn't brag about his story and when asked about it still didn't say much. He didn't expect or ask for any reward. The only reward he had was the ability to say he helped. He helped save lives, a privilege many don't have. It was in 2004 Knud was named a Righteous Among Nations hero. Over the years he has earned a few other recognition awards for his services in the Holocaust and saving the victims, but still stayed a very soft-spoken person.

In 2011 Knud died, at age 96, a humble and well respected man. I honor him today by writing this and for one other reason. To make sure a Holocaust never happens again and to make people aware of the one out of countless others who didn't stand silenced, and were heroes during the hectic time.

When I think of the Holocaust I no longer think of the bad Hitler and his followers had done. I think about the good others did to stand up and help the victims. For all the bystanders, I wish they would've helped knowing what big effect it would have on the world, or even our country itself. But if it happens again I'll know that I can make a difference. Even by saving one life, that's one less person dead.

Knud Dyby was a great person. He's a role model to me and inspires me to help during troubled times. It was seventy years ago he protected the Jews and other innocent people, and yet he is still is recognized today. He was a truly heroic person. The Holocaust is a tragic event in our history, but with the assistance of people like Knud Dyby we can prevent it from happening again

DR. PETER ZURCHER, HOLOCAUST HERO

Sofia A. Borrego

In our generation when someone says "hero" they might think of "Captain America," "Iron Man," "Super Man," or some other fictional character. Most people in the world do not realize that there are truly heroes in real life. Our heroes may not have super powers like flying, invisibility, transportation, laser eyes, etc. but it is all that we need in our world of no peace. We are all heroes who are not greatly recognized, but I would much rather be recognized by one person than not at all. Everyone and everything is a hero, in its own way, to the world and helps the universe keep its balance.

The Holocaust was a catastrophe to many Jews that no one will ever forget. Many innocent people feared Hitler and the power he had and controlled. The government took Jews and put them in extermination camps which were equipped with gas chambers for the purpose of exterminating the Jews. At extermination camps with gas chambers, all the prisoners arrived by train. Sometimes entire trainloads were sent straight to the gas chambers, but usually the camp doctor working subjected individuals to selections, were a small amount of people were considered fit to work in the slave labor camps. After the Jews died, dentist prisoners would extract the gold fillings in their teeth with pliers and cut women's hair. The government used the Jews for "medical" experiments. The most famous physician was Dr. Josef Mengele, who worked in Auschwitz. His experiments included putting subjects in pressure tubes, testing drugs on them, freezing them, attempting to change eye color by placing chemicals in children, and more. It reflected badly on the people of many states and had a very negative strong effect in the 1930's. With every mistake comes a great lesson, and many people saw the mistakes of the Holocaust. Eleven million people died for no good reason. Most died knowing and living what they believed. The people of the 1930's were not all bad, or made a big mistake. There were people who knew the good actions between the bad ones, and one of those people was Dr. Peter Zurcher.

Dr. Peter Zurcher was a Swiss businessman in wartime Budapest. In 1944, he was hired by Vice-Consul, Carl Lutz. Carl Lutz was the Swiss Vice-Consul in Budapest, Hungary from 1942 until the end of World War II. Carl is credited with saving over 26,000 Jews, the largest rescue operation of Jews of the Second World War. Peter worked in the Department for Safeguarding the Interests of Foreigners in the Swiss Embassy, and was able to save Jews from deportation. Peter risked his life for a woman named Maria Kromos. As soon as the Szalasi government seized power on October 15, 1944, the Jewish houses were closed, and Maria turned to Zurcher for help.

Zurcher then sent four men, dressed in Arrow Cross uniforms to arrest her. After the men in uniforms "questioned" her, she was released and accompanied back to Zurcher, who was waiting at the Swiss Legation. But he realized he could not hide her there. He took her to his own house and she stayed there for six weeks. Maira was then working for Peter as his secretary. Peter is credited with saving the Jews in the Swiss-protected houses in the ghetto when he found out that the Arrow Cross planned to evacuate and most likely murder the Jews. On October 22, 1998, Yad Vashem recognized Peter Zurcher as Righteous Among the Nations.

Peter has been admired for years because he had the bravery and faith of thousands of souls inside one man. Little do the people in our generation know about the heroes this world actually has. Even though you meet some people who seem like the hardest and coldest people, they were once as soft as water. So when you see someone doing a good deed, admire on how much respect and loyalty that person has inside of them. It might be the first or last time they help someone, but at least they did a good thing. If someone wants to be a hero, they should go and be a hero. No one can stop them, except for themselves. Being a hero is a person who is admired for courage, outstanding achievements, or noble qualities. The dictionary explains that a hero is a person invested with heroic qualities in the opinion of others. Being a hero is something a person achieves by an action.

We can all be mad, mean, frustrated, scared, irresponsible, etc., but that does not change who we can be if we really want it and do something about it. Sometimes if people in our world really tried and earned something, they could be unstoppable and accomplish what they believe in. No one would be able to discourage them, because they believed enough to not give up, and chased their dreams. Dr. Peter Zurcher was truly a hero who lived up to the opinion of many people who lived during the Holocaust.

HOLOCAUAST HERO

Sofia Bustos-Bennett

Paul Grueninger was nothing short of a hero. Instead of turning away, like most people did, this Swiss man faced the problem. He knew there would most likely be consequences, but he knew that he was saving many Jews from torture or death during the Holocaust. He has been honored in many ways and is recognized across the world for his brave actions. Anyone can look up to Paul Grueninger as a role model for our lives.

Paul Grueninger was born in Switzerland in 1891 on October the 27th. He was a Swiss Border police commander. He helped Austrian Jews when they didn't have the proper paperwork, instead of sending them back to Austria. He knew that sending them back to Austria would result in them feeling judged and persecuted. Antisemitism was the official state policy of Austria and they would most likely be persecuted everyday for their religion. His job was to send Jews wanting to cross the border without proper paperwork back to Austria. He soon realized that he was doing the wrong thing.

Grueninger realized how many Austrian Jews were scared and how much they wanted to come to Switzerland. His job was to send Jews wanting to cross the border without proper paperwork back to Austria. He began to notice the desperate Jews trying to cross the border illegally. Then Grueninger began to change the Jews' documents. He made it seem that the refugees had entered Switzerland before March 1938. March 1938 was when Switzerland became a restricted country to enter.

Grueninger then decided to do even more. He turned in reports that had flawed information. He lied about many things on the reports including the status of the Jewish refugees and how many arrived each day. Even after all that, Grueninger tried

373

to thwart plans of finding those who entered illegally. He truly tried his very best to help the Jews. At times, he even used his own things to help the desperate Austrian Jews. For example, he paid out of pocket to buy winter clothes to keep them warm. Grueninger was a brave man who risked himself for the goodness of others.

Of course, Grueninger had to know that there would be consequences if his actions were discovered. He did it anyway because he felt that his original job was wrong. He knew that sending them back to Austria would be painful for them mentally. He helped 2,000 to 3,000 Austrian Jews before getting caught. Once he was caught his life changed forever. Grueninger would never be physically punished or tortured, but the consequences were tough on him.

The Germans tipped off Swiss authorities to what Grueninger was doing. First off, they took away his job so he couldn't save anymore Jews. Next, they stripped him of his police rank and his pension. He had to move on with no pension, a payment from your employer after retiring, which was very hard on him. He lived in poverty in the years to come and even died a poor man. He knew that he was doing something wrong, but technically he was doing the right thing. Later in 1940 he was put on trial and was accused of breach of duty. He was then found guilty of breach of duty.

His life after that became difficult and a struggle, but Grueninger said he never regretted what he did to help the Jews of Austria. He even directly said his thoughts on his actions, "It was basically a question of saving human lives threatened with death. How could I then seriously consider bureaucratic schemes and calculations?" Grueninger said to explain his motivation to do what he did. A couple years later many people began to protest against the Swiss government. At the time, Grueninger was living a poor life. He struggled and tried to get jobs, but that was extremely hard in Switzerland with a criminal record. After some of the protesting the government knew they had to do something. The Swiss government decided to send Grueninger a letter. It was an apology letter that wasn't especially friendly. The letter wasn't rude, but it was to some extent reserved. However, they held back from reopening Grueninger's case. They also did not give him his pension back. Eventually, Grueninger died without ever receiving a pension or a clear criminal record.

About 23 years after Grueninger died, the Swiss government began to work toward clearing his criminal record. Some judges attempted to rehabilitate him, but the first try to do this was declined by the Swiss council. Another attempt was made and Grueninger was finally rehabilitated. It is sad that Grueninger never got to see his criminal record cleared, but at least it was cleared. Grueninger didn't deserve what happened to him, but it was expected since he did break the law.

Paul Grueninger was the true definition of a hero. He didn't wear a cape or have any superpowers, but he did stand up for what he believed in. He realized that the number of illegal Austrian Jews kept growing and growing. He also knew that he had to do something and he couldn't just be a bystander during the Holocaust. During the Holocaust, if you watched the horrible things happen you were participating in it. Grueninger would not tolerate it and he stood up for what he believed in. A hero is someone who risks themselves for the goodness of others and stands up for what they believe in. Grueninger did both of those things and many more hero-like things.

Even though Grueninger lived most of his life forgotten and poor, he still affected many people. He helped thousands of Jews who will always thank him. He can be classified as a Swiss border police commander, a football player, and a Righteous Among the Nations. Not to mention, a true, brave, and honorable hero. He may have been forgotten for a while, but he will never be truly forgotten for his life-saving actions.

KNUD DYBY: RIGHTEOUS AMONG THE NATIONS: THE STORY OF A TRUE HERO

Theresa Tran

The Holocaust was the "systematic, state-sponsored, bureaucratic persecution and murder" of millions of innocent people by the Nazi regime and its collaborators. The cause of this horrific event was the faulty conjecture that some groups of people were "racially inferior" to others and were therefore unworthy to live. Adolf Hitler, the leader of the Nazi regime and mastermind behind the Holocaust, spread this ideology and misled the Germans into butchering and oppressing the "racially inferior" people, the main victims being six million Jews living in Europe. This widespread massacre intimidated many people to turn a blind eye to the evil the Nazis were committing. However, a minority decided to break out of their roles of bystanders to become heroes who put their lives at risk to save the innocent and helpless. Knud Dyby was one of these brave and righteous people whose good deeds deserve to be remembered and commemorated today.

The main evil mastermind behind the Holocaust was Adolf Hitler. As Fuhrer, or chancellor, of Germany, Hitler was able to convince the Germans that they were superior to everyone else and that all unnecessary and non-idealistic people did not deserve to live. By wording his message craftily, Hitler spurred the Germans to take action to eliminate the Jews, Romas, sick, and disabled peoples, among others, living in Germany; age had not provided Hitler with a reason to show mercy, and both young and old people alike were slaughtered in gruesome ways. The German dictator was quite open minded to the many ways a person could be murdered, and the causes of his victims' deaths were of a wide variety. Death marches, hangings, gassings, malnourishment, sickness, gunshot wounds, and work "accidents" were only a few ways the Nazis killed the oppressed people.

Although many people supported the Nazi regime's message, many also disagreed with it. Despite this, the majority of the people who disagreed unfortunately decided to either ignore or become collaborators of the Nazis' crimes out of fear of being subjected to the same punishments as the oppressed peoples. This is why the heroes' and Knud Dyby's decisions to oppose the Nazi regime and the Holocaust were so remarkable. Even knowing the danger of death, the heroes decided to continue hiding and transporting the oppressed people away from Hitler's clutches.

Knud Dyby was born in Randeis, Jutland, Denmark on March 28, 1915. He was drafted into the military at the age of 20 and assigned to be a Guardsman at the Royal Palace in Copenhagen. Upon completing his military service, Dyby decided to join the national police force in Copenhagen. Little did he know that he could soon put his connections and skills as a policeman to use. While he was traveling around Germany in 1937 and 1938, Dyby saw first-hand the true nature of the Nazi regime. After witnessing the horrific actions the Nazis performed, Knud Dyby immediately joined several underground resistance groups, including the Danish-Swedish Refugee Service. Over the war years, Dyby used his status as a Danish State policeman to deflect attention from the Nazis away from himself and the Resistance and supply the Danish Resistance with intelligence information and documents about the Nazis' plans. Dyby also actively took part in sabotage operations and in the rescues and escapes of Danish Jews by way of boats. Since Knud Dyby was an avid sailor, he was able to smuggle many Danish Jews into fishing shacks. The Jews lived there until a skipper, or boat captain, could be found to transport them to a safer location such as Sweden.

As Dyby continued his underground operations, his actions eventually became known to the German authorities, and he became a wanted man. Nonetheless, Dyby decided to continue his relaying of information to the Resistance under his new changed name, Knud Dyby, which he used as his official name after the war. Until the war ended, Dyby continued his underground activities of sending nearly daily reports to the Resistance in Sweden, sabotaging the Nazis' plans, and assisting in the escape of nearly all of the Jews living in Denmark.

In 1945, as Allied forces marched further into Nazi-occupied territories, they stumbled upon many concentration camps with large ditches filled with bodies, rooms of baby shoes, and gas chambers with fingernail marks on the walls, all proof of the brutality of the Nazis and freed the captives from the SS soldiers. Had Knud Dyby not contributed to the rescue of Danish Jews, many of them would have most likely become a victim of that cruel fate of death. Although his actions may not have seemed like much compared to the whole resistance force against the Nazi regime,

Knud Dyby managed to save lives, every which one is precious, and earned the title of not only a hero but also of a righteous person.

Knud Dyby was honored by the U.S.A. and the U.K. in 1957. Many organizations like Yad Vashem recognized him as Righteous Among the Nations and a Hero of the Holocaust for his heroic deeds, courage, and humanitarian actions, which included not only the hiding of Jews but also the providing of assistance to downed pilots and escaped soldiers. His actions during World War II are remarkable examples for the future generations to look up to, follow, and imitate. Knud Dyby has shown the people how to live their lives by courageously standing up for what they believe is right and never allowing themselves to succumb to evil, so that another event similar to the Holocaust might never happen again.

ROSA NAEF: HOLOCAUST HERO

Alexis Dozier

The Holocaust was the terrible genocide of millions and millions of innocent Jewish people, homosexuals, the crippled, mentally insane, Jehovah's Witnesses, Slavic people, and Romas. This tragic event happened in 1933 and continued to kill until 1945. The Holocaust happened because one man, Hitler, was elected for Chancellor in Germany by the people of Germany. He and millions of followers, called Nazis, influenced people to take his heinous claims against Jews and the other oppressed people. He took advantage of his high position in the government to eliminate the people he did not think were not worthy to breathe his air. The Holocaust took place in all of Germany and many other places in Europe. Hitler's only solution was to exterminate these people.

Through all of this horrific tragedy, there were still many people who knew what Hitler was doing was wrong and cruel. One example of these kind hearted people was named Rosa Naef or Rosli. Rosa was born in Switzerland. As a toddler, Rosa knew as a toddler she wanted to help and heal people. When she was older, she helped Dr. Albert Schweitzer at his hospital in Lambarene, Africa. Afterwards she went to France, a few years of working at Dr. Schweitzer. She was put in charge of the Red Cross. The previous head of Red Cross, Mr. Frank, had brought about one hundred refugees from Austria and Germany to the hospital she ran in France, and the small place was overflowing with people. The hygiene of the hospital was not acceptable for Rosa. Children were quickly becoming terribly sick because of the poor upkeep of the hospital. Naef reported these conditions to Maurice Dubois, the director of another Red Cross near hers. He promptly moved everyone to a castle not far from the previous shelter.

This castle was a gold mine for Rosa and the children. It had big rooms and plenty of space for the children to roam and play. However, not all was perfect. The castle lacked the essentials of water, electricity, a proper sewage system, a clinic, and a schooling system. Nevertheless, Rosa still persevered and managed to fix these problems. She fixed the pipes and lights. Adults volunteered to work in the clinic and the children were provided school according to age.

The now permanent shelter was going great. The children excelled in their schoolwork, learning not only academics, but music as well. Unfortunately, on August 26, 1942, the castle received an unwanted visitor. During the night, gendarmes, or armed police officers, showed up in their cars ready to pick a fight. Six gendarmes trudged up the stairs to the dorms of the children and took down the names of all the children sixteen and older. Rosa then told the children to get dressed. She said they were going to another camp. The officers had arrested 45 children. Rosa quickly called Maurice knowing he would know what to do. She knew where the children were headed. Going to this camp was the first step until deportation to worse camps, like Auschwitz. So, she set out on her bicycle and her bike ran out of air. She found a taxi. The children were on a train to Portland and when the children saw her, they were ecstatic. They knew if she was there, everything would be okay. She had a calming effect on them. As they were about to board, Naef came running telling them they've been set free.

All was well until Germans invaded France in 1942. Rosa had a group of people to watch for gendarmes. There was a secret hideout in the attic above the church if the police got through. This was called the onion room because they used to dry onions there. The password to get into the onion room was "shortcut." The extremes that Rosa went through were not enough. She had to find a way to get the children out of France. She talked to people to give them homes before they crossed to border. Four children were scheduled to cross the border. The travels ended well. Rosa then continued to send out more groups of these children. On one travel with six kids, they were caught in the forest by police. Only one girl escaped across the border because the border police felt sorry for her. After Rosa heard of this failed mission she knew that the raids for the children would be more frequent from then on. She then hid the children in nearby farms and the onion room. Rosa was then dismissed from her job because of Switzerland's neutrality in the war. She was disobeying orders by hiding these children. Rosa moved to Denmark because she heard Denmark had saved most of its Jews. When Yad Vashem gave her the award of excellence she politely declined. At another ceremony Yad Vashem, presented her with the award she finally accepted. She died in 1996.

Rosa's magnificent act of selflessness saved so many innocent lives of children during the holocaust. Rosa's act of kindness inspires many people today to go against the majority and do what they think is right, even if it might be frowned upon by others. Rosa Naef is a true hero of the Holocaust.

ANNA CHRISTENSEN, A DANISH HERO

Ana Riley-Portal

The Holocaust was a horrific period of time in the recent history of the world. It touched the lives of many people all throughout Europe. In 1933, approximately 9 million Jews lived in the 21 countries that ended up under the occupation of Nazi Germany in Europe, during the Second World War. By 1945 two out of every three European Jews had been exterminated. Adolf Hitler was the leader who orchestrated this heinous genocide and he was aided by individual groups and entire nations motivated by racial hatred toward Jews. Hitler and the Nazis blamed Jews for all the social and economic problems. Hitler and his Nazi Party gave birth to the "Final Solution," a euphemistic way of referring to the systematic extermination of the Jewish population. Millions of Jews perished during the Holocaust, with very few surviving.

Among those heroes who helped those who survived was a woman named Anna Christensen from Nyborg, Denmark. Anna assisted in the rescue of 40 Jewish children. She was an active member of the International League for Peace and Freedom. After Hitler rose to power, Jewish refugees began to pour into Denmark from Germany and Austria, in the 1930s. A group was created whose mission was to save Jewish children from German government persecution. This group came to be known as Youth Aliyah. The group trained children for agricultural work in preparation for the move to Eretz, Israel. A number of these children arrived in Nyborg, Denmark. When the children first arrived in Nyborg, Anna Christensen enrolled them openly in the local school. On April 9, 1940, the Germans invaded Denmark; the Danish authorities were frightened about the fact that these Jewish children were enrolled in their schools. This caused Danish authorities to ban Jewish children from attending their schools. Because of this change, Anna Christensen decided to convert her cellar into a classroom for Jewish children.

Anna Christensen began to teach the children general subjects while the group leaders taught them other specific subjects. The German occupation of Denmark made the lives of Jewish people much harder and more dangerous. Jewish people were being taken to concentration camps and exterminated. When this happened, Anna Christensen began to organize different places for the children to hide in. She did this with the help of her friends. Anna inspected the homes where she would send the children to hide from the Nazis. She then would visit them twice per week and during festivals, continuing to teach them various subjects. Anna also cooked traditional dishes for the children to enjoy while hiding, so they would have some sort of normalcy in their lives at such a scary time. Anna Christensen was a kind and loving woman. She treated the children as a mother would treat her own young.

Anna made sure the children knew that she was always there for them. She did everything she could to encourage the children and lift their spirits.

In the fall of 1943, events took a turn for the worse for the Jewish people in Denmark. The Gestapo, the official secret state police of Nazi Germany, began to round up Jews in Copenhagen. The Danish police refused to assist the Gestapo in smashing down the doors of Jewish people and letters of protest were read at most churches to demonstrate that they were against this injustice. Danish Jews were more fortunate than Jews in other countries. The Danish people and their government refused to cooperate with the "Final Solution" and most Jews living in Denmark survived because the Danish people helped them escape to Sweden. The time came to help smuggle the children out of occupied Denmark. This was when Anna Christensen began to formulate a plan to take the children out of the country in order to save their lives. The Danish underground movement, a Danish Nazi resistance group, helped Anna to hide and smuggle the children out of Denmark into Sweden. Due to these efforts, Anna was able to save the lives of 40 Jewish children from extermination. After the war ended, Ana Christensen continued to have contact with "her children" through the years. She would send cards to them on the eve of every festival. She ultimately visited Israel in 1966 when "her children", now adults, invited her as their guest.

The Holocaust ended the lives of millions of innocent Jews. This time in history was a shameful event that the world can never repeat. Luckily, there were people like Anna Christensen who helped and protected the Jews during this time in Denmark. Anna Christensen was recognized as "Righteous Among Nations" by Yad Vashem on May 31, 1966. Yad Vashem is the world center for research, documentation, education, and commemoration for the Holocaust. There were many righteous people who helped save lives in this dark period of modern history. Brave people like Anna should never be forgotten. They risked their lives for the sake of others. It is also very important that this time in history is never forgotten. The Holocaust must never happen again. Those who forget history are doomed to repeat it.

A WORLD NOT TO BE FORGOTTEN

Andrew Monteverde

World War II, a time of sadness, and hatred brought to the world after World War I, especially for Jews, because of the Holocaust. The Holocaust was the brutal execution of 6 million Jews by the Nazi party during World War II. The Holocaust lasted about twelve years (1933-1945). Adolf Hitler, a German, was elected chancellor of Germany, led the Nazi Party, and practically started World War II. The Nazis believed that there were too many Jews in Germany, but eventually the party targeted all Jews, and

380

anyone who got in their way would be treated as if they were a Jew by the Nazis. The Nazis did not murder just Jews, they also killed Romas, or Gypsies, and mentally and physically disabled patients. Patients were killed because they would make bad slaves not able to do work. Basically anyone who could do work was kept as a slave, except children under the age of twelve were killed. The Nazis did not just murder Jews, but tormented and tortured them, and placed Jews in ghettos and concentration camps. For example, Nazis would shoot Jews, and let them fall in hole while they were still alive. This process continued until the hole was filled. Sadly, most people in the world knew this was happening to the suffering Jews, but didn't care or were not able to help, but there are people who did help, and prevented thousands of lives lost. Some of these people who helped were doctors who betrayed the Nazi party for the sake of Jews. Three people that did help Jews are Dr. Harald Feller, Gerhart Feine, and Georg Ferdinand Duckwitz.

One man who helped protect Jews was Dr. Harald Feller of Switzerland. In 1944 Dr. Feller became head of the Swiss legation after Maximilian Jaegar in Budapest, Hungary. Dr. Feller worked hard to protect and rescue Jews. He worked with other neutral legations by endlessly hounding the Horthy and Sztojay governments to stop killing, torturing, and deporting Jews. By giving fake passports and shelter to members of the Swiss legation, targeted by the Arrow Cross party, Feller saved many Jewish lives. The Arrow Cross party was very similar to the Nazi party, except they targeted mostly Jews in Hungary. Arrow Cross party members also wore green coats, and created their own version of the swastika. As the war was at its end, Feller hid Jews in the basement of the house he lived in, in Budapest, but was caught, arrested, and sent to prison in Moscow for one year, from February to February. Without a doubt, Dr. Harald Feller is a wonderfully stubborn man to risk his life to save hundreds of Jews.

Another person who saved Jews was a Swedish man named Gerhart Feine. Feine risked his life by betraying Minister Veesenmayor and SS Colonel Adolf Eichmann, two high ranking members of the Nazi Party, to save Jews. Eichmann and Veesenmayor had plans to murder and deport Jews in Budapest, but Feine told the neutral legations before the plans took place. Because of Feine's bravery, he made what would have been a very dangerous and challenging job much easier, and saved Jewish lives because Nazis would be an obstacle. Even after his betrayal towards the Nazis, Gerhart was never caught for this. Gerhart Feine took the biggest gamble he would ever portray in, risked his life, and won saving lives. Obviously, Gerhart Feine has also won the right to be a called a hero, not only for risking his life for Jews, but for being a role model.

A Danish member of the Nazi Party, Georg Ferdinand Duckwitz of Denmark, was a Trade Attache to the German Embassy in Copenhagen, Denmark. An attache is someone who is part of an ambassador's staff, or someone who has a specialized area of responsibility. He informed the Prime Minister of Sweden when he found out that the Nazi party was planning to deport Danish Jews. Because of this, Duckwitz was able to get a safe haven in Sweden going and saved over seven thousand Danish Jews. Most of these very same Jews lived past the day World War II ended. Just like any betrayal, Duckwitz risked his life, but unlike most betrayals, he succeeded. Georg Ferdinand Duckwitz was offered and became the German Ambassador of Denmark after World War II ended. Clearly, Georg Ferdinand Duckwitz did the almost impossible and saved thousands of Jews' lives.

The Holocaust was a dark time for Jews during dark times in the world. A time where Jews were targeted by Nazis for absurd reasons, and absurd results of killing millions of Jews. Jews were killed, tortured, and deported to concentration camps. Unfortunately, most people were afraid of the power of the Nazi party, joined the Nazi party, or simply did not care about the Jews, but some people cared and made a difference. Thankfully, Dr. Harald Feller, Gerhart Feine, and Georg Ferdinand Duckwitz saved, risked, and sacrificed their lives to save thousands of lives of not only Jews, but non-Jews too who were also in need. In conclusion, these three men are truly inspirational for the good they have done to the world, and for their perseverance. They have proven themselves true heroes of the Holocaust.

NEVER FORGOTTEN

Chantal Nguyen

The Holocaust began January, 1933. The Holocaust was a mass slaughter of several million Jews, Romas (Gypsies), and mentally or physically disabled. Nazis believed that the Jews were the reason for their economic crises, and that disabled people were simply not worthy of living. Under Hitler's command, the Nazis started their reign of terror by taking over Germany and expanding in other parts of Europe. Concentration camps, transit camps, forced-labor camps, and ghettos were set up for Jews that survived. Those who were put in camps were expected to work in tough conditions. They were also given very little to eat. Especially Jews were given little to nothing to eat each day. From 1941 to 1944, many Jews were moved from Germany to other parts of Europe like ghettos or extermination camps where they were eventually killed. Almost 6 million Jews and 7 million other victims of the Nazis were murdered as a result of the Holocaust. Even though there were numerous people that joined Hitler in this destruction throughout all Europe, there were also people who stood up for what was right. However, they were never fully recognized. Those people are known as the "unsung heroes of the Holocaust."

Elisabeth Eidenbenz was born on June 12, 1913. She was the daughter of a Zurich pastor. Elisabeth was a teacher in Switzerland and Denmark before she joined the

Asociación de Ayuda a los Niños en Guerra ("Association to Aid Children in War"). As a volunteer in an aid team she traveled to Madrid to help mothers and children amongst the Spanish refugees. Elisabeth was relocated to southern France She soon turned an old abandoned mansion into a maternity home for Spanish refugees. The château was in poor conditions and was renovated. She is the official founder of the Mothers of Elne (also known as *Maternitat d'Elna* in Catalan, *Maternidad de Elna* in Spanish and *Maternité Suisse d'Elne* in French). The hospital was completely finished by November 1939. Each room was named after a city in Spain to remind those who stayed there of their roots. As a nurse, she aided sick children and mothers. Elisabeth was a kind hearted and generous woman that wanted nothing more than to help those in need. But she was more than just a nurse or a volunteer. She was a hero.

In November of 1942, Germans invaded and began rounding up the Jews in Vichy, France, also known as the "Free Zone." As the Germans were in search of Jews, Elisabeth sent them into hiding the first time the Germans came to the hospital. However, the second time the Germans searched the hospital, they demanded to take away a Jewish mother named Lucie. They told Elisabeth that they would take her instead if Lucie refused to leave. Elisabeth would have selflessly sacrificed herself, but Lucie insisted on going instead. Through "strict neutrality" imposed by the Swiss Red Cross, Elisabeth was told to "give up Jews, Tziganes, and Spanish refugees if you are requested and do nothing to shield them from the roundups." Despite the orders Elisabeth continued to help victims flee from the invasion. Between 1939 and 1944 she saved almost 600 children, mostly the children of Spanish Republicans, Jewish refugees and gypsies.

Elisabeth Eidenbenz's heroic actions were finally recognized in 2002. Many books were written and published in her dedication. Just before Easter in 2002, Elisabeth was reunited with 60 surviving people that she had rescued. Over the years she has won many awards due to her brave and righteous actions.

Between 1933 and 1945 Hitler, the leader of the Nazi party, killed almost two out of every three Jews who lived in Europe as part of the "Final Solution." The "Final Solution" is referred to the mass extermination of Jews. The Nazis relocated most of the Jews to concentration camps. Several people joined the Nazi party fearing that the Jews would lead to their nation's destruction. There were hundreds of people that were too afraid of what might happen to stand up for what they knew was unjust. But there were also heroes like Elisabeth Eidenbenz. Elisabeth was a nurse, teacher, and a volunteer that helped others. After seeing the horrid sight of many sick and wounded refugees, Elisabeth built a hospital dedicated to women and children that sought medical attention. When the Nazis made their way to the hospital to round up Jews and others to put in camps Elisabeth risked her life to help hide and transport many people. The second time she tried however she was caught in the act. Elisabeth was well aware of the consequences of what might happen if she was seen trying to shelter the Jews, but even so she decided to help. She was courageous for standing up to the Nazi even other people would not. She was selfless enough to risk her safety for many others. Elisabeth shows the importance of rising up to unjust acts. Elisabeth's kind and loving heart touched the lives of many people. Her gallant actions will forever leave an imprint in this world and should never be forgotten. No one should ever again have to face such a harsh and difficult time like millions of victims of the Holocaust did.

HORRIFIC PAST

Christina Altamirano

The Holocaust and Hitler will be remembered for the persecution and torment of Jews. The Holocaust is a tragic event that happened in Germany begining in 1933. When Hitler and the Nazis invaded and took over Germany, they wiped out of two thirds of the population of Jews living in Europe, killing them one by one and making them all suffer. The Nazis burned down synagogues, secluded the Jews from the Christians, excluded them from all apartments, homes, and hotels, and forced them to work for the Nazis by threatening them. This mourningful time affected and killed many just for the sake of one person's opinion. The Holocaust is an event that is horrifying and something we will never forget. Two amazing heroes rose from the shadows and helped those suffering during this time, and these people are Henry Thomsen and Ellen Margerthe Thomsen.

The Holocaust was a time when many Jews were persecuted and victimized by the Nazis and Hitler himself. When Hitler had won his campaign, many Jewish families fled to protect themselves from what was yet to come. The Jewish men were transported during the "invasion" to several cities and countries. They were transported to concentration camps and forced to do back breaking labor. This labor was for the benefit of the Nazis. They would build structures for Nazis only, which was one way they killed off the Jews. The women and children were told that they would be sent to paradise where they can do whatever they pleased. Although they were told this, it was far from the truth, women and children were sent to killing centers and gas chambers because they were of no use to the Nazis or the slave work force. Jews were sent everywhere but Germany, for many different reasons. Even though the Jews were persecuted they did not give up or refuse to help other Jews that were in a difficult position.

Many people tried to help Jews and bring them back to their homes and save their lives. Two of these heroes were Henry Thomsen and Ellen Margrethe Thomsen. This couple were inn keepers in a village called Snekkersten. These two people saved about 1,000 lives. Their inn was a meeting point where Jews and fisherman met to transport the Jewish to and from Switzerland. The amount of Jews staying increased quickly. Soon enough Henry started to transport Jews to his home himself. While Henry was out transporting the Jews to and from Switzerland, Ellen stayed at the inn taking care of all the Jews in their custody. Although Henry Thomsen's trips had been going smoothly and had not been caught yet his operation came to a halt. One of his neighbors had reported to the police that they had seen a group of Jews on a boat. The police had caught many Jews at Henry Thomsen and Ellen Margrethe Thomsen's inn. They had also soon afterward caught Henry and other fishermen, along with many other Jewish people. The couple were interrogated and brought to court but had no evidence to prove them guilty. He continued his operation soon after the trial. Then in August 1944 he was arrested again and sent to a concentration camp and he lived four more months there before dying. He died at age 38. Henry Thomsen and Ellen Margrethe were two heroes who saved many lives and have a legacy that will never be forgotten.

Henry Thomsen was a Holocaust survivor as well as a Holocaust hero. He was born September18, 1906. He was born in Denmark and was an innkeeper as a profession. He had a middle name of Christian. Henry Christian Thomson was Jewish. This man died on April 12, 1944. This man also lived to be 30 years old. He was married to a woman named Ellen Margrethe who became to be Ellen Margrethe Thomsen. As well as Henry, Margrethe was also an innkeeper with her husband. She was also born in Denmark along with her husband Henry. She was born in 1912. No one knows how old she lived to be or when she died. Even though we do not how Ellen Mergrethe Thomsen helped in the process of saving these innocent Jews, we do know that she was involved in the process of saving the lives of many Jews, whether it was taking care of them in the inn or looking out for the police. Henry Christian Thomsen and Ellen Margrethe Thomsen were two Holocaust heroes, survivor, and incredible people who saved many Jewish lives.

The Holocaust was a terrifying time for Jews and also for some Gypsies. Many people were killed and many people's lives were endangered. One of those heroes of the Holocaust was a couple living in Denmark. This couple owned an inn and hid many Jews to give them a place to live. These amazing people were Henry Thomsen and Ellen Margrethe Thomsen. Many people made a difference for others during the Holocaust but Henry and Ellen Thomsen made a huge difference by rescuing about 1,000 Jewish lives. These two people were reliefs of this horrible massacre and made a huge difference during this time. This horrific event has made me think of all the horrible things I have done. After learning deeply about the Holocaust I have realized that I have to be more careful about my actions. Also that I have to treat everyone the same no matter who they are. The Holocaust was an event no one will ever forget.

JUST ANOTHER ONE OF THE HEROES

Claudia Isabella Campos

The Holocaust was a time when the Nazis wanted to execute and wipe out the Jewish population for the Germans' own hardship. Many people just watched as their friends, neighbors, teachers, workmates, classmates, and maybe even family members were being taken away to concentration camps where they were being starved, mistreated and eventually killed. These camps were run by the Nazis, who were mostly Germans. In the concentration camps, men and boys over ten years old were put to work on buildings and machinery. Women, if there were any there that were able to work, were forced to make the clothes, blankets, and any material items needed by the Nazis. Many people were killed in these camps, most were women and the children who were under the age of ten. The Nazis thought that women and children under ten years were not worthy of life, that's why they killed them. Some people did help the Jews escape Germany by giving them fake passports and enough money to flee. Some people hid the Jews in their own homes. If they were caught with a Jew in their home they were to be executed. Many people were brave enough to do this for plenty of Jews. The war betraying the Germans and the Jews later became into a World War. World War Two to be exact. The countries that were involved in the Second World War were Germany, Italy, and Japan on the Axis Power. The Allies were Britain, France, Australia, Canada, New Zealand, India, Soviet Union, China and The United States of America. The person responsible for creating this chaos and horrible unforgettable events was Adolf Hitler.

Hans Schaffert was one of the unnoticed heroes. Hans Schaffert had studied theology at Basel University. He was sent on a mission in South France to a concentration camp that was supposed to last about six months. The name of the camp was Gurs. Gurs was his first contact with the misplaced Jewish refugees. A great amount of Jews there were baptized Jewish Christians. They were all being transferred to a different camp. The new compound was being strictly guarded from the outside bordered with heavily armed forces. The police were told from time to time to go check nearby houses to see if any Jews were hiding there. If any were found they were taken into the camp and brutally beaten and put in a freight train to be never seen again. Hans Schaffert had witnessed those horrible events. Hans even tried stopping the events that went on, but sadly could not. His heart ached and hurt for the Jews. Stonewalled and frustrated, Hans decided to help the prisoners waiting to be deported by handing out food to them. He would wait with the prisoners until the train would come and pick them up. He was saddened about this cruel experience. He often worried for the safety of the Jews. Hans Schaffert wrote letters and warned Marc Boegner, a fellow pastor, about the horrible treatment of the Jews.

He wrote, "This tragedy was the most devastating experience of my life." He later wrote that he would devote all his resources and strength rescuing abused, harmed, hungry, and scared Jews. Hans arranged for many slaves to flee to Spain or Switzerland. He gave many Jews money, either the German currency or the place they were going to be flee to. The French police started becoming suspicious of him and asked him to leave and return back to Switzerland. After he returned back home, he started to tell the pastor about all the refugees that he had helped over the years. After building up great relationships with the Jews he helped, he thought God was looking down upon them when he met them back at Switzerland. In 1967, Hans received the Yad Vashem medal for being very kind to the Jews. He told the people that he was not worthy of it and that he should had done something even more to help. He told everyone, "I acted out of my deep theological conviction that whoever does wrong to the Jewish people is doing wrong to God's property."

Many people died in the Holocaust, either trying to save the Jews or being one of the people the Nazis were after. We must pray for the souls who had lost their lives in the Holocaust and for there not to be another Holocaust or World War. We also should aim to not make the same mistakes again. To prevent another Holocaust we all just have to be more caring and understanding towards each other. We have to protect each other, like the people who provided shelter for the Jews or helped them flee. With his heart of gold, Hans Schaffert tried to help as many Jews as he can by warning other parts of the world, collecting fruit for the Jews, and much more. We should all try to be more like Hans Schaffert.

"WITH FISHING BOATS TO SWEDEN"

Colin Ryan

The Holocaust was an event in fairly recent history where 6 million European Jews were systematically murdered by the Nazis for the purpose of purifying Germany. In a series of rapidly heating events, starting with the disgrace of Germany in World War I and the election of their political party in 1933, Nazis (National Socialists) claimed that they would make Germany great again. Their idea of greatness was ridding Germany of anyone who they deemed racially inferior, namely: the Jews. With the annexation of Poland and the Night of Broken Glass in 1938, the plot to exterminate the Jews, known as the Final Solution, was put into action. In the next seven years, two- thirds of Europe's Jews were exterminated. This number might be even bigger without the bravery and sacrifice of the individuals who risked their lives to rescue the Jews. One family who made sacrifices to rescue the Jews was the Thomsen Family of Denmark.

The Danish situation during the Holocaust was different than most of the other countries in Europe. When World War II began, Denmark wished to remain neutral. Germany wanted to keep Denmark as a financial ally during the war, so they respected this request. In 1939 German and Danish leaders signed the German-Danish Non-Aggression Pact. This pact lasted less than a year before Germany invaded Denmark, but during the occupation Germany allowed Denmark to continue to govern itself. For the most part, daily life in Denmark remained the same for about three years, until in 1942 when the German Foreign Ministry decided to start deporting the Jews in Bulgaria, Hungary, and Denmark. With this, Danish citizens such as Ellen and Henry Thomsen rose up to save the Jews.

Henry Christen Thomsen was born in 1906; his wife, Ellen, in 1912. In the early stages of the German occupation, Henry and Ellen were involved in illegal cargo shipments to Sweden. Most of the Swedish population opposed the Nazis. Later on, however, when the news of the projected deportation of Jews in Denmark was released, they decided to smuggle Jewish refugees to Sweden instead of the illegal goods. Henry joined the movement to rescue the Jews very early in the process. The family owned an inn, which became the headquarters for the fishermen who transported the Jews to Sweden in their boats. Because it was too dangerous for the local Jews to stay in the inn, they arranged which local homes the Jews were to stay in. When there were enough Jews to fill one of the boats, Henry arranged which boat they were to travel in. Eventually, there were too many people to be transported, so he bought a boat to make the journey himself.

Henry often played the role of a double-agent. The Gestapo, or secret police of Germany, would frequently come to the inn and question him. Henry would pretend to be friendly and help them, but in reality he continued to work against them. He collected information from the Gestapo and used it to save multiple lives. He was arrested by the Gestapo in 1943 on accounts of smuggling Jews, but was released, due to lack of evidence against him. He continued his illegal rescues until he was arrested by the Gestapo for the second time in 1944. This time he was convicted and sent to the Neuengamme Concentration Camp in Germany. He died there on December 4th of 1944. He was 38 years old.

Ellen also played a role in the rescue of the Jews, even though she had two young sons to take care of at home. Ellen cooked food for nearly all of the fleeing Jews, and made sure it was delivered to the correct houses at which the Jews were staying. Ellen survived while her spouse died. Later, in 1968, Ellen and Henry were given the title of "Righteous among the Nations" by Yad Vashem. That same year, Ellen traveled to Israel and planted a tree in the Avenue of the Righteous.

The Thomsens' heroism was described firsthand in 1993 by one of the people they rescued, a Jewish woman named Sarah Posin, who was transported to Sweden in 1943 by Thomsen; along with the rest of her family. She had come to Denmark in

1938 to visit her uncle and his family. In 1943, her family was given news that it was possible to escape to Sweden through North Zealand. She met a member of the resistance named Joergen Gersfelt, who directed them to the Thomsens. The Thomsen family directed them to a safe home. The next day, the Posin Family was sent back to the Thomsen Inn. Mr. Thomsen brought them to his fishing boat and hid them aboard, and they successfully reached Sweden. This firsthand account proves the extent of which Henry Thomsen organized under pressure the rescue of the Danish Jewish population.

Henry and Ellen Thomsen's finest achievement came at a time when most people turned a blind eye to the atrocities being committed all around them. In Denmark during the Holocaust, citizens saved 95 percent of their local Jewish people. This happened in a time where Nazis murdered two thirds of Europe's Jews. The Thomsens were crucial to this incredible rescue of these innocent people. By following their example, we can try to prevent an event such as the Holocaust from happening and make a difference if such a tragic event ever happens again.

A DOUBLE AGENT IN SWITZERLAND

Cristina Maetsu

On January 30, of 1933, in Germany, the Nazi party started executing a plan called the Final Solution to kill all the Jews, Gypsies, Hungarians, Romanians, Poles, Slavs, Russians, Czechoslovakians, and many more, including the crippled, blind, and the too old or the too young to work. This terrible idea of anyone who was not of German descent was inferior to the Germans was sponsored by the government due to the election of Adolf Hitler who became Chancellor of Germany in 1934. This started the catastrophe called the Holocaust. Eleven million people died during this disastrous event and 6 million of them were Jews. However, even though the Germans were neighbors with this peaceful people, only a few helped them escape, including people from other countries such as the Swiss. One of these people who contributed to the saving of the Jews was Anton Buhler.

Anton Buhler was head of one of the Aliens Police Forces that had to protect the boundaries of Switzerland between Austria and Italy from illegal immigrants. Switzerland stayed neutral in the war to not get involved in other countries problems. Because Switzerland was neutral, immigrants were sent back to their home countries, including Jews who were sent back to Germany and were then killed. Buhler didn't want immigrants to be sent back home for fear that the Jews would be executed. So, when the Federal Parliament had a meeting, in Bern, he expressed his point of view. But this was to no avail since the organization itself did not agree. He decided to take matters into his own hands after that.

Mr. Buhler started by helping four Viennese immigrants who had no visas into Switzerland. The Viennese helped him create a channel for the refugees who would get off at Martinsburg between Austria and Switzerland where they would be let in with the help of the police on Mr. Buhler's orders. Buhler saved at least 30 people by letting them slide through the border. He smuggled a family into the town he lived in, called Chur, to keep an eye on them and they became good friends. Since Chur is a small town, people started getting suspicious of Buhler so he moved them to an abandoned boarding house.

Over the course of the years, people became even more suspicious of Buhler of smuggling people across the border because he would not speak against Jews or illegal immigrants. Eventually, an investigation was done on him but nothing was uncovered. Despite the closed case, suspicion continued and he was called a Jew friend. Buhler was never able to get a promotion after the case. However, he was better off than another police officer who was caught smuggling refugees to Switzerland. That man was left without a job and was given a fine for court expenses. However, even after hearing this, it did not deter Buhler from helping Jews and other refugees through the border. By the end of World War II, he had helped a total of 350 people.

Anton Buhler risked everything he had to save the Jews, illegal immigrants, and refugees escaping to Switzerland. Without him, those families would have never survived. He had the courage that thousands of people didn't have during the Holocaust. My impression of Mr. Buhler is that he was very courageous and that many should follow his example of having your own opinion and not just going with everyone else's beliefs.

ANTON BUHLER: SWISS UNSUNG HERO OF THE HOLOCAUST

David Harris

The Holocaust was perhaps one of the worst moments in the history of mankind. It was the unsuspected and pointless slaughter of Jews, Gypsies, the physically and mentally challenged, homosexuals, and other innocent but different people. The Holocaust was centered in Germany but branched out to many European countries bordering Germany and other parts of Europe. The Holocaust was the main reason for the Second World War starting in 1939 and ending in 1945. The Holocaust was organized and conducted by the notorious Adolf Hitler, who won the favor of the Nazi political party, and later the favor of the majority of Germany. The "final solution" of the Nazis was to exterminate all people who differed from the Nazis, especially the antagonized Jews who the Nazis blamed for their defeat in the First World War, and for the killing of Jesus Christ.

Many people helped the Jews during the Holocaust out of sympathy and pure kindness. The people helping Jews, and everyone else who was persecuted by the Nazis during the Holocaust and World War II, were from many different countries and religious backgrounds. Most who helped did not do so out of obligation, but because of kindness and what they believed to be right. They helped those trying to escape the Nazi Party in many ways. They supplied those fleeing with visas to escape Nazi controlled regions of Europe into safer countries such as the United States of America, Great Britain, and other countries that were allied against Germany. They also brought food to those in concentration camps food, they hid those being persecuted. A Swiss man by the name of Anton Buhler, who was born in 1890, openly defied laws and the Nazis to do what he considered right.

Dr. Anton Buhler, a part of the Aliens Police Force in Switzerland, had to oversee the removal of aliens, or non-citizen inhabitants of a country. During World War II, part of his Job was to turn away Jews seeking to enter into Switzerland illegaly. The chair of the organization, Dr. Rothmund, was openly against letting the Jewish aliens into Switzerland, which would be considered as defying the Nazis. Not many people during the time of World War II would dare to openly go against the Nazi Party by deliberately helping the Jews. Buhler and his associate, Paul Gruninger, on the other hand, were in support of letting the Jews into the country, regardless of defying the Nazis and Swiss law itself. Buhler and Gruninger let the Jews who had escaped from the Nazis stay in Switzerland. They were not only risking their jobs, but they could also be found out by the Nazis in the process, which could result in either imprisonment or death.

Buhler helped the Jews by either sneaking them across the Swiss border or directly intervening by giving direct orders to his officers to let the Jews into Switzerland. Buhler also ordered his border police to allow refugees without visas from Vienna, Austria into the administrative capital of the country, and later met the refugees allowing them to stay in Switzerland until they could get American visas that he would provide for them. He helped a lot of people in this manner; allowing some in and helping get some out with his status and position in the police force. He was able to get the Jews out of the country by having them go to a border station at Martinsbruck where the police under his command would telephone him for his orders to let the Jews leave the country. He did all of this illegally, which endangered his job, but he wasn't removed from office, even though he was called Jew Friend and lost his promotion. Gruninger, on the other hand, was charged with "misuse of office," and was expelled from the force, paying fines and covering all of court expenses. Buhler saw all that happened to his colleague, but was still determined to help the Jews in any way possible.

Anton Buhler was a courageous man who not only risked his job, all of his money, but also his family and his life. Using his position of power for a good cause instead of turning his back on the persecuted people, as many others in his position would do, Buhler saved over 300 Jews. Buhler gave up his house, provided shelter at an old and unused abandoned boarding house, and gave free visas to anyone who asked for his help and did so without expecting to get anything in return. Although Switzerland was for the most part against the Nazis, it was still a brave thing for him to willingly defy the Nazis, knowing the price that might have to be paid in turn. Buhler was accused of helping the Jews but was never found guilty, and was able to keep his job, his family, and his life. Even though ordered to do otherwise, and his associate being caught for doing the same. Buhler still did what he believed was right and saved hundreds of lives in the process.

THE TRAGEDY AND HEROES OF THE HOLOCAUST

Gavin Alder

The systematic murder of over 6 million people, primarily Jews, is known as the Holocaust. In 1933, the German dictator, Adolf Hitler, ordered the harassment and eventually the assassination of Jews in Europe. The Nazis believed that the Germans were "racially superior" and that the Jews were "inferior." German authorities also targeted the disabled, weak, religious dissidents, and unwanted. The Nazi regime established concentration camps to contain their targeted enemies. By 1945, nearly two-thirds of the Jewish population was killed. Allied forces began to encounter and free concentration camp prisoners. The death marches led by the Schutzstaffelor Protection Squad ended in May 7, 1945, the day the German armed forces surrendered to the Allies. Although, this was a tragic event in history, there were many heroes of the Holocaust who sacrificed their lives to help others escape execution.

There are many stories of heroic people who helped the Jews escape execution, but one of the most recognized was Harald Petersen. Richard and Erna Hausmann were Jews who escaped Germany shortly before World War II in 1939. They first traveled to Sweden, but their residence permits would not be renewed and they could not stay. Next, they traveled to a farm in Denmark and found work, with other Jews, on a farm in South Zealand. Richard worked for a farmer named Harald Petersen in the parish of Kongsted. Richard and Erna found work at another farm about a year later, and then gave birth to a son named Herman.

Harald and his wife, Agnete, moved to a farm outside of Copenhagen located in Risby, Herstedvester. Once again, Richard and Erna went to see Harald Petersen for a job. Harald hired Richard to be a herdsman on his farm.

In 1943, the Germans were looking to arrest the Jewish people. Harald Petersen offered to drive the Hausmanns to Copenhagen, so they could escape to Sweden. However, he had no gasoline and it was strictly rationed. He was able to fill his tank with kerosene and drove them to Copenhagen. For three days they tried to find a fisherman to take them to Sweden. Mr. Petersen found a trustworthy fisherman to take them safely to Sweden for the price of DKR 3,000 in Danish currency. Mr. Petersen told the Hausmanns that he got the money from a benevolent woman who wanted to remain unknown. However, Mr. Petersen actually paid the fisherman with his own money. Mr. Petersen risked his own life to help the Hausmanns escape. When the war was over the Hausmanns contacted their rescuer and stayed in touch with him. On March 28, 1990, Yad Vashem awarded Harald Petersen as Righteous Among the Nations. He is on the Wall of Honor and the ceremony was organized by the Israeli diplomatic delegation in Copenhagen, Denmark. He also received a medal and Certificate of Honor on March 30, 1993. It is unknown when Harald Peterson was born, but he passed away on January 1, 1994.

Many Jews traveled to Denmark to escape going to the concentration camps. Denmark is approximately 570 miles from Germany. It is the southernmost country in Scandinavia. Prior to World War II, there were approximately 7,800 Jews living in Denmark. There were about 6,000 Jewswho were natives of Denmark, and the rest were refugees. On April 19, 1940, the German army occupied Denmark. Denmark did not challenge German control, so the Germans let them continue to run their government and army independently. Things were fine until the spring of 1943, when tension between Denmark and Germany was brought on because Danish resistance groups increased their activities due to the victories of the Allied forces.

Many Jews tried to escape to southern Europe by hiding under train cars, but their attempts failed. However, those escaping to Sweden by boat were mostly successful. In late August 1943, the Danish government resigned because they did not want to comply with the German government's demands to deport the Jews. On October 1, 1943, German police started to arrest Jews. It was later discovered that German sources leaked information to Danish groups so they could warn the Jews. The Danish people or Danes helped the Jewish people reach the beach where fisherman took them to Sweden. The Danish government and many leaders of the Danish churches objected to the deportation of the Jews. Within three weeks 7,200 Jews and 700 of their non-Jewish relatives were taken safely to Sweden. It is still recognized today how the Danes saved many of the Jewish people.

The Holocaust was a desperate time for the Jews and numerous other groups and this horrible event will never be forgotten. However, there were heroes during this difficult time in history. Harald Petersen was one of these people. He helped a Jewish family get safely to Sweden by using his money and risking his own life. The Danish government and religious leaders also helped the Jews escape execution. The Holocaust may have been a horrible time in history, but there were many brave heroes who risked their lives to save others.

HELP IN TIMES OF HELPLESSNESS

Ivanna Forero Pretto

The Holocaust was the mass murder and persecution of over 6 million Jews and over 5 million other "inferior" groups under the Nazi policy to exterminate the Jews in Europe, known as the "Final Solution," over a period of 12 years, from 1933 through 1945. The massacre was orchestrated under Nazi rule, who were the winning party for the elections, spreading from Germany to many areas across Europe. The leader of this tyranny was Adolf Hitler, who successfully had convinced millions that Germans were the superior race and that Jews were lesser and a threat to the German community. Therefore, they should all be eliminated. Though Hitler's mindset was convincing and the majority was under his influence, some still recognized that his doings were inhumane. Despite the risks, people like Fred Reymond did their part in helping Jews through this difficult time period.

Fred Reymond, born Christmas Day, December 25ʾ 1907, and lived in the small town of Le Sentier in western Switzerland for the majority of his life. As a young man, Reymond enjoyed sports and was actually a champion wrestler. His athletic history caused for him to maintain an excellent physique, and because of this, he enlisted in the Swiss Militia Army, as any Swiss man in fit shape would at the time. He was positioned as an intelligence officer, a person employed to collect, compile, and/or analyze information. When he married, he and his wife, Lilete, moved up onto Mont Rioud, or Mont Risoux, where he grew to know the mountain paths very well. At the age of 33, Reymond was authorized to observe the territory controlled by German forces in eastern France, which was adjacent to Switzerland. Because of his occupation as a watchman, Reymond crossed the border frequently and worked with different agents. He was in an ideal position to sneak people across to Switzerland, where the majority of the population strongly opposed Nazism.

Through his surveillance activities, Reymond was introduced to several persecuted victims, many among them being Jews, from the Vichy France regime, which was the government of Marshal Philippe Pétain's regime from 1940 to 1944, and also the German occupying forces in Northern France. He felt compassion for the Jews and made a decision to find a way to help. Reymond's French agents escorted escapees to a secret meeting place near the border, where Reymond would smuggle them in through a frequently unguarded gate. After that, there was the process of evading the Swiss patrols, which had the area under their watch to a great degree. Then, it was necessary to obtain train tickets and other papers to send the runaways off, giving them money along the way, for their journey still left ahead.

There were, of course, many risks in smuggling people across the border. Reymond was risking his life, the lives of his family, and the lives of his agents, who had assisted him and taken a significant part in the process. For the escapees, not only was it their lives and the lives of the people they loved at risk, but it was also what was to await them when they'd be forced to return if discovered. They would be forced into camps, to do grueling labor, have minimal food, or just be killed at once. The danger of their discovery was greater when moving during the daytime so Lilette Reymond took them into their household and housed them and hid the refugees for a day or two at most until it was deemed safe to move. Food and protection was also offered for the departure as well. Reymond frequently crossed the border, which amounted to difficulty and suspicion with the Swiss custom officials. They believed he was smuggling goods, not people, and he was fined more than once for it. Reymond used his being a "smuggler" as a cover for his actual illegal actions.

Reymond proved to be a true hero who helped many people. His actions were recognized years after the Holocaust when a Swiss newspaper uncovered his story and his secret rescue missions, which he had not shared with others. A journalist, who had heard of him and what he did, called to interview him and to reveal about his missions. The journalist called him in to tell how he and his wife hid refugees and arranged their transportations to safely arrive in Switzerland. There was it publicly announced the account of Fred Reymond and from then on he and Lilette were known as one of the numerous Holocaust heros, who endangered their lives to help others.

In conclusion, the tragic and horrific occurrence that is the Holocaust killed over 11 million people, 6 million being Jews, and 1.1 million were only children. Hitler's tyranny started in 1933, when he became chancellor of Germany, and ended in 1945, after occupying many other countries in Europe, when he cowardly committed suicide after being warned Russia was a day away from overtaking his chancellery. His dictatorship turned many good people into Nazis, so many were reluctant to help the victims of the Holocaust because it jeopardized their lives and the lives of their loved ones. Luckily, there were still many who could not stand the inhumane and unlawful actions done to others and gave up everything to assist in caring for the suffering people who were victimized during Hitler's rule.

HOLOCAUST ESSAY

Jackson Grogan

In "The Voices of Auschwitz" Bart Stern states, "So I was hiding out in the heap of dead bodies because in the last week when the crematoria didn't function at all, the bodies were just building up higher and higher. So there I was at nighttime, in the daytime I was roaming around in the camp, and this is where I actually survived, January 27, I was one of the very first, Birkenau was one of the very first camps being liberated. This was my, my survival chance." Mr. Stern was a survivor of the Holocaust. The Holocaust was the systematic, government-sponsored murder of millions of Jews, Gypsies, Poles, Russians, and others. When the Nazis came to power in Germany in 1933, the Holocaust began. Jewish families were sent to concentration camps including Auschwitz, where they were tortured, starved, over-worked and killed.

Over 9 million Jews were killed, but fortunately there were some survivors. Some of the Jews escaped, some left Germany to Spain for their own protection. In the final months of World War II, the camps were moved and the Jews were transported by train, or on foot. These was called "death marches," and the Jews had to walk through desert or mountains. Some Jews were transported to the largest concentration camp there had ever been. Millions of people died there, some survived and lived today, some died by starvation some were killed, or burned in gas chambers.

There were many people who helped Jews escape to safety or help the Jews to go to a different nations to escape the Nazis. Raoul Wallenberg (1912-1947) was a person who helped thousands of Jewish families. He was a first secretary in Budapest, where he used his diplomatic status to issue protective passports to thousands of Jewish families to identify them as Swedish citizens. Irena Sendler (1910-2008) was another hero who saved lots of Jewish families. A Jewish sympathizer since her own childhood, Sendler and her friends made thousands of false documents to help Jewish families. These documents helped hundreds and thousands of Jewish families to escape and hide from the Nazis.

When the Holocaust was finally over, many survivors found protecting in displaced persons camps runned by the allies who fought against the Nazis. Between 1948- 1951, 700,000 Jews moved to Israel. Some of the Jews went to America and other nations looking for a home. When the last camp closed down, all the prisoner were free. Even though the Jews were free, some still faced hard times. Some of the Jews were probably farmers and they did not get their farms back. The Jews did not have the same rights anymore or the same respect.

The Holocaust was the most horrible thing and event that has ever happened in the history of the planet. Millions of people died from the Holocaust, and the most who suffered during the war were the Jews. Even if it was the most terrible event that happened in history. The heroes, survivors, and the people who died during the Holocaust are still remembered in museums or websites of the Holocaust.

TWO REMARKABLE HEROES OF THE HOLOCAUST

Jamieson Avila-DaRosa

The Holocaust was the Nazi plan to exterminate the Jews, the crippled, and the Gypsies throughout Europe specifically in Germany and German occupied countries. The Nazis planned to do this by killing the Jews or sending them to concentration camps where they were worked to death and forced to march miles to other camps if the enemy forces were approaching the camp. The discrimination of the Jews began in 1933 when the Nazi political party was voted into office. One reason it began was because the Germans believed that they were racially superior and deemed the Jews a threat to society. The Nazis were led by Adolf Hitler who was the political face of the Nazis. When World War II ended in 1945 allied forces reached the few remaining concentration camps. The final camp to be liberated was Stutthof, which was liberated on May 10, 1945. In the time between 1933 and 1945 there were some great heroes. Several great heroes saved the lives of many Jews that were in trouble.

One of these heroes was Ernst Vonrufs. Ernst was a Swedish industrialist who was working in a textile factory in Budapest, Hungary. When the Nazis approached, he sent his family back to Switzerland and stayed behind to run his textile factory. The Swiss Ministry of Foreign Affairs put Ernst and another industrialist, Peter Zurcher, in charge of Jewish affairs. These two men did a great job of helping Jews during this war time. The German army was headed toward Budapest so Ernst and Peter began to send Jews to Palestine and Switzerland, which were both safe countries for Jews during the war. Ernst was giving the Jews papers, documents, and money to make it to their next home. This act protected many Jews from being taken hostage by the Germans. Not only did Ernst protect Hungarian Jews, but also foreign Jews in Hungary as well. On January 8, 1945 Ernst and Peter went to the house of Erno Vaina who was the last Arrow Cross head in Hungary. There the two began a conversation with Erno Vaina that saved several more Jews. The Jews who were saved by this were American Jews who had their papers taken away by the Gestapo. They were then forced into a Ghetto and could not leave since they were Jewish. Ernst and Peter convinced Erno Vaina to release them from the Ghetto so they could escape from the Nazis. The two continued to save Jews throughout Hungary. The two men were asked to stay in Hungary and help until the war was over and Hungary had regained all of its land that was occupied by the German forces.

In addition, Peter Zurcher was a Swiss businessman in Budapest, Hungary during the war. In 1944 he was employed to help with the Department of Safeguarding the Interests of Foreigners in the Swiss Embassy. In this position he was to help foreign Jews get documents and money to start a life elsewhere. He also made a plan to save a Jew who was not able to bribe her way out of Hungary. Peter decided to hide her in his house while he made fake documents for her so that she could get out of Hungary away from the Nazi forces. He was also involved in a plan with Ernst Vonrufs to save some American Jews who were trapped in a Ghetto.

Overall Ernst Vonrufs and Peter Zurcher were great men who were able to help many Jews escape from Hungary, and felt a sense of compassion toward these foreign strangers. Clearly, since they were able to help Jews, they were kind and brave, and they were great heroes who used their job positions to help many Jews in need of protection from the Nazis. Most certainly if Peter and Ernst had never helped the Jews, many Jews would not have made it out of Hungary and would have been captured by the Nazis. Peter and Ernst's plan to save the American Jews that had lost their papers proved that they were smart and were willing to do anything to save others even if it meant getting killed. Obviously they were heroes that need to be remembered for their actions.

Throughout the Holocaust there were many brave, heroic, courageous, and generous people. It was because of these people so many Jews were saved from the harsh treatment of the Nazis. However the reason this happened was because some people were too afraid to save the Jews because they were afraid of death. Clearly others were more selfless and were braver because they risked their lives to stop the pointless extermination of Jews. They had no intention of becoming famous, in fact they did not want to be known because what they were doing was so dangerous. These men Peter and Ernst are heroic because they fought for what they believed in even though they would be harmed.

FRIEDEL BOHNY REITER AND AUGUST BOHNY

Jason Paulo

The Holocaust was the name of the massacre of 6 million Jews by Adolf Hitler's Nazi party and the countries under his influence. German authorities believed that the Jews and other groups like the Roma, the disabled, the homosexuals, some Slavic people, Communists, Socialists, and Jehovah's Witnesses were not as valuable as they were.. The Holocaust started in 1941 when the Nazi Party ruled by Adolf Hitler was elected to be in control of Germany. Hitler then commanded to exterminate the Jews in Germany and nearby countries because they were considered to be "racially inferior" to the Germans. From 1941 to 1944 German authorities deported millions of Jews to ghettos, transit camps, extermination camps, and forced-labor camps.

The Holocaust was a horrible event that struck fear into the eyes of many people, mostly Jewish people. About 11 million people died in the Holocaust. Sadly 1.1 million of the deaths were people under the age of 18. More than half of the victims were innocent Jewish people. To be more concise, about 6 million Jewish people died during the Holocaust. Even though 11 million is a very depressing number, many people survived too. Examples of these heroes were Friedel Bohny Reiter (a nurse for Secours Suisse aux Enfants) and her husband August Bohny (the owner of L'Abric children's home that was sponsored by Secours Suisse aux Enfants).

Friedel Bohny Reiter was born in Switzerland. She was born in 1912. Her maiden name was Friedel Reiter but she added Bohny to her last name after she got married. She was an orphan because her parents died in World War I. Twenty nine years later in 1941 Friedel Reiter joined an organization that was founded to help kids during the Spanish Civil War. This organization was called Secours Suisse aux Enfants (Swiss Aid to Children). She helped rescue Jewish children in the French internment camp of Rivesaltes. She was sent to Rivesaltes by the Secours Suisse aux Enfants on November 12, 1941. Using the small amount of supplies she had she helped the kids by giving them clothing, food, and providing medical care for those who had serious injuries or illnesses. Next Spring, the tension in the Rivesaltes became tenser and, she realized that the best way to help the children was to get them out of the camp and into a house or shelter that would provide the adequate amount of physical care, emotional care, and mental care that the kids needed.

While she was looking for a place that the children could be sheltered in France, she met August Bohny, who was in charge of the L'Abric (The Shelter) children's home that was sponsored by Secours Suisse aux Enfants, in the village of Le Chambron sur Lingnon. August Bohny asked Secours Suisse aux Enfants to convert an old castle, called the Chateau de Montluel (Castle of Montluel) in Lyon, into a home for the children rescued from the internment camp called Rivesaltes. Friedel Reiter and August Bohny met for the first time when Friedel Reiter brought the first group of children to Castle of Montluel. They later got married.

Friedel Bohny Reiter and August Bohny saved over 100 children from the camps. Because of the large number of children saved, Friedel Bohny Reiter and August Bohny made a second Scours Suisse aux Enfants Children's Home that was called the Faidoli. They also created a furniture making workshop called Atelier Cevenol (Cevenol Workshop). There was also an agricultural training school for the children saved called Ferme Ecole.

In January of 1943, Friedel was sent to Le Chambron sur Lingnon to be the director of the orphanage with her husband. They lived at Le Chambron sur Lingnon until the end of 1944. In 1990, both were given the honor of being recognized as Righteous Among the Nations by Yad Vashem. While she was in Rivesaltes, Reiter recorded her experiences in a wartime diary, and the diary was published in 1993. The diary became the topic for a documentary made by Swiss filmmaker, Jacqueline Veuve.

Rivesaltes was located near the Spanish border. It was a military camp that could house up to 18,000 soldiers. In 1938 it was turned into a refugee camp for sufferers of the Spanish Civil War. In 1940, the camp was turned into a concentration camp. Rivesaltes had a maximum population of about 8,000. About 2,300 people were sent to a different camp where they were most likely killed. Only 600 children had left the camp alive.

Both Friedel Bohny Reiter and August Bohny were courageous people who risked their lives for a great cause. Because of their efforts, hundreds of children's lives were saved from the torture which was the camp of Rivesaltes. Friedel died in 2001 but her story lives on through her wartime diary which was published, the movie which was created, and most importantly in the hearts of the many people she saved from one of the worst events in human history.

OUR IRREVERSIBLE CRIME AGAINST THE HUMAN RACE

Jeong-hyun Nam

The Holocaust was an unforgivable persecution of innocent people. Between the day called "Kristallnacht," or "Night of the Broken Glass," on November 9, 1938, and Germany's surrender in 1945, Jews, Gypsies, and people such as the Poles were murdered. On Kristallnacht, the Nazis burned and looted Jewish synagogues, and Jewish stores and businesses, leaving so much broken glass in the streets. The Nazis also unleashed their terror and violence on helpless Jews, who were killed right on the streets, left behind with all the broken glass to be cleared away afterwards. The German Nazi Party, which was responsible for the Holocaust, believed all of these groups to have "racial inferiority" and opened death camps, especially in Auschwitz, which was more of a death factory. While other groups were targeted for political, behavioral, and ideological reasons, Jews were targeted as an alien threat and for their so-called "crimes" to the German racial community. Several death centers and concentration camps were opened in Germany, Poland, Austria, and Czechoslovakia. Six million Jews were killed by either disease or gas chambers. This was all part of the "Final Solution," which Adolf Hitler, the leader of the Nazis, planned as the annihilation of those who had supposedly "wronged" the Nazis at some point. However, there were some non-Jews who became heroes for saving Jews from the Nazis at the cost of their lives, such as Henry Thomsen and his wife Ellen.

Henry Thomsen was an innkeeper in Snekkersten, a small village in Denmark, along with his wife Ellen. When the Germans arrived in Denmark, the Thomsens made plans to begin to transport the Jews to Sweden, which was a neutral country. The Thomsens were ready to take the lead in the Snekkersten rescue operation to save Danish Jews by sea. Their inn was open to Jews who would leave for Sweden the next day. But, as the number of Jews continued to increase, Henry obtained a boat, and he would either drive Jews to the harbor where they could find a boat for their escape, or sail his own boat to Sweden with Jews. He and Ellen led the rescue organization at the cost of their lives. The Thomsens, however, were not alone in their cause to protect the Jews.

Many locals in Snekkersten helped the Thomsens in sending the Jews to Sweden. The Danish Resistance was a great help. For example, the German soldiers started using trained dogs to locate Jews on smuggling boats; Swedish scientists made a concoction from rabbit's blood and cocaine. Fishermen would carry the scent around on handkerchiefs so they could pretend they had colds when German soldiers came for an inspection. When the dogs smelled it, the cocaine in the scent numbed their noses and temporarily destroyed their sense of smell. The dogs would then be unable to sniff out any Jews on the boats, and as a result, the handkerchief saved many lives on boats. While many non-Jew anti-Nazi civilians were able to use many ways such as the handkerchief and see all their hard work to save the Danish Jews pay off at the end of the war, Henry Thomsen did not.

Henry Thomsen was unable to see the end of the war and all of the works to save so many Jews pay off. He was interrogated once based on the Gestapo suspecting him of ferrying Jews to Sweden. Despite all their efforts, they could not find any evidence that he had done so. After releasing him, he continued to work in the underground, ferrying more and more Jews to Sweden and freedom. But on August 9, 1944, the Gestapo arrested him again and this time, tortured him for his actions that saved more than 7,000 Danish Jews. After interrogation, he was sent to the Neuengamme concentration camp in Germany, where he died of pneumonia on Christmas Eve of 1944. Yad Vashem honored him and his wife as two of the Righteous Among the Nations in 1968.

World War II began in 1938 when Hitler began his work on his "Final Solution." The beginning of the Holocaust was on November 9, 1938, now known as Kristallnacht, or the Night of the Broken Glass. After hearing of the violence of Kristallnacht, the countries of the Allied Forces began to declare war on Germany. The U.S. joined the war after Pearl Harbor on December 7, 1941. Eventually, on April 30, 1945, Hitler and his wife Eva Braun committed suicide, as the Allies got closer to Berlin. Eventually, on May 8, 1945, Germany surrendered to the Allies, which became Victory in Europe Day (V-E Day), but the war did not officially end until Japan surrendered in August. The Holocaust was an outrageous persecution of Jews, Poles, Gypsies, the disabled, Communists, and homosexuals. They were all innocent and never meant to suffer this persecution. Yet there were heroes of the Holocaust who helped many of these victims as Henry and Ellen Thomsen did, and they are honored for their heroism and how they risked so much to save so many innocent people from certain death. These unspeakable and irreversible actions and mistakes of the years 1938-1945 must never be repeated again.

HANS SCHAFFERT, HOLOCAUST HERO

Joaquin Romero, Co-winner

The Holocaust was a truly horrific event orchestrated by the Nazis during World War II, in which millions of Jews were systematically killed. From 1933 to 1945 all throughout Nazi controlled Europe, Jews were killed in concentration and labor camps, as well as in closed off ghettos. Called the Final Solution by the Germans, the Holocaust came about after the Nazi party came to power in Europe and subsequently began invading neighboring countries at the start of the Second World War. The Germans wrongly deemed the Jews and others, including Roma, homosexuals, and Jehovah's Witnesses, inferior. The Nazis then began killing these and other minorities within their camps. At its end, more than 6 million Jews had been killed in the Holocaust, proving it to be one of the most devastating genocides ever committed.

Throughout Europe there were some people determined to save Jews from being killed in the concentration camps, some of which were not even Jewish themselves. One of these people was a man named Hans Schaffert. Shaffert was a Protestant minister originally from Switzerland. Schaffert felt very close to the Jewish community, a closeness that he developed while studying to be a minster. He worked with the Protestant aid organization Cimade, which, during World War II, helped displaced refugees in France many of which were Jewish. Over the course of about six months, he would save many Jews from Gurs, a concentration camp in southern France. While working in Gurs, Schaffert frequently would watch the Nazis march Jews from the camp into the town square. The prisoners would be then put onto a nearby train and then taken to another concentration camp, where they would almost undoubtedly be murdered. In August of 1942, Schaffert heard about mass deportations of Jews, much like the terrible deportations he had already seen. Schaffert tried speaking to both a commanding German officer, as well as church leaders of the area to make the deportations stop, but his attempts fell to deaf ears. After realizing that no one else would try to stop the deportations of the Jews in Gurs, Schaffert then dedicated himself to saving the Jews being persecuted around him.

As the deportations of Jews began in the Gurs camp, Schaffert gave food to prisoners, and stayed with them as they waited for the trains going to other concentration camps. Schaffert gave money to several Jews allowing them to flee to neighboring countries such as Spain and Switzerland. On many occasions Shaffert would personally see some refugees to the Spanish border, ensuring their freedom outside Nazi-controlled Europe. After doing this many times the French authorities noticed him. They became suspicious and requested that Schaffert return to Switzerland.

After returning to Switzerland, Schaffert continued to work as a pastor, and helped with other faith-based charities of the Swiss Evangelical Church. While doing this charity work, Shaffert would make sure that Jews staying at Christian churches could actively practice their faith, instead of having to conform to the rules of the place they were staying in. In fact, in several instances, Shaffert would have kosher food made so that Jewish refugees could follow their faith's dietary rules. His superior, Dr. Paul Vogt, described him as "showing courage, dedication and selflessness" only cementing the fact that Hans Schaffert cared deeply for those that he saved. In fact, much of his work in Switzerland helped the same people he had saved in France.

After the war, Schaffert was a founding member of an organization dedicated to friendly relations between Christians and Jews, further showing his feelings of solidarity towards both religions. On April fourth, 1967, Hans Schaffert was presented with the Holocaust remembrance organization Yad Vashem's Medal of Honor, and had a tree-planting ceremony in honor of his actions during the war. But despite his heroic actions, and the Medal of Honor only affirming them, Schaffert still felt that he was not worthy of the award. He did not feel he had done enough to save those prisoners being persecuted around him.

Hans Schaffert is just one example of those who ensured the safety of Jews when they were being persecuted during the events of the Holocaust. His actions in the Gurs concentration camp saved the lives of many Jews, and ensured their freedom in many other countries. He was caring to those that he had helped, and felt such solidarity towards the Jewish population, that he once said "Whoever does wrong to the Jewish people does wrong to the property of God and to God himself." Hans Schaffert was a helper and savior to those he aided, and he is truly an unsung hero of the Holocaust.

KNUD DYBY: A DANISH, AN OFFICER, A HERO

Joshua Gonong

To talk about the Holocaust, one must ask what the Holocaust is. The Holocaust was the persecution of Jews, Romas (Gypsies), and the physically and mentally disabled by the Nazi party. The Nazis thought they were far more superior than everyone else, which they believed to be inferior and a threat to German society. The Holocaust took place during World War II, 1939-1945, and occurred in Eastern Europe, mostly in Germany and Poland. Adolf Hitler, the dictator of Nazi Germany, and the Nazi party organized the whole plan. Thier final solution of getting rid of the Jews, Romas (Gypsies), and the physically and mentally disabled was to put them into concentration camps and burn all the camps, along with the victims in them. Though in an effort to help the suffering victims, there were people with a golden heart that tried to help the discriminated by escaping or helping them survive.

Out of many heroes that are not that well known for their good deeds and actions, one that stood out is a Danish man named Knud Dyby. He first encountered the Nazis in April of 1940, when Germany first occupied Denmark and tried to replace the Danish flag with their own. Dyby, being part of the King's Royal Guard, helped King Christian X, the current king of Denmark at the time, take down the flag that Germany was trying to raise. After leaving the Royal Guard, Dyby became a police officer and a member of the Danish Underground, a resistance against the German occupation. Being an officer, Dyby gained intelligence that was important to the Danish Resistance. For example, Dyby had knowledge regarding the German navy's patrol routes and the best lanes across sea between Denmark and Sweden.

After Dyby learned of the Germans' plan to gather the Jews and to deport them, he did his best to react quickly. He participated in the Danish-Swedish Refugee Service and in October of 1943, he helped to rescue almost 7,200 Jews. The Jews were then taken across Øresund, a narrow body of water connecting Denmark and Sweden. He used this to get the Jews to safety in Sweden. But until a boat arrived to take the Jews there, he helped the Jews to hiding places in hospitals for refuge. Dyby assisted about 1,888 people to Sweden, but not all the 1,888 were Jewish. The ships included other Danish people trying to escape the Nazis tyranical iron fist. The boats that made the trip had mail, money, weapons, intelligence data, and news.

In May of 1945, Denmark was liberated from the Germans. At that time Dyby ended his career as a police officer. He has been honored by a few organizations and moved to the United States after the war and lived there until his death in September of 2011 at 96 years of age.

Knud Dyby is a good example of the risk people would take to save the Jews of Europe. His knowledge of the German naval routes and refuge locations were an important part in saving the lives of the Danish Jews that he saved. His background as a sailor, military officer and police officer gave him important information to give to the Danish Underground and the Danish-Swedish Refugee Service about hiding spots for the Jews and the Germans' sea routes. His work with the Danish Underground and the Danish-Swedish Refugee Service was successful in saving most of the Danish Jews at the time. Knud Dyby, the officer of Denmark, had truly saved the lives of the Jews of Denmark. World War II and the Holocaust raged on for five more years until its end in 1945. The discrimination of Jews and others ended. But more troubles stirred in the world as conflicts started to rise with more dangerous wars ahead.

MAKING A DIFFERENCE
Katalina Wong

The Holocaust was a terrible time when about 6 million Jews were murdered and many other non-Jews were killed by a group called the Nazis. In 1933, the Nazi leader, Adolf Hitler came to power and put a belief into German minds. Hitler led them to believe that they could make the world perfect by killing those that they felt were not part of their superior group such as homosexual, Gypsies, the disabled, Poles, Russians, Jehovah's Witnesses, and especially Jews. The Germans believed that Jews were a threat to their race. The Nazi Party, the government that supported Hitler and his decisions, began to persecute all Jews. They tortured and murdered them. They created concentration camps where Jews would work and work until death. Jews worked and lived in terrible living conditions and were given little or no food until 1945 when they were liberated. Western Allies arrived in Germany and made the Nazi Party surrender, officially ending World War II. Though Hitler convinced many people to join him, there were few who tried to help and care for any unaccepted people. For example, Sister Jeanne Berchmans, a Swiss Hero, helped to keep some Jews out of Nazi hands. Sister Jeanne is just one of many who were considered Heroes of the Holocaust.

Sister Jeanne Berchmans was born in November 1897 at Bremgarten Switzerland. From a young age she decided to change her name from Marie Meienhofer to Jeanne Berchmans and dedicate her life to caring, supporting, and loving other people. In 1924, she made the decision to join the convent, Sacre- Coeur, or Sacred Heart. She became a Catholic nun who taught at her convent's school in Thonon-les-Bains. She taught students the languages French and German, as well as how to write and type at the college. About 400 ladies were attending this educational program. The school was very important to her because that was where she was hiding three Jews.

In 1944, Sister Jeanne was asked to hide a family of Jews somewhere in her convent by Father Rosay, a priest in a nearby town who was continually trying to save Jews from the Nazi soldiers. She was told to shelter and provide for the Wittels family. They were from Vienna and in 1938 left Austria after the Anschluss, when Germany and Austria decided to join forces. The Wittels family was Mrs. Wittels, her 21-year-old daughter Renée, and her nine-year-old son Bruno. Since Jeanne had been teaching German to her students, it was very simple to communicate with them. To explain their accents, Jeanne lied to the other nuns by telling them that they were people of Alsace who were forced to vacate their homes. They were hidden in a room on the third floor that was hardly ever used. The Wittels were given food, clothing, water, and all the essentials they needed to survive. They were treated like all the others but did not have to partake in religious rituals. Sister Jeanne considered the Wittels to be her family, and as a result she risked her life for them. For example, when German soldiers searched the convent for Jews, Jeanne lied to them. To keep the three hidden, Jeanne put them in a room with a "quarantine" sign on it. When the soldiers came to the room, Jeanne told them that this room was filled with patients sick with scarlet fever. Scarlet fever was a disease commonly in children and was severely contagious. The idea of coming down with this illness scared the Germans away. If Jeanne's plan did not work and the Germans found out that she was lying it could have taken her own life as well as the Wittels. The three family members survived and ended up staying at the convent until the liberation.

Sister Jeanne had a difficult time leaving the Wittels family after the war. She had grown a special bond with each family member. Although she was sad that they had to separate, she was overjoyed with a reassuring feeling that no one would hurt them anymore and was glad that they could continue their lives without living in fear. On October 6, 1991, Sister Jeanne Berchman was recognized as Righteous Among the Nations by Yad Vashem and was also added onto the Wall of Honor to acknowledge her work.

Sister Jeanne Berchmans is considered a hero of the Holocaust because she took care and loved the Wittels family. She provided them with shelter, food, clothes, and her friendship. She was that family's only friend for several years. The Wittels had no one except each other and Sister Jeanne. Without the help of Sister Jeanne, the Wittels most likely would have been captured, tortured, and or killed by the Nazis. Millions of civilians died from the effects of this horrible war. For about thirteen years, many people had to suffer the pain of being themselves and following their own religion, but certain people appreciated the diversity of others, so they tried to protect the unwanted. Those certain individuals saved probably thousands of lives from death or a life of misery. Sister Jeanne is considered a Hero of the Holocaust because of the impact she made on some Jewish lives, which is also why she is an incredible role model for children. She helped and cared for others but also risked her life in the process. I know that her sacrifices made a difference in the Wittels family and I hope I can make a change in someone else's life throughout my actions.

THE HEROIC JOURNEY OF FRIEDRICH BORN

Makenzie Jones-Dodd

During the time of World War II, many innocent people were exterminated because of their ancestry and religious beliefs. The Holocaust began in 1933 and took place in Germany. When Hitler, the leader of the Nazi Party, was elected, his goal was to eliminate all the Jewish origins, homosexuals, and Gypsies. He sent Nazis to the Netherlands, Belgium, Luxembourg, France, Denmark, Yugoslavia, Greece, Norway, and western Poland. Hitler mainly focused on Jewish men, women, and children. Most Jewish people were sent to concentration camps and experienced horrible living conditions along with very strict rules. This resulted in thousands killed. Some towns would not allow Jewish people to enter. Towns put up signs that said "JEWS ENTER AT OWN RISK." They were forced to work for the Nazis.

The story of Friedrich Born is particularly heroic. Friedrich was born June 10, 1963 in Hungary. He was forced to join the Red Army on May 1944. The Red army was a name for the Russian National Military Forces. The Red Army is also referred to as RKKA. The Red Army fought against the Nazis in Germany and helped rescue Hitler's victims. Born began to work in Budapest as a member of the Swiss Federal Department of Foreign Trade. Born found out about the deportation of Hungarian Jews, which began soon after the German Putsch in 1944. The German Putsch was when Germany attempted to overthrow its own government. This meant that more and more Jewish people were being deported from Budapest to Germany to be in Nazi extermination camps. Which meant Jews were being savagely killed.

Carl Lutz is the Swiss Vice-Consul. He had saved over 69,200 Jews. Born had followed Lutz's strategy, which was to hire all Jews and offer them protection from Nazis. He had recruited up to 3,000 Jews as workers for his offices. Born even designated several buildings that were protected by the ICRC. ICRC stood for the International Committee of Red Cross. The ICRC ensured protection and assistance to the victims of war and violence. Born amazingly pulled off to provide 15,000 protection documents for the Jews throughout Hungary. These protection documents prevented Hungarian Jews from being deported or being killed. After several months and years of following Lutz's strategy, Born rescued between 11,000 and 15,000 Jews in Budapest, Hungary. This so called mission saved half of the Jewish population of Budapest. The Jews survived with the help of Lutz and Born, and were able to stay safe and most of the Jews were able to remain with their families. So much work and effort went into protecting Hungarian Jews from deportation to Nazi extermination camps.

Nazi extermination camps were designed and built in Nazi, Germany during World War II. The purpose of these camps were to kill millions in awful ways such as being burned or gassed. Kids were ripped from the arms of their parents, wives were taken away from their husbands, and families were torn apart by deportation and death. All because the Nazis believed in something cruel. Nazis had the cruel idea that all those put into extermination camps were "life unworthy of life." The Jews and other various groups that the Nazis did not like, were treated awfully in these camps. People were starved, could not bathe, and were viciously beaten. Nazis began to establish different camps so they could kill a massive amount of people at once. The extermination camps were also called Death Camps. One reason people like Born and Lutz helped the Jews and fought against the Nazis, was because they were members of the Red Army. One of the Red Army's common enemy was the Nazis. They knew that being punished for being Jewish was wrong. They wanted to stop the Nazis and save them from being deported into extermination camps. After the war, Carl Lutz and Friedrich Born returned back to their normal lives and felt proud that they were able to save the lives of half the Jews in their town of Budapest. Twenty-four years after Born's death, in 1987, he was designated as Righteous Among the Nations by Yad Vashem. As for Carl Lutz, he died in 1975, and was given the same award as Born.

World wars are always a time of darkness for certain groups of people. The Jews were treated unfairly because they were not given the natural rights that everyone should have. People discriminated against the Jews for no better reason than that some one told them to. Sadly, millions were killed. Millions of homes were set on fire and destroyed. The worst action was when Germans destroyed the synagogues and all that was inside were destroyed with it. The Jews were punished for their beliefs and struggled to be active in their faith because people killed and beat them over it. Jews were humiliated in public for wearing yarmulkes. Even after the war and all that the Jews were put through, they still had trust in God. They rebuilt their communities and synagogues and prayed. Their faith in their religion helped them go through the dark, scary, depressing times of need.

CARL LUTZ: A HERO OF THE HOLOCAUST

Marta Maestu

The Holocaust was the insanity-driven disaster that caused the death of millions of Jews, the disabled, and Gypsies. This all took place in Germany starting in 1933 when Hitler came to power, just before World War II. Hitler believed that the Aryan race was racially superior and better than the Jews and the disabled, believing them to be nothing more than parasitic vermin. He held the extreme view that these people were unworthy to live. So Hitler decided to cleanse Germany of those who did not meet his status-quo by sending them to concentration camps, starving them, or working them to death. Most people stood by out of fear of the Nazis not out of hatred for the victims. Only a few people had the courage and valor to stand up to the Nazis and their regime.

One such hero was Carl Lutz, a Swiss diplomat who arrived in Budapest Hungary in January of 1942 to serve as the vice-counsel for Switzerland representing the United States, Great Britain, and many other countries that had cut ties with Hungary. Hungary had been a center of Jewish worship before the war. It then became a place of refuge for the people fleeing persecution and had housed 204,371 Jews before the Nazis occupied Hungary in March of 1944. Just over 100,000 remained when the war ended a year and a half later.

Lutz was appalled by the mass murder of Jews that had begun in Hungary and helped Jews escape persecution. Lutz began by attempting to persuade the Hungarian government to stop deporting Jews to concentration camps. This attempt failed, so Lutz tried working from a different angle. Lutz negotiated for protective letters from the Hungarian government. The protective letters gave the Jews permission to go to Palestine and put them under Swiss protection until they could leave the country. Switzerland was neutral, during the war making their protection extremely valuable unless Hungary wanted another enemy.

Soon Lutz had issued protective letters to over 1,000 Jews. Lutz was able to expand the protection offered by the letters to include the families of the people on the list. Lutz forged an additional 100,000 protective letters. Lutz forged so many letters because he felt desperate for the Jews to escape when the Arrow Cross Party came to power in Hungary in October of 1944. The Arrow Cross party rose to power with racist views and soon allied themselves with the Nazis. The authorities demanded that Lutz separate the legitimate protective letters from the false ones. In order to protect the precarious rescue operations, Lutz complied with the demands of the Hungarian authorities.

Lutz also freed many Jews from a death march to the Austrian border by showing documents that declared the Jews under Swiss protection. This was one of many exploits in which Lutz took part to free Jews from deportation centers and death marches. After freeing more Jews, Lutz went on to rent 76 houses in Budapest, Hungary where he housed the Jews who were under his protection. By now these numbers had reached near 3,000. Gertrude, Lutz's wife, helped provide the rescued with food and in some cases medical treatment. When the Soviets invaded Hungary in the January of 1945, he had to end his exploits to help the Jews and go into hiding with his wife. After the war he and his wife returned to Switzerland. Lutz died there in 1975.

Brave heroes like Carl Lutz and his wife Gertrude will always be remembered by those they saved and those who read about them for years to come, and perhaps forever, for their kindness toward the Jews and those who were to be persecuted. Lutz saved thousands of people and persevered were many others could not, or would not. Lutz proved that he indeed was a great hero through his many acts of bravery and genius.

HOLOCAUST: A TIME WHEN THINGS WEREN'T RIGHT
Maya Curiale

There was a time when people in the world were not kind to all races. When things like this happen, there are always bad results. One of these results is called the Holocaust. The Holocaust was a time when Jews, gays, and gypsies were discriminated in every way possible. During this time, even though there were many bad people, there were also good for example the Swiss and Danish.

Post World War I, Germany saw the rise of a radical leader named Adolf Hitler. Hitler promised the economically depressed nation that if they followed him they would return to their pre-war industrial and economic success. With fear and propaganda, Hitler convinced the nation to follow his leadership which was based on a belief system called Nazism. Hitler believed that for Germany to return to its former glory certain groups of people had to be exterminated. These people were Jews, Gays, and Gypsies. His way of exterminating these people was to build slave labor camps and crematoriums in which to gas and burn people. The Second World War in 1939 began as a world outrage to Hitler and his murdering of innocent people. At the end of World War II, over 5 million people had been put to death at concentration camps, such as Auschwitz and Dachau. All people who went to the camps were branded with serial numbers on their forearms. After the war, war trials were held at Nuremberg to punish Nazis who had partaken in the slaughter of these innocent people. Many of these war criminals escaped to South America and

410

were protected by many South American countries, such as Brazil and Argentina. The world wide search for these criminals continues to the present. Many novels and movies have been made documenting these horrors. Examples of these movies are Schindler's List, Sophie's Choice, and Life is Beautiful. Examples of novels are The Diary of Anne Frank, and Will to Meaning.

This horrible time in history also brought out the best in many people. There are many stories of brave citizens throughout Europe and Scandinavia. These people were justifiably called Heroes. These Heroes were people who hid the Jews and other victims in their homes, and fed them. Those who were caught doing this deed, were killed. One of those heroes was named Margareta Tobler. Margareta was born on December 1st in 1915. She was from Switzerland and she educated young children, worked in a children home, and survived the Holocaust. This home she worked in had taken in more than 100 Jewish children. These were children who had fled Germany, and were not able to contact their families. Margareta risked her own life for two young girls, Inge Bernhard who was 14, and Toni Rosenblatt who was 11. She took these two girls all the way to Switzerland before their visas expired. She saved their lives.

Oskar Schindler was a Swedish business man. During the war, he saved thousands of lives by providing passports for Jews and others persecuted people to leave from Germany to safer countries. A movie was made about him. A concentration camp was built in Italy in the town of Ferrara Monte. Germans sent Jews to this concentration camp for labor. The Italians did not execute anyone in the camp and smuggled many of the children out of the camp and placed them in Italian homes and orphanages to protect them from the Germans. Many people in France, England, Germany, Poland, and the Scandinavian Countries risked their lives in the Resistance to save the lives of persecuted people. World War II officially end in Europe on May 8, 1945.

After the war ended, many of the survivors found refuge in camps called Displaced Persons Camps run by America, France, Russia, and England. Survivors of the Holocaust lived in these camps until they could immigrate to safe nations. Seven hundred thousand Jews went to the new state of Israel. Other Jewish DPS went to the United States and other nations. The last DP camp closed in 1957. In total, over 5 million people lost their lives in World War II due to the atrocities committed by the Third Reich.

Today, many Germans deny that the Holocaust ever happened, although remains of concentration camps and crematoriums exist as well the memories and stories of millions of people. Neo-Nazism is a modern movement back in time to the basic principles of traditional Nazism. The beliefs of this group appear to be the same as the original Nazi doctrine. The belief is based on anti-Semitism and hatred of foreigners and immigrants. Today the main purpose of this political movement is to halt immigration and keep "race" pure. This movement is based on nationalism and hatred to those who are different.

These Neo-Nazis display many of the symbols that were used by the Nazis: the Swastika, the Nazi greeting (the outstretched right arm), and pictures of Hitler. These groups of Neo-Nazis meet to drink, play music especially white pride music, and sing old and new Nazi battle music. They arrange celebrations for important dates in Nazi history like Hitler's birthday. A number of these Neo-Nazi groups, particularly in Germany, also carry out violent assaults. Many people who are foreigners, people of presumed Jewish heritage and others have been assaulted and in many cases murdered. The Klu Klux Klan is based upon the teachings of the Nazi doctrines. The clan believes in "You ain't right if you ain't white," and that gay people and any foreigners don't belong in America. They too have also assaulted and killed many people. Hundreds of thousands of people in Germany opposed the Neo-Nazi party as well as hundreds of thousands opposed the Klu Klux Klan. The belief that decent people must never let this happen again is strong in the minds and hearts.

Today, most of the world acknowledges that the Holocaust took place in Germany. In many parts of the world today, many people are being killed due to fear, hatred, and ignorance. Genocide is happening in Africa, in China, and millions of lives have been lost. We must, as a people, always fight against injustice and tyranny. Many people were silent and stood by while the Holocaust took place. We cannot stay silent as innocent people are slaughtered.

THE UNKNOWN HEROES OF THE HOLOCAUST

Natalie Landeros Chan

When people hear about the Holocaust, most think back to a bad and unforgettable time in history. The younger generation might think, *what is the Holocaust* or *why is it such a terrible time?* Well, the Holocaust is such a terrible time because in Europe from 1939 to 1945 some Germans thought they were racially superior and the Jews were seen as outsiders to the German community. The Germans made a plan called the Final Solution. This plan was to send millions of Jews to camps where the Jews were fed 500 calories a day, put to exhausting labor, and separated from their families and homes. Unfortunately, other Jews were sent on death marches, put in camps where they were gassed and killed, and burned.

The Holocaust was an attack on the Jews by the Nazi regime. Between the years 1939-1945, 6 million Jews were killed. In 1933, Adolf Hitler rose to power in Germany and felt that the Germans were racially superior. Because of this animosity toward the Jews, 6 million people were sent to camps, death marches, and gas sites. It

412

is estimated that another 5 million people were publicly humiliated and tortured. During the Holocaust there were many people who gave refuge to the targeted, helped them escape, and lied so the Nazis would not kill them. There are a lot of Holocaust survivors who share their life changing stories with others, but there are also many heroes that did a lot for the Jews but go unrecognized like Carl Lutz a Swiss hero.

Carl Lutz is one of the many heroes of the Holocaust. Carl is a hero from Switzerland during World War II. He was born in Walzenhausen, Switzerland in 1895 and attended a school when he was old enough. When Lutz was 18 years old, he immigrated to the United States. When he arrived, he moved to Illinois, where he worked and stayed for 20 years. In 1920, he got a job at the Swiss Legation in Washington D.C. In 1926, he was assigned chancellor at the Swiss Consulate in Philadelphia. He decided to leave the United States in 1934 after being in the U.S. for more than 20 years. He was vice-consul to the Swiss Consulate in Jaffa, which was Palestine then.

In 1942, Lutz started cooperating with the Jewish Agency for Palestine. He issued many documents that enabled the safety of the Swiss citizens, and allowed 10,000 Jewish kids to immigrate. In 1944, Budapest was taken over by the Nazis and the Jews were being sent to death camps. Lutz was able to make a deal with the Nazis and Hungarian governments, so he issued 8,000 letters to Jews and helped them flee to Palestine. Lutz built 76 safe houses in Budapest and said the houses were Swiss annexes, making the houses off limits to the Nazis. One of Lutz's most memorable acts was when he jumped into the river to save a bleeding woman who was a Swiss citizen. Lutz would also stay up many nights and work for days to come up with plans to help save innocent people from facing public humiliation and public death. He was also able to successfully convince the Nazis and Hungarian governments to tolerate his plan to save some of the Hungarian Jews who were citizens. Lutz was supported by many until he had to leave due to government orders.

Lutz died in Switzerland in 1975. During World War II, he saved tens of thousands of people. Although he was not immediately recognized for his actions, he did receive some acknowledgement. Shortly after the war, he was criticized for exceeding his government authority. Later on, the government gave Lutz his credit and he was praised for his actions and was honored. In 1963, a street in Israel was named after him. In 1991, a memorial was dedicated to him in the Budapest ghetto. One of his most recent honors was in 2014 when George Washington University honored Lutz with a President's Medal during a ceremony attended by many, including his daughter. Carl Lutz is an example of one of the many unknown heroes of the Holocaust. Lutz did so much for so many people, and although he was not given his honor right away, he received the credit he deserved.

The Holocaust is a dreadful time in world history that will never be forgotten no matter how many years go by. The Holocaust changed the lives of many, and by hearing about it, it will impact many lives, like it did to mine. I learned so much including the fact that sometimes we take the luxury of not having to be criticized or mocked because our faith for granted. I also learned about one of the heroes of the Holocaust. Carl Lutz is one great example of a person who did so much for so many and is not as well known as other heroes. He knew that by helping the Jews get to safety and helping them take refuge could risk his life, but he was willing to risk his life for the safety of others. The Holocaust should be looked at with a lot of respect for the survivors, heroes, those who died because they risked their lives, and those who died with immense courage. Hopefully this generation can look back at the Holocaust and treat people better so this time in history never repeats itself.

HISTORY OF PAIN AND SUFFERING

Reet Chauhan

The Holocaust is one of the biggest crimes in history against humanity. The Holocaust took place in Germany beginning in the year 1933. Mindless murder of millions of human beings based on one person's ideology is unthinkable and one might think that this is fiction. The word "Holocaust" is used to describe a very dark event in human history. The Nazi party believed that they were superior and that they had the right to change and control others. Adolf Hitler was the mastermind behind the creation of the Nazi party. The Nazi Germans were the ones committing these awful acts of terror. Hitler believed in the superiority of the Aryan race and wanted to kill the people he did not consider pure. This belief of the superiority of their own race lead them to on the the task of systematic murder of Jews. The "final solution" to the Germans' "problem" was to put the Jews in concentration camps or kill them. Able bodied people were put to work in these starved to death. The sick, the old, and the too young were just put to death in gas camps and then chambers. In fact little babies were tossed into burning fires and just burnt to death.

There were mass graves of the murdered Jews and they were stripped of all valuable items before their bodies were burned or buried. It is estimated that millions of Jews were killed during the Holocaust.

Courage is something that people are born with; it can be mental or physical. Everyone has heroes that they look up to and wish that they had similar courage as their heroes. During the Holocaust there were thousands of people who risked their lives to help others. These people did not expect anything in return and helped others because they did not agree with the treatment of Jews. One such person is Rosa Naef, my Holocaust hero. She showed remarkable courage and compassion during this

414

hard period. She was born in Glarus, Switzerland 1911 and died in Glarus, Switzerland. She wanted to help children ever since she was a little girl and so decided to become a nurse. Her first job that is recorded is when she went to Africa to help Dr. Albert Schweitzer. When she returned back home she worked as head of the Red Cross children's home in France. There, she took care of the Jewish kids whose parents sent them away from Germany.

A couple years later Rosa decided to work at La Hille castle. There was no running water, electricity, proper sewage system, drainage, clinic, or school. But Rosa contacted some people and got all that repaired in a short time. All the children who stayed at La Hille castle loved it, but then French soldiers came and invaded their children's home. They accused Rosa of not maintaining discipline at the school and took away 45 older children. So Rosa sent all the remaining children to Le Vernet, and after a couple of days went there too. Though they tried to make the best of things, they missed La Hille castle. When Rosa finally got the notice that everyone could go back to their most prized children's home, everyone quickly packed what small belongings they had and left in a hurry. But a new surprise awaited them; German troops had taken over that area of France.

Rosa Naef and many others helped the Jews, some doing more daring things than they had ever done before. Rosa made every effort to save the children from being deported and taken to concentration camps. She planned their escape and also contacted local farms, so that they could hide the children. She organized escape routes for groups of people to Switzerland. News of her organization of escapes spread and she lost her position as warden of La Hille castle. After the war she decided to leave Switzerland and live in Denmark. The main reason for this being that she was upset by the way she was treated by the Swiss government. She had lost her job because she had tried to help children and people escape death in concentration camps.

It is true that good always triumphs in the end and the Nazi army was defeated by the Allies. The Holocaust is an important event and every generation needs to be aware of this black event that is a part of our history. This chapter of human history clearly demonstrates man's inhumanity to man. It is hard to imagine that one man shaped the mindset of an entire nation and used propaganda to further his end. It is said that the past can teach us many things and also show us the right path at times of confusion. What is important now is that we do not forget the lesson that we can learn from this tragedy. Kindness, compassion, and tolerance are traits that we need to encourage. It is our responsibility as the future generation to never let this sort of hatred and prejudice destroy our society.

HOLOCAUST ESSAY

Simon Bell, Special Award

Paul Grueninger was a police colonel in St. Gallen, Switzerland in the late 1930s, during a time when Nazism was rising all across Europe. He used the authority of his command as a way to help Jewish refugees fleeing the anti-Semitism in Austria. He is estimated to have saved about 3,600 Jews. For the risk he took, Paul Grueninger lost his job and his pension, was fined by the Swiss government, and died in poverty.

In 1938, Nazi Germany annexed its neighboring country, Austria. All Jews in Austria were forced to identify themselves as separate from other Austrians and Germans. They surrendered their passports to the new government of Nazi Germany. Their passports were returned stamped with the letter "J" to identify them as Jews. At first, the Nazis tried to make all of the Jews leave Germany and Austria, but later they were prohibited from leaving. At the time the Nazis began prohibiting Jewish travel, Paul Grueninger was a colonel with the Swiss border police, stationed in a town near the Austrian border. He was in charge of sending back Jewish refugees who tried to enter Switzerland, but did not have the proper permits. This was an important job since Jews who were in Switzerland legally would be taken to the Diepolsau camp, where they could receive help in finding a way to stay in Switzerland or in finding a new home in another country. Jews who were refused entry into the country would be turned back to face increasing restriction, discrimination, and violence back in Austria.

As a border guard, Grueninger was a dutiful civil servant. But he was also a man of empathy. While his specific orders were to turn away anyone who did not have proper papers to cross the border and enter Switzerland, Grueninger knew that to do so was to send them back to suffering, and possibly death. Knowing that hose Jews who could show they were in Switzerland prior to March 1938 were considered legal refugees and could seek permanent residency in Switzerland or in another country, Paul Grueninger deliberately disobeyed the instructions of his superiors and began to work out ways to help the Jews appear to be legal refugees.

To help out the desperate refugees, Colonel Grueninger began to falsify papers. He stamped passports to make it look like the owners had arrived in Switzerland before March 1938, and created false documentation to support their arrival. He also allowed some to enter illegally, not including their numbers in his accounts to those in charge. The dutiful policeman was breaking the law. Paul Grueninger turned in the fabricated reports, lying about the number of arrivals and potential crossings at the border, and the number of refugees in his district, legally or not. Since his superiors thought there were far fewer refugees in his district than there actually were, they found it increasingly difficult to trace the illegal entries. Grueninger also used his own money to buy clothing for refugees who had unexpectedly or suddenly fled their homes leaving everything they owned behind.

The Germans discovered what Colonel Grueninger was doing and informed his employer, the Swiss government. He was stripped of his badge and his military command. His benefits and pension were suspended, and he was charged with breach of duty for allowing 3,600 Jews to enter Switzerland illegally. He was also charged with falsifying registration papers for many refugees and helping some individuals avoid being found by the authorities and others to hide their valuables. His trial dragged on for more than two years before he was found guilty of breach of duty in March 1941. He lost all of his employment and retirement benefits, including his pension. He was forced to pay the cost of the trial and also a separate fine of 300 francs. Even though the court admitted that they understood he was trying to do a good thing, they said he should still have done as commanded and followed instructions to the letter.

For the rest of his life, Paul Grueninger lived in poverty, labeled as a criminal. His conviction made it difficult for him to get a job, but he never regretted helping all of the refugees. Later, in 1954, he said, "It was basically a question of saving human lives threatened with death. How could I then seriously consider bureaucratic schemes and calculations?" Yad Vashem bestowed on him the title "Righteous Among the Nations" in 1971 for his efforts to save Jewish lives. During his lifetime, the Swiss government never fully apologized to Grueninger. Only after his death did they reinstate his benefits to his survivors and annul his conviction.

Paul Grueninger was a great man who helped thousands of Jews escape the clutches of the Nazi Germans. Even though he risked humiliation and possible hatred for the rest of his life for his "crime," he followed his moral compass instead of hiding behind the idea of "just doing his job" – doing as the hierarchy told him to do. He may have not been recognized in his lifetime for his actions, but he will be remembered forever in history as a lifesaver to many people.

HANS SCHAFFERT, A MAN OF MANY DEEDS

Sydney Carlson

In 1933, one of the worst events in human history took place. The Holocaust was a senseless and horrible action. The Holocaust first began because the Nazi Germany party, led by Adolf Hitler, was voted in and they wanted a certain type of population. No Jews, no crippled, no Jehovah Witnesses, no gypsies, no sick or disabled. They only wanted people who were like themselves. This took place in Germany, but not all Germans are to blame. What was the Nazis' solution to their problem? Concentration camps, where only those fit enough to work survived andeverybody else had no value in the Nazis' eyes. While many died, there were some who managed to escape to safety thanks to some special heroes. These were people who were willing to put other people's safety before their own.

Hans Schaffert was a hero in many ways. He was a Swiss clergyman who did not agree with the Nazis and stood against them. In 1942 Hans went to the Gurs concentration camp in France with a Protestant aid organization. He was a protestant minister and social worker. He witnessed the harsh treatment of Jews as they were beaten and marched to be transported to the camp of Drancy. In a bold move, Hans asked the Commander in Chief and other church dignitaries to stop the Jews form being transported away. Unfortunately, he was unsuccessful. He decided to do something smaller, yet equally effective. He gave the prisoners food and company while they waited to be taken away. He gave Jews kosher food so that Jewish people could still remain faithful to their religion. In addition, he successfully helped many Jews escape to Switzerland and Spain and gave them money in hopes of having a better future. Hans himself escorted several prisoners on their way to Spain. He was very passionate about helping the Jewish people get through the war. He became good friends with the Jews and worked to ensure their welfare. After the Holocaust, Hans helped to found an association to create friendship between Jews and Christians. While we consider his acts heroic, in his mind he did these charitable acts out of the kindness of his heart and never felt as though he were a hero. When he was awarded the Yad Vashem Righteous Amoung the Nations medal of honor in 1967, he felt undeserving. Hans believed that by treating people well we are treating God well.

While giving out food is a small act, it had a huge effect. By giving out food to the Jews before they were brutally taken away they were given nutrients that they would need to complete the strenuous tasks that wait for them at the camps. Jews were never fed properly at the camps so the small amount of food made a big difference. Hans also waited with them until they left. In a time like that imagine what a difference it would make to have someone with you to talk to and comfort you. By helping the Jews escape to other countries Hans risked his life, to give someone a better life. He put others before himself and did not seek recognition. Escaping was dangerous but very helpful as it gave Jews a safe place and a second shot at life. Hans went as far as to make sure the Jews at the Christian church had kosher food so they could still practice their religion the same as before. Hans wanted to make sure the Jews felt at home and safe, he did big and simple things that made a tremendous impact on the lives of the people he touched. Whether he was giving out food or helping Jews escape Hans made sure to do all he could to ensure their safety. Hans

418

risked it all just to make sure others were treated nicely. That is the ultimate act of courage.

Throughout a time when such awful acts were committed there were still the people who were good, the people who did not see religion to be a barrier dividing us. It took people like Hans to make a difference. A person who was willing to give away his life for the better treatment of a friend, a family member or a complete stranger. It takes a strong person to commit an act of bravery, such as helping Jews escape, and yet not expect anything in return. Hans knew what he was risking, he knew he might die for his actions, but he did not care. Hans put others before himself without even questioning why. Hans was not deserving of the punishment he could have received, he was simply standing up for what he believed was right and just. The type of selflessness Hans showed is exactly what saved so many people. The stories we have heard about the holocaust, while horrific, would have been different without these types of Heroes. There would not have been those who were lights in the darkness, willing to lead others into the light. These were ordinary people just like you or me who did extraordinary things, and we will be forever grateful to them.

OPEN ARMS

Thien Tran

The Holocaust was an extermination of people deemed unfit to live ordered by Adolf Hitler, the leader of Germany's Nazi party during World War II. The plan was named the Final Solution, the extermination of every other race on the face of the Earth. The Nazi party believed that they were racially supreme, and considered others inferior, particularly Jews, Romas (Gypsies), the mentally and physically disabled, and homosexuals. The Nazis hunted and gathered these people including children from throughout Europe, and enslaved them in forced labor concentration camps to produce goods to fuel the Axis's war effort. Forced to live in squalid conditions facing starvation and harsh weather, those who were judged no longer able to work were summarily exterminated through inhumane manners like gassing them *en masse* in a gas chamber. Extremely merciless and brutal, the Nazis carried out the Holocaust throughout Europe, terrorizing the whole European population with this horrible act. Despite this there were still people who stood up and protected those persecuted. These unsung heroes have risked their own lives, fortunes, and families to save others. Among those was Auguste Bohny, a Swiss citizen who saved the lives of many children.

Auguste Bohny was born on July 9, 1919 in the Swiss town of Basel as the son of a tram conductor. Auguste attended high school in his hometown where he learned the piano and clarinet. Auguste joined the Service Civil International in 1937. He later attended teacher training college in 1939 and graduated in 1941 from the Swiss Army Recruit School. On May 1941, Auguste reported to the regional director of *The Association for War-Affected Children* in southern France, Mr. Maurice Dubois. Auguste was then assigned his post in Le Chambon-sur-Lignon, to build three more children homes. Auguste became the co-founder and administrator of three children's homes, *Guespy*, *Abric*, and *Faidoli* where approximately 200 kids each spent four to six months.

During the Holocaust, Auguste Bohny along with the assistance of Pastor André Trocmé used these children's homes as a refuge to rescue about 3,000 to 5,000 local people from being persecuted. Auguste and his fellow helpers forged identification papers, ration cards, and supplied people an escape route to other countries. Using these houses they saved over 800 kids. Nathalie Plessner, Hanne Hirsh, and Margot Wicki-Schwarzchild were three among the survivors confirmed by Yad Vashem.

In 1944, Auguste married Friedel Reiter. While working in southern France they fell in love. Friedel Reiter was herself an orphan in 1914 by losing her father at the front lines of World War I two years after her birth in Vienna 1912. She was accepted into a foster family in Kilchberg. She attended nursing school in Zurich and twenty years later she became a Swiss citizen. Knowing how being an orphan felt she joined the *Swiss Association for War-Affected Children* (SAK) like Auguste Bohny. She rescued children during lapses of attention of the Nazi officers on the railway platforms, and she brought them to storerooms till she could place them into families associated with the SAK. She disobeyed direct orders from the regional director and kept sheltering kids even when the French government was threatening legal action against the SAK. Together Auguste and Friedel worked to help kids and families in their region to escape the Nazi hounds and live better and safer lives.

When France was liberated they went back to Switzerland together and had four kids. Even after the war was ended, Auguste and his wife still donated to the cause of helping children to relocate from prison camps and begin a new life. Outside of these works, Auguste went on to pursue his career as a teacher. He later became a speech therapist and worked with challenged children. Auguste even furthered his service to the community by being the chairman of the Swiss National Association for the Blind from 1979 till 1995.

The Bohnys received two distinguished honors for their heroic actions. One award from Yad Vashem, for being The Righteous among the Nations in 1990, was given for specifically saving eight people. Another award that Auguste and Friedl received was the Moral Courage Award from the Jewish Foundation for the Righteous in 1994.

In the midst of the Holocaust, when Jewish families and particularly children were hunted and rounded up, not many of them could have thought that they could find help. But they did! Many people have been courageously involved in one way or another to save strangers who were being persecuted. These people risked and sacrificed their lives and fortunes to try their best to give a chance to the people that faced genocide. They did what they considered morally right for their fellow humans. They rescued the most vulnerable, the children who were victims of violence. These heroes should be respected. Selfless and brave, shielding and protecting the vulnerable, facing the worst of danger and terror, they showed us the utmost strength of human courage. These people were the best of us and they should go down in history as the people they are, heroes, like Auguste Bohny, Fridel Bohny-Reiter, and many others.

NOT YOUR AVERaGE HERO

Tyra Thompson

In 1933, the Germans, under Adolf Hitler's Nazi Party, murdered those of Jewish origin throughout Germany and other parts of Europe. Hitler and his collaborators believed that anyone that was a different race from them was a threat to Germany. Hitler and his followers exterminated not only Jews, but also homosexuals, Jehovah's Witnesses, the disabled, and their enemies. Unfortunately, Jews were the main target during the Holocaust and they were the most persecuted. The Germans tortured the victims and made life extremely difficult. The Nazis sent the victims to ghettos, concentration camps, transit camps, and forced-labor camps where they were eventually gassed or starved to death. The Nazis even convinced most of the Jews that they were being sent away to work camps but instead brought them to extermination camps where men, women, and children were systematically murdered. By the end of War World II in 1945, the Nazis had killed about 6 million Jews, which was one third of their population. This horrific historical event is called the Holocaust and as result over 9 million people died in total.

Thankfully, not everyone was as horrible as the Nazis during World War II. There were many citizens during the time who were brave enough to step up and help those who the Nazis were attacking and put their own lives and others at risk. For example, one of these heroes was named Sister Jeanne Berchmans. Born in 1897, Sister Jeanne Berchmans was one of the many Swiss heroes during the Holocaust who saved lives. She was born in Bremgarten, Switzerland and was christened Marie Meienhofer. At a young age, Marie decided to dedicate her life to loving and helping others and living as a disciple of God. She was a follower of Christ and knew she must be closer to God. So, in the year 1924, Marie joined the Catholic order of Sacred Heart and became a nun. She changed her name to Sister Jeanne Berchmans and taught as a teacher at the convent where she helped girls learn how to speak many languages, such as French and

German. During a time of persecution against the people of Jewish origin, she was asked by Father Rosay to give refuge to three Jews from Austria and keep them safe. She agreed and did her best to keep the Wittle family out of danger's way. The Wittles consisted of Taube, her daughter Renee, and younger son Bruno. They had fled from Austria in 1938. Meanwhile, Father Rosay, a priest in nearby Duovaine, was helping Jews everywhere to find safety. He was also one of many who dedicated a part of his life to keeping those in danger safe from the Nazis. She accepted his request and without any hesitation, and she hid the Wittle family in an unoccupied room. She treated them very nicely and made sure they were settling in fine. She put their needs before hers and gave them anything they were in need of. Soon, German soldiers came into the convent in search of any forbidden Jews. In a hurry, Sister Jeanne Berchmans quickly hid the Jews and put a sign on the door that said "Quarantine: Scarlet Fever" to trick the Germans. When the soldiers finally came across this particular room with the Wittle family inside, Sister Jeanne warned them that the people inside were sick and contagious. With little hesitation, the German soldiers left the convent in fear of catching the sickness. Because of Sister Jeanne's courageous act, the Wittle family later left and lived the rest of their lives in peace and away from the Germans.

Sister Jeanne Berchman was a wonderful person who saw beyond where people came from or what religion they practiced. She loved everyone and had a huge heart. She risked her life for the safety and protection of others and did everything in her power to keep them satisfied while they were with her. She was given the Yad Vashem medal in 1991 and was an inspiration to those around her. She truly was a hero of the Holocaust.

Sister Berchmans was not the only partisan who helped during the Holocaust. There were many others around the world and in Europe who voluntarily helped to successfully overthrow Hitler's tyranny. These people went to such measures as blowing up supply trains, destroying bridges, and freeing trapped Jews. These heroes dug tunnels underneath the ghettos and used that as an escape route to freedom and life away from the Germans for the Jews. These men and women dedicated their lives to fighting against Hitler and his campaign. If it were not for these lionhearted people, many of the survivors would not be alive today to tell their story.

The Holocaust teaches many that the world was not always a happy place and still to this day, some things have not changed, but simply decreased. For example, there is still murder and starvation today, but not as much as there was during the Holocaust. If it were not for the brave souls who took it upon themselves to risk their lives for those different from them, the world would not be same. As a result of Sister Jeanne Berchmans brave encounter, many Jews were saved. When looking back at all that Sister Jeanne had risked, one might acknowledge her bravery and dignity. Sister Jeanne Berchmans and many others were the true heroes of the Holocaust. May they and the Holocaust never be forgotten.

Sutter Middle School, Sacramento, CA

I have been teaching 8th grade English and U.S. history at Sutter Middle School for ten years. My commitment to teaching about the Holocaust came as a result of how poorly it was done in our anthology book. I have been on a quest to learn more every since. I am currently a fellow for the Central Valley Holocaust Educators Network and U.C. Davis. I have studied at the United States Holocaust Memorial Museum, the Museum of Tolerance and USC's Shoah Foundation. The underlying theme throughout my teaching is "What You Do Matters." I challenge my students to go deeper in their thinking during our study.

PAUL GRUENINGER

Callie Wong

The Holocaust was an atrocious event in which 6 million Jews were murdered because of a plan carried out by the Nazis. The Nazi party, or the National Socialist German Workers' Party, had very anti-Semitic beliefs and was lead by Adolf Hitler. The Holocaust lasted from 1933 to 1945. Jews were not the only ones targeted, as 5 million others were killed too. Those killed were also Jehovah's witnesses, Roma, homosexuals, political prisoners, handicapped, and political prisoners. While the Holocaust was a terrible result of the Nazis, many people realized the horrors that were taking place and decided to act against it even with their own lives were in danger.

Hitler had come to power in 1933 and immediately began restricting Jewish people's rights. Some had to leave their jobs, and others had their businesses boycotted. Books written by Jews were burned. New books were written, even children's books, which showed Jews as evil people. In 1935, Jews couldn't marry non-Jews, and they weren't even considered as citizens of Germany. Anyone who rebelled would be sent to a concentration camp. In 1938, Hitler decided to occupy Austria and Sudetenland. These countries had restrictions placed upon them, specifically placed on the Jews. They began to mirror Germany and the inhumane treatment of Jews. Jews' homes were looted, they were jailed or sent to concentration camps in Germany.

Paul Grueninger is an example of a true hero and of someone who was willing to rebel against the barbaric actions taking place around him. He was born in 1891 in St.Gallen in the North East of Switzerland. In August of 1938, Switzerland closed its borders so no refugees from Austria could enter. Grueninger was under orders to send back any people wanting to enter Switzerland that did not have the proper paperwork. In October 1938, Jews had a "J" stamped into their German passports after a meeting between Nazi and Swiss officials. Life for Jews in Austria was worsening, so more and more tried to illegally pass into Switzerland. Then at 47 years old, Grueninger had to decide whether to help the Jews pass and place himself in a dangerous position, or follow his orders and make them stay in Austria.

Grueninger made the selfless decision to help the Jews and face the consequences. Not only did Grueninger let the refugees enter Switzerland, he also lied in their records. Instead of saying the true date in which the refugees entered, he had their passports show that they had arrived before March 1938, when entry was still legal. These Jews were now "legally" in Switzerland. They were taken to Diepoldsau camp, where Jewish organizations helped them get temporary residency permits or find another final destination. Grueninger also gave false reports about the number of arrivals and helped stop attempts to find illegal refugees in Switzerland. He even used his own money to buy clothing for Jews during the winter.

Grueninger knew of the dangers that he faced while helping the Jews. A friend of his family even warned him, telling him that he was on the Gestapo's (Secret State Police) black list. However, he did not listen to the warning and instead kept helping the Jews. The Gestapo knew about him because of a Jewish woman he had helped; she had left her jewels in a hotel in Bergenz and asked him to help her recover it. He got in touch with Ernest Prodolliet who resided there. The women wrote to her relatives in Vienna, saying how nice Grueninger was and that he was going to get back her jewels. The letter was intercepted by the Nazis. The Gestapo took the jewels and put the hotel owner in prison. They then decided to watch Grueninger and later told the Swiss Federal Authorities.

Grueninger was fired in March 1939, and he was brought to trial. His crime was allowing about 3,600 Jews into Switzerland illegally. He was also charged with helping the Jews in other ways, such as helping them avoid detection. His trial was opened in January 1939 and lasted for two years. In March 1941, he was found guilty. Grueninger lost his retirement benefits and had to pay the fines for the trial. For the rest of his life he was poor, because it was hard for him to get a job with a criminal record. Even though he had been caught, Grueninger never wished he had followed his orders to sent the Jews back to Austria.

In December 1970, it was almost the end of his life and the Swiss government finally sent him a letter of apology. However, they didn't reopen his case until 1995, and he was completely absolved of all his charges in 1996. This was 23 years after his death. In 1971, the Yad Vashem Institute gave Grueninger a Medal of Honor as a Righteous Among the Nations. He died on February 22, 1972 at age 81. Grueninger's name appears in the plaque in the monument at Washington D.C. in memory of the Jews. Grueninger was the first Swiss person to be acknowledged by the United States.

Paul Grueninger was a courageous man in the midst of a systematic murder. Grueninger knew that helping the Jews would put himself in danger, but he did it anyway. He decided to take a selfless step and do what was right and not what others told him to do.

Bibliography

Tenembaum, Baruch. *The International Raoul Wallenberg Foundation*. The International Raoul Wallenberg Foundation. Web. December 28, 2014.
The Jewish Foundation for the righteous. The Jewish Foundation for the righteous. Web. December 29, 2014.
Yad Vashem. Yad Vashem. Web. December 30, 2014.

KNUD CHRISTIANSEN

Evan Chin, Co-winner

Knud Christiansen was used to being famous, as he was a Danish rower who competed in the 1936 Berlin Olympic games. Little did he know that later he wouldn't be earning a gold medal, but rather a spot on the list of legendary figures at the Yad Vashem Memorial Museum in Jerusalem.

During the Olympic Games, Knud had seen the infamous Adolf Hitler a few times, one of the times being when Hitler refused to watch African-American athlete, Jesse Owens, receive a gold medal. At that time, his future wife, Karen Rasmussen also was living in Berlin and was at a very prestigious cooking school. As a Jew, she had seen many other Jewish people being abused, so she quickly left and went to Denmark, where she met Knud. A few years later, Karen and Knud had two kids and lived in Denmark, which was being invaded by the Nazis at the time. He looked for any ways to help defend his country, so he had joined the Danish Resistance and a group of people called the Danish Freedom Fighters. Being a part of all those groups put him on a Nazi watch list, and he worried that being in those groups would put his family at risk. Since Knud was a part of the Danish Resistance, he heard about a big Nazi plan to arrest all of the Jewish people in Copenhagen. Copenhagen at the time had a majority of Denmark's Jewish population, so the Nazis referred to their plan as a convenient mass roundup. Knud was informed that the round up was planned on Rosh Hashanah at exactly 10 p.m. on Oct. 1 in 1943. At first, Christiansen ushered large groups of Jews to farmhouses, churches and city apartments, using every available shelter to safeguard the Jews from immediate arrest. His youngest daughter, Jytte, remembers her home was teeming over with guests in the living room, dining room and spare rooms in the back of the apartment.

Christiansen tried to save every Jewish person he knew; both close friends and even complete strangers. One night in late September, Christiansen rushed to his weekly bridge game and urged two of his friends to immediately go into hiding. One of the brothers insisted on going home first, ignoring Christiansen's offer to make arrangements for the brothers and their families. The next day Christiansen heard that the friend had been caught by Germans and sent to a detainment camp. Desperate to save his buddy, he went to a Danish Nazi who had his friend captive, and tried to convince him that he was only one-quarter Jewish, so technically he wasn't a Jew.

The commandant told Christiansen "too many Jews had slipped through the net," all the while refusing to release the friend. Taking considerable risk to his own life, Christiansen carried his request to the highest-ranking Nazi in Denmark, General Werner Best, who was known as the Blood Hound of Paris for sending many Jews to death camps.

Although nobody really knows what exactly happened, people say that the fact that Christiansen was an Olympic athlete contributed to the convincing of General Werner. In fact General Werner even asked him if he wanted to be part of a Nazi propaganda because he was "handsome gentleman."

For the rest of the war many Danish people helped Jews leave the country, but Christiansen and his family still stood out for saving the most lives. His father-in-law opened his home on the shoreline to shelter large groups of escaping Jews; his mother, the owner of a famous chocolate shop in Copenhagen, let the rescuers use her shop as a meeting place; and his younger brother acted as a lookout on the beachfront for Jews being taken across the channel from Denmark to Sweden.

His wife was in fact one of the most heroic members. For five years, Karen Christiansen, a highly educated woman, took a huge risk by publishing a newspaper called "Die Warheit" (The Truth), which translated BBC broadcasts from Dutch into German to inform Weirmacht soldiers of abuse being committed by the Third Reich and the more realistic accounts of the Allied advances in the war. Not only did she help by publishing newspapers, but she also helped wounded soldiers of the Danish resistance.

Christiansen also recalled that, "A lot of the Germans didn't want anything to do with the war," and that "They were very young and wanted nothing to do with the killing of Jews." He wished there was some way to have those soldiers join him, but of course they couldn't.

After 70 years, memories of the war now come to Christiansen in fragments. He recalls that he couldn't bear to watch the white buses of skinny, abused Jews returning from Theresienstadt detainment camp; the bittersweet feelings at the more fortunate parade of Jews returning from Sweden and dropping flowers of appreciation at his mother's floral shop; and the satisfaction of watching the Germans pack up and leaving Denmark. Christiansen says that the best memories he has of those terrible, desperate time is of his whole nation coming together to help a group of people.

In 2005, Knud and Karen Christiansen's names were added to a list of legendary figures—among them Raoul Wallenberg and Oskar Schindler—as "Righteous Among Nations" at the Yad Vashem Memorial Museum in Jerusalem. While Karen died in 1992, Knud Christiansen was 90 years old at the time of the honor.

HERMINE SANTRUSCHITZ GIES

Joseph Sison

Bravery. What do you associate with that word? Do you think of firemen or those who serve in our armed forces? Do you think of a time you conquered your fear? I would like to tell you about a woman who risked her life trying to save other people. This person should be an image we associate with bravery, because Miep Gies embodied bravery.

Hermine Santruschitz Gies was born in Austria in 1909. All of Austria suffered from food shortages after World War I. Hermine's parents sent her to Leiden, Holland, where she was taken in by a foster family. The foster family called her by the nickname Miep, and within a couple of years of taking her in they moved to Amsterdam. When she was 24 years old, she applied as a secretary and worked under Otto Frank, with whom she became good friends, as did her long- time fiancé, Jan Geis. Miep refused to join a Nazi women's association, and her Austrian passport was about to be invalidated; this would mean that she would need to be deported to Germany, which had annexed Austria. She and her fiancé got a quick marriage in 1941 so that she could obtain her Dutch citizenship and not be deported.

You have heard the story of the Anne Frank for sure. She was a Jewish victim of the Holocaust, and her diary helps us learn of all the torment that the Jewish people suffered. . When they were captured, she tried to buy their freedom, but that did not work. Miep could have been killed for her part in hiding the Jewish families, but she put their lives in front of her own, proving her bravery. This story is special to me because in the second grade I went to a B Street Theater play with my class to see "The Diary of Anne Frank." After seeing the play, I remember thinking about how much better this world would have been if more people were as brave and selfless as the woman who hid and took care of the Frank family. I thought that if more people petitioned for the rights of the Jews and stood up against what was bad, then the Holocaust might have never happened. Since watching the play, I always try to make it a point to stand up for people who are oppressed or are less fortunate. I want to make sure that nothing like the Holocaust ever happens again.

When I was in 3rd grade, I remember a time when two kids shoved me against a fence because they didn't like the way I looked. Fortunately, one of my friends was nearby and he stood up for me. I found what he did comforting. Because someone stood up for me then, I no longer was afraid to be different--because I knew my friends would be there for me, and I would never let any bully tell me how to live my life. This may just have been a small conflict that I had in my life, but I sometimes compare this to how it would feel to be Jewish during the Holocaust. People treat you differently in that you can't live how you want to live, etc.

Maybe if a lot more people were brave and stood up against the Jewish discrimination the Holocaust could have been prevented. When our teacher, Mrs. Cooperman, had a speaker who survived the Holocaust come in, he gave an example to help us better understand the persecution of the Jewish people. His name was Mr. Marks, and he gave the following example: Say you have a pencil, and your teacher takes it. Instead of arguing for it back, you say, "Whatever, it is just a pencil," and so you get another one. This sort of thing keeps happening, and the next thing you know you are told to stay in at lunch every day, and no one except you is given homework. This example that he gave compared the pencil and the other things taken away to the rights of the Jewish people, but he said if the Jewish people had protested more, they might not have gotten so many rights stripped from them. This analogy reminds me of what Edmund Burke's famous quote, "The only thing necessary for the triumph of evil is for good men to do nothing." And that is not what Miep Gies did.

Miep Gies makes me think of a hero because not only was she brave, but she was humble. "I don't want to be considered a hero. Imagine young people would grow up with the feeling that you have to be a hero to do your human duty. I am afraid nobody would ever help other people, because who is a hero? I was not. I was just an ordinary housewife and secretary." Her humility in denying herself as a hero only makes her seem more like one, for not being consumed with pride. Another quote that proves her humility was when she said, "I myself am just an ordinary woman. I simply had no choice." This also says that what she did was the right thing and the only thing that she could have done. For she would not wish to turn away help to those who needed it the most.

Not everyone in this world is a hero, but some people are. There were people who protested what the Nazis were doing to the Jews or who tried to protect the Jews, and they showed a lot of bravery. I hope that the example that Mr. Marks gave would inspire more people to be brave and go against an unjust government or even against a playground bully to protect other people or other kids. These people are heroes.

Bibliography

"Miep Gies." *Wikipedia*. Wikimedia Foundation. Web. 13 Feb. 2015. <http://en.wikipedia.org/wiki/Miep_Gies>.

DR. TINA STROBOS: DUTCH HOLOCAUST HERO

Quincy Johnston

When everyone is telling you something and the whole world believes it, how do you know right from wrong? How do you stand up and do something about it. You are, after all, only one person. Just one life like the rest of the world. How do you make a difference? The stories of Holocaust survivors show us that we can make a difference. It doesn't matter what anyone else thinks or what someone is telling you to do. No one controls you but yourself. You can stand up in the world and make a difference, even if it seems small at the time. Just one small action can do so much for a person. If you read and listen to people that were alive during the holocaust you start to understand the bravery and courage of people. It makes you want to stand up and do something, to make a difference in the world. I will be talking about one of the many heroes who stood up when the world was in peril. This woman did as much as she could to make a difference in the world she lived in. Her name was Dr. Tina Strobos.

Dr. Strobos was a woman who did what she could to help the world that was falling apart around her. She was born on May 19, 1920, in Amsterdam, Netherlands and died on February 27, 2012, in Rye, New York. She was just a young student who was studying medicine at the time, but she risked everything to help people in need. When the Nazis invaded the Netherlands, Dr. Strobos was studying at a university there. She refused to sign an oath of loyalty to Aldof Hitler along with the majority of the university and because of this the school was shut down. Dr. Strobos refused to do nothing about the awful things going on around her and joined the underground resistance movement. After armed resistance become too dangerous, she started to help by hiding Jews in her home. She hid more than 100 Jews even though it put her own life in jeopardy.

Dr. Strobos was interrogated by the Gestapo nine times. The Gestapo was the secret police of Nazi Germany. The Gestapo was brutal with her, and she was thrown up against a wall once and was knocked unconscious. Even though she was put through many hardships, she continued to do what was right. In spite of hiding Jews in her home, she also did a number of other things including carrying ration stamps on her bike to Jews in hiding, stashing guns and transporting radios to resistance fighters, and creating fake identity cards.

Perhaps the most heroic thing Dr. Tina Strobos did was hide Jews in her home. She lived with her mother and in their three story rooming house they ran a sanctuary for hiding Jews from the Nazis. The Dutch resistance sent a carpenter one day who came and built a hiding place in their home. The Dutch resistance was the underground resistance group Dr. Strobos joined and was a group that helped Jews

430

escape the Nazis. The hiding place held about four people. It was in the attic and had an escape route through a window. The escape route was necessary for the people hiding to be safe. The famous Anne Frank hiding place did not have an escape route and when the Gestapo came there was no way to escape. Dr. Tina Strobos' hiding spot was very well made and extremely hard to find.

Hearing stories of the Holocaust is horrifying. The pain and agony people went through was awful. They make you question life and what it means. The stories make you cry, and sometimes rejoice over the little victories of some survivors. There are many stories of people who hid in Dr. Strobos's attic. From a three year old child to a full family of five, she saved so many people. One of the lessons the Holocaust has taught us is that events like this can happen and the generations to come have to be aware so it will never happen again. While this might be a hard subject to learn about, is necessary.

It is people like Dr. Tina Strobos who we look up to. Someone that made a difference in so many lives by standing against something she thought was wrong. It didn't matter how many times the Germans searched her home, or how many times she was interrogated by the Gestapo. She stood up for what was right and that makes her the best kind of hero. Someone who stands up for what is right and what they believe in so that the world can prosper. Someone who doesn't mind making sacrifices for the good of mankind. We are all just people. We are all created equal, but there are some who have just a bit more bravery who do amazing things for the rest of mankind to enjoy.

KNUD CHRISTIANSEN

Sidney Fong, Co-winner

A horrible memory of an action that is recorded in history and is branded into people's minds can never be taken back or erased from the world. It leaves an imprint on people of all ages and cultures who have learned about this important, gruesome event, and reminds future generations to never repeat it again. This situation took place from 1939 to 1945, known as the Holocaust. The Nazi Germans exterminated innocent human beings, especially Jews, whose dignity was deprived from them. Certain groups in the world either were forced to join the Nazi Germans or went against them to save the Jewish people. Heroes who had rescued the Jews during the Holocaust and were willing to share their important stories with the world today, and risked their own lives to save many human beings from suffering gruesome conditions. One of the most important countries that helped the Jews escape the Nazis was Denmark. This country isn't a part of the list of the major, famous people who helped the Jews, but it was a country that wasn't attacked by the Nazis until later on in World War II. They protected the small population of Jews that were in Denmark during the Holocaust and didn't treat them poorly like other countries, such as Austria and Germany. The Jews were treated equally with other people in Denmark. When the Nazi Germans did come to take away the Jews, some Danish people risked their lives to develop rescue missions and made these missions successful.

After the tragedy of the Holocaust was over, many of the heroes and the Jewish refugees didn't come out to share their experiences, fearing to remember the horrific events that occurred during World War II. There were famous heroes in Denmark who made remarkable accomplishments to save hundreds of Jews. One of the little-unknown rescuers during the Holocaust was Mr. Knud Christiansen. When he was in his 20s, he discovered the Nazi brutality the first few years before the war started. He participated in the 1936 Berlin Olympics, as part of the Danish Rowing Team and married his wife, Karen Rasmussen. He also had a business that manufactured leather goods and the majority of the workers were Jews. In April 1940 to May 1945, Germany invaded their country, Denmark and other nations. During this time in history, Christiansen participated in the Danish Freedom Fighters, a group of people that protected the Jews from being taken from the Nazi Germans and participated in acts of destruction against the Nazi war effort. In order to protect the Jews, the Danish Freedom Fighters developed a rescue operation. They helped the Jews move into hiding places throughout the country and from there to the coast; fisherman then transported them to Sweden. These courageous Danish heroes, like Mr. Knud Christiansen, dedicated their time out of their daily life schedule to take part in this group until all the Jews were safe.

Christiansen helped rescue the Jewish refugees in various different ways. One of the most significant rescue missions he made was when he overheard a conversation between the upper ranks of Nazis in his neighbors' houses. Since he lived in a real estate area in Copenhagen, upper class Nazis chose these places for their headquarters. He discovered and learned their plan to arrest Jews in one "convenient" mass roundup. It was planned to be on Rosh Hashanah at 10 p.m. on October 1, 1943. They expected all of Denmark's 7,000 Jews to remain at home for this important, religious holiday. In order to keep these innocent people safe, he escorted them into farmhouses, churches, city apartments, his own house, and every available shelter. He rescued Jews who were his close friends to complete strangers. Another time was when he tried to warn his two friends who were Jewish brothers to go into immediate hiding after a weekly bridge game. Unfortunately, one of his friends ignored Christiansen's advice and went home to be captured by the Nazis. After hearing about this terrible news, Christiansen asked the Nazis to release his friend. With lots of persuasion involved, the Nazis finally set his friend free. Not only did he help the Jews escape, his extended family also had a

432

big part in it and had the same beliefs. For example, his father-in-law opened his big house to shelter huge groups of fleeing Jews. His mother allowed her chocolate shop to serve as a meeting place for rescue workers. His younger brother acted as a lookout on the beachfront for Jews to be ferried from Denmark to Sweden. His wife also helped block the information between Nazi soldiers by not publishing the newspaper that held the valuable information needed for the war. These courageous actions helped the Danish Jews in more ways than anticipated.

This scary time period dealt with racism against Jews and other cultures not under the Nazi standards of the people in the world. People around the world went against the Nazis' beliefs and fought against them to stop the persecution of innocent people. After reading about these Danish heroes and Mr. Knud Christiansen, it opened my eyes up to see ordinary people who risked their own lives to save many whom they care about and also ones who they didn't know. The Danish heroes fought for what was right and enforced that the Nazis' terrible actions were beyond cruel to exterminate a whole race of people. In Denmark, everyone treated each other with the same respect and didn't believe that anyone deserved extermination because of their race. They watched out for each other and developed friendly bonds. It was rare to see this kind of teamwork in such a country during this time. When reading more about the Danish heroes, I discovered that there were people outside of Denmark who didn't participate in rescuing the Jews and fight for what was right because they were scared to be involved in rebelling against the ruthless Nazis. It took bravery, cleverness, smart actions, and trust to save the Jews. These people stood up for the Jews when the Jews couldn't defend themselves from the Nazis. The Danish heroes worked together as a united country believing it was imperative to help save the thousands of Jewish refugees that lived in Denmark and fought against the Nazis to stop their heinous acts.

Mr. Knud Christiansen and the other Danish heroes risked their lives to save the Jews. They developed and succeeded in methods created to help save the Jewish refugees, believed in a goal to stop vicious people, and worked together as one to accomplish the important rescue efforts that were needed. I am amazed at how they devoted their time to do something that they believed was right and that human bloodshed should be stopped, despite endangering their own lives to help others. Many of the Danish heroes were not famous for their heroic efforts, but what matters are that people were being saved from extermination. We should learn from history so that we recognize the destruction of morality and respect for all humankind. Ironically, this period of history displayed how cruel human nature can be towards another, yet show the goodness and unyielding integrity to do what is right. The Danish heroes made a big impact on lives today and those who survived continue to share their stories of rescue, thanks to the brave individuals who had pride in humanity.

HOLOCAUST ESSAY CONTEST

Sidney Walthall, Runner-up

One of the darkest times in world history is during World War II. There were two major theatres to this war, one mainly in the Pacific islands called the Pacific Theatre, and the other in Europe called the European Theater. The European Theater included an eastern and western front, with the Russians fighting Germany from the East and the Americans and allies attacking from the West. The extent of the Holocaust was not well known outside of German held territories until Allied armies began overtaking German lands. Concentration camps were located mainly in Germany and Poland. These camps started out as horrific forced labor camps where Jews were forced to make weapons and materials for war. As time passed there became more and more death camps and fewer forced labor camps. The concentration camps became extermination grounds for the Jews. Gas chambers, starvation, and burning are just some of the ways Nazi Germans killed hundreds of thousands of Jews. Most countries were fighting against the Germans and people living in those countries helped many Jews escape the Nazi Germans. Some people stood by and watched the Germans exterminate Jews, but other honorable people like Per Johan Valentin Anger risked their lives to help the Jewish people escape Nazi Germany.

Per Johan Valentin Anger was born the oldest of three children on December 7, 1913, in Gothenburg, Sweden. Anger worked toward a law degree at the University of Stockholm and the University of Uppsala. Anger finally earned his law degree in November of 1939 the same day war broke out between Finland and the Soviet Union during World War II. That day Per Anger was drafted into the Swedish army. Not long after he was drafted, Anger was offered a trainee position at the Swedish legation in Berlin, Germany in the Swedish Foreign Department. Anger quickly finished his service in the army by January 1940 and by the end of January Anger had arrived in Berlin. While Anger was working in Germany for the Swedish foreign department he received underground information that the Germans had planned an attack on Denmark and Norway and that Sweden might be a part of the plan. Anger then sent a coded message of the planned attack to Stockholm, but it was not taken seriously. Later Anger received even more reliable information that the Germans were going to attack, and when he sent the second message it was taken seriously and Norway was warned. Oslo, Norway was attacked and captured by the Germans the next morning.

In 1941 Anger moved back to Stockholm where he became an official Swedish Diplomat and worked in the Foreign Department's trade center. He mostly worked on trade between Hungary and Sweden, until 1942, when in November he moved to

Budapest Hungary to work in the Swedish legation. In Budapest Anger continued to work mostly on Hungary and Swedish trade. Reports of liquidation and extermination in gas chambers in Poland began arriving in Hungary in 1942. Germany invaded Hungary on March 19, 1944. At this time there were about 750,000 Jews in Hungary. When Germany captured Hungary, Per Anger began to witness the Nazi persecutions of Jews in Hungary. Days after the persecutions began the Swedish Foreign Department set aside trade and started trying to save human lives. Anger came up with the idea to give out provisional passports to Jews with relatives or business associations in Sweden when a Jew named Hugo Wohl came to him in a very desperate state. These passports would protect them from deportation and internment. Jews with provisional passports were still required by the Germans to wear the yellow Star of David but were treated as Swedish citizens. Anger also came up with the idea to give out certificates to Jews who applied to be Swedish citizens. More than 700 provisional passports and certificates were provided to Jews in Hungary

In addition to saving Jews from behind a desk, Anger also worked with a man named Raoul Wallenberg who is recognized as a hero of the Holocaust. They worked together to save people from deportations at the train station. Anger would tell the German train commander that mistakenly there were Jews with protective passes on the train and that if the commander did not let them off then he would report the commander to Veesenmayer. Many people feared Veesenmayer so they would allow Wallenberg or Anger to go on the train and look for Jews with protective passes. In one instance Anger went on the train and found only two Jews with protective passes but was able to save 148 Jews without protective passes.

When Russians and Americans bombed the railroads and thousands of Jews were forced to walk to the border station called Hegyshalom, Anger was out in the real world directly helping Jews again. In 1944 Wallenberg and Anger began setting up safe houses for Jews. They disguised the safe houses as Swedish research institutes and libraries. That December, Wallenberg and Anger drove on the same route the Jews were forced to take to Hegyshalom. They distributed food to the Jews along the walk until there was none left. They also managed to save hundreds of Jews before they were handed over to a German SS commander at the border. About 37,000 Jews were forced to embark on the 180 kilometer journey and only 27,000 Jews made it to the Hungarian-Austrian border. Hundreds of them were saved but most of the 10,000 Jews died on the trip.

When the Germans neared Budapest, Anger and Wallenberg were given the option to go home along with the rest of the Swedish Foreign Department, but only one woman took the invitation back to Sweden. Anger and the others knew that if they left all the Jews they had saved would be vulnerable and their hard work would be for nothing. When the Germans invaded, Anger spent most of his time underground rather than above ground. At this same time Wallenberg disappeared. Anger last saw him on January 10, 1945, when Wallenberg refused to turn away from his work to go to a safe house. He was taken by the Russians on January 17, 1945, and to this day what happed to Wallenberg is a mystery. Anger was also taken by the Russians but after three months when the Swedish government intervened he was set free.

When the war was over Anger searched extensively for Wallenberg. Anger even convinced the German Chancellor in 1989 to call a Russian named Mikhail Gorbachev and ask him to free Wallenberg. The Russian refused to release him so Anger went to Moscow to speak with the man. Sadly Gorbachev refused again to free Wallenberg. After the war, Anger became Sweden's ambassador to Australia in 1970, Canada in 1976 and the Bahamas in 1978.

Per Anger was given several awards for his honorable actions during the Holocaust. In 1982 Yad Vashem and the State of Israel awarded him Righteous Among the Nations. This is an award that was given to people who risked their own lives to save the Jews. The Hungarian Republic's Order of Merit was presented to him by the Hungarian president in 1995. Anger was also honored by the Jewish Council of Sweden in 1996 and is honored by the Yad Vashem Holocaust Museum. The Swedish government also created the Per Anger prize for him in 2004. It honors people who have supported human rights and democracy. Per Anger has also had many books about him published. The first book about him was called _A Quiet Courage: Per Anger, Wallenberg's Co-Liberator of Hungarian Jews_ and was published in 1997. Per Johan Valentin Anger died on August 25, 2002, at 88 years old having made an incredible impact on the world.

Bibliography

"1995, Per Anger." _Wallenberg Legacy University of Michigan_. Web. 2 Jan. 2015. <http://wallenberg.umich.edu/medal-recipients/1995-per-anger/>.

"Heroes of the Holocaust - The Courageous Fighters against Hitler's Nazi Regime Genealogy Project." _Geni_family_tree_. Web. 2 Jan. 2015. <http://www.geni.com/projects/Heroes-of-the-Holocaust-The-Courageous-Fighters-against-Hitler-s-Nazi-Regime/953>.

"I Am My Brother's Keeper." _Per Anger_. Web. 2 Jan. 2015. <http://www.yadvashem.org/yv/en/exhibitions/righteous/anger.asp>.

Joffe, Lawrence. "Per Anger." _Theguardian_. 28 Aug. 2002. Web. 2 Jan. 2015. <http://www.theguardian.com/news/2002/aug/29/guardianobituaries>.

Lewis, Paul. "Per Anger, 88, a Diplomat Who Helped Jews, Is Dead." _The New York Times_. The New York Times, 28 Aug. 2002. Web. 2 Jan. 2015. <http://www.nytimes.com/2002/08/29/world/per-anger-88-a-diplomat-who-helped-jews-is-dead.html>.

"Per Anger." _Per Anger_. Web. 2 Jan. 2015. <http://www.jewishvirtuallibrary.org/jsource/biography/anger.html>.

European Schools

Christine Schären

Master Teacher, Collegé St. Croix, Fribourg, Switzerland
English Department

Juliana Almeida Brandáo

In 2011, I completed a bilingual degree in history and German, as well as teacher training for secondary education at the University of Freiburg, Switzerland. Since 2012 have been teaching history and German at the College of the Holy Cross (Sainte Croix) in Freiburg, Switzerland . In addition, I am working in the field of art education in Zentrum Paul Klee.

EINE ELISABETH EIDENBENZ – DER VERGESSENEN FRAUEN

Noemi Elodie Künzi

Stellen Sie sich vor, Sie würden einen Anruf erhalten. Die Person am anderen Ende der Leitung erklärt ihnen die schreckliche Lage, wie geflohene schwangere Frauen an Bahnhöfen auf Stroh ihre Kinder gebären. Im Land, in dem sich die Frauen befinden, herrscht gerade ein Bürgerkrieg. Die Person am anderen Ende der Leitung erklärt Ihnen, er brauche Ihre Hilfe. Sie sind jedoch nur zur Primarlehrerin ausgebildet. Was würden Sie tun? Würden Sie in das Land reisen, um den werdenden Müttern und Kindern zu helfen? Würden Sie dorthin reisen, um diese missliche Lage zu mildern? Was liesse Sie zögern ?

Eine der vergessenen Frauen erhielt genau einen solchen Anruf. Ihr Name war Elisabeth Eidenbenz. Am anderen Ende der Leitung erklärte ihr Karl Ketterer die damalige Lage während des Bürgerkrieges 1939 in Spanien. Elisabeth Eidenbenz hatte bereits ein Jahr zuvor mit Karl Ketterer für die spanische Kinderhilfe (SAS) zusammen gearbeitet. Ohne zu zögern folgte sie seinem Hilferuf.

Elisabeth Eidenbenz und weitere Frauen nennt man vergessene Frauen, aus dem einfachen Grund, weil man ihre grossartigen Taten vergass. Vergessene Frauen engagierten sich freiwillig. Es waren Kranken- und Kinderschwestern, Lehrerinnen, Kindergärtnerinnen und andere Helferinnen der Schweizer Kinderhilfe. Vergessene Frauen sind insbesondere diejenigen, welche während des Spanischen Bürgerkiegs halfen. Sie kümmerten sich um die Flüchtlinge, sorgten für Hungernde und arbeiteten in Kinderheimen. Aber weshalb sollte man die Taten solcher mutigen Frauen vergessen? Wie konnten wir nur diese Frauen vergessen, die auch dazu beitrugen, dass Menschen Kriege überlebten? Nur jene Menschen, denen geholfen wurde, haben sie nie vergessen. Aber vielleicht liegt es auch nur an der damaligen Sichtweise. Männer waren die Mutigeren. Männer waren die Stärkeren. Männer waren diejenigen, die in den Kampf zogen, an der Grenze standen und diese bewachten. Es sind Männer, die in den Kriegen kämpfen. Auch heute sind es grösstenteils Männer. Frauen können in der Schweiz freiwillig Militärdienst leisten. Aber während die Männer kämpfen, sich gegenseitig schwächen, was geschieht mit den Frauen und den Kindern? Vergessene Frauen haben sich für Frauen stark gemacht, die während Kriegszeiten litten. Besonders für die Kinder haben sich die vergessenen Frauen eingesetzt. Sie alle haben ein grosses Herz für Kinder und ein grosses Herz für die leidenden Frauen gezeigt. Zeigen Männer, die sich bekriegen, ein grosses Herz für Kinder? Sie kämpfen für das, an das sie glauben. Sie kämpfen darum lebendig zu ihren Familien zurückzukehren. Aber was waren die Frauen im letzten Jahrhundert ohne Männer? Sie waren schutzlos. Angreifbar. Manche sogar auf der Flucht. Sind es wirklich nur die Frauen, die damals ein grosses Herz gezeigt haben? Es sind Frauen, die sich damals schon um ihre eigenen Kinder gekümmert haben. Es sind Frauen, die den Haushalt erledigen. Auch in der heutigen Zeit sind es immer noch vorwiegend Frauen, die sich um die Kinder kümmern und den Haushalt erledigen. Auch werden in der heutigen Zeit noch Berufe wie Kindergärtner, Primarlehrer und Krankenpfleger mehrheitlich von Frauen ausgeführt. Schliesslich sind es ja auch wir Frauen, die die Kinder zur Welt bringen. Aus diesem Grund waren es wohl auch Frauen, die ein grosses Herz für Kinder gezeigt haben. Denn Kinder sind die Einzigen, die uns die Zukunft näher bringen können. Kinder sind unsere Zukunft.

Elisabeth Eidenbenz zeigte ein grosses Herz. Sie reiste nach Spanien, nur um den werdenden Müttern und Kindern dort zu helfen. Bescheiden nannte Elisabeth Eidenbenz auch den Grund in einem Interview 2006: „Warum ich das getan habe? Ganz einfach: Ich bin gefragt worden und habe Ja gesagt. Es war eine sehr interessante und notwendige Arbeit. Und eine Arbeit zu machen, die wirklich notwendig ist ... das ist was Wunderbares."

Aber auch Elisabeth Eidenbenz hätte man vergessen. Vielleicht haben Sie sogar noch nie etwas von ihr gehört. Vielleicht haben Sie sich noch nie mit vergessenen Heldinnen des vergangenen Jahrhunderts beschäftigt. Nur die Menschen, denen Elisabeth Eidenbenz geholfen hatte, hätten sich an sie erinnert, wäre da nicht ein Diplomat auf ihre besonderen Taten gestossen. 1991 suchte ein junger belgischer Diplomat jüdischer Abkunft seine Geburtsurkunde. Sein Name ist Guy Eckstein. Er fand seine Urkunde. Eine Urkunde des Amtes von Elne war es und auf der stand der Name der verantwortlichen Schweizerin. Elisabeth Eidenbenz. Guy Eckstein forschte nach ihr und machte ihre Taten bekannt. 1991 ist im Vergleich zu anderen „Helden" dieser Zeit spät.

Was genau hatte Elisabeth Eidenbenz für eine Tat vollbracht, dass sie als vergessene Frau gilt?

Elisabeth Eidenbenz ist am 12. Juni 1913 in Wila als evangelische Pfarrertochter geboren. Eine Ausbildung als Primarlehrerin im Lehrerseminar der Töchterschule Zürich absolvierte sie von 1923-1933. 1934 absolvierte sie eine Haushaltungsschule und unterrichtete Schwererziehbare in Winterthur und eine Klasse von fünfzig Kindern. Da sie das dänische Volksschulsystem faszinierend fand, reiste sie kurzerhand nach Dänemark um einen Sommerkurs 1937 zu besuchen. Von Dänemark reiste sie direkt nach Spanien, wo sie 1838 während des Spanischen Bürgerkrieges für die Arbeitsgemeinschaft für Spanienkinder (SAS) arbeitete. Im

Dezember 1938 kehrte sie zurück in die Schweiz. Dort erhielt sie den Hilferuf von Karl Ketterer.

Karl Ketterer hatte einen Hilfstransport zu spanischen Flüchtlingen in die Pyrenäen gebracht. Dort jedoch stellte er die schreckliche Lage für die schwangeren Flüchtlingsfrauen fest. Diese waren in grösster Not. So beschloss er, ein leerstehendes Schloss in Perpignan zu besetzten, um einen geschützten Ort für die Frauen zu eröffnen. Dazu brauchte er jedoch Hilfe von tatkräftigen Personen; so wie Elisabeth Eidenbenz. Sie hatte zwar keine Erfahrung oder Ahnung von Geburtshilfe, entschloss sich jedoch trotzdem zu helfen. Bei ihr seien die Frauen besser aufgehoben, als bei Niemanden, dachte sie sich. So gründeten sie in dem Schloss eine Mütterklinik. Schwangere Frauen aus Internierungslagern konnten ihre Kinder nun dort zur Welt bringen. 33 Kinder wurden von März bis zur Schliessung am 20. September 1939 in der Klinik geboren. Als der Krieg jedoch ausbrach, konnten die Hilfstransporte nicht mehr durch Frankreich reisen. Auf Anordnung des Besitzers musste die Klinik geräumt werden.

Maternité Suisse d'Elne

Elisabeth Eidenbenz kehrte kurz in die Schweiz zurück. Einen Monat später im November 1939 entdeckte sie ein leerstehendes Schloss in Elne. Mit grosser Willensstärke erlangte Elisabeth die Bewilligung, das Haus als neue Klinik zu nutzen. Elne liegt in Frankreich kurz nach der Grenze von Spanien. Mit Hilfe der SAK (Schweizerische Arbeitsgemeinschaft für kriegsgeschädigte Kinder) und Spenden aus der Schweiz machte sie das Haus bewohnbar. Das Schloss war vierstöckig. Jeder Raum in dem Haus benannte Elisabeth Eidenbenz nach einer Stadt in Spanien. „Es war ein grosses, schönes Haus mit einer Glaskuppel", erinnerte sich Eidenbenz. „Es gehörte zwei Bauern. Sie sagten mir, das Haus sei unbewohnbar. Das Dach rinne, und leider habe es keine Heizung." Spanische Flüchtlinge halfen ihr, eine Entbindungsklinik einzurichten. Die Entbindungsklinik sollte ein Zufluchtsort für Schwangere werden, was sie dann auch wurde. Flüchtlingsfrauen konnten ihre Kinder in Schutz gebären. Elisabeth Eidenbenz nahm sich den Schwangeren an und war bei all den über 600 Geburten dabei. „Jede Geburt war ein Erlebnis, eine riesige Freude. Haben Sie schon einmal eine Geburt erlebt?", fragte Elisabeth Eidenbenz an einem Interview. Der Interviewer hatte den Eindruck, als ob Elisabeth sich noch an alle Geburten erinnern könnte

Die Elne war ein Kinderheim, Entbindungsklinik und Zufluchtsort. Aber auch eine Insel des Friedens im Schatten des Zweiten Weltkrieges. Ein Kinderheim war es aus dem Grund, weil Elisabeth Eidenbenz schnell erkannte, dass vor allem Kinder die ersten Opfer in einem Krieg waren.

Als 1939 der zweite Weltkrieg ausbrach, waren ausserdem viele Juden auf der Flucht. Eine riesige Flüchtlingswelle hatte eingesetzt. Die Elne war eine rettende

Zuflucht vor Hunger, Not und Verfolgung. Die Maternité war die letzte Hoffnung vieler Flüchtlinge. Die Menschen sagten, solange es die Maternité gäbe, passiere ihnen nichts. Zu Recht aber auch. Elisabeth Eidenbenz verteidigte ihre Schützlinge, als wären es ihre eigenen Kinder. Elisabeth Eidenbenz betrachtete die Kinder auch als ihre eigenen. La Senorita, wie sie genannt wurde, wollte nie eigene Kinder. Weshalb sollte sie eigene wollen, wenn sie doch so einen wunderbaren Beruf ausübe, meinte sie dazu. Schliesslich hatte sie ja viele Kinder; die Kinder der Elne. Auch wollte sie nie heiraten, da sie das Gefühl hatte, keine gute Ehefrau zu sein. Nur dank Elisabeth Eidenbenz und den schweizerischen Helferinnens unermüdlichen Einsatz, ihres Willens und Mutes überlebten 600 Säuglinge, darunter auch Juden. Elisabeth Eidenbenz war es egal, dass es sich bei den Hilfesuchenden auch um Juden handelte. Sie nahm nicht Rücksicht auf Nationalität oder Vorschriften. Wer Hilfe brauchte, bekam Hilfe. 187 jüdische Kinder erblickten in der Oase des Friedens das Licht der Welt. Für Kinder und Mütter setzte sich Elisabeth mit grossem Herzen und Mut ein. Ganz besonders setzte sie sich für Jüdinnen ein, denn deren Kinder registrierte Elisabeth Eidenbenz unter einem falschen spanischen Namen. Sie verstiess dabei gegen das Gesetz. Dem neutralen Roten Kreuz war es verboten, in Frankreich ''politisch'' verfolgten Juden zu helfen. Manche Menschen sprechen bei dieser Tat sogar von der Eidenbenzschen List. Dies geschah in Anlehnung an Schindlers List.

Elisabeth Eidenbenz half nicht nur, sondern sie rettete auch Menschen.

Während des Zweiten Weltkrieges war es allen verboten, Juden zu helfen. Man verstiess dabei gegen das strenge Gesetz. Aber weshalb sollte man nach Herkunft und Glaube unterscheiden, wem man helfen darf und wem man nicht? Es sollte jedem geholfen werden, der auch Hilfe braucht. Den Juden hätte man während des Zweiten Weltkrieges helfen sollen, als sie verfolgt wurden. Doch wenn man einem Juden half, lebte man in ständiger Angst, sich dabei auch selber in Gefahr zu bringen. Dabei hätte es einfach gar nicht so weit kommen sollen, dass Menschen eine solch radikale Sichtweise entwickelten. Weshalb sollten Menschen weniger gut sein als andere? Wir sind alle gleich. Wir bestehen alle aus Knochen, Haut, Haaren, winzigen kleinen Zellen, Blut und Wasser. Man sollte Menschen weder durch ihre äussere Erscheinung, ihre Sichtweise, ihren Glauben, ihre Nationalität, ihr Geschlecht oder ihre Sexualität unterscheiden und dabei den schlimmen Fehler begehen Menschen auszuschliessen. Nur wenn jemand an etwas anderes glaubt, heisst das noch lange nicht, dass sein Glaube falsch ist. Nur weil jemand eine andere Sichtweise hat, heisst das noch lange nicht, dass seine Sichtweise verkehrt ist. Nur weil jemand eine andere Nationalität hat, heisst das noch lange nicht, dass seine Herkunft minderwertig ist. Man sollte weder rassistisch, noch radikal denken. Der Mensch ist ein Mensch, der Fehler macht. Nur sollten Fehler, die bereits passiert sind, nicht noch einmal geschehen. Menschen sollten ihre Sichtweise nicht auf andere Menschen aufzwängen. Menschen sollten nicht ausgeschlossen werden. Wir leben hier gemeinsam auf der Erde. Auf nur einem Planeten. Wenn Menschen einander ausschliessen und bekriegen, entsteht nie eine Gemeinschaft. Wir werden nie friedlich miteinander und / oder nebeneinander leben können, wenn Kriege weitergeführt werden. Und so etwas wie den Juden während des Zweiten Weltkrieges wieder verfahren ist, sollte und darf es nie wieder geben. Einen Völkermord, wie den Holocaust, darf es nie wieder geben. 6 Millionen Tote sind 6 Millionen zu viele.

Gegen das Gesetz zu handeln, gelang Elisabeth Eidenbenz jedoch nicht immer. Die Deportation einer Frau, war eines ihrer schrecklichsten Erlebnisse. Die Frauen in der Elne lebten in der ständigen Angst von der Gestapo abgeholt zu werden. „Man kann sich nicht vorstellen, wie es für die Frauen war, in dieser Angst zu leben", erzählte Elisabeth Eidenbenz in einem Interview. Das Abholen einer bestimmten Frau konnte Elisabeth nicht verhindern. Die Frau war eine deutsche Jüdin. Ihre ganze Familie war bereits deportiert worden. Unglücklicherweise erkundigte sich die Frau bei einem Besuch auf dem Kommissariat nach ihrer Familie. Nur so fanden die Behörden heraus, dass die Frau in der Maternité entbunden hatte. Ihr Kind hatte jedoch nicht überlebt und war bei der Geburt gestorben. Die Frau wurde später von der Gestapo abgeholt.

Kurz darauf kam das Ende der Maternité. 1944 musste Elisabeth Eidenbenz ihr Projekt nach der Invasion der Deutschen in Frankreich aufgeben. „Ich erinnere mich noch genau, es war an einem Gründonnerstag. Vier Offiziere kamen und sagten, wir müssten ihnen das Haus überlassen. Sie waren ganz nett, es tat ihnen selbst leid", erzählte sie in einem Interview. Das Schloss wurde vom deutschen Militär beschlagnahmt. Innert vier Tagen musste alles gepackt werden und sie zogen nach Montagnac um.

Elisabeth Eidenbenz zog 1946 nach Wien, wo sie in einer geräumigen Villa ein Kinderheim eröffnete. Dieses wurde 1948 vom Hilfswerk der Evangelischen Kirchen der Schweiz (HEKS) übernommen und erweitert. Bis zu ihrer Pensionierung 1975 arbeitete Elisabeth dort und zog dann nach Rekawinkel im Wienerwald. 2002 erhielt sie den Titel "Gerechte unter den Völkern". Weitere Auszeichnungen und Titel folgten. Drei Jahre bevor sie starb, zog sie in ein Zürcher Altersheim.

Sie starb am 23. Mai 2011 im Alter von 97 Jahren.

Anderen zu helfen, empfand Elisabeth stets als grosses Glück. Aber das liegt auch daran, dass Elisabeth eine Eidenbenz war. Diese Einstellung war im Stammbaum der Eidenbenz verankert, denn viele Angehörige arbeiteten eben gerade wegen dieser Einstellung als Hebammen, Krankenschwestern und Kindergärtnerinnen.

Ich gehöre zwar diesem Stammbaum nicht an, aber auch ich möchte Kindern und Menschen helfen. Als mich Bekannte vor einem Jahr danach fragten, wo ich mich in zehn Jahren sehen würde, antwortete ich: „In zehn Jahren sehe ich mich als Lehrerin in Entwicklungsländern." Und so sehe ich mich immer noch in neun Jahren.

Quellen:

http://de.wikipedia.org/wiki/Elisabeth_Eidenbenz (12.2.15)
http://www.frauennet.ch/index.php/frauen-geschichten/6-elisabeth-eidenbenz (12.2.15)
http://www.anglophone-direct.com/Elisabeth-Eidenbenz-and-the (12.2.15)
http://www.srf.ch/play/tv/srf-wissen/video/ein-herz-fuer-kinder-%C2%96-schweizer-retterin-im-zweiten-weltkrieg?id=344f69e5-9e67-49e2-af1c-6279ba2dd6a1 (12.2.15)
http://www.nzz.ch/aktuell/startseite/eine-der-vergessenen-frauen-1.10727796 (12.2.15)
http://www.gerechte-der-pflege.net/wiki/index.php/Elisabeth_Eidenbenz (12.2.15)
http://www.prospecttv.de/deutsch/Elisabeth_Eidenbenz.html (12.2.15)
http://regio.newsnetz.ch/bezirk-pfaeffikon/wila/600-Kindern-auf-die-Welt-geholfen/story/27858509 (14.3.15)
http://derstandard.at/2482086/Lebensretterin-ohne-Grenzen (14.3.15)
http://www.amazon.de/Vergessene-Frauen-Humanit%C3%A4re-Kinderhilfe-Fl%C3%BCchtlingspolitik/dp/3796526950 (14.3.15)

CARL LUTZ: VERGESSENER SCHWEIZER HELD DES HOLOCAUST

„Für mich gibt es nur Menschen, die ihr Leben retten wollen – es gibt keine Deutschen, keine Juden, keine Schweizer."

Nora Gnos, Co-Winner

Diese Worte richtete der Schweizer Diplomat Carl Lutz an SS-Obersturmbannführer Adolf Eichmann. Mit einer unglaublichen Zivilcourage setzte der Appenzeller sich im Zweiten Weltkrieg für die Juden ein – mit riesigem Erfolg. Aber wer war dieser Mann genau? In diesem Essay beschäftige ich mich mit diesem etwas in Vergessenheit geratenen Schweizer, aber auch mit Helden des Holocaust im Allgemeinen. Außerdem werde ich zum Thema Rassismus Stellung beziehen.

1. Carl Lutz:

Der ruhige Schweizer, welcher am 30. März 1895 in Walzenhausen (AR) geboren wurde, wuchs in einer frommen, christlichen Familie auf. Von seiner Stieftochter Agnes Hirschi wird er als zurückhaltend, sehr harmoniebedürftig und still beschrieben. Seinen eigentlichen Berufswunsch, Pfarrer, musste er aufgrund seiner Schüchternheit aufgeben. Stattdessen arbeitete er in der Schweizer Gesandtschaft als Konsularbeamter. 1942 wurde der damals 47-Jährige nach Budapest versetzt, um dort als Vizekonsul für die Schweizer Botschaft tätig zu sein. Bald fungierte er als Leiter der Abteilung „Fremde Interessen". So wurde Lutz zum Hoffnungsträger für die ungarischen Juden. Der Appenzeller konnte dem Geschehen in Budapest nicht länger zusehen. Er sprach bei Hitlers Gesandten in Budapest vor und kämpfte mutig für die Emigration ungarischer Juden ins sichere Palästina. Lutz hatte zuvor für die Deutschen gute Dienste als   Diplomat in Palästina geleistet. Er nutzte seinen guten Ruf in den Verhandlungen mit SS-Obersturmbannführer Adolf Eichmann aus – und hatte Erfolg. Seine Bemühungen zahlten sich aus. Ein Kontingent von 8000 Einheiten wurde vom Führerhauptquartier bewilligt. Aber 8000 gerettete Menschenleben waren nicht genug für Lutz. Er ergriff die Initiative und entwickelte ein Schutzbriefsystem. Ohne Absprache mit der Schweizer Botschaft bemühte er sich gemeinsam mit einigen Helfern um die Rettung von einer möglichst großen Anzahl von Verfolgten. Für Juden, die nach Palästina auswandern wollten, stellte er ab 1944 Schutzpässe und Schutzbriefe aus. Dabei handelte es sich um von der ungarischen Gendarmerie und dem Eichmann-Kommando akzeptierte Dokumente, welche die Juden unter den diplomatischen Schutz der Schweiz stellten. Damit wurden sie vor der Deportation nach Auschwitz bewahrt. Geschickt umging der Diplomat die festgesetzte Limite von 8000 Emigranten, indem er die Schutzbriefe immer nur von 1-7999 nummerierte. Die Rettungsaktionen wurden ohne Skandale und im Stillen durchgeführt – mit einer unglaublichen Effizienz. Durch den Einsatz von Carl Lutz wurden zwischen 50'000 und 70'000 ungarische Juden vor dem sicheren Tod gerettet. Das war ungefähr die Hälfte aller Juden in Budapest.

Nach dem Ende des Zweiten Weltkrieges wartete Lutz den Rest seines Lebens auf die Annerkennung seiner Verdienste durch die Schweizer Behörden.

Aber seine außergewöhnlichen Leistungen blieben von seinem Vaterland lange ungewürdigt. Stattdessen wurde ihm eine „Kompetenzüberschreitung" vorgeworfen, da er ohne Absprache mit der Schweizer Botschaft die Schutzbriefe ausgestellt hatte, und die Briefe zudem als „Schweizerbriefe" betitelt waren. Bis hin zu seinem Tode war Lutz aufgrund der Missachtung seiner Heldentaten frustriert. Am 12. Februar 1975 starb er einsam und verbittert in Bern. Erst im Jahre 1995 – rund 20 Jahre nach seinem Tod – wurde er durch die Schweizer Behörden rehabilitiert.

Ich habe bei meinen Recherchen den Eindruck bekommen, dass Lutz' Leistungen mehr oder weniger in Vergessenheit geraten sind. Lutz' aufgeschlossene Denkweise in einem sehr dunklen Kapitel der Menschheitsgeschichte war meiner Meinung nach vorbildlich und außerordentlich uneigennützig. Sein mutiges Handeln sollte vor allem von der Schweizer Bevölkerung viel größere Anerkennung erhalten. Niemand erinnert sich gerne an all die vergangenen Grausamkeiten, obwohl genau diese Erinnerungen von ungeheurer Bedeutung wären. Die Mitschuld am Holocaust wird gerade von Schweizern – zu Unrecht – oft nicht wahrgenommen und verdrängt.

2. Schweizer Grenzen im Zweiten Weltkrieg:

Carl Lutz gilt als einer der wenigen Schweizer, die im Zweiten Weltkrieg wahre Tapferkeit bewiesen haben. Die Schweiz trug in diesem Krieg zur Ermordung von schätzungsweise 100,000 Menschen bei. Dies ist ein umstrittener Wert, der gerade einmal die abgewiesenen Flüchtlinge beinhaltet. Tatsache ist: Die Verweigerung von Hilfe kostete unzählige Menschenleben.

Seit August 1942 waren die Grenzen für jüdische Flüchtlinge „nur aus Rassegründen", praktisch vollständig geschlossen. Von der Schweiz als „stark besetztes Rettungsboot", war die Rede. Illegale Einwanderer wurden in Wagen wieder zurück an die Grenze gefahren, den Nationalsozialisten übergeben und somit in den Tod geschickt. Aber auch schon im Jahr 1939 wurden auf schweizerischer Seite unfassbare Schandtaten begangen. Gleich wie in Deutschland wurden die Pässe der Juden mit einem „Juden-Stempel" / „J-Stempel", gekennzeichnet. Auch das Fotografieren in Grenznähe, wurde von den Behörden bald verboten.

Als grausames Beispiel für den schweizerischen Antisemitismus, ist der Fall des Wiener Juden Armin W. im Basler Staatsarchiv dokumentiert. Er floh 1939 illegal nach Basel. Er wurde nicht ausgeschafft, allerdings hatte man ihn einem Arbeitsverbot unterstellt. Um sich seinen Lebensunterhalt zu verdienen musste er aber etwas unternehmen – trotz des Verbotes handelte er mit Bleistiften. Ende 1939 wurde er erwischt und es wurde augenblicklich seine Ausweisung beschlossen. Um dieser zu entgehen, versuchte Armin W., sich mithilfe eines Drahts das Leben zu nehmen. Lieber wäre er auf diese Weise gestorben, als den Nationalsozialisten in die Hände zu fallen. Die Schweizer Polizei zeigte sich davon aber unbeeindruckt. Unnachgiebig wurde Armin W. zuerst das Leben gerettet, er wurde verarztet, und anschließend den Nationalsozialisten übergeben. Kurz darauf wurde sein Tod von der Deutschen Polizei bekannt gegeben. Armin W. sei an einer Zellgewebsentzündung verschieden – eine geläufige Umschreibung der Deutschen für die Morde in den Konzentrationslagern. Die Protokolle des Falles wurden gemeinsam mit dem Stück Draht, mit dem Armin W. sich das Leben nehmen wollte, zu den Akten gelegt. Beigelegt war noch eine Quittung über 3 CHF. – für die Reinigung des blutigen Zellenbodens.

Fluchthelfer, welche gegen die damaligen Gesetzte verstießen, wurden bestraft. Nur wenige Schweizer zeigten Menschlichkeit. Doch dann und wann bewiesen einige Einwohner Mut.

Vor allem die nahe an der Grenze wohnhaften Bürger widersetzten sich in einigen Fällen den Gesetzen, sie boten den Flüchtlingen Schutz – und brachten sich dabei teilweise in Lebensgefahr. Nach dem Krieg ernteten diese Helfer kaum Lorbeeren. Viele von ihnen wurden, wie Carl Lutz, erst einige Jahre nach ihrem Tod von den Behörden rehabilitiert.

Erst kurz vor Kriegsende, am 12. Juli 1944 hob das Eidgenössische Justiz- und Polizeidepartement die Weisungen von 1942 auf und bestimmte, „alle an Leib und Leben gefährdeten Zivilflüchtlinge aufzunehmen". Die Schweiz öffnete ihre Grenzen. Viel zu spät für viele Juden. Nachträglich beschrieb das Land sich als „Rettungsboot im Sturm". Als „gut ausgerüsteter Ozeandampfer" es sei die allgemeine Pflicht, alle „Schiffsbrüchigen" aufzunehmen. Von den tausenden Juden, die in den Jahren davor schonungslos abgewiesen wurden, sprach plötzlich niemand mehr.

1. Helden des Holocaust:

Vorbildliche Fluchthelfer wie Carl Lutz in der Schweiz oder Oskar Schindler in Deutschland, haben durch ihr mutiges Handeln tausende Leben gerettet. Sie haben sich selbst in Lebensgefahr begeben, ohne dafür eine Gegenleistung zu verlangen. Aber sie waren auch absolute Ausnahmefälle. Wie viele Menschen hätten gerettet werden können, wenn vor allem die europäische Bevölkerung mehr Zivilcourage gezeigt hätte? Es sollte sich jeder Mensch persönlich verpflichtet fühlen, Hilfe zu leisten, wo es möglich ist. Man muss in keinem Krieg kämpfen, um Gutes zu tun. Eher geht es darum, Menschlichkeit und Toleranz zu beweisen.

Bernhard Marks, ein Holocaustüberlebender, kam kürzlich an unsere Schule, um einen Vortrag über den Holocaust zu halten. Seine Schilderungen haben mich sehr berührt und ich bewundere seinen Lebenswillen. Herr Marks hat für mich eine immense Vorbildfunktion.

Meiner Meinung nach sind auch Menschen wie Herr Marks Helden des Holocaust. Sie haben unvorstellbare Schrecken überlebt. Und trotzdem wollen sie der Vergangenheit nicht einfach den Rücken kehren. Obwohl es viel schmerzhafter ist, als das Geschehene zu verdrängen. Mit seinen Reden erreicht Herr Marks jährlich tausende Schüler, wie er auch mich erreicht hat. Er bringt uns dazu, über den Holocaust nachzudenken und uns damit auseinanderzusetzen. Auch wenn jede Rede alte Wunden aufreißt. Es ist eine Kunst, sich seiner Vergangenheit in dieser öffentlichen Weise stellen zu können. Ganz und gar keine Selbstverständlichkeit! Herr Marks hat sich entschieden, die Bevölkerung für das Thema Holocaust zu sensibilisieren. Mit einem eisernen Willen verfolgt er dieses Ziel. Er hat aus einer furchtbar unmenschlichen Situation heraus eine Lebensaufgabe geformt. Selbst nach seinem Tod werden seine Reden in den Gedanken unzähliger Menschen verinnerlicht sein. Aber was, wenn es irgendwann keine Zeitzeugen für den Holocaust mehr gibt? Was können wir tun, um die Erinnerung lebhaft zu erhalten?

2. Vergeben und Vergessen?

Sicherlich ist es wichtig, nach solch fürchterlichen Erlebnissen einen Abschluss finden zu können. Was geschehen ist, muss akzeptiert werden. Durch Verdrängung wird dies aber unmöglich sein. Wir müssen erkennen, dass sich nicht alle Schuld auf Hitler und das nationalsozialistische Deutschland übertragen lässt. Auch alle umliegenden Länder haben sich schuldig gemacht. Die Verantwortung darf von niemandem zurückgewiesen werden. Es geht mir bei diesem Essay nicht um Beschuldigungen. Es macht keinen Sinn, nur zurückzublicken und sich schlecht zu fühlen – wir müssen handeln! Mein Ziel ist es, die Sensibilisierung der Bevölkerung für das Thema Holocaust zu unterstützen.

Wenn wir die begangenen Verbrechen verdrängen, werden wir sie irgendwann vergessen. Damit ist der Grundstein für eine Wiederholung gelegt. Durch Wegsehen wird nichts erreicht. Behalten wir die schrecklichen Geschehnisse aber in Erinnerung, sprechen darüber und beschäftigen uns damit, können wir daraus lernen. Der Holocaust ist eine grausame Erfahrung, welche die Menschheit gemacht hat. Diese Lektion muss unbedingt verinnerlicht werden, um ähnliche Ereignisse künftig zu verhindern. Es genügt nicht, die Vergangenheit zur Kenntnis zu nehmen und dann zu vergessen. Wir müssen unsere Konsequenzen daraus ziehen. Im Zweiten Weltkrieg wurden rund 6'000'000 unschuldige Juden aus sinnlosem rassistischem Hintergrund ermordet. Sorgen wir gemeinsam dafür, dass es nie mehr zu einer vergleichbaren Katastrophe kommt!

3. Holocaust aus heutiger Sicht

Der eigentliche Anstoß für mein Essay ergab sich schon vor Herr Marks' Rede. Wenige Minuten zuvor, genauer gesagt. Als ich mit meinen Freunden auf dem Schulweg war, wurde dem Besuch von Herrn Marks nämlich mit wenig Begeisterung entgegengesehen. Das Thema Holocaust hat jeder von uns schon mindestens drei Mal in der Schule durchgekaut. Man bildet sich ein, alles darüber zu wissen. „Das kann ja sowieso nie mehr passieren!", meinte eine Freundin von mir, „So dumm ist die Menschheit auch wieder nicht! Langsam sollten wir wirklich damit abschließen." Da wurde mir klar, dass wir es trotz der eingehenden Beschäftigung mit dem Thema immer noch nicht realisiert haben. Weil es gerade in diesem Moment wieder passiert. Rassismus; er hat nie aufgehört. Aber warum konnte so etwas Grausames wie der Holocaust überhaupt passieren?

Die Wurzeln von Diskriminierung und Rassismus aufgrund verschiedener Ursachen reichen weit in die Geschichte zurück. Die Einteilung der Menschen in verschiedene „Rassen" wurde vor allem im 18. Jahrhundert neu praktiziert. Wissenschaftler versuchten, eine Erklärung für die offensichtlichen Unterschiede zwischen den Menschen zu finden. Aber schon damals gab es Menschen mit anderer Meinung. Johann Gottfried Herder, ein deutscher Dichter, Schriftsteller und Theologe im Zeitalter der Aufklärung, schrieb:

„Ich sehe keine Ursache dieser Benennung. Rasse leitet auf eine Verschiedenheit der Abstammung, die hier entweder gar nicht stattfindet, oder in jedem dieser Weltstriche unter jeder dieser Farben die verschiedensten Rassen begreift. [...] Kurz, weder vier oder fünf Rassen, noch ausschließende Varietäten gibt es auf der Erde."

Folgen von Rassismus waren immer schon grausam. Eroberungen inklusive dem Völkermord an den einheimischen Urvölkern, die vollkommene Entmachtung einzelner Volksgruppen und deren Ausschluss aus der Gesellschaft, Sklavenhandel in all seinen Formen. Mit dem Holocaust und der systematisch geplanten Ermordung unzähliger Menschen, hat der Rassismus eine neue Stufe erreicht. Und trotzdem haben wir scheinbar nichts daraus gelernt. Rassismus existiert noch immer. Wir erobern den Luftraum, erfinden das Internet, besiegen Krankheiten. Aber ein Problem, welches besteht seit dem es Menschen gibt, das mit uns gewachsen ist, ignorieren wir mutwillig. Es ist ja auch ein furchtbar unangenehmes Thema. Warum die dunklen Seiten betrachten, wenn man sich auch auf das Gute im Leben konzentrieren kann?

Wir haben schon zu oft erlebt, wie diese dunklen Seiten uns eiskalt erwischt haben.

Menschen mit anderer Hautfarbe, anderer Sprache, anderer Religion, anderer Kultur, anderer Sexualität, anderen Geschlechts. Menschen mit einer Behinderung, mit anderen finanziellen Möglichkeiten.

Kurz; alles, was uns von einander unterscheidet, kann ein Auslöser für Rassismus sein. – Trotz unzähliger Organisationen und Abkommen, die gegen den Rassismus ankämpfen. Auch wenn wir schon zu oft die Auswirkungen von Rassismus zu spüren bekommen haben. Was muss noch passieren, damit wir uns ändern?

Nach Susan Arndt, einer deutsche Anglistin und Afrikawissenschaftlerin mit Schwerpunkt Literatur, ist Rassismus *„an gesellschaftliche Gegebenheiten geknüpft, die sehr widerstandsfähig und resistent, vielleicht sogar irreparabel sind."*

Auch in der Schweiz ist Rassismus nach wie vor präsent. Männer verdienen teilweise mehr als Frauen, immer noch werden Menschen beschimpft und herabgesetzt. Vorurteile sind tief in unserer Gesellschaft verankert. Aber die Gesellschaft besteht immer noch aus Menschen. Und Menschen besitzen die Fähigkeit sich zu ändern.

4. Rassismus im 21. Jahrhundert

Es ist ein absoluter Trugschluss, dass Rassismus nach dem Holocaust ein endgültiges Ende gefunden hat. Oft wird er jedoch heruntergespielt und verharmlost. Catherine Trautmann, ehemalige Bürgermeisterin von Strasbourg, Pressesprecherin und Kulturministerin der Regierung Mitterand, hat mit ihren Worten: *„Rassismus ist keine Meinungsäußerung, Rassismus ist ein Verbrechen!"*, *meiner Meinung nach genau ins Schwarze getroffen. Vor allem extremistisch-religiöser Rassismus, aber auch zahlreiche andere Formen des Rassismus sind im 21. Jahrhundert allgegenwärtig. Jeder von uns, wurde – bewusst oder unbewusst – schon mindestens einmal im Leben direkt mit Rassismus konfrontiert. Stichwort: Mobbing. Egal ob im Netz, am Arbeitsplatz oder in der Schule. Mobbing macht sich genau jenen Hochmut zu Eigen, der für den Rassismus typisch ist. Man stellt sich selbst über andere Menschen. Weil man selber mehr wert zu sein glaubt. Aber woher nehmen wir uns die Erlaubnis, uns über andere Menschen zu setzen? Wie und warum wollen wir den „Wert" eines Menschen überhaupt definieren? Für Carl Lutz hatte jeder Mensch den gleichen „Wert". Den Wert eines Menschenlebens. Wir haben gesehen, wie viele Leben diese Einstellung im Zweiten Weltkrieg gerettet hat.*

Egal ob man während des Holocaust Leben gerettet hat wie Carl Lutz und viele weitere mutige Menschen, die Bevölkerung sensibilisiert wie Herr Marks oder auch nur aktiv gegen Mobbing vorgeht – jeder kann seinen Teil beitragen, um den Rassismus zu stoppen. Es bringt nichts, diesen Text zu lesen, entrüstet den Kopf zu schütteln, und das Thema anschließend zu vergessen. Sehen Sie nicht stumm zu; schließlich könnten Sie der Nächste sein! Rassismus braucht keine nachvollziehbaren Gründe; die brauchte er noch nie! Martin Niemöller, ein deutscher evangelischer Theologe und führender Vertreter der Bekennenden Kirche sowie Präsident im Ökumenischen Rat der Kirchen, *brachte die Sache auf den Punkt:*

„Als sie die Juden holten, sagte ich nichts; ich war ja kein Jude.

Als sie die Zigeuner holten, sagte ich nichts; ich war ja kein Zigeuner.

Als sie die Kommunisten holten, sagte ich nichts; ich war ja kein Kommunist.

Als sie die Schwulen holten, sagte ich nichts; ich war ja nicht schwul.

Als sie die Sozialisten holten, sagte ich nichts; ich war ja kein Sozialist.

Als sie mich holten, war niemand mehr da, der etwas sagen hätte können …"

Helfen Sie einem Mobbing-Opfer, verbannen Sie rassistische Witze aus ihrem Repertoire und vor allem: Bemühen Sie sich um Toleranz. Beweisen Sie Zivilcourage, wenn sie gefordert ist. Weltweit werden oft verschärfte Gesetze und Strafen gegen den Rassismus gefordert. Aber das alleine reicht nicht. Es sind nicht die Gesetze, die sich ändern müssen – wir müssen uns ändern!

5. Quellen:

http://de.wikipedia.org/wiki/Schweiz_im_Zweiten_Weltkrieg#Asyl-_und_Fl.C3.BCchtlingspolitik (3.2.15)

http://www.3sat.de/mediathek/?mode=play&obj=46498 (3.2.15)

http://www.srf.ch/sendungen/dok/carl-lutz-der-vergessene-held (3.2.15)

http://de.wikipedia.org/wiki/Carl_Lutz (3.2.15)

http://de.wikipedia.org/wiki/Kriegstote_des_Zweiten_Weltkrieges#Opfer_deutscher_Massenverbrechen_im_Kriegsverlauf

http://de.wikipedia.org/wiki/Rassismus#cite_note-120 (2.3.15)

http://tbb-berlin.de/?id_menu=20&id_submenu=&id_presse=225 (2.3.15)

http://www.cube-mag.de/2011/11/rassismus-im-21-jahrhundert/ (2.3.15)

http://www.akdh.ch/ps/uek.pdf (2.3.15)

http://www.katriburri.ch/cms/upload/pdf/Microsoft_Word_b_-_Bilder_WWII_Web.pdf (2.3.15)

http://de.wikipedia.org/wiki/Johann_Gottfried_Herder (2.3.15)

http://de.wikipedia.org/wiki/Susan_Arndt (2.3.15)

http://de.wikipedia.org/wiki/Martin_Niem%C3%B6ller (2.3.15)

Arndt: *Rassismus in Gesellschaft und Sprache*. In: Susan Arndt (Hrsg.): AfrikaBilder. Studien zu Rassismus in Deutschland. Unrast Verlag, Münster 2001, ISBN 3-89771-407-8, S. 23

MUSYS LISTE

Robin Beglinger, Co-winner

Ende des Zweiten Weltkrieges reiste ein ehemaliger Schweizer Bundesrat nach Deutschland und vereinbarte mit Heinrich Himmler die Freilassung und die Ausreise in die Schweiz von über 1000 Juden. Diese Abmachung wurde später als Musy-Himmler Vereinbarung bekannt.

Doch wie kam es dazu, dass ein Politiker, welcher aus seiner Bewunderung der Politik der Achsenmächte nie ein Geheimnis machte, zum Holocaust-Helden wurde?

War Jean-Marie Musy überhaupt ein Held? Oder verdienen andere, im Hintergrund agierende Personen den Heldenstatus?

Über Jean-Marie Musy

Jean-Marie Musy wurde 1876 in Albeuve im Kanton Freiburg geboren. Seine Eltern, Jules und Louisa Musy, waren die Besitzer des Hotels „Auberge des Anges", welches noch heute in Alb euve in Betrieb ist.

Als Jugendlicher besuchte Jean-Marie das Kollegium Sankt-Michael in der Stadt Freiburg und das Kollegium Saint-Maurice im Wallis, wo er den Schwerpunkt Philosophie wählte. Später studierte er Rechtswissenschaften an der Universität Freiburg, wo er 1904 sein Doktorat erhielt.

Zwischen 1901 und 1905 übte er das Amt des Substituts des Staatsanwalts aus, parallel dazu bereitete er sein Anwaltspatent vor. 1906 heiratete er Julietta Meyer und eröffnete kurz darauf seine Anwaltskanzlei, welche er jedoch 1911 aufgrund seiner Wahl zum Staatsrat wieder aufgab.

Als Staatsrat, später als Staatsratspräsident, wurde ihm die Aufgabe zugeschrieben, die Staatsfinanzen, welche durch den Grossen Krieg von 1914 zusätzlich litten, zu sanieren und die Kreditwürdigkeit der Staatsbank wiederherzustellen.

1914 wurde Musy in den Nationalrat gewählt, wo er wiederholte Male seine Abneigung gegenüber dem Sozialismus ausdrückte. Später gelang ihm der Sprung in den Bundesrat, wo er dem Finanz- und Zolldepartement vorstand.

Trotz der unsicheren wirtschaftlichen Lage gelang es Musy, den Bundeshaushalt durch verschiedene Massnahmen (z.B. durch Anhebung der Zollgebühren) auszugleichen. 1924 war er Vize-Präsident, 1925 und 1930 Bundespräsident der Schweiz, 1934 gab er seinen Rücktritt bekannt.

Doch bereits 1935 wurde er wieder in den Nationalrat gewählt, wo er sich nun praktisch gänzlich seinem Kampf gegen den Kommunismus widmete.

In den folgenden Jahren engagierte er sich stark in antikommunistischen und nationalistischen Kreisen und Organisationen. In dieser Zeit trat er auch das erste Mal mit führenden Nationalsozialisten Deutschlands in Kontakt, darunter Heinrich Himmler, welcher später in der Musy-Himmler Vereinbarung eine wichtige Rolle spielte. Später, als der Zweite Weltkrieg ausgebrochen war und Musy aus dem Nationalrat abgewählt worden war, machte er aus seiner Bewunderung der Achsenmächte und seiner profaschistischen Einstellung (jedoch lehnte er die sogenannte Rassenlehre ab) kein Geheimnis mehr.

Bereits 1920 hatte ihn die Stadt Freiburg für seine Verdienste als Staatsrat, später als Bundesrat zum Ehrenbürger gemacht und benannte eine Strasse (Avenue Musy, Freiburg) nach ihm.

Die Rettung des Ehepaars Bloch

Im April 1944 wurde Jean-Marie vom jüdischen Ehepaar Lob kontaktiert. Sie wollten, dass Musy nach Frankreich reiste und die Befreiung von ihrem Schwager und ihrer Schwägerin, Herr und Frau Bloch (beides Juden, welche in Frankreich von den Nazis verhaftet wurden), erreichte.

Musy, der das Ehepaar seit langem kannte und dessen Söhne mit den Söhnen von Herr und Frau Lob im Militär gedient hatten, erklärte sich dafür bereit, nach Paris zu reisen und zu versuchen, das Ehepaar Bloch zu befreien. Trotz den eisernen Klauen des Nazi-Apparates gelang es Musy nach zahlreichen langen Verhandlungen einige Monate später, die Freilassung des Ehepaars durchzusetzen.

Wie kam es zur Musy-Himmler Vereinbarung?

Kurze Zeit später, im Oktober 1944, wurde Jean-Marie von Recha und Isaac Sternbuch, den Gründern eines Komitees, welches die Interessen der "Union of Orthodox Rabbis of the United States and Canada" vertrat, kontaktiert.

Recha und Isaac Sternbuch waren wohl auf Musy aufgrund seiner ungewöhnlichen Rettungsaktion in Frankreich aufmerksam geworden.

Die Sternbuchs fragten Musy, ob er bereit wäre, mit ranghohen deutschen Nationalsozialisten zu verhandeln, um die Ausreise von Juden aus verschiedenen Konzentrationslagern und Ghettos zu ermöglichen.

Trotz der Gefahren stimmte Jean-Marie zu und reiste kurze Zeit später mit seinem Diplomatenpass ins polnische Breslau, wo er sich mit Reichsführer Heinrich Himmler traf. Das Treffen hatte ein Vertreter des deutschen Auslandsnachrichtendienstes (Walter Schellenberg) organisiert, der aufgrund der drohenden Niederlage Deutschlands Kontakte zu den Alliierten aufnehmen wollte, um den Untergang Nazi-Deutschlands zu verhindern.

Die Musy-Himmler Vereinbarung

Als Himmler von den Absichten Musys erfuhr, liess er für das Treffen extra seinen persönlichen Zug anhalten. Doch wie ist diese grosse Bereitschaft des damaligen Reichsführers-SS zu solchen Verhandlungen zu erklären? Es ist anzunehmen, dass Himmler, den drohenden Untergang Nazi-Deutschlands vor Augen, in den Verhandlungen eine Chance sah, seine Schuld am Holocaust durch die Freilassung von Juden aus den Konzentrationslagern zu mildern und somit „seine Weste reinzuwaschen". (Was natürlich nicht funktionierte, Himmler wurde nach Kriegsende von den Alliierten verhaftet und beging kurze Zeit später im Gefängnis Suizid.)

Im Gegenzug für die Freilassung verlangte Himmler anfangs die Lieferung von Traktoren und Lastwagen von Seiten der Alliierten, worauf ihm Musy erklärte, dass sich die Alliierten nie auf einen solchen Handel einlassen würden. Bei einem späteren Treffen stimmte Himmler schliesslich einer Geldtransaktion zu. Das Geld für den Handel wurde von der "Union of Orthodox Rabbis of the United States and Canada" bereitgestellt. Bei diesem Treffen war laut Musy die Rede von bis zu 600'000 Juden, von welchen jeweils 1000-1200 alle zwei Wochen freigelassen werden würden. Laut Himmler konnte dies ohne die Zustimmung von Hitler erfolgen, der einen solchen Handel niemals toleriert hätte.

Nach diesem Treffen sammelten verschiedene jüdische Organisationen in den USA Dollars im Wert von 5 Millionen Schweizer Franken, welche auf einer Schweizer Bank deponiert wurden. Das Geld würde der deutschen Regierung jedoch nur überwiesen werden, wenn alle vereinbarten jüdischen Gefangenen freigelassen worden sind. Weil es nur zu einem einzigen Austausch von jüdischen KZ-Insassen kam, wurde bis Kriegsende kein einziger Rappen nach Deutschland überwiesen.

Erste Ausreise von jüdischen KZ-Insassen

Nach erneuten Treffen zwischen Jean-Marie Musy und Heinrich Himmler wurde schliesslich Walter Schellenberg, dem Himmler die Ausführung der Austausche übertragen hatte, damit beauftragt, bereits eine kleine Anzahl Juden aus den Konzentrationslagern freizulassen. Es ist anzunehmen, dass dies beschlossen wurde, um die „guten, ehrlichen Absichten" der Deutschen zu zeigen.

Schelling instruierte darauf Hermann Göring (Oberbefehlshaber der deutschen Luftwaffe), welcher trotz starkem Widerstand aus den Reihen des deutschen Militärs einer kleinen Anzahl Juden die Ausreise ermöglichte.

Die Befreiung von 1200 jüdischen Gefangenen

Am 5. Februar 1945 wurde beschlossen, dass ein Zug mit 1200-1300 jüdischen Insassen von Konzentrationslagern Richtung Schweiz fahren würde.

Bereits am Nachmittag des selben Tages setzte sich der Zug, begleitet von Hermann Göring persönlich, in Bewegung. 2 Tage später wurde der Zug von Truppen der Schweizer Armee in Konstanz in Empfang genommen und bis Kreuzlingen (Thurgau) gefahren. In Kreuzlingen wurden die Juden laut Zeitungsberichten „grossartig empfangen" und reisten danach weiter nach St. Gallen, wo sie in einem Schulhaus untergebracht und versorgt wurden.

Ein Journalist der Neuen Zürcher Zeitung schreibt am 8. Februar 1945 über die angekommenen Flüchtlinge: „Ihr Gesundheitszustand ist, soweit [sich dies] bisher feststellen liess, im allgemeinen gut und fast alle konnten den Weg zum Schulhaus [Hadwig-Schulhaus, wurde von den Behörden als Quarantänestation eingerichtet] zu Fuss zurücklegen, auch wenn sie einen sehr ermüdeten Eindruck machten und sich vielfach mühsam davonschleppten. Sie haben meistens einen länger daurenden Aufenthalt in Theresienstadt hinter sich und sind glücklich darüber, dem Konzentrationslager entronnen zu sein."

"Sie glauben, im Paradies zu sein, bloss weil man menschlich und teilnehmend und anständig mit ihnen spricht. Das Elend muss riesengross gewesen sein.", stellt der Arzt Hans Richard von Fels fest, der die Flüchtlinge in St. Gallen untersucht und behandelt.

Die Reaktion des Bundesrates

Der Bundesrat verkündete kurze Zeit nach dem Eintreffen des Zuges, dass Musy „in keiner Weise im Auftrag des Bundes" gehandelt hatte. Dies erscheint auf den ersten Blick rücksichtslos und wenig mitfühlend, doch man sollte die politische Spannung in der Schweiz zur Zeit des Zweiten Weltkrieges nicht vergessen.

Um eine Intervention von Seiten Deutschlands zu vermeiden und die Neutralität der Schweiz aufrecht zu erhalten, sah sich der Bundesrat während des Zweiten Weltkrieges wiederholte Male gezwungen, sich von Helden „zu distanzieren".

Wieso kam es nur zu dieser einen Freilassung von jüdischen Konzentrationslager-Insassen?

Nach dem Transport der 1200 Juden in die Schweiz sorgten Gerüchte und diverse Falschmeldungen von Zeitungen dafür, dass die deutsche Bevölkerung glaubte, die Juden wurden im Tausch gegen eine Schuldfreisprechung von SS-Offizieren bei Kriegsende freigelassen. Diese Meldungen waren komplett falsch und bewirkten, dass sich Adolf Hitler persönlich mit dem Thema auseinandersetzte.
Dieser war ausser sich vor Wut, als er von der Ausreise der jüdischen Gefangenen in die Schweiz und die darauf folgenden Gerüchte erfuhr und verbot mit sofortiger Wirkung sämtliche weiteren geplanten Austäusche.

Wieso setzte sich Jean-Marie Musy für die Freilassung der jüdischen Gefangenen ein?

Die Fahrten nach Deutschland zu den Verhandlungen, welche Musy jeweils mit einem Privatauto zurücklegte, waren nicht ungefährlich: Die Alliierten waren bereits in Frankreich gelandet und rückten nun weiter Richtung Berlin vor. Mehrere Male mussten Jean-Marie und sein Sohn, der ihn zu den Verhandlungen begleitete, die Fahrt aufgrund von alliierten Bombardierungen unterbrechen.

Später, als Hitler von dem Handel erfahren hatte, drohte er Musy mit der sofortigen Erschiessung, falls dieser erneut für Verhandlungen nach Berlin zurückkehren sollte. Doch aus welchen Gründen nahm Jean-Marie diese Risiken auf sich und reiste immer wieder nach Deutschland?

Bei dieser Frage scheiden sich die Geister. Laut Musys Biographen Gaston Castella handelte er aus rein humanitären und christlichen Motiven. Doch diese Motive wurden und werden heute noch immer angezweifelt. Obwohl Musy die sogenannte Rassenlehre der Nationalsozialisten in Deutschland ablehnte, machte er, wie bereits erwähnt, aus seiner Bewunderung für die Politik der Achsenmächte kein Geheimnis. Er fiel immer wieder durch profaschistische Äusserungen in den Medien auf und engagierte sich stark in antikommunistischen Kreisen. Auch wegen seinen engen Kontakten zu ranghohen Nazifunktionären wurde dem Alt-Bundesrat immer wieder vorgeworfen, er sei nazi-freundlich.

Viele Kritiker behaupten, Musy habe sich nur für die Rettungsaktion bereit erklärt, um sich selber, wie es wohl auch die Absicht von Himmler war, „reinzuwaschen". (mit einem gewissen Erfolg: „Was Herr Musy in dieser Sache getan hat, sei ihm gutgeschrieben", schrieb die Zeitung „Volksstimme" nach der Rettungsaktion.)

Andere vermuten, dass er aus rein politischen Motiven heraus handelte: Angesichts des schnellen Vorrückens der Amerikaner und ihren Verbündeten im Westen und der Sowjets im Osten wollte Musy die Alliierten und Deutschland an den Verhandlungstisch bringen, um die sogenannte „rote Gefahr" (Vormarsch der Sowjets) zu verhindern.

Welche Rolle spielte Recha Sternbuch in der Rettungsaktion?

Die Geschichte von Recha Sternbuch ist eine bewegende: Die 1905 als fünftes von neun Kindern geborene Jüdin interessierte sich bereits früh für die Studie der Thora und setzte sich intensiv damit auseinander. Später heiratete sie den Schweizer Isaac Sternbuch, der ein hohes Ansehen in orthodoxen Kreisen der Schweiz genoss.

Bereits vor dem Krieg war im Haus der Sternbuchs immer ein Bett für Menschen in Not parat. Bekannt wurde Recha, als sie kurz vor Ausbruch des Krieges mit Hilfe des Polizeichefs Paul Grüninger hunderten Flüchtlingen aus Deutschland und Österreich die Flucht in die Schweiz ermöglichte, indem sie z.B. Visen in die betroffenen Länder schmuggelte. Obwohl sie schwanger war, verbrachte sie mehrere Male Nächte in den Wäldern nahe der österreichischen Grenze, um ankommenden Juden die Einreise in die Schweiz zu ermöglichen.

Für diese Handlungen wurde Recha später inhaftiert, wobei sie ihr Kind verlor. Trotz diesem Verlust setzte sie, sobald sie wieder freigelassen wurde, ihre mutigen Rettungsaktionen fort und schmuggelte während des Krieges zahlreiche Visen in die angrenzenden, von Deutschland besetzten Staaten.

1944 war sie es, die zusammen mit ihrem Mann Isaac Jean-Marie Musy kontaktierte und so „den Stein ins Rollen brachte". Es ist erstaunlich, dass sie trotz den wiederholten profaschistischen Äusserungen von Musy in der Öffentlichkeit den Alt-Bundesrat kontaktierte und offensichtlich an das Gute in ihm glaubte.

Fazit

Als ich mit meinem Vater das Thema dieser Arbeit besprach, erzählte er mir von einem ehemaligen Schweizer Bundesrat, der während des Holocausts über 1000 jüdische KZ-Insassen rettete. Ich forschte im Internet nach und erfuhr dort mehr über den Alt-Bundesrat Jean-Marie Musy, welcher als Jugendlicher, genau wie ich heute, ein Gymnasium in der Stadt Freiburg besuchte.

Interessant fand ich, dass Musy sich von anderen Holocaust-Helden sehr stark unterscheidet. Ein Beispiel dafür waren seine persönlichen Kontakte zu Heinrich Himmler und anderen wichtigen Persönlichkeiten Nazi-Deutschlands. Aufgrund dieser Kontroversen ist man sich bis heute nicht einig, aus welchen Motiven Jean-Marie Musy gehandelt hat.

Ich stiess auf mehrere informative Zeitungsartikel, wovon einer am 8. Februar 1945, dem Tag der Ankunft des Zuges mit den jüdischen KZ-Insassen in St. Gallen, geschrieben wurde.

Nachdem ich möglichst viele Informationen gesammelt hatte, fing ich mit dem Schreiben der Arbeit an. Dabei wollte ich unbedingt auf die Motive eingehen, die Jean-Marie Musy dazu veranlassten, der Bitte des Ehepaars Lob und später dem Ersuchen von Recha und Isaac Sternbuch nachzukommen und diese durchaus riskante Rettungsaktion durchzuführen.

Nachdem ich mich nun während mehreren Wochen intensiv mit diesem Mann beschäftigt habe, glaube ich fest daran, dass Jean-Marie Musy, trotz den zahlreichen persönlichen und politischen Motiven (auch) aus Selbstlosigkeit handelte. Es ist jedoch nicht zu vergessen, dass Musy die Juden von Theresienstadt nicht im Alleingang rettete. Durch die Mithilfe zahlreicher mutiger Menschen, wie zum Beispiel Benoît Musy, der seinen Vater freiwillig mehrere Male nach Deutschland begleitete oder Recha Sternbuch, die zusammen mit ihrem Mann die Rettungsaktion initiierte, kam diese mutige, einmalige Heldentat zustande.

WE WILL NEVER FORGET

Translated From The Original French
Marion Conus

The Holocaust. This word makes me shiver. When the term is mentioned, we all have an image that comes to mind. Surely you would speak of the Second World War in and of itself, of Paris under German occupation, of atomic bombs launched on Hiroshima and Nagasaki.

For me, and I think for many others, I have the image of concentration camps.

Ever since youth, we were taught the story while speaking with others of what happened during the war of '39-'45. But our young age made it hard to completely become conscious of the callousness of what was happening in that era. As for myself, I understood it during lower secondary school when, with my class, we watched the documentary film "From Nuremberg to Nuremberg" by film director Frederic Rossif. Our teacher warned us of the harshness of these images. I remember that he told us that would be necessary to be shocked in some manner by the projected images so that, in this way, we would not ever possibly forget. My blood froze as soon as the images appeared on the screen and I understood, finally. So it was that which was inflicted on these people, so it was the hell of life in these camps, the hunger, the sadness, the despair. I had, from that point on, an understanding and I could never erase the image of these bodies bruised by hunger

456

and marked by pain. To forget was no longer possible, fortunately, for to forget would be the worst thing that could happen. To forget that these people died, forget that they were human beings like you and me who were murdered would be terrible. The generations that follow will have to have knowledge of these events that played out during this Second World War.

Toward the end of this film, there was an interminable list of names of people condemned to death or in prison for life for having assisted the Germans in some manner or another. At hearing that, I had the impression that the entire planet had contributed to the extermination of the Jewish people. But like often in the media today, one speaks more easily of people who have done harm. Violence, death, and pain is henceforward everywhere, in the newspapers, in video games, everywhere. This violence, under whichever form it takes, becomes commonplace and people become jaded.

Since youth still, we have been taught to live in an ideology that advocates love, friendship, and mutual assistance between all. Each individual, whatever their culture, has, normally, grown in this philosophy, without any other belief that our world is a world of peace and love. Yet what has come to pass is contrary to this. Since always there are wars, genocides, and attacks. I remember having read about requirements at the end of the First World War: "Never Again War." Following this war and to innumerable deaths in the trenches, the people swore to never again recommence such a massacre. The result? Nearly twenty years later, a Second World War. While I tell myself that this could maybe be an instinct to battle amongst Mankind, the human is programmed to do this, in spite of numerous teachings. I would enjoin to be convinced that the persons who had managed these extermination camps have had also, a teaching full of love. Thus how can one arrive at putting into place a massive system of extermination? The organization of these camps, the techniques used for killing, all were prepared in advance and calculated, all were industrialized. It is this industrialization of death that causes me anxiety. All of this necessarily was put in place by individuals and the question which I can't help but ask is "How did they possibly create such a system without thinking about other humans, of the millions persons who they were going to exterminate?"

But that which one unhappily has the tendency to forget, it is that on this Earth, there have been, there have been and there will always be good people, always ready for saving people, all ready for helping people go from peril to their own appropriate life. And nevertheless, we rarely call to mind these persons. A little of the gentleness in this world wouldn't have a bad effect on us. Thus today, we forget in a moment these persons who had scattered the evil and the terror around them and bring to the forefront these little known to the world people, but who saved the Hungarians from extermination camps.

Today, we are speaking of Giorgio Perlasca.

457

There was little information concerning the childhood of Giorgio Perlasca. He was born in Come in Italy, the 31st of January, 1910. Perlasca was a civil servant and man of Italian business, unknown, until he saved the lives of more than 2,000 Hungarian Jews during the Second World War.

Youthful, he joined the National Fascist Party and participated in the conquest of Ethiopia by Italy in 1935-1936. He equally participated in the Spanish civil war in 1936-1937. His cooperation with the army of Franco gave him a certificate of recognition – paradox? He would credibly assist Franco, a partisan of Hitler. In 1941, he left for a a business trip in Yugoslavia where he saw the degrading treatment the Jews were receiving. Yugoslavia was at the time invaded by Axis forces the 6th of April, 1941. Later, after 1942, he left for Hungary, to Budapest, the capital for his business. The 8th of September 1943, the day when the armistice between Italy and the Allies was signed, he refused to join the Italian social republic as he hoped to stay loyal to his oath against the king. For this reason, and for having a rather pronounced anti-Nazi side, he was rapidly researched and discovered by the Germans, who accused him of treason. It was in this way that he had to find refuge in the Spanish Embassy. This is how he received Spanish citizenship and a false passport. Giorgio Perlasca thus became "Jorge Perlasca". He worked with the Spanish diplomat Angel Sanz Briz to attempt to save the Jews.But in 1944, Sanz Briz left Hungary, leaving Perlasca on his own. This last did not discourage him, for even so and decided to present himself as the replacement of the old consul. From this moment, he would recover to aide and manage thousands of Jews hidden in the embassy or in safe houses, this with the aide of Raoul Wallenberg, a Swedish diplomat. From the 1st of December 1944 to the 16th of January 1945, Perlasca distributed thousands of false passports that gave Spanish citizenship to the Jews. He thus played well an ancient law that authorized Jews of Sephardic origins to return to Spain. He also aided the Jewish people of Budapest in bringing them provisions in spite of shortages. Finally, it was a few days before the taking of Budapest by the Soviet Union that Raoul Wallenberg, the Swiss Carl Lutz, and Giorgio Perlasca himself met the Minister of the Interior of Hungary to threaten him for the Allies that the Germans and the Hungarians would have a ban on touching the Jewish ghetto and the safe houses of Budapest. Thus, they were able together, again to save several people. After the war, Perlasca went back to Italy where he restarted his life of long ago. It would not be until 1987, nearly 40 years later that certain Hungarian Jews now living in Israel recovered a trace of him. They related then the enormous proof of courage and solidarity for which made proof that Giorgio Perlasca all throughout this war. The 9th of June, 1988 he was thus honored by Yad Vashem (Israeli organization, in memory of the victims of the Holocaust)an he received the title of "Righteous Among the Nations". Finally, it was at Padua, on the land of his origins that Giorgio

Perlasca, this Italian who passed himself off as Spanish in a unique goal which was to save people, that he died in 1992 at the age of 82 years.

Today what is left of this unbelievable journey of this man? There is still a bust of him sitting in Budapest. In the Museum of Yad Vashem in Jerusalem, there is a stone where his name has been engraved. There also has been a tree planted in an alley still at the museum, in his memory. Personally, I find that the tree, is very strong symbol and vehicle to send a big message to give homage to someone, thus, contrary to a statue or an engraved stone, a tree is living. It lives like the people who were able to be saved from an imminent death. The tree will pass through years, will be shaken by Nature but can continue to live. The tree symbolizes to us across thoughts, across history. We are all one of these trees. We appear futile, powerless faced with what comes our way, we believe we are powerless in the face of our destiny, and nevertheless, we are able to modify the course of things. Certain people say that everything is written ahead of time, that we are predestined. I don't think that this is true about the Just: we master that which happens, we are masters of ourselves. No one can dictate to us what one has to accomplish if they are not our conscience. A tree amongst a forest in all entirety can stand out from all the others by its rarity or still further by its beauty. Perlasca was one of these trees who knew how to stand out and to change history in this way in the lives of thousands of Jews.

What Men have made and lived over the course of their history, will continue, in spite of the people who have made nothing, in spite of those who are persuaded that the entire Holocaust has been invented and totally made up. For these people to understand, show them, make them visit, make them see the evil that we have been capable of inflicting on ourselves. Finally, maybe they will understand.

Men are the most cruel beings, who are capable of killing, without any pity. We kill ourselves, we detest ourselves and after we try to pick up the pieces to make as if none of it had ever taken place. But, how to remove the suffering of an entire people? How to remove these nightmarish memories that were lived by thousands of Jews? The trauma will always be present. I remember this book which I read not that long ago.: "Seule Venise" by Claude Gallay. This book profoundly marked me by the talent of the writing of its author and also by the evocation of this Slovenian painter, Zoran Music. She retold, in several lines, the life of this Jewish painter deported to Dachau from 1944 to 1945. I remember well these different passages where she explains the difficulty that Music had to lift the images of death from his life. To paint after the camps was impossible. The wound was still too fresh, too gaping, the pain too present. In these paintings now, one finds this pain. The horrors lived in these camps, the life next to death, the fear of the possibility of dying at each instant would mark forever his way of painting. I remain profoundly touched by his brushstrokes when I see what he was capable of painting several year later.

Sometimes, I dream of a better world. Of a world without wars, where everyone moves forward, hand in hand. But this utopia won't ever end up happening. Over the course of Human History there have been wars, man has always battled for a territory, for money, and he still battles to arrive at these ends.

The several lines recounted from the life of this man have to be an example for all. Here where many have thought that they no longer had any hope, Giorgio Perlasca came out of the shadows and fought to save the beings of another nation, of another culture, of another religion. This is proof that there will always be a little light in the night, a little joy in the sadness of the world to accomplish great things. There will be always hope, and you must never lose that view. The Just will always be present, discreet and yet they have marked us by their unbelievable generosity and their courage. Perlasca was the light, the hope, the Guardian Angel of these Hungarian Jews, and it is up to us now to be the Guardian Angel to someone.

Today, it is up to us to fight. We should never lose the memory of those who have perished before us and above all, never lose hope. Here where the night is the darkest, we look at the sky and its millions of tiny lights and we can smile because we live.

IDIOT?

Translated From The Original French
Martine Rouiller

There have been hundreds and hundreds of wars in the history of humanity. Life itself is a permanent combat. It is necessary to battle at first for one's birth. The body is obliged to breathe and to live. Soon after, a baby grows and fights for himself. One battles for an increase that allows him to be nourished and clothed. One battles to know who will get up during the night. One battles to make him go to sleep or to make him quiet. The baby does not finish this with being a child, who struggles with his homework or battles simply over going to school. If he has brothers and sisters, he will fight for his choice of bed, or for imposing his movie preference for DVD showing. Adults battle always. One battles to marry whom one loves, battles to attain a better work assignment, one squabbles with ones mother-in-law over the next vote. Then, as one ages, there is a battle with ones age. One fights with weakness. One battles with the little things that cause us to stumble, or the stairs that make old joints grind. One battles with hip prostheses, chairs that are too deep and remote controls. Sometimes, one battles with ones memory. Then, one struggles with death, to be able to combat again a little with life.

This constant fight between life and death, the war is the best means to remember it. Since antiquity, men have battled equally between themselves, for hatred, for jealousy, for want of power and wealth, for a need of glory, for love, for blood. One would believe men are uniquely driven by the need to kill one another. And to do this, Man has created multitudes of means to cause death, first of all to find nourishment for himself, but also for fighting. The first weapons were fists and stones, then objects fashioned of wood and bone. It was not long after that men began to employ metal to create deadly blades. Some would forget the possible crimes that could be committed by their arms, using them as objects of show and wealth. After this, man obtained powder, from which he made even more efficient arms. The castles of the Middle Ages and their deadly fleet recall to us a point at which man is eager for conquests. Then, firearms improved and became more rapid, more precise, and more deadly. Sub-machineguns and mines made their appearances. We arrive, finally, at the height of horror with the atomic bomb. Wars had very much evolved since the ancient world, but each seemed to forget that the same arms is the foundation of all wars: Man, himself.

Well then, since human beings are capable of studying the world and discovering each day innovations that allow for improvements on the living conditions of the species, one could ask why Man has always sought to improve his weapons to kill, torture, and to make suffer always more efficiently and such. When asking this question, one understands that war is the worst invention of Man, as much its immediate effects as its long-term effects.

We all know wars have an ending, but their memory is sometimes worse than the conflicts themselves. At the end of these conflicts, out of green meadows one sees cemeteries pushing up fields of white crosses. One sees then these pale trunks flowering with colorful bouquets, and on e reads there the stories of the soldiers. This one here had children, and they come every evening. That one there had only his mother, an elderly woman who couldn't offer much but a small bouquet during big celebrations. The three down there have the same name. Maybe they were brothers. From time to time, a monument replaces the tombs, a monument of which passersby read the inscriptions rapidly before going away. In this time of peace in Europe, war seems like nothing but a prisoner's bad dream in a thread of treaties and discussions woven between the nations. Nevertheless, Europe has been well-ravaged by the war and the horror of seventy years ago.

During the Second World War, death was everywhere. On the front, the fighting decimated bodies, spirits, and landscapes, still marked by it today. Death was united with life in a bloody marriage with monstrous offspring. Existence, that of others or one's own, was defended with ardor. In the camps, life appeared as nothing more than a corridor toward death. It is impossible to find words for the atrocities that were committed in the camps by the Nazis, who were concerned with the conditions of work and detention, or the medical experiences practiced on the detainees. The doors of Auschwitz have become the symbol of the horror and the darkness of their image can still make chills run down one's spine. Nevertheless, in spite of its numerous atrocities, the Second World War was able to make heroes out of ordinary people. Conscious of the stupidity of hatred toward the Jewish people, men and women who stood against the Nazis in order to protect the precious lives of people unjustly stalked. This war, as horrible as it was, allowed a resurgence of courage and kindness that was buried in certain people. Today, these individuals are called Just. Just in their conduct, just in their soul.

I often ask myself what are the qualities of being Just, or Fair. Would everyone merit this title? What is necessary to be Just? Does one have to be courageous? Must one like adversity or is it necessary to have a love of mankind? Does one have to be crazy or should one be noble? Is it required to be intelligent? Does one have to be part of a clandestine organization? Does one have to be Swiss? Or German? Does it require wealth? Or power? Is it necessary to understand the world and to know science? Does it require a confidence in one's core or to be sure of one's judgment? Does one have to believe in God, Allah, or oneself? Is generosity necessary? Must one have a love of glory?

All of the heroes I was able to research appear to have been endowed with all of all the qualities this world could offer, and that that they had saved four or hundreds of people. Today, I have chosen to speak about a small hero. Not the grand rescuers who would aide thousands of Jews, but a small man who achieved his peak by saving several lives. I had wanted to write about an accessible Just Person, a hero whom each could take as an example. A small hero who had all the big rescue qualities, if not looking solely at the number of persons whose lives he protected.

Today, I have found this hero.

He was a so-called idiot, generous and simple. One would have thought he was isolated, that he was making his own way. One would have thought him poor and deprived, but his heart was rich. One could believe he was feeble, but he demonstrated more tenacity and courage than anyone. No one followed his example when they should have been. They turned away from him. For a long time, he was left alone and unknown. Then, it was understood that he was Just.

I am going to speak to you of Anton Sukhinski.

Anton Sukhinski lived in Zborow, in Ukraine. This young man of small stature lived away from his neighbors, who patronized him and considered him like the village idiot. And why is that? Anton was endowed with an extreme patience and a very simple character, and he dedicated an infinite respect to all living creatures. In a testimony, Milek Zeiger, who represented amongst the Jews saved by Anton, explains that Anton respected the flies. Thus why he would save two foreign girls whom he did not know? Milek explained in the same testimony that his savior profoundly believed in the kindness of Man. For a long time, this character made Anton pass for an idiot, and isolated him from the other villagers. Misunderstood by his neighbors, Anton stayed as such throughout the entire war.

While the habitants of Zborow turned away little by little from their Jewish neighbors, delivering them to their deaths, Anton decided in spite of everyone to save lives, pushed by the conviction that God had ordered him to. The Just brought to the Zeiger family to his home, who counted as family members Itzhak and Sonya, parents of two sons: Milek and Munio. He saved as well a friend of this family, as well as Eva Halperin, an orphan alone in the world, and another adolescent of sixteen years, Zipora Stock. This was a very heavy responsibility for a man who was alone and poor, but Anton was determined. For a while he kept his protégés in his cellar. But soon, the neighbors learned of Anton's situation, and put pressure on him about the Jews he was taking in. Anton and those he was protecting complied with and submitted to the concerns of the villagers. The tension quickly became too strong for the father Zeiger, who rebelled against some villagers attempts of blackmail, and he refused to give them money. A gunfight ensued, and a friend of Zeiger was killed.

The Jewish refugees at Anton's decided to flee following the gunshot. But soon, the beating, freezing cold weather brought them back to Anton's who joyfully received them. The father of the family Zeiger and his protector

463

were conscious of the risks they would incur, and decided to change hiding places. They dug a small cellar in the garden, where the refugees could leave Anton's garret and hide for quite awhile. In this tiny hiding place where six people were squeezed, the tension was immense. The refugees were so terrorized that they didn't dare go out anymore and relied completely on Anton. The poor man already had a hard time to feed himself, and he was struggling like a madman to help his protégés. Happily, Anton's brother and his wife lived in the neighborhood and helped to nourish the Jews he was hiding.

The conditions were hard. Anton's protégés went through nine months inside this cellar, without ever setting a foot outside. The food was poor and rare, and the small man was sometimes obliged to be gone during several days to be able to eat or avoid the controls of the Nazis, who had come to threaten him several times. The bodies of the pursued Jews suffered as much from the hunger and loss of movement as from the fatigue caused by the stress and lack of nourishment. But more difficult still was the fear of constant danger. There was a constant risk of Anton's neighbors sending the Nazis who would break into the house, search and mistreat the small man who continually resisted them. From their hiding place, the Jews could hear them interrogating Anton and the searches of the Germans. They were motionless with fear each time during long minutes of silent prayer, just until the Nazis tired and left. The conditions little by little became intolerable, so much so that the mother Zeiger admitted that her children asked her at times for the right to surrender to the Germans. Happily, she was resisted by her husband, as well as by Anton, who persisted in spite of fear and misery. Time passed in the little cellar; life resisted and courage became firm.

Finally, one day, Anton opened the door the hiding place with a smiling face. The Russians had retaken Zborow. It was the liberation. After nine months, the Jewish refugees would from now on be purely free to go out in the sun. Anton Sukhinski, alone against all, had saved six lives.

After their cohabitation in this cellar, the six Jews stayed together for a bit. Then the Zeiger family moved the USA, Eva Halperin emigrated toward Uraguay, and Zipora Stock joined in Israel.

Anton Sukhinski was declared Just by the Nations in 1974.

Today, I wonder on this story. They took Anton to be the village idiot, but who was the most idiotic of Zborow? Anton, or his neighbors who let themselves be lulled by the rants of the Nazis? Anton might not have been a physicist, but he was given a heart of gold and unfailing courage. Is the brain more important than the heart? No. The warmth of a heart allows wonders that the rationale of a brain can't even imagine.

From my research, I asked myself numerous questions. A war is a horrible event. However, in spite of all the horror it can bring, war permits an evolution of humanity sometimes in a bad, but also in a good sense. It remains to be said, after the Second World War, "Never again." The atrocities of the Nazis provided the means for men to understand the absurdity of their behavior, and allowed heroes to be revealed to the world who inspire today's minds. There are hard lessons learned from these battles, but they are more useful than all the theories philosophers could write. Unfortunately, memories fade, and the ancient wisdoms disappear. For how much more time can the Second World War protect the fragile peace of Europe?

When I was little, I struggled to be once more in first place. When I become an adult, perhaps I will fight for peace.

MIEP GIES

Translated From The Original French
Cotting Coraline

In my essay I'll present a very remarkable woman, Miep Gies, the woman who protected Anne Frank as well as Anne's whole family during the Second World War.

Hermine Santrouschitz was born in1909, in Vienna, Austria. She was sent to Holland in December, 1920 at the age of 11 to escape the food restrictions enacted in Austria following the First World War and to restore her health because of tuberculosis. The host family lived in Leiden; this is the family whom the whole world soon came to know under the surname Miep. In 1924 her host family moved to Amsterdam, a city in which, in 1933 at the age of 24 she met Otto Frank who was looking for workers for his pectin and spice business, Opekta. At first she was responsible for claim forms [this has got to be wrong, what wholesale/retail business has a claims form department? Does the author mean a general accounting clerk?] But soon she was promoted to a more general administrative position, the secretary. [again this makes no sense: a secretary is not an administrative job] Shortly after she was she met Edith, Otto's wife and their two daughters, Margot and Anne. The young woman quickly became a friend of the Frank family. On July 16, 1941 Miep married Jan Gries, a year before the Frank family asked to be hidden. Marrying Jan Gries had given her an exemption from deportation to Austria for having refused to join the League of German Girls. [I'm assuming this is the group she is referring to: the girls association of Hitler Youth]

In the spring of 1942 the situation became more and more difficult for Jews in Holland, Miep Gies and her husband Jan immediately agreed to hide their friends. They created a secret annex in the rear of the Franks' business premises where the family could live well hidden. During the next two years they were joined by four other Jews, Victor Kugler, Johannes Kleiman, Miep Gies and Bep Voskuijl . Jan Gries the wife of Miep, and Hendrik Voskuijl, Bep's father were the only employees to know that the Frank family was hidden in the back of the office building. This was possible because the other employees suspected nothing and were ignorant of the hidden group who remained very quiet and made no noise during the day until noon [midi? does she mean quitting time, or the evening?] when the employees left the building.

Their hiding place was spacious enough to accommodate two families who could live with a measure of discomfort, dampness and the quirky layout of the space. The space was relatively well arranged with the necessities of life. It had several different spaces and occupied three floors. [does she actually mean "levels" with the word niveaux, or does she mean étages = floors as in first floor, second floor etc.], this living arrangement was exceptional if one compares it to other people who were more frequently hidden in cramped cellars, in confined underground spaces [sous-sol is usually the current word for basement, replacing cave which means cellar, but she already said cave/cellar so I assume she is using the older meaning for this word which actually means under the ground], or in old attics. On the first level there were two small spaces with a bathroom and an adjacent toilet. On the next higher level was a big open space with a small adjacent space in which there was a ladder leading to a small attic. For more security in case of evacuation by the German police, Johan Voskuijl, the man responsible for a safety system made a revolving shelving system. The entrance to the annex was hidden behind a movable bookcase that went unnoticed by anyone not having knowledge of it.

During these two years Miep Gies and her colleagues helped eight people to survive, and took care of the financial obligations and security. Each morning the young woman went into the secret annex to get a list of needed provisions before going to her office. Later she would buy the provisions and return to eat with Frank and the other refugees. The other people who protected the Franks would often join them for meals and keep the refugees current on the events of the war and recent political news. They were the sole contact between the refugees and the outside world. They used all their abilities to keep the refugees morale up during the most dangerous times.

On the July 13th, 1942, the Frank family were joined in the annex by the Van Pels family, Hermann, Augusta and their son Peter aged 16, and then in November by

Fritz Pfeffer, a dentist and friend of the family. Discretely obtaining enough food to feed all these people became more and more difficult for Miep Gies and her friends because with the newcomers there were too many people. [the end of this sentence in French makes no sense at all] In all, there were eight people in the annex. In the Frank family: Anne, strong willed and growing up; intelligent and somewhat reserved, who aspired to, one day, be a journalist and celebrated writer and was very wise for her age. Margot, at 16, was Anne's older sister she was sensitive and gentle with Anne. Otto, Anne's father, had a big heart, he was noble, patient and likeable, and he was a major support for Anne who was the most important person in the annex in his eyes. Edith, Anne's and Margot's mother was very talkative and frequently criticized her second daughter. Anne had [maintained?] a very bad relationship with her. Peter Van Pels was two and a half years older than Anne. He was a nice but timid boy. Hermann Van Pels, the father of Peter had the most realistic opinions and was the most accepting of all. [I'm not sure exactly what she meant in this sentence] Augusta Van Pells is described by Anne in her diary as very provocative [I'm sure she meant provocative and not provocatrice, totally different meaning] and the cause of all the discussions. [Does she mean: all the disagreeable discussions and animosity?] Fritz Pfeffer was a dentist who proved to be a grumpy man. Having new people in the annex was very pleasurable for the Frank family even if afterwards tensions began to create resentment in a group who were forced to live in what was becoming a very crowded space [environnement restraint?] which Anne frequently writes about in her diary. These tensions weren't an impediment when timid Peter Van Pells and Anne found they had feeling for each other and started a relationship. [? I can't think of a word that doesn't imply sexual relations]

This was how Miep Gies life developed during the two years until August 4, 1944 when the eight occupants as well as Victor Kugler and Johannes Kleiman were arrested following an anonymous tip. Only Miep and Bep, an employee of the company, escaped arrest because the interrogating officer like them was Austrian. Miep barely managed to save Anne's journal which she had not read. Later in August, 1944, Miep tried to free the arrestees by going to the office of the Sicheheitsdienst, the German police. They refused to release them and they were finally deported. About a year later on June 3rd, 1945, Otto Frank returned to Amsterdam alone and moved in with Miep Gies and her husband with whom he lived for a number of years. Later, he learned that he [author says: Otto] was the sole member of his family to have survived the concentration camps. Margot and Anne, their two daughters, died of typhus in the Bergen-Belsen concentration camp in February or March 1945. This is when Miep confided the news of Anne's diary to her father [to Otto] who published it in 1947. [in French this sentence is *really* strange]

In her diary, Anne had written, after hearing a speech on the radio from the Minister of Education, that after the war they would publish all written documents that contained references to the suffering of the Dutch people during the German occupation, [and?] that after the war she wanted to publish a diary that told the story of the [hidden Jews?]. Finally, it was for this reason that her father, after a period of much hesitation about the publication, decided to honor the wishes of his daughter [?] Anne had even begun with this idea by re-writing; correcting and removing some passages that she thought weren't interesting or were repetitive. She drew on her memory, comparing that to her original diary entries, until up to her last entry dated August 1st, 1944, three days before their arrest. [I paraphrased this sentence] In preparation for the publication of her diary Anne had already given the other occupants pseudonyms: Hermann Van Pells became Hermann Van Daan, Augusta Van Pells became Petronella Van Daan, Fritz Pfeffer became Albert Dussel, Victor Kugler became Harry Kraler, Johannes Kleiman became Simon Koophuis, Bep Voskuijl became Eli Vossen, Miep Gies became Miep van Santen, Jan Gies became Henk van Santen. Later Miep said that she had read Anne's diary after she found it and had removed [?] the compromising information it contained. Anne had received for her thirteenth birthday on June 12th, 1942 a notebook that she had shown her father a few days earlier, although it was a spelling book covered [?] in red and white cloth. The young girl had already planned to use it as an intimate diary. In her diary she talked about an imaginary friend named Kitty, she began to write and personally describe her family, her friends and her life at school. If the first entries were written in the style of a normal adolescent with a very ordinary life, the entries more and more addressed the changing experience and observations of a young girl during the ongoing German occupation. For example, she wrote about the yellow star that all Jews had to wear in public, and mentioned some of the persecutions and restrictions that upset [?] the Amsterdam Jewish population. On July 13t, 1952, Miep and Jan became the parents of young Paul. At this time Miep left her job at Opkta to devote her time to their son. Later, in 1987, she wrote a book *She Called Herself Anne Frank* in which she recounted the life and the hardships that had overcome the young girl. On January 26, 1993 her husband Jan was diagnosed with diabetes. Miep Gies died on January 11, 2010 at the age of one hundred. The couple innumerable prizes [?], their courage reaped many rewards and they became celebrated in Holland as well as around the world.

Of all of the people Miep Gies had protected [very paraphrased] apart from Anne and her sister Margot, and Edith, the mother of Anne and Margot, had fallen ill and died from hunger and exhaustion in the infirmary at Auschwitz-Birkenau on January 6th, 1945. Hermann Pels was, according to the Red Cross, gassed at Auschwitz the same day he arrived, September 6, 1944. According to other sources he had been spared in the first selection and died later. Augusta Van Pels died in Germany, or in Czechoslovakia, between April 7th and May 8th 1945, either on the trip to the Theresienstadt Camp, or after her arrival. Fritz Pfeffer was transferred from

Auschwitz to the Neuengamme Camp where he died in the infirmary on December 20, 1944 at the age of fifty-five. Peter Van Pels was transferred from Auschwitz to the Mauthausen Camp in Austria; he arrived on January 25th after an exhausting trip. Exhausted and sick he died May 5th, 1945, only three days before the liberation of the camp. Otto Frank, the father of Anne and Margot, survived the Auschwitz extermination camp. He died in Bale (Switzerland) in 1980 at the age of ninety-one.

I think that Miep Gies' success in saving Anne's diary was very beneficial for everyone. Reading the diary today lets us understand an adolescent during this period of persecution. The diary lets us see the misery of Jewish life at the time, and everything that was done in an attempt to stay alive. That this is an intimate diary of someone is good, because in the diary we can see the people's emotions, what they think, and the periods of distress [misery?] and of joy. We can better understand the conditions because it was written with touching and pregnant emotions. We can see a clearer reality of things. We cannot simply say: "Yes, it was horrible", there are emotions that truly touch us. We feel closer to the people, that they lived, we can better imagine the reality of the people unlike the history books in which we see what happened, but without delving into their thoughts of someone who had this life. The average book makes it possible to understand what happened, but in reading it we can only imagine the feelings of the people who lived [through this] and not the true reality.

I found that what Miep Gies , her husband and their friends, did was truly courageous. They ran many risks in hiding their friends in this manner, it was illegal, anyone hiding or aiding Jews was liable to be executed. This demonstrated a real proof of friendship and humanity; they overcame their fear to help save their friends while others in my opinion wouldn't dare break the law in this manner. I can use as an example the person who anonymously denounced the families living in the annex. This individual had to have acted under the influence of fear or of pressure but he had nothing to say, maybe that the lives had been spared, maybe the Frank family, and the other Jews with them would never have been discovered. Who could know that this would happen? It would be hard to lose nearly all your friends, she had succeeded is saving them for two years, and then she lost them, and she couldn't do anything to save them. The courage of this woman and her friends truly and greatly impresses me.

KARL PLAGGE

Translated From The Original French
Elsa Rohrbasser

There are some events that we must honor, that we perpetuate the memory of, and that above all we do not forget. These events destroyed cities, the landscape, families and entire populations, and somehow remade the world for the good of mankind since the beginning of time. The Second World War is a perfect example, Founded on a barbaric ideology, to destroy civilization as we knew it at the time, by a thirst for power, of money, or simply because of human dementia. And we somehow reconstruct it on the ruins of a senseless war. People are indoctrinated hearing absurd thoughts and commit irreparable acts believing they are doing good and ridding the world of vermin. However, in the middle of all these followers we can find heroes who even at a threat to their life, could rise up against these ideas and decide to protect Jews by hiding them in their own houses. We count tens of thousands of "The Righteous Among the Nations" in the world, and it is likely that we will neither know their names nor of their existence.

If I chose to write about Major Karl Plagge, it's to show that there were some people, even those well positioned, and who were members of the National Socialist Party of Adolf Hitler, who were capable of realizing the atrocities being committed around them, and who had enough courage to put their life and their position in danger to save some of the Jews. This man risked the loss of all that he had, but he knew that what he had to do was just. He did the best that he could, not enough according to him, yet it made it possible for a great number of Jews to go on living. Karl Plagge (1897-1957).

Commander Karl Plagge was born in Darmstadt, Germany, on July 10th, 1897. He was a German officer and a member of the Nazi Party (NSDAP) who during the Second World War employed between 1,000 and 1,200 Jews, of whom 250 to 500 men (the figure varies according to the source) were forced laborers. This assured them a much greater chance of surviving the extermination of Jews in Lithuania from 1941 to1943.

Karl Plagge was the son of a medical doctor who died when Karl was only six years old. A secondary school graduate he then enrolled in the army and served during the First World War He saw active service at the battles of the Somme, of Verdun and of Flanders. In 1917, he was captured by the British and held as a prisoner of war for three years. During this period he contracted polio, a serious [she uses: aiguë, meaning acute] and contagious illness, this left his with much weakened legs and a partial invalid.

At the age of twenty-three, Karl Plagge returned home and decided to enroll at The University of Darmstadt to study medicine. His family couldn't pay for medical school. Being financially constrained he chose the study of mechanical and chemical engineering. In 1924 he was awarded his university degree. In 1930 the whole world fell into a profound [economic] depression and Karl Plagge lost his job. He enrolled in a pharmaceutical chemistry course at the University of Frankfort on the Main and was graduated in 1932. He opened a small pharmaceutical laboratory in the basement of his mother's house; this permitted him to make a living for several years. Then, he married Anke Madsen. They had no children.

In 1931, Germany was suddenly in a grave economic crisis that resulted in the increasing popularity of the National Socialist Party of Adolf Hitler (NADAP). They promised a return to order and economic prosperity for the German people. Karl Plagge, like a number of other Germans, was attracted to these speeches filled with great promises that let the people imagine an attractive future for Germany. So, he rejoined the party in 1931. He was excited and enthusiastic about the idea of being part of the party that would reconstruct Germany from the ruins of the First World War and he volunteered to work for the purpose of the rebirth of Germany. However, he rapidly came into conflict and disaccord with the authorities of the party whose racial Nazi theories were for him, as a scientist, unacceptable and inconceivable. Karl Plagge was equally shocked by the manner in which the party treated their conquered adversaries. The party preferred to imprison these people, or assassinate them (during the Night of the Long Knives, June 30, 1934 for example) rather than accepting any cooptation. At the beginning of these events Karl Plagge thought that these problems were only aberrations that would be corrected in time with the popularization of the party. Sadly, he was wrong.

He accepted a position as a science lecturer at a party institute and was named head of the party's Institute of Technical Education. Never the less he refused to teach the racist theories of the Nazi Party. For him it was out of the question to take part in the ideological indoctrination, and he assured that the courses and the meetings at his institute remained solely scientific and not ideological. By 1935, these choices had resulted in him being accused of being a "friend of the Jews and of the Freemasons" and he was dismissed from all positions with the local National Socialist Party of Adolf Hitler. Karl Plagge, former idealist, ended up working against them.

In 1934, he found work in an engineering office owned by Kurt Hesse, whose wife was half Jewish. Kurt Hesse thought, however, that by hiring a member of the National Socialist Party he could protect his business from anti-Jewish boycotts organized by the Nazis. Plagge and Hesse, over time, became good friends.

In 1938, Germany became a more and more dangerous and threading place for Jews or the "impure non-Aryan races" living there. Karl Plagge protected his new friend and his friend's family and was made the godfather of the last Hesse child who was born a little after Kristallnacht and the destruction of the Darmstadt synagogues. In the spring of 1939, Plagge heard an inflammatorily vehement speech by a member of the party, and he realized that the Nazis, led by Adolf Hitler, would lead Germany directly to war [?]. In September 1939, the war started, Germany invaded Poland, and Karl Plagge found himself enlisted in the German army's Wehrmacht. Because of the weakness in his legs after having contracted polio, he was only posted to supporting services in positions behind the front line. At first he was an engineering officer, later was promoted to the rank of major. He was put in charge of a motor vehicle repair unit, the HKP-562, at Vilnius in Lithuania. There, he began to act, he obtained work permits for Jews, saying that they were indispensable, specialist workers; in reality they had no qualifications in this area. If the party authorities had discovered this blatant lie, Karl Plagge would simply have been executed. These work permits provided protection for the worker, and of his wife and two of their children, and permitted them to escape from the raids by the SS (the "Schutzstaffel") in the Vilnus ghetto. At the minimum, Karl Plagge, furnished 250 to 500 permits to the men, this provided protection for 1,000 to 1,200 people, including their wives and children from 1941 to 1944.

In 1943, the threat of liquidation hung over the Vilnius ghetto. As a result, the SS would execute all of the remaining Jews, whether they had a work permit or not. Plagge scrambled to create an independent work camp; he named the camp "Camp HKP-562", the name of his technical unit. Despite the efforts of the SS to counteract this attempt, the camp saw the light of day. On September 16, 1943, Karl Plagge will bring more than 1,000 Jews into the camp, Subocz Street, where their lives would be relatively secure when the ghetto would be liquidated by squadrons of the SS. The liquidation happened just six days after the workers evacuation.

The living condition in camp HKP-563 were just about right, the work was more suitable and the food more or less acceptable. Thanks to Plagge's orders, the civilians were treated with respect and almost without violence by the German soldiers. Here is a good example of his benevolence, Alfred Stumpff, one of Plagge's lieutenants testifies:

"One day, I saw by chance, a sergeant who came from Wiesbaden who was very angry with a civilian member of the SS. He was threatening a Jewish worker and stomped on his leg [author says: trampled on]. When I reprimanded the sergeant about his intolerable behavior he stated that: "The Jew had lied to me". Then he used National Socialist expressions like "All Jews are our enemies and aren't worthy of a German's protection." I said to him that it was shameful for a soldier to threaten and to shoot [?] a defenseless person and that it would be better that he fought the enemies of Germany; he

should be serving on the front. He declared that he was a SS member and threatened to complain to the local National Socialist Party administration about the incident. I immediately reported this matter to Major Plagge. He forcefully reprimanded the sergeant and transferred him to the inside of the park [?] where he couldn't come into contact with the Jewish workers. He also ordered a report to the administration (and for all that I know) he did. It's a situation in which M. Plagge defends his Jewish workers from the dangerous actions and behavior of these people."

Even though Karl Plagge was extremely helpful, the life of the Jews was in the hands of the SS. These two would later get into the camp where they would commit barbarous and inhuman crimes, taking advantage of times when Plagge wasn't there. For example, In November 1943, a Jewish family tried to escape from the camp, but Gestapo captured them, the man, his wife and their child were publicly executed at the center of camp HK-562, in front of all the prisoners who were forced to assist at the scene. Worse, on March 27, 1944, the SS took advantage of Karl Plagge's absence on leave in Germany, and entered the camp and made a raid only on the children; it was called "Kinderaktion" during which a great majority of the children were sent to their death.

In the summer of 1944, the Red Army was approaching Vilnius. Because of this, danger was constantly present, because before the Germans retreated they would take care to liquidate all the remaining Jews.

Faced with this danger on July 1, 1944, Karl Plagge gathered all the prisoners in the camp for an informal talk, in the presence of a single SS officer, during which he would inform them that both he and his men would be transferred to the East and that he couldn't get permission to take the workers with him.

Thanks to this barely concealed warning, most of the prisoners were able to hide themselves before the arrival of the SS squadrons. Only 500 Jews were there for SS roll call on July 3rd, 1944, they were immediately executed in the Paneriai Forest. The SS rummaged through the camp during the next three days, and managed to find most of the hidden prisoners, they were all shot at the center of camp HKP-562. When the Red Army arrived in Vilnius some days later they found about 250 Jews leaving their hiding places a few at a time.

In choosing to hire Jews instead of Poles for his unit, Plagge had managed to save the greatest number of Jews. The result, however, wasn't extraordinary, in the end his unit had to evacuate leaving the camp to the SS, who executed about 1,000 people, all of them only in the last three days of the German occupation in Lithuania. Only about 3-5% of the Lithuanian Jews hid in the forests, with friends or neighbors had survived, but about 20% survived thanks to the efforts of Karl Plagge. The Jews in his camp represented the biggest group of survivors of the Holocaust in Lithuania.

After the war, Karl Plagge returned to Darmstadt where he was tried as part of the de-Nazification program He was judged before a tribunal; its decision was positively and strongly influenced by the testimony of certain former prisoners. The tribunal would judge him to be innocent, however, he refused. He made a demand to be classed as a follower, a collaborator. He made this choice because, like the celebrated Oskar Schindler, he felt responsible for not having done more for the Jews, for not being able to save more. The Tribunal agreed with his demand.

Karl Plagge lived simply, peacefully and unceremoniously for the last years of his life and died in Darmstadt in June of 1957.

For more than fifty years, the surviving Jews of Vilnius and their descendants have searched for Karl Plagge to give him thanks for having been a great source of courage and morale for them, a light in the middle of total darkness. After 1945, the 250 HKP-562 work camp survivors relocated all over the world, in the end beginning a new life outside the camps. Over time those who survived the war and their descendants have come from Germany, the United States, Canada, Israel, France, Lithuania or even Russia trying again to find the great man. Their parents have told their stories, and about their losses, and principally their survival thanks to Major Karl Plagge; the identity and the incentive of the latter having stayed hidden for a number of years. Finally, in 2005, Yad Vashem conferred on him the title of Righteous Among the Nations, in February, 2006 the former Frankenstein barracks of the Bundeswehr in Pfungstadt, Germany was renamed The Karl Plagge Barracks, and finally there existed a prize: The Karl Plagge Prize scholarship to Lithuanian students engaged in the study of the history of Lithuanian Jews outside the school curriculum. The family of Karl Plagge and their friends supplies the funds.

Michael Good, the son of a survivor commented

For those amongst us who look back on this man and his life, there is much on which to reflect and much to learn. His example shows us that a just man can accomplish, even in an infinite ocean of darkness and despair. The good things that he accomplished are heard through decades, generations and a new century. For hundreds of us, living, the enjoyment of our life today, we speak our thanks and gratitude to his memory.

MIEP GIES

Translated From The Original French
Fanny Mulder

In this essay I would like to describe a very impressive woman who helped a well-known young Jewish girl. The woman's name was Hermine Santrouschitz, better known under the name Miep Gies. She helped Anne Frank and her family hide in an annex to avoid being found by the Nazis. She did everything possible to help this family; but, sadly couldn't manage to save them. To better understand this woman's story I will describe her life at the same time as that of Anne

Frank, a courageous young girl; a Jew who fought to survive.

Hermine Santrouschitz was of Dutch birth, born on February 15, 1909 in Vienna. At the age of eleven, after the First World War, she was sent to Holland, this as part of a program that helped children suffering from malnutrition and afflicted by tuberculosis to regain their health. At first she lived in Leyden with a foster family. This family named her Miep and this surname stayed with her until the end of her life. She asked her biological parents to allow her to say in Holland because she felt at home there. She was living with the same family four years later in Amsterdam.

The Frank family, who were Jewish, left Germany to escape Nazi persecutions they met other escaping Jews whose numbers were increasing, after Adolf Hitler came to power. Otto Frank left for Holland whereas Edith, Margot and Anne Frank were left behind to live with Edith's mother in Germany. In 1933, in Amsterdam, Miep met Otto Frank, Anne Frank's father, who was looking for personnel for the business he directed, Opekta. She was hired to be in charge of the claims and information office, and then she was promoted to a more general administrative position. When Otto Frank's business was doing well he found an apartment in suburban Amsterdam. Miep helped the Franks get settled in Amsterdam and rapidly became a close friend of the family. The two girls were enrolled in a Dutch school. Otto Frank's business was doing very well and he started another business in partnership with Hermann van Pels.

The situation rapidly became worse when Germany invaded Holland in 1940; a local occupation government was put in place and began persecuting Jews by establishing repressive and discriminatory laws. Even though Anne and Margot excelled in their studies the introduction of the new laws precluded them from attending public schools, thusly, they were enrolled in a Jewish school.

Thanks to Anne Frank's personal diary which she wrote both before and after she lived in the annex, and because of her tragic destiny, she has become one of the emblematic victims of the Holocaust. Anne began her diary two days after her thirteenth birthday and it ended several days before she was arrested. It was Miep who found Anne Frank's diary in a hiding place in the annex. She kept it in a drawer for Anne's return not having read it. She said in an interview that if she had read it she would have burnt it because of the compromising information it contained. When Anne Frank wrote in her diary, she was addressing an imaginary friend named Kitty. In her diary she described her family, her friends, and her life at school... At the beginning of the diary we read about the life of a typical young student, and then Anne gently portrays for us the changes that were happening during the growing oppression under German occupation. She tells us about the yellow star that Jews were required to wear in public, the enacted restrictions, and the shocking persecution of Jews in Amsterdam. Miep married Jan Gies on July 16th, 1941 when she was threatened with deportation to Austria because she had refused to join a Nazi association for young girls. And then Anne's older sister, Margot, received a warning of mobilization from the Central Bureau of Jewish Immigration, in July 1942, in which she was ordered to present herself to be relocated to a work camp. Otto explained a plan that consisted of them going to live in the annex he, and his most trusted employees, had prepared: Victor Kugler, Johannes Kleiman, Miep Gies and Bep Voskuijl, those whom it wouldn't bother if it was a little difficult. Anne described his wife, Petronella, as a challenging woman with days when it was better not to talk to her. And there was their son, Peter, fifteen and a half years old, whom she described as a gentle and timid boy. And there was Fritz Pfeffer whom she described as a grumpy man. Anne was very happy to have some new people to talk to; but, vary soon there was a lot of tension, that originated because of the crowded environment. Anne was always very close emotionally with her father because she found her mother distant during this period. However, with her sister there was a bond created; but, all the same there were a number of disputes. Peter made advances towards her, which at first she rebuffed, but later she realized she was starting to have feelings for him. In the annex Anne spent most of her time reading, studying and always writing in her diary. Her diary not only contained her observations, but also revealed her innermost fears of living in hiding, as well as her beliefs and ambitions. She wanted to become a writer or a journalist later in life and she thought she couldn't share these dreams with anyone. The more she would write the more confidence she had in her writing, and as time passed, she became more mature. Over time what she was writing became more and more abstract, she would talk more and more about her belief in God, about how it defined the nature of man, and her thoughts about the future of the Jewish people.

In the spring of 1944 Anne heard the Dutch Minister of Education, on the radio from London. After the war he wanted to collect everything relating to the suffering that Holland had undergone, and he gave one example: personal diaries. She decided to no longer write solely for herself; but, to publish a book after the war, her personal diary would serve as the model. So she rewrote her diary correcting and removing passages that she judged uninteresting. And added other things she drew from her memory. Despite the copy [despite the revisions?] she continued to write in her original diary.

On the morning of August 4, 1944, the security services of the German police, "Grune Polizei", discovered the Frank's annex because an unknown source had revealed the exact location to the commander, Karl Silberbauer. After the Franks were discovered, Miep Gies and Bep being Austrian, were not arrested because, Karl was an Austrian. Nonetheless, Victor Kugler and Johannes Kleiman did not have same luck. They were immediately arrested and put in prison. The eight illegals were transported to Gestapo headquarters where they were interrogated and held overnight. The next day they were transferred to the "Huis van Bewaring". Two

476

days later they were transferred to Westerbork, a collection and transit camp, where there were more than 100,000 Jews. Hidden Jews were considered criminals and were punished; they had to perform difficult and dangerous work like dismantling batteries to salvage the valuable metal.

On September 3rd, 1944, the group was deported to Auschwitz on the last convoy to leave Holland. After a three- day journey they were separated according to their sex to ensure that the women and the men would never see each other again. More than half of the 1,019 people were sent directly to the gas chambers where they died. All the people from the annex survived this selection. Not having been selected, the girls from the annex would be stripped to be disinfected; their heads shaved as a sign of humiliation, and an identification number was tattooed on their arm. The three Frank women stayed in a group in the same barracks. Otto Frank was successful in getting a job in the camp post office, where he was permitted, sometimes, to have more food. Meanwhile, the Pells were not put in the same barracks as the Franks'.

Anne and Margot were transported to Bergen-Belsen.. Edith remained behind, alone at Auschwitz. When the two young girls arrived at Bergen-Belsen, they were both exhausted from the journey in cattle cars. The number of prisoners in this camp continued to increase and was already overcrowded by the time they arrived. They began sleeping in tents. But when the tents began to fall apart all of the prisoners were crowded into the barracks. Illness was rapidly increasing because there were too many people in the barracks and they had contagious diseases, this increased the death rate.

Another transport from Holland arrived in Auschwitz at the end of November 1944 with Madame van Pels. Madame van Pells was to be transported to Raguhn several months later, however, she died during her transfer to the Theresienstadt camp in Chekoslovakia. Anne and Margot suffered terribly from the cold because it often snowed in Bergen-Belsen, their beds were beside the entry door and they were never warm. They suffered food deprivations over a long period of time, and they both became very sick with typhoid fever, this epidemic caused by lice spread through the camp. Margot was more gravely ill than Anne. The older sister soon died, the younger sister passed away a few days later. We can't be sure that they died from typhoid fever but certainly their weakened condition played an important part. They were interred in the common graves at Bergen-Belsen. They perished several weeks before the camp was liberated by British troops.

Otto Frank was the only one of the hidden group to survive the Auschwitz camp. Auschwitz was liberated by the Red Army on January 27th,1945. Otto Frank returned to Amsterdam with the hope of finding his wife and his daughters, but, he learned of the death of his family in June,1945. After having learned of the death of his family Miep Gies gave him Anne's diary. He decided to have it published since his daughter's dream was to be a writer. Anne Frank's diary was a great success and was translated into more than 70 languages. About 30 million copies were sold.

Miep was the last survivor who had helped Anne Frank and her family to hide from the Nazis during the Second World War. In August of 1944 she tried to bribe the Nazis in order to obtain the freedom of her friends, but it didn't work. When she got to the annex she found 300 manuscript pages scattered on the floor, she gathered them up and put them in a drawer. She also recovered the family's photo albums. Miep wanted to return it all to Anne after the war.

During the rest of her life she continued to broadcast the story of this young girl. She continually worked for Anne Frank's memory. She also wrote, in 1987, a book *She Was Named Anne Frank*. After the publication on Anne's diary, she and her husband received a number of international awards, including the Raoul Wallenberg prize for bravery and recognition as Righteous Among the Nations from the state of Israel, the Yad Vashem medal, and was ennobled by Queen Beatrix of Holland. She and her husband Jan had a son, Paul, born on July 13th, 1952 she resigned her position at Opekta. Her husband died on January 26th, 1993 from diabetic complications. Sadly, even with all she had done, she did not want to be thought of as a heroine, because for her, aiding a family who were her friends was a normal thing to do. She even says: "I only did what I could to help them".

I found this woman to be very courageous to help this family under pain of being put to death. I don't know if I would have been capable of this, I truly hope yes; but, I've not yet been able to understand the magnitude of the events of that time. I try to understand the ambiance of these wars, to know how people lived, and what they felt. Sadly, with all my efforts I can't begin to understand the severity of the situation. I just hope that had I been in Miep's place, I would have done the same thing.

HEROES OF THE HOLOCAUST: DR. EMANUEL RINGELBLUM

Translated From The Original French
Jill Nuoffer

Two years ago I went to Berlin for a semester of school. Besides visiting the city I went to the Sachsenhausen Camp and the Jewish Museum. These two visits were very impactful. The day we went to the camp the weather was threatening, a small disruption to our visit, but a good disruption. Thanks to the bad weather we experienced a good sense of what the inmates would have experienced. We were cold, the wind blew, our down jackets sufficed to keep us warm; but, only imagine the prisoners who had nothing but a thin shirt, thin pants, and wooden clogs as work boots. The museum was less intense than the camp but the photographic images of the metallic faces were an intense experience. Following the trip I wanted to meet an old prisoner of the camp in order to understand how he had lived there for five years while I, in just 2 hours, had more than enough.

I chose to write a piece about Emanuel Ringelblum. He was born in Poland, more precisely in Buczacz, in 1900, a city close to Stanislawow. He studied at the University of Warsaw. He wrote a thesis about the history of the Warsaw Jews in the middle ages. Because of this he received a doctorate in 1927. After receiving his doctorate, the still young graduate began his teaching career in a Jewish school. While teaching, Emanuel was also very active in politics. He had joined the group "Poalei Agudat Yisrael" at a very young age.

In 1930, Doctor Ringelblum took a part time job with the Joint Distribution Committee. Eight years later he was sent to Zbaszyn Camp with 6,000 Jews who were,, for the most part Polish citizens deported from Germany. During the five weeks when he was in the camp, he gathered evidence that the deported Jews gave him about the Third Reich. A year later, after the Germans invaded Poland, Emanuel Ringelblum took part in the activities of the coordination committee of organizations to help the Jews. While on this committee he became the head of the department dedicated to the promotion of mutual aid. This committee provided aid for the indigent, shelter for Jews who had come to Warsaw, and those whose houses had been destroyed. He was responsible for a network of dozens of popular soup kitchens that serviced thousands of impoverished people in the ghetto. In addition to these two important activities, Ringelblum also found time for two projects for which he is best remembered today. These were the Oneg Shabbat Archives and his personal chronicles.

Thanks to the Wolski family who lived in Warsaw, Emanuel succeeded in not being caught by the Nazis. They had a house with a garden that had a greenhouse under which they built a room. It was not luxurious but had everything needed for proper living. It was a small space 15 feet by 21 feet; on one side it had bunk beds, on the other a kitchen and in the center a table and bench. There was good evidence that there was sanitation as well, a door on one side of the kitchen led to a water closet. It had electricity and running water. This little space served to hide Jews who had escaped from the ghetto. Each of the family members had tasks to make sure the place was kept in good shape, like taking out the garbage and carrying in the food. But a major concern was the interaction between the Jewish refugees. There wasn't just one Jew, but around thirty in this little space. In an attempt to have a compatible group, they formed a committee to assign the tasks, like guarding the entrance, cleaning the space and so on. Of course, the refugees couldn't stay there and do nothing, so there were language courses or reading newspapers. The Wolski family children liked to show up in the evening to talk with the refugees, and stayed overnight. This was recounted by Wanda, the sister of Miezcyslaw. In the spring of 1944 (we don't know how they could have known) the Germans came to the Wolski house. The Germans loaded the Jews onto a truck and not only Doctor Emanuel Ringelblum but Mieczyslaw, Maria and Janusz. They were taken away; we don't know where. Several guards stayed behind. That afternoon they brought Mieczyslaw, Wanda's brother, back to the garden. He was weak and could barely stand up. On his body, if one could call it a body, he bore only a shirt. He stood up and looked at the house to say his last goodbye. The woman who had collected the Jews in order to protect them was quickly burnt. Her name was Krysia. Many days later the rest of the family returned to the house. Their house had been pillaged and the neighborhood treated them like criminals. But it was not only the neighborhood that treated them like that: their closet neighbors treated them like that as well.

But, the Oneg Shabbat Archives material and the personal chronicles of Doctor Rigelblum were rescued and slipped past the Nazis. Thanks, notably to the Wolski family who took the material and hid it. They were, for example, hidden in milk cans and underground in the Warsaw ghetto. The Oneg Shabbat consisted of testimonies, news and so on, of Jews in the ghetto. This book makes it possible for us to know how Jews lived. It's clearly evident how difficult it was to write at this time. With the aid of historians and other writers, Emanuel Ringelblum could assemble writings to make the Oneg Shabbat, the name of which came from the group that Emanuel had created. One testimony in this book is very interesting: the Grojanowski report. This report is that of a very old prisoner of the Chelmno extermination camp, Jacob Grojanowski. He was successful in escaping from the camp and was a refugee in the Warsaw ghetto in 1942. He gave the group detailed information about the camp.

Emanuel hadn't been able to directly save the Jews, but thanks to the written material he and his group had collected, other European countries like England could know what had transpired on the borders of the Third Reich. Doctor Emanuel Ringelblum deserves an entry about what he did, and not only him, but everyone else who had saved people during this very complicated period for the whole world. Without their courage maybe no one would know what happened in the ghetto or in the camps.

THE HOLOCAUST

Translated From The Original French
Luisa Jutzet

A tragic event of fear and death, filled with sadness. A difficult time that resulted in nothing. Only the odor of burnt cadavers and ashes carried away by the wind.

But some people didn't remain idle and do nothing. Some people fought. They helped the brutalized Jews, hid them, fed them, and saved them.

The Italian Schindler was named Giovanni Palatucci who saved more than 5,000 Jews from Nazi raids. Sadly, of all the help he provided, nothing can be found in any archive in the Croatian city of Rijeka, the former Italian city Fiume, where he had lived since 1937: Only his uncle who testified that he was responsible for saving many Jews and sending them to Southern Italy.

This protecting angel of the Jews was a Fiume police officer who, at the age of 31, was named chief of the Foreign Office at the beginning of the war in 1940.

He saved all the documented records of around 5,000 Jews, threatened with deportation, from destruction and provided them with false papers and funds.

The archivist, his uncle, transformed an internment camp in Campagna, a small city in the province of Salerne where he had influence, into a shelter for Jews. Later Giovanni refused a promotion that would have sent him to another city; this would have precluded him from carrying out his mission.

After 1943 and the fall of Mussolini's government, Fiume was occupied by the Nazis, but Palatucci continued to provide clandestine help and maintained contact with the Resistance despite the much greater risk of him being arrested.

His activities were finally discovered by the Nazis. This ended all his help for Jews.

Under German direction, the politics became totalitarian, bloody and anti-Semitic. The Italian Social Republic, or the Salo Republic, tried to create a nationalization policy composed of Catholics, socialists, communists, nationalists, conservatives ... all hostile to the German occupation.

Germany exercised intense military pressure against Italy; the resistance had trouble repulsing the German troops.

Helping the Jews became too dangerous. One of Palatucci's close friends, the ambassador from Trieste, offered him passage to his country, Switzerland, but Giovanni refused to send his Jewish fiancé there.

He was later arrested on September 13th, 1944. A death sentence awaited him, but the sentence was changed. He was sent to Dachau where he died a year later, in

February, 1945, at the age of 36: most likely from the epidemic of typhoid fever that swept Dachau, Bergen-Belsen and Ravenbruck. It was a veritable hecatomb.

There were a number of deaths that year. The evacuations due to the approaching Soviets consequently meant that nearly 250,000 Jews died of hypothermia, exhaustion or being shot. These death marches were very trying because the inmates had to walk dozens of kilometers a day while having almost no food.

Some Jews had escaped the massacre thanks to the help of people who risked their freedom and their lives to save people who were completely unknown to them. Giovanni Pelatucci was one of these people. In March of 1939, he had facilitated the exodus of a number of Jews to what was to be the future State of Israel.

There remain, however, some doubts about the aid that he provided. Is it true that this hero has been appropriately made part of history? The facts are that some Jews testified in his favor to this effect. But could he have been the volunteer executioner during the six years of the anti-Semitic racial laws, and could he have sworn allegiance to Mussolini's socialist republic, and collaborated with the Nazis.

The historian Marco Coslovich began to deconstruct his myth. After fifteen years his research has still not been successful. He called into question the testimony, and explains that these 5,000 Jews had been saved by the Allied troops who arrived in 1943. But how is it that anyone wouldn't have doubts about his subject for more than 60 years? Of course, it would be wise to study Palatucci more, but, his legend has fallen a little at a time because the documents, supposedly destroyed, have been rediscovered in the Fiume city archives.

According to Marco Coslovich, the Palatucci legend began in 1952, and was created by the State of Israel who wanted international recognition from the Roman Church, that was being attacked for the passive compliance of Pope Pius XII, and for the full expression of remorse for having followed the orders of the Fascist regime. The reason for his arrest was not the discovery that he had been aiding Jews but because of his collaboration with the Anglo-American secret service. 5,000 Jews could not have been found among the 500 inhabitants of Fiume. Palatucci would have sent 80% to Auschwitz, and the remaining 20% would have been sent to Campagna, but not under his command. His uncle, Guiseppe Mari Palatucci, also contributed to the forging of the legend.

Palatucci was active in the final solution according to the Holocaust Memorial Museum in Washington D.C.

The Italians wanted to believe in Palatucci so the deception was easy to believe in his acts of bravery and to see in him a national hero. They wanted to believe that they hadn't stood idly by and did nothing during the war. "We can imagine ourselves being different, better! Italians, the brave people, altogether. Now we discover that Palatucci, the Italian Schindler, was a man loyal to the Nazis, who hadn't saved thousands of Jews from deportation" sorry, La Stampa (one of the most widely distributed Italian dailies).

The Holocaust was a difficult period for a number of countries. Many people don't know what to do, and many try to forget: To forget what is past, to forget that the war happened. But what good is forgetting? What good is pretending that everything was fine?

"To forget the Holocaust is to kill twice"

Elie Wiesel

Yes, it's necessary to remember these past horrors because if we forget them nothing can prevent another war breaking out. Nothing will prevent more thousands of people being killed. We must build a world in which neither war nor hunger exists. But, what about this marvelous world? We must fight for a better world. We must make decisions that will change our future. We learn from our mistakes, go back to zero, and begin a new life. We can do many things for our planet. It's up to us to find the answers. It's up to us to build our ideal world.

"Remember the past to build the future"

Some people already understand that. Some people have already begun to fight for a cause that they know is far from won. But, they fight at the peril of their lives. They have managed to save people and know that it was worth the trouble.

Giovanni Palatucci was one of these people, Giovanni Palatucci was a savior. Sadly due to the accusations made by historians, nothing has been proved that this Italian hadn't actually saved numerous Jews and risked his life for these people. He remains a hero in the eyes of those who believe in him, who believe the numerous reported testimonies and the lack of information challenging his assistance for these rejected people. One such person, named Antonio Pagnozzi, attempted to gather evidence to show the heroic act that was the proof for Giovanni. That this, Righteous among the Nations, has made history is a fact. He's the most famous Italian. There have been streets, places, squares, fountains and even schools named after him. The numerous surnames attributed to him are the result of his benevolence.

His name was listed at Yad Vashem in 1990, and he was named a martyr by John Paul II in one of the stages in his beatification. No one is named "martyr" by mistake. He is, and remains, someone who lived during the difficult period of the Holocaust and who brought all possible help to people who needed it. We can hypothesize he collaborated with the Nazis; we can deny that he participated in saving all those numerous lives, but we can't close our eyes to the recorded testimonies. We can't refuse to believe in his involvement with the Jews who recounted his courage.

Giovanni Palatucci made it possible to oppose this mass crime, this absurd genocide which aimed to eliminate an entire population that was neither a political nor a military threat. This early eradication would have the effect of driving people to suicide.

This has changed how we think about people. Some people saw a need to worry about their own life and not pay attention to the fate of others. They think that if the war was won, all the persecutions would come to an end, and the deported people would return. They did not expect an attempt at the total annihilation of their own population.

The Jewish resistance had the privilege of attacks and sabotage rather than thinking about liberating the deportees. Sadly, they wanted to fight, knowing little of the use of weapons. This was caused by the numerous years of discrimination and of their religion which prohibits violence.

This war isn't finished. It was without pity but with a specific purpose. It was successful in the extermination of 2/3 of the European Jews, 40% of Jews worldwide, six million people were killed. Six million souls who asked only for life.

All were mocked, persecuted, humiliated All were starved and forced to work in the concentration camps, if they were not already there or shot and gassed, which was in full operation. There were only a bunch of traumatized survivors and skeletal cadavers to be discovered by the allied soldiers. Forced to live in ghettos after the German invasion of Poland, Jews had an abhorrent quality of life. They were forbidden from entering some stores, weren't allowed to be in the same places as the rest of the population; they had to occupy the worst places. Most were subjective and passive so as not to antagonize the Germans. They were never excluded from normal life; but, they were always terrorized. Who wouldn't be, in this situation?

This crime that was the Holocaust has left traces in the world. There weren't happy moments during this time. The only positive thought that the people could have was in waking up and realizing that they were still alive. Yes, the survival instinct was the only thing that kept them from going crazy, to not falling into depression.

Survive. Surviving in a world where war raged, surviving in a world where compassion had, it seems, disappeared. Survive. The Jews fought as best they could. They tried to stay alive until the war ended. They waited. Waited until this ordeal stopped. Waited until someone won the fight. Waited until a miracle happened. Their fight wasn't physical. It was mental.

And that was the most difficult battle.

The most courageous people during the Second World War were the people who gave everything for people they didn't know and made every attempt to save them.

This Italian whom the whole world considers to be a quisling, this savior fallen from his high status. He brings hope to the heart of the Jews unlike anyone else. How could they be reassured? Because the Yugoslavian Jews knew that they could find help in Fiume with a certain man, Palatucci, this in a testimony by Angello Picariello). But then, how to prove to the world that this man had brought help to the Jews? Simply by hearing the testimony of those who had lived the drama, of those who passed on the information. If no aid had been given, no one would have been able to pass on the story that one heard traveling through the countries with the allies.

Giovanni was a hero.

"There are two forms of heroism, the one stemming from an unexpected need or impulse, and Paltucci's: a daily heroism, which he repeated and confirmed in the face of the certainty of danger being risked... He acted knowing that he was moving toward his own sacrifice; for him, it was worthwhile to give his life for just one man." Amos Luzzatto

EN MEMOIRE DE LORENZO PERRONE

Translated From The Original French
Rebecca Fasel

"Forget the past, it's condemned to relive itself." – Primo Levi

A Jew. That's what all the Germans saw in him during the very famous Second World War. Primo Levi was a man before everything else. And maybe more human than certain others. He perhaps did not have a dreamy life but the proof of life that he gave could be an enormous lesson to all.

The 13th of December 1943. A date which I am sure has remained engraved in his memory until the end. It was this day that he was snatched from freedom. A little liberty stayed with him in any case. He was 24 years old when his hell commenced. First, to Fossoli, near the Austrian border, next to Auschwitz. He had lived more than 2 years in concentration camps. For the Nazis, he wasn't anything but a slave. A man, moreover that they were allowed to exploit. And it is in Auschwitz that he met Lorenzo Perrone. The man who saved his life. This one who allowed him to continue in spite of the past. Without which so much would be forgotten but while utilizing this he had as a life lesson to transmit to his next.

Lorenzo Perrone was a mason, labor-exchanged by the Italian Nazis for his construction abilities. That's what they told him, in any case, but in reality he was a forced laborer. Perrone was treated just as horribly as any other Jew. He built all day long with Primo Levi. These two men met each other on the building site. There, where the insults of the Germans came from all sides. There where each wrongly made gesture awakened a fear of seeing death approaching them.

One day, Levi had heard Perrone speak in the same dialect has his. One point in common which they had and sufficed to bring them closer together. In addition,

485

friends were scarce in the conditions. Maybe because of a fear to become attached and to lose everything. One more time. Or maybe for fear of having to share and then have less for oneself. The Jews had no power, no right. Death had become their companion.

From the time of this encounter, day after day, during six months, Perrone supplied, behind the backs of the Germans, a little more food for Levi. And just until December 1944.

The food that Levi received from Perrone saved his life. With the little that he ate that the German soldiers gave him, he would never have made it back home. Even with the small amount more he received, one could count his ribs easily. Levi didn't keep all the food for himself. Perrone had showed him a portion, and he did the same around him. His friends profited also from small extras received from Levi. Perrone had also given him a waistcoat which he could wear under his prisoner clothing to stay as warm as possible. It was maybe a patched waistcoat but one made do with what one had. And having clothing more than these striped, lightweight pajamas was already a great luxury of which not too many could profit. For Levi, Perrone had done an enormous amount. He had even accepted to send the letters which Levi had written to a non-Jewish friend. A Jew could be executed simply for writing to someone non-Jewish. Like that, Perrone risked his life each time he rendered this service. But Perrone had proved that in spite of all the atrocities they could endure, illnesses, hunger, gas chambers, arms pointed on them throughout the day, there remained a little humanity, with human warmth at the bottom of certain hearts. The letters sent arrived to the mother and the sister of Levi who had the chance to hide out in Italy. Someone protected them and took care of them. Other heroes were there, other humans having conscience and valor of mankind, whether they were Jewish or not. The mother and the sister of Levi were in contact with friends of friends friends and so on just until Perrone. It was thus they that sent Levi the extra food he had and also the waistcoat and other items which he had that helped him to stay alive. Each day, Perrone had fear of dying. He did all he could for Levi and never demanded anything in return and if this wasn't enough, he patched up his shoes broken on the worksite.

Perrone was an incredible man. He never lost hope. He persevered, he went to the ends of things. He was not maybe very religious but that meant nothing. He helped all the time his fellow man. It was a little like his motto.For him, to give meant more than to receive. And no one stayed indifferent in the face of what he was doing. Perrone shared and those who saw him did the same. Levi did the same. One night, when Perrone was taking a bowl of soup to Levi, a bombing struck Auschwitz. An explosion had seriously hit one of Perrron's eardrums. The ground had propelesand into the soup. He had to surely suffer but he gritted his teeth and continued on his path right to Levi. When he arrived, he said nothing to him about what had happened. He didn't want anyone to feel indebted toward him because he had come to skim past death for a bowl of soup. Yes okay, in these conditions abbowl of soup is very precious but nothing is worth more than a life. Perrone had kept this suffering to himself, well hidden. As he had learned how to do in this concentration camp when he had to work but as he did not have enough strength or when he had to battle without reason done in part for that entertainment of the Germans.

He had given the bowl of soup to Levi and then apologized. For the sand in the soup. He apologized. Perrone would have to complain or arrive in tears and asking for help, at least. But he preferred to remain discreet. He had restored his physical and morale and continued on his route. Perrone was a very humble man. Never did he demand anything is return for what he gave. He went so far as to refuse if someone proposed to him anything at all.

Perrone never lost hope and he repeated endlessly to Levi that there was a world outside of Auschwitz. A better world. A world where Just men existed. Good men who knew how to make goodness around them. Without predjudices, without categories. A world where everyone could find his place.

Without Perrone, Levi would never have been able to survive. He recognized this. He kept him alive. He had given him hope, day after day. Perrone had helped Levi, whether it was by feeding him or by bringing up his morale, while giving him a purpose, a will to live. He did this with all his heart, he lavished attention on his friend.

Saturday, January 27th 1945. Levi and Perrone were liberated. They had survived. It was over. The war was done. The shock had to have been immense. The Germans no longer had power over their lives. They could assert themselves, they could speak normally, they could go wherever they wanted. Ended were the strikes on the back or on the legs. Ended was the persistent work with no pay. Over were the dormatories with more than five in a bed. Finished. They went from indiscriminate prisoners to free men. How to go out again from it without any aftereffect?

Back home, Perrone had a hard time reconstructing, moving on and forging ahead. He began drinking and stopped working. The trauma he had lived through in the concentration camp had profoundly affected him. He had lost the desire to live. But Levi was there. He took care of his hero as he had done for him previously. Levi had tried to hospitalize him and heal him but there was nothing more that could be done. Perrone had given it all; all for those around him, for his friends. He had saved, I think, much more than a life. The others could not be brought out living but it doesn't mean anything. He had offered all that he could of himself. He touched hearts. He had helped heaps and heaps of people. He had turned over more than one life. In 1952, alcohol and tuberculosis took Perrone. Some people could criticize the way his life ended, the fashion with which he took care of himself, but I sincerely think that after having acted as he wished, after having given priority to others, no one has the right to say a word against him. In moments the most horrible that one could imagine, when no one had hope, he was there. He was not at all at the center of his world. On the contrary, he is perhaps somewhat forgotten. But he leaves even today a hard-hitting testimony. Pay attention to your neighbor. It was this that kept him going in his own life. It was his purpose. His generosity was stronger than the hatred of the German Nazis.

As for Levi, he got married to Lucia Morpugo and they had two children. In homage to Perrone, Levi named his daughter Lisa Lorenza and his son Renzo. He also wrote books of which an autobiography (*Si c'est un homme)* in which he speaks of Perrone, this generous worker who built walls and to whom he owed his life. In his book, Perrone is described like a saint. A natural and simple man. He was his hero, to whom he owed everything. Without Perrone, Levi would have forgotten the sense of friendship and love. But in 1987, Levi could do no more. He fell down the stairwell in his building. To see the people around him wanting to forget everything, seeing them become totally indifferent to what had happened made him suffer more than other things. He even wrote in one of his books: "To forget the past is to be condemned to relive it."

It is necessary to remember all that happened. It is necessary to learn from the mistakes of those who came before us, and not replicate that which was already done. Ignoring never leads to anything. But above all, we must memorialize these heroes like Lorenzo Perrone who gave their lives for others. The people who have taken care of those who needed it most during the worst moments of their lives.

They are so much more than that which one might think and that what they did is without a price. They should be honored for all that they have accomplished. Because simply they are heroes. They are our heroes.

C. K. McClatchy High School, Sacramento, CA

PAMELA RICE

B.A. Scripps College,
Claremont,California;
International Relations Junior Year
Abroad, University of Heidelberg,
Germany;
Masters in German, CSUS;
Credentialed in German and English.

Currently teaching German at
C.K. McClatchy High School,
Sacramento, CA

GERDA VALENTINER，谢谢您！

YongFen Lei (Sallay)

　　滴答，滴答，时间一秒一秒的过去，见证了多少英雄的崛起。古时北齐的神武帝高欢，曾留下"英雄莫问出处，富贵当思原由"的感想。可是，那些在历史上曾不惜一切代价救助过许多无辜人民的英雄就真的不**值**得我们这些世人去细细得琢磨与学习吗？是他们造就了现在的百姓，是他们造就了现在的社会，是他们造就了现在的世界。他们的存在是代表着正义的，勇敢的，和那段曾存在过的悲惨历史呀！

　　呼！呼！呼！

玻璃破碎的声音在德国，奥地利和苏台德区的大街小巷响起。一片又一片的玻璃犹如雪花般的掉了下来。这正是1938年的"碎玻璃之夜"，也称"十一月的迫害"。之所以被称为这两个名字是因为纳粹党把所有犹太人商店的玻璃给打破了，可恨的他们夺去了所有犹太人们的财产，袭击了所有犹太人们的家庭，和扫荡了所有犹太人们的教堂。一夜之间，全部的犹太人变得一无所有了。纳粹党竟然做出此等的迫害行为，难道他们就不会觉得内疚，不会觉得有愧于所有的犹太人们吗？那些行为岂是人类所为，简直就是禽兽都不如！

据官方公布的"碎玻璃之夜"死亡人数为91人，实际上却远远超过了这个数目。那夜过后，所有的犹太人被送进了所谓的"集中营"。起初的集中营只用于关押犯人，并不是用于屠杀。1939年后，集中营开始变了，变成了"灭绝营"，越来越多的犹太人被处死在里面。死亡手段十分残忍，包括烧死，苦役，劳动致死，枪杀或被送进毒气室等酷刑。

即使是能活下来的，也好不到哪里去，他们被迫受着日益残酷的虐待。无论是在肉体上还是心理上，都有极大的创伤。试想一下，如果你是集中营的一员，每天都过着没有灵魂般的生活，每天都要胆惊心颤地度过，最可怕的是你永远都不知道什么时候才是尽头，就只能盼啊盼，盼着自由之神的再次降临，终究可能盼到死恐怕还是盼不到，因为你永远都预测不了下一秒纳粹党会对你做出些什么可怕的事来。特别是那些可怜的孩子们，他们本该拥有的童年时光就这样白白得被夺去了，我为他们感到深深的不公与愤怒。

中国有句俗话说得好

"善人有善报"，就当犹太人们感到绝望的时候，一群又一群的人们为他们站了起来，给予他们温暖与希望。

我称这些人们为"英雄"，他们像是沙漠里的一片绿洲，草丛中的一眼细泉，石头下的一朵小花，黑夜间的一根蜡烛。他们临危不惧，在那千钧一发的时刻，不顾生命危险地为犹太人们争取属于属于他们的自由，尊严和一份对他们合理的解释。这般英勇行为，实在是令人心生敬佩，值得我们这些世人学习啊！

随着大屠杀一天一天地扩大，英雄随之一天一天地崛起。其中有一个名叫 Gerda Valentiner 的人令我印象十分深刻。她对犹太人们所做的事情让我感到一股深深的暖意。她不像其他人那样地去无视犹太人的存在与悲惨的遭遇，反而，她对他们伸出了援手，向他们雪中送炭，让他们寄有一丝的生存希望。她是多么一位值得后人学习及敬仰的女英雄呀！

接下来，让我们一起乘搭时光机回到Gerda Valentiner的那个年代。她是丹麦人，出生地是丹麦。纳粹党入侵丹麦的时候，她是一个老师，她的学生中有许多犹太人孩子，他们的衣服上都刺有一个黄色的星星，而这些黄色的星星是纳粹党为了容易辨认出哪些是犹太人而制造的，换而言之则是当时犹太人的标记。纳粹党还把所有的犹太人孩子赶出了学校，不允许他们接受任何教育，这对无辜的孩子们来说该是多大的打击啊！但其实，对他们更大的打击还在来临的路上。。。。。

　　在孩子们被赶出学校不久后，
已经有过百万的犹太人孩子被纳粹党给杀害了。当时在丹麦，人人皆感到惊讶和不安。大多数的丹麦人选择了放弃去帮助那些可怜的孩子们，统统都拒他们于千里之外。
不是因为他们没有能力，而是因为他们都害怕纳粹党会对自己的家人做出些惨不忍睹的事情。《三字经》常言，"人之初，性本善"，还是会有那么一群人无畏无惧，冒着生命危险地去向犹太人孩子们伸出援手的。毕竟，人类的心是肉做的，无论怎样还是会有感情的。

　　对于一位老师来说，他们的责任只是在教室里教育自己的学生道理和知识。但是，对于一位像 Gerda
Valentiner这样高尚的老师来说，她的责任不仅仅是在教室里教育自己的学生，还要尽全力的保护他们，即使要付出自己的生命也在所不惜。她是一位多么伟大的老师啊！

　　1943年十月份的某一个星期，准确的来说是一个决定犹太人命运的星期。Gerda Valentiner
尽她的能力把一部分的犹太人孩子们给集合起来安顿在她家。她在等一个时机，准备把那些孩子们送到瑞典，因为当时瑞典是一个安全的地方。

Gerda
Valentiner不仅仅尽了老师的工作，同时还负担起了父母的责任。她所照顾的犹太人孩子们有些是非常坚持于自己的宗教，所以根据犹太人宗教规则，他们只可以吃面包。Gerda
Valentiner也是一位宗教人士，她完完全全可以体谅那些孩子们的感受，所以她特意准备了一些专属的食物给他们。我相信，她为孩子们所做的一切都是出自真心的。同时，在孩子们的弱小心灵里，我想也是非常感激他们的救命恩人的。

当时，Gerda
Valentiner的举止还是鲜为人知的。直到有一天，一个叫Moritz
Scheftelowitz 的人告诉'以色列大屠杀纪念馆'关于她的英雄事迹。 Moritz
Scheftelowitz说他妹妹之前是Gerda
Valentiner的学生。他自己还清楚地记得1934年九月尾的那个夜晚，Gerda
Valentiner去他家告诉他父母危险即将到临。几日后，Moritz
Scheftelowitz和他的两个妹妹就搬到了Gerda
Valentiner的家里住。一直住到Gerda
Valentiner帮他们完成所有的迁离手续为止。他们前两次的离开都失败了，在第三次时终于如愿以偿，他们成功地离开了危险的丹麦。经过了一夜的船浪，他们终于到达了安全的瑞典。我为他们感到非常开心和幸运，但同时也有那么一丝的伤感，因为他们可能再也没有机会见到自己的父母，再

494

也可能回不到那个温暖的家了。那种感觉真的不好受，简直就是心如刀割！

按统计，Gerda Valentiner一共救了492个犹太人，大多数是小孩子。当她被问及救人时的感想，她只是很谦虚地说，"我只是做了作为一个丹麦人应该做的事而已，没什么特别的。我觉得帮助人们脱离致命的危险是一件很应该的事。"当我读到她说的这些话时，我完完全全地被她给征服了。她的言语与思想是多么的崇高，多么的神圣，多么的正气凛然啊！

在纳粹党被除去之后，她辞去了多年来老师的工作。接着的两年，她以社会工作者的身份默默地帮助在德国和奥地利的犹太难民营。在1971年，当时的她是68岁，已经是一名退休老人了。不过，她为了能体会到以色列风情，就亲自去了以色列，学习了希伯来语并在那里过了一年的生活。

从年龄上来算的话，Gerda Valentiner现在应该是112岁左右了。可惜的是，我并没有找到任何能够证明她是否还在世的资料。不过，我相信她的英雄精神是永远都不会消失的。我觉得我从她的英雄事迹中收获了许多我之前看不到的东西。是她！是她清楚地让我看到，
无论在何时何地，这颗地球上总是会有那么一群人犹如蜡烛般，虽然细弱

，但却在黑暗的夜里用仅存的力量温暖了别人，耗尽了自己。这种无私的奉献精神如太阳般地照亮着这个世界，让人永志不忘！

在此，我要向亲爱的Gerda Valentiner女士敬一个礼。她不仅仅是一个好老师，还是一位伟大的英雄！您永远都会存在于我们的心里，谢谢您！

GERDA VALENTINER, THANK YOU!
English Translation of Previous Essay

Tick ,tock, tick, tock, time passes by second by second. There are many stories of heroes, people who are selfless in heling others. An ancient northern emperor, Qi Gao Huan, famously said, "Never ask the truth of where a hero comes from. When you become rich, you should remember where you came from." History shows so many heroes rescuing innocent people at all costs, and it's worth learning and understanding how heroes created the present society and world, how they represent justice, righteousness, courage, and the sorrow of history.

Ping,ping, ping, the sound of shattered glass in Germany in the Sudentenland region. The broken glass looked like snowflakes all over the streets and allies. This was called the "Night of Broken Glass" or "Kristallnacht". In 1938, the Nazi party started to attack all of the Jewish people and sadly the Nazis took all of the Jewish property and the families had to sleep outside Jewish churches. Overnight, Jewish people lost all of their belongings. How can the Nazi party not feel guilty? Their behavior is inhumane. Not even animals would do it.

The official record of deaths during Kristallnacht was 91. However, the true number of deaths was not reflected in the record. After that night, all the Jewish people were sent to the so-called, "concentration camps". Originally, the camps were used to hold prisoners, not people doomed to be massacred. After 1939, the camps began to change into "extermination camps". More and more Jewish people were killed with extreme cruelty. Some types of torture included being burned to death, worked to death, shot, or sent to the gas chambers. Even if they were able to survive the torture, their lives were not easy and they endured more abuse. Jewish people suffered physically and psychologically.

Please imagine you are in the concentration camp. Living in fear on a daily basis and never knowing when it would end. We could only hope for freedom and hope God would come again. We would hope not to die and to be able to predict what the Nazis would do next.

Especially those poor children. Their childhoods were taken away from them. It makes me feel there was an injustice and I am angry for them.

A Chinese saying is, "A good heart will be well repaid". When Jewish people were in despair, groups stood up for the Jewish people and gave them warmth and hope. I call these people heroes: they are like an oasis in the desert, a watering hole in the grass, flowers under the stones, and the candle light in the darkness.

Their courage in this critical moment, risking their lives to fight for freedom, fight for their dignity, and demanding a reasonable explanation for them. The heroic act should be admired. We should learn from these people.

With the recognition of Holocaust Remembrance Day, we sometimes hear the word, "hero". One hero who impressed me greatly is Gerda Valentiner. Her actions on behalf of the Jews warmed my heart deeply. Unlike others who ignored the plight of the Jews, she lent a helping hand, and because of this, the Jews h ad a glimmer of hope for survival. She is worthy of future study and admiration.

Let us take a time machine back to Gerda Valentiner's era. She is a Dane, born in Denmark. When the Nazi's invaded Denmark, she was a teacher. Jewish children had yellow Stars of David woven into their clothing used by the Nazis to easily identify the Jewish children. In other words, it was the Jewish mark. The Nazis also expelled all of the Jewish children from school, forbidding them an education. Unfortunately, even more danger was in store for the children.

After the children were expelled from school, there were over a million Jewish children killed by the Nazis. This took the Danes by surprise. Most Danes chose to help the children. They helped even though they were afraid the Nazi Party would do terrible things to their own families. A *Three Character Classic* saying is that "Man's nature is good" or a group of people would be so fearless, risking their lives to change the fate of the Jewish children, lending a helping hand.

As for a teacher, their duty in the classroom is to educate their students about truth and knowledge. But for someone like Gerda Valentiner, a noble teacher, she took on not just the responsibility of educating her students in the classroom but also did her best to protect them, even placing her own life at risk.

One week in October 1943, a decision was made that affected the fate of the Jews. Gerda Valentiner set up Jewish children in her home. She was awaiting for an opportunity to prepare the children to go to Sweden because at that time Sweden was a safe place.

Gerda Valentiner not only did her job as a teacher but also took on parental responsibilities. Jewish children in her care were devout, so in accordance with Jewish religious rules, they can only eat unleavened bread. Gerda Valentiner was a religious person as well so she completely understood the feelings of those children, so she prepared appropriate food to give to them. I believe that everything she did is for the children and sincere. Meanwhile, in the children's minds, I think they were very grateful to their savior.

For a long time, Gerda Valentiner remained little known. Until one day a man named Moritz Scheftlelowitz told Israel's Holocaust Memorial about her heroic deeds. Moritz Scheftlelowitz told the story before his sister's, Gerda Valentiner's, students. He still clearly remembers the night at the end of September in 1934, Gerda Valentiner went to his house to live. Gerda Valentiner lived there to help his family complete all of the formalities until their escape. They tried twice before to leave but failed. On the third try, they got their wish and succeeded in leaving dangerous Denmark. After a night on the restless water, they finally reached the safety of Sweden. I am very happy for them, but also there is a trace of sadness because they might never have had the chance to see their parents again, and could no longer return to the warmth of their home. Feeling really upset, simply Xinrudaoge!

According to statistics, Gerda Valentiner saved a total of 492 Jews, most of them children. When she was asked to share her feelings, she just very humbly said, "I just did as a Danish person should do, nothing special. I think helping people out is a very deadly dangerous thing." When I read these words she said I was totally conquered. How noble her speech and I thought how sacred and how righteous, ah!

After the Nazi Party was removed, she resigned from teacher's work. The next two years as a social worker she quietly helped Jewish camps in Germany and Austria. In 1971, when she was 68 years old, she was already a retired old woman. However, personally she went to Israel where she learned Hebrew after a year.

From that time to now, Gerda Valentiner would be around 112 years old today. Unfortunately, I did not find anyone who can prove that she is still alive. However, I believe the spirit of our heroes never disappear. I think I learned a lot of things from her heroic deeds. She clearly let me see, no matter when and where, the Fengyun Earth will be a group of people like a candle, but in the dark of night, with the power only of the warmth of others, consumption do yourself. Such selfless dedication light the world, people will never forget!

Here, I would like to give dear Ms. Gerda Valentiner respect in ceremony. She is not only a good teacher, or a great hero! You will always be in our hearts, thank you!

Sheldon High, Sacramento, CA

Susan Abbott has taught English for over 30 years in the EGUSD school district. She has been named their 2016 Teacher of the Year, and in 2008 was named Carlston Family Foundation's Teacher of America.

DENMARK RALLIED TOGETHER: A NATION OF HEROES THAT SAVED THEIR JEWISH NEIGHBORS IN THE HOLOCAUST

Morgan Folger, Winner

 On September 29th, 1943, just a few days before Rosh Hashanah, the Jewish New Year, Leo Goldberger's life was turned upside down. Leo was a young Jewish boy, and lived in Denmark with his family during the beginning of the Nazi occupation in that country. He had been lucky so far—the Nazis had not yet acted on any major plans to fulfill martial law, and uproot him from his life—but all that was about to change. Leo's family received warning that the Nazis were planning to capture all the Jews in Denmark in just a few days. They had very little time to formulate an escape plan or decide what to take with them in their race for safety. Leo's family voyaged to Sweden, where they lived in safety until the end of the Nazi occupation. Leo's story is not particularly unique. Thousands of Jews like him left Denmark to find safety in Sweden, and thousands managed to survive. Their escape, however, would have been impossible were it not for the generosity of the Danish people. At every stop along the way to Sweden, Leo and the thousands like him were met with help from Danish people, many of them strangers. While atrocities occurred during the Holocaust all over Europe, the whole nation of Denmark rallied together in an ultimate expression of humanity by opening their homes, offering passage to safety, and logistically planning the transportation of thousands of refugees, to ensure the safety of their Jewish neighbors.

Unlike other European countries at the time, Denmark actively and collectively worked against Nazi brutality towards Jews, so much so that the entire country of Denmark is honored by Yad Vashem with the title of Righteous Among Nations (Weiss and Brachman). The quest to safety in Sweden that the Jewish people like Leo took was along what would later be called the Danish underground. The Underground became a necessity when, in Berlin, the Nazis decided that on October 1st, Rosh Hashanah Eve, "...the Gestapo would raid Jewish homes and seize the occupants," and those captured would be transported to Tereisendstadt, a Nazi concentration camp (Weiss and Brachman). This information was passed on to the Danish people by Georg F. Duckwitz, a Nazi official who empathized with the Danish resistance movement. Duckwitz shared the details of the Nazi raid with "friends, business acquaintances, and strangers wanting to help" (Holmskov Schluter). Duckwitz risked his life by sharing sensitive Nazi information to anyone who would listen, and thousands of Jews were saved because of his risk. The news of the raid spread exponentially, and Jews all over the country were advised to leave their homes by that day to save their families. In response to the news, a "part organized, part spontaneous rescue action was mounted" (Vogelsang and Larsen). The Danes worked to organize an effort to smuggle the Jews to safety in Sweden, which was neutral ("Rescue in Denmark"). They knew it would be difficult, and, even knowing that they were risking their lives, the Danish people refused to let the Jews of Denmark be transported to their death. Every single Dane was encouraged to participate in the liberation plan; church congregants were urged by their ministers to assist their Jewish neighbors, and even universities closed the week of Rosh Hashanah so that all students could participate in the rescue plan (Dolgin). The executed journey itself was difficult. Refugees were carried across the small channel of water between Denmark and Sweden in large fishing boats, rowboats, or even kayaks. Some were placed in freight cars that were brought to Sweden on ferries (Holmskov Schluter). All along the way, smugglers had to be wary of German officials lurking on the waters to snatch anyone guilty of smuggling. The Danish people navigated through the channel, and situated themselves at checkpoints to ensure the exiled made it to Sweden safely. Approximately 7,200 Danish Jews and 680 non-Jewish family members successfully journeyed to Sweden this way ("Rescue in Denmark"). Because of this, when, on Friday night, the Nazis raided Jewish homes, they found them empty (Weiss and Brachman). Every single traveller along the Danish underground owed their freedom to the Danish men and women who organized the mission, navigated the fugitives to safety, and opened up their homes as safe houses from the Nazis.

The journey by sea to Sweden was only half of the voyage for Jewish refugees. Jews traveling the underground had to first make it to the coast, but they were uprooted from their homes, and had no where familiar to go in their escape where they would be safe. Fortunately for them, Danes welcomed escapees into their homes with open arms, and promised their safety. Gilda Valentiner, a Danish teacher and secret member of the Resistance, was dedicated to providing refuge for the Jewish children that were uprooted. In trying to escape, many families were forced to split up. In the chaos and danger of the journey, it was thought that "separate hiding places for individual members of the nuclear family" was the safest mode of transport (Grimshy and Goldberger). Because of this, many children had to be separated from their parents. Gilda would approach families that she knew were in danger and offer to keep their children safe. She would protect the children in her home, while finding a way of passage for them to Sweden. Moritz Scheftelowitz testified to Gilda's operation. He remembers that Gilda had taken in his sisters, Dora and Rita, and arranged for their passage to Sweden ("Valentiner Family"). Gilda showed nothing but respect for the children she took in. For example, when Gilda learned that some

502

of the children were strictly observant of their religion, and were only able to eat the bread that was offered to them, she "brought them new dishes and food" that they could eat ("Valentiner Family"). Gilda played a crucial role in the lives of many Jewish children, but despite this, she remains modest. On July 28th, Gilda was recognized as one of the Righteous Among the Nations by Yad Vashem, the highest title offered to Holocaust heroes, but when asked about her extraordinary efforts, she only replied, "I only did what many Danes did, nothing special. We thought it perfectly natural to help people in mortal trouble" ("Valentiner Family"). After Gilda provided refuge and organized the transport of those they saved, they were in the hands of the many Danes who tasked themselves with navigating through the waters to Sweden.

Perhaps, while Gilda's children made their way to Sweden, they crossed paths with Knud Christiansen, a prominent Danish athlete and Holocaust hero. In 1936, Knud had competed in the Berlin Olympics as a rower for Denmark, where he lived and operated his business manufacturing leather (Dolgin). The leather industry of Denmark at the time was mostly operated by Jewish businessmen, and so, in his business, Knud came to know and be close with many Jews. After the occupation of Denmark, Knud joined the Danish Resistance, and worked to help his Jewish neighbors find safety. Knud helped large groups of Jews to churches, farmhouses, city apartments, and any other available shelter to keep them safe from arrest (Dolgin). From their, the refugees were carried by sea to Sweden. In addition to finding safeguards for Jews, Knud helped many across the channel. Knud brought Max Rawitscher, for whom he and his wife had opened up their home to, to Sweden from the shores of Denmark ("Christiansen Family"). Knud did this for various groups of Jews. He saved not only his close personal friends, but also "complete strangers" from Nazi arrest by going above and beyond for every single life (Dolgin). When Knud found out about the upcoming raid, he had warned the Philipson brothers, blacksmiths he had met, to go to his house instead of going home that night. Unfortunately, they did not believe him and went home anyway, where they were captured and thrown in a detention center. Knud refused to give up on them, and, by bribing officials and using his status as an Olympic athlete, he managed to have them freed ("Christiansen Family"). Like Gilda Valentiner, Knud was extremely modest about his heroism on the Danish underground. When asked about his work, he did not praise himself for getting involved and saving lives, but instead said, "It was something that needed to be done" (Dolgin). Much of the work Knud Christiansen and countless like him had done was improvised, however some, like Knud Dyby, helped to disseminate information and organize the transportation of refugees so that the journey went safely.

When, during German occupation, the Nazi flag was hoisted atop Amalienborg Castle, King Christian X was in an outrage, and demanded that the

Denmark flag be put back in its original position over the castle. Knud Dyby was on of the Denmark soldiers who removed the Nazi flag ("Knud Dyby: Denmark"). Thus began Dyby's efforts to resist the Nazi occupation. After his military service, Dyby became an officer in the Copenhagen national police force , and this position in the police force gave him the perfect opportunity to play a key role in the Danish underground ("Knud Dyby"). As an officer, Dyby gained access to vital information that benefitted the Resistance considerably. He knew the patrol routes of the German navy, and was able to distinguish the "best sea lanes between Denmark and Sweeden" ("Knud Dyby: Denmark"). Dyby shared his knowledge with members of the underground to use in their travels to Sweden. Because of the information Dyby shared, many more Jews made it to Sweden without detection than would have been possible—but his work did not end with that. Dyby played a key role in the organization of the underground. He was the lead in convincing and mobilizing countless commercial fishermen to participate in the underground ("Knud Dyby"). These fisherman smuggled Jews to Sweden on their ships, using the information Dyby gave them about where to navigate. On land, he "organized the city's taxi drivers" to transport Jews secretly to the Denmark coast, and even used his position as an officer to arrange the use of "state police cars" to assist in the transfer ("Knud Dyby"). Because of Knud's leadership, "close to 7,000" people were saved from the Nazi regime ("Knud Dyby").

Gilda Valentiner, Knud Christiansen, Knud Dyby, and the multitude of heroes for whom their stories represent risked their futures and lives for the Jewish people of Denmark, many of whom they had never met. How they managed to save so many is relatively simple: through the Danish underground. But why they did it is a completely different debate. The decision to save the Jewish people was a collective one. Knud Christiansen remembers, "The whole time people helped one another. People took risks they weren't normally take" (Dolgin). Because the fight against the Nazis was communal, the motivation for their efforts lies in the common Danish attitudes toward Jews at the time of the occupation. Before the Nazi's rose to power, Jewish Denmark citizens lived with relative ease—"for centuries, Denmark's Jewish community lived in tranquility, without discrimination or sense of alienation," and they were "protected like every citizen under law" (Weiss and Brachman). Such a long period of time without ethnic struggle led to a culture of acceptance and tolerance. Jews were not isolated, or thought of as others in Denmark. Peter Ilsoe, a member of the Danish resistance said, "We felt that the Jews were Danes like us, and we knew we had to help them" (Weiss and Brachman). After years of not being singled out for being Jewish, the "Jew" was no longer a significant part of Semitic Danish identity in society. This created a communal feeling between Danes and Jewish Danes. They were able to realize that they were all citizens of Denmark. Rabbi Ben Melchoir recalls his life in Denmark, and says, "The Danes consider us to be Danes. No one thought twice about the fact that I was Jewish" (Weiss and Brachman). The people of Denmark stood up to save their Jewish neighbors because they were their neighbors. They decided that it was more important to save their fellow Dane than to remain in silence, in safety, in immorality. For this reason Denmark was a shining example of humanity for the rest of the pitch-black, Nazi dominated Europe.

When the Nazis left Denmark, Leo Goldberger 's family left Sweden and returned to their homeland. Other Europeans were racked by Nazi occupation, and many Jews who returned to their home countries would find a mere skeleton of their previous life. Leo and his family, however, were met with "a universal celebration of welcome" (Grimsby and Goldberger). The family was able to joyously return to their pre-Holocaust lives thanks to their Danish neighbors, who saw to it that their home and workplace was cared for and remained exactly as it was left, and the Great Synogogue of Copenhagen, which his family had previously attended, was returned to its previous condition without delay. Through the dark abyss that was Nazi occupation, the Danish people managed to not only preserve the pieces of their Jewish neighbors' lives, but also to maintain their humanity. They saved thousands of Jews from detainment, and never lost hope for those who slipped through the cracks. In 1944, a "Danish delegation" was allowed to visit the Danes who had been captured, and eventually officials of Denmark accomplished the prisoner's deportation to the unhostile Sweden (Vogelsang and Larsen). Of the 500 who were deported, 450 survived (Rescue in Denmark). Today, Denmark is considered the only occupied country to outwardly combat the Nazi regime. The Dane's efforts were not perfectly successful, unfortunately, but even with the loss of around one hundred Danish Jews, Denmark acquired the "highest survival rate in Europe during World War II," and the entire nation is considered by Yad Vashem to be Righteous Among the Nations (Vogelsang and Larsen).

Works Cited

"Christiansen FAMILY." The Righteous Among Nations. Yad Vashem, n.d. Web. 28 Feb. 2015.

Dolgin, Robyn. "Danish Hero: One Rosh Hashanah Burns Bright in Holocaust." JewishPost.com. Jewish Post, n.d. Web. 28 Feb. 2015.

"Gerda Valentiner." "Their Fate Will Be My Fate Too.." Yad Vashem, n.d. Web. 28 Feb. 2015.

Grimsby, Liv, and Leo Goldberger. " Memory and Tragedy: The Life of a Young Danish Jew during WWII." Thanks to Scandinavia. Thanks to Scandinavia, 12 June 2012. Web. 28 Feb. 2015.

Holmskov Schluter, Hans. "Danish Resistance during the Holocaust." www.HolocaustResearchProject.org. Holocaust Research Project, 2007. Web. 28 Feb. 2015.

"Knud Dyby." Knud Dyby. Humboldt University, n.d. Web. 28 Feb. 2015.

"Knud Dyby: Denmark." The Jewish Foundation for the Righteous. The Jewish Foundation for the Righteous, n.d. Web. 28 Feb. 2015.

"Rescue in Denmark." United States Holocaust Memorial Museum. United States Holocaust Memorial Council, n.d. Web. 26 Feb. 2015.

Vogelsang, Peter, and Brian B.M. Larsen. "The Fate of the Danish Jews." The Danish Center for Holocaust and and Genocide Studies, 2002. Web. 28 Feb. 2015.

Weiss, Ruchama, nd Levi Brachman. "'Danes Saw Us as Friends, Neighbors, Not as Jews'" Ynet. Yedioth Internet, 03 May 2006. Web. 28 Feb. 2015.

"Valentiner Family." The Righteous Among Nations. Yad Vashem, n.d. Web. 28 Feb. 20

San Juan high School, Citrus Heights, CA

Shannon Barbarino
I have been teaching at San Juan High School in Citrus Heights for 8 years.
I grew up in Southern California, and attended California State University, Northridge for my BA English degree. Shortly after earning my degree, I moved to Sacramento for the credential program at Sacramento State University, and have been teaching in the area ever since. I enjoy working with high school students, and love it when their curiosity drives their learning. In those moments they truly have the ability to inspire and impress.

Ashley Beach has been teaching English and Drama at San Juan High School for three years. Ashley received her Bachelor's Degree from Cal Poly in San Luis Obispo. Ashley loves her job of working with high school students. She genuinely enjoys seeing them excited about school and learning.

507

HEROES OF THE HOLOCAUST

Bradley Cheungsomboun

The Holocaust is a time of great distress to many Jews and many other races. The fact of almost being pushed through mass genocide would have put Jews and others to the fact of hopelessness. The people who help and stood up for the Jews were and forever will be heroes. There was an abundance of Swiss heroes who aided the survival of Jews during the period of the Holocaust and the World War II.

There were many Swiss citizens who helped Jews survive the Holocaust. One person is Fred Reymond. He was born in the town of Le Sentier on December 25, 1907. Before the Holocaust he was an average watch maker. In 1940 Fred was commissioned to observe German occupying the foreign eastern French province. And that was when it all started to cause him to help Jews. He started his work with Jews due to his surveillance activity mostly to those who were persecuted by the Vichy regime. Which among the ones who were persecuted were Jews. Fred was one of the main leaders to the human smuggling in the Swiss Red Cross. He was the one who had the idea to help others just due to the fact of Fred felt a compassion to help when he saw the anguish and misery of the Jews, and decided to find a way to help. Since Fred was on both sides of the Franco-Swiss border he was ordered to run the rescue of the refugees, escaped prisoners of war, and marked members of the resistance as well as some British paratroopers and French youth. He brought the people he saved to a secret place at the border. The number of people he smuggled is unknown. There were many ways he helped the people saved. Ways such as giving them food, clothing them, house them, and even smuggling them to a better, safer place. He did this all under the pressure of being caught, prosecuted, or even being shot where he stood.

There are an unknown number for all the people Fred had saved. The world found out about Fred's good deeds due to the Yad Vashem representative in Geneva. There were times where Fred had been caught and prosecuted, but even though being caught and prosecuted he continued to save the men, women, and children that he had to for the greater good. He continued to help the Jews and others in the same way he did, but through different routes of the forest to get through to Switzerland. The effects of what he did are unknown as well as the whereabouts of what he did with his life after the war.

Fred had to go through many hardships during his time trying and succeeding in helping Jews in the Holocaust. He had to hide from many soldiers and border guards while making it through the whole forest to a specific place close to the border in Switzerland. As well as having to do all that stuff he was a very important person in the part in the starting of human smuggling during the Holocaust. His role during the whole time period of the Holocaust was major.

There were many Swiss who helped toward the survival of Jews during the Holocaust. One person who helped was Anne-Marie Im Hof-Piguet. Her date of birth and place where she was born is unknown. Her career was also unknown. Although she lived in Le Sentier, Switzerland at the time and she had volunteered into the Swiss Red Cross. She began a lot of her help on September 12, 1943. She helped them by smuggling others into Switzerland through a particular path, which eventually led to a house close to the border of Switzerland.

Anne helped the Jews by smuggling them in and out during the patrol of officers under the night. She also helped by housing the smuggled people, clothing, and feeding them. The amount of people she saved was also among the people who have their savior count being unknown. Anne saved those who wanted to get out of where they were. She saved the people by keeping them out of sight and unseen by other soldiers whocould deport them back. In the winter of 1943-1944 about ten to twelve other boys and girls sent out on the same route. But even though each route was the same, each new escape was just as dramatic as the others or even more.

The number of Jews saved is unknown as well as the others. Anne's whereabouts were spread to the world in November 28, 1991 by Israel's ambassador to Switzerland Raphael Giver. Anne was presented the Yad Vashem "Righteous Among the Nations" Medal of Honor. Anne was caught in the act of smuggling a few others by a Swiss guard who had appeared out of nowhere and stopped them. Yes as well as Fred they both continued with their work toward smuggling people. The effects of what they did have on her are unknown. What is also unknown is what she had done with her life after the war.

There were many Swiss who helped Jews survive the Holocaust. One such person is Paul Grueninger. His date of birth and origin of his birthplace is unknown. Although he was a part of the Swiss border police who was the commander of the Saint Gallen region, which also bordered Austria. In 1938, as a border guard he was permitted to stamp the "J" in the German passports signifying who were and were not Jews at the time. Even though being ordered to stamp he decided to disregard the official instruction and decided to let desperate refugees enter Switzerland.

Paul had helped many Jews and others enter Switzerland without stamping their German passports. He also falsified their passports so they would appear that they had entered Switzerland before March of 1938. Grueninger, as a policeman, decided to break even more rules and also turned in false reports about the number of arrivals and the status of the refugees within his district. At the time he appeared to save a lot of refugees. Paul decided to help and save any refugee, especially ones who were

Jewish or ones who were really desperate. Grueninger saved them in many ways. Ones especially where he had let refugees enter, making false reports about what went on in his district, and even spending his own money in order to buy winter clothes for needy refugees who had been forced to leave all their belongings behind.

The amount of Jewish refugees entered illegally were about 3,600 people. Germans informed the Swiss authority of what Grueninger was doing and he was dismissed from the police force in March of 1939 without any retirement benefits. His trial opened in January of 1939 and dragged on for two years in which after he was found guilty of breach of duty. After being caught he was unable to continue his work in both border police and being able to save and help Jews. Paul lived the rest of his life under difficult hardships, but despite the difficulties he never regretted his actions on behalf of the Jews.

In 1954 he explained his motives: " It was basically a question of saving human lives threatened by death. How could I then seriously consider bureaucratic schemes and calculations." After, in December of 1970 in result of protest in the media, the Swiss government sent Grueninger some sort of reserved letter of apology, but they had refrained from reopening his case and reinstating his pension. But, only after his death the steps were taken in order to rehabilitate him. The first attempt was rejected by the Swiss council, but in late 1995 the Swiss federal government finally annulled Paul's conviction. Yet before his death, the Yad Vashem had bestowed him the title of Righteous Among the Nations.

Paul Grueninger, in 1954 said: "I am not ashamed of the court's verdict, contrary I am proud to save lives of hundreds of oppressed people. Assistance to Jews rooted in the Christian world outlook... Was basically a question of saving human lives threatened with death. How could I seriously consider bureaucratic schemes and calculations." Intentionally exceeded limits of authority and often with owns falsified documents and certificates, but was done solely in order to afford persecuted people access into country personnel well-being, measured against cruel fate of thousands, so insignificant and unimportant, never even took into consideration.

There were many Swiss who had helped Jews survive during the Holocaust. One such person is August Bohny. His date of birth and place of origin are unknown. Bohny was a former warden. August and his wife Friedel helped kids and the special care to children who had lost their parents. In 1943 is when he started to make a larger effort towards helping.

He helped by renting two neighborhood farms and opening an agricultural college for the youth named Le Chambon. He had about 800 children at his college between 1941-1943. He saved about 800 youth at the time and gave them a type of education. August determined to save them by letting them live on the farm, as well as giving them an education, giving them food, and even clothing some of them. Although there was a house that was arrested and dispatched to concentration camps.

He also persisted and eventually saved and rescued those two boys that were first dispatched to the concentration camp. After the war August said: "With a certain measure of justified people, we dare say that we succeeded in looking after and protecting the young people who had been entrusted to us."

Bohny had saved about more than 800 people, mostly youth, who had been entrusted to him and his wife. Doctor Lucien Lazare recommended August to Yad Vashem for the "Righteous of the Nations" and had mentioned that he had saved "actively four members of the Schwarzschild family and a lot more Jewish refugees." Bohny hadn't exactly been caught, but a few kids he had looked after had been caught. Even though they had been caught he had tried all he could to save them and succeeded. He continued to help even after the war by keeping his farming college open. August kept his college going for a while even after the war. His agricultural college still has a large effect on a lot of people who would like to view his work and other Jewish youth work.

While recommending August Bohny, Dr. Lucien Lazar said he had: "Actively save four members of the Schwarzschild family and a lot more of Jewish refugees. As acting director of the Swiss children's homes at Le Chambon-sur-lignon, he received many refugees from the concentration camps and looked after them with fervor and dignity. When the French police had raided their homes, he actively arranged for the children to be hidden, and it was thanks to him and his efforts that the population of Le Chambon was ready to cooperate and receive the endangered children.

There have been a lot of Swiss and Danish people who helped Jews survive during the time of Holocaust. They all had done many great things such as smuggling them, permitting access, or even hiding them. There are a lot of other unknown Swiss or Danish saviors who had either passed away or have just gone unrecognized by others. But, the ones who are recognized will always have their names engraved in walls, remembered in minds, and rejoiced by their heroic deeds. A lot of their legacies and stories will live forever written in the books The Righteous of Switzerland: Heroes of the Holocaust, and The Righteous: The Unsung Heroes of the Holocaust. The Holocaust and other acts of genocide are beyond inhumane, indecent, and beyond forgettable. The acts performed by these men and women never shall be forgotten from the ages as we progress into the future. Acts from people such as Anne-Marie Im Hof-Piguet, Fred Reymond, Paul Grueniner, and August Bohny are one of the most heroic, close to superhero types of things hardly seen in humanity throughout the ages.

Work Cited

Paul Grueninger - The Righteous Among The Nations - Yad Vashem
www.yadvashem.org/yv/en/righteous/stories/grueninger.asp
Paul Grueninger - Holocaust Memorial Day Turst

http://hmd.org.uk/resources/stories/paul-grc3%BCninger
Paul Grueninger - Jewish Currents
http://jewishcurrents.org/tag/poul-grueninger
The Righteous of Switzerland: Heroes Of The Holocaust
https://books.google.com/books?isbn=0881256986
The Righteous: The Unsung Heroes Of The Holocaust
https://books.google.com/books?isbn=1429900369

THE LIGHT OF SWITZERLAND

Brian Gardiner

The Holocaust, the condemnation of selected groups under an individual influence on a nation of power. In other words Hell on Earth. This was undoubtedly one of the darkest times the world has witnessed, some more than others. However, in all darkness there is light, hope. The light source lies beneath the souls of those courageous enough to oppress the regime upfront. The righteous who pushed their efforts to helping the condemned, heroes. Due to the misfortune of lack of information, only few are widely known. I've chosen a handful of the thousands to share their acts with the public. In an attempt to voice these gentlemen, I'm hoping you listen.

Carl Lutz was a Swiss contributor to the scenes of Budapest. Born in Walzenhausen, he attended public school until the age of eighteen. Once an adult Carl had immigrated to the United States and began working in Illinois to pay for college, he would continue this for twenty years. Carl then was opted to leave the United States when he was assigned vice-consul of the Swiss Consulate General in Jaffa. He served up to 1942. As war began to brew, Lutz also took action. He began issuing safe-conduct documents which allowed Jewish children to emigrate away. Lutz was allowed 8,000 letters to give to the families of the community. Continuing his morale duties Lutz decided to actively participate on the "battlefield." As the Nazis were firing on Budapest, a woman was shot into a river. Lutz immediately dived under fire to escue her and return her to safety. The women then managed to give information on the fascists in Hungary. The very same river bears his name to this very day. In his effort's entirety,Lutz managed and credited for saving the lives of 62,000 Jewish people and died in Bern, Switzerland in 1975. He was 82 years old.

Another man of greatness named Harald Feller comes into play. Little is known about Feller's life before the war. He was born in Switzerland in 1913 and went on to replace Maximilian Jaeger as head of the Swiss legation in Budapest. Feller strongly supported Lutz in their acts of courage. Feller did not only rely on Lutz solely, he also had moments of glory of his own. During the end of the war Feller

512

decided to take more than political matters into his hands. Feller began hiding Jews in residences in Budapest when the heat reached its final flame. In his last effort to protect others than himself, Feller produced false passports for Swiss legation members targeted by the Arrow Cross Party (A side of the fascist who blatantly murdered 15,000 Jews in Hungary.) Feller died in 2003 after receiving his Righteous Among the Nations award in 1999. With his contributions Feller and Lutz saved more than 100,000 Jewish lives and stood in front of a bully's army to protect others than themselves. That's a pretty good definition of a hero to me.

Friedrich Born, born June 10, 1903, was yet another Swiss delegate stationed in Budapest. After learning of the Nazis' intentions, Born became concerned and decided to devote his time in Budapest to protecting the people from this massive power. Inspired by Lutz, Born hired 5,000 Jews as workers and had them stationed in buildings. Born then made the dire choice of submitting and distributing 15,000 protection slips that prevented the deportation of the given family, ultimately saving their lives. After the war Born went on to live his normal life, thinking back on his actions in Budapest quite often. Born died on January 14, 1963   at the age of 60. Twenty-four years after his demise, Born was designated as Righteous Among the Nations by Yad Vashem.

The next hero on this list is a popular Swiss known by many. Raoul Wallenberg, born August 4, 1912. After high school Wallenberg served in the Swedish military for eight months. After serving, Wallenberg was sent to study in Paris, but after a year had passed Wallenberg had moved to study in the United States in the state of Michigan and graduated with his degree in architecture in hand. However this did not allow him to become an architect in Sweden due to it being earned in America. Wallenberg possessed many occupations in his life as a result from his talents and intellect. He was an architect, businessman, humanitarian, and a diplomat. With no known direct connections to Lutz, Feller or Born, Wallenberg also protected those in Budapest by issuing safe documents to families. He is credited with saving 10,000 Jews in this instance. During the late stages of war Wallenberg was detained during the Siege of Budapest by the Red Army by presumed Soviet authorities. Without certainty Wallenberg was eventually presumed dead under Soviet imprisonment July 17, 1947. . Wallenberg beared the ultimate price to see the lives of many prosper and escape the hands of the Reaper himself.

To reflect, no matter how small or large, well-known or unknown, the efforts of all contributors were not in vain. In my eyes, not much can be told. These instances of horror were thankfully not during my time. In their showcases of valor, these unspoken heroes compelled me to use the utmost threshold of my interest and provide this information with the less enlightened. The problem with war is bias. And when a single figure has the influence of an entire nation, the worst circumstances can be expanded to beyond belief. To follow the beliefs of Man is a one-way trip of uncertainty. Not always intentional, Man destroys everything in his path for good or for worse. This leads to power-hungry individuals who never see an outcome but their own. To provide a name: Adolf Hitler. These lights in the darkness had the ability to become heroes, and the will of fire stood strong beside them as charging the oppression in its entirety. To be frank these gentlemen had the same power as you and me. The ability to take initiative and apply that under threatening instances segregate them from others.

So why does any of this matter? The answer is simple, but without clear definition it may seem unstable. The spine-chilling memoirs of surviving Hell itself may have never been produced if not for the heroes of the Holocaust. Elie Wiesel, Bernard Marks, and Primo Levi all have shared amazing stories of super-human strength and perseverance with the world. Possible only by themselves? Maybe so, but to blatantly disregard the efforts of these courageous few would be a felony against morale. In other words I don't believe these men had absolutely nothing to do with to liberation of those condemned in the camps. There are living examples of my pre-cursor on Earth today. These select few have the audacity to deny the Holocaust entirely. All due to the ignorance of a man with power. These people are only minor preventions of the idealist belief of "World Peace." In theory, if every single person in the world pursued an act of kindness there would be no negativity. We could all be "heroes" Although there is no doubt hatred will always arise out of any biased opinion, no matter how small that spark may be.

Though in times of complete darkness, the light will prevail through without waiver. In instances when it seems light will never fade, darkness with quickness and flare, will extinguish the luminescence. Hope and despair coexisting in one space. This happens on a global scale, although also in a single body everyday. The heroes of this specific despair-ridden spectacle of history managed to overcome their darkness and spread their light to hundreds of thousands of people with no beneficial motives other than the assurance of another human being. This allows those with embers to ignite and become overwhelmed with inspiration. Motivation to succeed in making this world a better place. Lutz, Feller, Born, and Wallenberg not only helped those facing the end during the Second World War, but provided their assistance in life seventy years later in the form of idols to many people today in 2015. Moreover the importance strands on to whether the inspired decide to act or sit in silence with pure intentions. Only the brave will be remembered and those who become heroes have stories to tell. This method of passing down intelligence has been going on continuously throughout the course of history. It's what keeps tradition and culture flowing along with mending society in relation to the normality of the time at hand.

With these beliefs in effect, the world may seem unfit to contain enough significance in order to continue our way of life. We hang on to the past instead of looking to the future and moving on too often. We use these gentlemen as figures to look up to yet never will we depend on them like the residents of Budapest. All we can do, as an entire united species, is attempt. As humans we naturally despise instability. The need of reassurance is dire in today's society. In Man's thirst for answers bias is formed. Thusly this recycles the previously negative actions of the past.

However never replicated they evolve to fit the normality of society. Our attempts cannot be sly. To provide subsidence to the situation, there is a need for example. We look to the remembered for guidance during our times of struggle, the heroes. In another 70 years there will be new examples for a new struggle. As long as we acknowledge those whose valor changed the world for the better, we stand a chance. It's an unpredictable world in everyone's grasp. The use of opinion is the answer. Power is everything, from influence to monetary.

Heroes have tremendous amounts of power, as do villans. What sets them apart is what their power stands for. Conflict is a popular resolution today. To the point where it has become a sport. The matter of opinion once again lays in opposition to customs. Many people enjoy, even admire, the witnessing of a brawl. A power struggle. While many despise the act and often despise the followers out of reaction. Sound familiar? Within this explanation I've managed lies hidden opinion. Which after all is only natural of humans. The cycle now begins with my own path to be examined, and possibly judged by those with opposing opinions. Creating an opportunity to inspire and enlighten others has also in return synthesized room for conflict.

In conclusion, the fact that heroes today have many methods of providing tinder for young sparks of hope, these righteous Swiss have provided long-standing inspiration for years now. Not only preventing harm to those who never deserved the manor of false accusations and punishment, but allowing themselves to consist in the lives of people for years to come. Doing so has made a select few grant themselves the ability to take their efforts into action. These men have undoubtedly made history within the darkest times of mankind. As the world faces other tragedies to come, who will step to the plate next? The answer, possibly you. In my final attempt to provide guidance like the men previously acknowledged myself. Will you rise to the occasion? I plead that you take the admiration of these heroes into your sincere consideration as I can provide a clear statement of reassurance. I was most inspired and had an amazing journey expanding my intelligence by learning the efforts these men went through to protect those in need. You could almost say it gave me faith that humanity may well be capable of peace. The emotions and respect I had for these heroes had deeply affected the way I go about day by day and personally allowed me to take action in my own society. How will you shine your light?

SWISS HEROES OF THE HOLOCAUST

Brittney Bell, Runner-up

Ask Yourself "Would I do what all these Swiss Heroes did during the Holocaust?" Would you? The Holocaust was a very unique event during the 20th century. The word "Holocaust" in Greek means "sacrifice by fire." It evolved slowly between 1933-1945. It was a state-sponsored persecution and murder of over 6 million Jewish people by Nazis. The Nazis thought that Germans were "racially superior" and that Jews were inferior. During 1933 the Jewish population of Europe was over 9 million. Most of the Jewish population lived where Nazis were soon going to take over or had influence during World War II. Two out of three European Jews were killed as part of the Final Solution. The "Final Solution" was the Nazi plan to exterminate the Jewish people. During 1941 the Jewish population grew to about 11 million Jews. In 1945 the Nazis killed over 6 million Jews and 1.5 million of these Jews were children. During the Holocaust it wasn't just the Jews who were killed. It was also Gypsies, the disabled, and Slavic people. Others were also killed for political and behavioral grounds and they were Communists, homosexuals, Jehovah's Witnesses and Socialists. It is just that the Jewish Community were blamed for many things and they were punished for it. There were many who helped the Jewish community during the Holocaust those including the Swiss and some of those people were Carl Lutz, Recha Sternbuch, Paul Gruninger, and David Frankfurter.

Carl Lutz   There were many Swiss who helped during the Holocaust. One such person was Carl Lutz. Carl was born March 30, 1895 in Walzenhausen, Switzerland. Carl was a Swiss diplomat in Hungary and also served as a Switzerland vice-consul. He was also in charge of representing the U.S, Great Britain and other places that were cut off from Hungary. Before all this he had immigrated to the United States when he was 18 years old and he lived and worked in the U.S for more than 20 years. Carl did all of his college studies in the U.S. Carl then got at the Swiss Legation in Washington D.C. He had also continued his education at George Washington University and received his Bachelor's Degree in 1924. Then in 1934 he left the U.S and got assigned to vice-consul to the Swiss consulate general. Carl began the process of helping Jews in March of 1944 when the Germans occupied Hungary and started to deport Jews to extermination camps. Carl then decided to try and persuade the Hungarians and Nazis to stop deporting the Jews. What Carl also did was he made group certificates to guarantee the Jews safety under Swiss protection until they made it out of Hungary. These were made for person and thousands of other people.

Carl Lutz did as much as he could to help the Jewish community. Carl from the beginning of when the Germans began to deport Jews. He really wanted to help the Jewish people by persuading the Nazis and Hungarians to stop and let the Jews go from Hungary to Palestine. After he tried to persuade the people he gave Certificates of Aliya (the art of going up)(progressing towards Jerusalem) which saved over 50,000 Jews. These certificates were not just for one person but for thousands of persons and their families. There was another event that occurred where Adolf Eichmann ordered the Jews from Budapest to march over the Austrian border. So what happened is that Carl and a few of his colleagues rushed to the rescue to pluck Jews out of the marching columns. Carl Lutz fought for the Jewish community trying to save them any way he could. Carl talked to the Nazis to get the Jews and he rushed into danger to pick the Jews out danger.

Carl Lutz has helped a total of about 62,000 Jews. The whole world found out about him probably in 1965 when he was "designated as Righteous Among Nations by Yad Vashem." Carl was the first Swiss person to be named Righteous Among Nations. Carl never really got caught while helping the Jews because everyone knew what he was doing; it was his job. After the war Carl was criticized by the government for 'having exceeding his authority." Also after the war Carls achievements were not immediately recognized in Switzerland but later they would be. When the Soviets invaded Budapest Carl and his wife fled. After the war they returned to Switzerland; that is when he was named Righteous Among Nations by Yad Vashem. Carl Lutz was very well known. He had a street named after him in Israel and there was a Memorial made for him in the old Budapest Ghetto.

Recha Sternbuch

There were many Swiss people who helped helped during the Holocaust but there weren't many like this person. This person who helped was Recha Sternbuch. She was born 1905 in Montreux, Switzerland. Recha and her husband Isaac were Swiss Jewish rescue activist. Recha was also the Swiss Representative of the Va'ad ha-hastsal (rescue committee of the American Union of Orthodox Rabbis). Recha Sternbuch was an orthodox woman. Recha had children and she was also pregnant with another and still helping Jews. Recha Sternbuch began helping Jews in 1941 with the "Relief Organization for Jewish Refugees in Shanghai" to rescue rabbis and students. Then changed the name to "Relief Organization for Jewish Refugees Abroad" and she would send aid packages.

When Recha was working with Paul Gruninger in 1938 they smuggled refugees into Switzerland. Recha Sternbuch was the head of the organization "Relief Organization for Jewish Refugees in Shanghai" this organization would help the Rabbis and Yeshiva studentswho escaped to Shanghai. Then they changed the "Shanghai" to "Abroad" with this organization and they would send aid packages to

Jews in Poland and Czechoslovakia. Recha would also try and rescue Jews by obtaining Latin American passports. Recha also negotiated with some Nazis on February 7, 1945 to let some Jews go from Theresienstadt to Switzerland. When Recha was working with Mr. Paul Gruninger they saved about 800 Jews. When Recha was negotiating she rescued about 1,200 Jews. Recha kept negotiating and rescued about 15,000 more Jews. While Recha Sternbuch was pregnant she spent her nights by the Austrian border to smuggle people in because Swiss border guards were not to allow anyone over 16 and under 60.

Recha Sternbuch saved a total of 17,800 Jews. The world probably found out about Recha Sternbuch when she was deemed Righteous Among Nations by Yad Vashem. When she was working with another Swiss hero Paul Gruninger she got arrested, got jailed, and she lost her baby and after a time she was let go and she continued her activism alone. After the war she did continue to help the Jewish community. Recha devoted herself to retrieving surviving Jewish children. Recha even kept tabs on what was happening throughout all of occupied Europe. In the end she never gave up on rescuing the Jews.

Paul Gruninger   There were many Swiss people who helped with the Holocaust. One such person was Paul Gruninger. Paul Gruninger was born October 27, 1891 at St. Gallen, Switzerland. Paul was a police commander at the Switzerland border. He was also a football player. Paul would start helping Jews after the Austrian Anschluss (the annexation of Austria to the Third Reich) in March 1938. Paul would let Jews through the Switzerland border even though he wasn't allowed to by making their papers look like they were in Switzerland before the borders closed down. Paul was doing this between August and December 1938.

Mr. Gruninger did everything in his power to help the Jews. He was not allowed to let anybody in the border without proper entry papers but he disregarded these orders. He would falsely dates on the Jews' papers to look like they were there in Switzerland before their borders shut down. Then to top the cake he would use his own money to buy clothes for the Jews who had nothing when they left their homes. During this time he helped about 3,600 Jewish refugees. There was no determining who to help it was everybody who came to the Switzerland border in 1938. Paul also worked with another Swiss hero Recha Sternbuch to smuggle refugees through the Switzerland border.

Paul Gruninger helped a total of about 4,400 Jews. The whole world found out what he was doing when his trial opened in January 1939. Yes, Mr. Paul Gruninger did get caught. Paul was discovered by some Germans who told Swiss authorities. He was arrested, put on trial and he had to serve time in prison. He also had to pay court cost and fines. Paul also lost his pension benefits. Paul could no longer help Jews after he was arrested and lost almost everything. Because Paul helped the Jews sneak in he lost almost everything. For the rest of Paul's life he lived with a meager income. Fifty years after the war and about more than 20 years after his death judges decided to lift the charges and Paul was fully rehabilitated by the Swiss government.

David Frankfurter   There were many brave Swiss people who helped during the Holocaust. One of these brave souls was David Frankfurter. David Frankfurter was born July 9, 1909 at Daruvar, Austro-Hungarian Empire. He was Jewish and his father was a Rabbi. David was a very sick child, he suffered an incurable periostitis (inflammation, tenderness and swelling around one or more bones). David went under seven surgeries. The doctors thought he wouldn't live a normal lifespan, but he did. He then went to complete his basic education. Then his father sent him to Germany to study dentistry. David first was studying medicine at Leipzig and then Frankfurt. David then went in 1934 to continue his study of medicine in Switzerland. He wasn't a Swiss citizen until he came to Switzerland to continue his studies. It was the year 1935 while David was in Switzerland some new things were going on. David was getting really tired of it so he decided to stand up and do something about it.

While David Frankfurter was studying in Germany some new racial Nuremberg Laws were passed and David was unhappy with these. David was mad that the Jewish people of whom he was very proud were being attacked. So David went to solve the problem by shooting the leader of the German NSDAP (National Socialist German Workers Party). There wasn't really a certain person he was helping. It was pretty much himself because he was tired of the Jews being attacked. What David Frankfurter did was amazing. When he was at his breaking point he found the leader's address in a phone book, went to the house, knocked on the door and the wife answered the door and led David to the leaders office and David waited. When the leader walked in David shot him five times in the head, neck and chest. He had just shot Wilhelm Gustloff.

David Frankfurter saved thousands of Jews. It was 1936 when he shot Gustloff, so that is probably when the world found out about David or when he was put on Yad Vashem. He called the police on himself after he shoot Gustloff. The police came, David got arrested and he was sentenced to 18 years in jail. He couldn't help the Jews while in jail. This affected him greatly; it ruined the rest of life. After the war he was pardoned but he could no longer be or stay in Switzerland. David went to live in Palestine. Twenty-four years later his expulsion was lifted. He was also elected Honorary Citizen of Switzerland.

All these Swiss heroes are very important. If they were not there to help the Jews there would never be an end to the Holocaust. I mean maybe if all the Jews died because of the Holocaust. If there wasn't saviors what would be of Europe. All I know life as we know would not be the same.

Works Cited

"David Frankfurter." Wikipedia.org. Wikimedia Foundation. 9 February 2015. Web. 12 February 2015. http://en.wikipedia.org/wiki/David_Frankfurter

"Frankfurter, David." YadVashem.org. Avner Shalev. 2015. Web. 12 February 2015. http://www.yadvashem.org/odot_pdf/Microsoft%20Word%20-%205862.pdf

"Gruninger, Paul." YadVashem.org. Avner Shalev. 2015. Web. 12 February 2015. http://www.yadvashem.org/odot_pdf/Microsoft%20Word%20-%206764.pdf

"Lutz, Carl." YadVashem.org. Avner Shalev. 2015. Web. 12 February 2015. http://www.yadvashem.org/odot_pdf/Microsoft%20Word%20-%206455.pdf

"Sternbuch, Recha." YadVashem.org. Avner Shalev. 2015.Web. 12 February 2015. http://www.yadvashem.org/odot_pdf/Microsoft%20Word%20-%206048.pdf

"Teaching the Holocaust with Primary Sources." Eiu.edu. Eastern Illinois University. Web. 12 February 2015. http://www.eiu.edu/~eiutps/holocaust_grueninger.php

HEROES OF THE HOLOCAUST

Cheri Taylor, Co-winner

The Holocaust was a period of terror and devastation. Jews were treated as less than human and made to suffer until their final breath. This was the time when heroes and saviors were needed most. And there were three such heroes.

This essay is not only going to bring light to heroes of the Holocaust that may not be well-known, but reveal the role that they played in it. Their heroic deeds and sacrifices along with their own moments of devastation will be retold. Their struggle to protect the innocent through obstacles and despite the severe consequences that awaited them. Their just actions will be re-lived.

The goal to meet in this essay is to address heroes of the Holocaust. While there are beyond many, not all will have their stories retold. However there are a few. Three to be exact. This essay will begin with the retelling of Paul Grueninger and then Carl Lutz, followed by Mr. Knud Christiansen, thus bringing things to a close.

There were many Danish and Swiss who helped Jews survive the Holocaust. One such person was a Danish hero by the name of Paul Grueninger. Grueninger was born on the 27th of October, 1891 in the city of St. Gallen, Switzerland. He worked as the Swiss border police commander of the St. Gallen region that bordered Austria.

It was his job to turn refugees back to their country where the official state policy was violent anti-Semitism. This caused him to begin the process of helping Jews. Due to annexation of Austria and Germany, Switzerland refused to let anyone into their country who had arrived without proper entry permits. In 1938, Grueninger decided to disregard official instructions and instead help refugees enter Switzerland.

He helped Jews in the Holocaust in more than just one way. He would falsify a refugee's registration in order to legalize their status so that their passports showed that they arrived in Switzerland before the time of March, 1938. Along with this, he would turn in reports that spoke falsely of the arrivals and status of refugees who were within his district. He would even interrupt and corrupt the efforts to trace down refugees who were known to have illegally entered Switzerland. Not only this, but using his own money, he would pay for winter clothing for those who had been forced to leave all of their belongings behind.

Grueninger initially saved around 3,600 Jews by falsifying their registration papers and allowing them to enter Switzerland by illegally permitting their entry. He saw how wrong it was to mistreat Jews just for who they were and for their free choice in choosing their religion. This led him to the understanding of who was in the wrong and who was in the right, leading to him helping individual Jews by protecting them from detection and his assistance in depositing their values.

The total number of Jews helped by him is at an estimate of 3,600. His action became known by the world from the Germans informing the Swiss authorities of his exploits. This led to him being put on trial and charged with accounts of permitting the entry of the 3,600 Jews illegally along with the falsified registration papers. The prosecution also added additional charges of him helping individual Jews from detection and the assistance of depositing their valued possessions. His trial opened in January, 1939, and it was held for over two years. In March of 1941, he was finally found guilty for breach of duty by the court. He was fined and forced to pay the costs of the trials along with his retirement funds being forfeited.

Despite the difficulties that surrounded him, he never once regretted his choice of actions on behalf of Jews. For the rest of Grueninger life he lived in difficult circumstances, being excluded and forgotten.

His actions had a lasting effect on the world, even if they might not be seen by all. However, the court did recognize his selfless and compassionate motivations and he received a reserved letter of apology. In 1995, his conviction was finally annulled by the federal government and in 1971, a year before his death, he was bestowed the title of "Righteous Among the Nations" by Yad Vashem.

Out of the many Danish and Swiss who helped Jews survive the Holocaust, another hero was a Swiss who went by the name of Charles "Carl" Lutz. He was born the 30th of March in 1895 in the area of Walzenhausen, Switzerland. His career was that of a Swiss diplomat. In March 1944, Germans began to deport Jews to extermination camps just weeks after their occupancy of Hungary. This caused Lutz to start the change of helping the Jews. He attempted to try and persuade the Hungarians in hopes that they would stop the deportations.

This was only the start of Lutz's way of helping Jews. During the time of the Holocaust, he saved around 53,000 Jews. Determining whether or not to help save the Jews was greatly reflected on by his career. Being a Swiss diplomat, he served as vice-consul for Switzerland. This meant that he was in charge of representing countries that had cut their ties with Hungary. Two of these countries being the United States and Great Britain. He was responsible for the issuing of four certificates of aliyah for each 1,000 people. These would allow for Jews to leave Hungary and travel to Palestine. As Swiss Consul, he represented both the British's interests that they had in Hungary and any issues they had that might regard the British Mandate located in Palestine. Not long after the certificates became augmented, not just one person but a person's family was allowed to immigrate. This lead to 50,000 Jews being put under the protection of the Swiss until their departure for Palestine.

The total number of Jews Lutz saved or helped is an estimate of 53,000. . In order to guarantee the safety of more Jews until they left for their journey to Palestine, he forged 100,000 more certificates and gave them to Jews. However, he was caught by the authorities along with his accomplice. Both he and Raoul Wallenberg were demanded to separate the legitimate from false papers. To keep their plans safe from the authorities and protect their rescue operation, they both decided it best to give in. Luckily, they were not charged or punished for their actions. Later, in January of the year 1945, Soviets had invaded Budapest. This resulted in Lutz and his wife Gertrud to flee from the country. They only returned later in 1964 after the war was long over. This same year after their return to Switzerland, they were both designated "Righteous Among the Nations" by Yad Vashem.

From the many Danish and Swiss heroes who were known for their part in the helping of Jews' survival during the Holocaust, there was a Danish by the name of Knud Christiansen. His birth was the year of 1915 in Denmark. His career consisted of him being a manufacturer of leather goods in an industry with a successful business. He was also a superior athlete in his twenties. He began his helping of Jews around the times of 1940 through 1945. He had already come across the cruelty of the Nazis years before the war had yet to begin. This gave him a small glimpse of what was in store for the future. When he began helping Jews, he was a member of the Danish Freedom Fighters and the Danish Resistance. This meant involving himself into acts of sabotage to slow down the Nazis' war effort. Along with this he was also part of the plan to put a rescue network into place to save most Jews that were escaping.

Christiansen was among the first to have learned of the plans the SS had made to arrest Jews at once, as one whole, making things incredibly easier for them. This would take action on the night of Rosh Hashanah on October 1, 1943. Knowing this, he began to usher Jews into any available shelter rather than let them go home where their terrible fates would be waiting for them. In order to keep them safeguarded from immediate arrest, they were placed in farmhouses ranging all the way to churches and even city apartments. Even Christiansen himself sheltered Jews through every room within his apartment with his family. On a single September night he rushed to a bridge game that was held every week in order to alert two of his friends of danger. His friends--two Jewish brothers--were to leave immediately and go into hiding in order to keep themselves protected from arrest. However, one of the brothers chose not to heed his words and was instead arrested by a Nazi and sent to a detainment camp. This lead to Christiansen taking a very high and extreme risk on his own life in order to save him. He managed to save him miraculously, though specific details aren't known. But in order to make his release possible, he had to carry his request to the highest-ranking Nazi in Denmark. He was General Werner Best and he was known for his title as "Blood Hound of Paris" for being responsible for the deportation of Jews from France to death camps. Yet, risking his very own life, Christiansen managed it. He managed to save the life of his friend. During this time, he helped over7,000 Jews. Knowing it was the right thing to do to save Jews during the Holocaust wasn't the hardest decision. During the 1936 Berlin Olympics, he watched along with many other athletes as Herr Hitler chose to exit the stadium rather that stay to watch as black athlete, Jesse Owens, received his medal. Along with that, his soon wife-to-be, Karen Rasmussen, would send letters to him. These letters would contain the words explaining that there was a terrible brutalization of Jews within the streets.

The exact number is unknown, but Christiansen was responsible for helping over thousands of Jews. His efforts to protect and save did become known. Not only was he known for his part in being involved in the Danish Freedom Fighters and the Danish Resistance, but due to his played role in the more exciting days of occupation, he earned himself a position on the Danish Nazis' "watch list." Though, surprisingly, he was never actually caught or ever even punished for these accounts. Long after the war was over, he and his wife along with three of their children immigrated to America in the year of 1970.   There he still maintained close relations with members of the Jewish Community. On any afternoon, he could be seen staying in shape using rowing machines at a local Jewish Community Center on Upper West Side. His story is a great reminder of the tremendous amount of moral courage it took to save the innocent from the corrupted. This courage was what one entire nation of people displayed all together. This is proof that this nation did what it could against high odds. This is proof that Christiansen did what HE could against the odds stacked against him. Within the year of 2005, both the names of Christiansen and his wife were added to the list of heroic figures as "Righteous Among the Nations" at the Yad Vashem Memorial Museum located in Jerusalem. For his courageous efforts, his known story takes a very special significance to others, especially on a special holiday that is very present in Holocaust history. It is the Jewish New Year.

Every person to have helped anyone subjected to the cruelties of the Holocaust is a hero. These three heroes are just a few out of many to have made a large impact in helping Jews and have their story told for it. Whether they are well-known or not, they have now been addressed for the people of the world to learn about. Paul Grueninger for his help in getting Jews into Switzerland for safety. Carl Lutz for the creation of certificates of protection allowing Jews to exit from Hungary and travel to Palestine. Knud Christiansen for his aid of sheltering Jews from arrest by the Nazis. Every role played was extremely crucial then and now. These are true heroes of the Holocaust.

Works Cited

"Rescue Story: Paul Gruninger." Paul Gruninger Holocaust Memorial Day Trust. Department for Communities and Local Government. Web. February 11, 2015. http://hmd.org.uk/resources/stories/paul-gr%C3%BCninger

"Tag Archives: Paul Grueninger." Paul Grueninger Jewish Currents. October 26, 2014. Web. February 11, 2015. http://jewishcurrents.org/tag/paul-greuninger.

"The Policeman who Lifted the Border Barrier." Paul Grueninger-Yad Vashem. Web. February 11, 2015. www.yadvashem.org/yn/en/righteous/stories/grueninger.asp

"Danish Hero: One Rosh Hashanah Burns Bright in Holocaust." Danish Hero: One Rosh Hashanah Burns Bright in Holocaust. Robyn Dolgin. Web. February 11, 2015. http://www.jewishpost.com/archives/news/Danish-Hero.html

"Carl Lutz." Carl Lutz Virtual Jewish Library. Web. February 11, 2015. http://www.jewishvirtuallibrary.org/jsource/biography/Carl_Lutz.html

SWISS HEROES OF THE HOLOCAUST

Desiree Chambers

World War II, which included the Holocaust, was a horrible time in our world's history. Nearly 11 million people were tragically murdered in this genocide. Although it is easy to reminisce on the villainous acts, it's important to keep in mind that there were so many people who had saved hundreds and thousands of lives. If it hadn't been for these heroes, the already immense number of deaths would have been even greater. The Righteous Among the Nations is an organization used to honor those who had put their own lives at risk to save the lives of Jews. Of the many Holocaust heroes, one that stands out is Friedel Reiter, later known as Bohny-Reiter. She was born in Vienna, Austria in 1912 and was orphaned during World War I. Reiter later moved to Switzerland along with others on a Red Cross orphan transport. As she grew older, she pursued a career in the pediatric medical field. Once the year 1941 came about, Reiter became a nurse for Secours Suisse aux Enfants, or the Swiss Aid to Children. While working there, they sent her on a mission to Rivesaltes Internment Camp in France.

With the few resources they had available, Reiter managed to provide many Jewish children with medical care, clothing, and food. During this time, she began to understand the importance of relocating these children. She started this journey by searching for places to move them to. Just when she needed it, she received help from August Bohny. August Bohny ran the L'Abric children's home as of 1941. This was sponsored by Secours Suisse, which is how they came to meet. Shortly after they met, they got married and worked together to save the Jewish children. They decided to use an old castle known by the name Chateau de Montluel. It soon became overly crowded, so the two had to find another place to shelter the orphans. Quickly, they stumbled upon another place called Faidoli to house them.

By the end of the war, they managed to save hundreds upon hundreds of orphaned Jewish children. Friedel Reiter and August Bohny were each recognized by Yad Vashem as Righteous Among the Nations in 1990. Reiter recorded all of the happenings in a journal which they later published in 1993. The book was then formed into a documentary in the year 1997. If they hadn't stepped up to help these innocent lives, those children would've died in the camps.

Benedikt Brunschweiler is another hero of the Holocaust. Born in 1910 in Switzerland, Beunschweiler lived a rather average life of being a businessman in Budapest since 1935. However, in 1944 he was nominated by Friedrich Born to be the Red Cross representative to the Benedictine Archabbey. The archabbey was an area made for refugees stationed on the mount of Saint Martin which included everything from a monastery to a school for boys.
Soon after that happened, Arrow Cross's power rose and authorities took over. While in their domination, they attempted to question and search the people of the archabbey. This is because it was clear that it was home to hundreds of Jews, refugees, and army deserters. Brunschweiler founded a home for the Jewish children which had at least 25 children. Meanwhile, the mothers and other Jewish refugees stayed in other shelters throughout the comlpex.

The red army soon invaded in 1945. During this time, Brunschweiler stayed in order to care for the refugees. He ended up being taken under arrest by the Russian Army but was quickly released. Until November of 1945, he remained loyal to his refugees and helped maintain the health of them to the best of his ability. After the war ended, he left Hungary and moved to the states. In 1950, he later decided to relocate himself to South Africa where he lived until death in 1987. In May of 2007, he was recognized for Wall of Honor for Righteous Among the Nations.

William Franken and his wife Laura Franken also assisted during the war. William was born in the Netherlands in 1889 and lived until the year 1962. He was a medical student in Switzerland and continued the career by being a family physician. Although they both lived in Switzerland, they spent a majority of their time at their vacation home in France. This is where they both were called in by the Brouzes, a family who lived near by, to help treat the ill Jewish refugees that had gotten trapped in the area in an attempt to escape. The Franken's managed to treat and cross over all 50 of the refugees. This selfless act inspired them. They decided to help any of the other groups passing through on their way to Switzerland as well. Soon, they had come to find out that the police were on to them. With that, they figured it best to shut it down, and return to their home in Switzerland before anything bad happened.

Laura Franken had been writing in a personal journal during her time in assistance to the refugees. In it, she wrote about a couple who had been passing through that they helped. This journal had subsequencially been published after the discovery that it had actually been the historian, Saul Friedlander's, parents. Later, in 1997, they were each recognized as Righteous Among the Nations. Along with the Franken's, Elizabeth Eidenbenz was a nurse who had helped during the war. She was born in Wila, Switzerland in the year 1913 and deceased a long time after in the year 2013. Eidenbenz was a teacher and a nurse. Being the caring woman she was, she decided to join the Association to Aid Children at War.

During war, many mothers who were pregnant were highly likely to lose their unborn child or die while giving birth. Another common cause of death was malnutrition and disease. Elizabeth Eidenbenz had decided to help these soon-to-be moms and became the founder of "Mother of Elne" in 1937, a maternity home for women and children. This foundation ran completely off of the generous donations of people in the area but once the war began, their income dropped and more refugees came in. Since they no longer had the money to house and care for these women, they were forced to associate themselves with the Red Cross. This made it harder for them because they now had to hide their Jewish refugees and abide by Red Cross's laws. They began to get harassed by the Gestapo and were even detained at one time.

By the end of her term, Elizabeth Eidenbenz had saved around 400 Spanish and 200 Jewish women and children. She came to the conclusion that it was her time to retire after. There had been several books written about her experiences throughout her time. She had also been recognized as not only the Honorary Citizen of Elne, but Righteous Among the Nations in 2002, Orden Civil de la Solidaridad Social and Creu de Sant in 2006, and Legion d'honneur in 2007 as well.

Another hero is Paul Gruninger. He was born in 1891 and passed away in 1972. Gruninger was a Swiss police commander in St. Gallen and was also a football player who won champion in 1915. Being an officer, he had full access to Jewish refugees' personal records.

He used this opportunity to saved nearly 3,600 innocent Jews. In order to make them legal, he would simply backdate their visas and falsify any other documents. This helped in indicating that they entered Switzerland during the legal time. When additional officers discovered what he was doing, he was fired from the police force. Gruninger was then convicted of official misconduct and fined 300 Swiss francs. When he was released, he was given no pension. Sadly, this led him to die in poverty. In 1995, the district court revoked all judgment and cleared his charges. Later, the government paid compensation to his relatives who were still alive. He had a street named Pisgat Ze'er and a stadium named Bruhl St. Gallen, both in his honor. In 1997 and in 2013 movies were made about him. Paul Gruninger was also recognized as Righteous Among the Nations.

Anne-Marie Im Hof-Piguet is, again, another Swedish hero of the Holocaust. She was born in 1916 and passed in 2010. Before the war, she was a Swiss flight attendant and studied history at the University of Lausanne up until 1940. After the war began, in 1942 until 1944, she decided to work at the Children's Aid of the Red Cross.

Once the Nazis began to take over, Anne-Marie managed to save a combination of 12 children and adults. In order to do this, she had to illegally bring them over the border to Switzerland. She and her family helped out with this. They had an underground type of system, which went through forests and multiple homes. During her scandalous helping, she had also helped more Jewish families get to Switzerland.

After the war ended, she began work as a teacher in Switzerland. There, she married a historian in 1947 named Ulrich Im Hof and together they raised their family. In 1959, she became the co-founder of Swisscontact. Later, in 1985, she published numerous memoirs of her incredible experiences. In 1990 she had been recognized as Righteous Among the Nations and in 1992, she won the prize of the Doron Foundation. Finally, she had launched the Academy of Human Rights in 1998, the same year she won the Human Rights Award of the Swiss Section of the International Society for Human Rights.

Lastly, Bill Barazetti risked his life in order to help Jewish children and adults during the war. Barazetti was born in Aarau, Switzerland in 1914 and died in 2000. When the war began, he was a philosophy student at Hamburg University. While studying there, he witnessed, first hand, all of the horrible things the Nazis did to his fellow Jewish classmates. This is what had inspired him to save the refugees. He became an intelligence officer in the Czech secret service where he later came back as a spy.

Barazetti arranged to have 3 separate areas to help Jewish families escape from Czechoslovakia and settle in British territory. During this time, he decided it best to live under an alias. He kept shelter mainly at the homes of families he was working with. Officers discovered his plan and he was almost arrested. Before they could capture him, he faked his death. To continue his work anonymously, he used another alias. The Gestapo found out and captured him and beat him nearly to death. A young woman named Anna had found him and helped him escape and nursed him back to health. Later they got married and had a child.

Barazetti wanted to continue even further into helping the Jewish. He sent his family away where he knew they would be safe. Now a wanted man, it made it tough for him to get around. He still managed to convince German officials to send three groups of children to him. Next, he sent them to pre-arranged foster homes in Britain. To do this, he had to forge visas for the children and organize a system for them.

Bill Barazetti saved nearly 700 children doing this. Once the war ended, he spent the rest of his life in Britain with his family. Barazetti was recognized as Righteous Among the Nations in the year 1993.

It is really important to always remember and study the Holocaust. This is primarily for the reason of not wanting this horrible atrocity to happen again. Many believe that history repeats itself, and this is a moment that would be horrible to see reoccur. There were so many amazing, selfless souls that, as a matter of fact, risked not only their own lives, but the lives of their families and people around them as well. If it wasn't for their benevolent acts, thousands upon thousands of innocent lives would have died of being in concentration camps, disease, or malnourishment. Thanks to those people, they had the opportunity to live.

HEROIC ACTS

Gradon Norquist

In 1939 a man by the name Adolf Hitler rose to power of the still economically devastated Germany and brought a feeling of normalcy to the people of Germany. But due to Hitler's totalitarian ideas and philosophies, a ghost of sorrow and death still lingers over Germany. That haunting memory is known throughout the world as the Holocaust. These chain of events would show the world the worst of humanity, but these events would show the greatness in people whether it be big or small. Whether being a war hero, politician, or a person who did a kind act to a Jewish refugee, there will always be evil but there will always be good to fight that evil, which will lead to many of the heroes of the Holocaust in this essay.

Paul Gruninger was a Swiss police commander who was ordered by the government to watch and deny any Jewish refugees who attempted to cross the border illegally. This was because the number of Jewish refugees entering Switzerland to escape Hitler's wrath was increasing at an alarming rate, and due to Switzerland's negotiations with Germany because all Jews' passports to be labeled with the letter "J".

Which because even legal Jews to be turned away at the borders to face Hitler's death camps. Which leaves Paul Gruninger with a very large moral unbalance whether to let the refugees pass to safety or to turn them away to look death in the face. Gruninger decided to disobey the orders given to him and help the Jewish people. He did this by changing the dates on the passports before 1938, when entrance to the country was restricted. Due to Paul Gruninger's action he has saved over 3,600 Jewish refugees. Eventually Mr. Gruninger's actions were figured out by German informants who had tipped off the Swiss government. His rank and retirement benefits were abolished and was fined 300 Swiss francs. After the trials and accusations made by the Swiss government Paul Gruninger lived in poverty most of his life. His charges were later uplifted after his death in 1972 and the government paid compensation to his family for their misjudgment. But he said "It was basically a question of saving human lives threatened with death. How could I then seriously consider bureaucratic schemes and calculations." Due to Mr. Gruninger's heroism and morality he was awarded the title of Righteous by the Yad Vashem organization in 1971. He never regretted his actions because he knew he had done the righteous thing.

DANISH AND SWEDISH HEROES OF THE HOLOCAUST

James McCarty, Special Award

During the Holocaust there were many terrible and horrific things that occurred which everyone knows about, but they do not know about the love and caring that also went on during this period. Danish and Swedish were just some on big scale of people that help during the Holocaust. I will be sharing some of their unbelievable journeys and daring quests with you.

Elisabetta Hesselblad

Elisabetta Hesselblad was one women who showed love and affection to Jews in a time when they were persecuted by the Germans and most people would be too scared to help the less powerful Jewish community. She was born June 4, 1870 and on that day the world got a little bit sweeter. She was born into a family with 13 children and still began to have an unbelievable life full of humbleness and grace. She came to the United States in 1888 she then studied to be a nurse.

She became very religious and she became a Catholic nun. This is where she then became intertwined with World War II. She took in people into her own home in Rome when the Nazi occupation was going on and she fed them and kept them warm.

By this kindness she was beatified by the Pope by John Paul II on April 9,2000. She was a very kind and beautiful women. She then returned home to Sweden in 1923 where she helped sick people and nursing them back to health. Many people tried to help in the Holocaust but the devastation of the amount of people that were killed way overshadowed these beautiful people such as Elisabetta Hesselblad. She risked her own well being and took in strangers and helped them through times of terror and fear. This is why she is a Swedish hero of the Holocaust.

Knud Dyby

Knud was born in 1917 in Denmark he didn't have much as a kid and knew he wanted to follow in his father's footsteps so began training to be a typographer. Once he had got done in the military he then became a police officer in Denmark. In 1943, Dyby learned about what the Germans were doing to the Jews and swore to help them. He then took in Jews and kept them at safe houses where they would be free from going to a concentration camp and all the agony that entails.

Knud carried thousands of Jews from Denmark to Sweden. He would take them on his fishermen boat and travel across the sea. He would even use his police car to transport the Jews to the boat. He was said to have brought nearly every Danish Jew safely to Sweden. He helped 7,000 people on his miraculous effort for the greater good and to help many people from hardship in the camps.

Dyby was a very well deserving man to be honored at the Israeli Holocaust memorial as one of the non-Jewish heroes of that era and will always be one. Dyby died in September 2011. He was 96 years old he lived a long life and made it worthwhile. He helped so many and in return he got a great memorable life.

Gerda Valentiner

Valentiner was born on January 29, 1903. She grew up in Denmark and knew she wanted to be a teacher. While she was a teacher she was very heavy in the Danish resistance during the German occupation. She took kids and adults into her home waiting for the right time to take them to the port to be transported to Sweden. She put her life on the line every day so that she could help save families and friends from the horrific events of the Holocaust.

She was a very inspirational person. She was a part of the good when so much was evil and she became an angel in the face of hell. There is one account of how brave and courageous she really was. Her sister's teacher was in danger of getting captured by the Germans and so she ran to their house and warned them of the danger approaching and allowed them to live with her.

After her saving of many people during this time she then took leave from her job and volunteered as a social worker for two years. In 1971 she retired. She came to Israel to spend her years and also helped many people then too just by sheer kindness and love. These factors of her life are the reason she was recognized by Yad Vashem as Righteous Among Nations.

Per Anger

Anger was born December 7, 1913 in Sweden. Anger went to a university and studied law. When he graduated, the war had began between Finland and the Soviet Union and as a result he was drafted into the war. He was finished with the war in 1940. He then went to Berlin to start his diplomatic career.

Anger was sending a telegram to Denmark and Norway telling them that the Germans were going to take over their station and incriminate those people. They did not believe Per and the next day the German official had taken over Oslo. Anger decided to take action once he became aware of Hitler's final solution. While the Jewish people were traveling to Sweden he issued non-legal passports so they would look as though they were allowed into the country when of course they hadn't had a passport so they would have been deported elsewhere

Anger also had an idea to issue special certificates to Jews who had tried to become members of the Swedish community. He gave more than 700 fake passports to Jews in need of a place to go to get as far as they could away of the horrific crimes going on. This man helped save many lives for no reason other than the knowing from right and wrong. He could have been prosecuted for disobeying German rule and sentenced to death. However he gave life to men and children alike for that he is a Swedish hero of the Holocaust.

Raoul Wallenberg

Wallenberg was born August 4, 1912 in Sweden. Wallenberg was an architect and businessman. He helped tens of thousands of Jewish people get out of their country and move to Sweden. He was a great man he housed many Jewish families in Swedish-owned factories.

Wallenberg was detained by the Soviets and disappeared never to be seen again. This shows the level of risk that helping people came within the time period. To help the enemy makes you the enemy and he helped many people and gave his life for what he believed. Wallenberg was a huge humanitarian and believed in equal rights for all. He was a huge help in the effort to help the Jewish people.

Raoul is probably one of the most heroes to be recognized because of the number of people he saved and the way he had disappeared after the Germans caught up with him. He was suspected of espionage and that's the last time anyone has heard or seen the graceful man.

Helga Holbeck

Helga is one of my favorite people to write about personally. Her birth date is not confirmed by any sources. Helga is a Danish woman and she was a worker in the international commission for the assistance of child refugees. In 1941 about 50 children were taken to an orphanage in the lower part of France. She was in charge of taking care of them. She then sent some to other orphanages throughout southern France and risked her life on a daily bases for the well-being of the kids that she tried to protect.

There is one instance when she offered a safe house to a famous Jewish painter and his wife. She gave people hope in times of despair and always found ways to give back even when she did not have the means to do so. She helped many people with giving them a safe house to live until the extreme genocide was finished. She then smuggled them into Switzerland to live the rest of their life.

Holbeck died in 1983. She did what she had to do to make other peoples' lives better also for them to even have lives to live. She was my favorite person to write about because she was really nothing. Nobody could even remember her birth date and she gave all her heart to strangers and victims of the Holocaust. She lived her life to the fullest when barely any people even recognized her as still living. These reasons are why she is a fabulous hero of the Holocaust.

Bill Barazetti

Bill was born in 1914 in Switzerland. Barazetti worked in the transporting. He transported many Jewish children. He became against Nazism when he was in college and he would see Jewish kids get beat up for no other reason but the simple fact that they were Jewish. Barazetti then knew he wanted to help the Jewish community in any way he could. In the course of three months he was able to transport three trains full of mostly Jewish children out of Prague.

Bill then tried to leave the country and was captured and beaten up and left for dead but his associate Anna found him. She took him in and nursed him back to health, and they eventually got married in Prague. Barazetti in 1938 went to Britain and joined the war office where he interrogated German police.

Barazetti helped thousands of kids and also helped people figure why the German police did what they did and there views on the Holocaust. He went through a lot to be an example as a figure to aspire to be and to look up to. He tried to help the most people he could and did a good job of it. Bill was a great man and died in 2000. Through his life people always recognized him as an idol and people wanted to be as kind hearted as him.

Dagmar Lustrup

Dagmar was born in was born in Denmark, and I could not find the date in which she was born. She was very into the women's peace organization and loved helping people. She was recognized though by the work she did in helping people escape the clutch of the Germans and getting them to safety. She ended up helping 20 teenagers get out of danger and into a new better establishment.

Though she was not the biggest contributor by helping 20 people still she helped 20 young teens in getting to continue their lives and to have kids and their kids will have kids and they will live on now because of her contribution to the Holocaust rescue effort.

Lustrup helped the kids try to get into Palestine by teaching them how to farm so they could live and maintain a good life in Palestine and continue their lives in happiness. Because they were not able to get into Palestine at that time they were brought to Dagmar's husband and he then got 3 homes for the ladies and they were still being taught how to farm so they would be able to eventually go to Palestine to get away from the violence.

The 20 teenagers who had nothing to lose were finally put on a boat to Sweden and then were on their way to Palestine. Through the courageous efforts of women that really had everything to lose and really nothing to gain except warmth in her heart these 20 teenagers were sent to Palestine and lived the rest of their lives at peace because one woman had enough of the brutality and violence.

All these courageous, loving, beautiful people are all heroes in their own way to help the same cause. They should that even in times of despair there can always be hope. These people were recognized by many organizations and were all great leaders to stand up in the face of darkness and turn on the small light with the good they did. I commend each and every person I wrote about because those are the type of people we need more of in our time. Even when most of them were not being prosecuted against they stood up for what they knew was right. These are the Swedish and Danish heroes of the Holocaust.

Works Cited

"Elizabeth Hesselblad." *Wikipedia*. Wikimedia Foundation, n.d. Web. 25 Feb. 2015.

"Knud Dyby." *Knud Dyby*. N.p., n.d. Web. 25 Feb. 2015

"Their Fate Will Be My Fate Too.." *Gerda Valentiner*. N.p., n.d. Web. 25 Feb. 2015.

"Per Anger." *Per Anger*. N.p., n.d. Web. 25 Feb. 2015

"Raoul Wallenberg." *Raoul Wallenberg*. N.p., n.d. Web. 24 Feb. 2015

"'I Have Come out of the Night, and You Fed Me.'" *'I Have Come out of the Night, and*

   You Fed Me.' N.p., n.d. Web. 25 Feb. 2015.

"The Poor Mouth." *: Bill Barazetti*. N.p., n.d. Web. 24 Feb. 2015

"The Righteous among the Nations." *Rescue Story*. N.p., n.d. Web. 25 Feb. 2015.

SWISS HEROES OF THE HOLOCAUST

Justine Peters

Crematorium, death, starvation and coldness. You may wonder what all these have in common, the thing that they have in common is called the Holocaust. Men and women were separated and the women and children were killed by the crematorium. The crematorium is a building of flames, when people get put inside, they die. Men younger than fifty were more important for work. Men that were older than fifty were sent to the crematorium. Teenage boys were sent to work if they were strong enough. This was a horrible experience for humans, but out of it came stories of amazing human beings. Such as Recha Sternbuch, Carl Lutz and David Frankfurter. These people are Swiss heroes of the Holocaust. Righteous Among Nations is an honorific used by the state of Israel to describe non-Jews who risked their lives to save Jews from Nazis. People became heroes when they did something heroic like save Jews from the Nazis.

There were many people who helped Jews survive the Holocaust. One such person as Recha Sternbuch. Recha Sternbuch was Swiss. She was born in 1905. She had a husband named Isaac. She started smuggling refugees while trying to invade the Swiss border, guards who had orders to turn back anyone under sixteen and over sixty years old. Recha started her rescue mission in 1938. She did this to save thousands of lives of Jews. Recha helped Jews by sneaking them out and fighting for them. If Recha didn't do these thousands of lives would not have been saved. At this time, Recha has saved 2,000 lives. The ways she saved Jews was by sneaking them out and how she would negotiate with people. When she negotiated with Dr. Musy to end the war he passed her four concentration camps. All together Recha had saved about 2,000 Jews from the Nazis. She tried to stop the war and save as many Jews as possible. We know she was wrong when she went to jail for smuggling 800 Jews and lost her child. After Recha was released she went right back to work alone and arranged a rescue mission for over 2,000 Jews and this affected her by losing her child and going to jail. Recha died in 1971. She affected the Holocaust greatly by saving more than 2,000 Jews from the Nazis. Recha Sternbuch was a Swiss hero of the Holocaust.

A second Swiss hero of the Holocaust would be David Frankfurter. He was born in 1909 and died in 1982. He is also considered a hero in the Holocaust because he killed one of the Nazi leaders named Wilhelm Gustloff. David went to medical school in 1929 at Leipzig and Frankfurt. He then moved to Switzerland. The Racial Nuremberg law was passed. This classified German people with four German grandparents as a German or kindred blood. People were classified as Jews if they

534

came from three or four Jewish grandparents. When the Nuremberg law was passed in Germany in 1935, David finally realized that what was going on was wrong. He then decided that he needed to take a stand against all Nazis and the killing of Jewish people. He decided to track down a leader of the Nazis named Wilhelm and followed him everywhere. On February 4, 1936 at Gusltoff's lodging at Famous Alpine Resort, David then shot him dead. He then surrendered to the police. Even though people were proud of his actions, the government was afraid of what he might do next so they punished him. The punishment that the government gave David was that German Jews would be getting tortured; the trial was called a murder case when it was an act of war. After 18 years the government gave David his freedom to leave. This pardon said that David would be banished to settling in Palestine for 24 years. Frankfurter was a Swiss hero of the Holocaust because he took a stand and killed a Nazi leader.

Another Swiss hero of the Holocaust is Carl Lutz. His real name is Charles; he was born in1895 and died in 1975. He was a Swiss diplomat in Budapest who saved Jews. In 1942 the vice consul charged of representing Great Britain and the U.S. In March 1944 Hungarians deported Jews to extermination camps. Charles tried to persuade Hungarians to stop. They offered to allow Jews to leave Hungary. Four group certificates of aliya were issued to 1,000 people. This represented British interests in Hungary. Expanding acceptance of people allowed no more than 50,000 Jews under his protection. Each person was given a letter that said they were protected by the Swiss. Once you left Palestine that would make you unprotectable. On October 1944 the Zionists youth activities were housed. They forged 100,000 documents for their own safety. Authorities demanded that Lutz and Raoul Wallenberg separate the legitimate from false papers. Buildings were built to house 3,000 Jews under Lutz protection. All but six survived. In 1944 Jews were marching out of Budapest when the Soviets invaded on January 1945. Lutz and his wife fled Switzerland and returned in 1965. They are designated as Righteous Among Nations by Yad Vashem. Carl Lutz was a Swiss hero of the Holocaust because he saved thousands of Jews by protection documents.

Yad Vashem is an official memory to those who were victims to the Holocaust. The law for Yad Vashem was passed Knessest. It is located on the Western slope of mount Herzl in the remembrance of Varselm. People who were Holocaust heroes were rewarded righteous among nations and given a spot on the hall of fame. The objectives of Yad Vashem are education, research, and commemoration. They organized courses for education throughout the world. Some of the prizes rewarded by Yad Vashem are for children's literature, painting of the Shoah, Annual Buchman Foundation memorial prize and Yad Vashem the international book prize. Righteous among nations is honoring non-Jews who risk their lives by saving Jewish lives. Over

24,300 have been recognized by righteous among nations. Yad Vashem is an organization in remembrance of victims of the Holocaust.

Another very important hero of the Holocaust would be Per Anger. He was a Swedish diplomat who assisted Raoul Wallenberg in the struggle to save Jews. This was going on during the Second World War. He was also an ambassador. Raoul was captured by the Soviets in 1945. Anger never went to go look for his friend. Anger's legacy will live on in all of these men and women who all risked their lives to save others who were afraid to face prosecution. The death of Per Anger upset the other Honorary Members of the Yad Vashem. He was a hero for over 40, although Per Anger will live on for many more years to come.

A very good hero of the Holocaust is Paul Grueninger. He was a Swiss police commander in St. Gallon, and righteous among nations member. He saved about 3,600 Jewish refugees by backdating their visas and falsifying other documents to indicate their entry of refugees was still possible. He was then dismissed from the police force and fined 300 Swiss francs. He then received no pension and died in poverty in 1972. He was hero of the Holocaust because he saved thousands of Jewish lives.

Also Raoul Wallenberg was an architect. He was Swiss and born on August 4, 1912 in Lidingo municipality, Sweden. He is very well known for saving tens of thousands of Jews in Nazi-occupied Hungary during the Holocaust. Wallenberg issued protective passports and sheltered Jews in buildings. He was on a mission to save the lives of nearly 100,000 Hungarians Jews. Raoul died at the Union of Soviet Socialist Republics on July 17, 1947. He was a hero of the Holocaust because he saved hundreds and thousands of Jews.

Another hero is Valdemar Langlet. He is a hero because he had a method to save Jewish people. Valdemar inspired Raoul by using the same method as he did himself. Valdemar was born on December 17, 1872 in Sweden. In 1965 Valdemar and his wife, Nina, were awarded Righteous Among Nations by Yad Vashem.

Also another hero of the Holocaust is Saly Mayer. He was born in 1892 in Sweden. He was a Swiss Jewish leader and a representative of the joint distribution committee. Mayer helped Jews by working with the Swiss government on the issue of Jewish refugees in Switzerland. He gave money to people who needed it so that he or she could rescue Jews. He saved thousands by giving people money to help save Jews. His responsibilities as a JDC representative was getting information from occupied Europe and passing it on to JDC headquarters in Portugal. He received $235,000 from the U.S. because he devised a way to sidestep American restriction on sending funds to occupied Europe. He later than died in 1950, he helped save thousands of Jews year and a half he didn't receive any funds because of Swiss restrictions. During the last year of the war he received $11 million. Sadly this amount was not even enough to help the Jews in occupied Europe. In the summer of

536

1942 Slovak asked for ransom money and kept asking to bring up the price. At first Mayer was suspicious but then changed his mind and sent the money by giving money to people to who needed it dearly.

Switzerland is a country in central Europe. When the years of Nazi power arrived the Swiss and instructions joined together under an umbrella institution. After Nazis came into power, thousands of Jewish refugees tried to get into Switzerland to escape from the Nazis. They tried to get into Switzerland by traveling in small groups. After that occurred thousands and thousands of Jews kept trying to get into Switzerland. During the war, Swiss tried to decrease the amount of Jews that tried to enter, in no offense to Germany or their people. Germany invaded central and Northern Italy on September 1943. However they allowed many Jewish people to enter Switzerland.

The Nazis killed about 6 million Jews during the time of the Holocaust. The Holocaust had the most killing during that time than any other war that ever happened around the world. In four years the Nazis murderd 6 million Jews. They were more successful during the months of April until November in 1942. About 250 during those months which they killed 2.5 million Jews.

The Holocaust was a time of terror and murder. It was not pleasant for the Jewish people. Heroes were people who helped Jews get to a safe environment. Heroes included people like David Frankfurter, Carl Lutz, Saly Mayer, Per Anger, and Paul Grueninger. Recha was an activist who helped refugees and Jewish children. Carl was a diplomat and saved thousands and thousands of Jews by documents of protection. David was a medical student who studied at Leipzig and Frankfurt then moved to Switzerland to kill a Nazi leader in 1936. Saly was a man who gave people money to save Jewish refugees and bring them under protection. Paul was a man who was a police commander. Per Anger was a Swedish diplomat who assisted Raoul Wallenberg in saving Jews. All these people are a part of the Righteous Among Nations. All these people saved thousands and thousands of Jewish lives. These people are heroes are the Holocaust because they all put an effort towards helping Jewish people live.

Work citations

http://en.wikipedia.org/wiki/Yad_Vashem

http://www.raoulwallenberg.net/press/releases/swedish-holocaust-heroe-dies

http://www.yadvashem.org/yv/en/holocaust/about/index.asp

http://www.yadvashem.org/odot_pdf/microsoft%20word%20-206048.pdf

www.Yadvashem.org/odot_pdf/microsoft%20word%20-%206455.pdf

www.Yadvashem.or/odot_pdf/microsoft%20word%20-%205862.pdf

www.raoulwallenberg.net/press/releases/swedish-holocaust-heroe-dies/

www.en.wikipedia.org/wiki.org/wiki/Yad_Vashem

DANISH AND SWISS HEROES AND HEROINES OF THE HOLOCAUST

Jacob Terhune

Five Million Nine Hundred Thirty Three Thousand Nine Hundred. This was the estimated death toll of the Jewish people after the perishment of the Nazi reign. Many more went unaccounted for because of the cruel ways of war. The Holocaust is one of the most horrendous events to ever happen to this very day, and it claimed the lives of many innocent people. Some victims have been named and some even brought justice, but many among those are forgotten. I will be telling the factual events from the lives of many well known, and some not so well known, heroes and heroines of the Holocaust. These people together helped over 100,000 Jewish people escape or hide from the Nazi regime.

Knud Christiansen

Knud Christiansen is among one of the most repeated names when the words "Holocaust Heroes" is typed into my search engine. Christiansen in his early twenties was living in Berlin. He had a career as a professional athlete, and in 1936 he competed in the Olympics there in Berlin as a member of a Danish rowing team. Humorously enough, his wife-to-be was also living in Berlin in the early thirties. There she attended a highly regarded cooking school and was known for sending letters home talking about the "terrible brutalization" of Jewish people there. When the Nazis invaded Denmark in 1940 and began to take over, Christiansen immediately took part in something called the "Danish Resistance." This was a brotherhood of Danish people who opposed the Nazi reign on Denmark.

During the Holocaust, he put his own life at risk by working in a leather manufacturing business which was mostly dominated by Jewish people. There he made a lot of Jewish friends. "It was something that needed to be done," he said. His apartment in Copenhagen put him in close proximity to the comings and goings of the high ranking S.S officials. This meant he was usually the first to unveil the secretive plans of the German S.S. He was then able to inform his Jewish acquaintances of any "mass roundups" that were being planned. One such "mass

538

roundup" was planned on Rosh Hashanah at 10 p.m. October 1, 1943. It was estimated that around 7,000 Jewish people were expected to be home, almost all of which lived in Copenhagen. To prevent the Jewish people from being arrested, he hid them in any place he could fine that was convenientid Jewish people in farmhouses, churches, and apartments to prevent them from being arrested.

His daughter Jyttte specifically can recall memories of the house full of guests. She was told to call them aunts and uncles to avoid any suspicion. One of the guests at one point was the director of the Danish national bank. Another rendition of a time he put forth effort to save Jewish people happened again on a late night in September of 1943. Christiansen was rushing on his way to his weekly bridge game when he suddenly insisted that two of his Jewish companions go into hiding immediately. One of the Philipson brothers agreed and proceeded to find shelter, but the other went home first. It was later found that the second brother who had gone home had been arrested and put in a concentration camp. Christiansen tried his hardest to get him out, even saying that he was only one fourth Jewish in hopes that the guards would reconsider. The commandant told Christiansen the too many Jewish people had already "slipped through the nets" and proceeded to refuse the release of the second Philipson brother. In one final effort, once again risking his life Christiansen took his request for release to the highest ranking Nazi official in Denmark. His name was General Werner Best, or better known as "The Blood Hound of Paris" for unforgiving deporting Jewish people from Paris into death camps. The second Philipson brother was eventually released. Many believe it was because General Best had respect for him considering he was an Olympic athlete previously. In addition, General Best referred to Christiansen as a "handsome gentleman with Aryan features." Christiansen was later invited to become part of a Nazi propaganda film which portrayed Denmark and Germany as friends. "The film was never made," Christiansen added.

No number has been accumulated for how many Jewish lives Christiansen saved. It has taken until recent years to fully uncover the story behind all that Knud Christiansen did. In 1970 his wife, his three children, and himself immigrated to the United States. Before he immigrated, his father-in-law, a physician opened a substantial size home on the shoreline to harbor Jewish people until they could escape. His mother, who owned a chocolate shop, allowed her business to be a meeting place for rescue workers. Knud Christiansen and his family have told their story and they did not disappoint. Their valor and courage in the tough time that was the Holocaust will always be remembered. In 2005, Knud and Karen Christiansen's names were added to a list of legendary figure. Among them Raoul Wallenberg and Oskar Schindler as "Righteous Among Nations" at the Yad Vashem Memorial Museum in Jerusalem. While Christiansen's wife died in 1992, He remained living until 2012 at the old age of 97.

Paul Grueninger

There were many Swiss who aided the Jewish people in their escapes during the Holocaust. One of these people is Paul Grueninger. He was born on October 27th, 1891. In 1938 Grueninger was working as a Swiss border police commander in St. Gallen. He began to notice that the Germans had begun to stamp the letter J on the passports of Jewish people. This is when Jewish people began to flee from Austria to other countries, but they were simply turned back. Grueninger was instructed to turn any fleeing Jewish people back toward their country, but he disobeyed the orders.

During the beginning of the Holocaust, Grueninger made a decision to begin falsifying passports of Jewish people and making it appear as if they had arrived before 1938. He also made an effort whenever he could to buy winter clothes for the incoming Jewish people. He was intent on helping them, but he could not falsify all of the fleeing Jewish passports so therefore he had to turn some down. After very little time, Germany informed the Swiss government of Grueninger's activities and in 1939 he was dismissed from the police force for official misconduct. It was estimated that in the end he saved about 3,600 Jewish people in his short time of rebellion.

The total number of Jewish people that Grueninger helped or saved is not known. The world came to know his story because he was sent to trial in 1941. He was found guilty of breach of duty, and was fined 300 Swiss francs along with the revoking of his pension. After this he became poor and gave up on the effort to help the Jewish people. In 1972 Grueninger died in poverty, only being remembered by those that he saved along the way.

Raoul Wallenberg

Raoul Gustaf Wallenberg was born August 4, 1912 in Lidingo Municipality, Sweden. He was a Swedish architect, businessman, diplomat and humanitarian. While being Sweden's special envoy between July and December 1944 Wallenberg made protective passports and sheltered Jews in buildings designated as Swedish territory. On January 17, 1945 during the siege of Budapest by the Red Army he was arrested by the Soviet authorities on suspicion of espionage. He disappeared soon after. He was never seen again.

Although he lived a short life and was captured during wartime, he was said to have saved tens of thousands of people in the time that he was active. Although, he left many lasting impressions as he was part of the Danish Resistance. He came to be "one of the most famous missing persons from the Twentieth Century."

Per Anger

Out of the many Swiss and Danish people who made efforts to help the Jewish people during the Holocaust, one such unrecognized person is Per Anger. Anger was born December 7, 1913 in Goteborg. He studied at the college of Stockholm and after graduating in 1939, he was drafted into the army. He was soon offered a trainee job at the ministry for foreign affairs in the legation in Berlin. He was assigned to the trade department but he heard about a pending Nazi attack on Norway and Denmark and soon began giving information to Stockholm. In 1941 he returned to Stockholm where he battled with trade relations between Sweden and Hungary.

After Germany invaded Hungary on March 19th, 1944, Anger became involved in efforts to aid Hungarian Jews. Anger came up with the idea of issuing Swedish provisional passports and special papers to protect Jews from internment and deportation. Seven hundred of these documents were issued at first. The legality of the documents was doubtful, but the Hungarian government agreed to recognize their authenticity. On July 9th, Raoul Wallenberg arrived in Budapest. He immediately improved Anger's idea, introducing colorful protective passes (Schutzpasse) and creating "safe houses" throughout the city. Anger and Wallenberg worked together, often literally snatching people from transports and death marches. After the Soviets invaded in January 1945, both Anger and Wallenberg were arrested. Anger was released three months later, but Wallenberg never was seen again.

Throughout the rest of his life, Anger tried to learn what happened to Wallenberg, even meeting personally with Soviet president Mikhail Gorbachev in the 1980s. In 2000, the Russian government finally admitted that Wallenberg and his driver died in Soviet custody in 1947, although the exact reasons for their deaths remain unknown. The Per Anger Prize was made by the Swedish Government to honor the memory of ambassador Per Anger and is awarded for humanitarian work and improvements in the name of Democracy. The prize is awarded to individuals or groups who have made something of themselves either in the past or in more recent times.

Carl Lutz

Another person who played a key role in the safety and security of thousands of Jewish people was Carl Lutz. Lutz was born on March 30, 1895 in Walzenhausen, Switzerland and attended local schools. He came to the United States at the age of 18, where he lived and worked for more than 20 years. He worked in Illinois to earn money for college, and started his college at Central Wesleyan College in Warrenton, Missouri. In 1920, Lutz found a job at the Swiss Legation in Washington, D.C. He continued his college there at George Washington University, where he got a bachelor's degree in 1924. While in Washington, D.C., Lutz lived in Dupont Circle. He continued to work for the Swiss Legation.

In 1942, he began distributing Swiss safe-conduct papers that let almost 10,000 Hungarian Jewish children emigrate. Once the Nazis took over Budapest in 1944, they started deporting Jewish people to the death camps. Lutz made a deal with the Hungarian government and the Nazis. He gained permission to issue protective letters to 8,000 Hungarian Jews for emigration to Palestine. It was said that during this time Lutz managed to save over 60,000 Jewish people.

Conclusion

As you can see, the extent that people would go to so they could save any amount of Jewish people were extreme to say the least. Those who aided the Jewish people during the Holocaust had opened their eyes to see the cruel uncalled for actions of the Nazi regime. It stands to this day that the people named will remain heroes and heroines of Holocaust through future years and their actions will always be remembered and cherished.

Works Cited

"Danish Hero: One Rosh Hashanah Burns Bright in Holocaust" JewishPost.com
The Jewish Post of New York.2013 On the internet
http://www.jewishpost.com/archives/news/Danish-Hero.html
"The policeman who lifted the border barrier" YadVashem.org
Yad Vashem The Holocaust Martyrs' and Heroes' Remembrance Authority 2015
On the internet
http://www.yadvashem.org/yv/en/righteous/stories/grueninger.asp
"Per Anger" Wikiepedia.com
This page was last modified on 6 January 2015, at 21:33.On the internet
http://en.wikipedia.org/wiki/Per_Anger
"Carl Lutz" Wikiepedia.com
This page was last modified on 12 February 2015, at 11:49.On the internet
http://en.wikipedia.org/wiki/Carl_Lutz

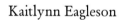

SWISS AND DANISH HEROES OF THE HOLOCAUST

Kaitlynn Eagleson

Many people know the horrific actions that took place during the Holocaust. People know the dictator, the camps, the hatred, and all the deaths and pain placed upon others. But one aspect few people know about are the heroes who risked their lives to save others during the Holocaust. The heroes range from young to old, rich to poor, strong to weak. They are not just one nationality or culture, but spread across the world. Though there are many notable heroes, some stories that come out of Denmark and Switzerland are powerful stories of selflessness, courage, perseverance, kindness, and hope.

Harald Feller

Harald Feller is one great example of a hero during the horrors of the Holocaust. Feller was born in 1913 in Switzerland. In his early thirties, Harald Feller worked as a Swiss diplomat. He began helping the Jewish when he met Carl Lutz, a Swiss vice-consul, in 1944. Harald Feller worked with other Swiss diplomats such as Wallenberg, Rotta, Perlasca, and Born. He was able to save Jews by giving many false passports after rescuing them from a transit camp. He provided them with food, water, and shelter in his basement of his consular residence in Budapest. The exact number of people he saved is unknown, but he was involved in "numerous" rescue operations. By the end of the war, Harald Feller had a great number of Jews hidden in his basement. When the war was over Harald Feller was arrested by an Arrow Cross Gang,A group of people who committed a reign of unpredictable terror against Jews of Budapest. He was tortured and kept until 1946 when he was released. On July 15, 1999 Yad Vashem recognized Harald Feller as a Righteous Among the Nations. Sadly, in 2003 Feller passed away due to natural causes. But, he left his mark on this world by saving lives.

Anna Christensen

Anna Christensen is another prime example of a hero during the Holocaust. She was born in the country of Denmark in 1865. Her occupation before the war is unknown. Anna was known to be "generous, caring, and loving"(unknown source). Like other heroes, Anna Christensen saved lives, but she also cared for them and their education. She had enrolled about 40 Jewish children in a local school before the war. When the Germans invaded on April 9, 1940, she transformed her cellar into a classroom for the children. She treated each child with "motherly affection." She encouraged them and lifted their spirits. Anna Christensen also assisted in the Denmark Underground Movement. She started to assist in autumn of 1943. She and others smuggled Jews out of the camps to safety in Sweden. They risked their lives to save others when doing so. It is unknown how many people Anna Christensen saved, but she was able to save men, women, and children. When the war was over, she was able to maintain contact with her "children." On May 31, 1996 Anna Christensen was recognized by Yad Vashem as a Righteous Among the Nations.

Friedrich Born

Friedrich Born is another wonderful example of a hero during the Holocaust. Friedrich Born was born June 10, 1903 in Langenthal, Switzerland. He was a Swiss delegate of the International Committee of the Red Cross, also known as the I.R.C, in Budapest. This was his occupation between May 1944 and January 1945. Because of his job he was forced to transfer to Hungary. When he was aware of Jews being taken to camps, he decided to set out and help. He gave Jews jobs working in his offices. They were given security in return for their work. They were protected by the International Committee of the Red Cross in designated buildings. He also gave out about 15,000 Schutzbrefe, protection documents from the I.R.C, to ensure protection of the Hungarian Jews. When the wars was over, Friedrich Born went back to his normal life like lots of other people. He kept his righteous actions to himself. At 59 on January 14,1963, Born passed away. He spent his last moments in Zollikofen, Switzerland. Twenty-four years after he passed, in 1987, he was identified as a Righteous Among the Nations by Yad Vashem.

Margaretta Tobler

Margareta Tobler, other known as Margaret, is an example of a hero in the Holocaust who may not have saved many, but risked her life to save few. Margareta Tobler was born in Switzerland. She was in early childhood teacher in France of Swiss nationality. She worked at Chateau de la Hille, a children's home. The children's home had about 100 Jewish adolescents who fled Germany and lost contact with their family.

Two girls in particular who she helped were Inge Bernhard who was 14 years old and Toni Rosenblatt who was only 11 years old. The two young girls had visas to enter Switzerland but had no funds to take the train trip and were not able to by themselves. So Margareta Tobler decided to aid in a specific rescue of those two girls. Margareta obtained 1000 francs, money of Switzerland in many other countries, from her uncle to use for the two younger ones. They secretly left on November 10, 1943. They risked being caught during the police checks on the train. They safely made it to Annemassee which was on the border of Switzerland. They were warmly welcomed to a Red Cross children's home, "Les Fuex Follets." After resting they tried to cross the border from France to Switzerland but were denied by French guards. At dawn they snuck out once again and successfully made it into Switzerland. The Swiss guards were very surprised. It is not known the exact number of people Margareta totally saved but at the least she saved two young children successfully. It is unknown what Margareta Tobler did once the war was over but before disappearing she saved lives. Margareta Tobler earned a Righteous Among the Nations on October 29, 2000.

Gerda Valentiner

Gerda Valentiner is an example of a teacher willing to save innocent children. Gerda Valentiner was born in Denmark. Before the war, she worked as a school teacher. But when the war broke out she began to save lives. In the weeks of October, when the deportation of the Jewish people was planned, she collected Jewish children from their parents and grandparents. She then took them to her home and took care of them until it was the perfect time to take them to the coast, where they would then be taken to safety in Sweden. Taking care of the children, she soon realized some were more "religiously observant" than others. Due to their religion, they were not able to eat some of the food Gerda Valentiner offered. The children who were more cautious were limited to the bread she had given them.

544

Once aware, she began to make dishes more suitable for the religiously cautious children. Once it was the perfect time to take the children, she took them to the coast and they were taken to the country of Sweden. When the war was over, Gerda Valentiner was modest of her actions. When asked about what she did she stated "I only did what most Danes did, nothing special. We thought it perfectly to help people in mortal trouble." Gerda took a leave of absence from her teaching job and volunteered as a social worker for two years at Jewish refugee camps in Germany and Austria. In 1971, when Gerda Valentiner was 68, she retired and went to Israel to see the beautiful county and to learn Hebrew, a goal she had in life. On July 28, 1968 Yad Vashem recognized Gerda Valentiner as a Righteous Among the Nations.

Bill Barazetti

The last but not least example of a hero during the Holocaust is Bill Barazetti. He was born in Aarau, Switzerland making him a Swiss hero. When Hitler came to power, Barazetti was a philosophy major at a school called Hamburg University, where he made friends with Jews, but then saw them taken away by Nazis.

In 1934 Barazetti moved to Czechoslovakia and became an intelligence officer. Whole spying in Hamburg after one year he was caught and was almost "killed" but luckily he faked his death. He made his way to Poland and was caught by Germans and almost beaten to death. When he tried to leave again he met a woman named Anna, a Czechoslovakian, and eventually married her, returned to Switzerland, and had a child named Nicholas in 1937. He did not approve of the Nazis' actions and he wanted to help.

He sent his son and wife back to Czechoslovakia and got involved in Nicholas Winston's rescue operations. Together, they raised funds, found foster families, arranged documents, and arranged train rides for Jewish children. Most of the children were sent to Britain on the trains he set up. He saved about 669 children.When the war was over Barazetti and his small family spent their lives in Britain. On October 27, 1993 Bill Barazetti was recognized as a Righteous Among the Nations.

If it were not for people like Harald Feller, Anna Christensen, Friedrich Born, Margaretta Tobler, Gerda Valentiner, and Bill Barazetti, Hitler would have reached his goal of eliminating the Jews. Though this moment in time shall not be forgotten, inhuman acts of genocide happen even in the present. But the bravery, selflessness, and kindness of others can help and or stop the problem.

UNDERGROUND AFFAIR

Shannon Negrete, Co-winner

Between 1933 and 1945, the Holocaust both began and ended. Much like some new form of the plague, it silently spread across the globe, killing many in its path. That is, except for the Danish, who refused to stand by and do nothing. As their affirmation and camaraderie flourished with each advance, it was as though they were foreshadowing the imminent invasion of the Nazis. In 1940, the Danish were infiltrated—but they showed no signs of surrendering. No matter the size of the task at hand, many brave Danish citizens risked their lives in the ultimate act of the famous Danish Resistance. In their humble stature, many believed it was merely their duty from one human to another, and go unnoticed to this day; while others have gone to such great measures, in this underground operation, that their presence could not be left unrecognized.

A family of these people are none other than the Marstrand Christiansens. Recognized in the year of 2005, Knud and Karen's work during the Holocaust touched the lives of many. During the year of 1930, Karen went to Berlin to learn in a prestigious cooking school. There she lived with a Jewish family and was exposed to the unfathomable horrors produced by the Holocaust. At one point, the brutality became too great, and Karen left halfway through her studies and returned home to Copenhagen, where Knud, her fiance, lived. Not long after, Knud, and his rowing team traveled to Berlin for the Olympics. There, he too saw the horrors described in Karen's numerous letters. Soon, Knud returned home, as Karen did, and thus began their tale.

When they married, in 1938, it seemed as though they had eluded the danger, but, as in surrounding countries, the original plan persisted. When the Nazis first came, they showed no signs of implementing the final solution. Despite this, many people continued to be alert, constantly watching for anything that might show signs of the onslaught. On October 1 of 1943, with Knud and Karen's spacious havengade apartment overlooking the Oresund Channel, it all began: Knud awoke that morning to the sight of two German freighters docked nearby. Immediately, Karen rushed to her underground press, which furtively updated the community after Denmark's occupation. Once the flyers telling Jewish families to hide and not go home that nigh, were printed, they were distributed among the endangered citizens. Still, Knud decided to personally inform his two Jewish friends, known as the Philipsons, after their weekly card game of bridge. Even so they, along with many others, dismissed the threat and retreated to their homes anyway. As they had warned, the Philipsons were taken. In Knud's desperation, he attempted to reason with the Nazis, only to have the threat of hanging bestowed upon him. After his defeat, he made his way to erner Best: the plenipotentiary or high-ranked Nazi. By offering a pro-German film to be made, he was able to persuade Best into releasing the Philipsons. Regardless of the absence of the film, the attempt was a success! Now was the time to go undercover.

Both Knud's widowed mother and Karen's father were in on the endeavor with Karen and Knud as well. All four played roles in rescuing the possible deportees. Knud's mother owned a chocolate shop, where they purposefully placed a soda pop bottle in the window; this signaled that it was a place that weapons and messages could be dropped, stored and distributed. In addition to this, Karen continued her underground press, known as the Fly Swatter, and produced the "Die Warheit" newspaper. This helped tell people where to go and who to talk to. Two of the administrators were Knud and Karen's father; both would chauffer, direct, hide, and smuggle people across the border. Knud single-handedly brought 17 Jews across, one by one, in his olympic boat. By this point, bigger boats were called in and more people began to join in.

One of these operations was headed by both Henry Christian Thomsen and his wife, Ellen Margrethe Thomsen. Both played active parts in the Danish Resistance. They owned both an inn and a seaside hotel; in both, they hid possible victims. At the inn they also held meetings with the fishermen involved in the operation and planned for their next transports. During the beginning, only illegal cargo transports passed from border to border, it wasn't until october that stowaways began to enter the scene. On October 2, Switzerland officially allowed the passage of Danish citizens into Swedish land. From there on out, nearly 8,000 citizens crossed land and water into the Swedish territory. With the help of many people, Henry and Ellen organized where people could stay and how many people would be clandestinely crossing the Oresund stretch. Eventually the amount of escaping citizens became too great, and Henry took matters into his own hands.

Henry got a license and a boat, which he named after his wife, Margrethe. He crossed the Oresund multiple times before the Gestapos noticed what was happening. He began to be questioned often until he was caught and arrested. After a week in jail, he was freed due to a lack of evidence. Despite his close call, Henry continued this perilous vocation. Even though Henry was as careful as could be, both pro-German citizens and the Gestapo kept him under close watch, and he was caught for a second time in August of 1944. This time, there was no evaluation. Henry was directly deported to Neuengamme concentration camp. Until dying of pneumonia during a transport between Neuengamme and Flensburg, on December 4, 1944, Henry lived and worked here. Even in Henry's absence, Ellen lived on and they were recognized in 1968.

During all of their travels, it is sure that Henry may have come in contact with Knud Dyby: another director in this grand plan. Though Dyby may have not have personally rescued more than 100 Jews, he helped in many ways.

When Dyby was 20, he was drafted into the military and eventually became a royal guardsmen, police officer, and avid sailor. Not all policemen were quite as experience as Dyby, but Werner Best knew that most Danish police were helping in the resistance and Best now wished to enforce his own policies, and that's just what he did. On September 04, 1943, nearly half of the Danish police force was captured and rushed off to jails and concentration camps, but Dyby was one of the many who were off that day and decided to not return to their positions. In their place, hundred of Gestapos took up residence and began to enforce the Final Solution in every way possible. Dyby knew just what to do, and thus he became a vital member.

Placing his own life in danger, Dyby joined the Danish Resistance. His years of experience were extremely important in the success of such operations. Knowing both the roads and boating schedule like the back of his hand and having connections with the Danish coast guards, he was able to organize missions with rarely any incident of disruption. Dyby knew the best places to hide and would often use fishing equipment shacks as hide outs. He also persuaded the coast guards to allow boats to make their way across the Oresund at nightfall and to tell him when and where German watercrafts were coming and going. This allowed Dyby to instruct five fishing skippers to make hundreds of trips, carrying 12 people each run. No person was left behind, and they brought about 1,888 people to safety, with only about 256 officers arrested and two ships lost. Even with everyone safely placed, Dyby continued his resistance until the very end. When all was done, Knud Dyby lived the rest of his humble life in peace, until he died in 2011, at the age of 96. Despite death, his story lives on, as many others' do.

Another of these stories is that of Helga Holbek. She was born into a wealthy family in Copenhagen, Denmark, and went on to live in Italy after graduation. After living in Italy, she moved to France; here Holbek directed a travel agency known as "International Holiday and Study Tours." At this agency, Holbek organized a place for teachers and students of different ethnicities and backgrounds to meet and form "international understanding and tolerance."1 When war turned her business sour, Holbek began her search for a new place to continue her service. Along her travels, she met a woman of the name Edithe Pye, who invited Holbek to talk with Howard Kershner. At this point, Helga Holbek became part of both the International Commision for the Assistance of Child Refugees and the American Quakers. Her work for the Kershners began in the form of child care and rescue.

Her work led her to rescue people of all walks of life. Whether they be for the Danish or not, Holbek proceeded with her dangerous duties, meeting her best friend, Alice Resch, along the way. Together, they took in children and hid them in childrens' homes both there and over borders. Often times, they would bring the children in trains, saying, with ice skates in hand, that they were going to the alps, when really they were illegally making their way across the Switzerland border. During one of these missions, Holbek met with Sigismund Kolozsvary, a famous artist, and his wife, and cautioned them to escape. Eventually, they agreed and, following Helga's instructions, crossed the border. They were not as successful as many other had been though, because, the next day, they were caught and sent back over the border, into an internment camp. As careful as ever, Holbek helped the pair escape over the border once more, completely successful this time. Eventually, the Kershners took a trip to the United States, and left Helga Holbek, their most qualified member, in charge of the 16 childrens' homes. Now with added responsibilities and duties, Holbek took charge and organized new objectives. One of these new tasks was creating something for all the new refugees who had fled to Toulouse, the base of the Quakers' center. After much thought, it was settled that a soup kitchen would be made. Many other tasks were carried out, but eventually the war concluded. This didn't stop Holbek from continuing her services, though.

As before, Holbek continued her previous work, but in a less dangerous way, and began to try and promote international friendliness again. After two succeeding wars, the world was exhausted though and merely wanted to stick to their own in cleaning up the ruins and, so, Holbek's plans of creating international halls were placed on hold. Holbek died in 1983 but her ideas and inspiration did not die with her, they were finally brought into fruition many years later, even though not many think of her as the founder of such an idea. Now, in recent times, International halls, building, and meeting places can be found all over the globe.

Such feelings of overall friendliness can be hard to forge but it is true that it's possible, even with their small scale, the Danish give a great example. Before the war, not much notice was given to the Danish, but, as the danger grew closer, their acceptance and community continued to grow both in range and feeling; they knew all humans were the same despite their differences and would not allow their thoughts to go unheard. There was even an account of a Jewish family compiling a book and sending it to the royal family, only to receive a letter of thanks to the Jewish Community the very next day. The Danish kept close bonds that they intended to keep and, instead of allowing the discrimination to proceed, acted upon the first threat.

The Danish Resistance was not made up of the mere 22 individuals, who have been recognized, but a great number of citizens working as one. This is the main reason that on various websites, the Danish Underground is requested to be shown as a group rather than individually. Even with this mindset in place, some citizens could not allow some heroes to go unnoticed for all they had done. After so many years, people have remembered these peoples' great acts of humanity, and, in return, have stepped forward and given these individuals the commemoration they deserve. Helga Holbek, Knud Dyby, Karen and KnudMarstrand Christiansen, and Henry Christian and Ellen Margrethe Thomsen are just some of the few who have had this service done to them. Despite their humble stature, their benevolent actions were bold and powerful. Those of the Danish Resistance helped many people, and their stories continue to live on in both the memories of those they helped, and those that come to discover them.

Works Cited

"Paying The Ultimate Price - Henry Christian and Ellen Margrethe Thomsen." IAm My Brother's Keeper. Yad Vashem The Holocaust Martyrs' and Heroes' Remembrance Authority. N/A. (Web). 16 February, 2015.

"With Fishing Boats to Sweden - Henry Christian and Ellen Margrethe Thomsen." The Righteous Among The Nations. Yad Vashem The Holocaust Martyrs' and Heroes' Remembrance Authority. N/A. (Web).16 February, 2015.

"Henry Thomsen." Wikipedia, den frie encyklopædi. N/A. 16 June, 2014. (Web).16 February, 2015.

"Knud Christiansen | Denmark." The Jewish Foundation for the Righteous. The Jewish Foundation for the Righteous. N/A. (Web). 16 February, 2015.

"A loser at the Olympics, he struck gold in Jewish hearts forever." The Copenhagen Post. Jaya Rao. October 6, 2012. (Web). 16 February, 2015.

"The Splitting Of The Sea, 1943." The Jewish Week. Jonathan Mark. 18 April, 2011. (Web). 16 February, 2015.

"Holbek Family." The Righteous Among The Nations. Yad Vashem The Holocaust Martyrs' and Heroes' Remembrance Authority. N/A. (Web). 16 February, 2015.

"Helga Holbek." ajpn.org. Patrick Cabanel. 2012. (Web). 16 February, 2015.Paldiel, Mordecai. (1993). The Path of the Righteous: Gentile Rescuers of Jews During the Holocaust. N/A: KTAV Publishing House, Inc. 17 February, 2015.

Resch Synnestvedt, Alice. (2005). Over the Highest Mountains: A Memoir of Unexpected Heroism in France During World War II. N/A: Intentional Productions. 17 February, 2015.

"Knud Dyby: One of the Righteous." Solly Ganor Remembrance. Solly Ganor. N/A. (Web). 16 February, 2015.

"The Rescue of the Danish Jews." The Holocaust. Louis Bülow. 2013. (Web). 16 February, 2015.

"Knud Dyby, Novato man who helped save thousands of Jews during World War II, dies at 96." Marinij News. Richard Halstead. 12 September, 2011.

Burgan, Michael. (2010). Refusing to Crumble: The Danish Resistance in World War II. North Mankato, Minnesota: Capstone Press. 17 February, 2015.

E. Werner, Emmy. (2004). A Conspiracy of Decency: The Rescue of the Danish Jews During World War II. Boulder, Colorado: Basic Books. 17 February, 2015.

Rees, Laurence. (2006). Auschwitz: A New History. New York, New York: PublicAffairs. 17 February, 2015.

Etling, William. (2005). Sideways in Neverland. N/A: iUniverse, Incorporated. 17 February, 2015.

Valley High School, Elk Grove, CA

Jess Furtell- Valley High, Elk Grove

ELSEBET AND JORGEN KIELER, KNUD DYBY

Camille Prasad, Co-winner

Elsebet Kieler was born on August 4, 1918 in Copenhagen. She was the oldest out of four kids. She has two younger brothers, Jeorgen and Felmming, and one younger sister, Bente. Elsebet and her siblings traveled and studied in England and Germany.

Before the war, Elsebet and her brother helped with publishing an illegal newspaper, "Frit Denmark." She was not married. Elsebet and her brother, Jorgen, were both members of the Holger Danske resistance group and were involved in the rescue of almost 1,000 Danish Jews.

In the beginning of the war Elsebet committed herself as a pacifist because of an experience she had on a trip to Germany. When she was in Germany, she saw a sign that said "Jews not wanted here" and that made her want to help Jews escape to Sweden.

Elsebet traveled the Danish countryside to collect over 1 million kroner from rich estates around Copenhagen. She and her brother Jorgen helped hundreds of Jews escape to Sweden and avoid extermination.

Elsebet and Jorgen were captured and imprisoned by the Germans. Jorgen was put into a concentration camp.

After the war Elsebet was reunited with her family. She came back to the United States to finish her graduate degree in comparative literature at Radcliffe College. She died in 2006. Her brother Jorgen went back to Denmark for a time and completed his studies in the United States. He became the director of research at Kraeftens Bekæmpelse (the Danish Cancer Research Institute).

Another rescuer was Knud Dyby. Knud Dyby was born in Randers, Denmark in 1915. He later immigrated to the United States. Knud worked in printing and advertising before Germany invaded Denmark in April 1940. In 1943, when Mr. Dyby learned that the Nazis were planning to round up Denmark's Jews and send them to concentration camps, he felt he had to do something. He played a big role in organizing fishermen in Copenhagen's North Harbor to take Danish Jews in small groups to safety in Sweden. Mr. Dyby had been a champion sailor since he was 16. He was a member of the King's Royal Guard and participated in removing the Nazi flag. Dyby was 26 at the time and a policeman. He came to this position through his experience as a Guardsman at the Royal Palace in Copenhagen. He was drafted into the military when he was 20, and assigned to the Guard because of his good looks and tall military bearing. As a police officer and avid sailor, he had access to information vital to the underground. He knew the best hiding places near the fishing coves. And he knew the patrol routines of the German navy along the best sea lanes between Denmark and Sweden. This information was critical in planning the hundreds of dangerous crossings that took place under his direction.

After leaving military service, Knud became a police officer and an active member of the Danish underground.

When the news spread of Germany's intention to round up Denmark's Jews, the county quickly mobilized. The evacuation began in dark and rainy October. Within three months (some accounts say two to three weeks) individual citizens and small groups were able to smuggle nearly all of the 8,000 Jews living in Denmark across the narrow body of water between Denmark and Sweden.

A number of underground organizations in both Denmark and Sweden worked together against the Germans. Ordinary Danish citizens played a major role in these efforts and sheltered Jews from the Gestapo in every conceivable nook and cranny. Hospitals were favorite hiding places, harboring approximately 1000 Jews.

Dyby was a member of the Danish-Swedish Refugee Service, a group responsible for transporting 1,888 people to safety. Not all of these people were Jews; there were Allied airman, saboteurs, Baltic refugees and others fleeing the Nazis.

When Denmark was liberated in May 1945, Knud ended his police career. After the war, Knud Dyby emigrated from Denmark, ultimately settling in the San Francisco Bay area. A year later he moved to the United States. Knud Dyby died in September 2011 at the age of 96.

Bibliography

"Kieler, Jørgen and Elsebet - The Jewish Foundation for the Righteous." *The Jewish Foundation for the Righteous*. N.p., n.d. Web. 02 Mar. 2015.

PAUL GRUENINGER

Dominic Cupps, Co-winner

Paul Grueninger was a football player when he was young but a hero as he grew older. He played for the local team, SC Bruhl, and helped them win their only Swiss championship. Paul Grueninger was born October 27, 1891 in St. Gallen, Switzerland.

After he finished school in Switzerland he grew up to be a police guard to guard the St. Gallen region border. He started to help the Jews by allowing them to cross the border illegally. He let them sneak across the border without proper permission. He did this secretly without anyone knowing. He never told anyone about what he was doing, because he knew the penalty was death if he was caught or told on.

Even though he knew the death penalty he still continued letting Jews escape. The question is why would he continue to let them pass by if he had so much to lose? He had decided to let the refugees cross out of the goodness of his heart. No one told him to and nobody asked him to. He took a stand to help these people were as other people sat there or joined in by torturing the Jews. He turned in false reports about all the people going through. And if that not enough he took his own money and bought them winter clothes.

Now even though people would have caught on eventually no one seemed to notice this until much later. But in March 1939 the 47-year old police guard was caught. The Germans informed the Swiss authorities. When this happened he lost all his benefits that the Swiss had given him. He also was brought to trial for letting 3,600 Jews in Switzerland and falsely turning in paper work.

Paul's case opened in January 1939 and lasted over two years. In March 1941 the court finally found him guilty and he was fined to pay all the trial costs. His retirement benefits were taken away for good. The court recognized his actions to be for good but, because being a state employee it was his duty to follow orders. So basically Paul helped so many people escape such a bad life and the court saw the goodness in his heart but because of him not following his orders he lost everything he had his money and his job.

Paul never once regretted helping the Jews where as most would have thought of not doing what he did at all. He was a true hero to many, not just Jews but to everyone. He's an inspiration to all who want to make a difference in the world. Many people shall remember his name for what he did to help the world for better.

Carl Lutz

Another Swiss hero is Carl Lutz. He was born in Walzenhausen, Switzerland on March 30, 1835. He was a chancellor at the Swiss in Philadelphia, United States. He got his bachelor's degree at George Washington University.

He was appointed vice-consul in Budapest, Hungary on 1942. He began cooperating with the Jewish Agency for Palestine. He gave out Swiss safe-conduct documents that enabled 10,000 Hungarian Jewish children to emigrate.

He helped many Jews escape a horrible life. He knew what he was doing was right in his heart. Even if he had the consequences he didn't back down from helping people even though most people wouldn't help in that situation. He was left with a decision that was hard to make but he chose the good one out of the kindness of his heart. And that made him a true hero. He did things that most people don't do on every day.

Sadly he passed away in 1975. He will always be remembered forever.

Bibliography

"Paul Gruninger." *Yad Vashem Righteous Among Nations*. Yad Vashem, n.d. Web. 02 Mar. 2015

"Lutz, Carl - The Jewish Foundation for the Righteous." *The Jewish Foundation for the Righteous*. N.p., n.d. Web. 02 Mar. 2015.

KNUD CHRISTIANSEN

Sandi Aguilar

Many Danish people did not agree with the decisions that the Nazis made in regard to the treatment of Jews. Denmark was a small country of 4 million people, with a history of hiding immigrants from the following countries: Germany, Poland, Sweden, and Holland. The Danish had found out that most of the 7,500 Danish Jews were about to be gathered together and deported to the German concentration camps. But the Danish made their decision that they were not going to let that happen and it did not happen. The Danish citizens gathered most of their fellow citizens and most were able to escape and become refugees. On the date April 9, 1949 Germany was then attacked by Denmark. Germany had then put Denmark under occupation. But the Danish and the Germans had worked out the terms of occupation which was that Danes had to supply rich agriculture produce and many other goods to the Germans. The following year the Danish resistance had started to slowly make its up way up until 1945. The Germans had commanded the Danish Jews to wear an armband with yellow stars. But the Danish never wore them. The Danish Jews ignored and were defiant of their occupiers. The date of August 1943 an emergency was proclaimed in Denmark. Nazis decided they would move against the Jews. Many of the Danes offered to locate and support places for the Jews to hide. In all parts of the country clergymen, civil servants, store owners, doctors, and farmers helped hide the Jews. Even the Danish police and the coast guards refused to help in the manhunt. Only about a fifth of the Danish Jew were able to make it to Sweden via this village. Over the course of many days, 7,000 Jews made to Sweden. But 481 Jews were captured and sent the Theresienstadt camp. That was not an extermination camp. The Danes had sent over 700 packages of food, clothing, and vitamins. Although 1 percent of the Jews were not rescued and did not survive the war years. One of the Danish people who took a big part of this would be Knud Christiansen. Knud Christiansen was a Danish man who was married to a woman who lived in Berlin. Knud had joined the Danish

556

resistance with many other Danes. Knud would ferry one Jew at a time across the Oresund. He earned a prominent position the Danish Nazis "watch list." He would engage in acts of sabotage. He even took the greatest risk ever and that was putting his family's life in danger. He had a wife and two kids at home during all of this. Putting his family in danger was a very big risk.

Bibliography

"Rescue of the Danish Jews." *Rescue of the Danish Jews*. N.p., n.d. Web. 02 Mar. 2015.

"Danish Hero: One Rosh Hashanah Burns Bright in Holocaust."*JewishPost.com* -. N.p., n.d. Web. 03 Mar. 2015.

"Christiansen, Knud - The Jewish Foundation for the Righteous." *The Jewish Foundation for the Righteous*. N.p., n.d. Web. 02 Mar. 2015.

PAUL GRUNINGER:

Unique Johnson

Most people write about people they know, but they don't know everyone. One person I'm going to write about is Paul Gruninger.

Paul Gruninger was born on October 21 1891 in St. Gallen, Switzerland. He was a football player and he played for SC Bruhl. After finishing school in St. Gallen he became a senior Swiss police officer. In 1915, he became a Swiss football champion. He was also a Swiss police commander in St. Gallen.

Paul Gruninger's actions saved thousands of people from being killed by a hateful dictator. Although Paul Gruninger did an illegal thing by entering undocumented refugees in Switzerland, he saved most of their lives.

Paul Gruninger saved 3,600 Jewish refugees by backdating their visas and falsifying other documents to indicate that they had entered Switzerland at the time when legal entry of refugees was still possible. In August 1938 the Swiss government sealed its borders prohibiting the entry of Austrian Jews into neutral Switzerland who were arriving without proper entry permits. In October 1938 negotiations between Switzerland and Nazi Germany led to the stamping of the famous "J "in German passports issued to Jews. As the situation of Jews in Austria worsened and the number of refugees who tried to illegally enter Switzerland increased, the 47-year-old official was faced with a monumental moral dilemma: turning the refugees back to their country where violent anti-Semitism was the official state policy, or facing the consequences of breaching the explicit orders of his government and suffering the consequences. At that time colonel Paul Gruninger was in charge of the Swiss border. He permitted two to three thousand Jewish refugees to enter Switzerland illegally.

He turned in false reports about the number of arrivals and the status of refugees in his district. Paul impeded the efforts to trace refugees who were known to have entered Switzerland illegally. As they were away Paul bought some refugees winter clothes because they were told to leave their belongings in their home.

Germans informed Swiss authorities about what Paul Gruninger had been doing. Gruninger was fired from police force in March 1939, charged with official misconduct and fined 300 Swiss francs. The following year he lost his police rank and all pension rights. His benefits were suspended and his retirement benefits were sforfeited because of his actions. Paul had an advantage to enter refugees in Switzerland that no one knew of. I acknowledge that Paul did what he did to save them from dying in Hitler's ways. So, he risked his life saving people he rarely knew to protect them. Gruninger was brought to trial on charges of illegally permitting the entry of 3,600 Jews to Switzerland and falsifying their registration papers. The prosecution added additional charges of helping individual Jews by shielding them from detection, assisting them in depositing their valuables. His trial opened in January 1939 and dragged for two years. He was fined and had to pay trial costs. In 1940 he was brought to trial and found guilty of fraud. The court recognized his motivations, but found that as a state employee it was his duty to follow his instructions.

Gruninger lived for the rest of his life in difficult circumstances. Despite the difficulties, he never regretted his actions on behalf of the Jews. In 1954 he explained his motives: "I am not ashamed of the courts verdict. On the contrary I am proud to have saved the lives of hundreds oppressed people. My assistance of Jews was rooted in my Christian world outlook... it was basically a question of saving human lives threatened with death. How could I then seriously consider bureaucratic schemes and calculations? Sure, I intentionally exceeded the limits of my authority and often with my own hands falsified documents and certificates, but it was done solely in order to afford persecuted people access into the country. My personal well-being, measured against the cruel fate of these thousands was so insignificant and unimportant that I never even took it into consideration." Gruninger served time in jail and was fined. After he got out of jail, he struggled to make a living because of his criminal record.

Paul Gruninger passed away in the year of 1972 at the age of 81. 23 years later in 1995, judges decided to reopen his trial and absolved him from the charges and the district rejected the judgment against him. The government of the canton of St. Gallen later paid compensation to his descendents. In December 1970 as a result of protest in the media, the Swiss government sent Gruninger a somewhat reserved letter of apology, but refrained from reopening his case and reinstating his pension.

Only after his death were steps to honor his name started. The first attempt was rejected by the Swiss Council, and only as late as 1995, the Swiss federal government finally annulled Gruninger's convictions. In 1996 Gruninger was completely rehabilitated by the Swiss government. In 1971, a year before his death, Yad Vashem bestowed the title of Righteous Among the Nations on Paul Guninger. A street located in northern Jerusalem neighborhood of Pisgat Ze'ev has been named after him. Also, Paul-Gruninger-Stadion is a football stadium in St. Gallen, Switzerland. The stadium is named after Swiss police captain and football player Paul Gruninger. It is the home of SC Bruhl and has a capacity of 4,200. The stadium had major renovations done during 2005 and 2006 and a new grandstand was erected. The grandstand has a capacity of 900 seats and the rest is 3,300 standing places. Although Paul Gruninger illegally permitted 3,600 people in Switzerland he saved their lives.

Bibliography

"Paul Gruninger." *Yad Vashem Righteous Among Nations*. Yad Vashem, n.d. Web. 02 Mar. 2015.

A Survivor's Voice

Bernard Marks was born in Lodz, Poland. Following the occupation by the Nazis in 1939, all Jews of Lodz were forced to move into the slum area of Lodz, a small area that formed the ghetto. Bernard spent four years working in a factory as a cloth cutter, while his father, Joseph, was the chief designer and pattern maker. In August, 1944, Bernard and his family were transported out of the Ghetto to Auschwitz. He never saw his mother or brother, or any of his 200 relatives, again.

When he and his father arrived at the selection ramp in Auschwitz, Joseph presented his young son's work permit and Gestapo registration to an S.S. officer to prove that Bernard had been working for the German government in the Ghetto. The officer then permitted Bernard to join his father at the selection ramp; both were assigned to work commandos in the Auschwitz/Birkenau camp. Later, it was learned that his father had been speaking to Dr. Mengele, the infamous doctor who performed hideous medical experiments on twins in Auschwitz.

Soon, Bernard and Joseph were transferred to the Dachau concentration camp and then to one of sub-camps to work as slave laborers building the Weingut II Bunker, an underground factory which was designed to produce Germany's ME262 jet planes. Beginning April, 1945 Bernard contracted Typhoid fever in camp Hurlach. (Kauferig IV)

On April 27, 1945, Bernard and his father were liberated by the U.S. Army 12th Armored Division. Bernard spent the next two years in Bavaria attending high school, trade schools, and university to catch up on studies he had missed during the five years living under the brutal Nazi regime.

Bernard Marks immigrated to Kansas City, Mo., in 1947 where he graduated for the second time from high school. He served in the US Army in Europe and Korea and was awarded the Army's Presidential Unit Citation, the Korean Presidential Citation and two Bronze Stars for bravery. He recently received a special medal from the President of Korea for the work he did with the local population, especially with children in need of medical attention.

Following his military service, Bernard graduated from Finley Engineering College in Kansas City, Mo., with a degree in Electrical/Nuclear Engineering.

560

In 1954, Bernard moved to Sacramento to work for the Aerojet General Corporation as a senior engineer on the Delta Rocket for the moon landing, Titan I and II ballistic missiles and various other research projects for both military and civilian applications.

Currently, Bernard is semi-retired as an environmental engineer, widowed, with two daughters and four grand children. In 2008, after 66 years of waiting for the right time and the right place, he finally achieved his goal of having a Bar Mitzvah at Congregation B'nai Israel., Sacramento.

Every year, Mr. Marks travels around the world to give presentations about the Holocaust from his first-hand perspective.

Bernie served for many years as President of B'nai Brith David Lubin Lodge, he is also a PP of Central California B'nai Brith District Grand Lodge #4, a recipient of the coveted AKIBA AWRD for community service.

Served in the U.S. Army with SHAEF Hdq. European theater as a translater and witness to the Dachau Trials. Also, served in Korea/Japan in the medical field. Recipient of the special Korean Presidential Medal for the work with children during the conflict. Recipient of many military medals including 2 bronze stars and the U. S. Presidential Unit Citation

Eleanor (Ellie), Bernie's wife of 56 years, passed away on April 15th, 2008. She served as President of B'nai B'rith Women, Sacramento Chapter #15.

Their daughters are active in Temple Beth El Sisterhood in Fresno, California.

Acknowledgments

I hereby wish to truly thank the teachers who encouraged their students to write these essays, the judging committee and proof-readers, editors and anyone else who helped with this project.

Judging Committees

Chief Judge:
Nadine Muench
Finance Operation, Leadership for Verizon Corporate

Mandy Greene, Administrator, Congregation B'nai Israel, Sacramento, CA

Steven Millner, Vice President, US Bank, Rancho Cordova, CA

Bernie Goldberg, Educator/Author/Activist

No picture

Shirley Lange, Retired

 Rachel Zerbo, Public Health Educator

 Laura Mahoney, Staff Correspondent for Bloomberg News

 Joel Schwartz, Senior Research Analyst, California State University, Sacramento

 Illene Carroll, Retired School Teacher

 Ann Owens, Librarian, Sacramento Public Library

 Elissa Provance, Assistant Director of Sacramento Jewish Federation

 Jessica Braverman-Birch, Director, Jewish Communications Relations Council of the Sacramento Jewish Federation

Heather Wilde, Administrative Assistant, Sacramento Public Library

Roxana Puerner, Administrative Analyst, Sacramento Public Library

Rachael Horsley -- State Water Resources Control Board, Associate Governmental Program Analyst

Carolyn Brokshire -- State Water Resources Control Board, Associate Governmental Program Analyst

Elaine Hussey has taught about The Holocaust for over ten years. She studied with the Museum of Tolerance in Los Angeles, and received a Fellowship to study at Yad Vashem. She primarily taught middle school children, and more recently has been giving lectures to adult study groups.

B. Carl Miller – Teacher/Author/Researcher

Elise Huggins - Teacher/French Translator

David Ayotte – Librarian/French Translator

Ken Chau – Library Services Assistant, Sacramento Public Library/ Chinese Translator

Bernard Marks - Author/Russian, German, French Translator

I am most appreciative to all the teachers and the judging committee for their dedication and work with the students from the many schools who contributed essays to this volume.

I am also greatly appreciative to the proof-readers listed below. And thanks to the Sacramento Public Library's I Street Press and Gerald Ward who helped assemble and publish all Volumes of these essays.

Laura Mahoney, Staff Correspondent for Bloomberg News

Gerald F. Ward, Librarian, Sacramento Public Library, I Street Press